COMMUNITY HEALTH, PREVENTIVE MEDICINE AND SOCIAL SERVICES

Sixth Edition

Brian Meredith Davies
MD (London), FFPHM, DPH

Formerly Lecturer in (Preventive) Paediatrics and in
Public Health, University of Liverpool
Formerly Director of Social Services, City of Liverpool
Director of Personal Health and Social Services, City of Liverpool

and

Tom Davies
MBBS (London), FRCGP

General Practitioner, Yaxley, Peterborough
Formerly Course Organizer, Peterborough Vocational Training Scheme

Baillière Tindall

London Philadelphia Sydney Tokyo Toronto

Baillière Tindall
W.B. Saunders

24–28 Oval Road
London NW1 7DX

The Curtis Center
Independence Square West
Philadelphia, PA 19106–3399, USA

55 Horner Avenue
Toronto, Ontario, M8Z 4X6, Canada

Harcourt Brace Jovanovich Group
(Australia) Pty Ltd
30–52 Smidmore Street
Marrickville
NSW 2204, Australia

Harcourt Brace Jovanovich Japan Inc
Ichibancho Central Building,
22–1 Ichibancho
Chiyoda-ku, Tokyo 102, Japan

First published 1966
Fifth edition 1983

A catalogue record for this book is available from the British Library

ISBN 0-7020-1380-3

Typeset by Colset Private Limited, Singapore
Printed and bound in Great Britain by Mackays of Chatham, PLC, Chatham, Kent

CONTENTS

PREFACE

This 6th edition marks an important change in authorship and in direction. For the first time my son joins me as co-author. This is aimed at both continuity into the future and at extending the readership, which it is hoped will increasingly include general practitioners and their primary health care teams, as well as those doctors who are undertaking general practitioner vocational training.

The National Health Service (NHS) has run into a difficult period, and the present uncertainty about the necessary changes has proved very unsettling for staff at all levels. It is important to understand why the changes, which started in the early 1980s, had to be introduced. Although complicated by the political emphasis placed upon them, the main reasons for altering the way the NHS and supportive social services were organized was the realization that efficiency in the utilization of these services was becoming more important. This is because of two main factors.

Firstly, there is a significant demographic change occurring within the population as the number and proportion of very old people (aged 85 years and over) rises dramatically. In 1978, 1 in 104 persons in the population were aged 85 years and over, by 1992 it reached 1 in 65 and, by the year 2000, it will be 1 in 50, and will peak at 1 in 44 by 2011. The increased demands of this age group for all types of health and social services — in the community, hospitals and in general practice — are well known. The trend not only increases the burden on all these services, but emphasizes the urgent need to prevent further problems developing within this and other groups of elderly persons. This is why there is so much emphasis on community care and the blurring of the boundaries between health and local social services.

Secondly, in the last 20 years, there have been many dramatic improvements in the treatment and prognosis of serious diseases which formerly resulted in early death — particularly among cancers, cardiac and vascular diseases. This has meant that a higher proportion of people are now living longer. This raises a further important question — how to improve the quality of life of those who have to cope with chronic disabilities and illness. This trend is bound to continue and will increase the need for further changes.

Preventive medicine is therefore becoming more important in solving the difficult dilemma of how to provide effective health and social services on an ever increasing scale. The most sensible way to approach this is to broaden the base from which prevention is provided, and this must mean greater involvement of general practitioners and their primary health care teams. When the NHS started in 1948, there were just over 20 000 general practitioners in the UK. This has now risen to nearly 32 000 with all new entrants spending 3 years in vocational training.

Most general practices now have highly developed primary health care teams available to them. There has been a great emphasis placed on training their own staff, and the advent of computers in general practice has facilitated much recall within primary care. The average general practitioner also now has a smaller list of 1890 patients.

If preventive medicine is to succeed, it must not only involve all medical staff in the NHS, but also must be accepted by the general public as being as important as the treatment of acute illness. This will never be easy, but one of the main priorities within the NHS during the next decade should be to achieve such acceptance. Although many approaches can help, one fact will always remain the same — the main point of contact between the NHS and the ordinary individual and family is, and will always be, the general practitioner and the primary health care team. This means that these professionals represent the greatest potential for extending preventive health care.

One of the main objectives of this new edition is to help extend preventive medicine in the NHS by providing a readable and clear account of its main features. There has been a complete revision and update of its contents with five new chapters. At the same time, an attempt has been made to widen the scope of the book by introducing a new approach from one of its authors (T.D.) who is actively working in general practice with the Royal College of General Practitioners and in vocational training in East Anglia.

The format of the book remains the same and is again presented in three parts. Part One covers Community Health and Preventive Medicine, Part Two Public Health and Social Services and Part Three Social Services. The number of chapters has been reduced from 28 to 25 although the length of the book is the same. The five new chapters cover medical audit (Chapter 2), AIDS and sexually transmitted diseases and viral hepatitis (Chapter 11), drug and alcohol abuse (Chapter 17), child physical and sexual abuse (Chapter 23) and homelessness (Chapter 25). Much of the contents of the new chapters (with the exception of medical audit and AIDS) was given in the earlier editions, but each has now been described in greater detail and each covers a whole chapter.

The chapters on the mentally disordered (those who are either mentally ill or have learning difficulties (mental handicap)) (Chapter 16) and on care of the elderly (Chapter 18) have been moved from Part Three to Part Two. This is because the care of such people can only be really effective by a joint approach by both health and social services working in the community.

Other chapter changes include an amalgamation of child health and school health services (Chapter 5) as this represents the modern approach. Also, the chapters on epidemiology of communicable diseases have been altered so that, after a short introductory chapter (Chapter 9), there is now a chapter on the epidemiology of common communicable diseases (Chapter 10) and one on the epidemiology of rare communicable diseases (Chapter 12), as well as one on AIDS, sexually transmitted diseases and hepatitis (Chapter 11).

Health education, environmental health and international health are no longer given separate chapters. In this edition, these subjects have been absorbed into other chapters (mainly in Chapters 7, 8 and 13). The final change has been to dispense with the separate chapters on management within the NHS which is now dealt with in Chapter 1 and with the chapter on management techniques, measurement of need and determination of priorities, which is now described in Chapter 2 on medical audit.

Chapter 1 covers recent changes in the organization of the NHS. Ever increasing demands and expectations continue to outstrip resources. New technology is also costly. To deal with some of these issues the government chose to follow an approach by creating an internal market with 'providers' of health care (hospitals, community services, etc.), separated from the 'purchasers' of such services (District Health Authorities (DHAs) and general practitioner fundholders). For the first time since the inception of the health services, DHAs have to attempt to define the health needs of their population, and then contract to purchase such services as are required. The resurgence of the Directors of Public Health was also a key factor in attempting to rationalize the provision of health care in the new NHS. The Independent Medical Advisors appointed by the Family Health Service Authorities also have a role in deciding priorities in primary health care.

No health service can succeed unless it constantly analyses its results. Medical audit has been developed throughout the NHS with this in mind. Chapter 2 describes the development of medical audit in hospitals, general practice and in community health and within public health since the mid 1980s. The main aim of medical audit must be to examine what is actually being achieved (in terms of patient care) rather than what is being provided by the service (by both staff and finance). It is encouraging to see more professional staff concerning themselves actively with medical audit and with the development of new and more effective ways of measuring the results of their work and how this could be improved. There have also been some laudable attempts to measure and improve patient satisfaction.

Chapters 7 and 8 are indicative of the new approach in this edition. Both have been completely rewritten and extended to describe the rapid developments which have taken place during the last 9 years. All aspects of primary, secondary and tertiary prevention have been fully discussed, with special emphasis on how general practice can provide many opportunities to extend practical preventive health methods. Immunization, prevention of accidents (especially within the home), mental illness and suicide, genetic counselling and the prevention of coronary heart disease are all topics covered in these chapters. Examples of health screening (secondary prevention) are fully illustrated and cover all stages of life — pregnancy, care of the newborn, children, adults and elderly persons. Under tertiary prevention, examples include the management of hypertension and medicinal drug surveillance — a subject that is growing in importance as the number of very old people (who are particularly susceptible) rapidly increases.

Chapter 8 deals with the role of the primary health care teams as well as those professionals who now are usually attached to such teams (health visitors, district nurses, midwives, school nurses, community psychiatric nurses, occupational therapists, physiotherapists, speech therapists and dieticians). The tasks of the practice manager, receptionist, practice nurses and dispensers (in dispensing practices) are also fully described. Chapter 8 also includes a brief discussion on the use and value of the computer in general practice. The Read Clinical Classification (now adopted by the Department of Health) is also briefly explained.

Drug and alcohol abuse are considered in depth for the first time in Chapter 17. Drug dependence is discussed in its widest sense including not only the illegal 'hard drugs' (heroin, cocaine, etc.), but also Type 3 dependence where a drug is initially prescribed medically and originally with no noticeable adverse effects. There is a section on alcohol abuse which especially considers the potential problems of heavy social drinkers and how such people may insiduously drift towards alcohol dependence. The 'unit of alcohol' approach is explained as this is most helpful in highlighting the possible dangers of alcohol.

Chapter 18 on elderly persons contains much new information. It starts with two interesting tables (18.1 and 18.2) which give the latest Office of Population Censuses and Surveys (OPCS) projections of the number of elderly persons over the next 30 years divided into different age groups. These show quite clearly where the main problems are likely to occur — with the very old aged 85 years and over. By the year 2000 this age group will rise by 40.6% compared with the numbers present in 1989 and then by 60.3% by the year 2011. From then to 2021 the numbers will fractionally fall. The consequences for health and social services are bound to be serious, for it is this age group who will always make the greatest demands for these services, irrespective of social class. The last 15 years has seen a large increase in the provision of many excellent pre-retirement courses, and details of their main contents are described. Reference is also made to the fascinating research carried out by Taylor and Ford in Aberdeen in 1980 on a random sample of non-institutionalized elderly persons. This research clearly shows that many of the popular assumptions made about elderly people are untrue. For instance, it did not find that those living alone or in poor financial circumstances or in remote places were necessarily at the greatest risk. A new section is included on confusion and dementia in elderly persons including Alzheimer's disease and the acute confusional state syndrome. A short account is given of the successful community care project introduced in parts of Kent. Many different types of residential care for elderly persons have evolved during the last 15 years and an account of these is given to complete what is virtually a new chapter.

The new Chapter 23 covers all aspects of child abuse (both physical and sexual abuse). Child sexual abuse became headline news in Cleveland in 1987–88, although there is plenty of evidence that it has existed for a long time. The chapter describes in detail the latest Department of Health's advice on child abuse—its recognition, diagnosis and treatment. The changes which followed the findings of the Lord Justice Butler-Schloss Inquiry, and which were enacted in the Children Act, 1989, are also described in detail.

In Chapter 24 on the care and rehabilitation of disabled persons, details are given of an important OPCS survey carried out in 1985–88 in Great Britain. This study estimates that there are 6.2 million disabled people in the country and that most live at home. These figures are a significant increase compared with the Amelia Harris survey of 1968–70. The relationship between disability and advancing years is striking — almost half occurs in those over the age of 70 years and this age group also contains most of the severely disabled persons. It is clear that the demographic changes already described will further increase the number of severely disabled persons in the community.

Chapter 25 now concentrates solely upon homelessness. This is a very complex subject and one which has increased in the last decade despite the 1977 Act which was introduced to control it. Special reference is made to two types of homelessness — that of young people and that of those who are mentally ill, many of whom have been discharged from hospital. Recent research into both of these disturbing trends is discussed.

The remaining parts of the book follow very much the pattern of earlier editions. There are, however, a number of important changes. In Chapter 3, wherever possible, vital statistics are given for the UK rather than for England and Wales. This has been made possible by a change in the pattern of statistics now published by the OPCS who now report much data as UK figures. A further change is the introduction for the first time of many health and social services statistics for Scotland. Many of these statistics come from a recent interesting publication *Deprivation and Health in Scotland* by Vera Carstairs and Russell Morris and published by Aberdeen University Press in 1991.

HEALTH OF THE NATION

An important White Paper, *Health of the Nation*, was published by the Department of Health in July 1992, just as this edition went into production. This introduced the concept of strategies and targets aimed at improving the health of the population during the next decade. The main objective is centred on five key areas and aimed at reducing the incidence and mortality of many serious diseases and accidents including:

coronary heart disease (CDH) and strokes;
cancers, particularly cancer of the breast and cancer of the cervix uteri in women
    and cancers of the lung and skin in both sexes;
mental illness, including a reduction in suicide rates;
HIV infections (and AIDS) and other sexually transmitted diseases (STDs);
accidents to children, young persons and those aged over 65.

Apart from various screening initiatives (see Chapter 7 of this book) and certain corrective treatments (for conditions such as hypertension), the main thrust planned is aimed at improving lifestyles now known to be associated with much preventable ill health including:

cigarette smoking (see Chapter 13);
fat consumption (see Chapter 13 and 14);
weight reduction (see Chapter 13 and 14);
excessive alcohol consumption (see Chapter 17);
sexual behaviour (see Chapter 11);
family planning, the main emphasis being to reduce the rate of conception amongst the under 16s (see Chapters 4 and 7);
reducing the percentage of injecting drug abusers (see Chapter 17).

The following is a brief summary of the main targets and suggested strategies for the next decade.

Coronary heart disease (CDH). (See Chapters 7 and 13.) The aim is to reduce the death rates from CDH in people under the age of 65 by at least 40% by year 2000 (from 58 per 100 000 population to 35 per 100 000). For those aged 65–74, to reduce the mortality by 30% (from 899 per 100 000 to 629 per 100 000).

Strokes. The target is a reduction of 40% for ages up to 75, that is, a fall from 12.5 per 100 000 to 7.5 per 100 000 for those aged under 65 and from 265 per 100 000 to 159 per 100 000 for those aged 65–75.

Cancers. Targets are (a) to reduce the death rate for breast cancers in women aged 50–64 invited for mammography screening (see Chapter 7) by 25% (from 95.1 per 100 000 to 71.3 per 100 000); (b) to reduce the incidence of invasive cancer of the cervix uteri by 20% (from 15 per 100 000 to 12 per 100 000 (Chapter 7); (c) to halt the increase of skin cancers (Chapter 7); and (d) to reduce the death rate of lung cancer by 30% in men under the age of 75 and by 15% in women under 75 by year 2010 (from 60 per 100 000 to 42 per 100 000 for men and from 24.1 per 100 000 to 20.5 per 100 000 for women (see Chapter 13).

Lifestyles closely connected with these diseases are smoking (CDH, strokes, cancers of the lung and cervix uteri) and fat consumption. The targets are to reduce cigarette smoking by all over the age of 16 to 20% of the population (a reduction of 35% for men and 29% for women), and for 11–16 year olds to reduce smoking by 33% by 1994 (from 8% in 1988 to less than 6%). For reduction of fat eaten, the target is to reduce the average percentage of food energy obtained from eating fat by 12% — this is most important to reduce the mortality from CDH and large bowel diseases.

Mental illness. The aim is to improve significantly the health and social functioning of mentally ill people. It is also hoped to reduce the overall suicide rate by 15% and the suicide rate in mentally ill persons by 33% (Chapters 13 and 16).

HIV/AIDS and other STDs. The main target is to reduce gonorrhoea by 20% by 1995. If this can be achieved, it is hoped it would indicate similar trends in the spread of HIV infection (Chapter 11).

Accidents. The main targets to year 2005 are to reduce death rates by a third among children under the age of 15, by a quarter for young persons aged 15–24, and by a third for people aged over 65 (see Chapters 5, 7 and 18).

Perhaps one of the most important features of the White Paper is the emphasis now officially placed on the importance of altering certain lifestyles. Permanent improvements are only likely if everyone recognizes that everyday habits are crucial to achieving good health. This includes not only avoiding such obvious hazards as smoking but also encouraging positive features of life such as healthy eating. It is hoped that this edition will help to emphasize the important messages contained in the White Paper.

Although this edition has been aimed at an extended readership, and particularly at those doctors who are undertaking general practitioner vocational training, great care has been taken to ensure that its contents should continue to meet the needs of the original group of readers — other doctors in hospital and general practice, medical students, health visitors, district nurses and other members of the primary health care teams and social workers. There is a real need for social workers not only to have textbooks on their own subjects, but also to be able to obtain a readable account of modern preventive and community health services. Many of these services are closely interwoven with their own work. Recent studies with child abuse, with disabled persons, with mentally disabled people and with elderly persons have emphasized the need for a better understanding between those working in the health and social services. It is hoped that this book will help to meet this need by providing an up-do-date account of preventive medicine, community health and social services.

We owe our grateful thanks to many people who have helped us with the preparation of this edition. We also particularly thank our wives without whose constant encouragement and support it would have been impossible to have completed this book.

Brian Meredith Davies,   Tom Davies
Liverpool   Yaxley, Peterborough

PART ONE —

COMMUNITY HEALTH AND PREVENTIVE MEDICINE

1

The National Health Service

The National Health Service (NHS) began in the UK in 1948. The NHS employed 793 000 in 1988 and 70% of its costs goes in staffing. The NHS at its inception cost £440 million; in 1990, it is estimated to have cost £29 billion, a four-fold increase after allowing for inflation.

Since 1948, there has been a number of reorganizations, the first major one being in 1974 with the reunification of the public health services and the establishment of the Family Practitioner Committees who took over the administration of general practice from the Executive Councils. Region Health Authorities, Area Health Authorities and District Health Authorities were also created. In 1982, the next major change occurred when the Area Health Authority tier was removed. By 1987 the Griffiths' NHS Management Report of 1983 had been implemented and this introduced into the NHS the concept of a management approach at all levels. Short-term contracts for managers and individual performance reviews and performance related pay for managers were also introduced.

The main objective of the NHS has remained the same throughout all these changes — the provision of a comprehensive health service covering hospital and consultant services, the family health services and the public health services free of cost at the time of need. Small charges are only made for certain features such as prescription charges (payable for less than 20% of prescriptions issued), eye testing and some dental treatment. There is no contracting out of the NHS and it is financed centrally by the Exchequer through general taxation and levies paid from National Insurance Contributions.

In 1988 the Department of Health and Social Security was divided into a Department of Health (DH) responsible for the NHS and personal social services (mainly provided by large local authorities) and a Department of Social Security (DSS), controlling all social security benefits. A separate Secretary of State with a seat in the Cabinet is in charge of each.

Towards the end of the 1980s a series of Green and White Papers (with their subsequent periods of discussion and consultation) were published eventually l~ to the passing of the National Health and Community Care Act, 1990, w' into full operation in the autumn of 1991.

This Act mainly changes the method of organizing the NHS. It also introduced a number of new features, which included:

- short-term contracts for some senior staff
- an extension of the management principle introduced by the Griffith report
- self governing hospital trusts
- new funding arrangements for some larger general practices
- regular medical audit.

This Act did not alter the main principle relating to the NHS mentioned above. This chapter describes the NHS and its organization and emphasizes in detail the more important changes introduced by the Act.

The reorganized Department of Health

Many changes have occurred since 1988 in the Department of Health (DH) and the present organization is illustrated in Figure 1.1.

SECRETARY OF STATE

Under the NHS Act, 1977, the Secretary of State is required to 'continue the promotion in England and Wales of a comprehensive Health Service designed to secure improvements in the physical and mental health of the people of those countries and in the prevention, diagnosis and treatment of illness'. The Secretary of State is responsible for all aspects of health including medical, nursing and dental services, hospital and other accommodation (e.g. health centres/clinics), ambulance services, facilities for the care of expectant and nursing mothers and young children, facilities for the prevention of illness, school health services, family planning services and such other services as are required.

The Secretary of State is answerable to Parliament for the conduct of the Health Services and any Member of Parliament may raise any issue, either as a parliamentary question, through debate or through investigation by one of the independent committees of the House of Commons. The Secretary of State must negotiate with the Treasury for the National Health Service Budget through the public expenditure survey process and should stimulate debate on health care by issuing Green Papers and consultative documents. After such consultation White Papers will be issued indicating the changes the Government wishes to make. Once decisions or new legislation have been passed details of the changes are communicated to Health Authorities and senior staff by Health circulars, Health notices or Executive letters.

The Secretary of State is responsible for liaising on health matters with other Government bodies such as the Ministry of Agriculture, Food and Fisheries, the

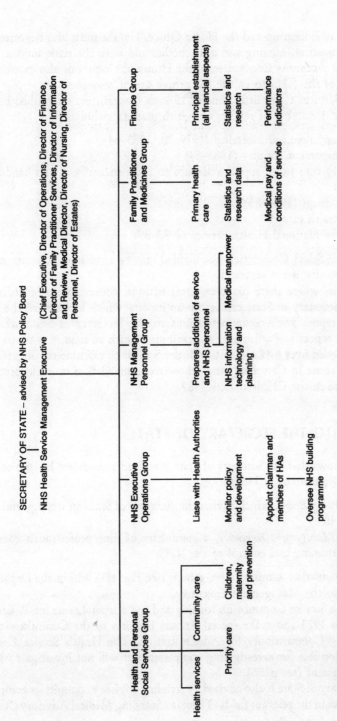

FIGURE 1.1 Organization of the Department of Health under the Secretary of State.

Department of Education and the Home Office. He/she must also negotiate with professional medical, nursing and other bodies and with the trade unions.

The Public Accounts Committee of the House of Commons also examines the expenditure of the NHS to ensure the proper use of resources.

A Social Services Committee, one of 12 such Committees established in 1979, has published a number of reports on health matters including:

- perinatal and neonatal mortality (1979–80, 1983–84)
- NHS management enquiry (1983–84)
- community care (with special reference to adult mentally ill and handicapped (1984–85)
- misuse of drugs (1984–85)
- primary health care
- funding the National Health Service (1988–89).

In 1991 the Select Committee was divided into two, to look at health matters and social security issues separately.

In addition, where there has been great national concern with regard to any subject the Secretary of State can set up an inquiry which looks at all the issues, publishes a report with recommendations to the Secretary of State who later presents that report to Parliament. An example of such an inquiry was one set up in 1987, presided over by Lord Justice Butler-Schloss to examine the allegations of child sexual abuse in Cleveland, and whose recommendation on child protection were included in the Children Act, 1989.

ADVISERS TO THE SECRETARY OF STATE

Figure 1.1 shows that the Secretary of State is assisted and advised by two committees at the Department of Health:

- *the NHS Policy Board*, which advises the Secretary of State on strategy and policy in the NHS
- *the NHS Management Executive*, a committee of nine professionals concerned with the running and control of the NHS.

There are five further administrative groups (see Fig. 1.1) within the Department who report to the Management Executive.

The Health Service Commission for England and a separate one for Wales were established in 1973 and make special Annual Reports to the Committee on the Parliamentary Commissioner for Administration. The Health Service Commissioner is responsible for investigating complaints but will not investigate issues of clinical judgement (see p. 35).

The Secretary of State is also advised by standing advisory committees comprising leading figures in the relevant fields. There is a Standing Medical Advisory Committee (SMAC), Standing Nurse and Midwifery Advisory Committee and a Standing Pharmaceutical Advisory Committee. The Secretary of State may also set up *ad hoc* committees to study special subjects and collect and consider evidence from many sources and to make recommendations in their reports.

A Health Service Commissioner for England, and a separate one for Wales was established in 1973 and is responsible for examining complaints in the health services. They are excluded from dealing with cases against individual doctors and nurses, any action which is dealt with by the central tribunal set up to deal with serious complaints (see p. 35) or any complaint which may lead to legal action.

Detailed organization of the hospital and community health services and general practice in England and Wales

Figure 1.2 illustrates the way hospitals, the community health services and general practice are organized in England. Wales is treated as one Regional Health Authority (RHA). It will be seen that there are a number of District Health Authorities (DHAs) in each RHA which are responsible for most hospitals, community health services and school health services in their area. The detailed differences in Scotland, Wales and Northern Ireland are described on pp. 18–21.

In addition, since 1991, there are increasing numbers of Hospital Trusts responsible for the self governing hospitals. The other large group responsible to the RHAs now consists of the Family Health Service Authority (FHSA), which in 1990 replaced the Family Practitioner Committees, and who are responsible for the general practice services and the dental, pharmaceutical and general ophthalmic services. The detailed organization and responsibilities of the RHA (see pp. 12–13), the DHA (see pp. 13–15) and FHSA (see pp. 21–23) are described later.

CHANGES INTRODUCED BY THE NATIONAL HEALTH SERVICE AND COMMUNITY CARE ACT, 1990 AND THE GENERAL PRACTITIONER CONTRACT, 1990

A number of important changes were made by the National Health Service and Community Care Act, 1990, and the General Practitioner Contract of 1990. They include the introduction into the NHS of:

- self governing hospitals
- funding and contracts
- practice budgets for some general practices
- Indicative budgets for all general practitioners (GPs)

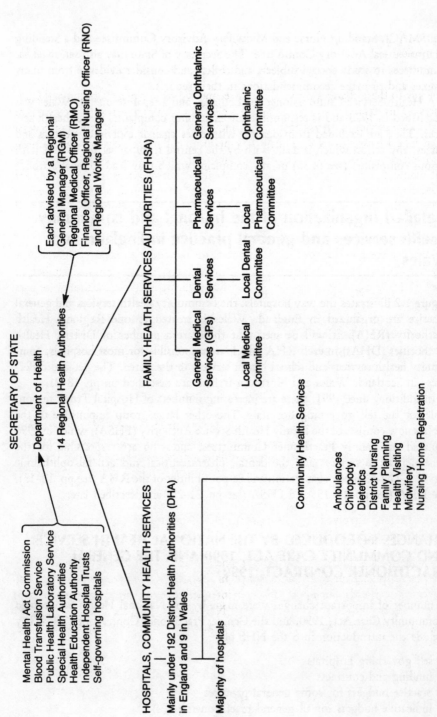

FIGURE 1.2   Organization of hospital, community health services and general practice in England and Wales (see also Fig. 1.1).

- capital charges
- medical audit
- a new chief executive post of General Manager for each FHSA.

The key to these changes is found in the second working paper 'Funding and Contracts'. This expressed a wish to create a clear division between the 'providers' of health care service (such as the hospitals and community units) and the 'purchasers' of such health care, usually a DHA. The intention behind this change was to create competition, which it was hoped would not only improve the quality of services but would also drive down costs and hence allow more services to be provided for the same budget sum. This 'purchaser – provider' arrangement has also been referred to as the 'internal market' within the NHS. A few small pilot studies were held prior to 1 April 1991, the starting time for the changes, but the effects of those changes are still largely unknown.

DHAs are responsible for the health care of their resident population and the purchasing of their care. The cost of treatment wherever carried out will be met by the DHA responsible for the place of residence of the patient (i.e. the money follows the patient). The budget of each DHA is allocated on a basis of their population adjusted for age, morbidity of the area and relative costs of providing that care. The provision of such services is to be arranged according to the need for health care rather than providing what is available. Contracts will be produced between 'purchasers' and 'providers'. There are three types of contract:

1. *Block treatment*, when an annual fee is paid for a predefined range of services, such as pathological services.
2. *Cost and volume contracts* when payments are made for a predefined number of treatments on cases, and extra cases in addition to that number would be funded on a cost per case basis. Costs will be agreed in advance, and for the extra contracted cases, may be at either the 'average' or more favourably 'marginal' cost.
3. *Cost per case contracts* are paid for where there is no existing contract either with the hospital involved, or the treatment is additional to one stipulated in the contract.

There are very precise rules as to how these contracts will be worked out. They must be realistically priced, not subsidized in any way, and will need to cover capital and other overheads. Such procedures are intended to allow direct comparisons between various providers, both within the NHS and the private sector.

Accident and Emergency Department's costs are borne by the hospital itself, but if admission results from attendance at the department for a patient not resident within that health district, the cost is charged to the district of that patient's residence. Complicated billing procedures, highly dependent on rapidly developing computer technology, will be essential to cope with all the work and contracts not covered by the block contracts.

Postgraduate training is protected to ensure that no savings can be made at its expense. Nurse, midwife and health visitor training is reimbursed by RHAs.

Self governing hospitals

These are separate entities and known as NHS hospital trusts. Such hospitals are able to acquire, own and dispose of assets. They have the power to borrow, subject to an annual limit, with the freedom to keep the surplus. They arrange their own management structure, and are able to employ as many staff as they wish. Pay and conditions of employment are left to the individual hospital to determine.

Practice budgets for general practitioners

General practices of greater than 9000 may apply to become General Practice Fund Holders (GPFHs). Such practices are given a budget to manage and spend on the three areas of (a) hospital costs (elective in-patient and day care treatments, out patient services and diagnostic tests), (b) prescribing costs (for drugs and appliances), and (c) a portion of staff costs. From 1 April 1993 most community nursing services (including district nursing and health visiting) will also be charged to GP fund holders.

In 1991 practices were given an allowance of up to £16 000 to prepare for holding a budget, and subsequently an annual allowance of £32 000 for continuing management costs. The total cost of computer hardware for fundholders is also reimbursed, along with 75% of the software costs. Any savings that the practice might make may be spent on improvements, as agreed with the FHSA, for example to enable the practice to purchase extra hospital/staff services. An overspend of up to 5% will be allowed over any one financial year, but the amount will be deducted from the next year's budget. An overspend of more than 5% will be investigated, and may mean the cessation of the arrangement. Exceptional patients, with treatments costing more than £5000 a year will have the excess amount paid by the RHA. In the first year (1991–92) there were 306 practices which elected to become fund holders.

Indicative drug budgets for general practitioners

RHAs are allocated a financial budget to cover expenditure on medicines for the family practitioner services within their region. FHSAs administer each budget, with the responsibility for calculating and allocating the money to the practices in their area. Each practice should receive monthly a computerized breakdown of their prescribing figures. FHSAs appoint doctors to oversee the prescribing in the practices, and visit those practices who do not keep to budget. If there are bona fide reasons for this, the budgets will be adjusted and no further action taken. If the doctor or practice continues to prescribe in what is considered an inappropriate way, the FHSA has the right (as they did under the old contract) to withold some of the doctor's remuneration.

Capital charges

In order to make the cost of health care provision provided under the NHS directly comparable with the private sector and thus facilitate competition between them, there is a consistent way that health authorities must deal with capital charges. Such charges are made up of two parts, capital depreciation and interest. All contracts with hospitals for the delivery of services must include both capital and revenue costs. Detailed asset registers must be set up and published. (Gifts are specifically excluded from such requirements.)

Medical audit

Introduced to cover both primary health care and hospital and community services, the main aim of audit is to enhance the overall quality of patient care within the NHS. Doctors with colleagues should regularly review aspects of their care and work to identify areas in which improvements could be made. Audit is defined as the systematic, critical analysis of the quality of medical care, including the procedures used for diagnosis and treatment, the use of resources, and the resulting outcome and quality of life for the patient. This is fully dealt with in Chapter 2.

NHS consultants, appointments, contracts and distinction awards

To facilitate a clearer understanding of the consultant's position and role vis-à-vis the District General Manager (DGM), the contract of all consultants was rewritten. RHAs are responsible for the appointment of consultants (with the exception of those working for Teaching Hospital Districts), but have delegated to DHAs the task of regulating their contracts. The DGM is responsible for ensuring that an adequate job description has been agreed upon with each consultant, and that it is reviewed annually. The DGM (and more than one if the consultant works in more than one health district) will in future always be a full member of the Advisory Appointment Commitee. Changes have also been made with Distinction Awards; these are for 5 years only and are reviewable. The consultant to hold such an award must show evidence of involvement in management. DGMs now also advise on the awards.

Detailed organization of NHS in England and Wales

REGIONAL HEALTH AUTHORITIES (RHAs)

The health services are administered peripherally through RHAs and DHAs. The Department of Health continues to exercise a great deal of control by financial, advisory and planning methods. Financially the Department supplies all funds, both revenue (for running costs) and capital (for constructing new buildings). Each RHA is given a budget and allocates to each DHA its financial resources. From 1991, hospitals have been given the opportunity of holding their own budgets by becoming NHS Hospital Trusts, and becoming self governing (and are not responsible to region — see p. 10).

Each RHA is administered by a Regional General Manager. The RHA is responsible for:

- allocation of resources, and overseeing the planning and budgets of the DHA, regulating the relationship between purchaser and provider, acting as arbitrators in the event of problems
- monitoring the performance of the DHA, FHSAs (responsible for GPs, dentists, ophthalmic services and pharmacists)
- holding the contracts of consultants, associate specialists and senior registrars (except for teaching hospital appointments), but delegating appointments to DHAs
- capital building projects
- postgraduate medical and dental training
- planning and education of non-medical staff
- ambulance services (unless delegated to DHAs or self governing trust).

Each authority has a Chairman and five non-executive members appointed by the Secretary of State, together with up to five executive members. The General Manager and Chief Finance Officer are ex-officio members. The other members are appointed by the Chairman, Manager and the non-executive members are appointed by the Secretary of State. The officers of the RHA, who advise the General Manager, include the Regional Medical Officer, Regional Nursing Officer, Regional Finance Officer, and Regional Works Officer. The 14 RHAs in England are responsible for populations of between 2 and 5 million and have a budget of £558 million to £1458 millions per year (1990–91). The RHA is not involved in the ordinary day to day running of the health services. Table 1.1 shows the size of each of the 14 RHAs in England, and the percentage of persons aged 65 and over, and Figure 1.3 (p. 14) shows a map of the RHAs.

The size of each RHA varies from 2.0 millions in East Anglia to 5.2 millions in the West Midlands. The percentage of persons over the age of 65 years is also

TABLE 1.1   Regional Health Authorities in England, total population and numbers of people aged 65 years and over, 1988

Regional Health Authority	Total population (millions)	% of persons aged 65 +
Northern	3.1	15.4
Yorkshire	3.6	15.6
Trent	4.7	15.2
East Anglia	2.0	16.1
N.W. Thames	3.5	14.4
N.E. Thames	3.8	15.3
S.E. Thames	3.6	17.7
S.W. Thames	3.0	17.1
Wessex	2.9	17.4
Oxford	2.5	12.6
South Western	3.2	18.5
West Midlands	5.2	14.7
Mersey	2.4	14.9
North Western	4.0	15.4

Data from refs 5 and 6.

different and varies from 12.6% in Oxford to 18.5% in the South Western RHA. This indicates that each RHA is responsible for different types of populations and will therefore require different types of medical services. The percentage of persons aged 65 years and over is 14.9 in Scotland and 15.8 in Wales, whereas in Northern Ireland only 12.2% of the population are in this age group.

DISTRICT HEALTH AUTHORITIES (DHAs)

DHAs are administered by the District General Manager. The DHA is responsible for the day-to-day management of the hospital and community health services. They have no responsibility for NHS Trusts services. Their main functions include:

- purchasing services for their residents
- day-to-day running of hospitals under their control
- maternity and child health services
- community nursing (district nursing and domiciliary midwifery)
- health visiting
- vaccination and immunization
- other community health services and after-care services (chiropody, dental clinics, family planning clinics, occupational therapy, physiotherapy, speech therapy, etc.)
- health education
- school health services

FIGURE 1.3   Regional Health Authorities, England.

- health centres
- ambulance services (where delegated by RHAs)
- appointment of consultants, associate specialists and senior registrars in districts where there are teaching hospitals.

Officers of the DHA

The District General Manager (DGM) is in overall charge of the Authority and is assisted by various Unit General Managers (UGMs) — see below. In addition, each

DHA has the following chief officers: the District Finance Officer, the District Medical Officer, the District Nursing Officer and two clinicians (one hospital consultant and one GP).

Directors of Public Health

The Acheson report, Public Health in England, 1988,[1] recognized that there was a need for the DHA to make decisions based on an assessment of the principal health problems of the population for whom they are responsible. There had been a confusion of the role and place of Community Medicine and Community Physicians, the Committee of Inquiry subsequently made a recommendation which was accepted that every DHA should appoint a Director of Public Health whose main duties would include:

- Providing epidemiological advice to the DGM and DHA, to enable planning of services, and evaluate the outcomes
- Developing policies with reference to prevention, health promotion and education
- Surveillance of non-communicable disease and environmental health problems
- Surveillance, prevention, treatment and control of communicable diseases
- Publishing an annual report for the DHA.

Units of management

DHAs are divided into units of management, looking after a group of hospitals, or the community services in a district. Each unit has a Unit General Manager (UGM), who has overall charge and is responsible for implementation of general management throughout the unit. The unit has a budget allocated and the UGM is responsible for the unit keeping within budget. Further developments, manpower and public relations are also part of the UGM's responsibility.

The structure of units in districts is variable. The community health services units may include:

Health Centre buildings   Dieticians*
District nursing   Child health*
Health visiting   Home nursing aids
Community midwifery*   Welfare foods
Speech therapy*   Incontinence service
Occupational therapy*
Orthoptics*
*Shared with hospital unit

SPECIAL HEALTH AUTHORITIES

There are a few special authorities that are directly responsible to the Department of Health and not to any RHA. They include:

- postgraduate teaching hospitals in London
- the Health Education Authority (HEA)
- the NHS Training Authority (NHSTA)
- the Special Hospitals Service Authority — Ashworth Hospitals (North and South), Rampton and Broadmoor.

OTHER SERVICES ALSO DIRECTLY REPORTING TO THE DEPARTMENT OF HEALTH

The following bodies and services also report directly to the Department of Health (see Fig. 1.1):

- The Mental Health Act Commission
- Health Advisory Service
- Public Health Laboratory Service
- Blood Transfusion Service
- Mental Health Review service.

COORDINATION OF NHS AND LOCAL AUTHORITY SOCIAL SERVICES AND EDUCATION

Important in the administration of each DHA is the identification of gaps in the health service and the development of ways to overcome them. Two types of multidisciplinary teams have been introduced to assist in the analysis of these problems, namely Health Care Planning Teams and Joint Care Planning Teams. The former is made up of professionals working in the district health services and the latter has joint membership between professionals of the DHA and the corresponding local authority services for social services and education.

Health care planning teams

Each DHA sets up health care planning teams to assess the needs of the health services. These may be permanent, looking at children, maternity services, mentally ill, those with learning disabilities (mental handicap) and the elderly. Others may be formed just to look at a specific issue, and will disband after making a report. Examples of this type of team include looking at such issues as day-case surgery and non-accidental injury in children.

Joint Care Planning Teams

Joint Planning was introduced with the reorganization of the Health Service in 1974 in recognition that services provided by local authorities have a considerable impact on health services and vice versa. The inter-dependence made it essential to have effective arrangements for joint planning to ensure the best balance of services and to make the most effective use of the resources available for such groups such as the elderly, the disabled, those with learning disabilities (mental handicap), the mentally ill, children and families, and for socially handicapped groups such as alcoholics and drug addicts. The Joint Care Planning Team comprises officers from the DHA and the local social and education services and reports directly to the Joint Consultative Committee (see below). With the full development of community care as outlined in NHS and Community Care Act 1990, which will be fully implemented by 1 April 1993, it is essential that the closest collaborative working is carried out.

Joint finance

It was recognized that under joint planning, development of certain services would be hindered if it were to be financed from the local authority's ordinary budget. Consequently 'joint financing' was introduced, by which limited and controlled use of resources available to Health Authorities was allowed to support selected personal social services spending by local authorities. Such monies were used to finance local authority projects with the health authority's support tapering off over a period of up to 7 years. Establishment of day centres, and community support centres for the mentally ill, and for patients with drug and alcohol related problems are examples of projects set up with monies from joint finance.

Joint Consultative Committee (JCC)

Each DHA and the corresponding local authority must set up a Joint Consultative Committee which has the responsibility of advising on the planning and operation of the health services and the social, environmental and education services run by the local authority. The FHSAs and voluntary organizations are also represented. The aim of such a committee is to improve co-operation between the services.

JCCs receive reports from the health and local authority services and, in particular, consider reports from the planning team, set up by both authorities. The JCC has no executive power, but has an increasingly important role giving essential advice on ensuring effective joint planning.

National differences within the NHS

In all instances the aims and objectives of the NHS in these countries are similar to those already described above.

SCOTLAND

The Scottish Home and Health Department is responsible to the Secretary of State for Scotland for the administration of the NHS in Scotland. Its head office is at New St Andrews House, Edinburgh.

There are 15 local Health Boards in Scotland which administer the local health services (except those carried out by the Common Services Agency — see below). These Boards take major policy decisions including the allocation of local resources and the long-term planning of services. Many of the day-to-day decisions are taken by the chief officers of each Health Board working together as an executive group.

The Secretary of State for Scotland is responsible to Parliament and there is a Scottish Health Service Planning Council set up to advise the Secretary of State on:

- the identification of health priorities in relation to the resources available and the necessary measures to meet them
- the implementation, review and evaluation of health planning in Scotland's national health services
- the integration of health care with other kinds of care to ensure a co-ordinated policy for the treatment of people in need.

The Council has set up a number of Advisory Groups.

The Common Services Agency

A significant difference in Scotland is that there is a central body, the Common Services Agency, to provide a range of specialized services which are more effectively organized on a national basis. These include dental estimates, ambulance and blood transfusion services, the purchasing of equipment and other supplies, the planning and design of health service buildings, legal services and health education. Responsibility for the administration of these services rests with a management committee appointed by the Secretary of State. The Common Services Agency whose headquarters are at Trinity Park House, Edinburgh, has several separate units including the Scottish Health Services Council, the Scottish Health Education Unit, the Communicable Diseases (Scotland) Unit, the central Legal Office of the Health Services in Scotland and the Information Services Division.

In addition there are:

1. A series of local area consultative committees to advise Health Boards on the provision of services in their area. These represent doctors, dentists, pharmacists and ophthalmic and dispensing opticians. Such committees advise on all professional matters.
2. University liaison committees which advise on undergraduate and postgraduate teaching and research.
3. A series of 48 local health councils which represent the 'consumer' interests of patients.

Integration of services

In the Scottish health services much emphasis has been placed on integration of services at patient level and not only at senior management level. All services are planned to meet the needs of patients and to make the best possible use of staff, financial and physical resources. Team work in all aspects of the health services is stressed as well as the involvement of doctors and clinical workers in management matters.

WALES

There are important differences between the health services in England and Wales. In Wales there is no regional tier of health authority. The Secretary of State for Wales has overall authority to Parliament for the health services in Wales. He has four main duties:

- to determine the health policies in Wales
- to allocate resources between the nine District Health Authorities in Wales
- to ensure that the objectives of the services are achieved
- to ensure that the standards of health service in Wales are satisfactory.

There are nine District Health Authorities in Wales (population figures in parentheses):

Powys (111 300)   South Glamorgan (390 400)
Clwyd (392 200)   West Glamorgan (369 700)
Gwent (440 100)   East Dyfed (225 100)
Gwynedd (234 100)   Pembrokeshire (107 500)
Mid Glamorgan (537 000)

These DHAs are responsible to the Secretary of State for Wales for all the day-to-day health services, with the exception of those undertaken by the Welsh Health Technical Services Organization (see below).

District Management Teams (DMTs) act in a very similar way to those in England with the addition that a senior member of each health profession is appointed locally to give advice to the DMT and to the DHA on all matters that are relevant to their profession.

The Welsh Health Technical Service Organization is directly accountable to the Secretary of State for Wales and has three main functions:

- the designing and building of all major hospital and other capital building works for the health services in Wales
- the control and running of a central computer service for the health services in Wales
- the negotiation of all central supply contracts for the health services in Wales.

NORTHERN IRELAND

In Northern Ireland a unified structure exists which is outside local political control dealing with the hospital, family practitioner, community health and social services. The probation and education services are not included. At provincial level, the DH acts as government agency and also like an English RHA, being responsible for policies and the allocation of resources. There are four Boards, each consisting of 30 members all appointed by the Secretary of State. Approximately one third are drawn from local government District Councils, one third from the professions and one third from industrialists, trade unions, voluntary bodies and the universities. Each Board is responsible for planning, delivering and monitoring the health and social services. Each Board has an Area Executive Team consisting of four chief officers of equal status, a Chief Administrative Officer, a Chief Administrative Medical Officer, a Chief Administrative Nursing Officer and a Director of Social Services. Each Board has from three to six Districts dealing with the day-to-day delivery of health and social services. District committees consist of local members of the public and are non-executive, but act as a focus for local opinion. Various district professional officers make up the District Executive Team and are individual subordinates to the corresponding Chief Officer at Board Level.

This combined structure has attracted much attention and has resulted in more positive moves towards multidisciplinary assessment and more flexible use of all the various facilities in each Board such as hospitals, homes, hostels, day care units, day nurseries. It has also resulted in better understanding between all those working in the health and social services.

The overall structure of the NHS is shown in Figure 1.2.

Community Health Councils (CHC)

These important bodies were introduced in 1974, following the NHS Reorganization Act, 1973. There is one CHC for each DHA in England and Wales. In

Scotland, Local Health Councils are the representative bodies and District Committees undertake their role in Northern Ireland. The Community Health Councils have three main aims to act as:

- the representative body for the general health interests of the resident population
- the NHS 'users' ' representative
- an independent and confidential advice agency for NHS 'users' (patient's friend)

Each CHC contains between 18 and 30 members. At least 50% are appointed by the relevant Local Authority, with a third of members appointed by the voluntary organizations. The names of the Chairman and members of the CHC must be publicized. The RHA will pay for the expenses of the Committee, and members of the RHA, DHA and FHSA are excluded from membership.

There should be friendly consultation between the DHA and each CHC, and there should be annual meetings between the two bodies. Members of each CHC are encouraged to visit or inspect premises under the control of the DHA, such as hospitals, offices, laboratories, health centres, clinics and staff residential accommodation. They may at any time publish reports on any matters they wish, and are required to publish an annual report, to be sent to the RHA and DHA and made public. The public are entitled to attend the CHC meetings.

The areas with which the CHCs may have an interest are summarized below:

- effectiveness of the health service provision
- planning of the health services
- variation in local health services
- closure of hospitals, or changes in arrangements for treatment
- collaboration with education, social and health services
- standards of services
- patient facilities such as waiting times, amenities for visiting, overnight stays, etc.
- catering standards
- complaints
- patient advice.

Administration of general practice in England and Wales – Family Health Services Authority

The Family Health Services Authority (FHSA) is responsible to the RHA for administering the following services:

- general medical services
- general dental services
- pharmaceutical services
- general ophthalmic services (see Fig. 1.2).

From 1 April 1991, the FHSA became accountable to the RHA, rather than as previously when it was directly responsible to the Department of Health. This was with specific aim of bringing primary care and hospital services together at a strategic level. There are 100 FHSAs in England, 15 in Scotland, 8 in Wales and 3 in Northern Ireland. Every FHSA consists of 11 members, all appointed by the Secretary of State. There is a Chairperson, a General Manager, five lay members and four professional members — a GP, a dentist, a pharmacist and a community nurse.

The General Manager is a full-time officer and is responsible for the day-to-day administration of the FHSA. An innovation (since 1991) is that the General Manager is a voting member of the FHSA. Like other general managers in the NHS, he/she acts as a chief executive and is on a rolling short-term contract.

Each FHSA must also appoint an Independent Medical Adviser (part-time appointment) whose main task is to help and advise the FHSA who must (a) assess the needs of their populations, (b) develop services to meet those needs, (c) ensure that quality services are provided efficiently and cost effectively, and (d) work closely with DHA and local authorities.

Doctors wishing to set up or join an existing practice to serve as a principal in the NHS must apply to the FHSA. In summary, the FHSA's role includes:

- administering the contracts of service of GPs and controlling the number practising in its area
- monitoring and auditing the behaviour of their GPs
- inspecting all surgery premises
- allocating funds for staff and for practice improvements
- supervising the registers of services provided by GPs in addition to general medical services; maternity, contraception, minor surgery and child health surveillance are the present examples
- holding the contracts of GPs who choose to become budget-holders, and have the responsibility of checking expenditure against budget
- setting up Medical Audit Advisory Groups (MAAGs) to support and monitor the medical audit procedures of its practices
- supervising the indicative prescribing budgets for GPs
- helping practices with the introduction of information technology; this includes the allocation of a grant of up to 50% of the costs, dependent on the practice size
- providing information to the public, and dealing with complaints made by patients.

The FHSA is required to meet at least four times a year and members of the public have a right to attend as observers.

GENERAL PRACTITIONERS

In 1989 there were 31 500 GP principals providing free medical care under the National Health Service in the UK. In addition there were 2292 trainee GPs. The

TABLE 1.2   Number of general practitioners in England; analysis by type 1967–89 as at
1 October

	1961	1967	1977	1982	1985	1990
All practitioners	20 865	20 026	22 327	24 835	26 190	27 523
Unrestricted principals						
Total	18 905	18 629	20 796	22 786	24 035	25 622
Single-handed	5337	4406	3419	2967	2915	2975
In partnerships of:						
2 doctors	6384	5310	4198	3922	3880	3865
3 doctors	4008	4647	4917	5102	4986	4581
4 doctors	1984	2640	3872	4380	4352	4543
5 doctors	715	890	2420	3220	3610	4107
6 or more doctors	450	736	1970	3195	4295	5551
Restricted principals						
Total	679	559	290	206	169	149
Assistants	1084	724	375	266	228	190
Trainees	197	114	866	1577	1758	1562

Data from ref. 4.

proportion of women GPs has doubled from 1968 to 1983 from 9.8% to 17.6%. The average list size for each GP continues to decrease by 30 patients a year. In 1989 the average list size in the UK was 1910. Of all GPs in the UK, over 75% work in group practices of three or more, and this compares dramatically with only 23% in 1948 (see Table 1.2). In rural areas a doctor may dispense medicines and certain appliances for those patients who live greater than a mile from a pharmacist. Approximately 11% of GPs provide dispensing services for around 7 million people.

Under the NHS every person has a right to be registered with a GP and 97% of the population are registered. The GP is usually the first point of contact for patients and most referrals to hospital and specialist care are from general practice. Each patient on average consults his doctor approximately four times a year, but there are noticeable differences according to age, sex and region. Regionally, Northern Ireland, Wales and Scotland have an average overall consultation rate of over five per year.

The FHSA is responsible for the registration of patients with a GP, and issue a medical card to the patient with the name of the doctor with whom they are registered and their NHS number.

GPs must offer adequate times when they are available to see patients in surgery, and these hours must be approved by the FHSA. They must practise from adequate premises, and render all necessary treatment of the type normally given by GPs. They must provide prescriptions where necessary, and also certain certificates according to the regulations. Sickness certificates must be provided free of charge, but others may be charged for.

Terms of service of general practitioners

From 1 April 1990, the terms of service for a GP were significantly changed in many respects.[2] Once a doctor has accepted a patient, he/she is required to render to that person all necessary and appropriate personal medical services of the type normally provided by general medical practitioners. A greater emphasis on preventive medicine has been incorporated into the terms of service. Thus, GPs must give advice, where appropriate, to any patient about their general health and especially on diet, exercise, smoking, alcohol and the misuse of drugs.[3] Every GP should also offer new patients a consultation and examination for the purpose of identifying those at special risk of disease or injury. Vaccinations should be offered where appropriate. The doctor must also give advice to patients so that they can take advantage of services provided by the social services department of the local authority.

The FHSA is required to keep a list of doctors practising in the area, the Medical List, which must indicate additionally which doctors provide contraceptive services, child health surveillance, minor surgery and maternity services (except in an emergency). These services are *not* part of the basic terms of service for doctors in general practice. This list is available at the local FHSA headquarters and main Post Offices and libraries, where it may be examined by any members of the public to help in their choice of a doctor.

A new feature (since April 1990) is that further medical examinations are also required to be offered to the following:

- newly registered patients (for patients aged over 4 years within 3 months of registering)
- patients aged 16–74 years who have not been seen within 3 years (to be offered each year)
- patients aged 75 years and over must annually be offered a home visit.

Every GP is responsible for ensuring adequate medical cover in their absence on holiday or for sickness. Every doctor must provide proper and sufficient surgery premises, including waiting room facilities for his patients. Rent which is assessed by the District Valuer plus full rates are directly reimbursed.

Records of the illnesses of the patients must be kept. The doctor must provide free of charge certificates needed under the National Insurance Acts and many other statutes. Charges may be made for other certification. GPs are also required to produce a practice leaflet and an annual report.

Practice leaflets

Since April 1990 a practice leaflet must be produced and made available to patients. This should contain full details of the doctors, including their sex, qualifications and first date of registration as a medical practitioner. The following practice information is also required:

- times that the doctor is available
- appointment system details, and how to obtain urgent and non-urgent appointments
- details how to obtain both an urgent, and non-urgent visit
- how to obtain repeat prescriptions or in the case of a practice that dispenses, the dispensing arrangements
- clinic details
- number of staff and their roles
- details of whether the doctor provides maternity medical services, contraceptive services, child health surveillance services and minor surgery services
- arrangements for the doctor or staff to receive patients' comments on the provision of general medical services
- geographical boundary of the practice
- details of wheelchair access for disabled patients
- if teaching of GP trainees or students takes place.

Annual reports

Each practice must also by the end of June each year send an annual report to the FHSA. The report should contain:

- information of all the staff assisting the doctor, their qualifications and training in the preceding 5 years
- changes in the practice premises in the preceding year
- referrals made to hospital, the total number referred as in-patients, the total number referred as out-patients. Such referrals are to be further subdivided according to the clinical specialty
- the total number of cases in which patients referred themselves to services under the NHS Act 1977 (usually Accident and Emergency departments)
- doctor's other commitments as a medical practitioner with reference to outside posts and description and annual hourly commitment of such work
- arrangements for the doctor or practice staff to receive patients' comments on the provision of general medical services
- information about orders for drugs and appliances, whether the doctor's practice has its own formulary, and the arrangements for the issue of repeat prescriptions.

General practitioner vocational training

Since 1982, all new principals to general practice must have completed an approved training scheme or be exempt because of equivalent experience. The training is either done through a formal 3-year vocational training scheme based on a District hospital, or may be organized individually, working in different hospitals with a year's trainee post in general practice. The formal vocational training scheme involves trainees spending a 3-year period divided between general practice, junior hospital training posts and day-release courses. Suitable hospital posts include general medicine, paediatrics, obstetrics and gynaecology, geriatrics, accident and emergency and psychiatry. The compulsory year's training in general practice is often divided between a short initial 2–3 months in one practice followed 2 years later by the final 9- to 10-month period.

Distribution of family doctors

The Medical Practices Committee (MPC) in London is responsible for the overall distribution of doctors throughout the country. Each area of the country is classified according to the number of doctors practising, as follows:

Designated — Where more doctors are required, with financial incentives given to start practice.

Open — An area where the doctor has an average list size of between 2100 and 2400 patients. Application to practise would be granted.

Intermediate — An area where the doctor has an average list size of between 1700 and 2100. Special circumstances will be considered before granting permission.

Restricted — An area where the doctor has an average list size of less than 1700. Additional doctors are not considered necessary and entry into practice is only through a vacancy in an existing partnership.

A doctor wishing to start a new practice, or apply for a vacant single-handed practice, must first apply to the FHSA, who after consultation with the Local Medical Committee (LMC), will forward it to the MPC with its recommendations.

Size of practice

A limit of 3500 is fixed on the total number of patients any single-handed doctor may have on their list. If a GP employs an assistant, and the permission of the FHSA must be obtained to do this, the limit of the allowable list size is raised by a further 2000 patients.

Choice of doctor

The public have a completely free choice of doctor and the doctor also is free to decide whether or not to accept the patient on to his or her list. Similarly the doctor is free to remove a patient from the list without having to give any reason. If patients have difficulties in finding a doctor to accept them, they can apply to the Allocation Committee (another sub-committee of the FHSA) which will then allocate them to a convenient doctor. A doctor thus allocated such a patient must look after them for at least 6 months.

Local Medical Committee (LMC)

One of the most important committees of any FHSA is the LMC which acts as the local medical advisory committee to the FHSA. It consists mainly of doctors practising in the area and the chairman is invariably a GP. There are representatives of the consultant services and it is usual for the District Medical Officer also to be a member. Any difficulties connected with particular practices or with local policies are usually referred to this committee which then advises the FHSA. In the same way, the Secretary of State may ask the LMC to investigate a complaint that a GP has not exercised sufficient care in certification. Other similar expert committees help with the administration of the dental services (the Dental Services Committee), the pharmaceutical services (the District Chemists Contractors Committee), and the ophthalmic services (Optical Committee) (see Fig. 1.2).

Remuneration paid to general practitioners

Payments paid to general medical practitioners may be classified as follows:

Practice Allowances
Capitation Fees
Items of Service Payments
Sessional Payments
Reimbursements
Grants.

Practice allowances

These include:

Basic practice allowance — payable to all GPs provided they have 1200 patients registered.
Designated area allowance — to encourage doctors to practise in under-doctored areas.

Limited practice allowance — (two types for maximum 4 years) to assist doctors setting up or filling a single-handed practice in a designated area.

Inducement payments — for GPs who have to practice in an area where the practice size is bound to be less than 1200 patients (i.e. a sparsely populated rural area).

Rural practice payments — paid to a doctor in rural areas if more than 20% of the patients reside 3 miles or more from the surgery.

Seniority payments — three-stage allowance, payable from the time the doctor has been in general practice, for 7, 14 and 21 years, respectively.

Other allowances — other allowances include the Associate allowance for single-handed (or job sharing) GPs, Assistants allowance for the employment of a full time assistant where the list size is large.

Capitation fees

Capitation fees (payment per person registered), are intended to account for 60% of the GP's pay.

Standard

The maximum number of patients for which a doctor is paid is 3500 (or the average number for a partnership). Differential payments are made for the following age groups: over 75 years, 65–74 years age group and those aged below 65 years.

Items of service fees

Immediately necessary treatment — paid where a patient who is not registered with the doctor is treated or advised.

Vaccinations and immunizations — this fee is paid according to the type of immunization given and dependent, in children, on a target figure of either 70% or 90% of children being protected (see below).

Emergency treatment fee — for treatment given in an emergency to a patient who is in the area for less than 24 hours.

Dental haemorrhage fee — for the arrest of a dental haemorrhage.

Night visit fee — is paid for visits requested and carried out to registered patients and temporary residents between 10.00 p.m. and 8.00 a.m.

Contraceptive services — payable quarterly for female patients receiving contraceptive services. Two fees payable, the higher rate fee for the fitting of IUDs.

Maternity medical services — the fee is dependent on the type of service provided and the length of time supervised. Higher rates payable to GPs with obstetrics experience and who are on the obstetrics list.

Temporary resident fees — two rates, payable for patients staying up to 15 days and up to 3 months.

Target payments

These were introduced in 1990 and are as follows:

	Higher	Lower
Cervical Cytology	80%	50%
Childhood Immunizations	90%	70%
Pre-school Boosters	90%	70%

Cervical cytology targets apply for women patients aged between 25 and 64 years in England and Wales (21–60 in years Scotland), who have been given an adequate smear test within the previous 5.5 years. Women who have had a hysterectomy are excluded from the target population. The test may have been taken by anyone, including agencies out of the practice (hospital, family planning clinics, etc.). These smears will count towards the target, but not towards the payment.

Immunization target payments are made for all children aged 2 years on the first day of each quarter. The children must have been fully vaccinated (three doses for diphtheria, tetanus, polio and pertussis, and one dose for measles or mumps, measles and rubella). Children immunized at local authority clinics count towards the target but not towards payment.

Pre-school booster target payments are made for all children aged 5 years on the first day of each quarter.

Sessional payments

These were introduced in 1990 and include the following.

Minor surgery

The GP must have applied to the FHSA and been accepted for inclusion on the Minor Surgery List. A minor surgery session comprises at least five surgical procedures (from an agreed list), performed at one or on separate occasions in the same quarter. This may be for the GP's personal list, or for his partner's patients. A GP *may only claim three such payments each quarter.*

Health promotion clinics

GPs may claim a fee in respect of any health promotion clinic provided for patients on their personal list, or any other patient registered with the practice. Clearly defined protocols should have been submitted to the FHSA who have discretion to determine which clinics qualify for payment. Generally these clinics should last at least an hour and attract a minimum of 10 patients. Activities which attract a separate fee (e.g. family planning, cervical cytology) do not qualify for payment.

Reimbursements

Drug tariff — payable monthly for drugs supplied to patients on doctor's NHS dispensing lists.

Rent, rates, water and sewerage charges — directly reimbursed to doctors owning their premises. In health centres, the District Health Authority is reimbursed by the FHSA.

Ancillary staff — previous to 1990 this had been limited to 76 hours per week staff time per doctor; 70% of the gross salaries together with 100% of employees contributions to National Insurance and some Superannuation costs were reimbursed. Each practice now must make its own case for what staff they wish to employ. The FHSA decides how much of the staff's salary it wishes to contribute to.

Grants

Improvement Grant — up to one third of the cost of buildings' improvement is payable, depending on set standards, with a minimum and maximum amount which can be paid.

Training Grant — payable to a doctor who employs a trainee GP and who is responsible for the training. The trainee salary is reimbursed and an allowance given for the motor car required.

Deprivation area payments

This new payment was introduced with the new GP contract in 1990 to reward GPs practising in less than favourable circumstances, and who are likely to deal with more difficult patients. These payments are made for each person living in a particular ward in England or Wales (postcode sector in Scotland) identified as having a Jarman index score of more than 30. Described by Professor Barry Jarman the score is based on eight variables obtained from the census data. In the first year, £25.5 million was made available for such payments; 9.1% of the population in England and Wales, and 11.4% of Scotland's population was covered by such payments. The eight variables (which reflect how the GP's workload is increased) are:

Old people living alone
Children aged under 5 years
Single parent households
Unskilled people
Unemployed people
Overcrowded houses
People who have moved house
Ethnic minority households.

Indicative Prescribing budgets

In order to place a 'downward pressure' on expenditure on drugs prescribed by GPs, in April 1991 the government introduced the Indicative Prescribing Scheme, whereby each practice is allocated a sum to cover the costs of drugs for that year. This money is initially allocated to the 14 Regions, and subsequently the money distributed to the FHSAs to calculate the set amounts for each practice. The sum chosen should take into account such factors as the previous prescribing history of the practice, its demographic pattern, the referral rates of patients to hospital, the number of patients in need of unusually expensive medicines. If RHAs and FHSAs exceed their firm budgets, this will not result in reductions in the provision of existing services to patients elsewhere as the drug funding is kept entirely separate from other NHS expenditure.

Each FHSA, through its own independent medical adviser, will advise practices on prescribing should they so wish. Each GP will receive monthly drug prescribing information. GPs who exceed the amount set for them will not be penalized unless there is clear evidence of excessive prescribing. Any such case is referred to a professional commitee of the FHSA, comprising three doctors. Where excessive prescribing is established, the FHSA may withhold remuneration from the practice, but this rarely happens and is used as a last resort measure.

Prescription charges

A prescription charge is made for every prescription, but those exempt include:

Women aged 60 years or over, and men aged 65 years or over
Children under 16 years, or under 19 years and in full time education
Those in receipt of Income Support, or Family Credit
Pregnant mothers, or women who have had a baby during the last 12 months
Those suffering from a defined list of conditions including:
   Permanent fistula requiring surgical dressings or appliances
   Epilepsy on treatment
   Continuing physical disability which prevents the leaving of the home alone
   Diabetes mellitus treated with either insulin or drugs
   Myxoedema
   Diabetes insipidus
   Hypoadrenalism (Addison's disease)
   Myasthenia gravis

Over 80% of all prescriptions do not attract a prescription charge.

Two pre-payment certificates may be obtained, one covering 4 months and one for 1 year. The 4-month certificate represents a saving if five or more prescribed items are needed in that time, and the annual one is cost effective if 15 or more items are needed in a year.

COMPLAINTS PROCEDURES

There is a central Tribunal set up by the Secretary of State with a chairman who must be a barrister or solicitor of at least 10 years' standing. The FHSA may refer cases of doctors, dentists, chemists and opticians, if they consider that such persons should no longer be employed within the NHS because of inefficient practice. The Tribunal holds an inquiry and, if it is satisfied that the report is serious enough, can suspend the person from practice within the NHS. In such a case, there is always a right of appeal to the Secretary of State.

Informal procedure for complaints — a proportion of complaints should be investigated informally and each FHSA must appoint one of its lay members to assist the General Manager of the FHSA to do this. This informal stage should not normally take longer than a week or two. If the complaint cannot be satisfactorily resolved informally, the formal procedure described below must be used. Some cases of complaint may, from the start, appear to indicate so serious a state of affairs that an informal inquiry would be inappropriate.

Formal procedure for complaints — each FHSA must appoint a Medical Services Committee which consists of a lay chairman from the FHSA acceptable to both sides, plus six other members, of whom three must be from the LMC. The Medical Services Committee has the responsibility of investigating any complaints raised by a patient about the service given to them by their doctor.

There is a set procedure laid down for the investigation of such complaints. The hearing is always in private and the doctor's name is never made public to avoid damaging their reputation, which could happen even if they were completely innocent and the complaint was frivolous. After the hearing, the Medical Services Committee reports its finding to the FHSA which then sends its decision to the Secretary of State. The doctor has the right of appeal to the Secretary of State. In the case of the proved complaint, one of the following actions can be recommended to the Secretary of State who then decides:

1. A sum be deducted from the doctor's remuneration to cover the expenses of the complainant only, and the doctor may be warned.
2. A further sum be withheld from the doctor's remuneration.
3. A special limit, as to the number of patients on the doctor's list, be imposed (this is rarely done).
4. Reference to the Tribunal that in the opinion of the FHSA the doctor should not be permitted to continue in the NHS. The Tribunal then decides on the facts.

The doctor may appeal to the Secretary of State against actions 1, 2 and 3 above, but not against action 4.

It is important to stress that the Medical Services Committee is only empowered to inquire into an alleged failure of a GP to comply with the terms of service under the National Health Service Acts. It has no power to deal with matters of civil or criminal law or with professional disciplinary matters dealt with by the General Medical Council (GMC).

The FHSA is also responsible for three other professional groups, namely the dentists, opticians and pharmacists.

GENERAL DENTAL SERVICES

In 1990, there were about 18 500 dentists providing dental treatment under the NHS in the UK. Over 40 million courses of treatment are carried out annually at a cost of £1.2 billion in 1990–91. Patient charges account for 38% of total general dental services and 43% of the cost was on conservative treatments (e.g. fillings, etc.).

A new dental contract was introduced on 1 October 1990, the first significant organizational change since 1948. Patients may now register with a dentist. Initially for adults this is for 2 years, and for children every year. Registration continues as long as the patient continues to see that dentist. Adults will receive more information about their treatment in the form of a written treatment plan. A patient who is registered on a dentist's list is entitled to free emergency dental treatment, although this will not necessarily be with the registered dentist personally. The dentist is obliged to inform the patient of what services are available and where in such an event. Replacement free of charge for certain restorations within a year is allowed for adults. A charge was introduced for adult dental examinations. The dentist is now paid a capitation fee for each child registered, instead of being paid solely by item of service for treatment given. They are also required to produce a practice leaflet.

The advantages to the dental profession include (a) a move away from 100% item of service payments (it is intended that 20% of their income will be accounted for by continuing care and capitation fees), (b) direct reimbursement of business rates from April 1991, and (c) new NHS payments for maternity leave, long-term sickness leave and a voluntary early retirement scheme.

Assessment of fees for approved treatment is done by the Dental Practice Board (DPB) based in Eastbourne for England and Wales, the Scottish DPB in Edinburgh and the Central Services Agency in Belfast. The introduction of the new contract has meant a reduction of some 95% in the number of treatment items for which the dentist needs prior permission. From April 1991 the boards have paid the dentists direct.

A voluntary vocational training scheme for dentists started in 1988, with over 400 estimated dentists on 37 regionally based programmes by the end of 1990.

People who are entitled to automatic free dental treatment include:

- children under 16 years (or under 19 years if still in full-time education)
- patients on Income Support or Family Credit

- pregnant mothers, or women who have had a baby during the 12 months before the treatment began.

GENERAL OPHTHALMIC SERVICES

The FHSA holds an ophthalmic list with names of ophthalmic medical practitioners (OMPS) and optometrists (opthalmic opticians). There are some 500 OMPS, 6300 optometrists and 3500 dispensing opticians in the UK. Much of the service has been deregulated, but only registered opticians may provide glasses for children under the age of 16 years. As from the 1 April 1989, free NHS sight tests are only available to the following groups of people:

- children under 16 years, or under 19 years and in full-time education
- those in receipt of Income Support, or Family Credit
- those with a valid Department of Social Security exemption certificate AG2
- those registered as blind or partially sighted
- diagnosed diabetic or glaucoma patients
- those aged over 40 years and the parent, brother, sister or child of a person with diagnosed glaucoma
- those people requiring a prescription for complex/powerful glasses
- patients of the Hospital Eye Service.

Other persons can apply for help with optical costs if they are on low income. Help with the eye test, and a voucher for some of the cost of treatment may be available.

PHARMACISTS

There are some 11 800 community pharmacies in the UK. Under the 1986 NHS (Amendment Act) each FHSA established a Pharmacy Practices Sub-Committee which considers applications for new dispensing contracts from both pharmacists and doctors and considers relocation applications. New contracts are only issued when the needs of the neighbourhood are not being met and the new pharmacy is 'necessary or desirable'. Patients are free to choose whatever pharmacist they wish to dispense their NHS prescriptions. Under their contract the pharmacist is obliged to dispense all prescriptions presented when they are open, maintain minimum hours of business and take part in a duty rota scheme where the FHSA or Health Board considers this necessary.

Community pharmacists are paid according to the number of NHS items they dispense, but some rural pharmacists may also claim a Rural Allowance. Payments for dispensing relate to the (a) 'net ingredients costs', (b) a dispensing fee, (c) a container fee, and (d) 'on costs'. The pricing is undertaken by the Pricing Bureau in

Newcastle, and payment made by the FHSA. Similar arrangements exist for dispensing doctors.

Health Service Commissioners (Ombudsmen)

Separate Health Service Commissioners for England and Wales have been set up by the National Health Service Reorganization Act 1973 to investigate complaints against the relevant health bodies. Both these Commissioners are only removable on an address from both Houses of Parliament and their salaries are paid directly out of the Consolidated Fund. They are therefore in the same independent position as High Court Judges.

The main functions of the Health Service Commissioners are to investigate:

- an alleged failure in a service provided by a relevant body — RHA, DHA, FHSA, Public Health Laboratory Service Board
- an alleged failure of a relevant body to provide a service which it was a function of that body to provide
- any other act taken by or on behalf of a relevant body in a case where it is alleged any person has sustained injustice or hardship in consequence of the failure or of maladministration.

It is important to note that the Health Services Commissioner is specifically excluded from dealing with:

- professional complaints against decisions of individual doctors or nurses in regard to individual patients
- any action which is dealt with by the Tribunal set up to deal with serious complaints
- any complaint which is subject to action in a court of law.

Complaints may be made to the Health Service Commissioners by the patient, his relatives or a friend or by a member of any hospital staff. The Health Service Commissioners will only investigate a complaint when the complainant remains dissatisfied after the health authority has had an opportunity to investigate the complaint and reply to it.

References

1. Public health in England: the report of the Committee of Inquiry into the future development of the public health function (Cm 289). London: HMSO. 1988.
2. Department of Health. Terms of service for doctors in general practice. Para 13.2 (a). 1989.
3. Department of Health. General practice in the National Health Service. The 1990 Contract. 1989.

4. Department of Health. Health and Personal Social Services Statistics for England, 1991. London: HMSO. 1991.
5. Central Statistical Office. Annual Abstract of Statistics. London: HMSO.
6. Central Statistical Office. Regional Trends 1988. London: HMSO.

2

Medical Audit

The National Health Service and Community Care Act, 1990, requires all doctors and other staff in the National Health Service (NHS), whether working in hospitals, in primary health care (general practice), in the community or in public health services, to carry out regular audit of their work from 1991.

The differences between medical audit and traditional review

The concept of medical audit is not new as all good doctors and other staff have always attempted to improve the care they provide for their patients by periodically assessing their work. It has long been realized that this can only be carried out effectively by analysing their results from time to time (traditional review). Yet the new system of medical audit being introduced into the NHS is different from traditional review in several important ways:

- medical audit is a more formal process which takes place simultaneously and continuously within all parts of the NHS
- it covers all aspects of the NHS
- it concentrates on measuring the practical results of the health services (outcome measurement).

Any methods of improving patient care have to be developed within the following three constraints:

- the financial services available
- the trained staff (doctors, nurses and other staff) working in the local health services
- the capital resources available locally — hospitals, clinics, day centres, equipment of all kinds, etc.

The differences between medical audit and traditional review can be summarized as follows:[1]

Medical audit	*Traditional review*
Explicit criteria are used for all measurements	Implicit judgements are mainly used by individual clinicians
Comparisons are converted into various forms of numerical measurements wherever possible	Not usually done
Comparisons are particularly made between similar health services	Rarely attempted
The aim is a clear identification at the end of each audit of the action needed to improve the particular health service being undertaken	Not undertaken in most reviews
A full formal recording of all information is made so that future annual medical audit can refer back to a base to estimate whether the service has improved	Such regular recording and comparison on an annual basis is very rare

Generally the traditional review is a very blunt instrument which only works well when sudden and dramatic improvements are made (such as the introduction of certain antibiotics) or when some near disaster occurs producing sudden and inescapable complications (such as serious side effects of some drugs).

Reasons for the present emphasis on medical audit

It is important for all health staff to realize the reason for introducing medical audit now after 45 years of the NHS. In spite of a steady development and improvement in the NHS, and although financial and staff resources are now greater than ever before, the shortfalls at present are large. There are many reasons for this including:

- The current demographic changes occurring in the population mean there are now more very old people alive in the UK. It is those over the age of 85 years who make the greatest demands on any health service. The numbers of people in this age group have increased since 1978 from 1 in 104 of the population to 1 in 65 by 1992 and will reach 1 in 50 by the year 2000.
- The many past successes in medical treatment in a number of different diseases (such as hypertensive disease, chronic bronchitis, neoplastic disease — the cancers) means that many more of the population now reach the age of 80, and an increasing proportion of these have chronic handicapping conditions which make a heavy demand on the health (and social) services.

- The emergence of completely new and very threatening diseases as natural mutations occur among viruses has added to this burden. The last decade has seen a classic example of this with the arrival of HIV and AIDS. This disease has not yet become a heavy medical and nursing burden on the NHS in the UK, but it has frightening potential and could produce heavy financial and staff problems during the next 15–20 years.
- There are ever increasing improvements in standards in society generally and people naturally demand better medical and nursing care.

All these features mean the NHS can never afford to remain static if it is to continue to meet the health needs of the nation. It is because the NHS has reached this critical stage that unless more effective measurements of clinical care can be evolved which will identify those services which urgently need improving, then any future development of the NHS is bound to be haphazard and disjointed, and probably will be unevenly spread throughout the UK. Medical audit is considered to be the most likely way that this dilemma could be resolved as it is aimed at testing all our health services and at demonstrating how the weakest ones could be improved.

None of this will be easy, especially the development of effective measures to quantify the results of clinical and nursing care (outcome measurements). Many have cynically stated that it will never be possible to measure fairly clinical care. However, doctors, nurses and other key staff working in the clinical field must lead the search for effective methods of outcome measurement for they alone fully understand the difficulties of clinical care. Solutions worked out by clinicians and nurses will be most likely to be accepted by the rest of their professional colleagues. The worst option would be the imposition of forms of audit by managers and other bureaucrats.

It is encouraging to see how many medical bodies have realized how essential it is for them to help develop effective forms of medical audit. These include the BMA, the Royal Colleges, the Universities as well as many individual consultants, general practitioners (GPs) and public health specialists.

The following parts of this chapter describe the progress already made in medical audit and gives details and examples of successful audits that are now taking place. Examples are given of medical audits in:

- hospital and consultant services
- District Health Authorities
- general practice and Family Health Service Authorities (FHSAs)
- public health medicine.

In addition, this chapter also covers:

- problems of medical audit
- educational value of audit
- outcome measurements.

Structure and features of medical audit

There is a classic cycle of medical audit illustrated in a report of the Royal College of Physicians[2] which includes four stages — the setting of standards, observation of practice, the comparison of standards and the implementation of change. Such a cycle repeated annually should ensure that the standards of all health care are checked each year and improved. This cycle illustrates many of the main principles of any learning process but, in medical audit, rarely is it as simple as the cycle suggests. The main difficulty is in the setting up of standards. It therefore seems sensible if a further cycle is added dealing with the setting of standards (see Fig. 2.1).

It will be seen that the two cycles join at the 'setting of standards' stage and, therefore, this should always be the starting point of any medical audit. This is important because it ensures that early in the process of any audit, the crucial question is always asked 'What is the main aim/objective'? But the answer to that question will differ depending on whose interests are being considered. And it can never be a satisfactory answer 'that the aim is to improve the quality of health care' for that only begs the question — is the aim in the interests of the doctor and other health staff, of the overall NHS (and Government who funds the service) or of the patient? Unless this dilemma is realized, the whole audit and its conclusion can become unreliable.

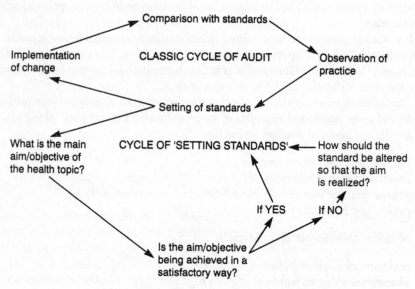

FIGURE 2.1   Modified cycle of medical audit. Redrawn from ref. 2.

STANDARD OF SERVICE

As medical audit is essentially a comparative process, it is important at the start to define clearly the standard of service (treatment, immunizations, etc.) to be aimed at. The new General Practitioner Contract introduced in April 1990 moved significantly in this direction by changing the basis of payment of immunization and cervical cytology so that is now dependent upon the results achieved. If 70% of children in any practice are immunized against certain diseases (diptheria, whooping cough, polio, measles, mumps and rubella) then a lower fee per immunization is paid rising to a higher fee when 90% and over are protected. Results below 70% do not now attract any fee. These levels have been agreed because little general community protection of children follows unless at least 70% are immunized. It is only when the 90% level is reached that these diseases become rare. A similar approach has been made in respect of fees for cervical cytology of women aged 25–64 years. Here the lower fee is paid when the 50% level is reached and the top fee when 80% are examined.

Linking such standards to the levels of payment quickly emphasizes how important it is constantly to aim at such results. It also reminds DHAs and FHSAs which areas of their districts need a special effort in health education to persuade the people living there of the importance of preventive measures.

The setting of standards of clinical care in general practice will never be easy, but it helps if more doctors have access to better information about their patients. Therefore, the introduction of computers into general practice will make medical audit easier. From April 1990, all patients aged 16–74 years must be invited to attend the practice centre for a medical check up, while for those aged 75 years and over, the GP must arrange an annual appointment (or visit) (see p. 24). GPs will for the first time, be able to carry out epidemiological studies in their practices as they will have far more information about their patients. As medical audit develops, the whole process of evaluation and enquiry will improve and this must be of benefit.

CONSTANT ANNUAL REVIEW

An annual repetitive review of all types of medical services is planned within the NHS and this should:

- identify health services which are not producing satisfactory results; this immediately raises the question of whether there is a better way to plan this service
- give an indication of the amount of work (and therefore, cost in terms of time, expertise and finance required) of different forms of health care
- identify which services should be given high priority; these will be services which give excellent results and may also be economical of staff

- assist postgraduate medical education because all repetitive evaluation and assessment is in itself very educative
- identify the inequalities of health care within any district or practice.

OUTCOME MEASUREMENT

It is most important that medical audit should measure exactly what is being achieved, not just what is being carried out in the health services. In the past, most reports on the NHS have stressed how much more money is now being spent or how more consultants, GPs or nurses are now being employed. Behind such statements lies the assumption that the more resources — staff of all kinds and capital (hospitals, health centres) and money — that are provided, the better will be the result. This is only partly true and the main reason for health audit is to test this assumption.

Results are the important feature of all medical audits and assessments. Therefore, how many patients have attended any out-patient department or have been in-patients in a hospital, or have been tested in some way (such as cervical cytology) or have been immunized is relatively unimportant compared with how much disease is now present and whether a higher proportion of patients are now being effectively diagnosed and treated successfully. Concentration on results is referred to as *outcome measurement* in contrast to the various forms of medical and nursing work undertaken in the NHS (*input measurement*).

The sudden burst of activity in all forms of medical audit within the NHS now being carried out by most doctors and other staff is encouraging for this is bound to lead to better forms of outcome measurement being developed. This is one of the most likely ways for the NHS to develop into a more effective service and one which will better meet the health needs of the nation.

Types of medical audit

There are four main types of medical audit:

- reviews of random selected medical records
- reviews of any health topic
- detailed analysis of all types of medical statistics with special reference to:
  - different parts of the UK
  - different socio-economic social classes within the UK population
- studies designed to ensure that the NHS is organized in such a way as to obtain the best value from its resources (staff, capital, available financial assets).

REVIEW OF RANDOMLY SELECTED RECORDS

Before any review of randomly selected medical records is started, it is important to agree first the format of the review.[3] This will usually involve pilot studies organized by a senior clinician assisted by colleagues (in any large hospital this means a wide range of specialties).[3, 4]

At an early stage full confidentiality is essential.[3, 5, 6] Complete trust must be created, for in any large group of professionals (such as a hospital with its various consultants), personal rivalries and ambitions will be present. An interesting by-product of successful medical audits is that trust improves[3] and with it the opportunity to make the audit more useful. But equally, an ill-conceived and badly planned audit will be likely to produce the opposite results. This is why careful and tactful preparation is so essential at the pilot stage.

One particular difficulty which always occurs is how to define 'adequate health care'. It may be necessary to revise definitions already agreed after any pilot study has taken place. Wherever possible, individual subjectiveness should be reduced to a minimum, although it may be impossible to exclude it completely. Any definition of 'adequacy of health care' should be based on an agreed aim or objective of the health service studied and particularly how certain types of patients should be treated. Unless this aspect is first carefully examined, results may be misleading as one clinician may treat a patient with a poor prognosis conservatively while another might attempt a more radical surgical treatment (with completely different immediate risks).[3] Unless this trap is avoided, the results of any medical audit may be difficult to rely on simply because the basis for comparison has been faulty as like would not have been compared with like.

In very large reviews involving many clinicians, even if the audit is carefully planned, inevitably one person may assess the same patient's progress differently, and in this way bias may occur. One method of reducing this problem is to measure the degree of change[3] rather than assessing the level reached. Rarely will experienced clinicians fail to agree on the direction of change (improvement or deterioration or unchanged), and if this is measured on some agreed numerical scale, the results will be comparable and the initial level into which the patient was placed will no longer be crucial.

A DETAILED REVIEW OF AN AGREED HEALTH TOPIC

This can be either a prospective or a retrospective study.[7] Any retrospective review must necessarily rely on the quality of the medical records available, and these can vary considerably. Two advantages of a prospective study is that it can be devised to record similar (and therefore comparable) material[4] and that it can include an assessment of patient satisfaction. Although this may be difficult to quantify, it can however be a vital part of any audit for such a study gives an indication of the degree of communication between clinicians and patient. This is important as the success of many treatments depends largely on the complete trust and co-operation of the patient.

Audits of specific health topics can be either in depth, or, as in the case of the Confidential Enquiry into Maternal Deaths[11] (see below), can be a regular continuous review over a long period.

AN ANALYSIS OF VARIOUS HEALTH STATISTICS

Medical audit also extends to studies of the level of health care in different areas and regions of the country. An analysis of such statistics forms the basis for health measurement (see Chapter 3). Much of this type of audit compares the health levels in either different parts of the UK and/or in different sections of the community based on the incidence of disease or its mortality. This gives a comparative indication of the rate of discovery of illness and the success of its treatment in different areas, occupational groups and social classes.

An example is given by comparing the perinatal mortality rates in various health districts over the years 1986–88. A wide variation is found with the lowest rates in Huntingdon (5.1) and Oxfordshire (5.3) to the highest in Burnley, Pendle and Rossendale (13.1) and Bradford (13.5).

The National Audit Office[8] commenting on these figures points out that such a range of low perinatal mortality rates cannot be explained by socio-economic factors alone. Such differences therefore indicate an urgent need for more active and positive audits on this topic, especially in areas which have shown a constant high perinatal mortality.

Differences between the various occupational groups (see p. 92) or social classes (see p. 91) have been well documented over many years. Even more disturbing is the recent 10-year follow-up of the findings of the Black Report[9, 10] which emphasized the inequalities in the health of sections of the population remain or are increased. There is certainly a need to improve and extend such public health audits of districts and to identify and define the action needed locally to remedy any health problems. The insistence in recent legislation for every Public Health Director in each DHA to submit in future an annual report on the state of public health is aimed at encouraging the development of new medical strategies locally. Such reports should also include periodically the results of audits of the success or failure of various initiatives of health education carried out locally.

Another example of a long-term and very successful community medical audit is the latest report on Confidential Enquiries into Maternal Deaths[11] in the UK from 1985 to 1987 (see pp. 108–109). This report is the longest running continuous medical audit (probably in the world) for it started in England and Wales in 1952 and has been published continuously covering 3-year periods. The latest report has been extended to include the whole of the UK. Originally each maternal death was carefully analysed by an independent consultant obstetrician and senior medical officer of health (now by a Director of Public Health). This audit has concentrated upon defining which maternal deaths were avoidable or preventable. The whole series makes fascinating reading because it has brought to light the repetitiveness of many of the mistakes as well as the dramatic fall in maternal mortality over the last 35 years (in 1955 the maternal mortality rate was 67.1 per 100 000 births whereas the rate for 1985–87 was 7.6 per 100 000 births — a fall of 883%). It seems most likely that this improvement must have been accelerated by these continuous audits which have highlighted errors — the importance of immediate careful follow-up of non-attenders at antenatal clinics, the unnecessary deaths from hypertensive disease of pregnancy, and the need first to resuscitate mothers after severe haemorrhage and in ectopic pregnancy before removal to hospital.

What is so significant is that, as maternal deaths are now extremely rare, without such continuous reminders, such incidents would almost certainly have been dismissed as unavoidable because they were 'very rare accidents' when, in reality, between 50% and 60% of these deaths are known to be preventable if only everyone concerned with the birth (including the mother) had followed the well-established guidelines governing maternity care in all its aspects.

PRIORITIES WITHIN THE NHS

It has already been suggested that, for many reasons, it is unlikely that the NHS will ever have sufficient resources to meet every need (see pp. 38–39). Therefore, priorities must become increasingly important. No system of priorities can become really effective until better information of the needs of the local health services is available. It is here that medical audit should show up the true value of the clinical and other work being undertaken. In other words it is most important to find out what locally is being done well and what is being done badly. Once such information is known then priorities usually set themselves, e.g. the main task is to improve the weaker parts without, at the same time, reducing the effectiveness of the better parts. If there is no effort made to find the priorities (i.e. changes are left to traditional methods of development), the most likely end result will be further improvements of the better parts of any health service leaving the weaker ones relatively unchanged. This is because the most effective parts tend to attract the best staff because of their reputation and because increased finances and resources (staff and equipment particularly) tend to follow the best examples of health care. Indeed, many great medical centres of excellence and research have developed in this way. This is fine for any University system or private or voluntary organization as no one would wish to stifle the best. But it cannot be the correct way to develop a nationwide general health service, such as the NHS, which should have as its main goals the development of an effective and sound health service covering all specialties, general practice and districts throughout the UK.

The most constant criticism about the way the NHS has developed during its first 45 years is that, although there have been many excellent examples of first class health care, these have been variable over different geographic areas and among various specialties, primary health care services and preventive health services locally.

A further advantage of any effective medical audit within, for example, a hospital service, is that communication between the different parts quickly improves as the various specialties become more used to working together.

Medical audit within the NHS – practical considerations

The present system of medical audit within the NHS is planned to:

1. Involve actively all parts of the NHS – hospital and consultant care, supportive health services (blood transfusion units, pathological and viral and bacteriological laboratories), community health services of all types, public health care, nursing services and ambulance transport as well as all the FHSA services – primary health care general practitioners), pharmaceutical and optical services.
2. Have constant link with the Royal Colleges all who have recognized[2] 'that resource management and medical audit are the cornerstones of better management and better patient care'. The Royal Colleges have also agreed that 'audit must remain the responsibility of clinicians and will continue to be a prime responsibility of the colleges'. It has also become the official policy of the Royal Colleges[7] to make regular medical audit a condition for the recognition of any hospital department for specialist training.

The Universities and research bodies have also come out strongly in favour of medical audit.

The Kings Fund set up a Medical Audit Programme in January 1989 which aims at identifying current activities (primarily in the hospital sector), disseminating practical information and establishing links with professional bodies by helping them draw up guidelines for audit. A publication *Medical Audit. A Hospital Handbook*[12] has been published by the Kings Fund who are also active in arranging workshops for local clinicians responsible for local audits. An audit exchange service is also available – details are obtainable from Dr Shaw, Director Medical Audit Programme, Kings Fund Centre, 126 Albert Street, London, NW1 7NF.

Central Government, especially through its Audit Commission[13] and the Health Advisory Service, has initiated certain enquiries and medical audits. The Audit Commission is mainly interested in implementing beneficial changes at local levels of the NHS. Special studies have already been held including day care and pathology services. Plans for 1991–92 include acute bed management and the integration of the community health services. In each study, a research team has been set up which particularly concentrates upon the variability of performance. Information and views are sought from the Royal Colleges, Universities and the Department of Health, as well as local clinicians and nurses (and staff interested in the study).

The Audit Commission is independent of those working in the NHS and its various reports have been circulated to all parts of the NHS, Royal Colleges, Universities and other experts who assisted with the studies. The first report on 'Day Surgery' was very well received as the Royal College of Surgeons acquired 12 500 copies to circulate to their members.

Examples of medical audit in the NHS

The following accounts illustrate recent successful examples of medical audit within the NHS:

In hospitals
In a DHA
In FHSA and general practice
In public health services.

Space does not allow many details to be included, but there are many successful medical audits now being constantly repeated in the medical press. The *British Medical Journal* (BMJ) has been publishing weekly a series of excellent articles since October 1990 under the heading 'Audit in Practice',[14] and all doctors should watch this feature for many helpful news items and topics on medical audit.

MEDICAL AUDIT IN HOSPITALS

A recent example of an interesting medical audit is that undertaken at the Central Middlesex Hospital in 1988–90 on medical in-patients.[3] After a 6-month pilot study which mainly concentrated upon medical records, certain defects were identified: the filing of medical records was poor, notes on drugs and allergies were inadequate, and information to patients and relatives was insufficient. On the other hand, the pilot study showed the standard of clinical management was high.

The main audit was launched in February 1989 at a general meeting of over 40 doctors drawn from all specialties and grades, and the interest also attracted geriatricians and paediatricians who attended. A scoring system (from 1 to 9) was agreed in an attempt to quantify results. During the main medical audit two meetings a month were held — a general meeting and one dealing with a specific medical topic. The meetings on topics proved more popular and covered pulmonary embolism, gastrointestinal bleeding, acute asthma, hypoglycaemia, strokes, myocardial infarction and overdose. Some interesting and vigorous differences emerged in these topic meetings on what was 'optimal clinical management'. There was no doubt that these meetings improved postgraduate education, especially for junior medical staff.

The lessons learnt included the development of 'a closely defined set of minimum standards for clinical notes that had the full support of the medical staff'.[3] Most staff agreed that following this audit there was a general improvement in standards. A follow-up controlled blinded study has been started to test whether this improvement can be attributed to the audit process. One valuable conclusion reached was that 'improved record keeping undoubtedly benefits continuity of care and serves as an important medico-legal requirement, as well as being a prerequisite for other forms of audit'.[3]

One of the most perceptive comments from this excellent paper is that 'the classic elegance of the audit cycle — observing practice, setting standards, improving practice and observing practice again — is far more muddled in the real world. The stages of the audit cycle interact in complex and subtle ways. For example, we inevitably used implicit standards in making observations; the very act of observation seemed to improve practice; and agreed standards were tempered by the feasibility of improvements.[1]

Such an observation sums up very well the experience of many others and should help to stimulate many more to persist in detailed medical audits however time consuming and difficult they may seem.

MEDICAL AUDIT IN A DHA

By 1991, as suggested by Working Paper 6 of the Audit Commission,[13] it is expected that all DHAs will have appointed a district medical audit committee. Such a body should foster medical audit within the district. The committee should be chaired by a senior consultant, have representation from all the major specialties, include a GP, have also a doctor representing the District General Manager and include a patient representative.

In Brighton DHA, medical audit started in the Royal Sussex Hospital in 1984, and the experience of this early audit committee proved to be very helpful in setting up the present one.[5] The choice of the right chairperson is crucial, it should be a senior consultant with in-patient beds (not a retired individual) who is prepared to spend sufficient time (about one session per week). The chairperson should be interested in medical audit and certainly not passive, or worse, obstructive. Examples of medical audit district topics which have been tackled by the present district medical audit committee in Brighton and the earlier one include:

- a district resuscitation policy to prevent overzealous resuscitation
- improving communication with GPs

- standardization of good clinical practice (with work manuals prepared for junior staff)
- steps to ensure that information given to patients and their relatives is better recorded
- ways to reduce excessive hospital stays
- promotion of day surgery.

An urgent district priority emerged — the setting up of effective mechanisms to correct deficiencies disclosed by the audit process and to monitor further results.

This medical audit, like so many others, soon identified a number of problems including:

- a lack of standardization of data
- how to ensure its accuracy and comprehensiveness
- co-operation from colleagues can be difficult, mostly because medical audit takes time — this can prove to be almost overwhelming in some instances.

If medical audit in a large hospital is to succeed, there must be complete co-operation and support from all the doctors concerned. Even at the lowest level, the 7 years of medical audit expertise in Brighton has shown that district medical audit improves efficiency and communication within the profession locally. A further bonus found is that it facilitates teaching in the hospital. However, as with so many other audits, this one concludes that it is vital 'that the present crude measures of appropriateness of medical treatment are developed'. However difficult, adequate time must be made available for effective medical audit — 'time to allow clinicians the luxury of really being able to think about the quality of care that they provide'.[5]

MEDICAL AUDIT IN GENERAL PRACTICE AND THE FHSA

From 1991, medical audit within general practice has been co-ordinated by a new medical audit advisory group (MAAG) which will be a committee of the FHSA.[14] In the MAAG there are 12 medically qualified members most of whom are general practitioner principals, appointed after consultation (to ensure they have the confidence of the local profession). The group should always contain doctors with recognized skills and experience of medical audit, and the group should also contain a consultant associated with audit activities in local hospitals, and a public health physician. There should also be a representative of local and regional educational organizations as liaison with those responsible for postgraduate education is important.

By 1992, it is expected that all GPs will be engaged in regular medical audit in some way within their practices. The local MAAG must:

- ensure that there are adequate procedures to protect complete confidentiality — this is very important

- arrange for mechanisms to remedy problems disclosed by the audit
- provide regular reports to the FHSA on the general progress and results of the audit programme.[14]

Detailed work of the medical audit advisory group (MAAG)

Apart from the three main tasks already described above, each MAAG may actively carry out audits covering all the doctors in any FHSA. One such survey was recently undertaken in Leeds[15] where 317 GPs helped with the survey (82% individual response, 88% practice response). Of these, 65% thought that medical audit would be a good way of improving the quality of care given to their patients. The survey showed:

- basic information systems were well established in the practices of Leeds; 86% of doctors had age and sex registers and 49% had a computer in their practice
- there was experience in medical audit amongst the GPs of Leeds
- some expertise was also present in drawing up disease registers, disease management policies and prescribing policies
- much data collection was, however, haphazard and little use had so far been made of the potential opportunities for medical audit from this data.

The main problems shown by the survey were that there was:

- a need to collect and compare all the facts from the various data collections in individual practices
- no forum for discussing the findings of audits undertaken and their implications
- a problem is that many GPs in Leeds do not have meetings with neighbouring practices; indeed a few did not even have regular meetings within their own practice
- an urgent need to organize peer reviews among colleagues where measured performance can be discussed; these were thought to be difficult to set up and that in a city as large as Leeds a skilled medical audit co-ordinator would probably be needed.

The planning of medical audit in general practice

The aim of medical audit in general practice is essentially the same as in other parts of the NHS — to improve the quality of care given to patients as well as encouraging all staff in the practice team to question constantly what is being done and achieved. However, because general practice is the first referral point for anyone to receive care, the relationship between all members of the practice team and the patient is always very important. Therefore, medical audit in general practice must not only concern itself with the quality of clinical care (diagnosis and treatment), but especially with all practical factors which may encourage or deter any patient from seeking help.[15] For instance, how available is the doctor and other practice staff (practice nurse, health visitor, district nurse, midwife) to any patient? Medical audit should, therefore, involve actively all members of the practice team — GP, practice manager, nurses and receptionists.

For many years, there has been general encouragement (strongly supported by the Royal College of GPs) to produce improvements in the smooth running of general practice which has been called 'quality assurance'.[12] In 1989, the more formal system of medical audit was introduced in every practice in the UK. The main difference between quality assurance and medical audit is that whereas during the 1980s the best and most progressive GPs were tentatively developing systems of improving their practices, medical audit introduces generally a system which will be a continuous analysis and review, on an annual basis, of the way any practice is run so that a constant check is being made on the quality of health care provided.

Steps in medical audit in any particular general practice

Many excellent short handbooks have been published describing different approaches to medical audit in a general practice.[3, 16-18] All stress the importance of following a set of well-tried stages which can be summarized as follows:

1. *Identification of various problems* — these cover a wide range: whether patients can easily obtain help (accessibility), non-attendance when patients fail to return (immunization, various follow-up examinations) whether certain methods of diagnosis produce results and why some treatments do not work properly.
2. *Setting the priorities* — as in many parts of the NHS, it is rarely possible to correct immediately all problems, so some system of priorities has to be worked out.
3. *Choosing the best methods of collecting information* — this is essential to enable problems to be discovered early and to remedy new difficulties. Sound sources of information should also make it possible later to check whether the changes introduced have succeeded in correcting the problem (see stage 5).
4. *The setting of standards and the checking of them* — this stage can be difficult and time consuming. Adequate standards can only be reached after much study and consultation, not only between members of the practice team but with other GPs (peers) and comparisons with the standards recommended by the Royal College of General Practitioners or those laid down in the contract.
5. *Comparing standards* — standards which are being reached within the practice with the standards decided in stage 4. This will enable a check to be made.
6. *Defects and deficiencies* — if defects and deficiencies are identified after the first five stages, then the practice team must decide what is the best way to correct them.
7. *Final stage* — the final stage is a further assessment to check whether the corrective action has been successful in remedying any deficiencies. At the same time,

a quick evaluation should take place to make certain the problem is unlikely to recur.

Where there are large numbers of GPs, it will be necessary for smaller local audit groups to be set up in addition to the MAAG. In all instances confidentiality will soon be shown to be very important. Because all audit is examining performance in practices, suspicion and uncertainty are bound to arise and deter some GPs from involving themselves too actively, especially in 'peer reviews'. It is therefore essential that audits are designed so that they are seen to be a positive force to help GPs rather than to inspect them and find faults.[19]

Undoubtedly as medical audit develops in general practice, the need to improve procedures which give GPs more information about their patients will become obvious. This should lead to universal age and sex registers and a further expansion of the use of computers to collect and analyse the medical records. Practice managers and their supporting staff will have a very essential part to play in most audits in general practice. Although the aim of audit in general practice is to improve clinical care, this can only be done if the delivery of health services is well organized.[20] Medical audit must, therefore, consider many features such as reducing the wait for routine appointments (i.e. improving access for patients to see a doctor or nurse), ensuring certain patients have regular reviews of their treatment, checking that various preventive targets are reached (immunizations, cervical cytology, mammography). All these would be in addition to checking that certain standards of clinical care are maintained (an example might include ensuring that all patients on hypertensive treatment are seen by a doctor at least annually).

One feature about medical audit in general practice is inescapable. It provides an opportunity for the GP to stimulate advances in clinical care and particularly to improve the one part of medical audit which is especially difficult — to develop effective outcome measurements of clinical care so that review and audit can show clearly exactly what is being achieved.

MEDICAL AUDIT IN PUBLIC HEALTH MEDICINE

Medical audit in public health medicine is similar in its process to the rest of the NHS but it has some marked differences.[8]

- most of the aims to improve public health depend on the co-operation and services performed by many other agencies or bodies; these can be in the clinical, preventive, educational, environmental, social or economic fields
- time periods over which results may be expected are usually much longer than in clinical areas of the NHS
- many different fields of medicine are involved — communicable disease control, child health, non-communicable disease control, maternity services, training,

community care, health care of elderly and physically handicapped and mentally disordered persons

Many public health physicians (PHPs) work in multidisciplinary fields covering both NHS and social services.

Structure of medical audit in public health medicine

Again many similarities exist — the same basic audit cycle (see p. 40) is largely appropriate. Most studies used are based on medical and sociological scientific methods. In these, all conclusions and results should satisfy three important criteria:

- validity
- reliability
- repeatability.

It is expected that, as experience develops in the field of audit of public health medicine, University academic departments will play an important role in the development and examination of such criteria.

Standards and guidelines[2]

As in all medical audits, the determination of standards and guidelines is very important and should be the starting point of any study. Some standards are universally accepted[21, 22] (national targets for immunization or cervical cytology), but others are more nebulous and need developing. As far as possible, all standards or targets should be capable of being expressed numerically (as with immunization and cytology) and then tested over the following years to see if they are achieving their purpose. This is the only certain way of developing effective outcome measurements.

Methods and types of medical audit in public health medicine

There are many kinds of audit carried out in public health medicine and these cover:

- examination of the annual planning cycle — many developments in the public health medical field depend on identifying particular local problems, such as why the screening for cervical cytology has a very low uptake in certain parts of a DHA, or why the concentration of accidents in children is unevenly distributed.
- priorities and the most important problems to be tackled locally
- review of the annual report of the Director of Public Health of each DHA — this should highlight various problems and how these should be reduced

- retrospective and prospective studies: the final analysis might cover any exceptional event which has recently occurred in the DHA — for example, a serious outbreak of some communicable disease which could indicate lessons to be learned and this could lead to modifications in standards and guidelines for the future
- examination in detail of any specific health project or topic in the DHA
- various training programmes: here the Faculty of Public Health Medicine advisors play a part as there is already a system of annual audit of training in all departments which also rules upon the suitability of certain posts for senior registrar in public health medicine.

Educational aspects of medical audit in public health medicine[8, 23]

As medical audit in public health medicine must always involve many other disciplines, it can act as a useful means of prompting the principle of prevention in all clinicians whether in hospital or general practice.

It also acts as:

- a method of continuing postgraduate education of public health physicians and trainees
- a reminder that consumers themselves (the general public) need constant encouragement to use effectively local preventive health services. Unlike in the case of acute clinical conditions, there is never the same urgency in preventing illness, and ignorance, procrastination, lethargy and unwillingness to use useful local preventive health services can be a powerful deterrent to the development of effective public health services. This is particularly the case in screening, such as cervical cytology, where the take-up is always very low in social class V (with a consequent increase in mortality — see p. 91).[21, 22]
- a reminder that as so many opportunities in preventive medicine depend on factors in other branches of the health services, successsful public health audit must always consider how better information can help to persuade colleagues to develop more preventive health care in their practices or specialities.

Outcome measurements

As with all other medical audits, effective outcome measurements are crucial and are generally considered to be very difficult to achieve.[18] Reference has already been made to a need to introduce a 'numerical approach'. Many public health activities are capable of being assessed in such a way provided the correct approach is made. Most medical screening can be assessed in this manner, but one needs to measure the degree of prevention in terms of three main factors:

- practicability
- population acceptance
- cost effectiveness

Annual medical audit provides the ideal opportunity to test out such measures, however artificial they may first seem to be. Trial and error is most likely to lead to advances in outcome measurement which can then become a general national method of finding out what are the most effective public health measures.

QUALITY OF LIFE AND PATIENT SATISFACTION

In the clinical field, many doctors have emphasized how difficult it is to measure outcome. Alan Williams of York University has called for long-term follow-up of patients' health in terms of improved life expectancy. That, of course, is relatively easy, but it is equally important to assess also the quality of life gained. There is increasing evidence that women, who consistently live longer than men, suffer from a greater degree of physical handicap in their last years. It would therefore seem helpful if the expectation of life of both sexes could be divided numerically into two groups — active life (with an assumed high quality of life) and relatively handicapped life, in which the quality of life is considerably lower.

Although initially many clinicians doubted whether patients (as consumers) could judge satisfaction adequately, and therefore such a measure should not be used as an outcome measurement, the views of many following medical audit experience is changing. As already mentioned earlier, patient satisfaction is not only useful as a measure of whether the patient is contented with the treatment, but also because where satisfaction exists it means that trust in and co-operation with the doctor will be at a high level.[20] This is always indicative that any treatment advocated will probably be carefully carried to completion.

In the NHS, there will always be patients, doctors and health staff, and 'the overall NHS' to consider, and it will never be easy to achieve a correct balance between all three interests. There is, however, an undeniable trend developing which was clearly reflected in the title of the White Paper 'Working for Patients' — that more consideration should be given to the interests of patients. This trend is likely to continue and to strengthen if the advice in working Paper 6 of the Audit Commission (1989)[13] urging district medical audit committees to appoint a patient representative is followed. The involvement of such a representative in the detailed consideration of all aspects of a medical audit may well be difficult, or even impossible, because of the need for absolute confidentiality. It remains, however, essential for all doctors concerned with detailed medical audits to realize the strength of this trend and always to consider the question of 'interests' from at least the patient, doctor, and 'NHS overall' in that order. In the long term, nothing less is likely to be acceptable politically.

References

1. Shaw CD. Criteria based audit. Br. Med. J. 1990, **300**: 649–651.
2. Royal College of Physicians. Medical audit – a first report, what, why and how. London: Royal College of Physicians, 1989.
3. Gabby J, McNicol MC, Davies SC, Spiby J. What did audit achieve? Lessons from preliminary evaluation of a year's medical audit. Br. Med. J. 1990, **301**: 526–529.
4. Bennet J, Shaw CD. Guidance on what should be in the clinical records for the Brighton Health Authority. Medical Record and Health Care Information Journal. 1987, **28**: 103–110.
5. Gumpert R, Lyons C. Setting up a district audit programme. Br. Med. J. **301**: 162–165.
6. Ellis BW, Sensky T. A clinicians's guide to setting up an audit. Br. Med. J. 1991, **302**: 704–707.
7. Conference of Medical Royal Colleges and Faculties. Building on the White Paper: some suggestions and safeguards. London: Conference of Medical Royal Colleges and Faculties. 1989: 17.
8. Faculty of Public Health Medicine. Report of a working group on the audit of public health medicine. 1989.
9. Black D, Morris JN, Townsend P. Inequalities in health. The Black Report. Harmondsworth: Penguin. 1982 (first published by DHSS in 1980).
10. Smith GD, Bartley M, Blane D. The Black Report on socioeconomic inequalities in health: 10 years on. Br. Med. J. 1990, **301**: 373–377.
11. Report on Confidential Enquiries into Maternal Deaths in UK, 1985–7. London: HMSO. 1991.
12. Shaw C. Medical audit. A hospital handbook. London: Kings Fund. 1989.
13. Audit Commission. Br. Med. J. 1990, **301**: 1265–1272.
14. Medical Audit in Family Practitioner Services – health circular HC(FP) (90)8.
15. Webb SJ, Dowell AC, Heywood P. Survey of general practice audit in Leeds. Br. Med. J. 1991, **302**: 390–393.
16. Baker R, Presley P. The practice audit plan. London: The Severn Faculty of the Royal College of General Practitioners. 1990.
17. Irvine D. Managing for quality in general practice. London: Kings Fund. 1990.
18. Hughes J, Humphrey C. Medical audit in general practice. London: Kings Fund. 1990.
19. Secretaries of State for Health. Wales, Northern Ireland and Scotland. Medical audit. Working paper 6. London: HMSO. 1989: 3–6.
20. Fitzpatrick R. Survey of patient satisfaction. Br. Med. J. 1991, **302**: 887–889.
21. Sharp F, Duncan ID, Evans DMH. Report of intercollegiate working party on cervical cytology screening. London: Royal College of Obstetricians and Gynaecologists. 1987.
22. Department of Health and Social Security. Cervical cancer screening. (DA (85)8). London: HMSO. 1988.
23. Batstone GF. Educational aspects of medical audit. Br. Med. J. 1990, **301**: 326–328.
24. Blair-Fish D. Medical audit: outcome measurements needed. Br. Med. J. 1989, **299**: 1361.

3

Measurement of Health

The assessment of the health of a nation or community can best be measured by the intelligent use of vital statistics. These can be defined as the study of various numerical data connected with the life and health of the population within the community. This includes information concerning births, marriages, deaths and the population, and the collection of data about the incidence of disease (morbidity) as well as the number of persons dying from diseases (mortality).

Sources of statistical information

The government office responsible for the collection and publication of vital statistics is the Office of Population Censuses and Surveys (OPCS).

There are many publications which act as the main sources of vital statistics. They include the following all of which are published by HMSO:

Population Trends (OPCS) — published quarterly, this gives the latest population and vital statistics for the UK and for the individual countries and various regions. In addition each issue contains four or five specialist articles on research projects and studies in the field of population and medical statistical topics.

Social Trends — published annually, this deals with many types of information about the population, leisure activities, personal incomes and wealth, health, social services, education, housing, environment, justice, law and public expenditure. It is an excellent publication to study before starting on any project as the information is presented in a helpful and readable way. It contains many tables and diagrams to point out and illustrate various trends. It also contains some excellent articles of current interest, several useful definitions of the many terms used, and a bibliography. It is compiled by the Central Statistical Office (CSO).

Health and Personal Social Services Statistics for England (Department of Health) — this annual publication is a collection of useful information about the NHS services and the personal social services. It gives many tables of vital statistics, standardized mortality ratios, costs of health and personal social services, community health services, psychiatric services, maternity and child health services, preventive medicine, morbidity statistics, and blood transfusion services.

Annual Report of the Chief Medical Officer of the Department of Health — titled 'On the State of the Public Health', this is a key document giving an outline of the health problems in the NHS and also covers any points of especial health interest in the year under review. In 1990, it reviewed the latest decade and gave an excellent short analysis of health achievements and problems.[1]

General Household Survey (OPCS) — published annually, this gives an insight into self-reported sickness and disability. It deals with acute illness (illness in the previous 2 weeks) and long-standing illness (illness over the last year) as well as information about the nature of such illnesses. It also includes data based on people's perception of their health (as opposed to sickness), and whether they have a sense of well-being.

Family Expenditure Survey (OPCS) — this is a continuous enquiry into the expenditure pattern of approximately 11 000 households.

National Food Survey (Ministry of Agriculture, Fisheries and Food) — this is a continuous enquiry into domestic food consumed and food budgets of 7000–8000 households.

Hospital In-patient Enquiry — jointly carried out by the OPCS and the Department of Health, this covers a 10% sample of in-patients in England and all in-patients in Scotland for non-psychiatric patients in NHS hospitals.

Mental Health Enquiry — this is an analysis of individual in-patient records of, admission to, and discharge from psychiatric hospitals and units.

Annual Report of the Health Advisory Service.

Report of the Mental Health Commission — annual report indicating the specific work of the Commission in the past year.

A recent important addition is the *annual report of each Director of Public Health* for each DHA. This is likely to become one of the most useful local reports and should indicate clearly any special health problems in the DHA. It should describe various medical audits carried out in the preventive health local services.

Additional information is available from:

- Census returns — the census is every 10 years with the latest being carried out in April 1991.
- Special studies carried out on specific topics — an excellent example is the *Report on Confidential Enquiries into Maternal Deaths* which usually covers 3 years. The report[2] published in 1991 covers the years 1985–87. These reports used to refer only to England and Wales, but now include all the countries of the UK and are jointly prepared by the Chief Medical Officers for England, Scotland, Wales and Northern Ireland.
- *Health Bulletin* — published quarterly by the Public Health Laboratory Service, this gives the latest information on communicable diseases, bacteriological and viral isolations and other epidemiological data.
- Special *ad hoc* enquiries and surveys such as the surveys into incidence of disability carried out in the UK from 1985 to 1988 by the OPCS (see p. 515).

- The reports of government comittees of enquiry: examples include the Report of the Enquiry into the Educational Needs of Handicapped Children and Young People (The Warnock Committee, 1987) (Department of Education and Science), and the Committee of Enquiry into Sexual Abuse of Children in Cleveland (1988, the Butler-Schloss report).[3]
- *Health Trends* — published by the Department of Health and Welsh Office quarterly, this is a collection of topical health subjects covering both national and international problems.
- World Health Organization (WHO) publications — there is a popular bi-monthly journal, *World Health*, which contains articles from all over the world on topical medical subjects. WHO publishes bulletins weekly on serious communicable diseases, an annual report and an annual volume of *World Health Annual Statistics* which gives the mortality rates of all diseases in member countries. WHO publications can be obtained from HMSO or they may be found in large reference libraries.
- In addition, various consultative papers (Green Papers) and White Papers covering health topics are the usual means that the government uses to inform widely of their plans for change. Also, the Department of Health and the Scottish Home and Health Department, the Welsh Office and the Department of Health and Social Services, Northern Ireland, all issue many memoranda and letters explaining fully the advice which the Department wishes to be followed, or explaining new legislation and other changes introduced.

Collection of statistical information

REGISTRATION OF BIRTH

The parent has a duty to register the birth of every child with the local Registrar of Births, Marriages and Deaths within 42 days.

NOTIFICATION OF BIRTH

This is for a different purpose and is mainly to ensure the local community and preventive services of the local DHA learn rapidly of every birth. This allows the infant health services to assist the mother without delay (i.e. enables the health visitor to call — see p. 126). Every birth or stillbirth must be notified to the Director of Public Health within 36 hours. It is usual for this notification to be carried out by the midwife or doctor attending the birth.

REGISTRATION OF STILLBIRTH

Every stillbirth must be registered with the local Registrar of Births, Marriages and Deaths. A special certificate from the midwife or doctor attending the birth must record that the child was stillborn. The definition of stillbirth is 'any child which has issued forth from its mother after twenty-eighth week of gestation and which did not at any time after being completely expelled from the mother breathe or show any other sign of life'. It is often referred to as 'a late fetal death: after 28 completed weeks of gestation'.

REGISTRATION OF DEATH

Any death must be registered by the nearest relative (or other person in charge) within 5 days of the death. The doctor who has attended the patient during the last illness must provide a certificate as to the cause of death. The cause of death on the death certificate provides the Registrar General with the official records of mortality and accurate certification is important.

STATISTICAL RATES

It is obviously desirable to refer to all vital statistics in terms of the same unit of population and this is usually per 1000 persons. The exception is the maternal mortality rate which is now expressed per 100 000 as maternal mortality is now a very rare event and this limit avoids quoting statistical rates in terms of small decimals.

ENUMERATION OF THE POPULATION

The first census ever taken was in 1801. The census is now carried out every 10 years with the last being held in April 1991. The responsibility for collecting the information is that of the Registrar General. The Census Act and various documents issued under the Act's authority give specific directions as to how the census must be carried out. An enumerator (recruited from the local authority and other staff) calls at each house and leaves the census form. This has to be completed by the head of the house for everyone resident in that house on census day. The enumerator then calls to collect the form and is able to give any advice as to its final completion. All information given in the census is completely confidential and may not be used for any other purpose.

SOCIAL CLASS

To help the study of statistics, especially mortality, the population is divided into six different social classes based upon the occupation of the chief wage earner of the family. These are as follows:

Class I Professional occupations (lawyers, doctors, directors, etc.); 7.8% of the population.

Class II Other professional and managerial occupations (teachers, nurses, managers, etc.); 23.5% of the population.

Class IIIN Non-manual skilled occupations (includes clerks of all types, shop assistants, etc.); 11.4% of the population.

Class IIIM A large group of skilled manual occupations (bricklayers, underground coal miners, etc.); 36.5% of the population.

Class IV Partly skilled occupations (postmen, etc.); 14.8% of the population.

Class V Unskilled occupations (porters, general labourers, etc.); 6.0% of the population, the smallest group.

The social class classification is particularly used when studying occupational mortality (see p. 91).

Vital statistics in the UK

In this edition, as explained in the Preface, wherever possible various measures of statistics (such as birth rates, death rates, infant mortality rates, perinatal mortality rates) have been quoted for the whole of the UK. This has been possible due to a gradual change taking place in the presentation of government statistics. However this change, which started about 5 years ago, is still incomplete. Most of the detailed analyses of vital statistics are still based upon the older 'England and Wales' numbers, and a few refer only to England. Separate statistics are kept and published for Scotland, Wales and Northern Ireland, but not quoted here because, in a book of this size, it is difficult to include all statistical details of these countries.

POPULATION OF THE UK

In 1990 the population of the UK numbered 57 411 000, consisting of 28 013 000 men and 29 398 000 women. There has always been an excess of females over males in the UK, although for every 1000 female births there are 1050 male births. However, the mortality of males is higher than females at all ages and, by the age of 52 years, there are more women than men alive. This preponderance of women increases until after the age of 90 years when there are nearly four women to every man.

Table 3.1 illustrates the population of the UK and indicates the distribution between England and Wales, Scotland and Northern Ireland.

Table 3.2 shows the population of the UK by sex and various age groups for 1991.

TABLE 3.1   Population of the UK, 1990 (thousands)

	Persons	Males	Females
England and Wales	50 718	24 765	25 953
Scotland	5 102	2 467	2 636
Northern Ireland	1 589	780	809
United Kingdom	57 411	28 013	29 398

Numbers are rounded and may not add to totals.
Data from ref. 21.

TABLE 3.2   Population by age groups and sex, England and Wales, 1990 (thousands)

Age groups (years)	Persons (%)	Males	Females
0–4	3380.0 (6.60)	1730.9	1647.1
5–9	3194.1 (6.29)	1637.4	1556.7
10–14	2992.9 (5.90)	1538.0	1454.9
15–19	3427.1 (6.76)	1759.5	1667.6
20–24	4001.3 (7.89)	2037.3	1964.0
25–29	4172.1 (8.23)	2108.9	2063.2
30–34	3598.9 (7.10)	1809.7	1789.2
35–39	3333.0 (6.58)	1668.6	1664.4
40–44	3674.0 (7.24)	1837.9	1836.1
45–49	3004.1 (5.92)	1507.4	1496.7
50–54	2751.1 (5.42)	1375.6	1376.5
55–59	2592.9 (5.11)	1285.4	1307.5
60–64	2564.1 (5.06)	1240.1	1324.0
65–69	2531.5 (4.99)	1172.0	1359.5
70–74	1930.1 (3.81)	833.2	1096.9
75–79	1672.3 (3.30)	650.9	1021.4
80–84	1114.2 (2.20)	373.2	741.0
85–89	554.1 (1.09)	150.9	403.2
90 and over	229.9 (0.45)	48.2	181.2

Numbers are rounded and may not add to totals.
Data from ref. 22.

The variation among the age groups in Table 3.2 reflects the changes in the birth rates in the past. In age groups up to the age 30 years, this is obvious from the figures; in older age groups, this effect tends to even itself out.

Since 1976, when the numbers of people over the age of 85 years represented 1 in 104 persons, the proportion of this age group in the population has risen steadily and by 1990 had reached 1 in 65. This trend is highly significant as those aged 85 years and over always present increasing care problems because very old people always need a high proportion of health (especially hospital) care and social services. (This problem is discussed in detail in Chapter 18 — see pp. 399–400).

BIRTH RATE

The birth rate is the number of children born per year per 1000 of the population. Another way of calculating this is:

$$\text{Birth rate} = \frac{\text{number of births in the year} \times 1000}{\text{mid-year population}}$$

In 1991, the birth rate in the UK was 13.8.

Figure 3.1 illustrates the variation in the birth rate in the UK which has taken place this century. The rate fell steadily until the end of the 1930s and since then it has fluctuated from a high of 21 in 1947 and another peak of 18.5 in 1964 to a

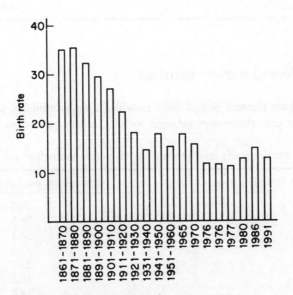

FIGURE 3.1   Birth rate in England and Wales, 1861–1991.

low of 11.6 in 1977. Since 1980 the figure has varied between 13.0 (1980) and 13.9 (1990) with the 1991 level being 13.8.

There are a number of important features of birth statistics including:

- social class variation in the birth rate
- births inside and outside marriage
- conceptions outside marriage
- age of mother at the birth of her first child in marriage
- variation in the birth rates between different countries of the world.

Social class variation in births

There is not a wide variation of births between the social classes (see Table 3.3). However, significantly more births occur in social classes I and II (the professional groups) compared with social classes IV and V (the unskilled section of the community).

TABLE 3.3   Social class and births inside marriage in England, 1989

Social class	% of population	% of live births
I and II	31	33.1
IIIN	11	10.9
IIIM	37	36.4
IV and V	21	19.6

Data from ref. 9.

Births inside and outside marriage

The Family Law Reform Act of 1987 provided a new definition of extramarital births. In the past these were referred to 'illegitimate births' (in contrast with

TABLE 3.4   Births outside marriage and age of mother in England and Wales, 1989

Age of mother (years)	Conceptions outside marriage (%)
All ages	28.0
Under 20	78.5
20–24	38.1
25–29	17.3
30–34	13.7
35–39	16.0
40 and over	19.0

Data from ref. 4.

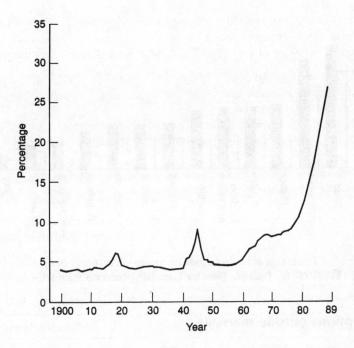

FIGURE 3.2   Percentage of births outside marriage in England and Wales, 1900–89. (Redrawn from ref. 4.)

'legitimate births' which took place inside a marriage). In future all births should be referred to either as 'births within marriage' or 'births outside marriage'.

During the 1980s, there was a large increase in the proportion of births outside marriage (see Fig. 3.2). In 1991 in the UK, births outside marriage numbered 235 200 (29.7% of all births). It will be seen that the percentage of births outside marriage rose from 11.8% in 1980 to nearly 30% in 1991. This rise has been most marked in the youngest age groups and especially in mothers under the age of 20 (see Table 3.4).

International levels of births outside marriage

Many other western countries have also seen a sharp rise in the percentage of births occurring outside marriage in the 1980s.[4] Apart from France and the Republic of Ireland where the rise was from a much lower level, the growth has been greater in England and Wales than elsewhere (see Fig. 3.3).

Note that in Sweden and Denmark, the rate of births outside marriage has consistently remained high, rising to 51% and 45% respectively, in 1988.

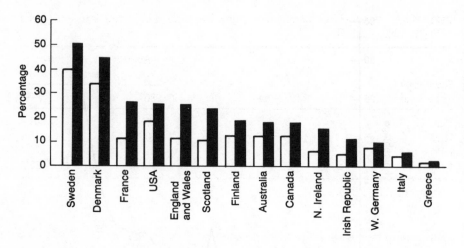

FIGURE 3.3   Percentage of births outside marriage: international comparison, 1980 (□) and 1988 (■) (1987 for Finland, 1986 for Canada). (Redrawn from ref. 4.)

Conceptions outside marriage

Conceptions outside marriage have also increased sharply. In 1990 in England, conceptions outside marriage formed 42% of all conceptions. As might be expected, the highest rates of conception outside marriage occurred in teenage women. Detailed analysis covers England where, in 1989, 98 697 maternities occurred in women under the age of 20 (61.8%).[4]

Age of mother at her first live birth within marriage

The average age of a mother at the birth of her first live child has been steadily rising during the last 20 years. There has always been a tendency for the age of the mother at her first live birth to be highest in social class I and II and then fall progressively as the social class moves towards social classes IV and V. Both these trends are clearly seen in Table 3.5.

Variations in the birth rates of different countries

Table 3.6 illustrates the wide variation in the birth rates of different countries. Note that well-established countries tend to have the lowest rates, whereas newer countries like Israel and the Third World countries the higher rates. In the past, Roman Catholic countries had consistently higher birth rates and although Poland (15.5) and Ireland (16.6) are higher than most European rates, Italy records the lowest rate in the world. The level of contraception plays an important part in keeping birth

TABLE 3.5   Average age of mother at first live birth within marriage in England 1970–72, 1980 and 1990

Social class of husband	1970–72	Average age of mother (years)	
		1980	1990
I and II	26.0	27.6	28.7
IIIN	24.9	26.0	27.4
IIIM	23.4	24.4	26.4
IV and V	22.4	23.1	25.3

Data from ref. 1.

TABLE 3.6   International birth rates, 1988 (unless otherwise stated)

Country	Birth rate	Country	Birth rate
Italy	9.9	USA	15.9
Greece	10.6[a]	Ireland	16.6[a]
Germany (Federal)	11.0	New Zealand	16.8[a]
Japan	11.0[a]	USSR	19.8[a]
Denmark	11.5	Israel	23.1(1986)
Netherlands	12.6	Mexico	29.0[b]
Sweden	13.3	India	32.0[a]
UK	13.8	Egypt	41.1[a]
France	13.8	Chad	44.2[b]
Canada	14.4[a]	Ghana	44.3[b]
Australia	14.9	Nigeria	49.8[b]
Poland	15.5	Rwanda	54.3[b]

[a] 1987.
[b] UN estimate, 1985–1990.
Data from ref. 10.

rates low, but some countries with very large populations (such as India) have adopted a central strategy to encourage lower birth rates as the best method of raising the standard of life.

DEATH RATE

The crude death rate is the number of deaths per year per 1000 of the population. Another way of expressing this is:

$$\text{Death rate} = \frac{\text{number of deaths in the year} \times 1000}{\text{mid-year population}}$$

TABLE 3.7   Causes of death at all ages in England and Wales, 1991

Cause of death	Number	(%)
Diseases of the circulatory system	261 834	(46.0)
(includes 150 090 deaths from ischaemic heart disease)		
Neoplasms	145 355	(25.7)
Diseases of the respiratory system	63 273	(11.1)
Diseases of the digestive system	18 508	(3.3)
Injury and poisoning	17 286	(3.0)
Mental disorders	13 500	(2.4)
Diseases of the nervous system and sense organs	11 889	(2.1)
Endocrine, nutritional and metabolic diseases	10 538	(1.9)
Diseases of the genito-urinary system	6 464	(1.3)
Diseases of the musculoskeletal system	5 417	(1.0)
Signs, symptoms and ill-defined conditions	5 208	(0.9)
Diseases of the blood and blood-forming organs	2 446	(0.4)
Infectious and parasitic diseases	2 406	(0.4)
Congenital anomalies	1 621	(0.3)
Diseases of the skin	930 ⎫	
Certain conditions originating in the perinatal period	250 ⎬	(0.2)
Complications of pregnancy	45 ⎭	

Data from ref. 11.

The crude death rate is of limited value, as the relative age of populations in districts and towns is rarely known accurately. Where there is a large proportion of elderly persons, the number of deaths in any community is bound to be high, irrespective of the living conditions. For this reason, it is not possible to deduce from a high crude death rate that the area is unhealthy. Therefore, it is better to use specialist mortality rates such as the infant mortality rate (see pp. 69–75) or the perinatal mortality rate (see pp. 76–77) or to compare the mortality in different years or in large different groups or occupations, the standardized mortality ratio (see p. 90).

In 1991 in England and Wales, the crude death rate was 11.2. The full details of the causes of individual deaths are given in Table 3.7. In 1991, 570 044 deaths occurred in England and Wales (277 582 men and 292 462 women).

It will be seen from Table 3.7 that the largest group of deaths was 'diseases of the circulatory system', responsible for 261 834 deaths (46.0%). This group contained 150 090 deaths from ischaemic heart disease (81 611 men and 68 479 women). Neoplasms formed the next commonest cause of death — 145 355 or 25.7% (75 853 men and 69 502 women). Diseases of the respiratory system caused 63 273 deaths (11.1%). The numbers of deaths from any other specific cause were considerably lower.

EXPECTATION OF LIFE

Very accurate estimations of the expectation of life are made by insurance companies as they base their premiums for life assurance on the expectation of life at different ages. Table 3.8 shows how the expectation of life has improved during this century and the estimated levels at different ages by the year 2001.

Until 1979, the expectation of life had been lower at birth than at 1 year reflecting the high infant mortality rate of previous years. However, since then, the infant mortality rate has fallen so quickly (see Fig. 3.4) that this trend has been reversed. Overall improvements in life expectancy are likely to continue in the foreseeable future. It is interesting to note that the highest expectation of life occurs in Japan where in 1988 there was a life expectancy of 78 years at birth.

Although the expectation of life is constantly increasing, it is important to realize that the expectation of life without disability remains largely the same. This is a particular problem in women, for although their life expectancy at birth is 5.6 years longer than men, because of the increased levels of chronic disability in women, the quality of the extra years is often impaired.

TABLE 3.8   Expectation of life by sex and age in the UK, 1901, 1989 and estimated for 2001

| | Expectation of life[a] | | | | | |
| | Males | | | Females | | |
Age (years)	1901	1989	2001	1901	1989	2001
At brith	45.5	72.8	73.9	49.0	78.4	79.8
1	53.6	72.4	73.4	55.8	78.0	79.3
10	50.4	63.7	64.6	52.7	69.2	70.5
20	41.7	53.9	54.8	44.1	59.4	60.6
30	33.8	44.3	45.1	35.9	49.5	50.8
40	26.1	34.8	35.7	28.3	39.8	41.0
50	19.3	25.6	26.7	21.1	30.4	31.6
60	13.3	17.4	18.5	14.6	21.7	22.7
70	8.5	10.9	11.9	9.2	14.2	15.1
80	4.9	6.2	6.9	5.3	8.2	8.8

[a] Further number of years a person could be expected to live.
Data from ref. 12.

INFANT MORTALITY RATE (IMR)

This is one of the most useful specialist death rates. It measures the number of infants under the age of 1 year who die each year per 1000 live related births.

Another way of calculating the IMR is as follows:

$$\text{Infant mortality rate} = \frac{\text{Deaths of infants under 1 year of age in year} \times 1000}{\text{number of live births during the year}}$$

In 1990, in the UK, the rate was the lowest ever recorded and measured 7.9 (8.9 in males and 6.8 in females). The way the IMR has fallen steadily and dramatically this century is shown in Figure 3.4.

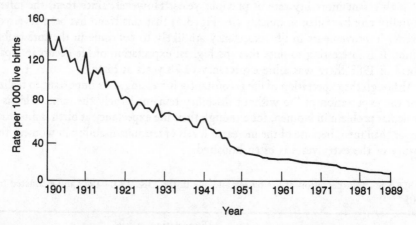

FIGURE 3.4   Infant mortality in the UK, 1901–89. From 1901–1921 rates are for Great Britain. (Redrawn from ref. 12.)

The IMR is one of the most widely used death rates as it gives an excellent indication of the living conditions in any area or in any section of a community. This is because the main factors influencing any infant's life and progress are very closely connected with their home. Where living conditions are poor the child is unlikely to develop to their full potential, and is more likely to fall ill or to have an accident, the consequences of which are likely to be serious.

The variation of the IMR in different RHAs is shown in Table 3.9. Note that considerable variations occur — the lowest rate is East Anglia with 6.7 and the highest is West Midlands (10.0). Many socio-economic factors affect the IMR including the level of unemployment and the prosperity of any community, as well as the distribution of social class in an area. Table 3.10 shows how the IMR varies between different social classes in England and Wales. The IMR is lowest in social class II (6.7), and then progressively increases to 11.8 in social class V. This clearly illustrates the additional hazards facing the infants of unskilled workers. This is the first indication in this book of the inequalities in standards of health in the UK which have been a constant characteristic since vital statistics were first studied in the 19th century. Many reports[5,6] have emphasized that these inequalities of health in the population have not diminished even though the overall rates have been

TABLE 3.9   Infant mortality rate (IMR) for Regional Health Authorities (RHAs) in England and Wales, 1988–90

RHA	IMR	RHA	IMR
East Anglia	6.7	Northern	8.3
Wales	7.5	Wessex	8.3
Mersey	7.6	Trent	8.5
South-west Thames	7.7	South-east Thames	8.7
North-west Thames	7.7	North Western	9.3
Oxford	7.7	Yorkshire	9.3
South Western	7.9	West Midlands	10.0
North-east Thames	7.9		

Data from ref. 13.

TABLE 3.10   Infant mortality rate (IMR): by social classes (births inside marriage only) in England and Wales, 1987 (all classes, IMR = 8.0)

Social classes	IMR
I	6.9
II	6.7
III N	7.1
III M	7.7
IV	9.6
V	11.8

Data from ref. 14.

reduced considerably — in 1951 the IMR was 30. There has therefore been a 380% improvement in the chance of a baby surviving in the first year of life since 1951, yet the differences between different social classes have not changed greatly.[5,6] Even the introduction of the NHS and the whole system of social security in 1948 does not seem to have disturbed these inequalities.

Birthweight and IMR

The weight of a baby at birth is an important factor in determining the risk that baby faces. It can be seen from Table 3.11 that the IMR and perinatal mortality rates (see p. 72) rise very steeply for tiny babies. Of the babies weighing less than 1500 g at birth, nearly one third die in their first year (the IMR for England and Wales for 1988 being 302.1). As the birthweight increases, infant mortality drops steadily; for babies weighing 4000 g or more at birth, the IMR was 3.1 in 1988.

TABLE 3.11   Infant mortality rates and perinatal mortality rates: by birthweight in England and Wales, 1981, 1986 and 1988

Birthweight (g)	Infant mortality rates[a]			Perinatal mortality rates[b]		
	1981	1986	1988	1981	1986	1988
Under 1500	345.7	302.4	302.1	422.0	345.5	319.2
1500–1999	72.5	61.1	53.2	122.6	85.0	82.7
2000–2499	24.7	19.7	19.9	32.8	27.3	24.1
Under 2500	72.1	65.3	66.7	105.5	86.4	82.0
2500–2999	9.5	8.0	8.0	7.5	6.6	6.6
3000–3499	5.2	4.8	4.6	3.0	3.0	2.7
3500–3999	4.7	3.9	3.4	2.4	2.0	1.9
4000 and over	4.5	3.7	3.1	3.9	2.7	2.5
All weights[c]	10.9	9.4	8.7	11.8	9.5	8.7

[a] Deaths of infants under 1 year of age per 1000 live births.
[b] Stillbirths and deaths of infants under 1 week of age per 1000 live and stillbirths.
[c] Includes others not stated.
Data from ref. 12.

The perinatal mortality rate shows a similar trend except there is a slight increase to 2.5 (1988) for babies weighing over 4000 g compared with a rate of 1.9 for babies weighing 3500–3999 g at birth. Note that both mortality rates improved during the 1980s — the IMR for all birthweights fell from 10.9 to 8.9 (a fall of 18.3%) while the perinatal mortality rate fell from 11.8 to 8.7 (an improvement of 26.3%).

Other specialized mortality rates in infants

These include the following:

- *neonatal mortality rate* — deaths in the first 28 days after birth
- *postneonatal mortality rate* — deaths from 29 days of life to 1 year
- *perinatal mortality rate* — the combined total of the stillbirth rate and deaths which occur in the first week of life
- *stillbirth rate* — late fetal deaths: after 28 complete weeks of gestation.

The IMR and all the above specialist rates are very much affected by whether the birth occurred inside or outside marriage (see Table 3.12). It will be noted that in all instances the mortality rates are significantly worse in births which occur outside marriage. This is a clear confirmation that the child born outside marriage faces extra risks. These include many different problems including lack of family support in some instances, possible homelessness or unsatisfactory housing combined with possible inadequate antenatal care.

TABLE 3.12   Specialized mortality rates in infants inside and outside marriage in England and Wales, 1987

	Inside marriage	Outside marriage	All
Infant mortality rate	8.0	12.3	9.2
Perinatal mortality rate	8.2	11.1	8.9
Neonatal mortality rate	4.7	6.1	5.0
Postneonatal mortality rate	3.4	6.2	4.0
Stillbirth rate	4.6	6.4	5.0

Data from ref. 14.

International IMRs

These vary considerably throughout the world (see Table 3.13). Note that Japan has the lowest IMR of 5.0. In Europe, Ireland, The Netherlands and France have the lowest rates, while Greece, Portugal and USSR have the highest rates. Most of the rates of Third World countries are high, with the worst rates being in Bangladesh (119) and Peru (122). Many of these countries have shown considerable improvements from 1973 to 1988, although any sudden catastrophe such as

TABLE 3.13   Infant mortality rates (IMRs) in different countries, 1988 (unless otherwise stated)

Country	IMR	Country	IMR
Japan[a]	5.0	New Zealand[a]	11.0
Ireland	7.4	Israel	11.4
Hong Kong[a]	7.4	Greece	12.6
Netherlands	7.5	Portugal	14.2
France	7.7	Yugoslavia	24.8
Canada	7.9	USSR[a]	25.4
Germany	8.1	Guatemala[b]	51.7
Denmark	8.3	Tunisia[b]	59.0
UK	8.8	Brazil[b]	63.0
Australia	9.2	Egypt	70.5
Italy[a]	9.5	Indonesia[b]	84.0
Belgium	9.7	Bangladesh[b]	119.0
USA	9.9	Peru[b]	122.0

[a] 1987; [b] United Nations estimate 1985–90.
Data from ref. 10.

drought, civil unrest and the consequent risk of starvation can quickly be accompanied by a marked rise in the IMR. There is no doubt that in this respect that IMR is the most sensitive indicator of a sudden deterioration in living conditions in any country.

Causes of infant mortality

As can be seen in Table 3.14, in 1987 sudden infant death syndrome (see pp. 124–126) was the largest single cause of death within the IMR. Deaths from this cause total 3.71 per 1000 live births out of a total for that year of 9.2 (40.3%). The next commonest causes are congenital anomalies which account for 0.75 deaths per 1000, diseases of the respiratory system (0.38 deaths per 1000), diseases of the central nervous system and slow fetal growth (each 0.20 deaths per 1000).

There are always significantly more infant deaths in males compared with females (in the ratio of 1.2 to 1.0). However, note that in the category of deaths 'sudden infant death syndrome' the ratio of male to female deaths rises to 1.5 to 1.0.

TABLE 3.14   Principal causes of infant mortality per 1000 live births in England and Wales, 1987 (infant mortality rate (IMR), all causes = 9.2)

Cause	IMR
Sudden infant death syndrome — males	2.23
— females	1.48
Congenital anomalies	0.75
Diseases of respiratory system	0.38
Diseases of central nervous system	0.20
Slow fetal growth	0.20
Infectious diseases	0.19
External causes of injury and poisoning	0.14
Hypoxia	0.11
Endocrinal diseases	0.04
Neoplasms	0.04
Diseases of digestive system	0.02
Diseases of genito-urinary system	0.02
All other causes	3.40

Data from ref. 14.

Infant mortality 1980–90 in England

Figure 3.5 shows the way the IMR and its two constituent rates (neonatal and postnatal rates) have fallen in 1980–90 in England. It will be seen that the steepest

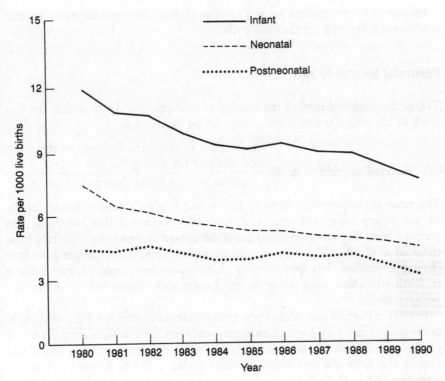

FIGURE 3.5   Deaths in the first year of life in England, 1980–90. (Redrawn from ref. 1.)

decline occurred in the first 5 years from 1980 to 1985, and was mainly a decrease of deaths in the neonatal period. In the decade, the neonatal death rate fell by 38%.

Neonatal mortality rate

The neonatal mortality rate is defined as the number of infants who die in the first 28 days of life per 1000 live related births. This can be expressed as:

$$\text{Neonatal mortality rate} = \frac{\text{infant deaths in the first 28 days of life during the year} \times 1000}{\text{number of live births during the year}}$$

The neonatal mortality rate for the UK for 1990 was 4.5. It is divided into:

- *early neonatal mortality rate* – deaths in the first 7 days of life (3.7)
- *late neonatal mortality rate* – deaths from 8 to 28 days of life (0.8).

Because of the exceptional hazards to young infants, the neonatal mortality rate is responsible for 48% of the total IMR.

Perinatal mortality rate

This is the combined total of the number of stillbirths and deaths within the first week of life per 1000 total births. This can be expressed as:

$$\text{Perinatal mortality rate} = \frac{\text{the number of stillbirths} + \text{deaths in the first week of life during the year} \times 1000}{\text{number of total births during the year}}$$

The value of the perinatal mortality rate is that it gives a good indication of the hazards to any baby in the period immediately before and after the birth. The perinatal mortality rate overcomes the disadvantage of separating stillbirths from those infant deaths which occur a short time after birth. A child might have little chance of survival, but exceptionally skilful midwifery could convert a likely stillbirth into a first week death; in either event such a death will be shown as a perinatal death.

In 1990 in England and Wales the perinatal mortality rate was 8.1 per total births as shown in Table 3.15. Note that the perinatal mortality rate fell during the whole of the period 1950–89, but that fall was relatively slow until the mid 1970s During the 1980s the rate of fall increased giving a 37.6% decrease in perinatal mortality rate in that decade.

TABLE 3.15   Perinatal mortality rate and stillbirth rate in England and Wales, 1950–90

Year	Perinatal mortality rate	Stillbirth rate	Year	Perinatal mortality rate	Stillbirth rate
1950	37.4	22.6	1971	22.3	12.5
1953	36.9	22.4	1973	21.0	11.5
1956	36.7	22.9	1976	17.7	9.7
1959	34.1	20.8	1980	13.3	7.2
1962	30.8	18.1	1983	10.4	5.7
1965	26.9	15.8	1987	8.9	4.6
1968	24.7	14.3	1989	8.3	4.5
			1990	8.1	4.5

Data from various OPCS Monitors in the DH series.

Factors affecting the perinatal mortality rate

There are three important factors which affect perinatal mortality: maternal age, parity and social class. Table 3.16 illustrates the way these three influence the rate.

TABLE 3.16   Perinatal mortality rate: by maternal age, parity and social class in England and Wales, 1987

Maternal age (years)	Rate[a]	Parity	Rate	Social Class	Rate	Stillbirth rate[b,c]
			Perinatal mortality			
Less than 20	8.6	0	9.0	I	6.8	3.5
20–24	8.3	1	6.6	II	7.0	3.8
25–29	7.4	2	8.5	IIIN	7.8	4.4
30–34	8.2	3+	10.6	IIIM	8.1	4.6
35+	12.5			IV	9.9	5.8
				V	10.9	6.3

[a] Perinatal rate all groups = 8.9.
[b] Stillbirth rate all groups = 5.0.
[c] Stillbirth rate by social class inside marriage only.
Data from ref. 14.

Note that the rate is higher in mothers aged less than 20 — probably because of the high rate of births outside marriage in this group. For mothers aged 35 years and over the rate is at its highest and is linked with the greater chance of haemorrhage and multiparous births in this group. Social class shows the classic lowest rate in social class I, but after that the rate rises progressively from 6.8 to 10.9 in social class V. This is a typical illustration of an inequality of health in the country. Stillbirth rates rise gradually from social class I to V.

Perinatal mortality rates for different RHAs in England and in Wales

The perinatal mortality rate varies between the different RHAs in England from the lowest of 6.7 in South Western and East Anglia to 9.9 in West Midlands (see Table 3.17). In Wales it varies between 8.3 in Clwyd to 10.9 in Powys.

STILLBIRTH RATE

The stillbirth rate is the number of stillbirths per 1000 total births. A stillbirth is defined as a late fetal death after 28 complete weeks of gestation.

In the UK in 1990, the stillbirth rate was 4.4. The stillbirth rate is lowest in Social Class I and highest in Social Class V as shown in Table 3.16 which gives the stillbirth rates by social class for England and Wales for 1987 (the stillbirth rate was then 4.6).

TABLE 3.17   Perinatal mortality rate: by Regional Health Authority (RHA) in England and Wales, 1990

RHA	Perinatal mortality rate	RHA	Perinatal mortality rate
East Anglia	6.4	Yorkshire	8.5
South Western	7.2	South-east Thames	8.6
South-west Thames	7.3	Trent	8.7
Oxford	7.4	North-east Thames	8.7
Mersey	7.8	Northern	8.7
North-west Thames	7.9	North Western	9.2
Wessex	8.0	West Midlands	10.1

Data from ref. 11.

MATERNAL MORTALITY RATE

The maternal mortality rate is a measure of the risk to the mother connected with childbirth. It is defined as the number of women who die each year from causes associated with childbirth per 100 000 births. This can be expressed as:

$$\text{Maternal mortality rate} = \frac{\text{deaths during the year in women associated with childbirth} \times 100\,000}{\text{number of total births during the year}}$$

Deaths are only counted if they are directly related to pregnancy. For example, death from renal failure which had commenced with a severe hypertensive disease of pregnancy would be counted as a maternal death even if the woman died years later. Death from a completely unrelated cause (such as a road accident or a medical or surgical emergency) would not be counted as a maternal death even if it took place during pregnancy.

This is the only rate calculated per 100 000 deaths. This is because it is now a very rare event. The maternal mortality rate in 1989 in England was 6.0 per 100 000 (a similar rate occurs for the other countries in the UK).

During this century, the maternal mortality rate has fallen in an entirely different way from the IMR. In 1900 it was 467 and during the next 35 years did not fall significantly — in 1935 it was 433. Following the introduction of chemotherapy for infections (the sulphonamides), followed shortly afterwards by penicillin and the start of universal blood transfusion in the early 1940s, it fell quickly (see Fig. 3.6).

Figure 3.6 shows that the maternal mortality rate reached 78 by 1951, 34 by 1961, 17 by 1971 and 11 by 1980. Its present level of 6.0 means that since 1935 it has improved 71 times — a more dramatic way of putting this is that the chance of a woman dying from causes associated with childbirth in 1935 was 1 in 230, while it is now 1 in 16 666.

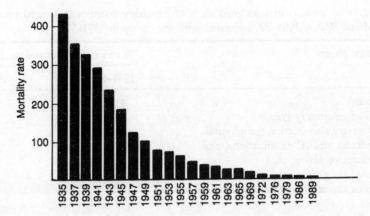

FIGURE 3.6   Maternal mortality rate (including abortion) in England and Wales, 1935–89.

Reference has already been made (Chapter 2, p. 44) to the role that early medical audit played through the series of Reports on Confidential Enquiries into Maternal Deaths to identify and highlight the high degree of substandard care still associated with such deaths.[2] For further details of the 1985–87 Report see Chapter 4, p. 109).

MORBIDITY

Much research has taken place in the last 25 years to improve methods of measuring the incidence of disease (morbidity). Two interesting projects were the large-scale studies of morbidity in general practice in 1971–72 and in 1981–82.[7] In the section below, details are given of the 1981–82 survey and these are compared with the earlier one.

The 1981–82 study covered 48 general practices, urban and rural, and a total of 332 270 patients. It included all types of general practice from single handed to those with four or more principals.

Seven main diagnostic groups were used to classify the reasons why patients consulted their GPs. The results are given in Table 3.18.

During the survey, which lasted 1 year, 71% of all patients consulted their GP. The age group which most frequently saw their doctor was the 'under 5-year-olds' — 98%. On average, each patient who consulted their GP, did so 1.5 times per episode of illness. Compared with the survey carried out in 1971–72, there was a considerable fall for the group 'mental disorders' and a marked increase for the group 'supplementary classification'.

TABLE 3.18   Results of a national study of morbidity statistics in general practice in England and Wales, 1981–82, compared with the survey in 1971–72

Diagnostic group	% of patient/doctor consultations	
	1981–82	1971–72
Remainder[a]	41.3	40.8
Diseases of respiratory system	16.0	18.7
Supplementary classification (prophylactic procedures, medical examinations, oral contraceptive advice, etc.)	13.9	10.5
Diseases of the circulatory system	8.9	8.5
Diseases of the central nervous system and sense organs	7.6	7.0
Mental disorders	6.8	10.3
Infections and parasitic diseases	5.3	4.2

[a] Remainder includes 'symptoms, signs and ill-defined conditions' which is the third highest patients consulting group. The most common conditions within this group were abdominal pain (29.8%), cough (25.0%), rash and skin eruptions (13.3%), headache (13.2%), malaise, fatigue and tiredness (12.7%), chest pain (12.1%), dizziness and giddiness (10.0%).
Data from ref. 7.

Age incidence

There were many instances where the consulting rates varied with the age of the patient. Figure 3.7 illustrating the incidence of Parkinson's disease, chronic bronchitis, migraine and acute otitis media shows three differences. The first two diseases show an incidence almost entirely in the age groups over 45. Migraine is at its maximum at ages 25–45 years and falls away in the very young and very old. Otitis media has a peak incidence in the 0–4 year age group. Acute bronchitis and asthma show further variations.

Sex differences

The most dramatic sex difference in consulting rates is shown in diseases of the genito-urinary system in which the incidence in women aged 15–24, 25–44, and 45–64 years is much greater than in any age group in men (see Fig. 3.8). The main reason is cystitis — women consult their GPs five times more often than men. Other common reasons why women consult GPs are excessive or irregular menstruation, menopausal symptoms and vaginitis.

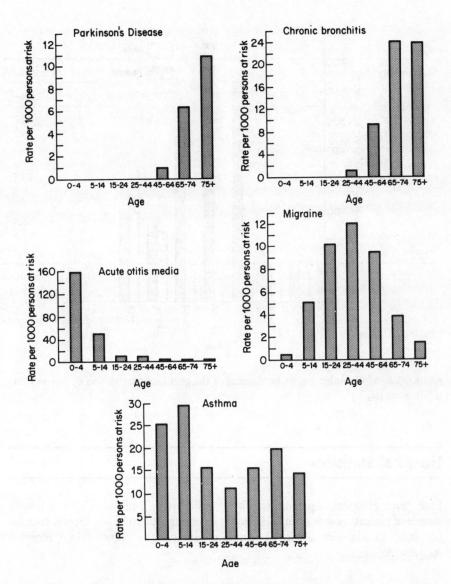

FIGURE 3.7   Patients consulting, by age, for selected disorders of the nervous system, sense organs and chest. (Data from ref. 7.)

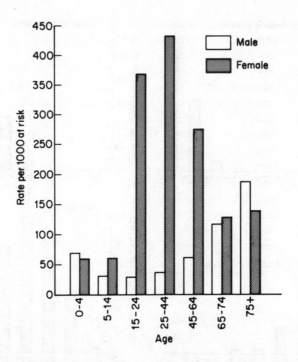

FIGURE 3.8   Consulting rates for diseases of the genito-urinary system by age and sex. (Data from ref. 7.)

Hospital statistics

Each year a Hospital In-patient Enquiry is published in England. This is a 1-in-10 sample of patient records from NHS hospitals in England excluding mental disorder hospitals. In addition, a 1-in-10 sample of day cases is collected in a Hospital Activity Analysis.

USE OF HOSPITALS

The pressure on NHS hospitals continues to rise. Table 3.19 shows the discharge rate per 10 000 population over the period 1979–85 in England. Between 1979 and 1985 the discharge rates overall rose by nearly 17%, but the increase in females was 2% more than in males. The 1982 figures were lower than could have been expected because there was widespread industrial action in hospitals that year.

The increase in women in the middle of life is partly due to the complications of childbirth and gynaecological conditions. Normal pregnancy statistics are not included.

TABLE 3.19   All discharges and deaths in NHS hospitals: estimated numbers and discharge rates per 10 000 population in England, 1979–85

	Year				Discharge rates		
	1979	1980	1981	1982	1983	1984	1985
All persons	919.5	961.5	984.8	980.7	1025.5	1053.7	1074.3
Males	890.5	927.5	950.3	950.1	988.1	1014.7	1032.1
Females	947.1	993.8	1017.5	1009.8	1061.0	1090.8	1114.5

Data from ref. 15.

TABLE 3.20   Discharge rates from hospitals (except mental hospitals) in England, 1985

Diagnostic group	Rates per 10 000 population
All causes	1074.3
Signs, symptoms and ill-defined conditions	145.3
Diseases of the circulatory system	124.0
Injury and poisoning	115.3
Diseases of the digestive system	108.0
Diseases of the genito-urinary system	99.6
Diseases of the respiratory system	97.9
Malignant neoplasms	85.5
Diseases of the nervous system and sense organs	62.7
Diseases of the musculoskeletal system	59.5
Benign neoplasms	32.4
Complications of pregnancy, childbirth and puerperium	31.1
Other reasons for contacting health service[a]	29.2
Diseases of skin and subcutaneous tissues	17.6
Endocrine, nutritional and metabolic diseases and immunity diseases	16.8
Infectious and parasitic diseases	16.3
Congenital anomalies	14.9
Certain conditions originating in the perinatal period	12.3
Diseases of the blood and blood-forming organs	9.7
Mental disorders	9.1

[a] Includes sterilization, housing, household and economic circumstances, and holiday relief care.
Data from ref. 15.

Table 3.20 gives the discharge rates for specific groups of diseases from NHS hospitals in 1985. Conditions within the groups of diseases in which discharge rates have risen more than average include carcinoma *in situ*, inflammatory disease of the pelvic cellular tissues and peritoneum, rheumatism, cataracts and low back pain. Reductions in discharge rates were recorded in obstetric complications, spina bifida and hydrocephalus, salpingitis and oophoritis, thyrotoxicosis and tuberculosis.

When the discharge rates from hospital are grouped into broad categories such as 'surgical cases', 'medical cases', etc., their representation graphically is shown in

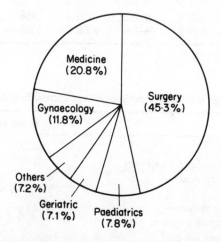

FIGURE 3.9   Percentage of discharges and deaths of in-patients (excluding mental disorders) in England, 1985. (Data from ref. 20.)

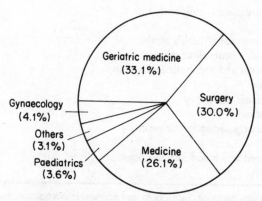

FIGURE 3.10   Percentage of hospital beds in daily use (excluding maternity and mental disorders) in England, 1985. (Data from ref. 20.)

Figure 3.9. Note that surgical cases easily represent the largest group followed by medical cases, gynaecology and paediatrics. Other conditions make up 7.2%, while geriatric cases are only 7.1%.

An entirely different picture is given if the daily usage of hospital bed is studied (see Fig. 3.10). Now geriatric cases are the largest group, followed by surgery, medicine, gynaecology, paediatric and other. This emphasizes the increasing hospital problem which an ageing population presents and this is made worse by the fact that many elderly in-patients have an extended hospital stay.

TABLE 3.21   Day cases and percentage of total cases treated in NHS hospitals 1982–85

Cases	1982	1983	1984	1985
Total day cases	684 930	787 470	863 440	938 330
% of total cases treated	13	13	15	16

Data from ref. 15.

TABLE 3.22   Total day cases and day cases as a percentage of total cases treated by select-ive causes in England, 1985

Diagnostic group	Estimated total day cases	Day cases as % of total cases treated
All causes	868 500	16
Diseases of digestive system	164 520	24
Signs, symptoms and ill-defined conditions	116 300	15
All malignant neoplasms	92 140	19
Diseases of musculoskeletal system	71 160	20
Diseases of female genital organs including breast	70 030	20
Prophylactic, observational and other contacts with hospital services	69 920	34
Diseases of skin and subcutaneous tissues	66 740	45
Benign neoplasms	58 170	39
Sterilization (male)	41 920	92
Diseases of genito-urinary system	30 080	23
Diseases of ear and mastoid process	28 470	28
Diseases of teeth and supporting structures	27 510	29
Pregnancy with abortive outcome	26 200	19
Diseases of eye	22 770	16
Injury and poisoning	18 670	3
Hernia	16 950	15
Diseases of male genital organs	16 480	16

Data from ref. 16.

DAY CASES

The proportion of persons being treated as day cases continues to rise steadily each year (see Table 3.21), currently reaching 16% of all patients. When the individual diagnostic groups making up the total day cases are analysed (see Table 3.22), it will be seen that the use being made of day admissions varies considerably. In male sterilization, 92% of patients are operated upon as day cases whereas in most other diagnostic groups day care is used for 15–45% of cases.

TABLE 3.23   Communicable diseases notified in England and Wales, 1990

Disease	Number of cases
Food poisoning	52 145
Whooping cough	15 286
Measles	13 302
Rubella	11 491
Viral hepatitis	9 005
Scarlet fever	7 187
Mumps	4 277
Respiratory tuberculosis	3 942
Dysentery	2 756
Acute meningitis	2 572
Malaria	1 478
Other forms of tuberculosis alone	1 187
Ophthalmia neonatorum	440
Meningococcal septicaemia (without meningitis)	277
Typhoid	178
Paratyphoid fever	93
Acute encephalitis	39
Leptospirosis	20
Cholera	19
Tetanus	9
Typhus	4
Diphtheria	2
Viral haemorrhagic fever	2
Relapsing fever	2
Anthrax	2
Acute poliomyelitis	1
Rabies	0

Data from ref. 17.

Communicable diseases

The total number of notifications of communicable diseases in England and Wales for 1990 are given in Table 3.23. Food poisoning notifications increased very rapidly from 1987 (29 331) through 1988 (39 713) to 1989 when 52 557 cases were notified. In 1990, notifications of food poisoning reduced very slightly to 52 145. Most of this increase was due to more outbreaks of *Salmonella enteritidis* food poisoning. A further marked increase was seen during the years 1987 to 1990 in the number of cases of virus hepatitis being reported. In 1987, 3379 were notified but this rose to 5063 in 1988 and to 7071 in 1989. There was a further increase in 1990 when 9005 cases were notified. The majority of this increase was in cases of hepatitis A which, in 1990, accounted for 7316 cases out of a total of 9005 (81.2%).

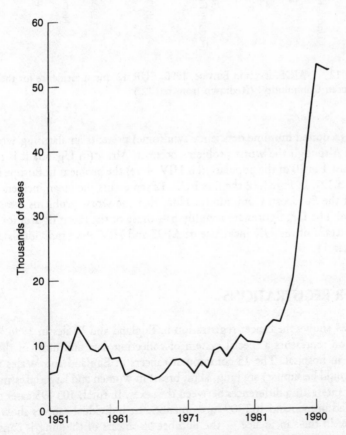

FIGURE 3.11   Formally notified cases of food poisoning in England and Wales, 1951–90. (Redrawn from ref. 12.)

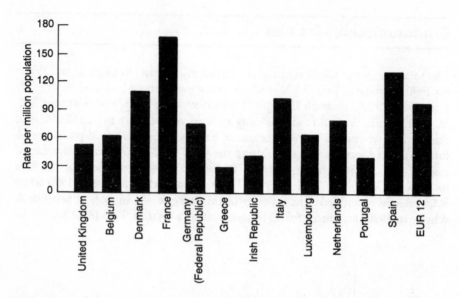

FIGURE 3.12   AIDS: levels in Europe, 1990. EUR 12, mean incidence for the whole of the European Community. (Redrawn from ref. 12.)

AIDS (acquired immune deficiency syndrome) presents an alarming world-wide increase. Although the worst problems occur in Africa (in Uganda it is estimated that at least 1 in 10 of the population is HIV +ve) the problem in Europe is serious (see Fig. 3.12). In Fig. 3.12 the line EUR 12 represents the mean incidence for the whole of the European Community. Note that the worst problems are in France and Spain. The UK figures are roughly half those of the mean figures for Europe. Further details of the UK incidence of AIDS and HIV +ve individuals are given in Chapter 11.

CANCER REGISTRATIONS

Table 3.24 shows the cancer registration in England and Wales in 1986.[18] Cancer registration represents a special system of collecting data and most of the figures originate in hospital. The 15 commonest cancers in England and Wales (the UK figures would be similar) are lung, skin, breast in women and large intestine. There are many interesting differences between the sexes. In total, 103 495 cases of cancer were found in men and 102 309 in women. Some individual cancers show marked differences in their incidence — the number of cancers of the lung is considerably greater in men, although the incidence is now falling in men but rising in women (see p. 281). The reason for the higher incidence of lung cancers which still occurs

TABLE 3.24   Cancer registrations and 15 main causes in England and Wales, 1986

Site of cancer	Males	Females
1. Lung	24 365	9 991
2. Skin	15 141	14 428
3. Breast	177	22 757
4. Large intestine (colon and rectum)	11 710	12 393
5. Stomach	6 624	4 029
6. Leukaemias and lymphoma	6 445	5 434
7. Prostate	10 180	–
8. Bladder	6 781	2 810
9. Pancreas	2 756	2 831
10. Ovary	–	4 507
11. Oesophagus	2 591	1 812
12. Cervix uteri	–	4 034
13. Uterus (other than cervix)	–	3 812
14. Eye, brain and other nervous system	1 757	1 312
15. Mouth and pharynx	1 791	936
Total cancer (including some very rare ones)	103 495	102 309

Data from ref. 18.

in men is the cumulative effect of the greater number of men who smoked in the past. There is also a greater number of men who develop cancer of the bladder (linked with an industrial cause in the past — see p. 291). Apart from the large numbers of cases of cancer of the breast in women, the incidence of most of the other cancers is similar in men and women.

MORTALITY RATES

Most mortality rates are very reliable as there is an obvious need for doctors to be very accurate when certifying death, even in the most primitive countries, so that mortality rates are widely used to compare international statistics of disease. WHO collects and publishes a comprehensive yearly report in which mortality rates are usually given in death rates per 100 000 population. Many of these international mortality figures are given in Chapter 13.

To ensure that every country and every statistician is using the same basis for including any particular disease, an *International Classification of Diseases, Injuries and Causes of Death* is used and each disease/cause of death is given an ICD number.

It is possible to compare mortality rates by giving deaths per 1000, 10 000 or 100 000, but for deaths in the UK a simpler and better way is to use the standardized mortality ratio (SMR).

Standardized mortality ratio (SMR)

The SMR is defined as the percentage ratio of the number of deaths observed in that year or group to the number expected from the age specific year or specialized group of the population.

The SMR is one of the most useful ways to compare quickly the mortality of different:

- years compared with the base year selected (see Table 3.25)
- social class (see Table 3.26)
- occupation (see Table 3.27).

Standardized mortality ratio for different years

A base year is first chosen (in Table 3.25 this was 1980). The SMR for all causes and for specific causes is called 100. An adjustment is then made for any changes in the sex/age distribution of different years and the SMR is then calculated for the year in question.

In Table 3.25, the SMR for diabetes in males is shown as 150 which means that 150/100 or 1.5 times the mortality from diabetes in males occurred during 1989

TABLE 3.25   Standardized mortality ratios (SMRs) of selected causes in England, 1984–89 (base year 1980 = 100)

Cause of death	Males				Females			
	1984	1986	1988	1989	1984	1986	1988	1989
All causes	93	92	87	86	94	93	90	90
Tuberculosis (respiratory)	77	72	75	55	84	87	76	80
Meningococcal infection	135	277	294	377	100	133	208	201
Cancer of stomach	94	88	82	79	89	79	76	73
Cancer of lung	96	90	87	83	115	117	123	124
Cancer of female breast	–	–	–	–	108	110	109	124
Cancer of cervix uteri	–	–	–	–	91	94	88	89
Leukaemia	102	99	103	97	107	104	101	110
Diabetes	129	162	166	150	130	153	140	148
Hypertensive disease	79	69	60	56	82	72	56	57
Ischaemic heart disease	97	94	90	92	102	100	89	93
Cerebrovascular disease	95	92	87	79	98	91	80	83
Bronchitis	63	50	35	29	76	65	46	37
Hyperplasia of prostate	89	74	59	56	–	–	–	–
Motor vehicle accidents	86	81	76	81	83	81	74	79
Suicide	106	105	110	100	85	72	68	55

Data from ref. 19.

compared with the mortality in the base year (1980). Likewise in women (SMR 57) mortality, during 1989, for hypertensive disease was 57/100 or 57% of the mortality from this cause in 1980. Table 3.24 enables a quick comparison to be made between the mortality rates for a number of important diseases in the years in question. The table also emphasizes whether a disease has increased, as in meningococcal infection, or reduced, as in bronchitis, and gives a clear indication of the degree of increase or reduction.

Note also the wide range of results. Some diseases from 1980–89 increased dramatically (meningococcal infections and diabetes in both sexes), some diminished significantly in both sexes (bronchitis and hypertensive disease). Suicide was an example of a cause of death which increased slightly in men but in women there was a considerable reduction.

Standardized mortality ratios for different social classes

The SMR can equally be used to compare the mortality between different social classes. This calculation is made every 10 years in a study called 'Occupational Mortality'[8] which is published by OPCS. The last such report was published in 1987 and covered the years 1979–80 and 1982–83. Table 3.26 compares the mortality of the different social classes using the SMR of each social class with that of the country as a whole.

It will be noted that social class I and II enjoy a greatly reduced mortality from most causes compared with social class V. Thus Table 3.26 shows that the mortality from all causes in men in social class I is only 66% whereas social class V suffers from 165% of the average mortality of the whole country (a difference of 2.5 times).

TABLE 3.26   Standardized mortality ratios: by cause and social class in England and Wales, 1979–80, 1982–83

Cause of death	Social class					
	I	II	IIIN	IIIM	IV	V
All causes — men	66	76	94	89	116	165
All causes — women	75	83	93	111	125	160
Cancer of the lung — men	43	63	80	120	126	178
Cancer of the lung — women	50	73	81	122	138	170
Cancer of the breast — women	109	104	106	101	99	94
Cancer of cervix uteri	29	60	73	112	124	186
Diabetes — men	67	76	113	100	123	155
Diabetes — women	47	59	92	114	145	247
Ischaemic heart disease — men	70	82	104	109	117	144
Ischaemic heart disease — women	46	75	80	122	144	194
Bronchitis — men	34	48	85	110	115	211

Data from ref. 8.

Recent work has shown that some of these figures (especially in social class V) are probably exaggerated due to bias, because of the OPCS decennial supplement method of comparing unlinked census figures and death registrations. A further method called the 'longitudinal study' has therefore been developed by the OPCS during 1971–81, and this shows a similar trend, but a smaller range — from SMR 70 for social class I to 125 for social class V for all causes of death (compared with 66 to 165 in Table 3.26).

Note that the one exception is cancer of the breast in women where there is a higher SMR for class I (109) compared with social class V (94).

Occupational mortality

Using the same source,[8] if the mortality of members of different occupations is compared, wide variations are found. Table 3.27 lists the SMRs for men aged 20–64 years by occupation for the years 1979–80 and 1982–83.

TABLE 3.27　Standardized mortality rates (SMR) for all causes of death for men aged 20–64 years in England and Wales, 1979–80, 1982–3

Occupation	SMR	Occupation	SMR
Local government administrators	64	Masons	100
Roadmen	67	Clergymen	102
Dustment	69	Librarians	108
Postmen	72	Bus and coach drivers	111
University academic staff	72	Judges, barristers and solicitors	113
Teachers (higher education)	73	Crane drivers	116
Board and paper workers	75	Waiters and bar staff	117
Physiotherapists	80	Pharmacists	121
Bookbinders	80	Police officers	126
Forestry workers	80	Environmental health officers	127
Teachers (main group of)	81	Miners (not coal), quarrymen	133
Ambulancemen	84	Butchers	134
Company secretaries	86	Actors	138
Hospital ward orderlies	87	Shoe repairers	146
Railway engine drivers	88	Prison officers	147
Dentists	89	Nurses	151
Rubber and plastic workers	90	Scaffolders	159
Textile workers	91	Musicians	181
Farmers	93	Steel erectors and benders	184
Carpenters and joiners	94	Fishermen	194
Coal miners (underground)	96	Printers	202
Medical practitioners	97	Brewery, vinery process workers	266

Data from ref. 8.

Even in the health services considerable differences occur in the mortality rates for all causes: physiotherapists (80), ambulancemen (84), hospital ward orderlies (87), dentists (89), medical practitioners (97), pharmacists (121) and nurses (151). Although the professional classes (social classes 1 and II) generally have low rates, within the group, many differences occur — local government officers are the lowest with an SMR of 64 whereas judges, barristers and solicitors are almost double with a SMR of 113. These different mortality rates do not only indicate particular hazards of different occupations, but are also influenced by the type of individual employed or who chooses such an occupation, and their life-styles.

Certain causes of death are commoner in some occupations. For instance, suicide is a particulary high risk in medical practitioners (a SMR for suicide of 202), nurses (a SMR of 275) and pharmacists (a SMR of 286). This connection is most likely to be due to the ease with which people in all such occupations can obtain lethal drugs.

Cirrhosis of the liver shows high SMRs in judges, barristers and solicitors (202), chefs and cooks (322), waiters and bar staff (367) and in brewery and vinery process workers (452). There is a tendency for people in all such occupations to have a high alcohol consumption.

Possible aetiological connections between diseases and social class are further discussed in Chapter 13.

References

1. Department of Health. On the State of the Public Health. Annual Report of the Chief Medical Officer. London: HMSO. 1991.
2. Report on Confidential Enquiries into Maternal Deaths in UK, 1985–1987. London: HMSO. 1991.
3. Department of Health and Social Security. Report of Committee of Enquiry into sexual abuse of children in Cleveland, 1987. [The Butler-Schloss report] London: HMSO. 1988.
4. OPCS. Population Trends. London: HMSO. 1991.
5. Black D Morris JN, Townsend P. Inequalities in health. The Black Report. Harmondsworth: Penguin. 1982 (first published by the Department of Health and Social Security in 1980).
6. Smith GD, Bartley M, Blane D. The Black Report on socioeconomic inequalities in health; 10 years on. Br. Med. J. 1990, 301: 373–377.
7. OPCS. Morbidity statistics in general practice 1981–2. Series MB5. London: HMSO. 1990.
8. OPCS. Occupational mortality. London: HMSO. 1987.
9. OPCS. Birth Statistics 1989. London: HMSO. 1991.
10. United Nations. Populations and vital statistics report 1988. United Nations. 1990.
11. OPCS. Monitor DH2 92/2. London: OPCS. 1991.
12. Central Statistical Office. Social Trends. London: HMSO. 1991.
13. OPCS. Monitor DH3 91/2. London: OPCS. 1991.
14. OPCS. Mortality Statistics 1987. London: HMSO. 1990.
15. OPCS. Monitor MB4 87/1. London: OPCS. 1987.

16. OPCS. Monitor MB4 873. London: OPCS. 1987.
17. OPCS. Monitor MB2 92/3. London: OPCS. 1991.
18. OPCS. Cancer registrations. London: HMSO. 1986.
19. Department of Health. Health and Personal Social Services Statistics 1991. London: HMSO. 1991.
20. Department of Health/OPCS. Hospital in-patient enquiry. London: HMSO. 1985.
21. Government Statistical Service. Monthly Digest of Statistics No. 559, p. 19. London: HMSO. 1992.
22. Government Statistical Service. Population Estimates. London: HMSO. 1991.

4

Maternity Services

In 1990 there were 706 140 births in England and Wales, which was the highest figure since 1972. The perinatal mortality rate, i.e. deaths of babies born after 28 weeks gestation and babies less than 1 week old, dropped to 8.1 per 1000 births (see p. 115). There have been dramatic changes in the provision of maternity services since 1960, and much of the change has been an excellent example of the close co-operation and co-ordination of the different parts of the health service. Table 4.1 shows some of the changes from 1955 to 1987 including a 10-fold reduction in maternal mortality. During this time there was also a four-fold reduction in the perinatal mortality rate, from 32.8 to 8.1. Table 4.2 shows the perinatal mortality rates by social class in England and Wales for 1987.

In 1970 a report of the sub-committee of the Standing Maternity and Midwifery Advisory Committee of the Central Health Services Council was published.[1] This was known as the Peel report and looked at the future of local health authority domiciliary midwifery services and the question of maternity bed needs for maternity patients. This report subsequently had a great effect on the development of maternity services in the UK. Its main recommendation was that sufficient facilities should be provided to allow all mothers to have their babies delivered in hospital. In 1964, in England and Wales, 31.2% of babies were delivered at home, and by 1990 the Peel recommendation had become a reality with only 1% of babies being born at home. The domiciliary midwifery services became amalgamated in 1974 with the hospital midwifery services. The Short report was published in 1980[2]

TABLE 4.1   Changes in numbers of births and maternal deaths from 1955–57 to 1985–87 in the UK

Year	1955–57	1964–66	1973–75	1982–84	1985–87
Births	2 521 804	3 040 377	2 239 233	2 183 151	2 293 508
Maternal deaths	1691	1011	408	203	174
Maternal mortality rate	67.1	33.3	18.2	9.3	7.6
Rates per 1 million women aged 15–44 years	41.7	23.8	9.0	4.7	4.2

Data from ref. 13.

TABLE 4.2   Infant and perinatal mortality by social class in England and Wales, 1987

	Social class					
	I	II	IIIN	IIIM	IV	V
Stillbirths[a]	3.5	3.8	4.4	4.6	5.8	6.3
Perinatal deaths	6.8	7.0	7.8	8.1	9.9	10.8
Neonatal deaths	3.9	4.1	4.4	4.5	5.6	5.9
Postneonatal deaths	3.0	2.5	2.7	3.3	4.0	5.9
Infant deaths	6.9	6.7	7.1	7.7	9.6	11.8

[a] Rates per 1000 total births; all other rates per 1000 live births.
Data from ref. 15.

and this led to the multidisciplinary Maternity Services Advisory Committee (MSAC) being established in 1981 to advise on matters relating to the maternity and neonatal services. One of the MSAC's first recommendations was to establish regional perinatal working parties and maternity services liaison committees in all health districts.

The Midwives Act prohibits, except in sudden emergency, any unqualified person who is not either a doctor or midwife (or student in training) from attending any woman in childbirth except under the personal direction of a doctor or midwife.

The UK Central Council (UKCC) for Nursing, Midwifery and Health Visiting

The UKCC for Nursing, Midwifery and Health Visiting was established in 1983 and maintains strict control over all midwifery services. Their rules are supervised locally by officers of the DHA and include:

- supervision over all certified midwives practising in the area both within the hospital and in the community. Midwives may not practise until they have given their notice to do so to the DHA
- power to suspend a midwife from practice if it is necessary to do so.

The UKCC lays down a code of practice and rules for all midwives. These specify the records they must keep, the standards they must follow in their midwifery practice, the drugs and the anaesthetics they can use, as well as defining the medical emergencies in which they have a duty to call in medical aid. The UKCC also insists that every practising midwife shall attend a refresher course once every 5 years.

Midwives for both the hospital and community services are provided by the DHA and are supervised by the staff of the District Nursing Officer. At present there are very few private midwives practising.

General practitioners

GPs who have special experience in obstetrics and who wish to provide maternity services to women under the National Health Service may apply to the FHSA to have their name placed on the Obstetric List. Such lists are kept in libraries for the general public to consult. Each practice must also state in their practice leaflets whether or not they provide such services. This may be provided for women who remain under the care of another GP for the rest of their health care.

Two types of care are possible: *complete care* where the GP with a midwife will supervise all aspects of the pregnancy including antenatal care, interpartum care and postpartum care; and *partial or shared care* where the GP and the midwife will supervise the ante- and postnatal care, but the interpartum care is under the control of a hospital consultant. Where the GP supervises complete care, the actual delivery is usually in a GP unit, which is ideally situated alongside or as an integral part of the consultant obstetrics unit in the District Hospital. Occasionally such GP units may be at an isolated location some way from the hospital, and even more rarely the mother may request and be accepted for a home delivery.

Home deliveries

Only 1% births now occur at home. When a mother wants a home delivery the GP will liaise with the midwife for sharing the care before and after, but no GP can be made to accept a woman for home delivery, whereas she has an absolute right that the DHA provides her with a midwife. When a woman who is booked for delivery goes into labour, the midwife visits, confirms that labour has started and arranges for any equipment, such as analgesic apparatus to be in the house. The GP is notified but the midwife remains with the patient and supervises the delivery. The GP is usually notified when the second stage starts. If during delivery, the midwife meets with any abnormality, she/he is required to send immediately for the GP. In very urgent and serious cases the midwife may send directly for the 'flying squad'.

The Domino scheme[3] (Domiciliary Midwife In and Out)

This scheme returns the mother home if all is well after some 6–48 hours. This has been one of the factors in the decline in home deliveries. To be in the hospital for the labour, where there is immediate help to hand, and then be home if all is well within 6 hours is an increasingly popular event. The domiciliary midwife is required to call on every woman discharged home early to continue the postnatal care of both mother and child. Extra help in the house should be available for all mothers discharged home early.

The obstetric flying squad

Each maternity hospital provides a mobile team, the so-called flying squad who will go to the home of a patient to deal with any emergency in labour or to any GP maternity unit. The team consists of an experienced obstetrician (consultant or senior registrar), anaesthetist, paediatrician, plus an experienced hospital midwife. Generally the flying squad is called out in about 1 in 70 domiciliary deliveries. The commonest reason is retained placenta (up to half the cases), as well as other complications of labour, such as an unexpected breech presentation. The flying squad is taken to the patient's home by ambulance which, after the patient has been resuscitated, can transfer her to hospital. An intravenous drip should be inserted and fluid replacement promptly started.

The MSAC's second report — Care during Childbirth[4] — highlighted the general discomfort that certain women felt with the inadequacies of care of healthy women during their pregnancies and the medical model of treating them as patients with illnesses. Emphasis was placed on the mother's wishes within the confines of safety of mother and child. Considerate explanation with regard to procedures involving the mother, and the joint formulation of birth plans have considerably helped to allay the anxiety. A feature which helped to forestall an increase of requests for home deliveries was the increasing use of the Domino scheme.

Aims of good obstetric care

The DH Maternity Services Advisory Committee have endorsed the following objectives for maternity care:[5]

- to reduce perinatal and neonatal mortality rates
- to eliminate disparities in the death rates between the different sections of the community
- to minimize impairment, disability and handicap
- to promote the social and emotional well-being of parents and children.

The King's Fund[6] listed the following four general objectives:

- to promote a safe and satisfying experience for pregnancy and childbirth

- to promote an environment in which the parents can participate actively during pregnancy and in the births of their children
- to minimize unnecessary medical intervention during pregnancy and labour
- to maximize easy access to maternity services for all ethnic and social groups.

Pre-pregnancy care

The GP is the ideal person, as an extension of their normal medical care, to provide information and guidance to a woman who is considering starting a family. This is the logical development of the GP's family planning role. Any relevant past obstetrics and family histories should be ascertained if not already known. Social factors, such as smoking, alcohol intake and diet (including weight guidance) should be discussed. The advantages of giving up smoking were stressed by the Chief Medical Officer in his 1990 report. Women who give up smoking before becoming pregnant have babies of the same average weight as those who have never smoked[7] and have a lower perinatal mortality rate. The presence or absence of antibodies against rubella should be checked. The date of the last cervical smear should be recorded.

Women with particular health problems (e.g. diabetes, hypertension), may be advised and drug therapies modified if necessary. Referral to an appropriate hospital may need to be made. Advice on prenatal diagnoses of inherited disorders, if there is a personal or family history (genetic counselling), can be given with referral to the Regional Genetic Advisory Specialist.

Antenatal care

For many years, antenatal care has aimed at providing good preventive and anti-cipatory care specifically looking for treating symptoms and problems of both the mother and fetus. It should also help to prepare the couple for the birth and raising of the child. Traditionally the frequency of visits to the clinic was based on a model outlined by Dame Jane Campbell in the 1920s.[8] There is a great variation between different countries (e.g. there is an average of five visits in Switzerland per pregnancy and up to 14 in The Netherlands).[8] Altering this time-established pattern has met with great resistance, from doctors, midwives and even the patients themselves. Such schedules need to be flexible and refined for individual needs. Clear instructions need to be recorded in the patient's notes and co-operation cards or the full notes need to be carried at all times (see Table 4.3 for the modern protocol).

TABLE 4.3   A summary of the modern protocol for antenatal care

Weeks	Primigravida	Multigravida	Done by	Reason
8	Mandatory	Mandatory	MW/GP[a]	Confirm pregnancy, past history, bloods, urine, book place of delivery
12	Mandatory	Optional	MW	Check blood results
16	Mandatory	Mandatory	Hospital	Detailed ultrasound scan
22	Mandatory	Mandatory	MW	Routine checks/classes
26	Mandatory	Optional	MW	
30	Mandatory	Mandatory	MW/GP	Blood tests/growth/blood pressure
34	Mandatory	Optional	MW/GP	
36	Mandatory	Mandatory	MW/GP	
38	Mandatory	Optional	MW/GP	Check weight, presentation blood pressure and growth
40	Mandatory	Mandatory	MW/GP	
41	Mandatory	Optional	MW/GP	
42	Mandatory	Mandatory	MW/GP	

[a] MW, midwife; GP, general practitioner.
After Marsh.[16]

Low risk mothers

These mothers have had previously uncomplicated pregnancies and deliveries, are in good health and are in the main suitable for GP complete care. This is the group which in the past would have been ideal for home deliveries.

Low risk pregnancy/high risk delivery

This group are in good health, had previously no complications prior to delivery, but had a complicated delivery such as caesarean section. Their care needs to be concentrated for the delivery rather than in the antenatal clinic.

High risk mothers

These mothers have a significant medical condition or a past obstetric history showing them to be at risk both during pregnancy and in labour. These women need very careful monitoring throughout their pregnancy.

OTHERS

There is, however, a miscellany of women who do run higher risks with their pregnancies. They include the very young, older mothers, unmarried, smokers, patients on drugs and with high alcohol intakes, irregular attenders, late bookers and those who have bled in the early stages of pregnancy. Although generalizations about care are impossible, amongst this group are the women who potentially and unpredictably could produce problems or who will default from clinic supervision. It is within this group that most good can potentially be done. All members of the team need to understand the problems of close surveillance, and when such a high risk person does not attend the clinic, attempts should be made to follow her up.

THE FIRST ANTENATAL EXAMINATION

Blood samples are taken at the booking clinic to check:

Haemoglobin (Hb)	to detect and provide treatment for anaemia
Blood grouping	
Wasserman or Kahn test	to detect syphilis (very rare)
Rubella serology	to detect antibodies and thus immunity from rubella (German measles)
Rhesus factor	only of concern if the mother is Rhesus negative and the father is Rhesus positive. If in such cases the child is Rhesus Positive (50% chance) there may be problems after the birth of the child, especially with second and subsequent pregnancies (see below)
Sickle cell test	for people of Afro-Caribbean descent and occasionally seen in Mediterranean and Middle East populations
HIV	for high risk women because of intravenous drug abuse, known sexual activity, etc. At present some women are tested anonymously for studies to establish the prevalence of HIV. More widespread HIV testing may be introduced

In addition to the blood tests a mid stream specimen of urine (MSU) is taken to detect infection and a cervical smear test may be taken, though this may best be left till after the delivery. A brief physical examination should be performed, looking particularly at the cardiovascular and respiratory systems and general fitness.

The examination should be completed by giving health education advice on diet and general management of the pregnancy. Risks associated with cigarette smoking and alcohol intake should be explained (according to the Health Education Council 1 500 babies a year die because the mother smokes). Ideally the midwife, GP and health visitor should all work together closely in the booking clinic. Arrangements are made for the expectant mother to attend mothercraft classes, usually held in the GP's surgery or health centre.

TRIPLE TEST

Wald[9] described how assays for oestriol, human chorionic gonadotrophin (HCG) and α-foetoprotein could be measured during weeks 16–18 of pregnancy and the results computed to make a risk assessment of the mother delivering either a child suffering from an open neural tube defect (anencephaly or spina bifida), or Down's syndrome. Many districts now routinely screen at around this stage, having accurately dated the pregnancy with an ultrasound scan, and the consultant or GP gets a computerized printout of the risk. Those who are at high risk (greater than one in 200) are then offered an amniocentesis.

CONTINUED ANTENATAL CARE

Subsequent attendances (see Table 4.3 for the modified attendance schedule) should always cover the following: (a) measuring blood pressure to look for hypertension, (b) measuring weight, and (c) testing urine for protein and glucose. Abdominal examination should be carried out, in the early stages to verify the size, but later to check the lie of the baby. General questions about the general well-being (physical and mental) of the mother should be made with opportunity given to exploring her questions and worries.

Ultrasound examination

Ultrasound examination is now carried out in most centres and this may involve up to three scans: the first at around 12 weeks to confirm the dates; a second detailed scan at around 18–20 weeks which is capable of looking for fetal abnormalities; and a third scan at 30–32 weeks to monitor the growth of the baby and to look for intra-uterine growth retardation. Debate still occurs as to the benefit of all three scans and trials are continuing.

Amniocentesis

This is offered to all women shown to be at increased risk from the triple test and is always performed in hospitals. If the triple test has not been carried out, it may selectively be offered to women aged 35 or over, or to those with a significant past obstetric or family history. For Down's syndrome the risks according to maternal

TABLE 4.4   Likely incidence of an affected fetus by age and condition of mother

	(years)	Risk of affected fetus
Advanced maternal age	35–36	1 in 213 ⎱ Risk of Down's
	37–39	1 in 148 ⎰ syndrome
	40 and over	1 in 52
Previous child with neural tube defect		1 in 20
Parent balanced chromosomal translocation carrier		1 in 4–10
Detectable metabolic disorder recessive inheritance		1 in 4
Mother carrier of X-linked disorder (e.g. Duchenne muscular atrophy, haemophilia)		1 in 2 male offspring

Data from ref. 17.

age are illustrated in Table 7.4. and the risks for some other genetically linked conditions are given in Table 4.4.

A needle inserted through the lower anterior abdominal wall and into the uterus is used to withdraw 5–10 ml of amniotic fluid. Ultrasound enables the needle to be safely guided away from the placenta and fetus. It is generally carried out between 16 and 18 weeks. The risk of abortion in experienced hands is in the order of 1 in 200. The test should usually only be offered to a woman in a situation where there is a greater risk of bearing a child with some abnormality. The fluid obtained is examined both microscopically and chemically.

Microscopic examination looks at the cells which have been cast off from the baby's skin and mucous membranes. This will identify the sex of the child, which is important in sex-linked conditions such as Duchenne muscular dystrophy and haemophilia. DNA analysis may also identify diseases such as sickle cell disease and thalassaemia. Examination of the cultured cells allows chromosomal analysis which detects abnormalities such as Down's syndrome (47 rather than 46 chromosomes — trisomy 21), and more rarely Turner's syndrome (45 XO) or Edward's syndrome (trisomy 18). It is also possible to diagnose enzyme deficiencies such as Hurler's syndrome.

Chemical analysis is done on the supernatant and usually the relevant chemical measured is α-fetoprotein (AFP), with a high level very suggestive of an open neural tube defect.

After amniocentesis there is an increased risk of respiratory difficulties in the fetus immediately after birth, and also orthopaedic postural deformities which may require treatment.

Screening tests to identify open neural tube defects

Before the triple test was introduced, routine AFP blood levels were estimated around the 16th week. If the level was high, it was repeated and if the second result was elevated the woman was referred for amniocentesis.

Chorionic villous sampling (CVS)

This was first caried out in China in the 1970s and its use has spread over the past few years. Its main value is as an alternative to amniocentesis in selected cases. The method has the great advantage of enabling a much earlier abortion to be arranged compared with amniocentesis if the diagnosis is positive.

About 10–50 mg of placental tissue is obtained, usually through the cervix, at about week 9 of pregnancy. Chromosomal analysis (for Down's syndrome, etc.) on a culture may be made as soon as 8 days later. DNA analysis may be made directly on the specimen. For high risk patients, with diseases such as thalassaemia, this may well become the method of choice. The MRC European trial[10] showed the risks of CVS to be significantly greater than amniocentesis. Of those sampled, 86% had a live baby that survived. Most of the loss was before 28 weeks gestation, and some of the detected abnormalities that were terminated would have spontaneously aborted anyway, before amniocentesis would have been performed. This makes the risks even greater when compared with amniocentesis. Reports from Oxford in 1991[11] suggested there may also be an increase in severe limb deformities in babies born to mothers having had CVS as a result of the procedure.

Counselling

Skilled counselling of both parents is important before screening. The risks of having a handicapped baby must be set against those of the procedure. Counselling is equally important after the screening procedure, and especially after a termination of pregnancy. Full details of the procedure must be given (written details are useful). In the event of a malformed fetus, the parents must be given every opportunity, both at the time of delivery and some time later, to discuss all their fears and worries. Blood tests can be performed on the parents to detect if they are carriers of certain diseases. Finally, the risks of likely recurrence in another pregnancy must be given where possible.

Dental care in pregnancy

Dental care in pregnancy is always very important as any expectant mother's teeth can deteriorate rapidly. Each mother should visit the dentist early in pregnancy for a complete check-up and treatment. All pregnant and nursing mothers (up to 1 year after confinement) are entitled to free dental treatment including, if need be, the provision of dentures.

Prevention of Rhesus incompatibility (rhesus iso-immunization) by immunization

It is possible to prevent many of the problems of Rhesus incompatibility by immunization with anti-D immunoglobin of Rhesus negative women immediately after their first confinement or miscarriage. However, there were still a reported 20 deaths from Rhesus iso-immunization in 1988, and 10 in 1989[12] (see Table 4.5). Rhesus iso-immunization occurs when Rhesus positive blood cells from the child cross the placental barrier, commonly at the time of birth or miscarriage. The Rhesus negative mother manufactures antibodies against these Rhesus positive blood cells and destroys them. However, in subsequent pregnancies these antibodies may increase and cross the placental barrier to enter the baby's blood stream thus destroying the baby's blood cells. Untreated, this may lead to a grossly anaemic baby or even a stillbirth. All Rhesus negative mothers must be given anti-D immuno-globin immediately following the delivery of a child, or miscarriage. The anti-D

TABLE 4.5   Classification of deaths registered by OPCS due to haemolytic disease of fetus and newborn, 1977–89

	1977	78	79	80	81	82	83	84	85	86	87	88	89
Prophylaxis not given during pregnancy[a]	85	68	64	54	26	33	16	12	16	17	10	8	7
Sensitized in first pregnancy	12	11	10	6	6	5	8	3	9	8	7	6	2
Failure of prophylaxis	9	7	12	11	9	6	9	9	8	5	10	6	1
Blood transfusion	0	2	1	1	0	0	1	1	0	0	0	0	0
Total	106	88	87	72	41	44	34	25	33	30	27	20	10
Deaths per 100 000 live births	18.4	14.6	13.5	10.9	6.4	7.0	5.4	3.9	5.0	4.5	3.9	2.9	1.5

[a] Pregnancies occurring before 1970, when anti-RH immunoglobulin was not widely available account for the majority of pregnancies in this group from 1983.
Data from various OPCS surveys.

immunoglobin then destroys any Rhesus positive red blood cells of the baby before there is time for the mother to develop antibodies.

The dose of anti-D immunoglobin for all Rhesus negative women, regardless of parity or blood group, is 100 μg. Further doses may be required for cases in which large transplacental haemorrhages have occurred. All Rhesus negative women having therapeutic abortions up to 20 weeks should be given 50 μg of anti-D immunoglobulin, and after 20 weeks the full 100 μg dosage should be given.

Social security benefits

Statutory maternity pay (SMP) is operated by an employer, there does not need to be an intention to return to work to claim. SMP is payable if the person has been in employment without a break for at least 6 months by her 26th week of pregnancy, and her average weekly earnings are above the amount where National Insurance (NI) contributions are paid. There are two rates of SMP. The greater amount is paid to a woman if she has been working at least 16 hours a week (full time) for at least 2-years, or at least 8-hours a week (part time) for at least 5 years. The first 6 weeks of SMP is paid at 90% of her average earnings. After that the lower rate is paid for the remaining time. SMP is paid for up to 18 weeks. For women who have been in the same employment for between 26 weeks and 2 years, the lower rate is paid for the whole period. At least 3 weeks notice of intent to take maternity leave must be given, and the employer is given the maternity certificate (form MAT B1).

Maternity allowance may be paid for up to 18 weeks to someone who has changed jobs, or become self employed provided the standard rate NI contributions have been paid for at least 26 weeks in the 52 weeks leading up till the 26th week of pregnancy. The maternity allowance is slightly less than SMP.

Maternity payment from the social fund (£85 for every baby expected, born or adopted) may be paid if the mother or partner are getting Income Support or Family Credit. The full amount is only paid if there are savings of less than £500. Applications should be made from 11 weeks before the baby is due until the baby is 3 months old. For an adopted baby the claim may be made up to the time he/she is 1 year old.

Prescription charges — exemption certificates are issued by the FHSA to all expectant mothers which provide for free prescriptions and dental care until their babies are 1 year old. Form FW8 (available from the GP, midwife or health visitor) must be completed.

Free milk is available to expectant mothers and all children under school age where the family income is below a certain level, i.e. on Income Support or Family Income Supplement. Free milk is also available to all handicapped children aged 5–16 years who are not registered at school and to children attending a registered day nursery.

Care of the mother and child during the puerperium

The midwife has full responsibility for the domiciliary care of the newly delivered mother and child during the puerperium. Midwives must visit for a minimum of 10 days and a maximum of 28 days, and usually also visit in the evenings for the first 3 days. Records of pulse and temperature are maintained. If a temperature of 38°C (100.4°F) occurs or a reading of at least 37.5°C (99.4°F) on 2 successive days, medical help should be sought.

Blood for the Guthrie test (to discover phenylketonuria) and to test for hypothyroidism is collected by means of a heel prick by the midwife from the baby between the 6th and 14th day.

Breast feeding should be started whenever possible and much patience, encouragement and care will be needed to do this. In the puerperium the midwife helps the mother with all aspects of mothercraft which she has learnt in her health education classes — how to bathe the baby and generally care for the newborn child.

POSTNATAL CARE

A careful examination of every mother delivered in hospital should be undertaken before her discharge home. The baby should also be fully checked. A further postnatal examination is carried out 6 weeks after delivery, usually by the GP, but this may be at the hospital when there has been an abnormal delivery or caesarian section. Decisions about the next pregnancy, place and mode, are often best clarified at this stage when recent events are still clear. Clarification can be obtained from the hospital records about such aspects as pelvimetry (measurement of the size of the pelvis) in a woman who has had a breech delivery, blood sugar series in pre-diabetic women, etc. By this time the health visitor should be liaising with the mother. The baby also should have a 6-week check performed.

Family planning

Ideally discussion should already have taken place regarding the use of further contraception. The choices available for the woman include:

Combined oral contraceptive which stops ovulation. Taken for 3 weeks out of four, may suppress breast feeding, and therefore not often used in mothers who are breast feeding.
Progesterone only pill which needs to be taken every day, can be used with breast feeding. Does not stop ovulation. Women may experience irregular bleeding or amenorrhoea. Less effective than combined pill.

Injectable progestogens — licensed only for use after rubella immunization has been given when certain contraception is essential. Is effective for 3 months in full dosage. Cycle control can be affected, and once given cannot be reversed.

Intra-uterine devices ('the coil') — usually copper-coated, the modern coil can be left for up to 5 years. Best fitted after 6 weeks and possibly 3 months. Risks include perforation of the uterus, infection and heavier bleeding.

Diaphragm which needs special measuring, best used with a spermicide.

Female sterilization either immediately in the postnatal period or after an interval of 3 months. The fallopian tubes are either cut and tied or clips placed on them. Often done through the laparoscope.

The male may also use the condom, or be sterilized (vasectomy). Coitus interruptus (withdrawal) and the rhythm method are still greatly used, though not particularly recommended in view of their potentially high failure rates. New methods such as the progesterone impregnated ring pessary are being evaluated at the present time.

Confidential enquiries into maternal deaths, 1985–87

Beginning in 1957, there have been reports published in England and Wales every 3 years relating to confidential enquiries into maternal deaths. Scotland started reporting such details from 1965 and North Ireland from 1956. Different time intervals were selected. The figures were combined and a total Report for Deaths occurring from 1985 to 1987 was published in 1991.[13] All such deaths are reported on form MCW 97 and sent through community physicians/directors of public health to a central committee before sending them to the national assessors. The confidential enquiries should be required reading for all professionals involved in the care of pregnant women. In the most dramatic way possible they highlight the dangers and problems and stop any possible complacency in the provision of maternity care.

The last report covered a total of 265 maternal deaths in the 3-year period — 212 in England, 18 in Wales, 25 in Scotland and 10 in Northern Ireland. Of these deaths, 16 were late 'deaths', i.e. more than 6 months after pregnancy and delivery. With each report clear recommendations are made and these should be widely disseminated. Subsequent reports have only too often pointed to lessons previously known but not acted upon. Close collaboration with anaesthetists and general medical colleagues is a vital prerequisite of optimum care. The report also pointed out potential problems with staff providing obstetrics and gynaecology services on different sites and called for a reappraisal of the total staff, medical and midwife, available to provide adequate cover on a 24 hour basis.

Table 4.6 shows the changes in the maternal death rate over 3-year periods spanning the 18 years from 1970 to 1987. Hypertensive disease of pregnancy and

TABLE 4.6   Direct maternal deaths by cause, rates per million pregnancies in England and Wales, 1970–87

	1970–72	73–75	76–78	79–81	82–84	85–87
Hypertensive diseases of pregnancy	14.9	13.2	12.5	14.2	10.0	9.4
Pulmonary embolism	17.6	12.8	18.5	9.0	10.0	9.1
Anaesthesia	12.8	10.5	11.6	8.7	7.2	1.9
Ectopic pregnancy	11.5	7.4	9.0	7.9	4.0	4.1
Amniotic fluid embolism	4.8	5.4	4.7	7.1	5.6	3.4
Haemorrhage	10.4	8.1	10.3	5.5	3.6	3.8
Abortion	25.3	10.5	6.0	5.5	4.4	2.3
Sepsis (excluding abortion)	10.4	7.4	6.5	3.1	1.0	2.3
Ruptured uterus	3.8	4.3	6.0	1.6	1.2	1.9
Other direct causes	6.9	8.5	8.2	7.5	8.4	7.5
All deaths	118.7	88.0	93.4	70.0	55.0	45.6

Data from ref. 13.

pulmonary embolism are the two main facts responsible for maternal deaths in the latest report. There have been dramatic decreases in reported deaths from abortion (73 to 6) and from anaesthesia (37 down to 6) over the 17-year period.

HYPERTENSIVE DISEASE OF PREGNANCY (PRE-ECLAMPSIA)

Despite recent advances in the control of hypertension and convulsive disease, the report stresses that hypertensive disorders remain a major cause of death. Recommendations made in the two previous reports to implement specialized regional teams to assist in the treatment of these difficult cases have not been followed, and the death rates from pre-eclampsia in England and Wales remained the same between 1970 and 1972 and between 1985 and 1987 compared with a fall in deaths and death rates from eclampsia. The influence of age, particularly over 35 years, is apparent from such figures. The percentage of maternal deaths where care had been judged to be substandard rose from 72% to 81%, but this might just reflect higher expected standards. The natural desire of a woman who may feel well to stay at home must be recognized. However, it is essential that effective supervision of that patient is maintained to detect early signs of deterioration. The woman must be fully involved in the decision making and immediate admission to hospital facilitated when required. The role of the consultant obstetrician at this crucial stage is stressed, and junior staff should not be expected to make treatment decisions. Because such conditions are relatively rare, supervised teams of obstetricians, anaesthetists and physicians specializing in renal medicine/hypertension hould be consulted. Half the eclamptic fits in the report occurred in women already under medical care in hospital. There is evidence that the use of low dose aspirin in pre-eclampsia is beneficial[13] and this is undergoing further trials.

THROMBOSIS/THROMBOEMBOLISM

Venous thromboembolism is a major cause of maternal deaths in the UK. There were 30 such deaths from pulmonary emboli reported, with 16 deaths occurring during pregnancy including eight deaths before 17 weeks of gestation; 14 such deaths occurred after delivery. Most of the antenatal groups had unrecognized deep venous thrombosis, and where the diagnosis had been considered investigations were negative in four cases which had provided a false sense of security. The report states the potential dangers of anti-coagulant therapy seem to have been exaggerated. Pulmonary embolism was often mistaken for infection. Most of the postnatal group were active and had already been discharged from hospital. Risk factors for such complications include past history of thromboembolism, obesity, immobilization, operative delivery and lupus anti-coagulant (shown on routine blood grouping).

ANAESTHETIC DEATHS

There were six anaesthetic deaths (and two late deaths) reported in the 3-year period, and 16 further deaths in which anaesthetic factors were considered to have contributed to the deaths. The endotracheal tube lying in the oesophagus was the most common reason. Patients who might be more difficult to anaesthetize include the obese. Only one woman died of aspiration of vomit and associated pneumonitis. The routine use of ranitidine for all patients in labour must not be forgotten.

ECTOPIC PREGNANCIES

There were 22 direct deaths before 28 weeks which included 16 due to ectopic pregnancy, four to spontaneous abortion, one to ruptured uterus and missed abortion and one to legal abortion. Of the 16 who had ectopic pregnancies there was a history of tubal damage and abnormality in seven cases. Too many cases of ectopic pregnancy are missed because the medical attendants had not considered the diagnosis of pregnancy and a previous history of sterilization is a particularly hazardous trap. The ready availability of β human chorionic gonadotrophin (HCG) for the detection of early pregnancy should enable the diagnosis of pregnancy to be readily and immediately ascertained. Ultrasound scanning can make an important contribution to the management, but is not reliable under 6 weeks gestation, and its use out of hours for emergencies is also problematic. Delay in considering the diagnosis must be kept to a minimum with immediate hospitalization and assessment on arrival in hospital by a senior doctor.

HAEMORRHAGE

There were 10 deaths from antepartum (APH) and postpartum haemorrhage (PPH), four from a placental abruption and six from a PPH. The fact that there were no deaths from placenta praevia might be attributed to the use of routine ultra-sound scanning. Assessment of blood loss is often underestimated, and delays in obtaining blood for replacement is inexcusable.

INFECTIONS

There were six direct deaths reported and three deaths where infection had played a major role. The β haemolytic streptococcus was the causative agent in four such cases and *Escherichia coli* the agent in two. The problem with these infections is the insidious nature of their onset, often mimicking flu-like symptoms, and their rapid fulminating progress.

CARDIAC DEATHS

In the last survey these ranked third in the list and involved 23 cases. In six cases pregnancies had preceded against strong medical advice, and with eight deaths the severity and implications of the problem had been underestimated and the lack of team co-operation evident.

MATERNAL DEATHS FROM CONGENITAL HEART DISEASE

These rose from 22% in the early 1970s to 43% of the total maternal deaths in the last survey. There are also special anaesthetic problems to be noted in women with cardiac disease and the prophylactic use of antibiotics should be prerequisite at delivery.

Conclusion

It is clear that much has been done over the past few decades to improve services for pregnant women in the UK. The GP and community midwife have a large part to play, with careful antenatal care, working closely as a team. The National Audit Office[14] emphasized the skills of the midwife, and stated that they had tended to be underused in maternity care. Careful audit, both in hospital and general practice must continue to look closely at the services provided, with women themselves being closely involved with the discussions about their care.

References

1. Central Health Services Council. Domiciliary midwifery and maternity bed needs (Peel Report). London: HMSO. 1970.
2. House of Commons Social Services Committee. Second Report: perinatal and neonatal mortality. London: HMSO. 1980.
3. Maternity services. Pulse 14 January 1989; 49(2): 65–70.
4. Department of Health and Social Security. Second report of the Maternity Services Advisory Committee. Maternity care in action. Part 2 — Care during childbirth. London: HMSO. 1984.
5. Department of Health and Social Security. First, second and third reports of the Maternity Services Advisory Committee. Maternity care in action. London: HMSO. 1984.
6. The Nation's Health. A strategy for the 1990s. p. 260. London: King's Fund. 1988.
7. United States Department of Health and Human Studies. The health benefits of smoking cessation: a report of the Surgeon General 1990. Rockville, MD: Office on Smoking and Health. 1990.
8. Chamberlain G. ABC of antenatal care. Br. Med. J. 1991, 302: 774.
9. Wald NJ. Maternal serum screening for Down's syndrome in early pregnancy. Br. Med. J. 1988, 297: 883–887.
10. Medical Research Council. MRC European trial of chorionic villous sampling. MRC working party on the evaluation of chorionic villous sampling. Lancet 1991, 337: 1491–1499.
11. Frith HV et al. Severe limb abnormalities after chorionic villous sampling at 55–66 days gestation. Lancet 1991, 337: 762–763.
12. Hussey RM, Clarke CA. Deaths from rhesus haemolytic disease in England and Wales in 1988 and 1989. Br. Med. J. 1991, 303: 445–446.
13. Report on confidential enquiries into maternal deaths in the United Kingdom, 1985–87. London: HMSO. 1991.
14. National Audit Office. Maternity services. London: HMSO. 1990.
15. OPCS. Mortality Statistics, England and Wales, 1981. 1990. London: HMSO.
16. Marsh GN. Modern obstetrics in general practice.
17. McNay M. Br. J. Hosp. Med. 1984, 31: 406–416.

5

Child Health Services

The health of the children of the country should be of the greatest concern to us all. Almost one fifth of the population of the UK is under 15 years of age. Much has been done during the past 90 years to develop effective medical services for young children, more than for most other groups in the community. By 1990, the perinatal mortality rate had fallen to 8.1 per 1000 births and the infant mortality rate to 7.9 per 1000 births (see Chapter 3 for further details). However, large variations still exist throughout different regions of the country and between different social classes.

Role of parents

The role of the parents in the upbringing of their children is crucial. The health care needs of a child are inextricably linked to the social care needs of the family. Behavioural patterns of the parent are likely to be copied by the child (smoking and drinking habits are obvious examples). The effect of marital breakdown of the parents, neglect and abuse also have major effects on the child. It is less clear, and little data exists to enable comment, what effect the child has on the health of the parents.

The Children Act (1989) introduces the concept of parental responsibility (see Chapter 22), and in health the advent of the parent-held record (see later), clearly places the parent at the centre of the care of the child. This has also been clearly recognized by the recommendations for parental attendance at case conferences. The legal right to see medical records held by doctors will enable involvement.[1]

Organization of child health care services

The primary health care team obviously plays the central part in providing health care services, both to the child and the family. Since April 1990, GPs have been able to register to provide child health surveillance to children aged under 5 years on their list. The surveillance (or watching over) of the health of all children can only be successfully carried out with the closest co-operation between the many professionals likely to be involved and the parents.

The community child health services came under the control of the DHA in 1974. In most districts these services are under the general supervision of a paediatrician with a special interest in community child health. Senior clinical medical officers (SCMOs) and clinical medical officers (CMOs) help carry out some of the surveillance. Immunization is the responsibility of a designated doctor in each district.

The school health service is also the responsibility of the community child health services (see later). District handicap teams, formed to bring together a multidisciplinary team to assess, treat and support the family, were introduced following the recommendations of the Court Report (see later). Such teams are still only present in about two thirds of districts in England and Wales.

There will be numerous occasions when the child with a specific problem comes under the divided care of the hospital service. In addition, in all instances where there is a health or social handicap, those in the educational and social service fields are required to be concerned from an early age (1981 Education Act − see p. 132).

Over the past two decades, the key community worker in the preventive child health services has been the health visitor usually attached to a health centre or large group practice working very closely with GPs. Details of the role of health visitors are discussed later (see p. 126).

Care in the neonatal period

The first month of any child's life (and especially the first week) is one of the most critical. Table 5.1 shows the number of stillbirths, perinatal and infant mortality statistics for England and Wales in 1990. The number of live births increased by

TABLE 5.1   Births, perinatal and infant mortality statistics for England and Wales, 1990

Live births	706140
Stillbirths	3256
Deaths under 1 week	2498
Perinatal deaths	5654
Perinatal mortality rate[a]	8.1
Deaths under 4 weeks	3221
Deaths under 1 year	5564
Infant mortality rate[b]	7.9

[a] Perinatal mortality rate per 1000 births.
[b] Infant mortality rate per 1000 births.
Data from ref. 10.

2.7% in 1990 compared with 1989. The perinatal mortality rate (stillbirths and deaths under 7 days expressed per 1000 live and stillbirths) was 8.1. The rate for regions ranged from 5.9 per 1000 births in East Anglia to 10.2 for the West Midlands RHA. Of all births, 7% were low birthweight babies (under 2500 g). These low birth weight babies accounted for 60% stillbirths and 50% of infant deaths.

Nearly all babies (over 99%) are now born in hospital or a similar maternity unit, but most of these will be home within a few days (some indeed being discharged after 6 hours; see p. 97). Therefore the care of the child in the neonatal period occurs both in hospital and in the community and staff from both must work closely together. Every newborn infant should be fully examined by a doctor before leaving hospital. Ideally parents should be present at this examination and certainly the doctor should always personally communicate the findings to the parents. Where any abnormality is found or where there is a social problem, both the GP and the health visitor should be informed.

In addition to feeding and general care difficulties, there are four special problems found in the neonatal period:

(1) haemolytic disease of the newborn
(2) neonatal cold injury
(3) care of low weight (premature) babies
(4) congenital malformations.

Screening tests are also carried out to exclude phenylketonuria, hypothyroidism and congenital dislocation of the hip.

HAEMOLYTIC DISEASE OF THE NEWBORN

Reference has already been made to this disease and its prevention (Chapter 4, Table 4.5) In the presence of the slightest jaundice, a blood estimation of bilirubin (obtained by a heel prick) should be done before discharge. Fop those children at home who appear jaundiced, the midwife carries a simple perspex device (an icterometer) for estimating quickly the depth of jaundice in the newborn child and in cases of doubt will arrange a bilirubin blood test at the local hospital and appropriate treatment where necessary.

NEONATAL COLD INJURY

All newborn infants may suffer from neonatal cold injury, but the danger is greatest in low weight babies. If any baby, in the first few weeks of life, becomes seriously chilled, its body temperature may fall dangerously low (to 32.2°C (90°F) or lower). The infant then becomes quiet and difficult to rouse or feed. There may be a deceptively florid complexion, but the skin surface is much colder than usual and later the child becomes oedematous. This is a dangerous condition which can prove fatal.

Prevention depends on ensuring that the temperature of the room in which the baby is sleeping does not fall below 18°C (65°F). Most midwives carry a wall thermometer which is used to record the maximum and minimum temperatures of the room. This check is needed both in winter and in summer when unexpectedly low temperatures may occur at night.

CARE OF LOW BIRTHWEIGHT (PREMATURE) BABIES

Approximately 7% of all live births involve a baby of low birthweight, less than 2.5 kg (5.5 lb).

Special care baby units for low birthweight babies

About 1–2% of all live births require a period of prolonged care in a special care unit until their weight is satisfactory. Approximately 14–15% of other live births are admitted to such units for a short time after birth for observation and resuscitation. Special transport arrangements are necessary to enable a very low birthweight baby to be safely transferred to such a unit.

There are special aspects of care in the case of low birthweight babies, namely:

- incubator care
- feeding
- prevention of infection
- prevention of hypoxia
- prevention of the complications of prematurity.

Incubator care

Babies in Special Care Baby Units (SCBU) are normally nursed in incubators. This allows the temperature, relative humidity and supply of oxygen to be controlled. The risk of too high an oxygen level, which may damage the eyes of the newborn (retrolental fibroplasia), is minimized by monitoring the levels of oxygen in the blood.

Feeding

Human breast milk, obtained from breast milk banks, is the feed of choice for such babies. Inadequate sucking and swallowing reflexes in the baby born before 34 weeks gestation may mean that the feeding must be done through a tube passed into the stomach (nasogastric tube) or intravenously by a drip.

Prevention of infection

The immune system is relatively deficient in the premature baby, as is the response of the white blood cells. This decreased inflammatory response may be the reason that there are often very few clinical signs to accompany serious, life threatening infections. Great care must be taken to minimize the risk of infection in such units. The risk of developing neonatal sepsis and meningitis is about four times greater in the premature baby compared with the full term infant. Strict isolation techniques, including the use of gowns and masks, should be applied.

Prevention of hypoxia

The respiratory centre in the brain is immature in the premature baby, which results in periodic breathing and apnoeic spells. Sophisticated ventilation methods are used and the oxygen in the blood strictly monitored (to prevent retrolental dysplasia, see below). The brain itself (particularly around the *ventricles*) is particularly prone to haemorrhage in pre-term infants. Ultrasound scans may be used for early diagnosis of such problems.

Prevention of the complications of prematurity

Other complications that pre-term babies are likely to develop include respiratory distress syndrome (RDS), jaundice, intracranial haemorrhage and gastrointestinal problems such as necrotizing enterocolitis. Vitamin K is recommended for all babies (to lessen the risks from haemorrhage).

The active involvement of the parents in the nursing and care of even very premature babies and the use of photographs of the babies have helped overcome some of the worries regarding 'bonding' in children who previously might have been in incubators for many weeks and had only the minimum contact with their natural parents. However, the strain on parents whilst their child is being cared for in a SCBU should not be underestimated. They will need to be given every opportunity to discuss their feelings and fears.

CONGENITAL MALFORMATIONS

About 1 in 48 babies is born with a congenital abnormality.[2] These vary from serious defects such as myelomeninigocele (spina bifida), intestinal obstruction or some kind of congenital heart disease to foot defects and cleft lips. In the worst cases, immediate specialized hospital care is essential, but in others a plan of future action needs to be discussed. In all instances, there should be sympathetic and full communication with both parents and a full explanation given. The health visitor and GP should be involved at an early stage so that the mother may know to whom she can turn for day-to-day advice. In all cases of the birth of a child with an inherited abnormality, whether of an anatomical type (spina bifida, cleft palate) or of a metabolic origin (phenylketonuria), the parents should be offered genetic counselling.

In all cases where a permanent disability is likely, the district handicap team (see p. 128) should be involved at an early stage and the parents clearly made aware of the wide range of professionals and services ready to help.

Morbidity of congenital malformations

A scheme of voluntary notifications of all abnormalities observable at birth (or found within 7 days after birth) was introduced in the UK in 1964 to enable continuous monitoring of congenital malformations following the thalidomide tragedy. The doctor or midwife completes the notification of birth form and states on

TABLE 5.2   Principal causes of congenital malformation by site in England and Wales, 1986

Site	Number	Rate (per 10 000 live and stillbirths)
Talipes	1944	29.3
Hypo- and epispadias	1036	15.6
Cardiovascular malformations	882	13.2
Ear malformations	661	9.9
Polydactyly	638	9.6
CNS malformations	637	9.6
Cleft lip	611	9.2
Syndactyly	519	7.8
Down's syndrome	445	6.7
Reduction deformities	276	4.2
Cleft palate (excluding lip)	275	4.1
Spina bifida	267	4.0
Anal atresia/stenosis	159	2.4
Hydrocephalus	138	2.1
Exomphalos, omphalocele	127	1.9
Eye malformations	102	1.5
Tracheo-oesophageal fistula and oesoephageal atresia and stenosis	94	1.4
Anencephalus	52	0.8

Data from ref. 2.

it whether any abnormality was apparent at birth. The District Medical Officer will then find out from the GP or hospital concerned the precise diagnosis. The completed form is then sent to the Office of Population Censuses and Surveys (OPCS) which maintains a national register. This scheme is designed to detect changes in frequency of reporting rather than to estimate the absolute incidence of malformations.

In 1986, just over 13 000 babies in England and Wales were notified with one or more congenital malformations. Approximately 84% of the children had one, 12% two, 3% three and 1% four or more malformations. The age and parity of the mother are also factors in determining the levels of incidence; the lowest rates are in the younger mothers having their second child while the highest rates are in mothers over 40 having their fourth child. Table 5.2 shows the principal conditions recorded by site in England and Wales in 1986.

Talipes is the commonest malformation followed by hypospadias and epispadias, cardiovascular malformations and ear malformations. More abnormalities occur in boys than girls, by a ratio of 5 : 4, but this is mainly due to the external genital abnormalities.

SCREENING TESTS

Four important screening tests should be carried out on newborn babies. These are to detect: phenylketonuria, neonatal hypothyroidism, congenital dislocation of the hip, and deafness (during the period 3–8 months).

Phenylketonuria

This is a rare inherited metabolic disease. Faulty metabolism results in poisonous phenylalanine metabolites being produced which can lead, after a few months, to markedly retarded mental development and severe mental handicap. Only if the disease can be diagnosed within a few weeks of birth and the child given a special diet can mental deterioration be avoided. To ensure that every case of phenylketonuria is discovered early enough, a Guthrie test is carried out on a specimen of blood taken from the baby between the 6th and the 14th day of life. Several spots of blood from the young infant are collected from a heel prick on to specially absorbent filter paper. In the laboratory a small disc is punched out of each of the blood-impregnated filter papers and up to 100 individual discs are placed on a special agar plate containing a spore suspension of *Bacillus subtilis* and an inhibitory substance. Phenylalanine acts as an antagonist to the inhibitor and, after incubation, growth of the organism will be observed around blood discs which contain phenylalanine.

Neonatal hypothyroidism

The incidence of neonatal hypothyroidism is calculated at one in 3937 births (1 in 6640 male and 1 in 2756 female births).[3] Undetected it can cause permanent brain damage and retardation. Provided the condition is treated before the 3rd month of life, 74% of those with this condition will achieve an IQ of 90 or better. If the diagnosis is delayed until the 4th to 6th month, only 33% come into this category. The test is done on the same blood sample as the Guthrie test (see above). The test involves measuring by radioimmunassay the thyroid hormone (T4) which comes from the pituitary gland and is present in the baby's blood. The thyroid stimulating hormone (TSH) may also be measured, is more specific, but requires a further specimen of blood. It is always measured to confirm the diagnosis. All births are now screened for neonatal hypothyroidism. With full screening it has been estimated that about 150 infants a year will be prevented from developing brain damage and mental handicap.

Congenital dislocation of the hip

This is a condition which if diagnosed very early can be effectively treated. If, however, diagnosis is delayed, it is much more difficult to correct and may lead to permanent disability.[4] The main cause of this condition is inadequate development of the acetabulum of the pelvis. There is a simple test (eliciting Ortolani's or von Rosen's sign) which should be carried out on all babies at 6–14 days after birth and at monthly intervals until the child is 4 months old. This test consists of manipulating the hip of the child from the adducted to the abducted position while the thigh is flexed. A positive or abnormal result is indicated by a 'click', or snap, being produced during the test and corresponds with the dislocated femoral head moving into the proper position in the acetabulum.

Whenever this test is abnormal, the child should be immediately referred to an orthopaedic surgeon. Confirmation of the diagnosis is now done by ultrasound examination. Treatment is simple and consists of maintaining the hips continuously in abduction by application of a plaster spica or special splint. This produces constant pressure by the head of the femur in the centre of the acetabulum and causes it to deepen and develop normally. After 6–9 months of such treatment the danger of permanent congenital dislocation of the hip has passed. Diagnosis within a week or two of birth means that treatment can be completed before the infant would normally have reached the stage of standing.

Deafness

The diagnosis of congenital deafness in an infant is best made by carefully observing the pattern of sound production and vocalization of the child between the 3rd and

8th month. During the first 2 or 3 months of life, any child will make reflex noises — crying loudly if uncomfortable and gurgling if content. This stage is similar in both normal and deaf children. By the 4th month, the first attempts at vocalization are made in the normal child and by 7–8 months, the infant babbles away loudly and tunefully and has a very definite ability to listen. It is at this stage of development that the deaf child's reflex vocalizations begin to diminish and, by the 8th month, he/she is making fewer and fewer attempts to produce sounds.

Because of this change, the health visitor should be careful to observe all children from 3 to 8 months of age, and particularly those in the high risk groups which include: family history of deafness, low birth weight, birth asphyxia, jaundice in the neonatal period, infections such as rubella, cytomegalovirus or neonatal meningitis and malformations of the face, external ears and cleft palate.

The 6% of newborn infants at high risk includes 60% of those subsequently found to be severely deaf. The acoustic cradle may be used in the maternity hospital with the baby's head resting in a moulded headrest to detect turning and reactions to sounds. Babies who 'fail' such a test will then require further assessment. The incidence of severe sensori-neural deafness in children aged 4 years and under has been calculated by Taylor[5] to be 1 in 2000.

FEEDING

Wherever possible, breast feeding is recommended and much patience and perseverance may be needed to establish it. Encouragement is often required to allay the fears of mothers that their breast-fed babies are not getting enough milk. The increased tendency for mothers to return to work after 2 months and the ease and convenience of artificial feeding have tended to increase bottle feeding. There is, however, plenty of evidence to show that breast feeding gives a child the best possible start in life and the incidence of all types of infection (particularly infantile gastroenteritis) is significantly lower[6] (see also Chapter 14). The personal bond between mother and the breast-fed child is very close. From the mother's point of view, the incidence of carcinoma of the breast seems to be lower in women who have breast fed their children. When breast feeding cannot be established the health visitor advises the mother on artificial feeding. Dried and evaporated milks are used, being reconstituted just before the baby's feed.

Child health surveillance

The aim of child health surveillance is to:

- help each child to reach his/her full potential
- detect early all delays in development
- ensure each child receives periodic developmental screening tests looking at

(a) physical development, (b) hearing language and speech and (c) social skills, including the ability of the child to make satisfactory human relationships
- provide health educational advice and support to parents including training in parenthood
- link the preventive health services with treatment sought for illnesses or accidents
- prevent communicable diseases by immunizations.

DEVELOPMENTAL CHECKS

Much of the preventive health services for young children depends on recognizing the normal stages in a child's development. Considerable variation occurs and no reliance should ever be placed on stereotyped tables of progress, but usually a baby will double their birthweight by five months and treble it by a year. Regular weighing is useful only to indicate in general a change in progress — a sudden loss of weight or a halt in the gain of weight calls for further investigation. Care must always be taken not to overstress the baby's weight, for it should never be a mother's main guide to progress. Some of the fittest babies are those who have been breast fed and these are usually lighter than average although very active and alert.

The frequency of checks has been the subject of some debate. The recommendations of the Hall Report[7] are outlined in Table 5.3. It recommends the times which are especially important and these include: birth, 6 weeks, 8 months, 18 months, 2 years and 3 years. If problems are discovered then it will be necessary for the team to assess the child even more frequently. No opportunity should be missed, however, to assess a child's development on each occasion it is seen by a health care professional.

During the whole assessment, it is essential to involve the parents as actively as possible. In fact, it will often be found that the parents are the best source of information about their child's progress. The best possible way to involve the parents is to encourage them to assess and to teach their child; aiming to build the partnership with the parents. The parent-held record will also help in this respect.

The healthy infant normally sits with support by the 3rd, or 4th month of life, and will sit alone by the 6th or 7th month. By the 8th or 9th months he/she can usually stand with support and will probably stand without support between 10 and 14 months, and walk soon after. Crawling and creeping often occur at about 9 or 10 months, but may not always do so.

Weaning from either the breast or from the bottle usually commences between 4 and 6 months. Once started, it is wise gradually to extend the range of foods used so that the child becomes accustomed to different tastes.

The development of speech is a very important stage. The normal child learns to speak by imitating what he/she hears and by 18 months of age he/she should be using simple words and sentences. A slow development of speech always calls

TABLE 5.3   Suggested core programme of surveillance for all children

Age of child	Examination[a]
Neonatal	Height*, weight*, head circumference*, full physical CDH*, testes*, eyes (red reflex)*, consider high risk group for hearing assessment (ARC/BSER)
Discharge (10 days)	CDH*
6 weeks	Height*, weight*, head circumference*, CDH*, eyes*, refer high risk hearing
8 months	Eyes (? squint)*, hearing (distraction test)*, CDH*, testes*
21 months	Walking with normal gait*, saying words and understands
39 months	Height*, testes* (if not checked before)
5 years (school entry)	Height*, weight*, eyes (Snellen chart)*, hearing (Sweep test)*
School	Height (if parental concern), eyes (visual acuity at 8, 11 and 14 years)*, colour blindness test (11 years)*

[a] At all examinations parental concerns must be asked about, and those of teachers, etc. where appropriate.
* Procedures that fulfil the criteria for screening.
Modified from chapter 17 of ref.7.
ARC, auditory response Grade 1; BSER, brain stem evoked response; CDH, congenital dislocation of hip.

for investigations to exclude: (a) deafness and (b) children with learning disabilities (mental handicap). Diagnosis of either condition may be extremely difficult in the very young child. If deafness is suspected, an immediate audiometric test should be carried out at the local specialist unit. Special equipment and soundproof rooms are essential to define the extent of the deafness. Children with learning disabilities (mental handicap) show delay in all stages of development — sitting, standing, walking — as well as a retarded development of speech.

Sphincter control of the bladder of the baby is slow to develop and may not be completely reliable until the child is 2½–3 years old. It is important that the mother realizes this fact. Between 10–20% of 5-year-olds and 5–6% of 10-year-olds still wet at night.

CHILDREN AT SPECIAL RISK

There is a need in some infants for more intensive oversight of their health and for special monitoring of their development progress. Such children represent about 15–20% of all births in whom either the prenatal, family, perinatal or postnatal history are in some way abnormal. The group will also include families known to be living in poor social conditions (problem families). The selection of such a group to receive care should be flexible, but should certainly include those with a history of:

- low birthweight
- any congenital malformations
- history of rubella in the mother during pregnancy
- history of maternal hyperemesis or hypertensive disease of pregnancy
- difficulties in the neonatal period, e.g. anoxia, convulsions
- those infants with any marked illness postnatally.

The occurrence in other members of the family of hereditary disorders or markedly abnormal behaviour should also be warning signs for extra care. Such children are known to be at special risk. Particular attention should be paid to potential deafness.

PARTICULAR HAZARDS OF THE POST NEONATAL PERIOD

Apart from the continual dangers from serious congenital malformations already being treated, there are two main hazards facing an infant in the first 9 months of life — respiratory diseases and sudden infant deaths syndrome (SIDS, cot death; see Table 5.4) In some cases, these conditions are connected.

TABLE 5.4   Sudden infant deaths: by age at death, 1988 and 1989, England and Wales

			Age at death (months)					
Year	All	under 1	1	2	3	4	5	6–11
Number								
1988	1593	83	294	374	294	188	128	232
1989	1326	69	253	337	243	160	92	172
Percentage of all SIDS under 1 year								
1988	100	5.2	18.5	23.5	18.5	11.8	8.0	14.6
1989	100	5.2	19.1	25.4	18.3	12.1	6.9	13.0

Data from ref. 8.

Sudden infant death syndrome (SIDS, cot death)

Sudden infant death is a most distressing event with the sudden death of a child who had previously seemed to be completely fit and well. In 1988–89, 62% of the deaths were among male infants, and 70% occur in infants aged between 1 and 4 months.[8] It is rare beyond the first year of life. No one cause is responsible.

Causes which have been postulated are many and include:

- sleeping in the prone position (face down)
- overwhelming infection
- allergy (possibly to cow's milk)
- mechanical obstruction, e.g. laryngeal oedema, smothering
- cardiac arrhythmias
- metabolic causes (e.g. calcium, sodium and magnesium metabolism)
- overheating
- hypothermia
- disorder of the respiratory control centre in the brain (this may cause prolonged apnoea).

At post-mortem examination there is usually little to find. There may be evidence of an upper respiratory tract infection in approximately one third of cases. More deaths occur in the winter months compared to the summer months.

Although SIDS has been thought to occur without warning, retrospective analysis shows that in quite a number of instances symptoms have been present in the child for a day or two before death. These may have been mild or their significance been unrecognized by the parents. Such symptoms include snuffles, coughs and wheezing, diarrhoea and vomiting, and non-specific symptoms such as irritability, drowsiness and lethargic behaviour. Boys are affected more than girls. There is a higher risk in very low birthweight babies and where a previous sibling has died from SIDS. Babies of opiate addict mothers have up to an 80 times greater risk. Other risk factors include:

- number of children in the family
- young mothers
- maternal urinary tract infection in pregnancy
- history of difficult labour
- twins
- babies where there has been difficulty in establishing artificial feeding.

'Near miss' infants who have been found moribund and successfully resuscitated continue to be in a high risk group and much attention has been focused on these children. Such occurrences are greater in families of socio-economic classes IV and V.

Prevention studies in Sheffield suggest that it may be possible to identify families whose children may be at potential risk. Such families need concentrated and good antenatal, perinatal and postnatal care. Advice on the hazards of smoking, and encouragement to breast feed should be given. Home respiratory monitoring with an alarm system to indicate apnoea (apnoea alarms) are being used increasingly for the 'high risk' infants. Reservations that the device would only increase parental anxiety have been shown to be incorrect, and parents appreciate the added security they feel with such an arrangement.

The Foundation for the Study of Infant Deaths (FSID) has been responsible both nationally and locally for much public education and awareness of the problem. At the end of 1991, with the endorsement of the DH, the FSID through health authorities wrote to all GPs with a four-point guide to reducing risk. The advice, similar to that given in New Zealand where the cot death rate has been halved, is as follows:

- place the baby on its back or side to sleep
- avoid smoking, and keep the baby out of smoky atmospheres
- do not let the baby get too hot
- if you think the baby is unwell, contact the GP.

The earliest results are most encouraging. There was a dramatic fall in the number of SIDs in the first 3 months of 1992: OPCS reported 130 deaths during January to the end of March 1992, compared with 365 and 321 deaths in 1990 and 1991.

A sudden infant death is a family tragedy. Much support of the parents will be needed to help them with their feelings of guilt, anger and grief. Explanations, including post-mortem findings when available, and discussions about the future need to be given. Long-term support of the family by the health visitor and GP is essential.

ROLE OF HEALTH VISITOR

During the puerperium the midwife is responsible for the care of the newborn infant. At the end of this period the health visitor becomes the main health education adviser helping with advice on such things as infant feeding, prevention of accidents, and immunization. The health visitor ideally should already have met the mother during pregnancy at the mothercraft classes.

One of the most valuable aspects of a health visitor's work (see also Chapter 7) is that she/he visits the home regularly where she/he can give practical health education advice about frequency of feeding, clothing, the temperature of the baby's room and general hygiene.

The health visitor usually works from a health centre or group practice, but may visit a child health clinic set up separately. After the initial home visits, she/he endeavours to persuade the mother to bring the baby to be seen at the health centre or clinic (at approximately 6 weeks). Most mothers attend regularly, especially during the first year of the baby's life. The fact that the mother comes to a health centre or clinic does not mean that the health visitor ceases to visit the home, although the frequency of visiting is usually reduced.

As the child grows older the health visitor continues to advise and help the mother. Apart from general health education, specially important aspects include:

Immunization schedules — these are checked and everything is done to encourage completion of all immunizations and their booster doses. This is most important. *Any serious illness* should be carefully followed up by the health visitor. The health visitor, in the follow-up, checks on the child and if need be, arranges for the GP to examine the infant. Hearing difficulties, chest problems and squints should be checked for.

Advice to parents with disabled children — the health visitor has special responsibilities to assist and advise all parents with disabled children. The health visitor should provide a point of contact for the parent of every child who has been found to have a disability or who is showing signs of special needs or problems.

The prevention of home accidents in young children is becoming relatively more important as other causes of child deaths (such as infectious diseases) have diminished. Table 5.5 shows causes of deaths in children from accidents.

TABLE 5.5   Accidental deaths by cause, age and sex[a] for England and Wales, 1984

Cause	Age (years)								
	0–4		5–9		10–14		All ages		
	M[a]	F	M	F	M	F	M	F	Both
Road accidents	57	32	105	57	129	68	291	157	448
Fires	34	19	13	9	8	6	55	34	89
Drownings	27	9	13	0	10	5	50	14	64
Inhalation/ingestion	23	21	3	1	4	0	30	22	52
Falls	20	6	12	1	17	2	49	9	58
Suffocation	16	12	1	1	19	0	36	13	49
Electrocution	0	1	4	0	3	2	7	3	10
Poisoning — medicine	4	4	0	0	0	1	4	5	9
Poisoning — other	1	2	1	2	12	2	14	6	20
Scalds	5	3	1	0	0	0	6	3	9
Other accidents	25	15	15	2	16	9	56	26	82
All accidents	212	124	168	73	218	95	598	292	890
Deaths per 10 000 population	1.3	0.8	1.1	0.5	1.2	0.5	1.22	0.63	0.93

[a] M, male; F, female.
Data from ref. 11.

Child health clinics

From 1974, the running of these clinics passed from the care of the local authority to the health authority. Clinical medical officers (CMO) may attend these clinics on a sessional basis. The services at the clinics include sales of infant foods, including suitable dried milks, concentrated orange juice, vitamin supplements and certain other baby foods, often at lower prices compared to retail outlets.

Education is a most important function of such clinics, and may include both the health visitor and midwife in mothercraft classes. The health visitor may advise on all sorts of minor problems as they arise.

Court Committee Report

A comprehensive review of the child health services in the UK was carried out by a special committee under the chairmanship of Professor Court in the mid 1970s. Its report[9] made many recommendations which were mostly accepted by the government (with the exception of those advocating the creation of specialist health visitors and child health nurses, consultant community paediatricians and GP paediatricians).

The main themes of the report stressed that:

- Child health shows a changing pattern with more chronic illness and handicap as well as an increase in child psychiatric problems.
- Much ill-health in children is preventable and social and geographical factors are very significant; there is considerable variation in local infant and perinatal mortality and morbidity.
- More importance should be paid to health and social care within families, and this involves a need to promote a better partnership of care between parents and professional staff of all kinds.
- An unmistakable interrelationship exists between the health, educational and social needs of all children.

More integration of child health services was considered to be essential, particularly between prevention and therapeutic care and between hospitals and the community services. Health visitors were seen as key personnel in achieving this better integration and their work with children and families should become their top priority. The specialist paediatric services should be increasingly extended into the community and all GPs should have adequate training in child health and, in future, undertake more preventive work with children under 5 years of age. The committee stressed the importance of helping the children in greatest need.

DISTRICT HANDICAP TEAM

The Court Report recommended that a special multidisciplinary team called a 'District Handicap Team' should be established in each health district and based on a district general hospital. Their functions should include:

- investigation and assessment of all individual children with complex disorders, and co-ordination of their treatment
- professional advice to parents, teachers, child care staff and others who may be directly concerned with their care and guidance to them in their management of their children

- encouragement and help for all professional field work staff in the management and surveillance of handicapped children locally; each team should act as part of a common service to the health educational and social services
- provision of primary and supporting specialist services to the local special schools.

The following professionals should always be members of any District Handicap Team:

- paediatrician
- clinical school medical officer
- nursing officer for handicapped children
- specialist social worker
- psychologist
- teacher
- supporting administrative staff.

Health of the schoolchild

The progress of any child at school depends on many factors including parental, environmental and domestic. The intelligence of the child and the school are also important. Ill health or a serious physical or learning disability may soon produce educational problems. In recognition of the importance of health, special arrangements are made to look after the health of the school child. Each DHA, in conjunction with the relevant local education authority must organize a school health service.

AIMS AND OBJECTS OF THE SCHOOL HEALTH SERVICE

The objects and functions of the school health service are:

- to make certain that every schoolchild is as fit as possible so that each may obtain the maximum benefit from his or her education
- to promote positive health in all children attending school; every child should be as fit as possible
- to help with the ascertainment and treatment of various groups of handicapped children and those with disabilities so that every child can gain the maximum benefit from his or her education.

ORGANIZATION OF THE SCHOOL HEALTH SERVICE AND INTEGRATION WITH THE PRE-SCHOOL AND PRIMARY HEALTH CARE SERVICES

Each DHA must designate a key doctor who is a community physician experienced in child health who, with the senior nursing officer, has direct responsibility to the local education authority for the organization of health services to schools. This ensures that there is a sound day-to-day link between the primary health care team and those working in the school health services. The community physician responsible for dealing with child health problems should always ensure that there is a satisfactory system to exchange essential information (some of which will be confidential) between the doctors in primary health care teams and those in the school health services. Similarly there should be a sound system for sharing essential information with other professionals working in the education services, especially with teachers and those who can help with information about home conditions (health visitors, education welfare officers, specialist careers officers or social workers). Special steps are also taken to ensure that there is integration of the child health services for the pre-school child and schoolchild. Every DHA must appoint a senior nursing officer who is accountable to the district nursing officer for all child health nursing including that within the school health service. She is professionally responsible for all the nursing staff employed in the field of school health (school nurses) and must collaborate with the community physician responsible for child health.

NURSERY SCHOOLS

The normal child can gain much from attending a nursery school from the age of 3 years to when they start school, at $4\frac{1}{2}$ or 5 years. Most of the value of such schools, which many children only attend for a half a day, is in the social contact made and in easing the start of attendance at primary school. Just under 50% of children in the UK aged 3 and 4 years attend nursery schools. The medical supervision of children in nursery schools is the responsibility of the school health service.

THE SCHOOL NURSE

There were 2473 registered school nurses in England and Wales in 1987. They play the key role in supervising the health care of children at school. They liaise closely with teachers, parents and the health care professionals. Co-operation with the primary health care team, the health visitor and GP in particular is very important.

Pre-school examination

The initial examination usually takes place shortly after the child has been admitted to the infant school, but it may be performed as a pre-school initial medical examination. A check on the immunization received is made and, if any are needed, these can be given before entry into school.

School medical examinations and inspections

The present basis of the school health service is a combination of full routine examinations of all children around the time of entry into school and selective examinations during school life. There is a full examination at 14 years of age. The school nurse may complete an extensive questionnaire on each child before the examination at 5 years old. This covers developmental history, social development, general physical condition and home conditions. Specific problems will be asked about.

Selective medical examinations may subsequently be carried out on children who have suffered particular illnesses. Such examinations are carried out by the school doctor, who visits regularly, and problems raised by parents, teachers and school nurses may also be dealt with. Parents are invited to attend if they wish. The emphasis of the service changed during the late 1970s and 1980s, from one of providing just regular examinations to one which fostered a closer and more continuous link between school health staff and teachers.

The first full medical examination pays particular attention to eyesight and hearing. The eyesight test checks on visual accuracy, colour vision and muscle balance. If any defect is found, a full ophthalmic examination is arranged, often with an orthoptist performing an initial assessment. Appropriate treatment (glasses, orthoptic treatment for squints) may then be arranged if required. The hearing of each child should be tested individually by the school nurse using a sweep test with a pure tone audiometer. This is a light portable machine producing sounds of varying volume at frequency ranges from 128 to 8000 cycles per second. Each ear is tested independently. Tests are carried out at each frequency starting with a loud volume of sound and gradually reducing the volume until the child can no longer hear anything. This level indicates the hearing threshold — the lowest volume of sound at that particular frequency which the child can hear. This test is repeated for each frequency so that a pattern of hearing is established for both ears at different frequencies of sound. It is important to test hearing at different frequencies as there may be a loss of hearing at one particular part of the sound scale (such as a high frequency deafness). Testing the hearing of a 5-year-old should take about 3 minutes. About 2% of those tested fail. The test should then be repeated having treated the child if any immediate cause, such as wax or infection, has been found. If still abnormal such children should be referred to an Ear, Nose and Throat Department for further investigation and treatment. The DHA is responsible for the provision and repair of behind-the-ear hearing aids or, where necessary, body-worn hearing aids required by schoolchildren.

Any other disability discovered at the first full medical should be assessed regularly to check on progress.

There are special particular responsibilities of the school doctor and school nurse in respect of promoting positive good health among the children:

- *Investigation of all communicable diseases in the school* — for example, if a case of tuberculosis occurs within a school, complete examination of all contacts (staff and children) must be carried out to make certain that an unsuspected case has not been the cause. Contacts over the age of 15 years are X-rayed. Younger contacts are tuberculin tested; chest X-rays are arranged on any positives.

- *Immunization* — immunization should always be encouraged in children and the immunization status of every new school entrant should be checked. BCG vaccination against tuberculosis should be offered to all school children aged 10–12 years who are tuberculin negative. Vaccination against rubella should have been given to all school girls at the age of 13 years if they have not already been protected against rubella.
- *Health education* — this is one of the most important functions of the school medical officer and school nurse. Examples of topics include sex education, AIDS and family planning, smoking and health, alcohol and drugs, heart disease and prevention of disease by immunization. Much of this health education should be integrated naturally into the ordinary curriculum of the school. The role of exercise should be discussed and exercise should be encouraged for all children.
- *Hygiene* — the hygienic conditions of the school should be inspected periodically by the school medical officer and school nurse and should include examination of buildings, the heating plant, washing and lavatory facilities and the kitchen premises.

The nurse may also check children for various conditions, including the common problem of headlice. About 2% of schoolchildren are found to have evidence of infestation with headlice, mainly in the form of nits which are the eggs of the head louse. Treatment of all the family is essential to prevent recurrent re-infestations. Reported headlice infestation in England and Wales has fallen from 189 200 in 1981 to 94 600 in 1986. Scabies is occasionally found in schoolchildren. Treatment with benzyl benzoate is rapid and effective, but again only if all infected members of the family are treated simultaneously.

EDUCATION ACT 1981

The discovery, classification and care of handicapped schoolchildren is a most important role of the school health service. The Education Act 1981 introduced the concept of special education based on the special educational needs of the individual child. Previously children were categorized by handicap, which did not necessarily indicate the educational needs of the child. Separate education for such children had been the emphasis.

About 16–17% of the school population (one in six) at any time (or 20% or one in five at some time during their school life) require some form of help, which might take the form of special teaching techniques or equipment, a specially modified curriculum, or help with social or emotional problems. The term 'handicapped children, has been replaced by 'children with disabilities or significant difficulties'.

The term 'educationally subnormal, has been replaced by the term 'children with learning difficulties', which includes slow learners.

Under the Education Act 1981, a child is considered to have special educational needs 'if he has a learning difficulty which requires a special educational provision to be made to meet those needs'. The term 'learning difficulty' is defined to include not only physical and mental disabilities, but also any kind of learning difficulty experienced by a child provided it is significantly greater than that of most children of the same age. It does not include a learning difficulty caused by a child speaking a foreign language.

Under Section 2 of the Education Act 1981, the principle was established that all children for whom the local education authority (LEA) decide that special educational provision should be made should be educated in ordinary schools so far as is reasonably practicable. This principle is subject to:

- an account having been taken of the views of the parents
- the ability of the school to meet the child's special educational needs
- the provision of efficient education for other children in the school
- the efficient use of resources by the LEA.

IDENTIFICATION OF EDUCATIONAL SPECIAL NEEDS

Every LEA has a duty to endeavour to identify children with special educational needs between the ages of 2 and 16 years. The parents must always be notified of the intention of the LEA to make an assessment and be given information about the assessment procedure. The LEA must also provide the parents with the name of an officer from whom they may obtain further information. The Education Act, 1981, empowers the LEA, with the consent of the parents, to assess the special educational needs of children under the age of 2 years and the LEA must do so if the parents ask for an assessment.

The LEA must, for a small percentage of children who have severe or complex learning difficulties, make a 'statement' determining the appropriate provision to be made in respect of individual special educational needs. The LEA is then under a legal duty to arrange special educational provision in accordance with the statement. Parents have a right of appeal against the proposed special educational provision, first to a local appeal committee and finally to the Secretary of State for Education and Science.

Responsibilities of DHAs to facilitate early discovery of children with special educational needs

Every DHA and its professional staff has a duty to inform the parents and the appropriate LEA when they form the opinion that a child under the age of 5 years has, or is likely to have, special educational needs. The parents must be informed before the LEA, but if the parents do not agree with the health authority or do not take up the offer of a discussion, the LEA will nevertheless be informed of the health authority's opinion.

Independent schools

If an independent school wishes to accept LEA placements of children in respect of whom a 'statement' has been made and maintained, then the school must, in future, meet similar standards in respect of premises, qualified staff, education and care to those required in maintained and non-maintained special schools.

Professional advice

The LEA in preparing an assessment and 'statement' must seek medical, psychological and educational advice. The LEA may at their discretion seek advice from other professionals in the health or personal social services. This may include health visitors, school nurses, occupational therapists and social workers.

Principles applying to the care of children with disabilities or significant difficulties

There are five important principles applying to the care of children with disabilities or significant difficulties:

- The degree of disability, e.g. deafness, should be diagnosed and discovered as early as possible. It is important that the diagnosis be made within the first year of life.
- Special education and care must be started early — in deafness, as soon as diagnosed, in blindness between 1 and 2 years of age.
- The aim should always be to make each child as independent as possible.
- The best solution for any schoolchild with a disability or significant difficulty is always the one that is as near normal as possible.
- The after-care of the child with a disability or significant difficulty when school is left should never be forgotten. If possible, special vocational training and/or work preparation should always be arranged.

The child with a disability or significant difficulty may be educated in a number of environments. The aim is to try and keep them in an ordinary school, although it may be that they are in a special class, or indeed the school shares a site with a normal school so that there is a mixing and sharing of facilities. For those more seriously affected, they may need to be in a residential special school. Some children who are medically ill, may need to receive their education in the hospital where they are being treated, or at home.

Discovery of disability and disclosure to parents

The importance of early discovery of any disability or difficulty has already been stressed. Once a problem has been discovered an explanation to the parents must be carefully and sensitively undertaken. In the case of a serious disability, most parents find it difficult to grasp the full meaning and implications, and are in need of continuous support and will require information, advice and practical help. Parents also should know the one person whom they can contact at any time for advice and help and one individual professional should be designated the key worker (or the 'named person') to act in this way. Voluntary and self help organizations provide much written material which may be of great help.

The health visitor is ofter the key worker for the pre-school child. When at school, the head teacher, or other teacher, may be the key worker for the child with educational difficulties. As children near school-leaving age it will ofter be appropriate for the Specialist Careers Officer to act in this way.

The Special Advisory Service of each LEA should be available to every parent of a disabled child who should always be told in writing how to contact members of this service if necessary during the school holidays.

Range of special education provided

In most severe disabilities, and especially if the child has already attended a primary school and made little progress, attendance at a special school may be required at least for an initial period. Many different types of special school have developed, run either by education authorities or voluntary bodies, and some have been in existence long before there was any statutory special education for very disabled children.

In practice, special schools are needed for three groups:

- *children with very severe or complex physical disabilities*, including blindness or deafness, to children with severe congenital disabilities (spina bifida and the severe types of cerebral palsy), to children with grave progressive diseases such as certain muscular dystrophies
- *children with severe emotional or behavioural disorders* who have difficulty in forming relationships with others or whose behaviour is extreme or unpredictable
- *children who for various reasons do badly in ordinary schools* and who need the more intimate atmosphere of small teaching groups to make educational progress.

Even with very severely disabled children, the aim should always be to increase the integration of such children with normal children. Integration may allow some mixing of disabled and normal children for some aspects of their school activities.

The disabled child who has attended a special school for many years will need to experience some degree of social and functional integration during the last 2–3 years of formal education.

Special problems of the disabled child in the transitional period from school into adult life

All children with disabilities or significant difficulties are likely to suffer special problems on leaving school. Their transition into adult life will probably be more difficult than that of a normal child for they are likely to find it less easy to get a job or to be accepted for higher education. A careful re-assessment takes place during the child's last 2 or 3 years at school (certainly never later than when the child is aged 14 years). This re-assessment should involve not only the teaching, psychological, medical and nursing staff, but also include careers guidance officers, disablement resettlement officers (DROs) and social workers from the social services department. The parents must be closely consulted and involved in decisions being made, and the help and support required estimated. The child may be advised to stay longer at school, or the child may attend a linked course planned jointly by schools and colleges of further education in which the pupils spend up to 2 days at the college being introduced to the possibilities of further education and generally widening the child's horizons.

Another arrangement to help with the transition is 'work preparation' whereby disabled young people still at school are placed in simulated working conditions by both visiting factories or work situations or by work experience in the form of a planned period of supervised employment in industry, commerce or in the public services. Such work preparation should be carefully planned as part of the school curriculum for such disabled children. For those over school leaving age, there are also Employment Rehabilitation Centres.

Assessment of a specific vocational kind should, wherever possible, be carried out locally, but there are specialized residential units to which the child may go, such as the Queen Elizabeth's Foundation at Banstead Place.

Careers guidance

Special guidance is needed in the choice of career for all disabled children and involves their parents, with teachers, the Specialist Careers Officers, members of the school health service and the social services department. A link must also be maintained with the DROs who help with the employment of disabled adults.

Some young people on leaving school, especially if their disability is a learning disability (mental handicap) type, will be transferred to adult training centres run by social service departments and, hopefully, later to sheltered workshops. Some very severely physically disabled young persons may likewise move on to special day centres or rehabilitation units run by social services departments.

Children who are blind or partially sighted

Blind children have no useful sight and must be educated by non-visual methods. In practice this means that children whose sight after correction is worse than 3/60 will usually be classified as blind. Such children start their training when they are 2 years old, either in special local units or the Sunshine Homes run by the Royal National Institute for the Blind. Education in most cases takes place in residential schools during the earliest years, except in the largest cities where other facilities may be available. For older children, carefully planned integration is possible and helpful as it prepares the blind young person more completely for adult life.

Partially sighted children includes children whose visual acuity after correction is 3/60 to 6/24 . Children with progressive myopia come into this category. Classes must be small (containing not more than 10 children) and special equipment is needed. Wherever possible, partially sighted children are taught in special day schools or special classes in ordinary schools so that there is as little interference with the normal education programme as possible.

Children who are deaf or have only partial hearing

Deaf children are those who cannot be taught by auditory methods. It is most important that their education and training be started very early (as soon as diagnosed). Very specialized tuition is needed which translates the teaching of sounds into a visual exercise, and by such methods it is possible to teach totally deaf children who have never heard human speech to talk. Without such tuition, the totally deaf child would always be dumb, as speech is normally learnt by a process of copying sounds.

Most deaf children are educated in special residential schools until they have acquired speech and a good mastery of lip reading. Some form of integration should then be encouraged, especially in secondary schools, although some extra personal teaching supervision will always be needed. Children who have partial hearing, provided they are assisted with special apparatus, can be taught by aural methods. It is usual for such children to be taught in small classes. These can be in special units in ordinary primary and secondary schools. Only the more severe or those with multiple disabilities need to be taught in special schools.

Children with epilepsy

The majority of children with epilepsy can be educated in an ordinary school provided that: (a) the fits do not occur too often, (b) the emotional stability of the child is reasonably normal and there is no marked behavioural difficulty, (c) there is a sympathetic teaching staff who realize that no other child in the class will be harmed by witnessing an occasional epileptic fit. Good liaison between the school doctor and teacher can help considerably. If the child has very frequent major fits, admission may have to be arranged to a special residential school for children with epilepsy for assessment and treatment. In most cases, it should be possible for the child to return to a normal school.

Children with learning difficulties

This is a very large group and includes children with a low IQ. Educational performance depends on the intelligence of the child and on his/her application. The IQ (Intelligence Quotient) is calculated by dividing the mental age by the real age and multiplying by 100. Such assessments are usually carried out by an educational psychologist. For example a child aged 10 years who has a mental age of 7.5 years would have an IQ of 75. The distribution of IQs in the community gives a parabolic curve when plotted. In terms of usual performance, IQs will be found as follows:

over 125	university entrant
115–124	highest stream
90–114	middle stream
80–89	lowest stream
55–79	children with learning difficulties
Under 50–55	children with special learning difficulties for their intelligence is very limited (i.e. those with learning disabilities (mental handicap)

IQ must only be used as a rough guide. Performance is the decisive factor and depends on a combination of IQ and application, which in itself is affected by mental stability, concentration and to a minor degree training. Great care is needed in assessing such children and repeated tests should be regularly carried out. Physical causes, such as deafness, should rigorously be looked for.

Children with learning difficulties usually need to be educated where the pace of teaching is slower, but can be integrated into ordinary schools provided special help is available. A special problem with children with learning difficulties is that they are more likely to show behavioural problems than normal children. This may bring some into trouble with the law, and unplanned pregnancy is a danger for girls.

Children with special learning difficulties (mental handicap)

This is a group of mentally handicapped children, whose education since 1970 has been the responsibility of the education services. Such children are usually taught in a special day school. Some form of transport is used to collect the children from convenient meeting places near their homes to carry them to and from the school. Emphasis is always placed on encouraging independence and self-reliance. Occasionally in rural areas 5-day residential special schools for such children are used at which the children stay from Monday to Friday, returning home for the weekend.

The aim of each special school is to educate these children in the widest sense and later on prepare the child for workshop employment. This includes social habit training, including eating, care of clothes, and personal hygiene. Later rudimentary lessons of arithmetic, reading and writing are held, but a number may never reach this stage. Most learn to recognize simple letters and figures, handle money, and a few can do simple sums. The education should include cooking.

These children are usually educated in small mixed schools (60–70 children). The children are divided by aptitude rather than by age. The level of intelligence of an entrant to such a school varies, but most have intelligence quotients between 45 and 55.

Children with severe emotional or behavioural problems

This child presents a really difficult problem and may show many features of maladjustment and may become retarded educationally. Such a child often has a normal or higher than average intelligence. Many different factors cause behavioural problems including psychological disorders, unstable home conditions, victim of physical or sexual abuse and marital difficulties between parents including divorce or separation. The Child Guidance Clinic where a child psychiatrist, psychologist and social worker function as a team may be used to investigate and treat such children. Special educational treatment may be indicated for maladjusted children with unsatisfactory home conditions in small residential schools containing 50–60 children.

Other groups of disabled children

There are other groups of disabled children such as:

Children with a physical disability, such as cerebral palsy, or spina bifida. Their education will largely depend upon the degree of the problem; many can be integrated into the ordinary school, but the more severe and complicated cases need specialized care, often in separate residential units.

Children with autism present a small but difficult group. In the early stages of diagnosis and assessment, special schools are needed, but the least affected children should be able to return eventually to ordinary school.

Children with dyslexia can easily be misdiagnosed as 'unintelligent'. Dyslexia shows itself in a series of ways affecting spelling, reading and other language skills. There is always a marked discrepancy between the mental potential of the child (usually normal) and his/her educational level. The incidence is as high as 3% although many minor cases are missed. Many children with dyslexia do well if the condition is recognized early. Dyslexic children and those with speech defects may often develop emotional difficulties from the frustration of being unable to keep up with other children or to make themselves readily understood. Special help with remedial teaching or speech therapy should be available. Speech therapists are employed in every school health service.

In all the above instances, it is essential to emphasize how important a specialized multidisciplinary assessment is to unravel the real causes of a child's problem, and how important it is that good effective communication exists between the various professional groups.

References

1. Access to Medical Records Act. 1991.
2. OPCS. Monitor MB3 87/1. London: OPCS. 1987.
3. Grant DM, Smith I. Survey of neonatal screening for primary hypothyroidism in England, Wales and Northern Ireland 1982–4. Br. Med. J. 1988, **296**: 1355–1358.
4. Dunn PM, *et al*. Congenital dislocation of the hip. Early and late diagnosis and management compared. Arch Childhood **60**: 407–414.
5. Taylor IG. The prevention of sensori-neural deafness. In: *Disorders of auditory function*. 3rd edn, eds IG Taylor, A Markides. London: Academic Press. 1981, pp. 25–31.
6. Howie *et al*. Protective effect of breast feeding against infection. Br. Med. J. 1990, **300**: 11–16.
7. Hall DMB. Health for all children — a programme for child health surveillance. Oxford University Press. 1989.
8. OPCS. Monitor DH3 91/1. London: OPCS. 1991.
9. Committee on Child Health Services (Chair Prof SDM Court) Fit for the Future. Vols 1 and 2. London: HMSO (Cmnd 6684). 1976.
10. OPCS. Monitor DH3 91/2. London: OPCS. 1991.
11. OPCS. Mortality Statistics: Cause, 1984. London: HMSO. 1985.

6

Immunization

In many communicable diseases an attack is followed by a varying period of immunity from further attacks. Not all communicable diseases are followed by such an immunity (e.g. the common cold), but in many the length of immunity is substantial and may last many years or even a lifetime. Whenever people develop immunity in this way, they do so by manufacturing special disease-resistant bodies in the blood called *antibodies*. It is possible to copy this mechanism artificially by introducing into the human body modified bacteria, viruses or their products so that the individual does not suffer from the disease but does develop antibodies and, therefore, an immunity to a natural attack. Artificial immunization and vaccination rely on this principle.

Diphtheria and poliomyelitis are probably the best two examples of the success of immunization in this country. During the 1930s there was an average of 61 000 cases of diphtheria, with approximately 3000 deaths per year. Within 20 years of the introduction of a vaccine the incidence had fallen to just 16 cases in a year with two deaths (see Table 6.1).

In the 5 years preceding immunization, poliomyelitis had an average notification rate of 2800 cases per year with 300 deaths. Within 6 or 7 years of the introduction of the vaccine, some 19 million people had received two doses of the vaccine. This resulted in a hundred-fold decrease in notifications between 1957 and 1963. Unfortunately, however, not all vaccination programmes have been so successful.

TABLE 6.1   Diphtheria in England and Wales, 1920–80

Year	Cases	Deaths
1920	69 481	5648
1930	74 043	3497
1940[a]	46 281	2480
1950	962	40
1960	49	5
1970	22	3
1980	5	0

[a] Immunization introduced in the mid 1940s.

Before 1970, epidemics of measles occurred every 2 years, but the introduction of the vaccine in 1968 altered this to yearly outbreaks. In 1961 there were 788 800 notifications, this had dropped to 155 000 by 1971 and to 26 000 in 1990. However, throughout the 1980s measles and pertussis (whooping cough) continued to be troublesome and occasionally fatal diseases; Table 6.2 outlines the decrease in Great Britain since 1979. Only approximately two thirds of the children had been vaccinated against either disease. Such low immunization rates do not enable herd immunity to protect those that are not immunized. The percentage of the population that needs to be vaccinated for herd immunity to play a part in the control of that disease is different for individual infectious diseases. For scarlet fever, for example, it is 75%; for measles 85–90%; for pertussis it is not known. The Faculty of Public Health Medicine[1] have stated that by 1995 total notifications for measles in Scotland and England and Wales should be 5000, reducing to 1000 by the year 2000. Table 6.3 shows the current vaccination rates for England, Wales and Scotland. By February 1991 it was estimated that the national averages for immunization coverage for England were 90% for diphtheria, tetanus and polio, 89% for MMR (mumps, measles and rubella), and 85% for pertussis.[2] The government publication *The Health of the Nation* [2] announced new national immunization targets of 95% by 1995.

In 1991 the World Health Organization (WHO) reported that 80% of the world's children were now immunized with BCG, diphtheria, polio, pertussis, tetanus and measles.[3] This compared to 50% having been vaccinated in 1987 and just 5% in 1974. As a consequence of such vaccination they estimated that the WHO's immunization programme had prevented more than one million deaths

TABLE 6.2   Measles notifications in England, Wales and Scotland, in 1979–90

Year	England and Wales	Scotland	Total
1979	77 386	10 324	87 710
1980	139 485	6 646	146 131
1981	52 974	4 698	57 672
1982	94 195	10 581	104 776
1983	103 700	6 193	109 893
1984	62 080	4 897	66 977
1985	97 408	4 595	102 003
1986	82 061	7 073	89 134
1987	42 155	2 695	44 850
1988	86 001	2 258	88 259
1989	26 801	3 359	30 160
1990[a]	13 302	2 006	15 308

Data from various OPCS Monitors in the MB2 series and from the Scottish Common Services Agency.

TABLE 6.3   Immunization acceptance rates for children under the age of 2 years in England, Wales and Scotland, 1979–89

	Diphtheria/Tetanus		Pertussis		Polio		Measles	
	E&W[a]	S[b]	E&W	S	E&W	S	E&W	S
1979	79	76	34	48	79	75	50	56
1980	81	79	40	52	81	79	52	52
1981	83	80	45	54	82	82	54	54
1982	84	83	52	58	84	82	57	57
1983	84	83	58	60	84	82	59	60
1984	84	85	64	69	84	84	63	64
1985	85	87	65	69	85	85	68	73
1986	85	86	68	71	85	85	71	76
1987	87	87	73	74	87	87	76	77
1988	87	88	75	76	87	88	80	84
1989		90		80		90		
1990		93		85		93		

[a] E&W, England and Wales.
[b] S, Scotland.
Data from ref. 1.

from measles, neonatal tetanus and pertussis. It was also estimated that over 175 000 cases of poliomyelitis a year were being prevented in the developing world.

Immunization target payments

Under the new general practitioner contract from 1 April 1990, GPs were paid separately for achieving immunization targets. Two targets, an upper and lower target, were for 90 and 70% respectively. Payments are paid for two groups, childhood immunizations for 2-year-olds and pre-school boosters for 5-year-olds. The upper target for childhood immunizations requires that 90% of children aged 2 years in any one quarter must have been fully vaccinated with three doses against diphtheria, tetanus and polio, three doses against pertussis and one dose of measles, or the combined MMR vaccination. The lower target figure, which pays a third of the upper figure, is paid if 70% of the target group have been fully vaccinated. Children vaccinated other than in general practice may count towards the percentage figure, but payment is reduced according to the numbers. In the first 6 months of the scheme, 55% of general practitioners reached the upper target and 25% the lower. By October 1990, 70% had reached the upper target, with a further 17% reaching the lower figure.

Artificial immunization

Artificial immunization can be either *active* or *passsive*. In active immunity a special product of the bacterium or virus (antigen) is introduced into the body, usually by injection, occasionally by mouth, and this stimulates the human body to manufacture its own protective antibodies. The immunity produced usually lasts a long time. Unfortunately, however, there is a delay of 1 or 2 months before such immunity is built up.

In passive immunity, antibodies which have been made by immunizing an animal or man are then used to protect the individual. The great advantage of passive immunization is that it is effective immediately, but only lasts a relatively short time, usually between 4 and 6 weeks. It is used either to help treat someone with the disease, for example, giving diphtheria antitoxin to someone with diphtheria, or to give temporary immunity to someone who has been in close contact with the disease and who may be incubating it. The other main disadvantage of passive immunity is that the person may easily be sensitized to the protein of the animal or human from whom the antibodies came, and this may cause serum sickness. A more satisfactory passive immunity is obtained by using immunoglobulin, the active constituent of human blood which contains antibodies.

In preventive medicine much greater use is made of active immunization than of passive immunization.

ACTIVE IMMUNIZATION AND VACCINATION

Communicable diseases attack in two main ways: (a) by a direct invasion process usually of a certain part of the body, and (b) by producing a very powerful poison (toxin) as they multiply in the body. Examples of the former include the inflammation of the lung in whooping cough, of the small intestine in typhoid, or in part of the central nervous system in poliomyelitis. Toxins are produced by diphtheria, tetanus and some food poisoning bacteria.

The first group of diseases can be prevented (1) by immunizing with an antigen of a *dead* or modified bacteria or virus (*killed vaccine*) or (2) by using a *live* vaccine made from a bacterium or virus which has undergone a mutation, which means it cannot now produce the real disease in humans, but can still produce antibodies and therefore an immunity (*attenuated vaccine*), and (3) by a recently available technique which has become available where a component of the microorganism which is not toxic is used ('*component*' *vaccines*).

In the second group of diseases it may be possible to inject a modified toxin (toxoid) prepared by the action of formaldehyde on the toxin. Toxoid is harmless but has retained the antigenic properties of toxin so that its injection results in the person actively developing their own antibodies which can counteract toxins.

TABLE 6.4   Types of vaccine in use at present

	Viral vaccines	Bacterial vaccines
Live	Yellow fever Measles Rubella Oral poliomyelitis (Sabin) Mumps Mumps, measles and rubella	BCG
Inactivated	Influenza Polio (Salk) Hepatitis B Hepatitis A	Hib Typhoid Cholera Pertussis Pneumococcal Meningococcal
Toxoids		Diphtheria Tetanus

Toxoid may be used to prevent tetanus and diphtheria, but is of no use for toxin food poisoning.

Table 6.4 shows the main groups of vaccines which are at present available. After immunization the levels of antibodies present (and therefore the level of immunity) may vary in different persons. Over several years, protection wears off gradually as the level of antibodies declines. Blood tests may be used to measure these protective antibodies and to see if vaccination is required (e.g. for rubella vaccination in the adult woman). Most diseases are usually prevented in 90% of people immunized, and an attack after immunization is usually very mild.

Vaccination policies and the eradication of the fatal infectious diseases, such as poliomyelitis and diphtheria, did tend to lead to a complacency regarding immunization. Many myths and incorrect ideas exist,[4] and these include:

- *The need for immunization.* Measles and whooping cough are not considered by some people to be serious diseases which require prevention. Measles is fatal in about 1 in 5000 to 1 in 8000 cases (there was one fatal case in 1990 in England and Wales) and whooping cough is fatal in 1 in 10 000 cases (with seven deaths in 1990 in England and Wales).
- *Contraindications to giving an immunization to an infant.* It is essential that all professionals involved in immunization are well-informed about the risks and benefits and be positive in their recommendations. In the 1970s when the vaccination rate was disappointingly low, there was much misunderstanding in relation to immunization. Vigorous campaigns to educate all professionals involved have helped remove a lot of these myths. The following are examples of reasons why vaccinations were not given but in fact are *not* contraindications:

Premature baby	Breech delivery
Respiratory distress syndrome	Eczema
Asthma	Being breast-fed
Hay fever	Nappy rash
Congenital heart defect	Cystic fibrosis
Adopted mother	Jaundice as baby
Under 2 kg	On antibiotics
Discharging ear	Down's syndrome
Snuffles	Mother pregnant
Grandparent, cousin or aunt/ uncle have fits	Child too old
	Previous infection of measles, mumps or rubella

Immunization is best postponed if the subject is suffering from an acute illness and has a fever and is systemically unwell. There is a minimal raised risk of a febrile convulsion if such an individual is vaccinated, but confusion may arise between deciding if certain symptoms arise from the vaccine or illness. Minor infections in the absence of fever or systemic upset are not contraindications. However, there is an important group for whom the administration of live vaccines is contraindicated.[5] It includes:

- HIV positive individuals
- patients receiving high dose steroids (2 mg/kg/day) for *more* than a week
- patients on immunosuppressive therapy including radiotherapy (there should be a delay of 6 months after finishing treatment)
- patients suffering from leukaemia, lymphoma or Hodgkin's disease or other tumours of the reticuloendothelial system
- other patients with known impaired immunological mechanisms.

Such high risk patients should be given an injection of immunoglobulin as soon as possible after exposure to measles or chickenpox. Children on lower doses of steroids for less than 2 weeks, and those on lower doses on alternate day regimens may be given live vaccines. Children using inhaled steroids for asthma can be immunized. There should be a delay of 3 months administering live vaccines to any individual who has received immunoglobulin because the immune response may be inhibited.

JOINT COMMITTEE ON VACCINATION AND IMMUNIZATION (JCVI)

Set up in 1962, this body advises the Health Minister on all the medical aspects of vaccination and immunization. They also produce the excellent and authoritive booklet 'Immunization against Infectious diseases'.[6] It was as a result of their suggestion that a single schedule of immunization was introduced in 1968. In 1985 the

JCVI recommended that each Health Authority should designate a particular person to take a special responsibility for implementing improvements to immunization programmes at a local level. Several modifications have been made to the schedule over the years. The last two major changes were the introduction of the MMR vaccine in 1988, and the rescheduling of the first three vaccinations earlier in life to the 2nd, 3rd and 4th months, respectively, from May 1990. Since October 1992, Hib vaccination (see p. 150) has been offered to all children at the same time as the triple vaccination.

ROUTINE IMMUNIZATION SCHEDULE

The schedule was changed in 1990 as a response to research carried out in 1989 by the Department of Health and others to look at why immunization rates vary so much throughout the country. The accelerated vaccination schedule was introduced in an attempt to reduce the dropout rate between the first and third doses (from the previous $7\frac{1}{2}$ months to just a 2-month gap), to have uniformity across health districts (and thus help people moving around the country), and to attempt to combine immunization with child surveillance. Table 6.5 summarizes the routine vaccinations available for children in the UK (see p. 148).

REACTIONS TO IMMUNIZATIONS

About 15% of babies have a mild reaction to diphtheria, tetanus and pertussis (DTP) within 48 hours of the injection. There may be some local swelling or a mild general reaction such as a slight temperature, headache, and general malaise. Such a reaction should never be a reason for not having future injections. About 30% of children may have a mild reaction 7–10 days after a measles injection, and up to 10% of girls experience mild joint pains and generalized reaction after rubella vaccination.

Severe reactions are, fortunately, very rare, but are a contraindication to further vaccination. Anaphylaxis must be anticipated with the correct drugs (adrenaline/hydrocortisone) immediately to hand, ideally in a specially prepared pack. The emergency care for someone suffering from anaphylaxis is as follows:

- place the patient on their left side
- insert airway if the patient is unconscious
- give adrenaline 1/1000 intramuscularly (see Table 6.6 for dosage)
- give oxygen
- send for a doctor
- start cardiopulmonary resuscitation if necessary
- 100 mg hydrocortisone and possibly 2.5–5 mg of chlorpheniramine maleate (piriton) may be given by intravenous injection
- repeat the adrenaline if necessary up to a maximum of three doses.

TABLE 6.5   Routine immunization schedule in Great Britain, 1989

Age	Vaccine[a]	Dose[b]	Notes
Primary immunization			
Birth	BCG	0.1 ml intradermally	For Asian babies and babies of those with tuberculosis
2 months	Polio	3 drops	Unvaccinated parents should be given vaccine at the same time
	DTP	0.5 ml IM/SC	
	Hib	0.5 ml IM/SC	
3 months	Polio	3 drops	
	DTP	0.5 ml IM/SC	
	Hib	0.5 ml IM/SC	
4 months	Polio	3 drops	
	DTP	0.5 ml IM/SC	
	Hib	0.5 ml IM/SC	
15 months	MMR	0.5 ml IM/SC	For children not already protected, to be given before infant school (4–5 years)
15 months	Measles	0.5 ml IM/SC	To be given if MMR refused or may be used from 6 months in a measles epidemic and repeated at 2 years
Secondary immunization			
4–5 years	Polio	3 drops	
	DT	0.5 ml IM/SC	
Tertiary immunization			
10–14 years	BCG	0.1 ml intradermally	If tuberculin negative
10–14 years	Rubella	0.5 ml IM/SC	Girls only who have not received MMR
School leaving	Polio	3 drops	
	Tetanus	0.5 ml IM/SC	

[a] D, diphtheria; T, tetanus; DTP, diphtheria, tetanus, pertussis; MMR, mumps, measles and rubella.
[b] IM, intramuscular; SC, subcutaneous.

All cases should be admitted to hospital for observation, and the reaction should be reported to the Committee on Safety of Medicines using the Yellow Card system (see Chapter 7).

TABLE 6.6   Recommended dosage of adrenaline for use in anaphylaxis

Age (years)	Dose of adrenaline (ml)
Less than 1	0.05
1	0.1
2	0.2
3–4	0.3
5	0.4
6–10	0.5

ROUTINE IMMUNIZATIONS

Tetanus

The vaccine is a suspension of purified toxoid prepared by formalin detoxification of the clostridium tetanus exotoxin. The adsorbed vaccine, which is thought to be more effective, is prepared by adsorbing the toxoid onto aluminium hydroxide. Protection from tetanus toxoid vaccination lasts for at least 10 years. More frequent boosters greatly increase the likelihood of severe local reactions.

Pertussis

Unfortunately there was much adverse publicity about pertussis immunization in the 1970s (down to 31% acceptance in 1978), and many myths have come to be established in people's minds which are proving hard to shake. The only absolute contraindication to pertussis vaccination is a previous *severe* local or general reaction. A severe local reaction is when most of the circumference of the arm, or most of the thigh is swollen with erythema. A severe general reaction would include anaphylaxis, collapse, fever higher than 40.5°C. and convulsions within 72 hours of injection. Special consideration (i.e. the risks should be balanced) is needed when deciding whether to vaccinate children who had cerebral irritation in the newborn period, those with neurological disease or developmental delay and where the parents or siblings have a history of epilepsy. There are probably very few children who ought not to be vaccinated — less than 5%. Pertussis vaccination is not usually recommended after the age of 5 years.

Diphtheria

This is the third constituent of triple vaccine, but may be given separately to high risk people including health care staff working in a communicable disease unit, family contacts, and those going abroad to work in an underdeveloped country. A reinforcing dose of dilute low-dose vaccine can later be used for such people and is sufficient to recall immunity without the risk of an adverse reaction, commonly found when the full strength vaccine is used in the adult.

Hib disease

A new vaccine was introduced nationally in the UK in October 1992 against *Haemophilus influenzae* Type b (Hib). This organism is the main bacterial cause of meningitis in children under the age of 5 (peak incidence 11 months). The type b strain may also cause epiglottitis, septicaemia, arthritis and pneumonia. The vaccine is an inactivated conjugated polysaccharide vaccine. It is important to realize that it is ineffective against other haemophilus strains such as those that cause middle ear infections, and also that it has no protective effect against other bacterial types of meningitis such as meningococcal meningitis.

Three doses of the vaccine are given to children under 1 year old, ideally at the same time as the Triple vaccine and poliomyelitis vaccine (2, 3, and 4 months). Children over the age of 1 who missed the first course should have just one dose given, and it may be given simultaneously with MMR (at a different site).

Poliomyelitis

The oral live Sabin vaccine has replaced the inactivated Salk vaccine, which was given by injection and this produces an immunity not only to a clinical attack of poliomyelitis, but also to a carrier state in the intestine. It can be given to close contacts to reduce the danger of an epidemic. All three types of poliomyelitis virus, Types 1, 2 and 3, must be included in the immunization which should be offered to all the population up to the age of 40 years. It is usual to give three doses of a trivalent vaccine (containing all three types of virus). Each dose seeds the small intestine. One of the types of poliomyelitis virus then grows rapidly and colonizes in the villi of the intestine. This produces a marked immunity against that type of virus. Once the intestine has been seeded by the poliomyelitis virus of a particular type it cannot be colonized again with the same type. So the second dose leads to colonization of one of the other two types and the third dose to colonization and protection against all three types. It is thus essential that all three doses are given to ensure complete protection. The vaccine is conveniently given on a lump of sugar. Very occasionally vaccine-associated paralysis may be a complication of vaccination. The risk is in the order of 1 per 5 million doses. The risk is greater in people over 50 years of age. The injectable (inactivated) Salk vaccine should preferably be given to this group if required. The Salk vaccine is also the preferred choice in pregnancy and for people who are immunosuppressed.

Measles

Live viruses only are now used to produce active immunity as the killed vaccines failed to produce long-lasting protection. The Schwarz strain of live vaccine is used. Official recommendation suggests that human immunoglobulin should be given concurrently for children with a personal or family history of convulsions, but there is no evidence that this is necessary. The vaccine may be used to control outbreaks of measles. If given under the age of a year in such circumstances, a booster should be given at the age of two. The risk of serious neurological reaction to measles vaccination is probably in the order of 1 per 100 000 doses. This is significantly less than with the disease itself.

Rubella

A single dose of freeze-dried live attenuated virus of the Cendehill strain is used. The vaccine has a storage life of 1 year at 2–8°C. Introduced in 1970, rubella vaccination is offered to all girls aged 10–14 years irrespective of whether or not there is a past history of German measles. For older women, serological testing carried out by the Public Health Laboratory Service should be done to detect immunity. Vaccination should then be offered to those who are sero-negative (not immune). Surveys of girls and young women show that 90% or more have demonstrable immunity.[7] Table 6.7 shows the notifications of the congenital rubella syndrome in the past 10 years. In 1986 and 1987, 362 infections in pregnancy were confirmed by Public Health Laboratories in England and Wales.

Very close surveillance in Britain, USA and Germany has failed to find any

TABLE 6.7   Cases of congenital rubella syndrome reported by year of birth

Year	England and Wales	Scotland	Total
1980	30	4	34
1981	12	1	13
1982	29	2	31
1983	43	4	47
1984	30	3	33
1985	17	1	18
1986	18	3	21
1987	23	1	24
1988	13	5	18
1989	4	1	5
1990[a]	4	3	7

[a] 1990 figures are provisional.
Data from various OPCS Monitors in the MB2 series, and from the Scottish Common Services Agency.

instance of a case of congenital rubella syndrome following inadvertent vaccination shortly before or during pregnancy. There is no evidence that the vaccine is teratogenic. Accidental vaccination in pregnancy would not now necessarily be considered a reason for the termination of the pregnancy. However, it is still recommended that pregnancy should be prevented for 1 month after the vaccination.

Mumps

This is a live attenuated vaccine used extensively in the USA but not previously thought to be worthwhile using routinely in the UK. It should not be used in children under 1-year-old. By the end of 1988 it began to be used routinely for all children in the UK in combination with measles and rubella (see below).

Mumps, measles and rubella (MMR)

In October 1988, the Government introduced a combined measles/mumps/rubella vaccine (MMR) with the intention to vaccinate all children between the ages of 1 and 2 years, both girls and boys, against measles, mumps and rubella. Hence it is hoped to eliminate these diseases and their consequences. To achieve this, the target for vaccination remains that already set for measles, i.e. 90%. The mumps component has been included because at present some 1200 admissions to hospital a year are as a consequence of mumps. Mumps is the commonest cause of viral meningitis and it may cause permanent deafness.

MMR is a freeze-dried preparation to be stored between 2–8°C and protected from light. The dose is 0.5 ml given by intramuscular or deep subcutaneous injection. For parents who decline MMR, the ordinary single antigen measles vaccination is recommended. MMR will be given to all children about to start primary school (4- to 5-year-olds) unless they have a valid contraindication or unless they already have received the MMR vaccination. Consequently, at present MMR vaccine should be given irrespective of previous measles vaccine or history of measles, mumps or rubella infection. Mild reactions may occur as with measles after a week, and mild parotid swelling seen after about 2 weeks. Such children are *not* infectious.

Tuberculosis

Immunization against tuberculosis is undertaken using a live vaccine of the Bacillus-Calmette-Guérin type (BCG). This is a modified (attenuated) bovine strain of *Mycobacterium tuberculosis* which has lost its power to cause disease in man, but can still produce a small trivial skin lesion. The vaccine is inoculated intradermally and, after a short period, an immunity against tuberculosis develops. BCG immunization is only used on people who are tuberculin negative, that is persons who have no skin sensitivity to tuberculin as shown by the Mantoux or Heaf test. Four main groups of people are immunized:

- close contacts (i.e. other members of the family) of a person with tuberculosis; this group includes the newborn baby if either parent has tuberculosis
- schoolchildren who are tuberculin negative aged 11–13 years
- nurses and medical students who, in their occupations, are liable to run a greater risk of infection from tuberculosis
- children of certain immigrants (especially Asians); all groups should be tuberculin tested and those who are negative immediately vaccinated with BCG

The JCVI have recommended that the current school BCG vaccination programme continue until 1996, when the policy will be reviewed and future policy reconsidered. BCG should not be given to children with active eczema, local sepsis or if they are HIV positive. If the injection produces a chronic ulcer (probably because of incorrect technique with the vaccine being given subcutaneously instead of intradermally), then a paste made up with isoniazid powder may be applied to aid healing.

SPECIAL GROUPS

Anthrax

Immunization against anthrax is available for all workers at risk. A killed vaccine is used and primary immunization should be carried out by three doses of vaccine injected intramuscularly at 3-week intervals and a fourth dose after an interval of 6 months followed by an annual booster dose.

Influenza

Inactivated influenza vaccines are prepared from egg-grown viruses of both A and B types which are expected to be prevalent in the forthcoming season. The formulation is reviewed annually, and dependent on what changes in antigen have occurred (antigenic drift), the composition of the vaccine is altered accordingly. Such antigenic drift may be quite marked following large winter epidemics. In the 1989 epidemic (the worst since 1975–76, due to the strain H3N2), over 5 million doses of influenza vaccine were given to groups considered to be at risk. A single injection is usually sufficient for adults. Three types of vaccines are available:

- whole virus vaccines, which are unsuitable for under 12-year-olds
- split virus vaccines, which are derived from the virus particles
- surface antigen, or subunit, vaccines where the antigen subunits are separated from the virus particles and adsorbed onto aluminium hydroxide.

Those at risk for whom it is recommended to consider influenza vaccine include:

- the elderly
- those with chronic cardio-vascular respiratory or renal diseases
- diabetics or those with other endocrine diseases
- all people who are immunosuppressed
- people living in long-stay institutions or hospitals, and
- health service staff in high risk areas.

Hepatitis B

Current vaccines are prepared from surface antigens extracted from human carriers. These have been purified and made free from the infectious HB virus. Genetically made antigens are now being produced in yeast cultures and are available. They have been shown to be perfectly safe and effective. Both vaccines contain 20 μg of hepatitis B surface antigen per 1 ml dose. Three doses are required: the second after 1 month and the third 6 months after the original dose. Booster vaccinations should be offered every 3–5 years.

Hepatitis B is spread by blood, saliva, semen and vaginal secretions, and the following people, if in frequent contact with blood and needles, should be considered candidates for hepatitis B vaccine:

- personnel working in renal dialysis units
- personnel working in units that deal with known carriers of hepatitis B
- personnel working in haemophiliac units or blood transfusion units
- renal dialysis patients who when travelling abroad will receive haemodialysis outside the UK
- personnel in laboratories
- nurses, medical and dental students
- dentists and dental nursing auxillaries

Other people at high risk for whom vaccination should be considered include:

- those working in institutions for people with special learning disability (mental handicap) where there is a high risk of hepatitis B
- health care personnel working in areas of the world where there is a high prevalence of hepatitis B
- non-immune regular sexual contacts of hepatitis B carriers
- active male homosexuals
- parenteral drug abusers
- infants of mothers who are hepatitis B carriers

Of those over 40 years old, 10–15% do not respond to the vaccination. Younger people are more responsive. Post-vaccination screening for antibody response should be done 2–4 months after the course of injections. Non-responders should be revaccinated, but the response again may be poor. Such individuals should be advised that hepatitis B immunoglobulin (HBIG) may be necessary for protection if exposure to infection occurs, for example those individuals accidently inoculated by blood products from an infected person or for sexual consorts of recently diagnosed hepatitis B sufferers (seen within 1 week of the onset of jaundice) (see below).

Meningococcal vaccine A and C

Meningococcal vaccine is a purified heat-stable, lyophilized extract from the poly-saccharide outer capsule of *Neisseria meningitidis*, and is effective against serotype A and C organisms. It does not protect against Group B meningococcal infection, which is responsible for about 60% of all cases of meningococcal septicaemia/meningitis which occur in this country. Children under 3 months fail to respond to the Group A polysaccharide and a similar lack of response against the Group C is noted in children under 18 months. Immediate family or close contacts of Groups A and C meningitis cases should be given meningococcal vaccine in addition to chemoprophylaxis.

It is recommended that travellers to endemic areas, such as the sub-Saharan belt of Africa be vaccinated against Group A. The risk is greatest during the dry season and stops with the onset of the rains.

Pneumococcal vaccine

This is a polyvalent vaccine given to individuals at special risk (e.g. patients who have had a splenectomy). It is best given prior to operation if possible. It should not be used under the age of 2 years. Newer and more effective vaccines are at present being developed.

Rabies

Active immunization is arranged immediately after a patient has been bitten by a rabid animal. Human diploid cell rabies vaccine is used and the course consists of 14 daily subcutaneous injections into the abdominal wall with a booster dose 10 days later and a final booster dose 20 days after that. For persons at special risk (i.e. handling animals that may be rabid), two immunizations are used and are given 4–6 weeks apart. Booster doses follow 6 months later and subsequently every 3 years.

IMMUNIZATION FOR PERSONS TRAVELLING OUTSIDE THE UK

Typhoid and paratyphoid fevers

Typhoid and paratyphoid fevers can be prevented by giving a course of typhoid and paratyphoid ABC vaccine (TAB) which is a suspension of killed typhoid and paratyphoid bacteria. Two doses are given at intervals of not less than 10 days or more than 2 months. Booster doses should be given every 5 years.

TAB immunization should be given to all who are going to travel in countries in which primitive water supplies are common. These include all tropical countries, in the Indian sub-continent and Italy, Spain and Africa. It is also a wise precaution if camping in Europe.

It is usual to suffer from a mild reaction after TAB inoculations — the patient complains of a headache and has a slight pyrexia for a few hours.

Cholera

Cholera vaccine is of less value in controlling the spread of cholera than in conferring some temporary protection against clinical illness in individuals who travel to countries where the disease occurs. Immunization against cholera is only necessary for travellers visiting certain parts of India or other countries where cholera occurs. The immunization is by means of a vaccine (a suspension of killed cholera bacteria in equal parts of Ogawa and Inaba serotypes prepared from smooth cultures of the classical biotype of *Vibrio cholerae*), and consists of two inoculations with at least 2 weeks in between each dose. Moderately severe reactions may follow this inoculation. Recently the effectiveness of such vaccines has been reported by WHO to be low and to last for only 3 months.

Yellow fever

Yellow fever is a serious tropical disease which is limited to a narrow band of countries in mid-Africa and central South America. A most effective immunization is given by injection of a live attenuated strain of virus which produces immunity. Very stringent storage conditions are essential for this vaccine which is freeze-dried. For this reason, special centres have been set up in this country to give yellow fever vaccination and it can only be given at such centres. Immunization is only necessary for persons visiting those parts of Africa or South America where the disease occurs, but for all such travellers, immunization against yellow fever is compulsory.

TABLE 6.8   Rapid immunization schedule for travellers from Great Britain

Day	Vaccine
1	Cholera (1)
	Typhoid (1)
	Tetanus (1)
	Oral polio (1)
2	Yellow fever
13	Cholera (2)
	Oral polio (2)
28	Typhoid (2)
	Tetanus (2)
	Oral polio (3)

Data from ref. 9.

Japanese B encephalitis

This disease occurs throughout South-east Asia and the Far East mostly during the monsoon season. The mosquito that transmits the illness dwells in rice fields. Visitors to such risk areas should be offered vaccination. Two injections, should be given 7–14 days apart. Full immunity takes a month to develop. A third reinforcing dose is recommended after a year. This vaccine is available on a named patient basis.

Tick-borne encephalitis

Warm forested parts of Europe and Scandinavia in the late spring and summer harbour the tick that transmits this virus. The killed vaccine is available on a named person basis. The full course is three injections, the second after 4–12 weeks and the third 9–12 months after the second.

Table 6.8 shows the emergency vaccination schedules for travel abroad. Advice on prophylaxis against malaria even for travellers spending just a few hours in a port or airport in an endemic area must be given at the same time as the immunization.

Passive immunization

Individuals who have suffered from certain diseases continue to have antibodies in their blood. Preparations from this plasma may be used to obtain immediate but temporary protection against these infections. Two preparations are available, human normal immunoglobulin and human specific immunoglobulin.

HUMAN NORMAL IMMUNOGLOBULIN

This is used as a protection against hepatitis A and is used for individuals at particular risk, namely:

- travellers to tropical countries
- individuals in institutions during an outbreak
- households of contacts who are particularly vulnerable, such as an immunosuppressed child with leukaemia or other malignant disease

The dosage is 500 mg or 250 mg if under 10 years old. Human normal immunoglobulin may also be used to prevent infection in a woman who has been in contact with rubella in the first 12 weeks of pregnancy and who is not immune. A large dose of 2 g of immunoglobulin is required. The other main reason for passive human normal immunoglobulin vaccination is to prevent the onset of measles in a child who is already unwell and in hospital. The normal protecting dose of immunoglobulin is 0.4 g for children under 2 years old and 0.75 g for older children.

HUMAN SPECIFIC IMMUNOGLOBULIN

These preparations have a high antibody content being prepared from sufferers of recent infections or immunizations and are used for high risk groups as outlined below. At the present time four are available against the following:

Hepatitis B virus immunoglobulin. This is used to protect people at risk such as after injuries from a needle (needlestick injuries) or bites from an infected person, and for babies born to hepatitis B positive mothers.

Anti-tetanus immunoglobulin. This was made available through the regional transfusion centres in 1979 and is used to prevent tetanus in patients with seriously contaminated wounds.

Anti-rabies immunoglobulin. This is given with the vaccine to persons bitten by animals known to have, or suspected of having, rabies.

Anti-varicella immunoglobulin. This is used primarily for children with leukaemia and on immunosuppressive therapy who have been in contact with chickenpox.

The Public Health Laboratory Service hold such immunoglobulins (in Scotland the Blood Transfusion Service holds supplies).

INTRAVENOUS IMMUNOGLOBULIN

Over the past 10 years, immunoglobulins have been given to patients, initially to allow an increasing dose of immunoglobulins to be given to sufferers from primary hypogammaglobulinaemia (15 g every 2 weeks compared to 2 g per week intramuscularly). Subsequently such therapy has been tried on patients in whom an immune mechanism is not immediately apparent. Patients with asthma, recurrent miscarriages, myalgic encephalomyopathy, HIV and after bone marrow transplants have all apparently benefited, though trials continue.[8]

Vaccine damage payments scheme

This scheme was introduced in 1979 and allows for a tax-free lump sum of £20 000 (increased from £10 000 in June 1985) to be paid to any child or adult who has been severely damaged by vaccinations recommended for the benefit of the community. The claim must be made within either 6 years of the date of vaccination, or for babies, by the time they reach the age of 8 years. Claims have to be submitted with medical evidence to be assessed by a panel of doctors. Appeals against claims which are not successful may be made to an independent tribunal whose decision is final. By June 1987, 3266 claims had been filed with 839 awards made.

References

1. Faculty of Public Health Medicine of the Royal College of Physicians. UK levels of health. London: Royal college of Physicians. 1991.
2. Health of the Nation (Cmnd 1523) London: HMSO. 1991.
3. Gillen D. Immunising children. Br. Med. J. 1991, 303: 875.
4. Nicoll A. Contraindications to whooping cough immunisation — myths or realities? Lancet 1985, i: 679–681.
5. Contraindications to childhood immunization. Drugs Ther. Bull. 1988, 26: 81–84.
6. Joint Committee on Vaccination and Immunization. Immunization against infectious diseases. London: HMSO. 1990.
7. Miller CL et al. Effecting selective vaccination on rubella susceptibility and infection in pregnancy. Br. Med. J. 1985, 291: 1398–1402.
8. Webster ADB. Intravenous immunoglobulins. Br. Med. J. 1991, 303: 375.
9. Protection and Prevention. London: Wellcome Medical Division. 1984.

7

Preventive Medicine in General Practice

The role of the primary health care team has moved increasingly into the field of preventive medicine since the late 1970s. The new GP contract of 1990 emphasizes the role of prevention. In the contract, several new requirements were placed on the GP, these included the offer of annual examinations for persons over 75 years old, the offer of medicals for patients not seen for 3 years, and the introduction of health promotion clinics. Much of the work done in these clinics is of a preventive nature.

There are three types of preventive medicine:

1. *Primary prevention* which aims at the complete avoidance of disease. Examples include all forms of immunization, and many practical aspects of health education in which individuals are persuaded to avoid or change potentially harmful habits such as smoking and drug abuse. Fluoridation to prevent dental decay is another example.
2. *Secondary prevention* is concerned with the early detection of disease in patients who have no symptoms. Many opportunities occur in general practice such as screening of babies and toddlers, the detection of early hypertension in adults and cervical cytology. Secondary prevention is synonymous with *screening*.
3. *Tertiary prevention* is concerned with discovering complications of a disease before its effects have resulted in disability or handicap. Careful management of many chronic diseases such as diabetes mellitus, asthma and high blood pressure should prevent many long-term complications.

The responsibility of the primary health care team never ends. Although the demands on professional time in busy general practice are great, with proper organization and records, many opportunities will present themselves to advise, check and, hopefully, modify potential harmful factors. Nurses are playing a much greater part in supervising such care and running many prevention clinics in general practice. Table 7.1 represents the relationship between integrated preventive and therapeutic care and general practice. Anticipatory care is the attempt to identify and prevent problems before they happen, and is relevant to primary, secondary and tertiary prevention.

TABLE 7.1   Relationship between the integrated preventive and therapeutic care and general practice

Symptom free	← →	Symptoms
Health surveillance	← →	Clinical care
Health education	Developmental assessment	Ordinary care
Primary prevention e.g. immunizations	Secondary prevention e.g. screening, presymtomatic detection of disease	Tertiary prevention e.g. preventing complications	Diagnosis and management of acute and chronic

Modified from ref. 25.

Primary prevention

CHILD HEALTH

It is with infants and children that the primary health care team has the best opportunity to prevent illness and practise primary prevention. It may be possible to anti-

TABLE 7.2   Neonatal and postneonatal mortality rates per 1000 live births, by social class, in Scotland

Class	Mortality per 1000 live births			% decrease	
	1946	1960	1975	1946–60	1969–75
Neonatal mortality					
I	16.7	13.0	7.6	22	41
II	25.0	17.2	8.7	31	49
III	29.3	17.1	11.1	42	34
IV	31.1	20.7	10.8	33	38
V	36.9	21.0	14.6	43	30
Postneonatal mortality					
I	5.5	2.2	1.8	51	33
II	12.8	4.3	3.8	66	12
III	22.0	7.2	4.7	67	35
IV	29.3	10.2	5.1	65	50
V	36.1	12.8	10.8	64	16

Data from ref. 1.

cipate which children will be at the greatest risk. The Black Report — *Inequalities in Health*[1] — highlighted the fact that at birth, and during the first month of life, twice as many babies of unskilled manual parents as of professional parents die, and in the next 11 months of life *four* times as many girls and *five* times as many boys die. The report also clearly showed that the differences in morbidity (especially self-reported incidents) closely followed those of mortality. Prevention achieved for children is particularly satisfying as the results can last a lifetime. The impact of the

TABLE 7.3   Possibilities for prevention: some of the target conditions for which prevention of cause, early detection or health education are, or may be, worthwhile

---

Surveillance of pregnancy

Blood group incompatibility	Neural tube defect
Down's syndrome	Rubella
Sexually transmitted disease	Excess tobacco and alcohol use
Drug abuse	Hypertension
Diabetes mellitus	

Children

Neonatal hypothyroidism	Phenylketonuria
Maldescent of testes	Squint
Congenital dislocation of the hip	Child abuse
Iron deficiency anaemia	Developmental delay
Abnormality of colour vision	Growth retardation
Accidents	Poisoning
Cystic fibrosis	Diphtheria
Tetanus	Whooping cough
Measles	Poliomyelitis
Dental caries	Visual and hearing defects
Psychosocial maladjustment	Scoliosis

Adolescents

Rubella	Accidents (at work and at home)
Smoking	Alcohol and drug abuse
Unwanted pregnancy	

Women and men aged 16–64 years

Complications of pregnancy	Motor accidents
Smoking	Alcohol and drug abuse
Rubella	Hypertension and ischaemic heart disease
Cancer of cervix and breast	Suicide

Women and men aged 65 years and over

Hypertension	Dental caries
Loss of autonomy	Feet problems
Dementia (partial)	Visual defects
Hearing defects	Influenza (particularly for those at risk)

Modified from ref. 6

free GP services since 1948 (the start of the NHS) did, until 1960, reduce the inequality, but for the period 1960–75 social classes I and II generally improved their mortality considerably more than social class V (see Table 7.2). The mortality rates for boys and girls of all ages between 1 and 14 years in social class V are over twice those in social class I for boys and one and a half times greater for girls.

These figures emphasize the continuing problem for GPs and the primary health care team keen to practise preventive medicine. Table 7.3 summarizes conditions for which prevention of causes, early detection, or health education, are worthwhile. The way that such care is provided may alter between practices, indeed one practice may choose several methods. Special clinics or sessions run in conjunction with practice nurses or health visitors may be set up. Management schedules of protocols clearly defining both the aims and procedures to be followed should be established. However, each consultation should also be used as as an opportunity to check on the general development of the child.

Most general practitioners have registered for child health surveillance (see pp. 121–122). With assistance from the health visitor, the routine testing at regular intervals of hearing, eyesight, motor and social developments should identify those children with problems and enable early referral for action (see Chapter 5).

High risk groups

The ablility to identify those at particular risk enables special care to be given. The risk factors that have been identified include prenatal, perinatal and postnatal factors including:

- congenital deformities
- respiratory problems
- jaundice
- convulsions in the postnatal period
- familial disease
- social class V
- permanent or temporary (more than 3 months) separation from parents
- parental factors such as chronic illness, mental instability and unstable employment.

The ability to identify patients by social class, particularly those of classes IV and V, would mean that more attention might be paid to those at greater risk. Many GPs have operated age/sex registers, which identify patients by age and sex, for some time, and many are now computerized, but few would be able at present to identify patients by socio-economic class. New software for such computers would present all sorts of opportunities (see Chapter 8).

Child abuse can, in some instances, be prevented by exceptional vigilance on the part of the GP and the primary health care team. The condition and its diagnosis and management are discussed in Chapter 23. The GP may be called to treat an injury in a young child and may, therefore, be in an excellent position to suspect and diagnose this condition. Similar opportunities exist when there is a suspicion of child sexual abuse. It is particularly important that early warning signs of this condition are recognized and understood. In all instances of serious doubt a case conference is called and a check is made whether the child or family is on the Child Protection Register.

NUTRITION

As nutrition today is usually very satisfactory, it is easy to ignore the important part it plays in maintaining health. With expectant and nursing mothers and young children, health visitors advise on nutrition and many welfare foods and vitamin additives are provided to assist in this work. The importance of folic acid in the prevention of neural tube defects is discussed in Chapter 14.

IMMUNIZATION

The prevention of disease by immunization is one of the most valuable examples of primary preventive medicine carried out by family doctors. A full schedule of immunizations for children is given in Chapter 6. It is important that all courses of immunizations are completed. If the mother fails to bring the child for second and third doses, the health visitor should be asked to call on the mother to ensure that the course is completed. Some district health authorities allow vacination to be given in the home. With proper care to explain and educate, greatly improved immunization uptake figures can be obtained and so improve the herd immunity (see Chapter 6).

INTERNATIONAL TRAVEL

With increasing numbers of people going abroad, GPs have an important role in the immunization of travellers. It is particularly important for the GP to realize that *the majority* of cases of typhoid are caused by holidaymakers neglecting to be immunized, especially those going to the Indian subcontinent, the Middle East, Africa, Spain, Italy, Yugoslavia and Portugal, especially on camping holidays in rural areas (see Chapter 6).

PREVENTION OF ACCIDENTS IN THE HOME

In 1987 there were 4178 deaths resulting from accidents in the home or residential homes.[2] In addition there was a total of 2145 deaths as a result of accidents (falls, poisoning, burns and drowning) occurring elsewhere. Most accidents in the home are preventable. Health visitors in their routine visiting of families are always attempting to teach how such accidents can be avoided, and GPs have an excellent opportunity to do similar work while carrying out home visits (see also Table 5.5).

All doctors prescribe potentially dangerous drugs in their practice. If patients carelessly leave them lying about, children can easily mistake them for sweets, with tragic consequences. Not all patients realize that *any* medicine or drug may be dangerous, especially if taken accidentally by a child. The introduction of 'child-proof' tops, not only for medicines but also for dangerous household chemicals such as bleach, has been an important measure in reducing accidental self poisonings. Everyone should take care how and where they store drugs. Grandparents visited occasionally by grandchildren may not have child-proof tops on their drugs, and an innocent game by a grandchild during one visit can easily turn to tragedy. The drug companies and food manufacturers also have a responsibility — unfortunately too many drugs and sweets look similar.

Safety gates preventing the child falling down stairs should be encouraged. Bedding for cots should be chosen with care to avoid a situation where accidental suffocation or strangulation might occur. Plastic bags should never be left where a young child could get them.

THE ELDERLY

The elderly are clearly the highest risk group for accidents, particularly with falls. A fall is always more serious for the elderly than one in a younger person because (a) it is more likely to result in serious injury, especially fractures, and (b) so often a fall is the start of an elderly person going into a decline. Women are more liable to falls than men, and the tendency increases with age. Reasons for the increasing tendency to fall include poor sight, vertigo and a lack of balance as well as the increasing tendency to trip.

Most falls can be prevented if the old person is taught suitable precautions. The likelihood of an increased tendency to trip should always be explained, and care taken to ensure that floor fittings, carpets, rugs and linoleum are securely fastened. If the old person is living with a family, the children should try not to leave toys where they can be tripped over. Loose electric flex across the floor is another hazard to avoid. Learning to walk with some support from a solid object — banister, handrail, walking aid — will also help if the person suddenly feels giddy. Many old people take drugs, including sleeping tablets and these may increase their tendency to fall.

Very old people depend increasingly on sight to maintain balance as the labyrinthine function is often faulty. This dependence increases as age advances and is most important over the age of 85 years. An elderly person who is quite steady in daylight may be very liable to fall in the dark. This should always be explained to the elderly and their carers, as it is essential that there is adequate light in any room or passage used by them. If the old person has to get up at night, a bedside lamp should be turned on before they leave the bed or a hand held electric torch should be used.

Osteoporosis

This is the reduction of bone mass per unit volume with normal mineral and chemical composition. A mainly female condition, it is found in one in four women over the age of 60 years. Unfortunately no easy test exists to either predict or detect those who will be affected. Clinically, three common fractures occur in people with osteoporosis:

1. *Femoral neck fractures* of which there are some 40 000 a year in the UK leading to 6000 deaths. This represents much suffering and handicap and also means 5000 hospital beds are occupied annually at a cost to the NHS of an estimated £500 000 000.[3]
2. *Vertebral crush fractures* causing pain, loss of height and kyphosis (widow's hump).
3. *Distal radius fractures* (Colles' fracture).

Risk factors for osteoporosis include increasing age, female sex, thin physique, early menopause, excess coffee and alcohol ingestion, cigarette smoking, certain drugs such as steroids, and prolonged immobilization. Prevention includes dietary measures (particularly early in life), exercise, and hormone replacement therapy for women at risk. Once established, the process of osteoporosis cannot be reversed, only the effects slowed down.

Hypothermia

This is a serious condition found mainly in elderly persons in which the body loses heat and cannot maintain correct temperature control. It is discussed fully on p. 404. It is important that the condition is recognized early as treatment is then much more satisfactory. It is not always understood that hypothermia can develop quickly in an old person who has suddenly been taken ill (such as during an attack of pneumonia). GPs should therefore be vigilant in such circumstances.

ROAD ACCIDENTS

In the UK in 1987 there were 10 169 transport accident deaths (5175 male and 5094 female). The Department of Transport estimated the cost of each fatal road accident in Great Britain in 1986 at just under £300 000 (including costs for lost output of £151 000 and an allowance of £145 000 for pain, grief and suffering).[4] Road accidents accounted for nearly 40% of all accidental deaths, and 34% of all deaths in the 15–24 years age group.

Compulsory seat belt legislation was introduced for front seat passengers on 31 January 1983, and became permanent in 1986. It has been estimated that at least 200 deaths a year have been saved with the introduction of seat belts, as well as greatly reduced morbidity. Most accidents occur between 5 and 6 p.m. with a secondary peak between 8 and 9 a.m. reflecting the heaviness of traffic at these times. Almost as many adults are injured between 11 p.m. and midnight as between 8 and 9 a.m., and the role of alcohol in many of these accidents is well recognized. One in three drivers killed on the road has a blood alcohol level above the legal limit, and this rises to two out of three killed between 11 p.m. and midnight.

It is right that there is great concern regarding traffic accidents but Great Britain now has one of the lowest rates of road deaths in the world. In 1909 when statistics were first kept there were over 1000 fatal accidents for 100 000 vehicles on the road. Seventy-six years later the number of motor vehicles had increased 215 times but the numbers of fatal accidents just 4.6 times.[5]

SMOKING

It has been estimated that each week over 2000 people die prematurely from the effects of cigarette smoking, the most common diseases being cancer, bronchitis and emphysema, ischaemic heart disease and peripheral artery disease. Some 34 190 people died from cancer of the lung in England and Wales in 1991. If every GP managed to persuade 5 people a year to stop smoking over 150 000 people a year would stop and a reduction in the rate of premature deaths would soon be apparent.

The trends of the last 10–15 years have been encouraging with smokers now in the minority in all socio-economic groups. In 1988, 68% of the adult population were non-smokers. However smoking in children continues to be a major concern and in 1988 more schoolgirls (9%) than boys (7%) regularly smoked. The rates of decline in children have been less than for adults. Public awareness campaigns about the health risks may be effective but the small amounts spent in relation to the huge budgets of the tobacco companies (£56 million in 1985 for advertising) show the problem. The cost of smoking to the NHS in 1991 was estimated by the Health Education Authority at £437 million.[6]

The GP and other members of the primary health care team have an excellent opportunity through their work to educate and hopefully *prevent* their patients from starting to smoke. The difficulty with children and adolescents is trying not to come over in too authoritarian a manner which probably only increases the adolescent's desire to rebel (and hence possibly smoke). GPs should know (and record) the smoking habits of all their adult and adolescent patients. They are ideally placed to offer advice and monitor the attempts of patients to stop smoking (with the use of the appropriate literature). The degree of ignorance of the long-term side effects of smoking is still surprising, and much satisfaction is to be gained by helping young persons to stop.

In *Health of the Nation*,[7] the government stated that they wished the targets for the year 2000 to be that the prevelance of cigarette smoking should be reduced to 22% in men and 21% in women (from 33% and 30% in 1988, respectively).

MENTAL ILLNESS

Over 10% of consultations in general practice are for emotional disorders, and the rate may be significantly higher. The GP, consulting for short periods of time, may miss important clues if care is not taken. Traditionally the GP's role has been with physical illnesses which have required prescriptions, and caution is needed so as not to prescribe inappropriately for patients with emotional problems.

At risk

There is evidence that there is a genetic element in some psychiatric illnesses. For neuroses this is only slight with twin studies revealing an increased correlation of neuroticism and anxiety. However, the psychoses have a significantly greater genetic element. The mode of inheritance for schizophrenia is strong, but the mechanism uncertain. Manic depressive psychosis is thought to be inherited by a single autosomal dominant gene, with bipolar disease having a greater tendency to be inherited than unipolar depressive disease.

Other risk factors for mental illness include:

- separation from a mother, especially in the crucial first few days (bonding) and for longer periods at a later age
- parental loss before the age of 17 (especially the loss of a mother when under 11)
- three or more children aged 14 year or under at home (for women)
- poor marriage
- unemployment.

Treatment options as well as drugs, whose role may be very limited, include psychotherapy (individual, group or family), and marital therapy. Sexual therapy may be chosen for sexual problems which are not uncommon, especially after a myocardial infarction, sterilization in females, or abortion.

Counselling

The GP may personally undertake counselling or refer to psychiatrists, clinical psychologists, community psychiatric nurses, social workers, counsellors, marriage guidance (Relate) or Samaritans. Other members of the primary health care team especially health visitors, have a crucial role to play, particularly in cases of mothers with young children.

BEREAVEMENT

It is important to provide support for the natural mourning process which may conveniently be considered in four stages. The first stage is that of numbness and denial. The second is one of yearning which may include anger. The third is the stage of disorganization/despair, and the last is that of reorganization. Knowledge of the four stages is helpful, but often there is a considerable overlap between the phases and the phases are seldom distinct. It is essential that prompt notifications of deaths are given to those who look after the relatives. This should be a two way process, with both the hospital notifying the GP, and the GP notifying the hospital for patients dying at home.

SUICIDE

On average, each 3–4 years a GP will have one patient who commits suicide. Once the GP has made a diagnosis of mental illness, care must be taken to consider the risk of suicide. The fear that to mention suicide might introduce the idea to the patient is unfounded. Most patients are only too pleased to be able to discuss their feelings and fears. Denial of suicide, however, in the very depressed patient should not be relied upon.

Risk factors, which should be closely marked on the medical record (possibly in confidential code), as well as including history of previous psychiatric disorder, depression, previous suicide attempt, alcohol abuse, and living alone (single or divorced). There is a higher risk in the over 45 years age group, and there is a higher risk in men than women. Suicide is commoner in the spring.

PEOPLE WITH SPECIAL LEARNING DISABILITIES (MENTAL HANDICAP)

Severe special learning disabilities (mental handicap), that is with an IQ of less than 50, occurs in two to three people per 1000 population. Mild special learning disabilities (mental handicap), when a patient has an IQ between 50 and 70, occurs more frequently. In school age children, approximately 25 per 1000 are thus affected.

Most such handicapped persons are diagnosed in childhood. Generally the greater the handicap the earlier the diagnosis. Causes of such handicap is often not always known, but can include:

- *Prenatal factors* such as chromosomal abnormalites (e.g. Down's syndrome), metabolic causes (e.g. ketonuria, hypothyroidism), infections (including cytomegalovirus), drugs (including alcohol), rhesus incompatibility and exposure to X-rays.
- *Perinatal factors* such as hypoxia, trauma and haemorrhage.
- *Postnatal factors* such as trauma, meningitis, encephalitis, poisons (lead/mercury) and nutritional factors.

Prevention of special learning disabilities (mental handicap)

Most cases of special learning difficulties (mental handicap) are caused by developmental abnormalities, by birth injuries or by chromosomal abnormalities. Very occasionally the condition will follow a severe infection of the brain or meninges (encephalitis or meningitis), and for this reason it is essential that no delay ever occurs in diagnosing and treating such conditions.

Methods of prevention can be summarized:

- *Genetic counselling.* This is usually only possible after the birth of one affected child or where there is a history of a possible familial tendency to transmit a hereditary disease likely to lead to disability.
- *Amniocentesis.* Amniocentesis was previously offered to pregnant women aged 35 and over. Following research by Wald[8] and others, it has been shown that by screening the blood serum of all pregnant women at 16 weeks for α-fetoprotein, unconjugated oestriol and human chorionic gonadotrophin, it is possible to detect up to 60% of affected pregnancies while requiring only 5% to undergo amniocentesis. Many districts introduced such a programme in 1991 with a computerized assessment of the calculated risk. The risk of a woman having a Down's syndrome baby in relation to her age is shown in Table 7.4.

TABLE 7.4   Incidence of Down's syndrome by age

Woman's age	Risk	Woman's age	Risk	Woman's age	Risk
20	1/1923	30	1/885	40	1/109
21	1/1695	31	1/826	41	1/85
22	1/1538	32	1/725	42	1/67
23	1/1408	33	1/592	43	1/53
24	1/1299	34	1/465	44	1/41
25	1/1205	35	1/365	45	1/32
26	1/1124	36	1/287	46	1/25
27	1/1053	37	1/225	47	1/20
28	1/990	38	1/177	48	1/16
29	1/935	39	1/139	49	1/12

Data from ref. 27.

- *Rubella immunization.* This at present is done for girls aged 11–14 years, but now also with MMR for all children aged 18 months.
- *Immunization with anti-D immunoglobulin* and proper diagnosis and care of the child at risk of haemolytic disease of the newborn will reduce the chance of kernicterus and of subsequent special learning difficulties (mental handicap).
- *Improved antenatal and perinatal care* will reduce the risk of asphyxia and hypoxia in the newborn and possible brain damage to the child. Approximately 45% of children with cerebral palsy have also some degree of mental handicap. The association between hypoxia during birth and subsequent cerebral palsy is not however clear-cut.
- *Improved intensive care for babies of low birthweight* during the neonatal period.
- *Neonatal screening* for phenylketonuria and hypothyroidism (see pp. 119–120).

ABORTION

Since the Abortion Act, 1967, GPs are consulted on many occasions by patients requesting an abortion. The present law allows a pregnancy to be terminated by a doctor if two registered medical practitioners are of the opinion, formed in good faith:

- that the continuance of the pregnancy would involve risk of the life of the pregnant woman or of injury to the physical or mental health of the pregnant woman or any existing children of her family, greater than if the pregnancy were terminated
- that there is a substantial risk that if the child were born it would suffer from such physical or mental abnormalities as to be seriously handicapped.

In 1987 there were 174 276 abortions carried out in England and Wales. This was an increase of 1.2% from 1986, but the numbers of abortions carried out on foreigners were reduced by a quarter to 18 085. There were almost 39 000 terminations carried out on teenagers (3765 under 16).

It is clear that the responsibility of the doctor as set out in the Abortion Act is essentially a preventive medical one involving the likely result of the pregnancy on the health of the mother and child. The implications for improved family planning for those women at risk of unplanned pregnancy are obvious. The timing of the abortion is also crucial from a safety point of view and to minimize risks to future pregnancies. Just over 75% of abortions were carried out for women 12 weeks or less pregnant, but still approximately 25% were carried out with the woman over 12 weeks pregnant and it is in this group that there is most risk.

The law was changed in 1990,[9] with termination of pregnancy on medical grounds being permissable up till just 24 weeks when the grounds for termination as a risk to the physical or mental health of the pregnant woman or her existing children. The old 28-week limit still applies when there is a risk of grave permanent injury or death to the mother or a substantial risk of serious handicap in the child.

FAMILY PLANNING

(See also Chapter 4, pp. 107–108 and Chapter 8, p. 201.)

GPs have an important preventive medical function in relation to family planning and patients seeking such advice should either be dealt with directly (the doctor may prescribe for his patient), or be referred to a clinic run by the DHA.

OCCUPATION AND DISEASE

There are many special industrial health problems, and the GP should always be aware of the main industrial processes in his/her area and their special hazards. There are about 50 prescribed industrial diseases and 16 notifiable industrial diseases. The Inspector of Factories has a role in the prevention of such diseases and in matters of compensation in the form of Industrial Benefit which can be paid to sufferers. About a third of workers in the UK have a full occupational health service, about one third have a partial one (often provided by GPs) and one third have no service at all. The functions of an occupational health service include:

- immediate treatment at the workplace
- monitoring of toxic substances used in the factory
- health education
- the prevention of accidents
- employment rehabilitation and advice
- diagnosis of occupational diseases.

Occupational diseases include:

Lung diseases such as pneumoconiosis in miners, occupational asthma, byssinosis (from cotton, hemp or flax).
Skin diseases. Over 60% of all new certified incapacity for Industrial Injury Benefit is payable for skin diseases. Causes of such diseases include biological and chemical agents, physical effects (e.g. vibration, cold, etc.).
Cancer.
- lung cancer from arsenic, nickel and chromium exposure; also from radon exposure in certain mining groups
- bladder cancer from aromatic amines (rubber and dyestuff industries)
- liver angiosarcoma from exposure to vinyl chloride (manufacture of PVC)
- myeloid leukaemias in radiologists exposed to excess X-irradiation.
Deafness. Exposure to noise in excess of 60–80 dB will alter the threshold for hearing, which can become permanent with repeated exposure. Domestic noise, such

as domestic appliances, and leisure noises, hi-fi and pop concerts, may play a significant part in the development of deafness.

Central nervous system. Poisoning by heavy metals, such as lead, mercury and manganese, may cause encephalopathies, neuropathies or even psychotic symptoms.

PREVENTION OF CORONARY HEART DISEASE

Coronary heart disease (CHD) is the greatest single cause of death in the UK. A third of all male deaths and a quarter of all female deaths are due to coronary heart disease. The mortality is higher than in most other countries and is particularly high in Scotland, Wales and Northern Ireland (see also Chapter 13). The strategies for prevention recommended by the British Cardiac Society Working Group on Coronary Disease Prevention (1987)[10] were:

- altering the mass characteristics of lifestyle which are the underlying causes of the disease, e.g. prevention in whole population (WHO[11])
- identifying and helping individuals at special risk within the population
- providing better emergency services for cardiopulmonary resuscitation
- preventing recurrences and progression of disease, e.g. secondary and tertiary prevention.

The following factors are important in the aetiology of CHD and are discussed more fully in Chapter 13:

- cigarette smoking
- blood pressure
- diet
- obesity
- physical activity
- cholesterol
- diabetes mellitus
- oral contraceptives
- stress.

ADVERSE REACTIONS OF DRUGS

In 1987 there were 397 million prescriptions issued from general practice. More and more powerful drugs are being used, and several have quite significant side effects. The Committee on Safety of Medicines (CSM) is responsible for monitoring suspected adverse drug reactions. A yellow card system has been in operation for years, for doctors to complete when they suspect symptoms reported by the patient are or may be due to an adverse drug reaction. For new drugs, all reactions should be reported (such drugs are shown by an inverted black triangle in the British

TABLE 7.5   Numbers of suspected adverse drug reactions reported to the Committee on Safety of Medicines in 1987

Organ	Reaction		
	Most important	Serious	Fatal
Skin	4 991	524	5
Cardiovascular	280	266	57
Central nervous system	2 351	736	7
Auditory, vestibular and visual	323	68	0
Blood	543	479	28
Collagen/vascular	351	187	18
Endocrine/metabolic	500	177	2
Reproductive (male and female)	304	31	2
Gastrointestinal	2 471	641	72
Hepatic	573	484	32
Muscular/skeletal	384	29	0
Psychiatric	985	332	1
Respiratory	717	415	21
Urinary	292	148	23
Others	1 366	432	12
Total	16 431	4 949	280

National Formulary) or serious reactions in older established drugs. Since 1986 these forms have been available at the back of the FP10 prescription pads and at the back of the British National Formulary, which is issued twice yearly to all GPs. This yellow card system makes a significant contribution to the safety assessment of marketed drugs, but adverse reactions are still grossly under-reported and often unrecognized. Table 7.5 shows the numbers of adverse reactions reported to the CSM in 1986 and 1987 according to the system affected.

Since 1987, every time a new drug is prescribed, the prescribing doctor is sent a special yellow card with a red triangle on it. This is kept with the patient's record and the doctor is asked to fill in and return it if the patient suffers a serious reaction or dies while taking the drug. The CSM have the power to withdraw a drug's licence if its side effects are considered to be too great. This is balanced with the reasons for which it is being prescribed.

Secondary prevention

SCREENING

One of the more effective ways for the GP to undertake secondary prevention is by screening. Screening may be defined as some form of questioning, examination, or investigation of an individual who is symptom free with a view to discovering the presence or absence of disease. Screening may be done on the whole population (mass screening) or with individuals presenting to the GP for other unrelated problems (case finding or opportunistic screening). *Anticipatory care* also incorporates case finding.

Before the 1960s, very little screening was carried out in the UK on the general population. The experience of World War II, however, in which so many had been conscripted and therefore had had to undergo a series of medical screening tests before entry into the forces, had emphasized how much latent pathology was present in the community. The value of discovering such pathology early enough to enable effective treatment to be started became recognized. The advent of screening, particularly with cervical cytology, caused some of the more conservative clinicians to point out that such tests produce much fear and anxiety. Some doctors are still not keen to encourage widespread screening (e.g. for high blood cholesterol levels, etc.) because they fear that little permanent value will be achieved and a great number of persons as well as being made to feel very anxious, may also be given a false sense of security which could lead a patient to ignore subsequent symptoms which might later develop. However, with patients being given more information about their health and lifestyles, advice about their weight, exercise, smoking and alcohol consumption will enable individuals to make important choices.

The principle behind screening is that certain diseases and pathological conditions can often be recognized by some fairly simple test long before any serious disease has developed or before symptoms have occurred. Occasionally it is possible to diagnose a precancerous condition and effectively treat it before any malignant growth has developed. This is the basis for the cervical cytology test which discovers what is thought to be a precancerous condition of the cervix uteri. In other instances abnormal metabolic or endocrine diseases can be identified very early, which enables effective treatment or diet to be started so that serious damage to the brain can be avoided. Examples include screening for phenylketonuria and hypothyroidism. In all such cases, it is important to understand the principles behind screening and the criteria which must be met to make any screening test acceptable and effective. Wilson[12] described the basis for screening, and the following is a synopsis of the points made:

1. The disease being searched for by screening should always be a reasonably serious one, and have a recognized latent or presymptomatic stage.
2. The screening test itself should be simple to carry out and unequivocal in interpretation. It is no use, therefore, using screening tests which are complicated (and expensive), or whose results are difficult to intepret, or which may give false positives and so be misleading.
3. As far as possible the screening test should be an objective rather than a subjective test. This may take the form of:
   - the demonstration of a chemical which is normally not present (e.g. phenylketonuria), or an abnormally high level which indicates an abnormal state (e.g.

an open neural tube defect which is accompanied by a higher level of
α-fetoprotein)

- an abnormal physical sign (e.g. a clicking or clunking hip in congenital dislocation of the hip, a high blood pressure or the presence of sugar in the urine).
4. The test should always be completely safe and should produce as little anxiety
as possible in the people tested. To do so might be counter-productive. For this
reason it is important to counsel the persons to be screened so that they fully
understand the nature of the test. It is especially important to try and explain
the limitations of such screening, and how a negative result does not guarantee
the absence of disease. Significant symptoms must still be taken seriously.
5. Effective treatment must be available for the abnormal condition or disease identified by the screening test. Such treatment preferably should be easy to carry out
and relatively cheap (both in terms of money and health personnel).

Table 7.6 summarizes the questions one should ask before thinking about
screening.

TABLE 7.6   Summary of the questions to be asked before screening

Is the disease being screened for important?
Is the natural history of that disease known?
Is successful treatment available?
Is the test safe and reliable?
Does the test discriminate well, with few false positives or negatives?
Will the test reassure those in whom it is negative?
Can the target population be easily reached?
Is the cost of the test reasonable ('cost benefit' both of the test and treatment)?
How often should the screening be performed (should not be only once)?

EXAMPLES OF SCREENING

Pregnancy and the newborn

Most antenatal care work is essentially screening, either of all women or of some
high risk groups. Examples of screening of all women include screening for anaemia
and hypertensive disease of pregnancy. Screening for chromosomal abnormalities
(e.g. Down's syndrome), open neural tube defects, and rhesus incompatability are
examples of selective screening (see p. 102).

Screening of the newborn is essentially mass screening and involves blood tests
for (a) phenylketonuria, and (b) hypothyroidism. Examination of the newborn may
discover congenital dislocation of the hip, maldescended testes and congenital heart
disease. A great deal of anxiety may be produced with 'innocent' cardiac murmurs,
but they do require proper evaluation. Identification of congenital deafness by not
later than 8 months is important.

Children

Screening in childhood is done routinely at varying intervals, mainly by the health visitor with the help from either the GP or the clinical medical officer at DHA clinics. This may continue with the school nurse for the child at school (see also child health surveillance, Chapter 5). These developmental screening tests concentrate upon five main areas of an infant's normal function:

- locomotion including posture
- muscle function and control
- speech and language development
- growth
- the social development of the infant.

Adult screening

The general opinion now is that there are many valuable screening tests which adults should be encouraged to have, but that these need always be accompanied by some balanced health education and counselling. Care must be taken not to create undue anxiety. Conditions considered worthwhile screening for in adults include carcinoma of the cervix, breast cancer, obesity, ischaemic heart disease, hypertension and large bowel cancer.

Carcinoma of the cervix

Cervical cytology was introduced by Papanicolau in 1943 and has been used in Britain with a national screening programme since 1966. The technique is simple. A vaginal speculum is passed and a direct smear obtained from the cervix by sweeping a wooden spatula through 360 degrees. The wooden spatula is then wiped on to a glass slide. The specimen is fixed with a dilute alcohol fixative and sent to the laboratory for histological determination. The first indication of abnormality is the appearance of abnormal changes in the nuclei.

The whole basis for cervical cytology is the belief that there is a progression from dysplasia to carcinoma *in situ* which subsequently leads to invasive carcinoma of the cervix. Dysplasia or cervical intraepithelial neoplasia (CIN) is classified as mild, moderate or severe (CIN I, II, or III). Progression to carcinoma *in situ* is not inevitable and there is no absolute evidence that all carcinomas *in situ* will become invasive. Smears which show mild dysplasia will need to be repeated in 6 months, and all other patients with abnormal smears should be referred to a gynaecologist.

Colposcopy is now the method of choice for investigating and managing all forms of dysplasia and carcinoma *in situ*. The colposcope is a low-powered microscope which views the cervix which has been treated with an application of acetic acid. This is normally carried out by a gynaecologist. The patient is examined on her back with her legs in stirrups. Passing a speculum allows direct visualization of the abnormal areas of the cervix. Biopsies may be taken and clearly identify areas of dysplasia. These may be very precisely treated by cryocautery or laser treatment. The whole procedure may take some 15–20 minutes. More extensive lesions may require a cone biopsy or hysterectomy.

In 1986 over 4.25 million smears were examined (see Table 7.7). The number of positive cases has increased from 5.1 cases per 1000 in 1976 to 9.2 per 1000 in 1986. In 1985, Regional Health Authorities introduced computerized recall systems in co-operation with the Family Practitioner Committees to improve the national recall scheme. In 1990 GPs were encouraged to perform more cervical smears in women aged 25–64 years by being paid a fee, dependent on whether they achieved a 50% or 80% 'target' (see Chapter 1).

TABLE 7.7   Cervical cytology in Great Britain, 1971–86

Year	Smears examined (thousands)	Rate per 100 000 females	Positive cases per 1000 smears	Deaths from cervical cancer
1971	2205	8	–	2551
1976	2803	10	5.1	2420
1981	3293	12	6.9	2218
1986	4270	15	9.2	2203

Data from ref. 4.

Cervical smears should be offered to all women. The first smear should be done within a year or so of her beginning to have sexual intercourse. Ideally the smear should be repeated after a year to minimize the chance of a false negative result. Repeat smears should be taken every 3 years until the age of 35 years, and then every 5 years until the age of 65 years.

Risk factors for carcinoma cervix include:

- sexual transmission – probably viral; annual smears are recommended for women who suffer from genital warts
- number of sexual partners (and number of partners the male has had)
- age at first pregnancy and parity
- method of contraception (barrier methods protect)
- occupation and social class (six times the risk for social class V compared to social class I)
- cigarette smoking.

It is very difficult to separate individual factors, and the same factors are often significant in several of the above, if not all. By being aware of the risk factors, females at higher risk may be identified. Every effort must be made to encourage women from socio-economic class V to come for the test (see also Chapter 3).

Breast cancer

Self-examination of the breasts is a technique which can be quite easily taught by the practice nurse or the health visitor. It is important that every lump found is reported as soon as possible. However, by the time a lump becomes fully palpable, if it is a carcinoma it has probably already been present for some time. Ideally such lesions are best discovered and treated before they are clinically palpable.

Mammography

The Forrest report in 1986[13] stated that all studies had shown the value of screening by this method for women over 50. High quality single mediolateral oblique view mammography was considered the preferred option for the development of mass population screening. Regional Health Authorities were responsible for the introduction of the NHS Breast Screening Programme from 1987. All women aged 50–64 years are called for routine mammography every 3 years. Women who have had one carcinoma of the breast have a four- to six-fold risk of developing a primary breast cancer in the opposite breast.

Obesity

Recognition (and treatment) of impending obesity is one of the simplest and most valuable screening tests which can be carried out. Many diseases, including ischaemic heart disease, diabetes and degenerative arthritis (osteoarthritis), are commoner in obese persons. The association of gross obesity with a reduction in life expectancy is well known, and everyone should be encouraged to watch their weight carefully especially between the ages of 35 and 50 year (see Chapter 14).

Ischaemic heart disease and hypertension

Shaper and colleagues (1987)[14] recommended the use of a simple scoring system to try to predict those men in the practice population at greatest risk of ischaemic heart disease. The system is outlined in Table 7.8.

TABLE 7.8   Scoring system to predict risk of coronary heart disease for men

Smoking years	×7.5
Systolic blood pressure	×4.5
Doctor diagnosis of ischaemic heart disease	+265
Doctor diagnosis of diabetes	+150
Current angina	+150
Death of a parent from 'heart trouble'	+80

Data from ref. 14.

Totalling the risk scores produces a figure, from which one can calculate the risk. As a rule of thumb, anyone with a score of 1000 or more should be considered to be at risk, and advised accordingly. Guidelines are produced to make adjustments for age. Hence a 40–44-year-old man to be in the top 20% would have a score of 870 or over, a 45–49-year-old a score of 950 or over, a 50–54-year-old a score of 1035 and over and a 55–59-year-old a score of 1095. Such a basic screening system used opportunistically would identify 54% of the major ischaemic heart disease events which will occur in the 5 years following screening. The use of a more detailed screening procedure (intermediate) including measuring blood cholesterol increased the yield to 58%, and the full scoring system with an electrocardiogram (ECG) to 59%. GPs should thus aim to identify the top 20% of their practice population at risk from ischaemic heart disease.

GPs should aim to record the blood pressure in each of their patients at least every 5 years. There are no symptoms caused by raised blood pressure, hence blood pressure must be measured regardless of the apparent well being of the person. Mass screening or opportunistic screening may be used. Automated sphygmomanometers are now available which will measure blood pressure from a finger. Early treatment can do much to prevent further illness.

The main problem in hypertension is to decide the level at which hypertension is defined. The British Cardiac Society Working Group on coronary heart disease prevention recommended treatment above the level of 100 mm Hg at fixed diastolic pressure.[10] The threshold should be higher for women (because of their reduced risk of cardiovascular complications) and lower in younger subjects. The decision whether to treat or not will also depend on other risk factors, such as smoking, significant family history and lipid profile, diabetes, and if there is any evidence of damage to specific end organs, for example left ventricular hypertrophy, fundal changes in the eye, or kidney problems. It is also possible now to screen for other cardiovascular conditions. Ultrasound has been used to diagnose abdominal aortic aneurysms presymptomatically, thus enabling prophylactic surgery with much safer results.[15]

Cholesterol

The 20% of people with the highest cholesterol levels are three times more likely to die of heart disease than the 20% with the lowest levels. Practically speaking, measurement of cholesterol levels should concentrate initially on those scoring highly on the Shaper index. Levels should also be taken from those with a family history of premature coronary heart disease and first degree relations of those with hypercholesterolaemia.

Cancer of the large intestine

This is the second commonest cause of death from cancer and is the fifth commonest cause of death under 65 year of age. Prognosis for the condition has not altered over

40 years, which reflects little change in the stage at which diagnosis is made. High risk groups, although of overall small numbers, include familial polyposis coli and sufferers of chronic ulcerative colitis. Studies in Nottingham[16] have shown the feasibility of screening general practice populations for occult blood loss in the stools. Further investigations of the positives with colonoscopy and radiography may lead to earlier diagnosis and a better prognosis. Carcinoma of the bowel is under-publicized for such an important malignancy, and health education regarding the significance of abnormal symptoms, particularly bleeding, is important.

Other cancers

Ovarian and uterine cancer may be discovered by routine pelvic examination. They will already be quite large by the time they are detected. Attempts are being made to evaluate ultrasound examinations in asymptomatic women.[17] Experiments are also taking place at the moment to test the use of the marker CE1 in the blood. If present, the use of selective ultrasonography for carcinoma of the ovary might be the appropriate method.

Diabetes

Mass screening is not cost effective, but early diagnosis for an individual is very important in order to begin treatment and hopefully prevent long-term complications. Urinalysis of high risk groups (obese, those with a family history, or on various medications), should be done regularly by the GP. Such urine testing is now also done by the GP at new patient medicals, and 3 year medicals.

Tuberculosis

Detection of TB is now concentrated on high risk groups. These include families of recently arrived immigrants from the Indian subcontinent, and single men, older than 45 year, living alone or in hostels. There is an association between alcohol dependency and tuberculosis in this latter group. Other individuals who should have chest X-rays as a preventive measure include those who work with young children (i.e. teachers, day nursery staff and those involved in children's homes), and those wishing to adopt or act as foster parents. Tuberculosis in individuals who are HIV positive is also becoming more important clinically.

The elderly

The following conditions may be screened for in the elderly:

- nutritional disorders and anaemias
- hypertension

- hearing impairment
- visual impairment (cataracts, glaucoma and accommodation problems)
- dental caries
- feet problems
- loneliness
- dementia.

All general practitioners must offer yearly home visits to all patients over the age of 75 years. The role of the health visitor in such assessments is very important. In some practices a health visitor for the elderly will concentrate solely on this group. Quality of life rather than longevity is important.

Prevention of blindness

It is particularly important to watch for an early developing cataract as so much can be done early in the disease. A history of rapidly failing sight, of seeing better in a dim room or of having to change spectacles frequently should always be fully investigated by an ophthalmic surgeon. Glaucoma may be detected by testing and recording the intraocular tensions. This is usually done by opticians, but new pulsed tonometers with digital readouts are available and being used in some general practices. All first degree relatives (of any age) of someone with glaucoma should be screened. Measurement of the visual fields may also detect early signs of glaucoma.[18]

All elderly persons should have an eye test every 2 years, but some will need help in making arrangements. The health visitor or social worker should be asked to help, and this may involve arranging transport for the old person in certain instances. It is essential to assist frail old people living alone in this way.

Nutrition

A number of elderly patients living alone at home fail to eat proper meals, and recent investigations have shown that approximately 20% of those admitted to geriatric hospitals are suffering from 'latent' malnutrition. For this reason, it is wise for the GP to assume that all elderly patients living alone, and especially those with limited mobility, may be borderline as regards satisfactory standards of nutrition. If further investigation confirms this, doctors should arrange for a meals-on-wheels service or for a care assistant to be employed (see p. 415). Such social help should prevent serious degrees of malnutrition.

Multiphasic screening

This involves subjecting individuals to a battery of tests in the hope of finding some abnormality which can then be pursued. This has never been shown to be of proven value. Studies in both America and Great Britain show no difference in major disabilities 7 years later. Many of the results may be equivocal. Screening is usually done in isolation and independently with the results sent to the GP. A false sense of security is only too easily created by such procedures, with the priorities for patients confused, and main risk factors such as smoking and lack of exercise, pushed into the background by concern for some minor biochemical abnormality.

HAZARDS OF SCREENING

Care should be taken to keep a sense of priorities when screening. Unnecessary investigations, provoking much anxiety, should be kept to a minimum. It is easy to give a wrong sense of proportion to the patient, who may begin to worry unduly over a mild hypertension or raised cholesterol but fail to stop smoking. In any screening programme, well-educated, well-motivated people will be more likely to attend (often social classes I and II) with those at greatest risk (groups IV and V) more likely to fail to attend. There is also an implication for the use of resources with the introduction of any screening programme. Cost effectiveness and overall benefit should be clearly proven before any new method is introduced.

Tertiary prevention

Tertiary prevention is synonymous with the management of chronic disease. The aim is to prevent complications and handicap. More and more GPs, often with practice nurses, run clinics for patients with various medical conditions such as diabetes mellitus, asthma, hypertension, etc. The use of predetermined protocols (management strategies) to help in the monitoring and management of disease certainly improves effectiveness of care. The Medical Research Council mild hypertension trial[19] showed quite clearly the ability of a nurse to co-ordinate the management of mild hypertension in general practice using structured guidelines. The community diabetic sister works closely with the GP and hospital clinics, and undertakes home visits which has meant that in many instances insulin may now be started very effectively at home without the need for hospitalization.

PREVENTION AND SOCIAL CIRCUMSTANCES

Housing conditions

Poor housing conditions not only predispose the individual to attacks of diseases (particularly communicable diseases in children, bronchitis, rheumatic fever, high level of accidents) but may also be a most important factor in the correct management of illness. A patient with severe angina of effort or a chronic cardiac condition should ideally avoid stairs. In a modern house it is usually possible to do this by turning a downstairs room into a temporary bedroom, especially if there is a downstairs lavatory, but in an old house this could be impossible and the management of such a case made difficult. A patient with malignant disease finds poor housing conditions a great handicap: for instance, it is difficult to look after a colostomy in the absence of a bathroom, internal lavatory and proper washing facilities. Most local authorities give special priority for urgent rehousing for important medical reasons. Doctors should acquaint themselves with these so that they can help their patients in this way. Full details are available from the local Director of Public Health.

Reference has already been made to the importance of living conditions in reducing problems in the elderly. It is particularly important that full use is made of supporting social services provided to help patients in their own homes such as home helps, meals service, chiropody and the installation of various aids and adaptations. The soiled laundry service may be invaluable. Occupational therapy providing activity and a sense of purpose is important.

Personal aids, adaptations and telephones

Aids, adaptations and telephones are available from all social services departments for those who are seriously disabled. Voluntary organizations may also be approached for the provision of such equipment. Full descriptions of such services are given on p. 525.

DISTRICT NURSING

DHAs provide district nursing (including nursing aids). Each district nurse is a fully trained State Registered Nurse having also undertaken a special course in district nursing. Special equipment such as hoists, special beds, wheelchairs, handrails, walking aids, etc., are usually lent by the DHA when needed. All forms of nursing are carried out and, in the most serious cases, two visits a day can be paid to the patient's home. The home nurse always works in close collaboration with the GP. To assist the bathing of patients who are bedridden but do not need full nursing services, many authorities employ State Enrolled Nurses (SEN) and bathing attendants (see Chapter 8 for further details about district nursing and community hospitals).

REHABILITATION

The chronic patient should be encouraged to keep active even if the eventual prognosis is poor. It is useful to arrange attendance at either a handicapped persons' handicraft centre or an occupational therapy centre run by the social services department or by the DHA. Transport is a problem for many of these chronic cases, but most social service departments now provide special transport: personnel carrier vehicles and vehicles with mechanical lifts attached to carry patients in wheelchairs. Doctors requiring such facilities for their patients should contact the Director of Social Services.

COMPULSORY REMOVAL OF ELDERLY AND OTHER PERSONS

The way in which such patients can be removed to hospital or hostel by section 47 of the National Assistance Act, 1948, is described on p. 424.

CONVALESCENT CARE

There are two forms of convalescent care provided by the DHA: that carried out in special convalescent hospitals as a final part of a hospital treatment process, and convalescent holidays. Details will be provided to any GP on inquiry to the District Medical Officer. Many voluntary organizations also have centres where holidays can be arranged, helping both the cared for and the carers.

HEALTH EDUCATION

Health education units

Virtually every district in England and Wales now has a Health Education Unit.[21] Their role is to provide support and back-up in the form of leaflets, posters, films and videos. They liaise with all members of the primary health care team and have important links with the Social Services, Community Health Council, and are becoming increasingly involved with schools. More recently, Health Education Officers (HEOs) have become involved in more promotional work with the media, local radio, etc. (see also Chapter 8, p. 201)

HEALTH PROMOTION

The Royal College of General Practitioners has described how health promotion can be developed at five levels in general practice,[22] namely:

Level 1 *Reception area*. Use of brochures, posters and other visual and audiovisual techniques

Level 2 *Example*. Making premises no smoking areas

Level 3 *Consultation*. Opportunistically asking and recording smoking habits, alcohol intake, diet and family history

Level 4 *Patient follow-up*. Special arrangements may be made to determine progress and modify subsequent management

Level 5 *Special clinics*. Antenatal clinics, child surveillance clinics, family planning clinics and those for specific disease management such as hypertension and diabetes.

Confusion exists about the use of the terms health education and health promotion, although the differences may not seem obvious and may indeed not be so. Health promotion will be of no use unless there is the educational opportunity to produce a change in behaviour. Back-up facilities and material for distribution must be available and a balance drawn between high profile glossy advertising and the continuing local work.

Nurse facilitators

In 1982, the Oxford prevention of heart and stroke project appointed a nurse facilitator whose job was to help GPs and the primary health care teams extend preventive medicine in general practice.[23] Together with the team, the nurse facilitator discussed priorities for preventive medicine and made plans of how best to screen the practice population. The practice nurse was trained in methods of prevention, particularly with blood pressure recording, and smoking and dietary advice. Risk cards, reminder labels and letters were produced, and recall systems established. Meetings with other staff members and receptionists were arranged and a system of audit to measure progress continues. There were, by the end of 1988, over 70 health districts who had appointed such facilitators covering a population of almost 22 million. FHSAs have also appointed their own facilitators, and in a few districts doctors themselves (usually GPs) have functioned as facilitators.

SELF-EDUCATION PROGRAMMES

Part of health education and health promotion involves the use of self-education programmes, conducted with the help of the media, and with production of learning aids such as leaflets, video recordings and lectures. Over the past few years there have been campaigns relating to:

Skin cancer (malignant melanoma). There has been much publicity recently informing the public about this cancer and encouraging earlier detection which allows curative treatment.[24] There has been an increase in the incidence of this tumour in the past few years. People are advised to consult their GP if:

- there is any change in the size or coloration of an existing spot, or of any new spot or nodule
- bleeding, itching, and/or pain in any old or new mole
- irregularity of the edge, or variation in colour of the mole make it especially suspicious
- ulceration of existing moles, and the appearance of further nodules in the surrounding tissues.

Testicular cancer. All men should be taught the importance of regularly examining their testes and reporting any change in size. Teratomata and seminomas, the two common cancers of the testes, have a greatly improved survival rate if detected early.

Breast cancer. All women should be encouraged to examine regularly their breasts once a month and report any suspicious lump or abnormality.

Rectal cancer. The importance of rectal bleeding is often underestimated. Campaigns to educate the public to present earlier with potentially important symptoms may have a major impact on the prognosis of a lesion if detected early.

It is important that all members of the primary health care team are made aware of such campaigns before they are announced publicly, so that they are ready to respond and that they do so in an appropriate fashion.

Medical records

It is obvious that for successful preventive medicine to be carried out there must be adequate and proper medical records. The information must be easily recognizable and reliable. Important family history should be noted, particularly first degree relatives suffering from ischaemic heart disease, carcinoma, glaucoma, asthma, etc. There should be a history of past and present occupations, immunization data, baseline of physical measurements such as weight, blood pressure, and a statement of the recognized risks. The increasing use of computers in general practice will be a tremendous help to all wanting to practise preventive medicine, but great care should be taken with the accuracy of the data stored.

References

1. Department of Health and Social Security. Research working group on inequalities on health: inequalities in health — Black Report. London: DHSS. 1980.
2. Department of Trade and Industry. Home and leisure accident research. 11th annual report home accident surveillance update. 1987 data. London: DTI. 1989.
3. Spector TD. The epidemiology of osteoporosis. Osteoporosis. Update Post Graduate Series. 1991.

4. Central Statistical Office. Social Trends, Vol. 18. London: HMSO. 1988.
5. Doll R. Major epidemics of the 20th century from coronary thrombosis to AIDS. Social Trends, Vol. 21. London: HMSO. 1991, pp. 13–21.
6. Health Education Authority. The smoking epidemic — counting the cost. London: HEA. 1991.
7. Health of the Nation (Cmnd 1523) London: HMSO. 1991.
8. Wald NJ. Maternal serum screening for Down's Syndrome in early pregnancy. Br. Med. J. 1988, 297: 883–887.
9. Warden J. Abortion time limit reduced. Br. Med. J. 1990, 300: 1155–1156.
10. British Cardiac Society. Report of the British Cardiac Society working group on coronary disease prevention. London: British Cardiac Society. 1987.
11. WHO. Community prevention and control of cardiovascular diseases. Report of a WHO expert committee. WHO/DVD 85.2. Geneva: WHO. 1984.
12. Wilson JMG. Surveillance and early diagnosis in General Practice. In Proceedings of Colloquium Teeling-Smith G (ed) pp. 5–10 London: Office of Health Economics. 1966.
13. Breast Cancer Screening (Sir Patrick Forrest, Chairman). Report to the Health Ministers of England, Wales, Scotland and N. Ireland. London: HMSO, 1986.
14. Shaper AG et al. A scoring system to identify men at high risk of a heart attack. Health Trends, Vol. 19. London: HMSO. 1987, pp. 37–39.
15. Collin J et al. Oxford screening programme for abdominal aortic aneurysm in men aged 65–74 years. Lancet 1988, ii: 613–615.
16. Hardcastle JD et al. Controlled trial of faecal occult blood testing in the detection of colorectal cancer. Lancet 1983, ii: 1–4.
17. Campbell S et al. Transabdominal ultrasound screening for early ovarian cancer. Br. Med. J. 1989, 299: 1363–1367.
18. Hitchings RA. Screening for glaucoma. Br. Med. J. 1986, 292: 505–506.
19. Medical Research Council. Principle results. MRC trial of treatment of mild hypertension. Br. Med. J. 1985, 295: 97–104.
20. Committee of Safety of Medicines Update. Br. Med. J. 1988, 296: 1319.
21. DHSS Task Force. Health Promotion in the NHS. A report on visits by a DHSS task force. Health Trends, Vol. 19. London: HMSO. 1987, pp. 27–29.
22. Royal College of General Practitioners. Combined Reports on Prevention. London: RCGP. 1984.
23. Fullard E et al. Facilitating prevention in primary care. Br. Med. J. 1984, 289: 1585–1587.
24. Doherty VR, MacKie RM. Experience of a public education programme on early detection of cutaneous malignant melanoma. Br. Med. J. 1988, 297: 388–391.
25. RGCP. Healthier children. Thinking prevention. Report No. 22. London: RGCP. 1982.
26. Council of Europe. Organization of Prevention in primary health care. Strasbourg: Council of Europe. 1986.
27. Hook EB, Chambers GM. Birth Defects 1977, 3A: 123–141.

8

The Primary Health Care Team and other Community Health Services

The primary health care team concept has evolved since the start of the National Health Service (NHS). The attachment of community nurses, health visitors and midwives strengthened the view that delivery of good and efficient primary care depended on close co-operation between the various health professions and occupational groups. The joint working party on the primary health care team (the Harding Report)[1] stated the concept of the primary health care team is viable and should be promoted wherever possible in the interests of improved patient care. Care must be taken that the advantages of the team approach are advantages for the patients and not just for the team itself.

Members of the primary health care team

The following personnel may be considered as part of the primary health care team (the list is not exhaustive):

Staff employed by general practitioner (GP)	Attached staff from District Health Authority (DHA) (from 1 April 1993, Fundholding GPs may purchase some of these services)	
Practice manager	District nurse	Speech therapist
Receptionist	Health visitor	Community psychiatric nurse
Practice nurse	Chiropodist	Orthoptist
Dispenser	Physiotherapist	Dietitian
Counsellor	Occupational therapist	School nurse

Practice premises and health centres

The great drive to build health centres occurred in the 1970s, but the number now being built has fallen dramatically. Health centres are units where family doctor services, child health (including school health) and health educational services are carried out side by side. Each DHA has the responsibility of providing and servicing health centres (including the provision of caretaking staff and cleaners). In most, GPs employ their own receptionists and secretarial staff. The Department of Health now encourages GPs to build their own purpose-designed surgeries and payment for the building is made through the cost rent scheme. The modern surgery, whether it is a DHA health centre or a practice owned surgery, should be the focal point for the provision of primary health care services, acting as a natural meeting place for other community services, including social services. In some there is partial attachment of a social worker to the primary health care team.

Teamwork

Unfortunately in too many health centres and surgeries, teamwork is not achieved. Individual members may be very isolated, may never meet or talk to each other. In others, meetings may be held, but because of the poor understanding of each other's respective roles, little meaningful communication occurs. Important factors in determining if a team is likely to function well include:

- size of the partnership
- numbers of attached staff
- the time that each may spend in the building
- numbers of cross referrals
- regular interdisciplinary practices meetings, where each member can feel on equal terms and have a say in policy decisions
- clinics held where members of the primary health care team work side by side
- shared access to medical records.

Staff employed by GPS (see Table 8.1)

PRACTICE MANAGER

As the business of modern general practice has become more difficult and more people are involved in the primary health care team, either as direct employees or attached staff, the role of the practice manager has evolved to provide administrative support for the GP in respect of staff, premises and finance. Duties will include:

1. Employment of staff, their contracts, holiday leave and sickness leave, dealing with the increasingly complicated legal implications of employment law.

TABLE 8.1   Practice staff employed by general practitioners, 1979–89[a] (thousands)

	1979	1986	1987	1988	1989	% change 1979–89
Total number of staff	35.6	52.1	55.7	60.4	65.7	84.3
WTE[b] staff by type						
Total	21.4	31.3	33.1	35.8	39.9	86.3
Secretary	2.3	3.3	3.3	3.8	4.2	82.3
Receptionist	8.6	13.7	13.7	16.0	17.6	104.7
Secretary/Receptionist	5.4	6.2	5.9	6.3	6.4	18.4
Dispenser	0.2	0.4	0.4	0.4	0.6	148.0
Nurse	1.1	2.6	2.9	3.7	4.9	366.2
Combination of above	3.8	5.1	5.0	5.6	6.2	63.2
WTE staff per unrestricted principal	0.94	1.20	1.25	1.33	1.46	

[a] Staff employed on qualifying duties for whom direct reimbursement is allowed under paragraph 52 of the Statement of Fees and Allowances.
[b] WTE, whole time equivalent.
Data from ref. 9.

2. Training for staff, ideally both in the practice and by arranging attendance at purpose-designed courses. Such staff training is now obligatory.
3. Health and safety at work and the associated legislation.
4. Financial matters, petty cash, PAYE and claims for reimbursement sent to the FHSA for items of service payments and other allowances.
5. Initial investigation of any complaints either by a patient or a staff member.
6. Organization of regular meetings with the partners and all members of staff, with documented minutes at such meetings.
7. Collection of statistical information. He or she may co-ordinate the administration of the audit activities being undertaken in the practice.
8. Consideration of long-term plans for the development of the practice.

In fundholding practices, there may well be another manager, the contracts' manager, who will manage the budget and contracts held by the practice for the care of its patients. In some areas, practices have made joint appointments.

RECEPTIONIST

A good receptionist is essential to the proper running of modern general practice and the functioning of the primary health care team. Responsibilities include making appointments for the doctor and practice nurse and getting notes ready for surgery. The receptionist may take messages on behalf of other members of the primary health care team, passing them on directly or entering details into relevant books.

Medical records are an essential part of good medical practice. Files should ideally have a summary card on to which various risk factors (such as smoking, obesity, high blood pressure) have been noted. The receptionist may be asked to highlight when certain procedures are due, for example, check blood pressure, cervical smear. This will enable opportunistic screening (see Chapter 7) to occur. Explanation of the reasons why such methods are used will make the receptionist feel more involved.

The advent of computers (see p. 204) requires that the receptionist be vigilant on checking registration details, and transferring patients in and out appropriately. Protocols for such duties need to be established in practices to avoid duplication or confusion.

PRACTICE NURSES

The title practice nurse has come to be applied to nurses directly employed by GPs. They work mostly in practice treatment rooms in contrast to community nurses who do most of their work in the patient's home and who are usually employed by the DHA. The number of practice nurses has doubled in the past 6 years to approximately 4000, and their role is developing very fast. The practice nurse may make the first assessment of a patient attending, advising on such matters as first aid. She is trained to perform various nursing procedures such as dressings, injections, venepuncture, urine tests, and record ECGs. She may help or perform minor operations such as suturing, treating warts and changing pessaries.

The practice nurse has increasingly become involved with chronic disease surveillance. They have often become the key person in running clinics for specific illnesses such as diabetes, asthma, and hypertension, as well as screening procedures such as cervical cytology and breast examinations. Family planning is increasingly being carried out by nurses who have been appropriately trained. The nurse will usually give immunizations and advice, and is increasingly becoming involved with counselling. The nurse is also responsible for the management of the treatment room, ordering supplies and laundry, sterilizing equipment and supervising adequate disposal of sharps and clinical waste.

In the USA since the late 1960s, nurse practitioners have been trained to act as surrogate physicians acquiring skills of diagnosis, investigation and treatment of common ailments. Experience of the nurse practitioner in this country has shown that the nurse can be as effective as a doctor in making initial assessments of patients, diagnosing and treating certain mainly acute illnesses (otitis media, sore throat, vaginal discharge) and supervising chronic disease care and therapy (e.g. hypertension). They can also be effective in the rehabilitation of the elderly after surgery.

DISPENSERS

Rural GPs are allowed to dispense medicines to their patients (for anyone living more than 1 mile away from a pharmacy). The dispenser is responsible for making up prescriptions and advising patients on how best to take the medicine and to warn about any relevant side effects. Training may be carried out with day release courses which cover such aspects as pharmacology, physiology and maths.

Staff attached to the primary health care team (see Table 8.2)

COMMUNITY NURSING

A comprehensive district nursing service must be provided by each DHA to assist in the treatment of disease at home. There are approximately 19 500 nurses (whole time equivalent) in employment as district nurses (community nurses) in the UK.[2] Many work full time, but there are also a number of part-time nurses. Their work, which has continued to show a marked increase over the last 5 years, is spread between different age groups of the population with the major proportion being for the elderly.

TABLE 8.2   General practitioner attached staff: numbers

	District nurses		Health visitors		Midwives		Community psychiatric nurses (CPNs)	
	1981	1989	1981	1989	1981	1989	1981	1989
England	14 523	15 235	9 244	10 051	3 406	4 076	1 083	3 379
Wales	1 244	1 130	559	555	193	282	80	239
Scotland	2 318	2 317	1 488	1 579	143	194		53
Northern Ireland	637	686	440	464	57	148		116
United Kingdom	18 722	19 368	11 731	12 649	3 799	4 700	1 163	3 787

Data from ref. 2.

Traditionally, district nursing provides nursing care for the patient being treated at home by the GP. Comprehensive nursing care is provided for both acute and chronic patients. Special late night visits may be arranged to assist very ill patients. In some areas a special service has been provided to enable continuous care to be given at night to patients very ill at home — often to persons suffering from a terminal illness.

With elderly chronic patients who may be incontinent and bedridden, a special soiled laundry service has been developed in conjunction with the district nursing services for daily changes of clean linen to be provided. This is a great asset to relatives looking after any bedridden incontinent patient and enables the elderly person to remain at home for a longer time.

In some practices the district nurse or community nursing sister still does some work, mostly dressings or injections, in the treatment room at pre-arranged times.

DISTRICT NURSE TRAINING

In 1981 a new extended training scheme was introduced for district nurses. The course covers 6 months study and, in addition to lectures and tutorials, includes four assignments which the student must complete during the course:

1. *A patient care study*. This includes a record of an individual patient's care and management, the objectives of the care, the social and economic family background, the relevant medical history, the plan, implementation and evaluation of the nursing care (2000–2500 words).
2. *A project of the student's choice* aimed at studying in depth an aspect of community care of particular interest. This is in the form of an illustrated essay of about 2000 words.
3. *A health centre/general practice study* aimed at focusing attention on primary health care provision in the UK. It covers many aspects including the role of each member of the primary health care team, the communication system and the various opportunities for health education. This is an illustrated essay of about 2500 words.
4. *An analysis of either a teaching or management problem* encountered on the course (800–1000 words).

This new extended course is aimed at equipping the district nurse to be able to cope with what is becoming an increasingly important role in the present-day health service.

The nursing process

Towards the end of the 1970s, with the development of the nurse's professional role, there was a great debate about the concept of the nursing process. Essentially the nursing process consists of assessing and identifying problems in conjunction with the patient, and defining goals. These agreed measures are then implemented and assessment made to see if they have been successful. This is very far removed from the role of the nurse where the doctor instructed the nurse to undertake some procedure. It is obvious that clear recognition of the role and function of each member of the health care team will minimize misunderstanding, thus avoiding resentment and the underuse of expertise.

Day surgery

There has been a marked increase in patients undergoing day surgery over the past 10 years. Some 794 000 day procedures are now carried out per year.[3] This activity has added quite considerably to the district nurse's work. The nurse may visit before the operation to assess the patient's suitability for such surgery and give preoperative advice. A visit on the evening of the operation soon after return to home may be required. Early discharge following conventional surgery is becoming more common, and needs important input by the district nursing service.

In some districts, patients may be discharged as soon as 24 or 48 hours after major surgery. In Peterborough, elderly people are being discharged back to their own homes within this period of time after hip fracture surgery. This is arranged in connection with the Hospital at Home Scheme[4] which in effect provides a hospital bed in the community. The district nurse is the leading member of the Hospital at Home team and will decide on the patient's suitability for early discharge and subsequent management.

Day hospital and community hospitals

The district nurse is the key person to liaise between such hospitals and the primary health care team. Community hospitals occupy similar buildings to the older cottage hospitals but function in quite a different way. They are staffed by the practice health team. The GP will provide the medical expertise and the district nurse the nursing expertise. A community hospital is linked to a health centre and has a small number of in-patient beds in a day ward. It receives various groups of patients, including physically and mentally handicapped patients and those in need of social support. Patients treated at such hospitals include medical patients not requiring intensive medical care, pre-discharge postoperative patients, certain geriatric patients, holiday admissions (respite care), certain chronically handicapped and elderly persons and terminal care patients.

MIDWIVES

The European Economic Community (EEC) midwives' directives brought about the lengthening of midwives' training from 1 year to 18 months from September 1981. There are three periods of training for Registered General Nurses (RGNs): (1) an initial period concerned with the physiology and psychology of normal childbirth, (2) a period in the community of not less than 12 weeks and up to a maximum of 18 weeks, and (3) a final period when the student is introduced to her/his role as a practising midwife.

Midwives are independent professionals in their own right. They are responsible for the overall supervision of antenatal and postnatal care of all women booked for hospital delivery, GP unit delivery and occasionally home delivery, and for supervising mother and child for up to 10 days, and sometimes 28 days, after delivery. Practising midwives are allowed to use pethidine on their own responsibility. The safekeeping of pethidine is spelt out in the Misuse of Drugs (Safe Custody) Regulation, 1973 (see also Chapter 4). There are approximately 4700 community midwives in the UK.

HEALTH VISITORS

Much of the health visitor's role has already been described (see Chapter 5, Child Health Services). There are approximately 10 000 health visitors (whole time equivalents) in practice in England and an estimated 2500 in practice in Scotland, Wales and Northern Ireland. The health visitor is an RGN with midwifery or obstetric training, who also holds the Health Visitor Certificate. This is gained from a 1-year course (or 2-year part-time course) which covers human growth and development, social policy and administration, social aspects of health and disease, and the application of such knowledge to the principle and practice of health visiting. Grants to fund such training may be provided by the Local Education Authorities (LEAs) or by scholarships from some associations and commercial firms.

The health visitor's role in health education aims at the prevention of illness and promotion of health. This is done in antenatal classes, child health clinics and by visiting families at home. More recently they have also been running their own clinic-based activity in health centres or GP surgeries. There is close liaison with other members of the primary health care team, particularly the GP, the district nurse (community nursing sister), school nurse and social worker. Shared access to notes greatly helps communication. The health visitor's role in advising and encouraging uptake of immunization is all-important. The health visitor is increasingly becoming the key person in the health services for suspecting and dealing with children who have been neglected or abused.

The health visitor also has a very important role in the care of the elderly. Indeed health visitors with a specific interest in the elderly are being appointed in some districts, and some being employed directly by GPs. A health visitor visiting the elderly in their homes and giving simple advice about heating and nutrition, and helping to arrange other services such as care assistants or meals-on-wheels, may make a great difference to an elderly person's existence.

SCHOOL NURSE

The school nurse has the overall responsibility for promoting positive attitudes to health within the school setting and will give advice to the school staff and attend to the needs of schoolchildren if required. There are approximately 2500 registered (and 162 enrolled) school nurses in England. Duties include making hygiene inspections, screening checks (hearing, eyesight), advice about immunization (particularly rubella and BCG), identifying children with special needs, carrying out home visits to specific children, being aware of the possibility of child abuse and attending case conferences on schoolchildren. The nurse deals with outbreaks of infection in schools in consultation with the teachers, environmental officers, and school medical officers and also undertakes emergency first aid where necessary and liaises closely with other members of the primary health care team. The nurse assists the school medical officer at various medical examinations. Their role is a wide but important one, the main problem being that in any secondary school there may be children with up to 20, 30 or even more GPs so that close liaison with them might be difficult (see also Chapter 5).

COMMUNITY PSYCHIATRIC NURSE (CPN)

The CPN is in the unusual position of working in the community, but being employed and paid for by the DHA as part of the consultant psychiatrist's team. Technically speaking, therefore, he/she might be considered as part of the secondary health care team, but undoubtedly functions most effectively when working closely with the primary health care team. There are approximately 3400 qualified CPNs working in England, and a further 400 in Wales, Scotland and Northern Ireland (see Table 8.2).

CPNs are registered mental nurses who have undergone one year's training, usually at a Polytechnic. Their course covers sociology and psychology, and includes project work and various attachments to the social services and other agencies. The CPN assesses, treats and monitors pyschiatric patients in the community. With the Department of Health firmly committed to treating more and more such patients in the community, the CPN is central to the whole process. The CPN may well acquire specialist skills in such areas as family therapy and counselling.

CUMBERLEGE REPORT (1986)

This suggested that each DHA should identify neighbourhoods consisting of 10 000–25 000 people and set up a Neighbourhood Nursing Scheme for each.[5] This should be led by a manager and be based on the community. There has been much discussion whether this would improve or handicap the function of the primary health care team. However, the problems of inner city care with patients of any one practice scattered far and wide have to be acknowledged and the efficient use of resources considered.

The Cumberlege Report also recommended that the UK Central Council

(UKCC) for Nursing, Midwifery and Health Visiting and the English National Board (ENB) for Nursing, Midwifery and Health Visiting should include a common training course for all first local nurses wishing to work outside the hospital.

PROJECT 2000

In 1985 the UKCC set up a project team to look at nurse training. Their report was published in 1986 and was entitled Project 2000.[6] Their proposals were that nurse education should be more closely associated with higher education. Its introduction was partially as a result of the changes occurring in health care which included demographic changes, the greater emphasis on a holistic approach to nursing, health education and the increasing importance of illness prevention. Government accepted the proposals in 1988. By the end of March 1991, Project 2000 had been started at 30 sites in England.

The course lasts 3 years, with the first 18 months being a common foundation programme, providing a general introduction to nursing. After 18 months, there is a choice of one of four structured programmes in: (1) adult (general) nursing, (2) mental health nursing, (3) learning disability (mental handicap) nursing and (4) children's nursing. The profession agreed that there should be just one level of qualified nurse, with no more enrolled nurses being trained. In the second 18 months the student nurses will provide no less than 1000 hours of service provision, most of which will be in their final year.

CHIROPODIST

Chiropody services are provided by DHA for the elderly, handicapped persons, children, diabetics and pregnant women.

Most old people suffer from a variety of minor foot defects such as ingrowing toe nails, corns, hallux valgus and hammer toes which lead to much pain when walking, and to some degree limit movement. This may even result in the old person being made housebound with all the subsequent problems, e.g. difficulty with shopping, leading eventually to malnutrition. Most of these foot defects can be considerably helped by regular chiropody. Diabetic patients need to pay particular attention to the care of their feet. Arrangements vary in different districts, but there are five main ways of providing chiropody:

- chiropody sessions in health centres, funded by the DHA
- domiciliary treatment service provided for the seriously ill and the housebound
- special chiropody sessions are arranged in clinics and old people's clubs
- chiropody treatment may be carried out at the private surgeries of chiropodists with the DHA meeting the cost
- the GP employing the chiropodist, but having the expense covered by the FHSA

considering it to be a health promotional activity, and realizing payment as a clinic session.

To obtain maximum value, chiropody treatment must be carried out regularly, once every 6–8 weeks.

There are approximately 2650 chiropodists (whole time equivalents) employed by DHAs seeing over 1.75 million persons. Of these, 1.59 million are elderly.

SPEECH THERAPIST

There are approximately 2600 speech therapists (whole time equivalents) working in the NHS in England. Their training involves a 4-year degree course at a university or polytechnic. They take referrals from health visitors, GPs and hospital consultants. A speech therapist diagnoses, assesses and treats all disorders relating to communication. Much of their work is concerned with children in special education. Their work with adults includes helping the rehabilitation of stroke patients. Conditions treated may be summarized under the following categories: (a) articulation problems, (b) language problems (use and understanding of spoken and written word), (c) voice problems, e.g. after laryngeal surgery, and (d) disorders of fluency (e.g. stammering).

OCCUPATIONAL THERAPIST (OT)

Over 4600 OTs are employed by the health services, and some 1000 by social service departments in England and Wales. OTs are trained to help people cope with day-to-day living. Such daily activities include bathing, feeding and retraining for work. Home visits are often carried out to advise on small adaptations that may be required to help with daily living and the need for rehousing for physically handicapped people. Much of their work involves the care of those with a physical and/or learning disability (mental handicap) and the mentally ill. Their job has two main functions, physical therapy and, increasingly importantly, psychological therapy. Training consists of a 3-year full-time course leading to a diploma in occupational therapy from the College of Occupational Therapy.

PHYSIOTHERAPIST

The physiotherapist's main function is to help temporarily or permanently disabled people regain as active a life as possible after illness. This may be with short-term problems after injury, such as with sports injuries or falls, but also with the long-term disabled such as those with a learning disability (mental handicap), or victims of conditions such as a stroke or a serious road traffic accident. Early intervention by a physiotherapist in the care of a patient suffering a stroke may prevent permanent loss of the use of a limb. In hospital, they are also used to treat patients with chest conditions, to aid the drainage of the lungs (e.g. postoperatively, and with patients suffering from pneumonia or bronchiectasis).

Physiotherapists may use equipment such as infra-red and ultrasound machines, traction equipment and small weights. They may use manipulation techniques in the treatment of musculoskeletal conditions. They are also increasingly being taught relaxation techniques. Many GPs now enjoy direct access to the services of a physiotherapist based at the District General Hospital. In some surgeries the physiotherapist may be employed by either the DHA or the practice on a sessional basis. Training consists of a 3- to 4-year degree course. To become a chartered physiotherapist, a person must pass the Diploma of the Chartered Society of Physiotherapy (MSCP). There are approximately 9300 physiotherapists (whole time equivalents) working for the NHS in England.

DIETITIAN

Dietitians working in the NHS advise on all health matters concerned with food and diet. They have a role in local campaigns on healthy eating, advise hospital caterers about the nutritional aspects of food presented in hospital and also see patients. Community dietitians will take referrals from GPs and are increasingly running clinics in doctors' surgeries/health centres. Patients referred have conditions such as diabetes, coeliac disease, obesity (particularly children) and raised serum cholesterol and lipids. A 4-year course in nutrition, dietetics or both is required to become a dietitian, and includes 1 year working in hospital under supervision for registration. There are approximately 1200 dietitians working in the NHS in England.

ORTHOPTIST

Orthoptists diagnose and treat complex disorders associated with binocular vision. Most of the work of an orthoptist is with the very young. As many as 8% of all children in the first 7 years have impaired vision and 3–5% have an established squint. The orthoptist often screens children in the community for such disorders. Many physically and handicapped children have visual defects. It is important to detect all such disorders as soon as possible to instigate treatment before permanent vision suffers. There are approximately 500 orthoptists working in the NHS in England. The recommended ratio for orthoptist provision is one for every 50 000 population. The training involves a 3-year course to obtain the Diploma of the British Orthoptic Council (BOC).

Other community health services

FAMILY PLANNING

Free family planning advice, treatment and supplies (those relating to female methods of contraception) are supplied by the NHS through GPs, hospitals and family planning clinics. At present in England GPs deal with more family planning consultations (2.45 million in 1985) in the ratio of approximately 3 : 2 compared with hospitals and family planning clinics (1.48 million in 1985); 14 000 patients were seen at home in over 51 000 visits by family planning staff on domiciliary visits.

The methods of contraception used in this country for various age groups are outlined in Chapter 4 on pp. 107–108. Condoms are only prescribable through family planning clinics. GPs are entitled to offer contraceptive services to patients even when that patient is registered with another GP for general medical services.

ENVIRONMENTAL HEALTH OFFICER (EHO)

The EHO's role is to ensure that the environment in which we live is suitable for us to remain free from disease. The environmental health officer will supervise commercial food preparation and working conditions and will inspect premises which may be considered unfit for human habitation. They are responsible for monitoring levels of noise and pollution in the atmosphere and may be called in when there has been an infestation of rats, mice, lice, etc. An EHO could also be involved in an investigation of outbreaks of infectious diseases.

HEALTH EDUCATION OFFICER (HEO)

Many of these professionals have a dual training of nursing/health visiting and teaching. Their function is the organization and promotion of health education within a district in a variety of ways. They may be involved with the training of other members of the primary health care team. They liaise closely with teachers, collecting and distributing suitable material and information, and make regular assessments and evaluations of the impact of the health education undertaken. National and local campaigns will be organized by the local health education department under the supervision of the HEO. There are approximately 580 HEOs in post in England and Wales. About half the HEOs hold the Diploma of Health Education which is a 1-year full-time course. The Certificate of Health Education is obtained after a part-time course.

FACILITATOR

In the past 5 or 6 years, over 70 facilitators have been appointed, either by the FHSA or DHA to help GPs and their primary health care teams extend preventive medicine in general practice. The facilitator discusses priorities for preventive medicine and makes plans of how best to screen the practice population and train the practice nurse in methods of prevention (see also Chapter 7).

AMBULANCE SERVICES

Until 1990 the ambulance service was administered by 45 separate health authorities in England, eight DHA administered services in Wales and a single Scottish Ambulance Service administered by the Common Services Agency. In England there were six metropolitan services administered by Regional Health Authorities (RHAs), 38 area services and the London Ambulance Service administered by the South-west Thames RHA on behalf of the four Thames regions. From April 1990 a small number of ambulance authorities applied for status as NHS trusts. There are approximately 19 000 ambulance personnel employed in England. There are also over 3000 ambulance officers and control assistants.

Ambulance services transport ill persons from home to hospital (or hospital to home) or from the scene of an accident to hospital. Their *medical condition* must be sufficiently serious to prevent them from travelling by public transport. Two types of ambulance are normally used: stretcher ambulances and sitting case vehicles. The former carry ill patients to and from hospital and the latter are used to transport sitting patients to hospital out-patient, physiotherapy or occupational therapy departments. In large cities and towns, separate stretcher ambulances are manned to deal with accidents and emergencies.

All ambulance personnel are trained in first aid and each ambulance should carry modern automatic oxygen resuscitation apparatus. Skilful first aid, such as properly conducted mouth-to-mouth breathing, followed by oxygen therapy can be a life-saving procedure in emergencies such as drowning, gas poisoning or electrical shock. Defibrillation for ventricular fibrillation in a patient with a coronary can be life-saving. An additional £3.8 million was provided by the government in July 1990 for all ambulances to be equipped with a defibrillator.[7] It was the intention that all qualified ambulance staff would be trained in cardiopulmonary resuscitation and in the use of a defibrillator by the end of 1991. Special arrangements are usually made to meet a large emergency due to a major civilian disaster such as a train accident. Large supplies of medical and nursing equipment are always available at ambulance headquarters to rush to the scene of the disaster, and mobile medical teams from hospitals may need to be called out to the scene of the accident.

Each year approximately 18 million people are transported by ambulance services.

Another 3.25 million are carried by the hospital car service. Of all cases carried by ambulances, 11% are for emergency cases (999 calls).

By 1996 some 60% of all qualified ambulance staff will be trained to paramedic standard. This will hopefully enable every emergency ambulance to be staffed by at least one fully trained paramedic.

PHARMACISTS

There are approximately 12 000 dispensaries or chemist contractors, in contract with FHSAs throughout the UK. Approximately eight out of 10 NHS patients consulting their family doctor are given a prescription for at least one medicine as part of their treatment. Pharmacists in contract with the NHS, FHSA or equivalent Scottish and Irish bodies are required by their terms of service to supply medicines and certain appliances ordered on NHS prescription forms. Dispensing must be performed by a qualified pharmacist and all medicines must be of a quality specified. The pharmacist is a very important figure in the community, being ideally placed to give advice on self medication and directing the patient to the GP if the symptoms warrant it. He/she will check the prescriptions issued and clarify any question of the wrong dosage or possible interaction occurring with other medication.

Prescriptions

In 1986, some 397 million prescriptions were dispensed. This represents seven items per person, an increase of 50% since the NHS started. Of all prescriptions issued in 1986, 82% were exempt from prescription charges. Children under the age of 16 years, or under 19 in full-time education, women over 60 and men over 65, those on Income Support or receiving Family Credit are exempt from paying prescription charges. Others who are also exempt include people suffering from a variety of medical conditions, such as epilepsy, diabetes mellitus and thyroid disorders requiring thyroid replacement. If someone has a handicap which means they are unable to leave the house without the help of another person, they also are exempt from prescription charges.

Voluntary services

Full details of local voluntary services are available from the local Voluntary Service Council or the local Citizens' Advice Bureau. Voluntary services are a very important supplement to the other primary health care services. They may help in the various groups that are formed to deal with medical problems. Such problems include alcohol abuse, autism, physical or learning disability (mental handicap), cancer, care of the blind and deaf, general help for children of one parent families, and counselling for bereavement and other crises.

Voluntary services may also organize facilities for the elderly, such as companion clubs and day care. Other agencies such as Red Cross, St John Ambulance and Women's Royal Voluntary Service have a important role in general health and first aid care.

Computers in general practice

By March 1991, according to a Department of Health study, 6130 general practices were computerized (63%) compared with only 942 (10%) 4 years previously.[8] Much of modern general practice lends itself to computerization, and the introduction of targets in the new Contract in 1990 persuaded many that computers would be indispensible; 97% of practices have their age sex register and other registration details on computer. Over 90% do their authorized repeat prescriptions by computer. Each practice has on average 4.7 visual display units (VDUs) 2.1 VDUs for a single-handed to 9.2 VDUs for a six or more partner practice. Fundholding practices have an average of 10.6 VDUs. The average purchase cost (1990–91) was £10 369, with average maintenance costs of £1342 per annum.

The ability to be able to recall patients with certain medical conditions, or for preventive health checks, generating automatic personalized letters is a major use for the computer. Fund holding practices could not function without computerization, and need extra sophisticated programmes to monitor their work. Other tasks for which the computer is being used include audit (59%), acute prescribing (48%) and clinical note recording (56%). Practice accounts may also be done by computer. A few practices are putting appointments on the computer. Dispensing practices may produce automatic labels for the drugs and stock control by use of the computer.

The computer will increasingly enable GPs and others in the team to have access to large databases for a variety of medical information. This may be accessed through a modem from afar, or be stored on a CD-ROM within the surgery. The computer may act as a prompt/aide-memoire in the consultation and direct the doctor or nurse through a predefined practice protocol for care in certain conditions (e.g. diabetes). Patient instruction screens may be used to reinforce certain information, and the computer could generate a printout for the patient. Programmes enabling interactive learning also exist for the computer.

Audit of such things as workload, types of consultation, diagnoses, drugs prescribed, and follow-up and outcome may all easily be done. Referrals are an essential area for the practice to monitor. Office functions such as word processing with customized letters, handouts, information leaflets and even the production of patient newsletters are possible.

Many practices have been producing annual reports for several years, and the computer is a very powerful tool to collate much of the data required in such reports. Under the 1990 contract all GPs are required to produce an annual report (see Chapter 1). Some practices modify their annual report for different audiences, for example the FHSA, patients, staff and the doctors.

Communications to other NHS computers will enable much of the administration to be streamlined. Pilot studies looking at communications with hospitals, for laboratory and X-ray information, out-patients and other departments are taking place and being evaluated. For the GP, a link to the FHSA would enable patient registrations, claims for item-of-service payments and target information to be done automatically. Eventually there is no reason why practices shouldn't have direct links with the NHS Central Register, RHAs, DHAs, other GPs and other health care professionals.

READ CLINICAL CLASSIFICATION

Designed by Dr James Read, a GP in Market Harborough, and greatly refined over the past 6–7 years, the Read Clinical Classification and has been bought by the NHS and been established throughout the NHS as the system to use. It is a fully comprehensive classification, hierarchical at five levels. The codes have five characters, based on the 58 alphanumeric characters 0–9, A–Z, a–z, (i and o have been excluded to avoid confusion). Hence there are 58^5 options, i.e. 656 356 768 possible codes. The codes are cross-referenced to other existing classifications such as ICD-9, ICD-9-CM and OPCS-4.2. It is a far more comprehensive nomenclature than any existing system. It is always possible to go from a Read Code to an exact ICD-9 or ICD-9-CM equivalent but it is not always possible to go the other way. The core of the coding system is a nomenclature of 'terms', each term represents a specific concept — be it a disease, occupation, drug, operation, etc. There are at present 100 000 of these 'preferred terms' in the Read Codes. There are 58 possible 'chapters'. Those starting with an upper case letter (A–Z) represent diseases, those with lower case prefixes (a–z) drugs, and the digits (0–9) a miscellany, including occupations, history/symptoms, examination/signs, diagnostic procedures, laboratory procedures, preventative procedures, operations and other therapeutic procedures.

The Read Codes are dynamic, fully flexible and have monthly updates. The ASCII hierarchy helps aggregation, analysis, manipulation, and data retrieval. Management in the health service requires such information as demographic and morbidity patterns, waiting lists, prices, referrals, in-patient episodes, out-patient visits and tests, and the monitoring of contractual agreements, and this is best done with powerful computers analysing the data.

All practices using computers must be registered under the Data Protection Act. A few practices have already moved to the paperless record using the computer for all their recording. For this to be acceptable several prerequisites are required:

- there must be 100% confidence in software and hardware
- ability to store and keep all history
- all entries must be dated with user's name
- there must be a legally valid audit trail to establish when recordings were made, and by whom.

Some forms used at present require patients' or doctors' signatures and hence still require some manual recording. All members of the primary care team should be able to log on and use the system. Special printouts, relevant to each individual, should be able to be produced.

Computers have arrived at a much faster rate than anyone would have predicted in general practice. By the turn of the century, links to hospitals and FHSAs will be well established. Patients themselves may well have small smart cards which are plastic credit card-sized cards on which electronic computer information can be stored. Significant clinical information, including therapy, will be stored on such cards, and given to any health professional at the time of consultation to be called up into the computer system being used.

References

1. Standing Medical Advisory Committee and the Standing Nursing and Midwifery Advisory Committee (Chair W. Harding). The Primary Health Care Team. Report of a joint working group. London: DHSS. 1981.
2. Central Statistical Office. Regional Trends, Vol. 26. London: HMSO. 1991, p. 125.
3. Audit Commission. A short cut to better services. London: HMSO. 1990.
4. Anand JK, Pryor GA, Morgan RR. Hospital at home. Health Trends, Vol. 21. London: HMSO. 1989, pp. 46–48.
5. Community Nursing Review (Chair J. Cumberlege). Neighbourhood Nursing – A focus for Care. Report. London: HMSO. 1986.
6. United Kingdom Central Council for Nursing, Midwifery and Health Visiting. Project 2000. A New Preparation for Practice. London: UKCC. 1986.
7. Department of Health. On the State of the Public Health for the year 1990. Annual Report of the Chief Medical Officer of the Department of Health for 1990. London: HMSO. 1991.
8. Department of Health. Report. Computers in General Practice. London: HMSO. 1991.
9. Department of Health. Statistics for General Medical Practices in England and Wales, 1979–89. Bulletin 4(4) 191.

9

Epidemiology of Communicable Diseases

Communicable or infectious diseases are those which can be spread either from person to person or from animal or insect to a human. Such diseases are caused by infection of the body with bacteria or viruses or their products. Epidemiology is the study of all the factors connected with the incidence and spread of such diseases — it includes the causation of the illness (aetiology).

When many cases of the same communicable disease occur simultaneously, an epidemic is said to exist. A series of similar epidemics throughout the world is a pandemic. Scattered cases of communicable disease with no connection between them are said to be sporadic. When such disease is constantly present in any area, it is said to be endemic.

Classification of communicable diseases

One of the best methods of classifying communicable diseases is by their mode of spread. There are six main groups.

- **Air-borne or droplet infections**
  Bacterial diseases
    Streptococcal infections — scarlet fever, erysipelas, puerperal fever, tonsillitis, rheumatic fever
    Staphylococcal infections — pemphigus neonatorum
    Diphtheria
    Bacterial meningitis
    Whooping cough
    Tuberculosis
    Pneumonia
    Legionellosis
  Virus diseases
    Influenza

Encephalitis
Measles, rubella, mumps, chickenpox
Glandular fever
Viral meningitis
Viral respiratory infections
Common cold
Herpes simplex
Herpes zoster
- **Faecal-borne or gastrointestinal infections**
Bacterial diseases
Typhoid and paratyphoid fevers
Bacillary dysentery
Food poisoning
Botulism
Infant gastroenteritis
Campylobacter enteritis
Cholera
- **Water-borne infections**
Typhoid fever
Cholera
Cryptosporidiasis (protozoal disease)
- **From animals**
Anthrax
Leptospirosis
Rabies
Q fever
Toxoplasmosis
Via milk — brucellosis, bovine tuberculosis
Viral haemorrhagic diseases
- **By contact**
Human to human
Sexually transmitted diseases — syphilis, gonorrhoea, non-specific urethritis, some forms of viral hepatitis, chlamydia, genital warts and herpes
Acquired immune deficiency syndrome (AIDS) — normal heterosexual intercourse and anal intercourse, especially in homosexuals
Via blood
Viral hepatitis (some forms) — see Chapter 11
AIDS
Skin Contact
Scabies
By injury
Tetanus

- **From insects**
  Plague
  Malaria
  Yellow fever
  Typhus

Epidemiological investigation of communicable diseases

A full investigation of all serious communicable diseases should always be undertaken to find the cause of the infection and to study the factors which contributed to its spread. A successful investigation will often prevent further cases by defining a continuing source of infection. Epidemiological investigations should include a careful history of the patient and close contacts, and any link between the patient and other cases should be investigated. If the disease is not normally present in the country (e.g. cholera) it is important to establish if the patient has recently travelled abroad. In gastrointestinal infections (typhoid fever or food poisoning) which are usually the result of food contamination, a complete record should be collected of the food eaten.

INCUBATION PERIOD

In all communicable disease there is a latent period between infection and the first symptoms or signs of the disease — the *incubation period*. For example, a person infected with typhoid fever will show no symptoms for 14 days and an accurate knowledge of this incubation period is most important as it allows investigations to be concentrated on the food eaten 14 days before the first symptoms, for this was the time of infection.

Incubation periods are never easy to remember and may vary in the same disease. They can most conveniently be divided into four groups.

- Very short incubation periods, 2–18 hours
  Staphylococcal food poisoning (2–4 hours)
  Clostridium perfringens food poisoning (10–20 hours)
  Salmonella food poisoning (12–18 hours)
- Short incubation periods, 2 to 9 days
  Streptococcal infections — scarlet fever, erysipelas, puerperal infection, tonsillitis
  Staphylococcal air-borne infections — pemphigus neonatorum
  Pneumonia
  Diphtheria

Influenza
Meningitis
Dysentery
Infantile gastroenteritis
Paratyphoid
Anthrax
Gonorrhoea
Legionellosis
Leptospirosis (usually 7–10 days, but occasionally up to 19 days)
- Long incubation periods, 10–25 days or longer
    Typhus — usually 8–14 days
    Viral haemorrhagic fever — usually 10 days
    Chickenpox — usually 17–21 days
    Rubella — usually 17–20 days
    Measles — usually 12 days
    Whooping cough — usually 14 days
    Mumps — usually 17–20 days
    Typhoid — usually 14 days
    Poliomyelitis — usually 11–14 days
    Q fever — usually 19 days
    Syphilis — usually 21–25 days (in exceptional cases can be up to 90 days)
    Rabies — 14–42 days
    Hepatitis 'A' (infective hepatitis) — usually 18–45 days and some non-A and non-B
    Hepatitis 'B' (serum hepatitis) — 60–105 days and some non-A and non-B
- Exceptionally long incubation period and variable
    AIDS — very variable, probably more than 2 years in most cases; American experience suggests even 7–10 years is possible.

Bacteriological or virological investigations

These are most important in all investigations of communicable disease. They aim at:

- confirming the diagnosis
- discovering which close contacts are carriers
- demonstrating a source of infection, e.g. a contaminated foodstuff in food poisoning.

If possible, the pathogenic organism should be isolated. This may be by blood culture (typhoid, meningococcal septicaemia), nose and throat swabs (streptococcal infections, diphtheria), sputum (tuberculosis, pneumonia), faeces (typhoid, dysentery, poliomyelitis) or throat washing (influenza).

In air-borne bacterial disease, nose and throat swabs are taken. In tuberculosis, sputum tests, both by direct examination and culture, should be carried out on all patients. In faecal-borne disease specimens of faeces or rectal swabs of patients and contacts should always be examined. In most outbreaks, it is usual to find a symptomless carrier. If such a person works with foodstuffs, he/she may easily cause further infections. In some virus diseases, electron microscopy is used to study the morphology of the virus particles.

Blood tests on antigen–antibody reactions often provide valuable diagnostic aids. These include precipitation tests as in grouping and typing of streptococci, or agglutination tests, e.g. Widal tests for salmonella infections. Usually, such tests only give a retrospective diagnosis. This is because a positive result depends on demonstrating a rising titre of antibody in the patient's blood in specimens collected (a) very early in the disease and (b) about 6 weeks later.

In AIDS the original infection is diagnosed by the demonstration of antibodies against the human immunodeficiency virus HIV. The actual diagnosis of the disease of AIDS is a clinical one (see Chapter 11) as at present there is no laboratory confirmatory test available.

CARRIERS

In some instances, the source of infection may be a human carrier. A carrier is a person who is harbouring and excreting the pathogenic bacteria or virus without suffering from any symptoms. Human carriers are of two kinds:

1. *Convalescent carriers*. These have had the disease recently and, during their convalescence, still excrete the causative organism. In many infectious diseases, such as diphtheria, streptococcal infections, typhoid fever, dysentery and poliomyelitis, convalescent carriers are common. Such carriers are usually temporary and excrete organisms for a few weeks only. Occasionally, convalescent carriers may become permanent. An example is a chronic typhoid carrier who will intermittently excrete typhoid bacilli in the faeces all his/her life.

2. *Symptomless carriers*. These are people who have never suffered from the disease or had any symptoms, but who are excreting the pathogenic organism. Such carriers probably have had a subclinical attack of the disease. Examples include typhoid, dysentery, salmonella food poisoning and poliomyelitis. Symptomless carriers may be temporary or permanent. Carriers may be further classified as:
   - nasal carriers – streptococci and staphylococci infections, diphtheria
   - throat carriers – streptococcal infections, diphtheria, meningococcal infections
   - faecal carriers – typhoid, poliomyelitis, dysentery
   - urinary carriers – typhoid
   - HIV – individuals carrying HIV in their blood who can infect others by

blood contamination (including needle stick injuries) and by sexual intercourse — see chapter 11).

Before any investigation can be started, it is essential to know the location of
every case. For this reason, most communicable diseases are compulsorily
notifiable — they must be reported immediately to the 'proper officer' i.e. the
Director of Public Health of each DHA. A small fee is paid for each notification.
The complete list of notifiable diseases is:

Anthrax	Plague
Cholera	Poliomyelitis (acute)
Diphtheria	Rabies
Dysentery (amoebic or bacillary)	Relapsing fever
Acute encephalitis	Rubella
Food poisoning	Scarlet fever
Leptospirosis	Tetanus
Leprosy	Tuberculosis
Malaria	Typhoid and paratyphoid fevers
Meningitis	Typhus
Meningococcal septicaemia (without	Whooping cough
meningitis)	Viral haemorrhagic fever
Measles	Viral hepatitis
Mumps	Yellow fever
Ophthalmia neonatoram	

Any changes to this list are always mentioned in the MB2 series of OPCS Monitors.
It is helpful to remember the few communicable diseases which are *not* notifiable:

AIDS	Influenza
Common cold	Pneumonia
Chickenpox	Sexually transmitted diseases

Note that AIDS and sexually transmitted diseases have never been notifiable in
the UK because it is feared that to do so would result in much concealment of infections and thus encourage further spread. Certainly countries who have insisted on
notification of sexually transmitted diseases generally have higher rates of infection.

Factors connected with the development of communicable diseases

There are three main factors which determine the development of communicable
disease:

1. Environment. The ease of spread of communicable disease depends on the
   environment. Air-borne infections are commoner in winter time when cold

conditions encourage overcrowding in houses with a subsequent greater risk of aerial infection. Gastrointestinal diseases, on the other hand, are commoner during the summer months when warm weather assists bacterial multiplication in infected foodstuffs or when insects, such as flies, are found. This seasonal incidence is an example of the effect of environment.

Bad housing conditions, including overcrowding and lack of adequate ventilation, will further aid the spread of communicable diseases. Many tropical diseases are spread by insects and the presence or absence of such vectors determines the level of disease.

2. Properties of the infecting bacteria or viruses. The main two factors are the virulence of the bacteria or virus and the size of the infecting dose. With a bacteria of high virulence, the size of the infecting dose will be small and vice versa.

3. Characteristics of the patient being attacked. This is mainly connected with the resistance of the patient to the disease and depends on both local and general immunity, which may be natural or artificial.

In an individual subject with a risk of infection, the end result may be development of serious attack, development of mild attack, development of subclinical attack, development of a symptomless carrier state, or escape of infection. Which of these five possibilities occurs mainly depends upon the relative importance of the environmental factors, the properties of the infecting organism and the immunity of the patient. In very adverse conditions where there are bad environmental or living conditions, or where very virulent bacteria or viruses attack a person with no immunity, a serious case of the disease will probably develop rapidly. On the other hand, an infection with a mildly virulent bacterium in a person with a good resistance will probably result in no development of disease. Between these two extremes all types of result may follow — a normal attack of the disease, a very mild attack which may not be recognized (subclinical attack), or the development of a carrier state.

Complete avoidance of the risk of infection is not usually possible with many common infectious diseases, but in some instances (e.g. viral haemorrhagic fever) avoidance of importation of the disease or control of any imported source (travellers who have been in contact with the disease) is one of the best ways to prevent the disease.

The virulence of the bacterium or virus is always important. The sudden emergence of a new strain of a bacterium or virus with an increased invasiveness can be a major factor in producing an epidemic. The unexpected development of a serious streptococcal septicaemia is usually explained by accidental infection with a very virulent organism.

The size of the infecting dose is also important and varies in different infectious diseases. In chickenpox, measles, typhoid and cholera, the minimum dose of organism which will lead to infection is small. In such diseases, the threshold of infection is said to be low — the diseases are extremely infectious. In other illnesses, such as whooping cough or salmonella food poisoning, the threshold of infection is higher — it is necessary for the minimum infecting dose to be much bigger and, consequently, such diseases are not as infectious.

Local resistance can be lowered by factors such as injury or cold. The development of a common cold after chilling in winter is probably due to a temporary lowering of local resistance. However, the most important factor is the presence or absence of general immunity. Natural immunity may be genetic, for there are differences in the resistance shown by different races in the world. Such immunity is connected with genetic factors and these are responsible for much variation in the natural resistance of different members of the same race. Thus, some families and individuals seem naturally to escape attacks while others readily fall victims to many communicable diseases. Artificial immunity has been discussed in Chapter 6.

In AIDS, the development of the disease is characterized by an interference with the body's immune system. Although antibodies may be present against many pathogenic bacteria or viruses, they are rendered useless and the individual has no resistence. This means that the individual is extremely vulnerable to all types of infection (see Chapter 11).

References

1. OPCS. Monitor Series MB2. Infectious Diseases (published quarterly). London: OPCS.

10

Common Communicable Diseases

Bacterial and viral diseases caused by air-borne infections

STREPTOCOCCAL INFECTIONS

Causative organism: Streptococcus haemolyticus Group A.
Incubation period: Short, 2–7 days.

These include such varied diseases as scarlet fever, erysipelas, puerperal fever, tonsillitis, cellulitis, septicaemia and rheumatic fever. Infection usually spreads from another case or from a nasal or throat carrier either directly by droplets or indirectly by infected dust. It is most important to realize that the same type of streptococcus may cause scarlet fever in one patient, tonsillitis in another and puerperal fever in a recently confined woman.

Scarlet fever

Scarlet fever is still commonly seen in the UK, but is usually mild. In 1990, there were 7187 cases notified in England and Wales (this figure is above average).[1] It is commoner in winter than in summer and is caused by infection with a strain of haemolytic streptococcus which produces an erythrogenic toxin in a patient who has no immunity to this toxin. If the patient has an immunity to the erythrogenic toxin, no skin rash develops, although other symptoms (e.g. tonsillitis) will occur. Such a case can readily infect another person who, if he/she has no immunity, will develop a rash and be diagnosed as having scarlet fever. For this reason, the source of infection may be a carrier, a patient with tonsillitis or another case of scarlet fever.

Method of spread

Scarlet fever is spread by air-borne infection via droplets and dusts.

Control

Home isolation is sufficient except in severe cases or unless there are special dangers of further infection, e.g. a home attached to a food shop or dairy. Children can return to school as soon as complete clinical recovery has occurred.

Secondary streptococcal infections

Secondary streptococcal infections used to be a major problem in puerperal pelvic infection and in cross-infection within hospitals. Because of the sensitivity of streptococci to antibiotics and chemotherapy, secondary streptococcal infections are now far less serious than staphylococcal and other infections (see below). The danger is still present and is greatest in surgical wards where great care must be taken in dressing wounds. No wound should be dressed shortly after the ward has been cleaned or beds made because of the danger of circulating infected dusts.

Since many normal persons carry pathogenic streptococci in their noses and throats, it is still most important to maintain aseptic conditions in surgical theatres and in midwifery practice. Sterile masks, caps, gowns and gloves must always be worn by doctors and midwives attending deliveries in the home or in hospital. Special sterilized packs are supplied free for all home confinements. No midwife with a nasal or throat infection should attend a mother in her confinement. In such circumstances, the midwife must remain off duty until bacteriological examination of her nasal and throat swabs are normal. If an unexpected puerperal infection occurs, the nasal and throat swabs of all who attended the birth must be examined to exclude carriers.

STAPHYLOCOCCAL INFECTIONS

Causative organism: Staphylococcus aureus
Incubation period: 4–7 days
Staphylococcal infections are responsible for pemphigus neonatorum, for a number of cross-infections in hospitals, some cases of bacterial infections and for a small proportion of toxin food poisonings (see p. 236).

Pemphigus neonatorum

This highly infectious and dangerous disease is fortunately rare, but mortality from complications may be considerable in some outbreaks. It is spread by:

- contact with a person with a purulent staphylococcal lesion or
- air-borne infection.

It is important to isolate the infant immediately, away from the maternity unit if possible; it is best to admit the mother and child to an infectious disease hospital.

Prevention

The following are important preventive measures:

- early diagnosis to enable prompt isolation — all skin blisters in infants should be swabbed
- early discharge home of remaining mothers and babies to reduce the chance of cross-infection
- in outbreaks which are not immediately controlled, new admissions to the maternity unit should be stopped.

Hospital infections

Hospital infections still remain a problem. They mainly affect:

- other patients (cross infection) especially very small babies and others who are immune-suppressed i.e. being treated with corticosteroid and cytotoxic drugs.
- certain members of the staff nursing and caring for patients. This is a special problem in dialysis units and for those dealing with certain communicable diseases. It can also be a special problem in casualty departments with diseases capable of being spread by blood (AIDS, viral hepatitis).

Strains of *Straphylococcus aureus* that are resistant to antibiotics, *Pseudomonas pyocyanea* and infections with *Klebsiella aerogenes* are the worst hospital infections. Staphylococcal infections can be reduced by ensuring that special clothes are always worn in operating theatres. Under no circumstances should street clothes be worn in such units even for short visits there. Surgical gowns should always be changed between operations as there is increasing evidence of considerable infection of these from patients. *Pseudomonas* infections are often spread by fluids and therefore liquid soap containers (particularly if corks are used) and any standing water on wards should be avoided.

Protection of staff

In extreme cases when nursing very infectious patients (i.e. viral haemorrhagic fever) a physical barrier should be used to separate staff from patients. This is the principle of the Trexler plastic isolator which is a large airtight plastic tent with two compartments (one for the patient and one for supplies). These are joined together once the patient is inside. Air pressure is kept below atmospheric pressure to reduce the danger of leakage and the extracted air passes through filters to remove any infected particles. Staff can treat and nurse patients through specially protected portholes.

Investigation of hospital infections

Whenever cases of hospital cross infection occur, a full bacteriological survey must be undertaken. It is also important to isolate the patient, as removal of the source of bacterial infection is essential to control further infections, especially in cases of *Pseudomonas pyocyanea.*

It is helpful to appoint a Hospital Infection Control Officer who may be a bacteriologist or hospital sister who co-ordinates the work of controlling the spread of infection. The function of such an officer includes:

- collection of records of hospital infections
- encouraging prompt recognition and isolation of infected patients
- checking ward techniques (barrier nursing)
- supervising routine checks of staphylococcal carrier rates in staff in operating theatres
- following up and co-ordinating with the investigation of discharged patients. In this respect close links must be built with the local Director of Public Health.

MENINGITIS AND/OR ENCEPHALITIS

Causative organisms: various bacteria and viruses.

Bacteria

A full list of the bacteria responsible for attacks of meningitis is given in Table 10.1. *Neisseria meningitidis* causes 39.3% of attacks (meningococcal meningitis) followed

TABLE 10.1   Bacteria isolated in cases associated with acute meningitis or encephalitis in England and Wales, 1990. (Based on information from laboratory reports to the Communicable Disease Surveillance Centre)

Type of bacteria	Number of cases (%)
Neisseria meningitidis	966 (39.3)
Haemophilus influenzae	618 (25.1)
Streptococcus pneumonia	438 (17.8)
Streptococcus other	141 (5.7)
Other bacteria	128 (5.2)
Staphylococcus aureus	66 (2.7)
Escherichia coli	56 (2.3)
Staphylococcus epidermis	25 (1.0)
Listeria monocytogenes	23 (0.9)

Data from ref. 1.

by *Haemophilus influenzae* (25.1%) and various other bacteria. Note that *Listeria monocytogenes* (causing listeriosis which is often characterized by a meningitis) only represents 0.9% of cases of bacterial meningitis.

Viruses

Causative organisms: Table 10.2 shows that Echoviruses cause 41.7% of viral attacks of meningitis or encephalitis followed by Cocksackie A (26.0%) and Cocksackie B (18.0%) in England and Wales in 1990.

TABLE 10.2   Viruses isolated in attacks of meningitis or encephalitis in England and Wales, 1990. (Based on laboratory reports to the Communicable Disease Surveillance Centre)

Type of virus	Number of cases (%)
Echovirus	95 (41.7)
Cocksackie A	59 (26.0)
Cocksackie B	41 (18.0)
Herpes simplex	13 (5.7)
Mumps	10 (4.4)
Adenovirus	2 (0.8)
Measles	2 (0.8)
Varicella zoster	1 (0.4)

Data from ref. 1, based on information from reports to the Communication Disease Surveillance Centre.

Incubation period: various, but mainly short, 2–7 days.

Since 1985, meningococcal meningitis has shown a marked increase in England and Wales (see Fig. 10.1). In the period 1987–90, a concentration of cases of meningococcal meningitis occurred in the Stroud area of Gloucestershire. Fortunately the 1989 figures showed no further signicant rises. Group B strains predominated in these attacks, but there has been a marked decrease in Group C strains. Vaccines against Group A and C strains are now licensed and available in the UK. Vaccine should be given to travellers to countries where the risk of meningococcal meningitis infection is high, and also to close contacts of Group A and C infections.[2]

Early diagnosis of meningococcal meningitis is important because:

- antibiotic treatment at that stage is usually effective
- close contacts of cases caused by Group A and C strains may be vaccinated.

In the Chief Medical Officer's annual report for 1990, it was stated 'The winter upsurge of meningococcal meningitis started earlier than usual in December 1989,

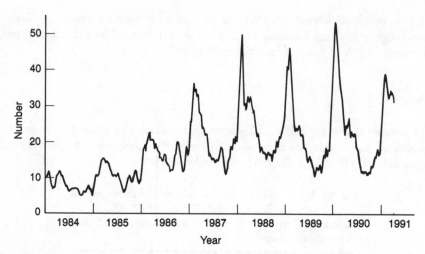

FIGURE 10.1   Cases of meningococcol meningitis in England and Wales, 1984–91 (data from ref. 2).

and reached higher levels than had been seen in the previous peaks of the present upsurge. It is probable that the influenza epidemic of the winter of 1989 exacerbated the transmission of meningococci and lowered individual's susceptibility . . . Group B strains of meningococci continued to predominate (60%) while Group C showed 30% approximately.'[2]

Prevention: in October 1992, a new vaccine (Hib vaccine) was introduced against *Haemophilus influenzae* Type b (see p. 150).

TUBERCULOSIS

Causative organism: Myobacterium tuberculosis.

Incubation period: unknown but probably weeks.

The annual numbers of notifications of tuberculosis fell steadily up to year 1987 when they had reached 5086 in England and Wales. They rose to 5164 in 1988, to 5432 in 1989 but fell back again to 5204 in 1990. The impact of AIDS has certainly contributed to the increase especially in London and Edinburgh. During 1990, 3942 cases of respiratory tuberculosis were notified in England and Wales. For many years more cases have been reported in men then in women, usually in the proportion of 58–60% to 40–42% in women. Approximately 57% of the male cases were aged 45 years and over whereas, in women, only about 45% of cases came into this age group.

The fall of tuberculosis in England and Wales for 1982–87 is shown in Fig. 10.2 which also illustrates the small increase from 1987 to 1990. In England and Wales, the highest rate of tuberculosis occurred in 1990 in persons whose ethnic origin is

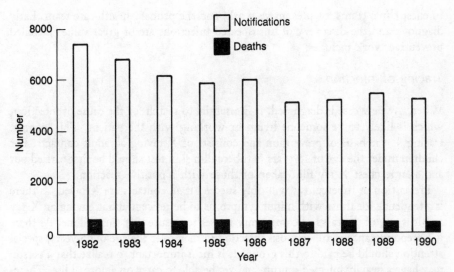

FIGURE 10.2   Notifications and deaths from tuberculosis in England and Wales, 1982–90 (data from ref. 2).

in the Indian sub-continent.[3] The next group with the highest rate of tuberculosis is those over the age of 65 years.

Another group which has a high rate of tuberculosis are AIDS patients. In the UK by 1990, 4% of persons with AIDS were diagnosed as also suffering from tuberculosis and a further 4% had other mycobacterial infections. Clearly further careful monitoring of all individuals known to have been infected with HIV is important as there is likely to be a high rate of tuberculosis infection, and such people will be sources of infection to others.

Method of spread

Spread of tuberculosis in the UK usually occurs via infected sputum from a known or an unsuspected case. As bovine tuberculosis has virtually disappeared from the UK, milk is no longer a vehicle of infection. However, in countries with a bovine tuberculosis problem, milk can still be an important source of infection if it is drunk raw. Consumption of infected meat can also spread tuberculosis, but sound meat inspection should prevent that problem.

Prevention of tuberculosis

The responsibility for prevention of tuberculosis rests with chest physicians, Directors of Public Health, community physicians, specially trained health visitors, community nurses sometimes called tuberculosis visitors, who are usually attached to chest clinic teams for preventive work, and the primary health care team. Early diagnosis and the discovery of unsuspected infections are of great value. Detailed preventive work includes:

Tracing of infection

When any new case is diagnosed, it is essential to search for the cause of infection, which is likely to be someone living or working with the patient. This 'contact tracing' is the basis of prevention and consists of X-raying all adult contacts. For children under the age of 15 years, a tubercullin skin test should be first carried out and a large chest X-ray film taken of those with a positive reaction.

Prevention of tuberculosis will only succeed if *all* contacts are X-rayed, as there is a tendency for those with minor symptoms to be reticent about having an X-ray and it is one of the tasks of community nurses to ensure that this is done. As there is a preponderance of tuberculosis infection in men over the age of 45 years, special attention should be paid to this group. It is most important to realize that a person may have a heavily infected sputum and yet be able to carry on a normal life. Therefore, the absence of any symptoms should never be used as an excuse to dispense with an X-ray in a contact.

Housing

Overcrowded housing and sleeping accommodation produce conditions favouring the spread of tuberculosis. Each patient should always have his/her own bedroom unless married. Where the patient is married, the couple can share the same room, but should use twin beds. It is most important that no parent who has had tuberculosis should ever sleep in the same room as a child. If the home of the patient is not large enough to allow a patient to have a separate bedroom, immediate rehousing is essential to avoid infection spreading through the family. Most local authorities have special priority housing schemes which enable such patients to be rapidly rehoused.

Occupation

Special precautions are taken to ensure that no one with tuberculosis is employed in an occupation where he/she is likely to spread the disease.

All entrants to Teachers' Training Colleges must have a clear chest X-ray. Routine chest X-rays are advised for nursery nurses, and other persons working with young children, including teachers and child care staff.

It is illegal for a person with open tuberculosis to be employed in the food trade.

Follow-up

All patients should be carefully followed up for at least 5 years after infection and this should include:

- visits to a chest clinic for a clinical check with X-rays
- home visits to ensure that social factors there have not deteriorated, for if this happens a relapse is more likely.

Chemoprophylaxis

The use of drugs to prevent infection is now widespread. *Primary chemoprophylaxis* is the use of drugs to prevent infection in those particularly at risk, e.g. newborn babies of mothers with positive sputum. *Secondary chemoprophylaxis* is the use of drugs in tuberculin-positive persons who have no clinical evidence of the disease, to prevent the development of clinical tuberculosis. In the treatment of clinical cases, the use of drugs is effective both in curing the individual and in reducing infectivity at an early stage. Constancy of drug treatment is essential. Recent studies have shown that many patients may fail to take their drugs regularly, and this not only reduces the efficacy of the treatment, but increases the chance of drug resistance developing.

Immunization with BCG

The ingestion of live *Mycobacterium tuberculosis* may or may not result in a recognizable clinical infection of tuberculosis. In many instances the patient develops sufficient resistance and immunity to prevent a clinical infection, but in every case a skin sensitivity develops. If later a minute quantity of old tuberculin or purified protein derivative (PPD) is introduced into the skin of such a person by intradermal injection (Mantoux test) or by multiple puncture (Heaf test), a sharp reaction or flare occurs. This is called a positive tuberculin skin test. It means that, at some time in the past, the patient has ingested live *Mycobacterium tuberculosis* and all such persons should be X-rayed, as occasionally a latent infection will be found. If no disease is discovered, it can be assumed that there is enough immunity to resist infection. In this way, the tuberculin skin tests, although tests of hypersensitivity, can be used as indicators of immunity to tuberculosis.

Immunization should be offered to all negative reactors in the following groups:

- all family contacts of cases
- all medical students and nurses
- all schoolchildren aged 11–13 years
- children of immigrants (and especially newborn babies) in whose communities there is a high incidence of tuberculosis irrespective of their age.

In 1990, the Joint Committee on Vaccination and Immunization recommended that, until more is known of the likely impact of the HIV epidemic on the incidence of tuberculosis in the UK, BCG immunization in schoolchildren should continue.

INFLUENZA

Causative organism: influenza viruses — now typed into three strains, A, B and C. Most epidemics are caused by strain A; strain B is a secondary cause; strain C does not cause epidemics.
Incubation period: 1–3 days.

Incidence

Influenza is endemic in winter. Epidemics occur irregularly every 2–3 years and are often world-wide in distribution (pandemic). The disease is spread by droplet infection.

In the winter of 1989–90, there was a severe epidemic of influenza which was the worst outbreak since 1975–76. The strain was $A(H_3N_2)$. Figure 10.3 shows the weekly cases. Note that the peaks of both epidemics in 1975–76 and 1989–90 occurred in week 8 (towards the end of February). It was estimated that the outbreak in 1989–90 resulted in nearly 30 000 deaths, mainly in persons over the age of 75 years and 43% in people aged over 85 years.[3]

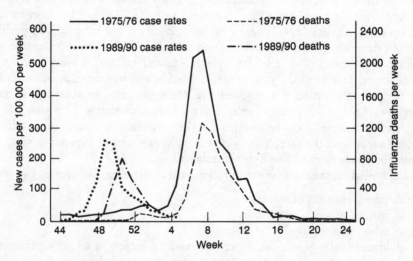

FIGURE 10.3   Weekly new cases and deaths for epidemic influenza in England and Wales, 1975–76 and 1989–90 (data from ref. 3).

Prevention

The rather limited success of active immunization has in the past been due to vaccine being prepared from strains which are different from the virus causing the current epidemic. Recently viruses have been developed by genetic recombination of naturally occurring strains of influenza A virus with a low yield in laboratory culture with high yielding laboratory-adapted strains. These recombinant strains are indistinguishable from the naturally occurring parent and are used to prepare vaccine. The advantage of this process is that vaccines can now be prepared reasonably quickly after the appearance of a new variant of influenza A virus. WHO plays an important role in influenza prevention. Recently many new variants have first appeared in the southern hemisphere or Far East and this has enabled vaccines to be prepared against these new strains to protect individuals in the UK.

Even with new techniques effective vaccines may be in short supply, so essential workers should be protected first together with other 'at risk' groups of the community (see p. 153).

MEASLES

Causative organism: a virus.
Incubation period: 10–14 days (usually 12 days).

Incidence

Large-scale epidemics still occur among children with a peak usually every 1–3 years, especially in large towns. Since the introduction of measles vaccination, there has been a marked reduction in measles incidence in the UK (see Fig. 10.4). For instance, there were 97 408 cases in 1985, 82 061 in 1986, 42 165 in 1987, 86 001 in 1988, 26 222 in 1989 and 13 302 in 1990.

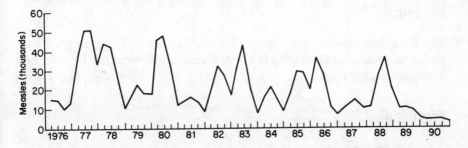

FIGURE 10.4   Corrected quarterly notifications of measles in England and Wales, 1976–90 (data from ref. 11).

Prevention

This is by immunization with measles vaccine now part of MMR (mumps, measles and rubella, see p. 152). Two interesting figures (Figs 10.5 and 10.6) from the Chief Medical Officer's Report of the Department of Health, show the encouraging effect of MMR vaccine on the incidence of rubella and measles.

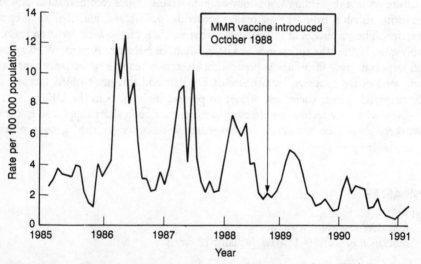

FIGURE 10.5   Effect of MMR on rubella: 4-weekly reports of rubella from RCGP's general practices, England and Wales, 1985–91 (data from ref. 3).

RUBELLA (GERMAN MEASLES)

Causative organism: a virus.
Incubation period: 17–20 days.

Incidence

This is a mild disease and the only problem resulting from it is the danger of congenital malformations developing in a baby if a mother develops rubella in the first 3 months of pregnancy.

Prevention

This involves the following:

■ MMR vaccination (mumps, measles and rubella immunization) for all children aged 15 months (see p. 148)

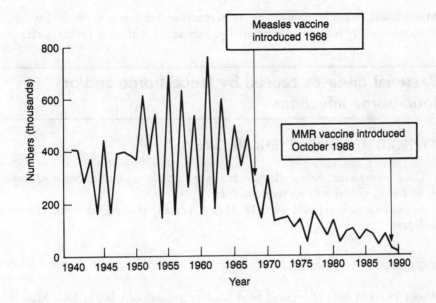

FIGURE 10.6   Effect of measles vaccine and MMR on incidence of measles in England and Wales, 1940–90 (data from ref. 3).

- active immunization of any girl aged 11–13 years who has not previously been immunized
- avoidance of contact by any mother early in her pregnancy with any case of rubella
- if a mother in the first 3 months of pregnancy has inadvertantly been in contact with a case of rubella (perhaps an older child in the family), passive immunization using immunoglobulin can be attempted, but the dosage must be high (2.0 g)
- if any older woman is immunized actively, it is essential to ensure that pregnancy does not take place for at least 3 months following vaccination.

MUMPS

Causative organism: a virus.

Incubation period: usually 17–20 days.

This is a mild disease, but it is important to prevent mumps because of the danger of the following complications:

- meningitis and/or encephalitis as mumps is responsible for 4.4% of all viral causes of this condition
- orchitis which can be an unpleasant complication in males.

Mumps was formerly thought to be responsible for much male sterility, but although sterility may occur temporarily, permanent sterility is probably rare.

Bacterial diseases caused by faecal-borne and/or food-borne infections

TYPHOID AND PARATYPHOID FEVERS

Causative organism: *Salmonella typhi* causes typhoid fever and *Salmonella paratyphi* A, B and C give rise to paratyphoid fever.

Incubation periods: typhoid fever, 12–21 days, (usually 14 days); paratyphoid fever, 2–7 days.

Incidence

About 140–180 cases of typhoid fever are reported annually in the UK. Many of these occur in small isolated outbreaks. Usually 80–85% of typhoid fever occurs in travellers who have contracted their infections abroad, especially in the Indian sub-continent. Others come from the Middle East, Africa and some European countries, especially Italy and Spain (water and food-borne infections contracted in isolated villages or when out camping or in a mobile caravan). In 1989, 89% of paratyphoid cases occurring in the UK were traced to infections from abroad, and most of these were caused by food-borne transmissions. Carriers play an important part in the spreading of typhoid and paratyphoid fevers.

Method of spread

The eventual source of most infections is the faecal matter of a human case or carrier. Typhoid fever has a low threshold of infection which means that it can quite easily be spread by water. Paratyphoid fever, on the other hand, has a much higher threshold of infection and therefore cannot easily be spread by water. The methods of spread include:

Direct transmission

This is rarely seen but there is always a danger in typhoid fever that anyone nursing a patient may become infected. For this reason, all cases of typhoid fever should be treated in an infectious disease hospital by staff previously immunized against typhoid fever. It is hazardous to treat typhoid fever patients in a side ward of a general hospital.

Indirect transmission

This can be, for example, by water, or by food.

Water

In the last century, this was the most usual method of infection, but with the control of water supplies, it is very rare in well-developed countries to find such an outbreak, although it is still the usual method of spread in more primitive communities. The last serious water-borne outbreak of typhoid fever in this country was in Croydon in 1937 when 290 cases of typhoid fever occurred. It was caused by a urinary carrier contaminating the water supply while he worked on a deep well. In 1963, a water-borne outbreak in Zermatt, Switzerland, resulted in 434 cases.

Food

This is the main vehicle of infection today for both typhoid and paratyphoid fevers. Any foodstuff may be involved, but prepared/cooked meat products are among the commonest. Much publicity was given to the 1964 Aberdeen outbreak, which was caused by a 6 lb tin of corned beef which became infected with *Salmonella typhi* through the use of unchlorinated water during the cooling process following sterilization. Canned foods generally are a rare cause of typhoid fever. Foodstuffs are most commonly infected by a carrier working in the kitchen and contaminating food. Ice cream can cause typhoid if contaminated with typhoid bacilli during manufacture (Aberystwyth outbreak in 1945). Compulsory pasteurization of ice-cream in the UK has prevented a recurrence of this method of spread.

Shellfish growing in polluted water may contain typhoid bacilli as it is usual for them to filter large quantities of water through their shells. Any bacteria in the water will remain in the shellfish. Subsequent consumption may lead to typhoid or paratyphoid fever.

Milk. Since widespread pasteurization of supplies, milk-borne typhoid fever has never been reported in this country, but paratyphoid fever has occurred rarely following the drinking of raw milk. With primitive production methods, typhoid fever could be spread by milk contaminated directly or indirectly by a carrier.

Flies may, in primitive conditions, contaminate food by carrying *Salmonella typhi* from human faeces to foodstuffs. This is only likely where there are very primitive methods of faecal disposal such as trench latrines.

Accidental cross-infection in a gastroenterological unit

In 1977 in England, an interesting episode occurred at a gastroenterology clinic: one subclinical and three clinical cases of typhoid fever occurred in patients being medically treated for gall-stones. They were thought to have contracted the infection from contaminated duodenal tubes. The source of infection was another patient who had been intubated several times at the clinic and was shown to be a faecal and biliary excreter of *Salmonella typhi*. After a review of procedures at the clinic, disinfection and re-use of the tubes was abandoned in favour of use on one occasion only.

Period of infectivity

As long as *Salmonella typhi* or *S. paratyphi* are excreted in either the faeces or the urine, the patient is infectious. It is usual for an uncomplicated case to excrete bacteria in the faeces for a few weeks, but about 5% continue to do so for 3 months and about 2% become chronic carriers. Faecel carriers far outnumber urinary carriers, who are rare. Faecel carriers are invariably intermittent, carrying for a short time, then ceasing to carry for a few weeks (in rare cases for as long as 26–27 weeks) so that routine random sampling will discover few chronic carriers.

Prevention

It is essential that all typhoid patients should be admitted to an infectious disease hospital. Early diagnosis is an important factor in prevention. Laboratory aids to diagnosis include:

- *Blood culture.* The best time is the first week of disease when over 80% of cases are positive. Subsequently the number of failures increases. Collect 5–10 ml of blood.
- *Stool culture.* Positive results are found in the second week.
- *Urinary culture.* In a minority of patients, a positive culture in the urine is obtained usually during the third week.
- *Agglutination tests (Widal reaction).* Agglutination tests are considerably less valuable in diagnosis than culture of the organism in the blood, faeces or urine. To be conclusive, a rising titre of H and O agglutinins must be demonstrated. Blood must be collected as early as possible (first week) and compared with the results of samples collected 4–6 weeks later. This means that conclusive diagnosis is only possible retrospectively by this method. In an uninoculated person, an H titre of 1 in 50 and an O titre of 1 in 100 are highly suspicious of infection. It is most important to realize that previous inoculation (TAB) can cause ambiguous results especially with H agglutinins. The 'Vi' agglutination used to be considered useful in tracing carriers as often a carrier will have a high Vi titre (1 in 10), but the 1964 Aberdeen outbreak clearly showed it is not a reliable test for Vi antibodies were not then found in chronic carriers.

In tracing the source of infection, a knowledge of the phage type of typhoid or paratyphoid organism responsible is essential. There are now over 145 different phase types of *Salmonella typhi* and *Salmonella paratyphi*. Isolation of the organism in blood, stool or urine enables this typing to be carried out.

Prevention

The prevention of typhoid and paratyphoid fevers depends on:

- full immediate investigation of cases to discover the cause
- control of chronic carriers
- food control — sampling at docks, pasteurization of milk and ice cream, prohibition of infected shellfish
- sterilization in food preservation
- environmental hygiene
- immunization of holiday visitors to the Indian sub-continent, Far East, Middle East and Africa and to Italy, Yugoslavia, Portugal and Spain (if travelling in country areas).

Carriers are responsible for many infections, and any carrier who handles food of any description or who is employed by a water supply department may be most dangerous. For this reason, whenever a case of typhoid or paratyphoid fever occurs, a complete investigation must immediately be carried out to find the cause of the infection. A careful history is taken to discover what food was eaten by the victim and close contacts at the start of the incubation period, which is 14 days before the first symptoms in typhoid fever, and 7 days in paratyphoid fever.

Immediate stool examinations must be carried out on all close contacts and especially on kitchen personnel. If a carrier is discovered, the typhoid bacteria are identified and typed by phage typing. This is then compared with that causing the outbreak. If the type is different, the carrier could *not* be the cause of the infection, but if it is the same, the carrier *may* have been responsible. The discovery of a carrier of the same type does not prove the cause, and further epidemiological investigations are necessary.

The only certain method of finding carriers is to follow up every case for many months after infection by regular fortnightly sampling of faeces and urine. By this means the chronic intermittent carrier will be identified.

Once a carrier is diagnosed, a careful check is kept on his/her occupation and family. By law, no chronic carrier of typhoid or paratyphoid may be employed in the food trade. Nor should a carrier be allowed to work in any kitchen, water department, school or similar institution.

Constant sampling of foodstuffs, pasteurization of milk and ice cream supplies and cleansing of shellfish are all important preventive measures.

Clean sterilized water must be used to cool tins in canning processes. This is because tiny pinholes could enable typhoid bacteria to gain entry as happened in the Aberdeen typhoid outbreak in 1964.

Careful methods of sewage disposal, and purification and sterilization of water supplies have reduced the likelihood of any further water-borne outbreaks in the UK. Any failure to maintain such standards can be disastrous, as was illustrated by the 1963 Zermatt outbreak of typhoid fever.

DYSENTERY (BACILLARY)

Causative organisms: there are four types of *Shigella* bacteria responsible for dysentery attacks: *Shigella sonnei* (71.7%), *Shigella flexneri* (24.6%), *Shigella boydii* (3.0%) and *Shigella dysenteriae* (1.3%).
Incubation period: 1–7 days.

Incidence

In England and Wales in 1990, there were 2756 notifications of dysentery (i.e. clinical attacks), but during the same period, there were 3441 bacteriological identifications of dysentery bacteria reported. Bacillary dysentery in the UK is usually mild and is only serious in young infants or in debilitated elderly people.

Method of spread

Sonnei dysentery is spread by direct contamination from person to person. In a closed community, such as a ward or nursery, it spreads slowly at first, but as soon as a substantial proportion of the community is infected, the outbreak develops more quickly.

Prevention

Outbreaks of dysentery can be prevented by:

- *Early diagnosis of first cases.* This is especially important in day nurseries and hospital wards. All cases of diarrhoea, however mild or transient, should be bacteriologically examined (stool specimens or rectal swabs) to make certain that early cases are identified. It is usual to find a proportion of symptomless carriers among close contacts, but this carrier state only lasts from 2 to 3 weeks. Chronic carriers are unknown.
- *Home isolation of cases and symptomless (contact) carriers.* Provided action is taken early, careful investigation and isolation of all sources of infection (cases and carriers) will prevent a serious widespread outbreak. If a widespread outbreak has already developed, isolation will achieve little.

FOOD POISONING

In 1990 in England and Wales, 52 145 cases of food poisoning were notified. This is slightly less than the record high figure of 52 557 reported in 1989. Figure 10.7 clearly illustrates the rapid rise in the numbers of food poisoning notified since 1987 and how the levels have remained at this level.

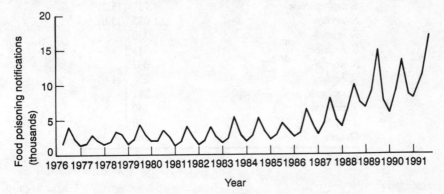

FIGURE 10.7   Corrected quarterly notifications of food poisoning in England and Wales, 1976–91 (data from ref. 1).

There are two main groups of food poisoning:

- infective food poisoning − salmonellosis
- toxin food poisoning − caused by staphylococci, *Clostridium perfringens* and botulism. Most food poisonings are caused by salmonellosis and this cause is now considered in detail.

SALMONELLOSIS

Salmonellosis is a true bacterial infection in which the small intestine is attacked by salmonella organisms.

Causative organisms: Many types of salmonella bacteria can produce food poisoning and the number of different serotypes now identified exceeds 1000. These are classified at the Division of Enteric Pathogens at the Central Public Health Laboratory Service (PHLS) at Colindale. In 1989 the number of isolations of salmonella bacteria totalled 29 905 and Table 10.3 shows the main types.

Methods of spread

There are five main sources of infection:

TABLE 10.3   Types of salmonella bacteria in food poisoning outbreaks in England and Wales identified by the Public Health Laboratory Service in 1990

Type of salmonella	Number of cases (%)
Salmonella enteritidis	26 203 (72.7)
S. typhimurium	4 757 (13.2)
S. virchow	1 083 (3.0)
S. infantis	330
S. heidelberg	313
S. newport	307
S. hardar	236 (4.8)
S. montevideo	211
S. panama	160
S. agona	158
Others	2 268 (6.3)

Data from ref. 1.

- poultry, especially chickens
- poultry products — mainly eggs of chickens in the cases of infections of *Salmonella enteritidis*; duck eggs are potentially more likely to lead to infection and should be eaten only after extensive cooking
- pigs — a number of outbreaks of *Salmonella typhimurium* have been traced to pork pies and similar products
- human cases and carriers
- rodents.

The large increase of *Salmonella enteritidis* infections in 1987 was connected with chickens and the eggs of chickens. Chickens are affected by *Salmonella enteritidis* and careful review of the methods of feeding at battery farms has reduced the incidence.

Prevention

Fortunately the threshold of infection of salmonellosis is high — very large numbers of bacteria need to be ingested to produce clinical attacks of food poisoning. This means that the method of storing chickens, especially after being cooked, is crucial. All such foods should always be stored in refrigerated conditions. The observed seasonal increase in outbreaks of food poisoning in the summer months is nearly always due to the more serious effects of poor storage when the ambient temperature is high which encourages rapid multiplication of bacteria in food not stored under refrigerated conditions.

A complete epidemiological investigation must be undertaken whenever an outbreak of salmonellosis occurs. Specimens for bacteriological examination should be collected from all close contacts and kitchen personnel, and any salmonellae isolated must be typed. If a carrier is found, it must *not* be assumed that he or she is necessarily the cause, for such a carrier may also have been infected in the outbreak. Any carriers who are food handlers should be kept away from work until they are clear. It is rare for salmonella carriers to become chronic as the carrier state usually lasts for only a few weeks.

Duck eggs are particularly liable to become heavily contaminated and should only be eaten as hard-boiled eggs (10 minutes boiling). Cases have been traced where duck eggs have been used for making cakes — the cooking may not completely destroy any salmonellae due to poor conduction of heat in cake mixtures. Egg products such as imported egg albumen should be pasteurized as laid down by the Liquid Egg (Pasteurization) Regulations, 1963. Similarly, coconut products are best heat-treated.

The risk of salmonella food poisoning can be reduced by the following:

1. Careful storage methods must be observed. Refrigeration of foods liable to contamination is most important to reduce the multiplication of any contaminating bacteria. This is especially important with prepared meat products such as meat or pork pies and cooked meats. In shops such foods should be kept constantly in refrigerated conditions and special refrigerated display cabinets make this possible.
2. Very careful complete defrosting of frozen chickens before cooking is essential. Unless this is carried out there is a danger that any salmonella infection deep in the chicken joint may never be destroyed in the cooking. Then, if the storage after cooking is careless (i.e. in a warm kitchen overnight rather than being refrigerated), and if the chicken is subsequently served cold, heavy contamination can occur. Many serious salmonella outbreaks have been caused in this way.
3. Extreme care must be taken in the handling and preparation of food, as this reduces the chance of a faecal carrier accidentally contaminating food.
4. Immediate bacteriological investigation of any diarrhoea or gastroenteritis, however mild, among food handlers. While awaiting results, such personnel should stop working.
5. Avoidance of unnecessary storage of prepared foods. If all prepared foods were eaten promptly, or if any left over portions were thrown away (*not* stored), a considerable reduction in such food poisoning would result. Thus, it is most unwise to prepare the sweet today for lunch tomorrow unless it can be stored in a refrigerator.
6. Gamma radiation from a cobalt-60 source has been shown to be very useful in destroying salmonellae in frozen whole egg, coconut, imported meats and animal feeding stuff.
7. Pasteurization of liquid milk — raw milk has been traced as the infecting agent in about 2–3% of cases.
8. Avoidance of eating raw or lightly boiled eggs.

TOXIN FOOD POISONINGS

Toxin food poisonings are those in which the poisonous substance ingested is a bacterial enterotoxin produced by prior bacterial multiplication in the food. Once this toxin is present, the further role of the bacteria is unimportant and subsequent destruction of the bacteria (by heat — pasteurization) will not usually destroy the toxin (which is heat stable) or render the food safe.

STAPHYLOCOCCAL TOXIN FOOD POISONING

Cause: ingestion of food containing an enterotoxin which has been produced by the multiplication of certain strains of staphylococci.
Incubation period: very short, 2–4 hours.

Incidence

Although varying from year to year, usually 1–2% of food poisoning episodes are traced to this cause. Fatalities have resulted from staphylococcal toxin food poisoning but are very rare.

Method of spread

In most instances, human staphylococcal lesions such as abscesses, paronychia, nasal infections or infected nails are the source of the contamination.

The foods which are most often implicated in staphylococcal food poisoning are prepared meats. All types of cooked meats have been traced as vehicles of infection, the commonest being ham. Other foods which may be involved include canned foodstuffs (meats, fish and vegetables) and, much less commonly, unpasteurized milk and its products.

Staphylococcal toxin food poisoning can occur only after a combination of the following events:

1. Contamination of the foodstuff with a strain of *Staphylococcus aureus* which is capable of producing an enterotoxin. Fortunately only a few strains can do this.
2. Food must provide a suitable culture medium — cold meats are a good medium for staphylococci, and growth is not inhibited by the presence of salt in the meat.
3. Food has to be stored at a sufficiently high temperature, 10–49°C, to encourage growth of the staphylococci — enterotoxin is produced during multiplication of staphylococci in the food, and multiplication for 8–12 hours is necessary for production of a substantial amount of toxin. Once staphylococcal enterotoxin

has been produced in any food, it is difficult to destroy as it is heat stabile. This means that even boiling a foodstuff already contaminated with enterotoxin would only destroy a small and insignificant amount of that toxin, although all staphylococci would be destroyed.

Although the simultaneous combination of factors 1, 2 and 3 occurs only infrequently, the fact that over 10% of persons carry staphylococci in their noses means that potentially dangerous pathogenic bacteria will accidentally contaminate foods on occasion.

Prevention

Staphylococcal food poisoning can best be avoided by: (a) consuming foodstuffs within 2 hours of preparation whenever possible; (b) where this is not possible, food must *always* be stored in cool, refrigerated conditions which are too cold for bacterial multiplication (if no multiplication occurs, toxin will not be produced); (c) by ensuring scrupulously clean conditions while handling or preparing foods. A high degree of personal hygiene is important. Hands must be frequently washed and habits avoided which would encourage transfer of staphylococci from the nose and mouth of the food handler to foodstuffs.

CLOSTRIDIUM PERFRINGENS (CL. WELCHII) TOXIN FOOD POISONING

Cause: Clostridium perfringens is an anaerobic spore-bearing bacterium which on multiplication can produce a heat stabile toxin which causes a mild food poisoning. There is increasing evidence that heating the spores tends to activate their germination. This 'heat shock' may well explain why so many outbreaks of this food poisoning follow heating up of precooked foods.

Incubation period: 10–20 hours.

Incidence and method of spread

The spores of *Clostridium perfringens* are very widely disseminated in earth and faeces. Anaerobic conditions are needed for multiplication and toxin production. Meat dishes (stews, soups, boiled meats) are usually found to be the cause, especially if prepared some hours before consumption.

Prevention

It must be realized that it is almost inevitable that spores of *Clostridium perfringens* will gain access to kitchens on raw meat. This means that infection can only be avoided if the following strict rules are followed:

- avoidance of precooking of meats
- avoidance of storage of any food between 10°C and 49°C for more than 3 hours
- if meats have to be precooked, it is essential that they are rapidly cooled and maintained below 10°C in a domestic refrigerator
- care should always be taken when gutting animals such as rabbits to avoid contamination of the flesh with faeces in the intestines.

BOTULISM

Causative organism: Clostridium botulinum (an anaerobic bacteria which produces spores).
Incubation period: short, 12–72 hours.

Incidence

Cases are usually very rare in the UK (until 1978 there had been no cases for over 40 years).

In 1978, four cases of botulism occurred (with one fatality and three other very serious paralysed cases) following consumption of a tin of red salmon. Cases are still reported in America and Europe. In 1982, there was a repetition of botulism traced to cans of red salmon imported from Alaska and restrictions were placed upon the sale of such products.

Most botulism in America has been traced to home-bottled vegetables in which there is inadequate sterilization resulting in anaerobic conditions. Prevention includes avoidance of bottling of any vegetables and proper control of commercial canning.

In the UK in June 1989, another outbreak of botulism occurred which affected 27 persons with one fatality. The source of the intoxication was a hazelnut conserve used as added flavouring in yogurt. To kill the spores of *Clostridium botulinum* the conserve needed to be processed at a high temperature. The outbreak emphasized the importance of using correct techniques in all food processing, particularly for canned food products with a low acid content.

The Department of Health have subsequently advised all environmental health officers to arrange visits to manufacturers of canned products and other anaerobically packed products to ascertain whether adequate procedures are used. A Government

Code of Practice on low acid canning is available and this has been emphasized to producers.[4]

LISTERIOSIS

Causative organism: Listeria monocytogenes.
Incubation period: probably 7–30 days.

Incidence

In 1990 there were 25 cases of listeriosis recorded in England and Wales. This represents a large reduction in the numbers reported in 1988 (29) and in 1989 (250). In the last 4 years considerable interest and concern has centred on the spread of listeria infections. The aerobic bacteria is widely found in soil, in animals and in poultry and, in certain circumstances, can cause disease in humans.

During 1988 and 1989 a number of surveys were carried out by the Public Health Laboratory Service which showed that 60% of raw chickens and 10% of soft cheeses were contaminated with *Listeria monocytogenes*. Also, 12% of precooked, ready-to-eat poultry and 18% of chilled and cooked meals were found to be

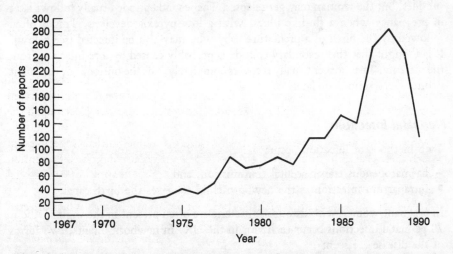

FIGURE 10.8   Reported cases of listeriosis, England and Wales, 1967–90. For the years 1967–79 the number of reports includes those from Northern Ireland. For the years 1980–90 it includes reports from England and Wales only. For the years 1967–82 the number of reports includes only those to the Communicable Disease Surveillance Centre (CDSC). For the years 1983–90 it includes those to CDSC and the Division of Microbiological Reagents and Quality Control (DMRQC).

contaminated.[5,6] Significantly, the bacteria seems able to multiply when stored under refrigerated conditions.

Carriage in humans, as in animals, is widespread and surveys have shown that *Listeria monocytogenes* may be found in up to 29% of the faeces of healthy persons. There were 291 cases of listeriosis recorded in England and Wales in 1988 and a slight reduction to 250 cases in 1989. However, during 1990 there was a dramatic fall in the number of cases reported with the total for that year being 116 (see Fig. 10.8).

As the Chief Medical Officer of the Department of Health noted in his 1991 annual report 'This is very heartening and it is hoped that this downward trend will continue'.[3]

Types of listeriosis

During pregnancy

When the disease attacks pregnant women, it usually shows two or more febrile episodes. The woman has some or all of the following symptoms: headache, general malaise, pharyngitis, conjunctivitis, diarrhoea, abdominal or low back pain. Occasionally the febrile attack may be misdiagnosed as pyelonephritis. Blood culture at this stage is usually positive. If ampicillin is given promptly, the fever quickly subsides, but the woman may get relapses. The second episode usually follows later in pregnancy when a flu-like illness with a low pyrexia develops. This is often followed by the birth of a premature baby who may also be infected (see below). It is thought that this secondary episode is probably caused by a re-infection from the placenta. The mother usually recovers completely, but the outlook for the infant is often very serious or fatal.

Neonatal infections

Two methods of infection occur:

- haematogenous transplacental transmission, and
- intrapartum infection as the newborn child traverses the birth canal.

In pregnant women with listeriosis, bacteria are often present in the vagina. About 70 perinatal infections occur each year in the UK. In newborn infants, two forms of the disease are seen:

- a septicaemia within 2 days of birth, the premature baby is particularly likely to show respiratory distress and rashes may occasionally also be seen
- a meningo-encephalitis may develop after the fifth day following the birth.

Occasionally, a slowly developing hydrocephalus may also follow.

Up to a third of infected babies are stillborn. Provided prompt treatment is given with ampicillin, approximately 50% mortality can be expected in the remainder. With late or no treatment the mortality is likely to reach 90%. Provided any surviving infant was at least of 36 weeks gestation when born, sequelae are most unlikely.

Disease in adults other than pregnant women

Central nervous system infections are the most likely forms of listeriosis seen in adults other than pregnant women. Fever of a low grade is usually present and focal neurological signs may develop such as cranial nerve palsies or hemiparesis. Occasionally there is a progressive loss of consciousness eventually leading to coma.

In immunosuppressed adults who develop any form of meningitis, infections with listeriosis are among the commonest causes. Treatment is ideally with ampicillin and this should be continued for at least 1 week after all fever has subsided. The prognosis for adult forms of listeriosis is usually good provided treatment is started promptly.

Prevention

The main problem of listeriosis is that three groups of the population are at special risk:

- pregnant women
- their newborn babies
- adults who are receiving immunosuppressive treatment.

Prevention is primarily aimed at preventing infection spreading to these groups.

Because of the rising numbers of cases of listeriosis, the Department of Health through its Chief Medical Officer early in 1989 advised that individuals in the above vulnerable groups should avoid eating soft ripened cheese such as brie, camembert and the blue vein types, and to reheat any cooked ready-to-eat foods until piping hot rather than eat them when cold.[7] Later in 1989, the Chief Medical Officer gave further advice,[8,9] that vulnerable persons should not eat pâté after samples of pâté in two Welsh districts indicated that the product might be contaminated with Listeria monocytogenes.[2]

CAMPYLOBACTER ENTERITIS

In 1977, Skirrow[10] described for the first time an enteritis caused by Campylobacter. Since the late 1970s the Communicable Disease Surveillance Centre has

TABLE 10.4   Laboratory reports of *Campylobacter* faecal isolates to the Communicable Disease Surveillance Centre in the UK and Channel Islands, 1979–80

Year	Total reports
1979	8 514
1980	9 477
1981	12 479
1982	12 878
1983	17 327
1984	21 122
1985	23 706
1986	24 952
1987	27 465
1988	28 971
1989	32 646[a]

[a] Provisional data from the Communicable Disease Surveillance Centre.

undertaken bacteriological tests for this pathogen, and these are now carried out routinely in most laboratories (see Table 10.4).

It is now recognized that *Campylobacter* is one of the most frequently isolated causes of bacterial enteritis. The full epidemiology of the disease has not yet been unravelled, but it is already clear that in only a proportion of these isolates is there a connection with a known food source.

INFANTILE GASTROENTERITIS

This is a general description of a mixed group of severe gastrointestinal infections in young infants. Most have short incubation periods of 2–5 days. Approximately 18 serotypes of *Escherichia* have been specifically involved, especially O 26, O 55, O 11, O 125, O 126, O 127, O 128 and O 129. Many enteroviruses (Echo and Coxsackie B viruses) have also been identified as causes.

The disease is fortunately much less common now than it was 50–60 years ago. The incidence is greater in bottle-fed babies than in breast-fed children. Poverty and the associated conditions are important factors, for most cases of the disease occur in the overcrowded homes of social classes IV and V. Infantile gastroenteritis can be a very serious problem in paediatric hospitals and maternity units.

Prevention

Encouragement of breast feeding can do much to reduce the incidence of infantile gastroenteritis and every effort should be made to keep breast feeding going if the infant develops an illness. If the baby must enter hospital his mother should also be admitted so that breast feeding may be maintained.

The risk of hospital outbreaks can be minimized by arranging for all young babies to spend as little time as possible in hospital as there is no doubt that many attacks result from cross-infection from infant to infant in the ward. It is therefore important that any infant with diarrhoea is immediately isolated and that no child with a history of diarrhoea is admitted to a clean infants' ward, such children should be sent to an isolation unit.

There is a particularly dangerous type of unidentified gastroenteritis which occasionally breaks out in the nursery unit of a maternity ward. As soon as such an attack is confirmed, all new admissions to the maternity ward should be stopped and the ward emptied as soon as possible with mothers and babies being discharged home early. By this action, the danger of widespread infection will be reduced.

Attempts to control the spread of infantile gastroenteritis by strict barrier nursing usually fail, probably due to the intensity of infection, the physiological incontinence of infants and the role that infected dusts play in spreading the disease.

References

1. OPCS. Monitor. Infectious diseases. MB2 92/3. London: OPCS. 1992.
2. Department of Health. On the State of Public Health. Chief Medical Officers Report for the year 1989. London: HMSO. 1990.
3. Department of Health. On the State of Public Health. Chief Medical Officer's Report for the year 1990. London: HMSO. 1991.
4. Department of Health and Social Security. Food Hygiene Codes of Practice No 10. The canning of low acid foods: a guide to good manufacturing practice. London: HMSO. 1981.
5. Pini PN, Gilbert RJ. The occurrence in the UK of Listeria species in raw chicken and soft cheeses. Int. J. Food Microbiol. 1988, 6: 317–326.
6. Gilbert RJ, Miller KJ, Roberts D. Listeria monocytogenes and chilled food. Lancet 1989, i: 383–384.
7. Department of Health. Advice to the public on listeria and food. (Press release 89/60). London: Department of Health. 1989.
8. Department of Health. Listeria found in pate. (Press release 89/299). London: Department of Health. 1989.
9. Department of Health. Advice to vulnerable groups on pate standards (Press release 89/369). London: Department of Health. 1989.
10. Skirrow MB. Campylobacter enteritis: a new disease. Br. Med. J. 1977, 2: 9–11.
11. OPCS. Monitor. Infectious diseases. MB2 92/1. London: OCPS. 1992.

Control of Aids, Sexually Transmitted Disease and Viral Hepatitis

Acquired immune deficiency syndrome (AIDS)

The acquired immune deficiency syndrome (AIDS) is caused by the human immuno-deficency virus (HIV), a retrovirus that inhibits cell-mediated immunity. AIDS was first diagnosed in Los Angeles in June 1981. The HIV virus was first isolated in France in 1983 and was previously known as the human T cell lymphotropic virus type III (HTLV III). The virus multiplies within certain body cells such as lympho-cytes, monocytes and macrophages. It seems likely that the virus originated from Central Africa. The effect of AIDS in certain African countries is nothing less than devastating. In 1985 a second virus, HIV II, was diagnosed in West Africa, which suggests the evolving nature of the disease.

The actual illness of AIDS can only be diagnosed clinically when either:

(a) the patient develops an infection which is usually harmless to man, but because the immune mechanism of the body has been damaged by the HIV virus has now become a recognizable and dangerous disease (opportunistic infection) or

(b) the patient develops unusual forms of cancer.

(a) *Opportunistic infection.* Diseases that indicate some underlying lack of cellular immunity, often presenting with chest infections, central nervous system (CNS) infections or gastrointestinal symptoms. These include:

- *Helminthic and protozoal infections* such as *Cryptosporidiosis* causing diarrhoea, *Pneumocystis carnii* causing pneumonia, *Strongyloidosis* which can cause pneumonia or affect the CNS, and toxoplasmosis causing pneumonia.
- *Fungal infections* such as aspergillosis and candidiasis affecting the oesophagus or lungs, cryptococosis and histoplasmosis.
- *Atypical bacterial infections* such as the atypical mycoplasmoses.

- *Viral infections* including disseminated herpes simplex infections, and cyto-megalovirus infections

(b) *Cancers*. The best known is Kaposi's sarcoma which presents with a reddish-purple lesion, either flat or raised, on any part of the skin or hard palate. Other malignancies include cerebral lymphoma, non-Hodgkin's lymphoma and lympho-reticular malignancy which presents more than 3 months after an opportunistic infection.

The data for AIDS are collected by the Communicable Disease Surveillance Unit in England and the Communicable Disease Unit in Scotland under a voluntary system of monitoring which started in 1982. AIDS is not a notifiable disease. The strict criteria for the definition of AIDS as laid down by the US Centres for Control in Atlanta are recognized and used in the UK. Table 11.1 provides a breakdown of AIDS cases in England till December 1990. The vast majority so far are males (95.5%) and of these 85% have been classified as homosexual/bisexual males with a further 2% homosexual but also intravenous drug abusers. Haemophiliacs who

TABLE 11.1   Cumulative totals of AIDS cases by exposure category in England to 31 December 1990

Probable virus aquisition route	Number of cases			
	Male	Female	Total	%
Sexual intercourse				
Between men	3086	0	3086	81
Between men and women				
'High risk' partner	11	17	28	1
Other partner abroad	128	59	187	5
Other partner UK	10	12	22	1
Injecting drug use (IDU)	77	24	101	3
IDU and sexual intercourse				
between men	60	0	60	2
Blood				
Blood factor	202	3	205	5
(e.g. haemophiliacs)				
Blood or tissue transfer	24	37	61	2
(e.g. transfusion)				
Mother to child	15	17	32	1
Other/undetermined	31	4	35	1
Total	3644	173	3817	100

Data from ref. 8, based on information from CDSC.

TABLE 11.2   HIV antibody positive reports, AIDS cases and known deaths, by exposure category in England to end December 1990

Exposure category	Number of reports				
	Males	Females	Unknown	Total	%
Sexual intercourse					
Between men	8 130	0		8 130	63
Between men and women					
'High risk' partner	20	130		150	1
Other partner abroad	324	242	7	573	4
Other partner UK	30	36	2	68	<1
Undetermined	124	113	—	237	2
Injecting drug use (IDU)	725	331	5	1 061	8
IDU and sexual intercourse between men	152			152	1
Blood					
Blood factor (e.g. haemophiliacs)	1 095	6	1	1 102	8
Blood or tissue transfer (e.g. transfusion) abroad/UK	63	58	2	123	1
Child of at risk/infected parent	54	35	3	92	1
Other/undetermined	1 071	748	78	1 297	10
Total	11 788	1099	98	12 985	100

Data from the Public Health laboratory Service, CDSC.

received infected blood/blood products comprise the second largest grouping (205 cases).

The prevalence of the virus in the community is very variable, and the true figure is not known. In autumn 1988, the government announced that anonymous unnamed blood testing would be carried out in an attempt to discover more accurate prevalence rates.[1] This is a problem which is not only confined to London, although 78% of AIDS cases (2948), and 71% (9254 cases) of HIV antibody positive results occurred in the four Thames Regions. Table 11.2 summarizes the patient characteristics for the 12 985 HIV positive cases reported in England up till December 1990. Homosexual men account for 62.5% of such cases, 8% were known intravenous drug abusers and 8% haemophiliacs.

METHOD OF SPREAD

The spread of all the reported cases of AIDS or HIV seroconversion has been by (a) sexual transmission, (b) blood to blood or (c) by the materno-fetal route. HIV has been identified in blood, breast milk, cervical and uterine secretions, saliva and tears. However, HIV is a weak virus that survives poorly outside the human body, and its presence in some body fluids may not be significant regarding transmisson. AIDS is not spread by droplets or from insect bites.[2]

CLINICAL PROGRESS

After exposure to the HIV virus the patient usually experiences no symptoms at all (subclinical infection). When seroconversion occurs it may be symptomless but, if symptoms occur, these may be non-specific and be very similar to those of glandular fever, namely malaise and lethargy, fever and a sore throat. There may be a transient skin rash and swollen lymph glands. Antibodies develop about 6 weeks after exposure, but can take much longer (delayed seroconversion). The antibodies provide no resistance to the disease. Their detection only identifies carriers of the virus.

Patients who are seropositive generally progress to a chronic state of infection which may be asymptomatic. The percentage of HIV patients who will go on to AIDS is unknown. Present estimates (which are constantly being changed) is that one third will progress.[2] However it may be as high as 75%.[3] For those with symptoms these show varying degrees of severity and include persistent generalized lymphadenopathy (PGL), AIDS related complex (ARC), various neurological illnesses and AIDS.

PGL

This is defined when there are lypmph glands, greater than 1 cm in diameter, at two or more sites, persisting for 3 months or more. Inguinal lymph nodes are excluded and the glands must be non contiguous (not side by side). Most patients with PGL seem to remain well, but possibly 10–30% of patients progress to AIDS.

ARC

This is more serious than PGL and indicates evidence that the immune system is beginning to be impaired. The disease criteria are summarized in Table 11.3. These patients are unwell and have a high risk of progressing to AIDS.

Neurological involvement

The effects of the virus are not confined to the immune system. HIV can attack the brain directly and cause such symptoms as headache, depression, seizures and

TABLE 11.3   Criteria for diagnosis of aids related complex (ARC)

Symptoms/signs	Laboratory abnormalities
Continuous/intermittent fever >38°C	Lymphopenia, leucopenia
Weight loss >10%	Thrombocytopenia
Persistent lymphadenopathy	Anaemia
Intermittent/continuous diarrhoea	Reduced ratio of CD4:CD8 (>2sd)
Fatigue reducing physical activity	Reduced T helper cells (>2sd)
Night sweats	Reduced blastogenesis
	Raised globulins
	Cutaneous anergy

Data from ref. 2.

ultimately dementia. The spinal column may be affected, as may the peripheral nerves. These symptoms can occur with no evidence that the patient's immunity has been affected. The effects may not become evident for many years after exposure to the virus, and make long-term prediction about the disease even more difficult.

AIDS

This is the most severe consequence of HIV infection. It is almost inevitably fatal. The development of oral candidiasis (thrush), constitutional symptoms and herpes zoster (shingles) are significant predictive symptoms for the development of AIDS. Blood tests showing anaemia, cytopenia (low white blood cell count) and a raised erythrocyte sedimentation rate (ESR) are also significant.

TREATMENT

This is concerned with dealing with the major complications of the disease. Infections should be diagnosed as soon as possible and fully treated. This is particularly important for *Pneumocystis carnii* pneumonia which can be fatal within days, but with effective treatment can prolong the life of an AIDS patient very significantly. Radiotherapy and chemotherapy may be used for Kaposi's tumours and may induce remission, but have not been shown to alter survival. Quality of life is all important. Zidovudine (Retrovir) was licensed in 1988 for management of patients with advanced HIV infection (ARC or AIDS). In 1990 the product licence was extended to include patients with early symptomatic HIV disease and asymtomatic but progressive disease. The *Drugs and Therapeutics Bulletin* in October 1991[4] concluded that zidovudine should be offered to any patient with HIV infection who has developed symptoms, but treatment for asymtomatic patients was still controversial. There was no evidence that prophylactic treatment with zidovudine for needlestick injuries was of any value.

PREVENTION

In 1986 the British government started a massive publicity campaign to educate the general public about the dangers of AIDS. Over £20 million was spent on advertising which included leaflets being delivered to every household (23.5 million) in the country. Spread by heterosexual intercourse is still rare, but will become more common as the numbers of infected people increase. In England, 1028 HIV positive cases had been acquired by heterosexual intercourse and reported by the end of December 1990. Heterosexual spread is becoming an increasingly significant problem. The use of a condom to avoid coming into contact with possible infected secretions is advised, but ultimately monogamous relationships with uninfected partners will be the only guarantee of not catching AIDS through sex.

The problem of HIV positive women and pregnancy is also increasing. Not all women will want to be offered a termination. The initial indications of the risks of the child being affected seem to have been overestimated. In the European Collaborative Study[5] on children born to women with HIV infection, it was calculated that the risk of one of these children being affected is less than one in seven. Some HIV positive women actually seek help with infertility.

Contaminated blood products, imported from the USA at the beginning of the 1980s were responsible for the high numbers of haemophiliacs becoming HIV positive. All Factor VIII and Factor IX are now heat-treated before injection. All blood donors are screened for HIV and those in high-risk groups (homosexuals, intravenous drug abusers) are asked not to donate blood. During 1990 screening of blood donations with the anti-HIV-1 + 2 combined test commenced in the UK; 33 donations were found to be HIV positive. There had been a total of 184 positives by the end of 1990 in the previous 6 years of testing.

AIDS IN THE USA

The first report issued by the National Commission on AIDS published in 1991 outlined the size of the problem in the USA.[6] At the time of the report 120 000 people had died, with a projected figure of 350 000 deaths by the end of 1993. Of these cases, 20% occurred in people aged 20–29 years and new cases of HIV infection in 1991 were running at between 45 000 and 200 000 a year.

THE FUTURE

The virus is continuously changing its structure, and the development of new strains may serve to hamper efforts at producing a vaccine. In October 1991 in

Florida, plans were laid down to establish clinical trials in Uganda, Rwanda, Thailand and Brazil.[7] Trials are also planned for the USA.

The changes in the virus may also affect its infectivity, so it may become more infectious, but this is unknown. It is difficult to discover if people are changing their behaviour. Certainly there is evidence (less gonorrhoea, the slowing rate of HIV seropositivity) in homosexuals which suggests that they are altering their lifestyles, but with other groups it is less clear. The British pharmaceutical industry is at present estimated to be spending some £40 million on AIDS-related research.

Sexually transmitted diseases (STD)

The three common STDs endemic in the UK are gonorrhoea, non-specific genital infection (or non-specific urethritis; NSU) and syphilis. Cytomegalovirus, trichomoniasis, pediculosis pubis and genital warts are common and are also sexually transmitted. Herpes (genitalis), hepatitis A and B, and beta haemolytic streptococcus are organisms increasingly implicated as being sexual transmitted. Table 11.4 shows the common micro-organisms that can be sexually transmitted.

The most common symptoms of a STD are urethral and vaginal discharge, dysuria (pain on micturition) and genital ulceration. Accurate diagnosis is essential

TABLE 11.4   Micro-organisms that can be sexually transmitted

Bacteria
    Chlamydia trachomatis
    Neisseria gonorrhoeae
    Trepenoma pallidum
    Gardnerella vaginalis
    Group B haemolytic *Streptoccocus*
    Haemophilus ducreyi
    Shigella species

Viruses
    Herpes simplex types 1 and 2
    Wart virus
    Molluscum contagiosum virus
    Hepatitis A and B virus
    Cytomegalovirus
    Human immunodeficiency virus

Others
    Mycoplasmas, e.g. *Ureaplasma urealyticum, Mycoplasma hominis*
    Parasites, e.g. *Sarcoptes scabiei*, and *Phthirus pubis*
    Protozoa, e.g. *Trichomonas vaginalis, Entamoeba histolytica, Giardia, Lamblia*
    Fungi, e.g. *Candida albicans*

before treatment is started. Proper microbiological testing must be scrupulously carried out. Unless this is done many diagnoses will be missed. The patient should ideally be referred to a clinic specializing in STDs unless there are good facilities for microscopy available. The implication with STDs is that there will always be more than one patient who will need treatment. Contact tracing of a patient's sexual partners and their treatment can prevent the disease spreading further. More than one disease may be acquired at the same time, and hence if only one is treated and the others not checked for, either at the time or later, serious disease may be missed. This is particularly true of syphilis which has a long incubation period.

Table 11.5 shows the number of new cases of STD in England in 1989. None of these diseases is notifiable, but accurate records are kept by all departments of genito-urinary medicine by filling in the form KC60. There are 230 such departments in the UK. Confidentiality for the patient is essential in the treatment of STD. No information is released to a third party without the patient's permission. A separate system of records from the general hospital notes helps ensure that this confidentiality applies to hospital care as well. All treatment prescribed from a clinic for STD is free from prescription charges.

CHLAMYDIA AND NON-SPECIFIC GENITAL INFECTION – NSGI (NON-SPECIFIC URETHRITIS, NSU)

This is the most common diagnosis made in STD clinics in this country. Since 1987, chlamydial infection, pelvic infection and epididymitis and NSU have been included under separate headings on form KC60. In 1989, of the 120 014 reports made for NSGI, chlamydia was identified or suspected in 48% of women and 22% of men in this category. Other organisms suspected of causing the condition include *Ureaplasma urealyticum*. Other causative organisms are rarely isolated. The incubation period for NSGI is between 10 and 28 days. The male patient usually presents with a urethral discharge, but in women over 90% are symptom free. Treatment is usually started with tetracycline which is the antibiotic of choice. Follow-up should be undertaken after 3 weeks to assess treatment, and again after 3 months to eliminate the risk of a double infection with syphilis. Occasionally NSU in males may become chronic, and affect the prostate. In women, NSGI is the commonest cause of pelvic inflammatory disease (PID) and subsequent infertility.

GONORRHOEA

Gonorrhoea is caused by the bacterium *Neisseria gonorrhoeae*. It has an incubation period of 2–7 days (usually 5 days). In the male it usually presents with dysuria and purulent urethral discharge, but 5–10% of cases may be asymptomatic. In women, up to 60% may have no symptoms. The rest will have a discharge. Most women

TABLE 11.5   All cases of STD seen at genito-urinary clinics in England, 1989

Condition	Males		Females	
1. All syphilis	923		488	
Infectious syphilis		269		122
2. All gonorrhoea	11 346		8 415	
Post-pubertal uncomplicated		10 708		6 986
3. Chancroid/donovanosis/ lymphogranuloma venereum	67		21	
4. Other chlamydia (excludes 5 and 7)	16 081		20 880	
Post-pubertal uncomplicated		12 752		17 515
5. Pelvic infection and epididymitis	1 326		4 954	
6. Non-specific genital infection and related diseases	57 894		19 366	
7. Chlamydial infections/NSGI with arthritis	456		44	
8. Trichomoniasis	316		7 437	
9. Vaginosis/vaginitis/balanitis	8 539		30 865	
10. Candidiasis	9 811		48 382	
11. Scabies/pediculosis	5 344		2 142	
12. Herpes — all	9 906		9 382	
Herpes simplex — 1st attack		5 792		6 611
Herpes simplex — recurrence		4 114		2 771
13. Wart virus infections — all	45 804		32 342	
Wart virus infections — 1st attack		27 448		23 506
Wart virus infections — recurrence		18 356		8 836
14. Viral hepatitis	548		59	
15. HIV/AIDS	7 130		470	
16. Other conditions requiring treatment	38 861		31 466	
17. Other episodes not requiring treatment	74 179		56 797	
18. Other conditions referred elsewhere	4 549		6 353	
Total new cases seen	293 080		279 863	

Source: collated by the Department of Health from returns of Form KC60.

diagnosed present as a result of their partner having been diagnosed. PID is the most important complication in women. If there is delay in diagnosis or treatment there is a long-term risk of infertility (due to blocked fallopian tubes), ectopic pregnancy and chronic PID.

Penicillin is the treatment of choice in gonorrhoea. In some clinics patients are also treated with tetracycline because they are assumed to have NSGI in addition to gonorrhoea. Tetracycline and co-trimoxazole may be used for patients who are allergic to penicillin. Up to 50% of patients develop a post-gonococcal urethritis (PGU). This is usually due to *Chlamydia trachomatis* (in 80% of cases).

Penicillin-resistant strains

These were first reported in the UK in 1977 with a subsequently steady increase in numbers reported, but recently these have stabilized. World-wide, it remains a problem, particularly in the Far East, Africa, North America and Scandinavia.

SYPHILIS

Syphilis is caused by *Trepenoma pallidum*. In 1989 there were 269 cases of infectious syphilis seen in men in STD clinics in England (923 cases in all). This represents a decrease from 2291 cases reported in 1977, and compares with the peak in the post-war period when almost almost 28 000 cases a year were seen. About 19% of cases of infectious syphilis were homosexually acquired. There were 122 infectious cases in women.

The incubation period for primary syphilis is between 9 and 90 days (mean 21 days). The first presenting feature is a single painless sore at the site of inoculation. This may be extragenital. Secondary syphilis (usually in the form of a skin rash) appears 4–8 weeks after infection. Just over half the cases have a generalized lymphadenopathy. About 35% of people with untreated syphilis may develop late non-infectious complications of the CNS and cardiovascular system.

Diagnosis of syphilis includes microscopical examination of material from the original lesion. Serological tests, which may take about 3 months after exposure to become positive, are helpful. The Venereal Disease Research Laboratory test (VDRL) has replaced the Wasserman reaction (WR) test. This detects non-specific antibodies and becomes positive 10–14 days after the appearance of the primary chancre. This test is positive in 75% of cases of primary syphilis. The *T. pallidum* haemagglutination test (TPHA) detects antibodies for pathological trepenomata (including yaws) and is the better test for late or latent syphilis. It is positive in only some 50% of cases of primary syphilis. Abnormalities of the cerebrospinal fluid (obtained by a lumbar puncture) at any stage of syphilis may prove the diagnosis.

Penicillin remains the treatment of choice, with erythromycin and tetracycline being used for patients who are allergic to penicillin. There are now very few early congenital cases of syphilis a year.

Other sexually transmitted diseases

CYTOMEGALOVIRUS (CMV) INFECTION

This infection is caused by members of the herpes virus group. As well as in man, CMV occurs in dogs, sheep, monkeys, pigs and rodents. CMV is spread by kissing and sexual intercourse. Some 40–70% of pregnant women are immune, hence up to 60% may not be immune. Primary infection in pregnancy has up to a 50% chance of resulting in congenital infection. The incidence of congenital infections is in the order of 1 in 200 pregnancies. If the CNS is involved, up to 90% of affected children will be mentally retarded. Major problems encountered include spastic quadriplegia, microcephaly, psychomotor retardation and sensorineural deafness and blindness. Of infants suffering from congenital infection, 45% will show signs at birth or later. This is not always recognized as the result of CMV infection. Non-specific long-term handicap, clumsiness and a lower than expected IQ may be the only findings.

The initial infection with CMV is usually so mild it is rarely diagnosed in the adult. However, CMV infections in pregnancy are more important than rubella, syphilis or herpes. At the present time routine screening for antibody levels is not feasible. The long-term answer would seem to rest with the development of an effective vaccine.

GENITAL HERPES

The herpes simplex virus is a double-stranded DNA virus. This is the commonest cause of genital ulceration in the UK. There are two types, type one (HSV-1) and 2 (HSV-2), both with a short incubation period of under 7 days. HSV-2 is by far the more common. In 1989 there were 19 288 cases of genital herpes seen in departments of genito-urinary medicine in England; 35% of these were for recurrences. The problems with genital herpes are many. The incidence is increasing rapidly, there is no cure, it may be recurrent, it may be associated with cervical dysplasia and carcinoma and it can cause fetal and neonatal infections.

The initial symptoms may be confused with those of cystitis, namely pain on passing urine. This is not a urethral pain, but occurs with urine coming into contact with the vesicles external to the urethra. The first sign is redness, vesicles then progress to ulcers and finally crusting. The whole process may last up to three weeks. The cervix will be involved in 80–90% of cases in women. Visualization of the cervix however may be difficult because of the intensity of the discomfort. In the primary infection there are usually enlarged inguinal lymph glands present. Diagnosis may be confirmed by taking cultures (the specimen is placed in a special viral culture medium) and sent to the laboratory for culture. Other diseases such as gonorrhoea, chlamydia, trichomoniasis and syphilis should be excluded.

Treatment is unsatisfactory. The anti-viral agent acyclovir is used and helps in shortening the length of the primary attack, but does not alter recurrence rates. Prevention is only possible with abstinence during the time that lesions are present. The sheath does not necessarily prevent transmission. The Herpes Association which acts as a counselling and information resource may help sufferers.

GENITAL WARTS

These are caused by a small DNA virus of the papovavirus group. The incubation period is variable and ranges from 1 to 6 months. Sexual transmission is the method of spread. It is rare for other skin warts to be transferred to the genitals. They may present to genito-urinary departments (78 146 cases in 1989), surgeons, gynaecologists and dermatologists as well as GPs. Their incidence is increasing. The diagnosis is a clinical one as the virus cannot be cultured. Warts may suggest other STD infections and these need to be excluded by routine testing.

Treatment is with 10–25% podophyllin solution, two to three times a week. Glacial trichloracetic acid may be used if podophyllin has had no effect. Podophyllin is contraindicated in pregnancy. Cautery or surgical excision may be needed if the warts are very large or numerous.

MISCELLANEOUS STDS

Candidiasis or thrush is due to the fungus *Candida albicans* and is frequently sexually transmitted, but in recurrent infections the male partner may be the carrier (and is often asymptomatic). Symptoms in the female include an intense irritation and white creamy discharge. Treatment is with pessaries, nystatin, clotrimazole, miconazole or econazole. Recurrent infections may be due to candidiasis being present in the bowel for which oral nystatin may be used. It is a very common complaint, and often occurs after treatment with antibiotics. When such antibiotics have been given for other reasons they will kill the protective bacteria (including lactobacillus) usually present in the vagina and the fungus, which is not affected by the antibiotic, then grows without competition. Thrush is also more common in pregnancy, in women on the oral contraceptive pill, and just before a period is due. It is more common in diabetics, indeed diabetes may present in this way (particularly in males). Most thrush is treated by GPs.

Trichomoniasis (TV) is caused by the protozoon *Trichomonas vaginalis*. The vaginal discharge is more greenish and foul smelling. Treatment is with metronidazole (flagyl) orally (400 mg twice a day for 5 days). The male partner should be examined and treated at the same time. TV may well mask gonorrhoea. In genito-urinary departments, 19% of patients with TV have gonorrhoea as well.

Pubic lice and scabies are also examples of genital infestations. The pubic louse, *Phthirus pubis*, is a different species from the head and body louse. It is not spread by sleeping in infected sheets or wearing infected clothing. The louse is unable to survive away from the body and body heat. The patient may be asymptomatic, or complain of irritation. Treatment is with Gammexane or 0.5% malathion.

Scabies, due to the mite *Sarcoptes scabiei*, presents with intense itching some 2–6 weeks after contact. Burrows are made by the female in the top layer of skin to lay her eggs. Spread is by close physical, but not necessarily sexual, contact. Diagnosis may be made on clinical grounds, with skin scrapings being examined under the microscope for the mite. Treatment is by 1% gamma benzene hexachloride (Quellada/Lorexane). The head and face are not affected. Treatment may be repeated after 2 weeks if necessary.

Viral hepatitis

The generic name 'infective jaundice' covers both infectious hepatitis (hepatitis A) and serum hepatitis (hepatitis B). The condition is notifiable in England and Wales. Since March 1987 records have separated the types of hepatitis. In 1990 there were 7214 reported cases of hepatitis A in England. There was a provisional total of 526 cases of hepatitis B reported to the Communicable Disease Surveillance Centre (CDSC) from England in 1990. Other forms of hepatitis include hepatitis C (the so called non-A, non-B hepatitis), hepatitis D and hepatitis E (previously known as the epidemic form).

HEPATITIS A

This is caused by a small RNA virus. The incubation period is 3–5 weeks. Hepatitis A occurs endemically in all parts of the world. Spread is by the faecal–oral route, commonly by person to person contact and is more common with poor sanitation and overcrowding. Many food-borne epidemics have been reported and traced to food handlers who are infected. There is a large shedding of the virus in the faeces during the incubation period of the disease. In the UK there is an increased prevalence in autumn and winter. When sexually transmitted, spread is by oral–anal contact and occurs usually between homosexual men. Serological tests will detect specific IgG antibodies, which only last a short time and hence indicate recent infection. Immunity is shown by the presence of IgG antibodies which persist for many years. Often the infection may be subclinical. Although the course of the acute infection may be prolonged, hepatitis A never progresses to liver failure, and recovery is normal. The patient is usually treated at home. A vaccine against hepatitis A was introduced in the UK in 1992. Passive immunization with immunoglobulin may be given to close personal contacts with hepatitis A and for controlling outbreaks in institutions such as nursery schools and homes for persons with learning disabilities (mental handicap).

HEPATITIS B

This is caused by a DNA virus. The incubation period is variable and may be between 7 and 15 weeks. Transmission is through blood products and other body fluids such as semen, vaginal secretions, saliva and breast milk. Transmission may occur through accidental inoculation of tiny amounts of blood during various surgical or dental procedures. Needles, shared by drug addicts or used in tattooing and ear-piercing have been implicated in the spread of hepatitis B. Sexual intercourse, both heterosexual and homosexual, is another important cause of transmission. It has been estimated that up to 5% of all those attending STD clinics may be carriers of hepatitis B. The carrier state may be life-long and occurs in 5–10% of infected adults. In some parts of the Far East and Africa, up to 20% of the population may be carriers. In the UK the carrier rate is of the order of 0.1%.

The clinical features of the disease will be as for any non-specific viral illness to begin with, namely fever, headache and fatigue with jaundice following. A careful history including recent travel, intravenous drug abuse, tattoos, transfusions and sexual history will be important. Detection of the hepatitis B surface antigen (HBsAg) will indicate acute infection. Great care must be taken in both taking the blood and sending it to the laboratory. The specimens should be labelled 'high risk'. Of patients, 5–10% will develop a chronic infection, which is determined by the persistence of HBsAG in the blood for more than 6 months. Other STD diseases must be looked for if intercourse is thought to have been the method of spread. Long-standing infection is associated with cirrhosis and primary hepatocellular carcinoma.

Treatment includes the use of a low-fat, high energy diet. No alcohol should be drunk until the liver function tests are normal. Much effort has been put into the prevention of hepatitis with vaccination of at-risk groups becoming more important (see Chapter 6). Other hygiene precautions, especially when handling blood and other contaminated body secretions from infected patients (or suspected infected patients), cannot be stressed too greatly.

HEPATITIS C (NON-A, NON-B HEPATITIS)

This is now the most common form of hepatitis following blood transfusion in some parts of the world (possibly up to 90% of post-transfusion cases where screening for hepatitis B surface antigen is done). Up to 30% of patients have abnormal liver function tests for more than 6 months. Severe chronic liver disease may follow.

HEPATITIS D

This gives a very high risk of severe acute and chronic liver disease. The causative agent is the delta particle and is only found in hepatitis B carriers. It is very prevalent among intravenous drug abusers.

HEPATITIS E

Previously known as the epidemic form, this virus closely resembles hepatitis A, but carries a 20% mortality rate. It is a particularly severe disease in pregnant women. The virus is found in the Soviet Union, the Indian subcontinent and Algeria.

References

1. Department of Health and Social Security. Report of a working group on the monitoring and surveillance of HIV infection and AIDS. London: DHSS. 1988.
2. Adler MW. ABC of AIDS. London: BMJ. 1988.
3. Anderson R, May R. Plotting the spread of AIDS. New Scientist 26th March, 1987.
4. Zidovudine in HIV infection. Drugs Ther. Bull. 1991, 29 (21): 81–82.
5. Eades A *et al*. European Collaborative Study. Children born to women with HIV infection: natural history and risk of transmission. Lancet 1991, 337: 253–260.
6. Tanne JH. American Plan to combat AIDS. Br. Med. J. 1991, 303: 803.
7. Roberts J. Trials of HIV vaccine planned for developing countries. Br. Med. J. 1991, 303: 1219–1220.
8. Department of Health. On the State of Public Health. Chief Medical Officer's Report for The Year 1990. London: HMSO. 1991.

12

Rare Communicable Diseases

Diphtheria

Causative organism: Corynebacterium diphtheriae.
Incubation period: 2–7 days.
This disease is now very rare with few cases being notified — one in 1988, two in 1989 and two in 1990 in England and Wales. This compares with an annual average of 55 000 before immunization was introduced in 1943.

PREVENTION

Widespread active immunization of all children is essential to maintain the present very low levels. Over 90% of children should be immunized.

ACTION TO BE TAKEN ON DISCOVERY OF A CASE

Immediately a case is reported, an investigation should be started to discover the source of the infection, which is usually another case or carrier. Nasal and throat swabs should be taken from all close contacts (members of the same household or class). Other children from the same family should be excluded from school until bacteriological tests are completed. Any close contacts who are food handlers should be excluded from work. Child contacts who have been previously immunized should be given an immediate booster immunization. Adult contacts should be Schick tested (all Schick positives are susceptible). All susceptible contacts should be given a small dose of antitoxin (500 units).

Poliomyelitis

Causative organism: a virus with three distinct types.
Incubation period: 10–16 days.
Since mass immunization was started in the early 1960s, cases now occur only rarely — there were two in 1988, one in 1989 and one in 1990. This virtual disappearance of the disease is dependent on a continued high rate of immunization in young children. Poliomyelitis has a very marked seasonal incidence with most cases occurring in late summer and early autumn.

METHOD OF SPREAD

Poliomyelitis is a faecal-borne disease spread mainly by close human contact. The following factors may precipitate attacks:

1. Tonsillectomy or tooth extraction if undertaken while the patient is carrying the virus in his/her throat or faeces. For this reason, in serious epidemics, or in close contacts, it is usual to suspend such operations.
2. Certain prophylactic injections if carried out while the patient is incubating the disease. This type of attack, often called 'provocation' poliomyelitis, is not often seen and is usually mild, only affecting the group of muscles into which the injection was given. Lumbar puncture is contraindicated.
3. Violent exercise can lead to a more serious attack if undertaken in the early meningitic phase of the disease. Because of the danger of close contacts developing poliomyelitis, it is wise to limit violent exercise in the close contacts during the incubation period.

PREVENTION

Active immunization using live attenuated virus vaccine (Sabin) is the most effective way of preventing poliomyelitis. Efforts should be made to immunize all young children and to give them booster doses at 5 and 15 years old. In 1990, in the UK, at least a 90% immunization of children and young persons was achieved.

ACTION TO BE TAKEN IF A CASE OCCURS

The following persons should immediately be given an oral dose of poliomyelitis vaccine whether previously immunized or not:

- all contacts at home, work or school
- all persons living within an approximate radius of a quarter of a mile.

This serves not only to boost their immunity, but also blocks the entrance of 'wild' or epidemic virus into their intestines, and thus reduces the chance of further infection.

Anthrax

Causative organism: spore-bearing *Bacillus anthracis*.
Incubation period: 2–5 days.

INCIDENCE

Anthrax is primarily a disease of animals (sheep and cattle). It is not commonly found in animals in the UK, but is widespread in many Middle East and Eastern countries. Most cases of anthrax in the UK are associated with imported animal products such as wool and hair, bristles, hides and bone meal. It is primarily an industrial disease, affecting those who run special risks attached to their occupation. Those working in wool sorting, dockers handling hides, abattoir workers and those working with bone meal products are most likely to develop the disease.

Very few cases of cutaneous anthrax have been reported recently in England and Wales — two in 1988, 1989 and 1990. Cases of the more dangerous pneumonic form are extremely rare. *Bacillus anthracis* rapidly produces spores on contact with oxygen and these spores then become widely disseminated in air and soil. In countries where the disease is endemic, infection spreads via such spores.

SEGREGATION OF PATIENTS

All patients should be treated in an infectious disease hospital. Because of the difficulty in diagnosis, cases may accidentally be admitted to general hospitals. Fortunately effective antibiotic treatment is usually prescribed early and the danger of cross-infection is virtually non-existent.

PREVENTION

As anthrax is a special hazard in the occupations mentioned, it is important to ensure that such workers understand the dangers they face. Diagrams illustrating symptoms are prominently displayed so that if anyone develops the skin lesion of anthrax, it is more likely to be recognized and diagnosed early. In addition, all workers at risk carry a small 'identification type' of card on his/her person to show to any doctor attending them so that the doctor is warned of this industrial hazard. Early diagnosis is most important as modern antibiotic treatment can quickly cut short an attack. Further preventive measures include:

- a cleansing treatment of wool imports carried out at centres close to the mills
- wearing protective clothing when handling hides and bones; evidence suggests that handling wet hides is safer than handling dried hides
- conforming to special regulations regarding the disposal of carcasses of animals who have died from anthrax (Anthrax Order 1938); if any animal has died from a disease suspected to be anthrax, a veterinary surgeon should confirm the diagnosis by collecting a specimen of blood from the ear. Once anthrax is confirmed, it is most important that no autopsy is performed as this would encourage widespread formation and dissemination of spores. Carcasses of animals should be burned or buried deep in quick lime
- immunization against anthrax (see Chapter 6, p. 153).

Rabies

Causative organism: a virus.
Incubation period: 2–6 weeks, but occasionally longer.
Many different wild animals can be infected (foxes, badgers, otters and many rodents) as well as domestic dogs and cats. About three quarters of all animals on the continent of Europe found to be infected have been foxes or badgers, with the remainder being domestic animals.

Rabies is very rare in the UK and during 1976 to 1989, only eight cases were reported.[1-3] Recently, one case was notified in each of the years 1986, 1987 and 1988, but no case was reported in 1989 — all cases had been infected abroad. The case in 1987 was in an 8-year-old boy who had been bitten by a dog in India,[2] while the 1988 case was in a man who had been infected in Bangladash.[3] Both cases died.

Recently a successful scheme to immunize foxes and badgers has been introduced in six European countries (Austria, Belgium, France, Germany, Luxemburg and Switzerland) (see Fig. 12.1).[4] Oral vaccine has been added to baited meat and this has proved to be a successful way of immunizing these wild animals.

Although rabies is not usually transmitted from man to man, the longer survival times now reported from intensive care units and the nature of the treatment given there raises the possibility that hospital staff are now more exposed to the risk of infection than previously. In the event of a number of cases being

FIGURE 12.1   Areas of Europe where oral rabies vaccination has been introduced (data from ref. 4).

treated at a specialist hospital, key nursing and medical staff may require immunization.

RABIES ACT 1974

Under this Act,[5] there is a cumpulsory 6-month quarantine for all animals entering the country. Effective precautions must also be taken against the transmission of the disease within quarantine kennels. All dogs and cats entering quarantine must be vaccinated on entry with a proved potency-tested inactivated vaccine; they must also be revaccinated after 1 month in quarantine to extend immunity.

Dogs and cats are allowed to enter Britain only at a limited number of ports. Animals landed illegally may be destroyed on landing and the Act provides severe penalties, including up to 1 year's imprisonment for offences against the orders under the Act.

Further orders provide for a wide range of measures to control any outbreak of rabies in Britain. These include destruction of foxes, controls on the movement of domestic pets and their vaccination, the seizure of strays and the banning of hunting and cat and dog shows.

VACCINATION AGAINST RABIES

Prophylactic vaccination against rabies (see pp. 155–156) should be offered to all persons at risk in their work including:

- those employed at quarantine kennels
- those working in quarantine premises in zoos
- agents authorized to carry such animals
- those working in research and acclimatization centres where primates and other imported mammals are housed
- those working in ports regularly importing animals
- those working in ports as veterinary and technical officers of the Ministry of Agriculture, Fisheries and Food.

Booster immunization should be given every 2 or 3 years.

Leptospirosis

Causative organism: a spirochaetal bacteria, *Leptospira*, which is subdivided into various serotypes — *L. icterohaemorrhagiae*, *L. hardjo* and *L. canicola*. Infection usually takes place through the skin or mucous membranes from water which has been contaminated with the urine from infected animals.
Incubation period: 4–19 days (usually 7–10 days).

INCIDENCE

Approximately 48–112 cases of leptospirosis have occurred each year in the British Isles during the 1980s[6] (see Table 12.1).

No cases of *Leptospirosis canicola* disease were recorded in 1986–89. *L. hardjo*, is mainly an occupational disease found in farm workers who have picked up their infections at work. Many of those with *L. icterohaemorrhagiae* are also infected at

TABLE 12.1   Leptospirosis in the British Isles, 1979–89

	1979	1980	1981	1982	1983	1984	1985	1986	1987	1988	1989
L. icterohaemorrhagiae	23	27	39	22	38	25	16	20	18	34	21
L. hardjo	17	14	18	12	54	29	54	41	49	42	16
L. canicola	5	2	4	7	8	4	4	0	0	0	0
Others/not established	9	5	9	13	12	14	22	9	12	17	10
Total diagnoses	54	48	70	54	112	72	96	70	79	93	47

Data from ref. 6.

work, but a few cases are caused by recreational activities such as swimming in a river or pond which has been contaminated with the urine of rats. Most cases of leptospirosis occur in men, but this is due to the greater chance men have in contracting these infections through their employment.

PREVENTION

Personnel at risk should always be warned of the dangers of infection and the method of contamination. It is useful to provide each worker with an 'identification type' card giving warning symptoms and ask him to show this to any doctor he consults. Such an arrangement helps early diagnosis.

It is important that workers liable to contamination use protective clothing. Rubber gloves and rubber thigh boots should be worn by sewer workers especially when they are working in an area known to be heavily rat infested.

The public, and especially children, should never be allowed to wade or bathe in a ditch or pond known to be rat infested. Occasionally infections have been traced to bathing in slow-moving rivers. Every effort should be made to destroy the rats.

Legionellosis

Causative organism: a bacteria, *Legionella pneumophila*.
Incubation period: 7 days.

INCIDENCE

This is a serious respiratory disease which has a mortality rate of 10–15%. A National Surveillance Scheme for legionellosis has been set up at the Communicable Disease Centre. During 1989, 232 cases were recorded with 30 deaths — a mortality rate of 12.9%; 88 of these cases were associated with travel abroad.[7]

Several serious outbreaks have been recorded during 1985–91, including one at Stafford District Hospital in 1985 involving 101 cases with 28 deaths.[8] In 1988 at least 60 persons were infected with legionellosis at the British Broadcasting Corporation (BBC) headquarters in London.

METHOD OF SPREAD

Legionella pneumophilia is found in natural and artificial water supplies and is spread by air-borne droplets. Domestic hot water systems, jacuzzis, showers, industrial-based coolants and water-cooled air-conditioning systems have all caused outbreaks.

PREVENTION

All cooling towers require regular cleaning and treatment with biocides and hot water systems should use calorifiers to ensure storage temperatures are above 55° C. A Department of Health Code of Practice for engineers working in the NHS hospitals was issued late in 1988 in an attempt to make safe potentially dangerous sources of infection in hospitals.

Malaria

Causative organism: malarial parasite, four types, Plasmodium falciparum, Pl. vivax, Pl. orale or Pl. malariae.

Incubation period: Pl. falciparum 12 days, Pl. vivax and Pl. orale 14 days, Pl. malariae up to 30 days.

INCIDENCE

Since 1985 the annual number of notifications of malaria in the UK has decreased. In 1990, 1493 cases were notified. In December 1989 changes were made to the form of certificate used by doctors to notify cases of malaria such that the name of the country where the malaria was contracted must now be stated. Cases of malaria are almost invariably contracted abroad, although in 1983 two cases of Plasmodium falciparum occurred which were thought to have been contracted in England.

METHOD OF SPREAD

Malaria is spread through the bite of an infected female Anopheles mosquito. The malarial parasite has two cycles, an asexual one occurring in man and a sexual one in the mosquito. Thus, the mosquito is not only the vehicle of infection, but is necessary for the completion of the life cycle of the malarial parasite.

The period of communicability in an infected human is as long as the infective gametocytes are present in the bloodstream. This period is, of course, dependent on the treatment given.

PREVENTION

For many years, anyone visiting and working in areas of the world where malaria is endemic has been advised to take prophylactic drugs. However, there is now increasing evidence of the emergence of resistant strains of *Pl. falciparum*. It is important for visitors to realize that it is still therefore possible to acquire *Pl. falciparum* infections of malaria while taking prophylacic drugs.

Cholera

Causative organism: *Vibrio cholerae* including Eltor biotype, serotype Ogawa and serotype Inaba.
Incubation period: short, 1–3 days.

INCIDENCE

Cholera last occurred in a serious epidemic form in the UK in 1866. It was virtually absent from most westernized communities until the recent Eltor outbreaks. It is endemic in India, Burma, Pakistan, Bangladesh and the Philippines. Since the 1970s considerable epidemics of the Eltor strain have spread to parts of Africa, Middle East, Turkey and some parts of Europe. In England and Wales odd cases have occurred in most years from 1980 as shown in Table 12.2. It is clear that air travel has facilitated its spread.

TABLE 12.2   Cholera cases notified in England and Wales, 1979–90

Year	Number of cases	Year	Number of cases
1979	0	1985	7
1980	4	1986	9
1981	9	1987	13
1982	1	1988	17
1983	5	1989	13
1984	3	1990	19

Data from various OPCS Monitors in the MB2 series.

METHOD OF SPREAD

Contaminated water in the early stages of an epidemic and direct contact from cases later both contribute to the spread of the disease. Flies may also be responsible. The disease becomes epidemic in areas in India and the Far East during the hot, moist seasons before the rains and then rapidly subsides.

PERIOD OF INFECTIVITY

This depends on the presence of cholera vibrios in the stools — usually for 14 days, but occasionally up to 3 months. Recent work in Eltor epidemics has shown that many infections with this serotype have no symptoms and that some may excrete the organism for up to 4 years.

PREVENTION

This depends on purification of water supplies and safe disposal of sewage, and it is this factor which has been responsible for the disappearance of the disease in highly developed countries. In epidemics, water or milk should be boiled (unless pasteurized) and careful segregation of all patients arranged with terminal and concurrent disinfection.

Active immunization should be arranged for those at special risk (doctors, nurses) and for travellers. Immunization provides approximately 50% protection for a short period (few months). Re-immunization is, therefore, advisable for those at risk after 6 months. Under International Sanitary Regulations, the validity of a cholera vaccination certificate lasts for 6 months beginning 6 days after the first injection of vaccine.

Mass vaccination has proved of limited value because of the short period of protection and the cost.

References

1. OPCS. Monitor MB2 87/4. London: OPCS. 1987.
2. OPCS. Monitor MB2 88/1. London: OPCS. 1988.
3. OPCS. Monitor MB2 89/2. London: OPCS. 1989.
4. World Health Organization. The Work of WHO. Biennial Report of the Director General of WHO 1986–87. Geneva: WHO.
5. Rabies Act 1974 London: HMSO.
6. Department of Health. On the state of the public health. The Chief Medical Officer's annual report for the year 1989. London: HMSO. 1990.
7. Legionnaires Disease Surveillance. England and Wales 1989. Communicable Diseases Report Vol 4, p. 5 1990. Public Health Laboratory Service.
8. Department of Health. On the State of the Public Health. The Chief Medical Officer's annual report for the year 1985. London: HMSO. 1986.

13

Epidemiology and the Prevention of Non-communicable Diseases

Epidemiology

Diseases can only be effectively prevented if all the various factors which cause them are fully understood. In previous chapters, it has been shown how communicable diseases can be prevented by understanding the qualities of the various infecting organisms (bacteria or viruses) and the reaction of the human body when invaded by them.

With non-infectious illnesses the greatest barrier to prevention is that often little is known about the cause of disease. Yet, even when the exact cause of the disease process is imperfectly understood (as with a neoplastic disease), much can be learnt about it by a study of the many factors that influence it. The complete study of these various complex factors is called epidemiology. As well as covering the causation of disease (aetiology), epidemiology includes the following:

- Variations of the disease in time, which covers a brief study of the way the disease has altered in incidence and severity over the past few generations.
- Present-day morbidity (or incidence) of the disease including comparisons between different countries, different areas of the same country and in different strata of the same community. The following factors are connected with morbidity:
  - (a) seasonal incidence
  - (b) the effect of heredity or race including the changes in incidence noted in migrant groups when individuals of one nationality permanently move to live in another country
  - (c) geographical factors
  - (d) predisposing causes — these may be either in the occupation of the patient or connected with his or her social and recreational life or habits. There may be a marked delay between exposure to the cause and the development of the disease (often called the 'latent period')

(e) sex differences

(f) the personality of the patient — psychosomatic factors.

- Social factors in the disease.
- Mortality of the disease.
- Estimation of the chances of an individual developing the disease.
- Methods of preventing the disease.

In this short chapter, no attempt will be made to discuss even briefly the epidemiology of all groups of non-communicable diseases. Instead, a few selected diseases will be discussed which illustrate many of the fascinating aspects of epidemiological study and how methods of prevention may be developed.

Epidemiology often concentrates attention on a disease because of some significant change in its incidence. This leads to more research which brings to light further features, and finally an important causative factor may be defined. Cancer of the lung is an example. Because of its marked increase since 1950, increasing research has been undertaken and a connection with cigarette smoking has been demonstrated. Such a causative factor could never have been discovered by the investigation of a series of single clinical cases — a study of the whole community was needed to bring this factor to light.

Epidemiology can also be said to help define the problems of disease. In most cases, there is a multiplicity of factors affecting its incidence. The clinician studies the various pathological factors concerned, but the treatment must fit into the life of the patient. The social factors in the patient's environment are all important and may well be responsible for a relapse (a good example is given by duodenal ulcer). The field of epidemiology enlarges the scope of investigation into disease. It also covers many more patients than could ever be seen by any individual clinician.

Ischaemic heart disease

INCIDENCE AND MORTALITY

Deaths from ischaemic heart disease have increased dramatically during this century. The exact range of increase has been difficult to calculate because methods and standards of diagnosis have improved markedly since 1930. However Sir Richard Doll[1] in *Social Trends 1988* notes that 'a large increase in the incidence of coronary thrombosis has occurred over the last 100 years. If all diseases of the coronary arteries are classed together, we obtain the picture shown in [Fig. 13.1] where the age standardisation rates for both men and women are seen to have increased fifty fold until the early 1970s' . . .

Further epidemiological evidence that major increases occurred during the 1950s

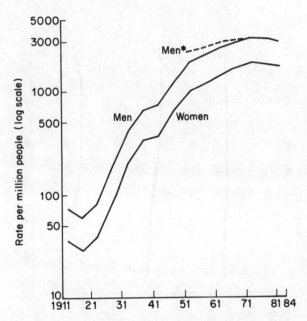

FIGURE 13.1   Mortality rates from coronary artery disease: by sex in England and Wales, 1911–84. Mortality from angina pectoris, coronary thrombosis and other diseases of the coronary arteries, standardized for age. *Rate for coronary artery disease plus myocardial degeneration in the presence of arteriosclerosis. (Data from ref. 57.)

and 1960s is given in Fig. 13.2.[1] This shows that the increase was most marked in age groups under 60 years in which the standard of diagnosis would be likely to have been most precise. From Fig. 13.2 it can be seen that the number of deaths from ischaemic heart disease in the UK have now levelled off and begun to fall. However, ischaemic heart disease is still the main cause of death in UK. In 1991 in England and Wales 150 090 people (81 611 men and 68 479 women) died from this cause. There was a peak incidence in 1985 with a total of 163 104 deaths, but since then the numbers have fallen by 7.6%. However, deaths during 1985–89 have fallen faster in men — a fall of 9.6% compared with a fall of 4.9% in women.[2]

Coronary heart disease is a good example of an illness which affects all sections of the community, but in which the highest mortality is in men and women of manual classes[3] and in men and women of Asian origin.[4]

There is a marked difference between the death rate (and incidence) of ischaemic heart disease in men and women of middle age (35–50 years). The rate in men is five times greater than that in women. From the menopause onwards the death rates in women rise progressively until at age 70 years the rates in the sexes are roughly equal.

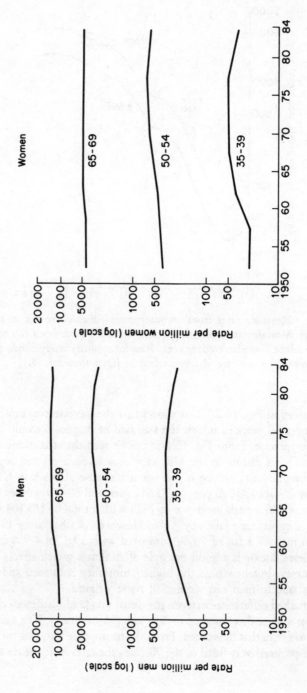

FIGURE 13.2 Mortality rates from coronary thrombosis: by sex and age in England and Wales, 1911–84. (Data from ref. 57.)

SEX DIFFERENCES

In the past there has always been a male predominance in this disease, but this is gradually changing as shown in Table 13.1 which gives the deaths from ischaemic heart disease in England and Wales over the period 1961–90.

TABLE 13.1   Deaths from ischaemic heart disease in England and Wales (rates per 100 000) 1961–91

Year	Males	Females
1961	297.3	210.1
1966	324.3	222.8
1971	349.8	239.2
1976	373.5	268.2
1980	373.9	265.5
1986	351.1	261.2
1991	329.8	263.8

Data from various OPCS Monitors in the DH2 series.

Note that from 1961 to 1980 there was a greater increase in men than in women — 24.5% compared with 21.8%. However in the last 11 years there has been a greater fall in male deaths than in female deaths.

SOCIAL CLASS

There is an increased gradient in the level of ischaemic heart disease in both sexes as the social class falls from Class I to Class V (see Fig. 13.3). This gradient is greater in women than in men.

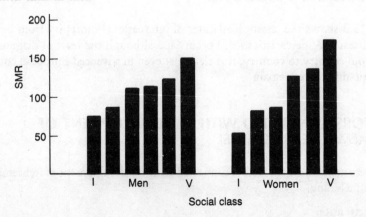

FIGURE 13.3   Mortality from ischaemic heart disease for men and women aged 20–64 years in England and Wales, 1979–80, 1982–83. (Data from ref. 55.)

REGIONAL DIFFERENCES IN MORTALITY

In both England and Wales and in Scotland there are marked differences in the mortality of ischaemic heart disease as shown by Table 13.2.

TABLE 13.2   Standardized mortality ratios (SMRs) for ischaemic heart disease by Regional Health Authority (RHA) in England and Wales, 1989, and by Health Board in Scotland, 1980–85

England and Wales, RHA	SMR	Scotland, Health Board	SMR
Oxford	83	Lothian	92
South-east Thames	84	Borders	92
East Anglia	85	Grampian	93
North-west Thames	85	The Islands	94
North-east Thames	87	Tayside	96
Wessex	88	Highland	98
South Western	99	Forth Valley	98
West Midlands	106	Greater Glasgow	100
Wales	107	Fife	102
Trent	108	Dumfries and Galloway	105
Mersey	114	Ayr and Arran	108
Yorkshire	114	Argyll and Clyde	108
North Western	121	Lanarkshire	113
Northern	123		

Data from refs 16 and 46.

INTERNATIONAL INCIDENCE

Table 13.3 shows the latest calculations of international mortality from ischaemic heart disease. Wide variations still occur, and although the level of diagnosis may vary from country to country, it is clear that even in advanced European countries, dramatic differences remain.

FACTORS CONNECTED WITH THE DEVELOPMENT OF ISCHAEMIC HEART DISEASE

There are many different factors connected with the development of ischaemic heart disease including:

- hypertension
- cigarette and small cigar smoking
- obesity and diet (fibre levels)

TABLE 13.3   Deaths from ischaemic heart disease per 100 000 population in various countries, 1986 (except where indicated)

Country	Deaths	Country	Deaths
Japan	49.5	Canada	213.8
Hong Kong	52.9	USA[a]	237.1
Spain	111.1	Australia	257.8
Argentine[a]	116.5	Germany (Federal)	265.4
Portugal	121.7	New Zealand	270.2
Yugoslavia[a]	134.2	Malta	271.5
Mauritius[b]	144.8	Netherlands	284.5
Italy[b]	150.0	Australia[b]	290.0
France[b]	155.4	Ireland[a]	382.1
Bulgaria	160.1	England and Wales	427.5
Israel	187.2	Scotland	547.7

[a] 1984, [b] 1985.
Data from ref. 47.

- high blood lipid levels (e.g. high blood cholesterol levels)
- lack of physical activity
- genetic factors — these may be linked with blood cholesterol levels
- other diseases (e.g. diabetes mellitis)
- socio-economic factors.

Hypertension

Recent work has confirmed that there is a direct association between the level of diastolic pressure and coronary heart disease — the higher the diastolic pressure the higher the risk. Prolonged reductions in the diastolic pressure of 5, 7.5 and 10 mmHg were found to be associated with at least a 21%, 29% and 37% less risk of coronary heart disease, respectively.[5] In a further study, the results from 14 trials of antihypertensive drugs, showed that a sustained reduction of 5–6 mmHg in the diastolic blood pressure over 2–3 years resulted in 14% less coronary heart disease.[6]

Smoking

Cigarette and small cigar smoking is the largest single preventable cause of all disease and premature mortality in the UK, and this includes coronary heart disease.[7] It is likely that the differences in mortality from ischaemic heart disease between social classes (see Fig. 13.3), regions (see Table 13.2) and sexes (see Table 13.1) is also connected with the level of smoking in the group or area.

Obesity and overweight

There is a greater risk of coronary heart disease in people who are overweight, and the greater the degree of obesity the greater the risk of developing coronary heart disease. The usual modern method to determine overweight is to calculate the body mass index (BMI; see p. 318). Any person who has a very high BMI — over 30 — will, according to the Royal College of Physicians,[8] have twice the risk of coronary heart disease compared to individuals with a BMI of less than 22. Diets high in fats (especially animal fats) should be avoided. High intake of fibre reduces the risks of heart disease.

High blood cholesterol

Generally, the higher the level of blood cholesterol the greater the risk of coronary heart disease.[9, 10] The usual level of blood cholesterol which is connected with moderate levels of coronary heart disease is a level of 5.2 mmol/l, while a level of less than 4.2 mmol/l is associated with low levels of ischaemic heart disease. However, a recent dietary and nutritional survey of British adults[11] aged 16–64 years showed that 68% of men and 64% of women had a serum cholesterol level above 5.2 mmol/l. A raised blood cholesterol level probably only becomes critical when it is associated with other 'at risk' factors, i.e. high blood pressure, smoking, obesity.

Lack of physical activity

Many controlled prospective studies have shown that individuals whose work or leisure involves regular vigorous exercise are between one third and one half less likely to die from coronary heart disease compared with people who lead sedentary lives.[12, 13]

Diabetes

Individuals with diabetes mellitus are more likely to develop ischaemic heart disease. Those with diabetes are often overweight (up to 90% of persons with diabetes are overweight). It is now recognized that diabetes is fairly common among Indian immigrants who have settled in the UK. This may explain the higher death rates in Indians in the UK.[14]

Socio-economic factors

Working class men are over 3.5 times more likely to die from heart disease than professional men, and this association continues after other risk factors are taken into account.[3] A marked difference in the standardized mortality rate (SMR) for ischaemic heart disease exists between social class I and V (see Table 3.26, p. 91). Unemployment or the risk of unemployment can also have an adverse effect. Recent Swedish research[15] showed that the risk of unemployment increases the serum cholesterol concentration in middle aged men. This study also found that the increase in blood cholesterol was more pronounced where there was also a sleep disturbance.[15]

Work in Scotland by Carstairs and Morris[16] has emphasized the association between ischaemic heart disease and deprivation. The SMRs for individuals aged 0–64 years was 63 for the most affluent group studied, but rose to 123 for the most deprived.[16] Comparison by social class in persons aged 20–64 years showed the SMR range from social class I to V was 66–158.

PREVENTION OF ISCHAEMIC HEART DISEASE

Steps to reduce the various risk factors mentioned above should lower the chance of contracting ischaemic heart disease. Because the causal relationship is essentially multifactorial, it is almost impossible to calculate the risk to an individual of one factor. Work in Iceland has shown that the incidence of myocardial infarction in men under the age of 75 years decreased by 23% during the period 1981–86.[17] Three major factors are considered to have produced the improvement in Iceland: a decrease in smoking, lowering of the systemic blood pressure and a reduction in the serum cholesterol level by 10%.

Generally it is considered that hypertension, smoking, gross overweight and lack of exercise are the most useful factors for individuals to concentrate upon, as well as having a diet with a high fibre content and a reduced fat content. Probably at least one blood cholesterol test should be carried out to identify that very small group of people with very high levels. Repeat blood cholesterol tests in persons whose levels are normal are unlikely to achieve further prevention. The tests may well be difficult to interpret and can cause unnecessary worry to anxious persons. This itself increases stress and may thus have adverse effects. It is better to concentrate upon the five factors — hypertension, smoking, overweight, lack of exercise and a diet low in fats and high in fibre — that are linked with lifestyles and therefore can be readily understood by everyone.

The cancers

Cancers are the second commonest cause of death in the UK. The complete causation of cancers is not yet fully unravelled, although just over 70% of all cancers can be attributed to two causes:[18]

- diet (about 31%)
- smoking (about 31%).

Although a number of industrial processes have been identified as possible causes of cancers, these only represent at the most 1–2% of all cancer deaths. There is also no evidence that any such carcinogenic substances constitute a cancer risk outside the workplace. Asbestos which can cause lung cancer is one of the best known examples of an industrial cancer risk, yet asbestos is only responsible for less than 5% of deaths from cancer of the lung. It is estimated that the risk of asbestos-related lung cancer is increased by 10 times if the individual also smokes.[18]

INCIDENCE AND MORTALITY

The annual number of cancer registrations in England and Wales is in the region of 220 000 (see Table 3.24 p. 89). The mortality figures for 1991 are shown in Table 13.4. In this year, the cancer deaths from all causes totalled

TABLE 13.4   Principal causes of cancer deaths in England and Wales, 1991

Site	Males	Females
Lung	23 308	10 882
Stomach	5 122	3 305
Breast (female only)	–	13 786
Colon	5 283	6 103
Rectum	3 196	2 516
Oesophagus	3 178	2 088
Pancreas	2 941	3 068
Prostate	8 570	–
Lymphatic and haemapoietic tissue	5 207	4 687
Ovary	–	3 866
Cervix uteri	–	1 668
Uterus (other)	–	1 494
Bladder	3 335	1 545
Kidney and other unspecified urinary organs	1 506	1 057
Leukaemia	2 033	1 654

Data from ref. 48.

145 355 (75 853 in men and 69 502 in women.)

Most of these mortality figures are fairly constant from year to year although the overall numbers are falling gradually. Leukaemia is an exception for there was an increase in deaths during the 1980s. Between 1980 and 1991, leukaemia deaths in England and Wales increased from 3340 to 3687 (an overall increase of 10.3%) The rate of increase in men was greater than in women (11.1% compared with 9.5%).

It will be seen that there are many differences between the sexes. More men than women die from cancer of the lung (although male deaths from this cause are now falling while female deaths continue to rise). Men also show more deaths from cancers of the bladder, stomach and rectum. In women, breast cancers form the largest group — in 1991 there were 13 786 deaths from cancer of the breast in women. Cancers of the colon are also commoner in women than in men.

REGIONAL INCIDENCE

Considerable regional differences occur in the mortality from all cancers in England and Wales and in Scotland (see Table 13.5).

TABLE 13.5   Standardized mortality ratios (SMRs) for all cancers by Regional Health Authority (RHA) in England in 1985, and by Health Board in Scotland, 1980–85

England, RHA	SMR	Scotland, Health Board	SMR
South Western	92	The Islands	79
East Anglia	93	Dumfries and Galloway	87
Wessex	93	Borders	88
Oxford	94	Grampian	93
South-west Thames	94	Fife	94
North-west Thames	96	Highland	95
South-east Thames	100	Tayside	96
North-east Thames	100	Ayr and Arran	97
Trent	100	Forth Valley	98
West Midlands	101	Lothian	100
North Western	106	Lanarkshire	101
Northern	108	Argyll and Clyde	102
Mersey	110	Greater Glasgow	113

Data from refs 16 and 49.

SOCIAL CLASS

All cancers show a marked variation in incidence and mortality within social classes. Men show a greater variation than women. Generally mortality is lowest in social class I and highest in social class V. One of the largest differences is recorded in

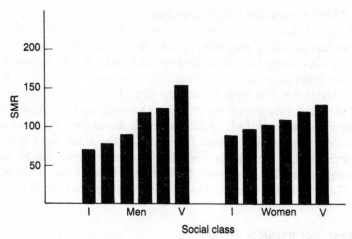

FIGURE 13.4   Mortality from malignant neoplasms by social class in men and women aged 20–64 years in England and Wales, 1979–80, 1982–83. (Data from ref. 55.)

cancer of the cervix uteri (see Table 3.26, p. 91) where the lowest SMR is 29 in social class I and then rises progressively to an SMR of 186 in social class V. Leukaemia is the one exception and shows no definite difference between the social classes (see Fig. 13.12).

TABLE 13.6   International cancer death rates per 100 000 population, 1986 and 1987

Site	USA[a]	Austria[b]	France[a]	Netherlands[a]	UK[b]	Australia[a]	Japan[a]
Stomach							
Male	7.2	29.3	16.0	19.5	23.5	10.9	50.6
Female	4.4	24.9	10.6	12.6	14.8	6.3	29.3
Lung							
Male	72.5	67.2	64.4	104.6	102.0	54.4	38.7
Female	32.7	18.6	8.6	13.7	40.7	16.8	13.9
Breast							
Female	32.8	42.1	33.6	41.3	52.4	27.2	8.5
Cervix uteri	3.7	5.8	3.1	4.2	7.3	4.4	2.9
Leukaemia							
Male	8.1	7.3	9.6	7.4	7.7	7.3	5.6
Female	6.3	7.0	7.4	6.0	6.5	5.5	3.7

[a] 1986, [b] 1987.
Data from ref. 50.

INTERNATIONAL CANCER MORTALITY

It is interesting to compare the differences in cancer mortality throughout the world. Table 13.6 shows the cancer mortality rates per 100 000 of the population for seven developed countries.

CANCER OF THE LUNG

A dramatic increase in deaths from cancer of the lung occurred during 1947–71 (see Table 13.7). This represented an increase of 234% in the number of lung cancer deaths. Since 1971 the rise has been more gradual and the peak mortality was reached in 1987 with 36 729 deaths (the rate of increase from 1971 to 1987 slowed down to 19.4%). Deaths from lung cancer fell in England and Wales from 1987 to 1991 to 34 190 (a fall of 6.9%).

TABLE 13.7   Deaths from cancer of the lung in England and Wales, 1947–91

Year	Deaths	Year	Deaths
1947	9 204	1971	30 754
1951	13 347	1975	32 831
1955	17 272	1979	34 730
1959	22 063	1983	35 572
1963	24 434	1987	36 729
1967	28 188	1989	34 351
		1991	34 190

Data from ref. 2.

Trends in lung cancer mortality in the sexes

There are still many more lung cancer deaths in men than in women — in 1991 in England and Wales there were 23 308 deaths in men and 10 882 in women. Yet lung cancer deaths in men are now falling steadily, but the rate in women is rising — see SMRs in Table 3.25, p. 90. This shows that during 1980–89, the SMR in men fell to 83, but rose to 124 in women (1980 SMR = 100). In 1991 cancer of the lung deaths were 30.7% of all male cancer deaths, but in women the figure was lower at 15.7%.

The different mortality trends in the sexes are very clearly shown in Fig. 13.5. Note that the rate of increase flattened out in men in the mid 1970s and now has started to fall. However in women the rate has steadily increased. Indeed, in Scotland by 1984 the acceleration of lung cancer deaths in women had resulted in the deaths from this cause exceeding those from breast cancer for the first time. In England and Wales, there are still markedly more deaths from breast cancer in

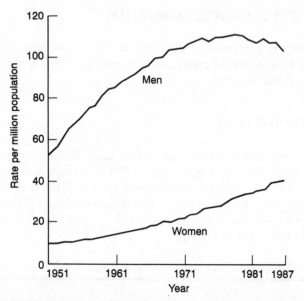

FIGURE 13.5   Mortality rates from lung cancer in the UK: by sex. (Data from ref. 58.)

women than lung cancer (see Table 13.4), but lung cancer deaths over the age of 55 years are now approaching those for breast cancer.[7]

Although there are now encouraging falls in lung cancer deaths in men, the original rates were so high in the UK that this rate is still much higher than most other countries (see Table 13.6). Scotland has an even worse record and still has the highest rate of lung cancer deaths in the world.

Social class

There is still a well-defined social class gradient in mortality from lung cancer (see Fig. 13.6). Carstairs and Morris[16] also found a steep mortality gradient between the SMRs of the most affluent group in the community (SMR 58) and the most deprived group (SMR 179 in people of all ages in Scotland). This was also mirrored by the variation in the SMRs for lung cancer in Scottish local authorities — SMR for Glasgow and Cumbernauld was 144 and 132, respectively, compared with the lowest for Shetland and Skye (46 and 49).

Factors connected with the development of lung cancer

In men 90% of lung cancer can be attributed to cigarette smoking.[7] There is also roughly a 30-year gap between commencing smoking and the development of lung

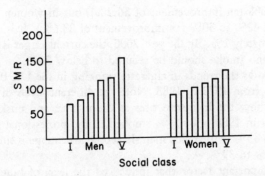

FIGURE 13.6 Mortality from lung cancer in men and women aged 20–64 years in England and Wales, 1979–80, 1982–83. (Data from ref. 55.)

cancer, and past and present trends in smoking reflect the numbers of cases in the sexes. Most men started smoking from 1920 onwards and this was followed by a rapid increase in lung cancer in the 1950s and 1960s. Then important changes occurred — once it had been clearly demonstrated that smoking causes lung cancer the numbers of men smoking began to fall. From 1972 to 1988 smoking fell in men

TABLE 13.8 Cigarette smoking (%) in Greet Britain by sex and socio-economic group, 1972–88

	1972	1976	1982	1986	1988
Males					
Professional	33	25	20	18	16
Employers and managers	44	38	29	28	26
Intermediate and junior					
non-manual	45	40	30	28	25
Skilled manual	57	51	42	40	39
Semi-skilled manual	57	53	47	43	40
Unskilled manual	64	58	49	43	43
All aged 16 years and over	52	46	38	35	33
Females					
Professional	33	28	21	19	17
Employers and managers	38	35	29	27	26
Intermediate and junior					
non-manual	38	36	30	27	27
Skilled manual	47	42	39	36	35
Semi-skilled manual	42	41	36	35	37
Unskilled manual	42	38	41	33	39
All aged 16 years and over	42	38	33	31	30

Data from ref. 51.

from 52% to 33% (an improvement of 36.2%), but in women the fall was less marked — from 42% to 30% (an improvement of 28.6%). It is now falling each year by approximately 1%. By the year 2000, the current target is that the proportion of adults who smoke should be reduced to below 20%.[40]

Table 13.8 shows the trends in cigarette smoking in the UK by sex and socioeconomic group from 1972 to 1988. Note the different levels of smoking in the population and how the incidence rises as the manual and unskilled groups are reached. In men in 1988 only 16% smoked in the professional groups, but the incidence rose to 43% in unskilled men. In women the range is similar but slightly less — from 17% to 39%.

The second important factor that influenced the level of lung cancer was the change in the composition of cigarettes. The tar level in cigarettes first fell in the 1950s and then later (between 1965 and 1984) fell more steeply (by 54%).

Concern at present is being expressed about the proportion of secondary schoolchildren who regularly smoke. By 1982, 11% of boys and girls smoked, but by 1986, the percentage of boys still smoking had fallen to 7%, but the number of girls had risen to 12%.[7]

Passive smoking

Recently concern has not only focused on the risks of smokers later developing lung cancer, but on the risk to non-smokers who inhale other persons' smoke (passive smoking). American and Australian research[19, 20] has shown that the inhalation of other peoples' smoke can cause lung cancer in non-smokers. In a review of the probable implications for non-smokers in the UK, Wold and Namachabel[19, 20] suggested that one quarter of the lung cancer found in non-smokers — approximately 600 cases annually — could be caused in this way.

Other forms of nicotine and tobacco use (such as sucking) have been shown to cause cancers of the mouth and throat[22] and the use of such products has now been banned in the UK.

CANCER OF THE LARGE BOWEL (COLON AND RECTUM)

It is convenient to discuss the epidemiology of cancers of the colon and rectum together (under the collective term large bowel cancers) because the factors which determine their incidence are similar. In 1991 in England and Wales there were 17 071 deaths from large bowel cancers (8452 men and 8619 women). These figures were made up of 11 386 deaths from cancer of the colon (5283 men and 6103 women) and 5685 deaths from cancer of the rectum (3169 men and 2516 women).

There are marked variations in the incidence of large bowel cancers in the world — these cancers are eight times commoner in the UK (and many other

TABLE 13.9   Standardized mortality ratios (SMRs) for large bowel cancers (colon and rectum) for all ages by Regional Health Authority (RHA) in England in 1989, and by Health Board in Scotland, 1980–85

England, RHA	SMR	Scotland, Health Board	SMR
North-west Thames	83	The Islands	85
South-west Thames	90	Fife	92
South-east Thames	91	Lanarkshire	93
North-east Thames	92	Lothian	93
East Anglia	93	Dumfries and Galloway	96
South Western	94	Argyll and Clyde	97
Wessex	95	Borders	98
Yorkshire	102	Forth Valley	99
Oxford	104	Greater Glasgow	104
Trent	107	Ayr and Arran	105
North Western	110	Grampian	107
Mersey	110	Tayside	107
West Midlands	110	Highland	108
Northern	114		

Data from refs 16 and 46.

westernized countries) than in North Africa and South Asia.[23] There are also differences in the incidence of large bowel cancers in the UK (see Table 13.9).

The range of cancer registration of large bowel cancer in local government districts in Scotland is even more varied (all Scotland ≡ 100). In the case of cancer of the colon the lowest rates are found in Orkney (62) and Dumbarton and the highest are in Inverness (146) and Aberdeen City (131). For cancer of the rectum, the lowest figures are in Sutherland (59) and Caithness (71) and the highest in Aberdeen City (128) and in Bearsden and Milngavie (126).[16]

Causation of large bowel cancers

There is now a large amount of evidence that the main reason for the wide variation in incidence of large bowel cancer throughout the world is connected with diet. Many studies have shown that the major factors are a diet which is:

- high on total fat content
- high in meat consumption
- low in fibre
- high in refined carbohydrates (sugar).[24]

It is known that in many of the African countries with very low rates of large bowel cancers, the intake of fibre is seven times greater then in many westernized

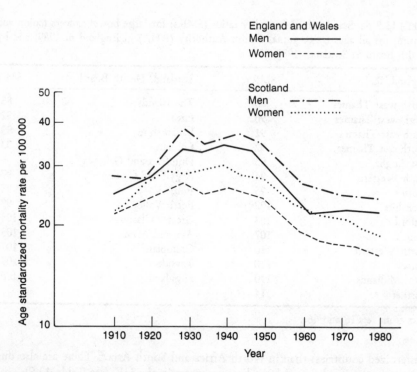

FIGURE 13.7   Trends in mortality from large bowel cancer in the UK, 1910–80. (Data from ref. 59.)

countries. The association is unlikely to be genetic as after some years rates rise rapidly in immigrants to America and Europe who settle and adopt the local eating habits.[1] The rates of large bowel cancer in Britain are known to be associated with the daily intake of fibre — where this is consistently high the large bowel cancer rate is low.[25]

The levels of large bowel cancer in men and women in the UK from 1910 to 1980 are shown in Fig. 13.7. Note that there was a steady increase in large bowel cancers from 1910 to 1930 (this increase started later in Scotland). A consistently high rate then persisted for 12 years, but after 1942 there was a striking decrease which was probably connected with the change in eating habits in the UK during World War II (1939–45) when there was a dramatic increase in consumption of dietary fibre coincidental with the doubling of cereal consumption.[26]

Prevention of large bowel cancers

Probably the most certain way to reduce large bowel cancer incidence is to ensure that diets include less fat, a reasonable limit on meat and, especially, a high fibre content. The screening for large bowel cancer is discussed in detail in Chapter 7 (see pp. 180–181).

CANCER OF THE BREAST IN WOMEN

In England and Wales, cancer of the breast is the commonest cancer in women — about 22 000 women develop this disease every year with approximately 13 750 deaths. No specific causes have been discovered, but there is strong circumstantial evidence that the cancer is linked with environment and life-style. Table 13.6 shows that British women are six times, Dutch and Austrian women five times, and American women four times more likely to die from breast cancer than Japanese women. Genetic factors are unlikely to be the explanation for the differences as black women in America and Japanese women in Hawaii have similar rates to their white American compatriots, but a much higher rate than their country of origin.

Hormonal factors may be important and the incidence of cancer of the breast is particularly high in women who have an early menarche and a late menopause. Also the incidence is greatest in women who have their first child late and least in those who have their first child early. It is three times greater in women who have their first child after the age of 35 years compared with those whose first child is born before they are 18 years old. Another factor which is being researched now is the possible relationship between the use of the oral contraceptive pill — some studies have suggested that breast cancer may be commoner in women who start taking the pill under the age of 25 and who continue to take it for more than 8 years.[27-29] It used to be thought that breast feeding in some way protected women from a later cancer of the breast, but this has now been disproved.

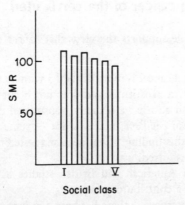

FIGURE 13.8   Mortality from cancer of the breast in women aged 20–64 years in England and Wales, 1979–80, 1982–83. (Data from ref. 55.)

Social class

Unlike most neoplasms, cancer of the breast in women shows an atypical social class gradient in that it is inverse — deaths are slightly higher in social classes I and II than in IV and V (see Fig. 13.8.)

Breast cancer deaths have been slowly increasing for much of this century. The reasons are uncertain but it is thought that social changes which have resulted in women tending to postpone the birth of their first child may be responsible. This could also explain the inverse social class gradient as women in social classes IV and V tend to have their first child 3.6 years later than women in social classes I and II (see Table 3.5, p. 67).

Prevention of breast cancer in women

The modern method of screening for early breast cancer — mammography — will be available everywhere in the UK NHS after 1993 when it is hoped to persuade women aged 50–70 years to attend regularly for screening (see p. 179).

CANCER OF THE CERVIX UTERI

Cancer of the cervix uteri was responsible for 1668 deaths in England and Wales in 1991. The death rate has been gradually falling, but this may not continue. Although the death rates fell in women over the age of 40 years during the 1980s, death rates from this cancer have increased in women between 25 and 34 years old in the UK.[24]

Factors connected with cancer of the cervix uteri

Most of the evidence available supports the view that cancer of the cervix uteri is connected with:

- *Sexual intercourse* — cervical cancer is more likely if a woman has multiple sexual partners. It is commonest in prostitutes and does not occur in nuns. It is also more common if a woman also has a sexually transmitted disease.[31]
- *Presence of varients of human papilloma in the vagina* — some of these can cause genital warts. Because of this finding, it has been suggested that this cancer can be indirectly sexually transmitted.[30, 31]
- *Cigarette smoking* — both American and British studies have concluded that cigarette smoking can be a contributory factor.
- *Change in methods of contraception* — there has been a reduction in the use of the barrier methods of contraception — condom and diaphragm use has diminished in favour of the pill. Some researchers have suggested, therefore, that indirectly

the pill may have been responsible for an increase in the incidence of this cancer especially among younger women. No certain conclusion is possible for this view and further research is necessary.

- *Glomerulonephritis* — recent research in Norway[32] has shown that cervical cancer is commoner in women with glomerulonephritis. The increased occurrence was independent of the use of immunosuppressive treatment, but when this therapy was used it was more advanced. The authors recommended that women with glomerulonephritis should have regular cervical smears.

Incidence

Cancer of the cervix is the commonest cancer found in women in Africa, Asia and Latin America. It is, however, less common in Europe and North America. It has always been rare in Jewesses and this used to be thought to be due to male circumcision, but recent work has shown that this is unlikely to be true. Certainly cleanliness is an important preventive factor as the disease is rare in communities who practice ritual ablution before and after sexual intercourse.

Social class

There is a well-marked social class gradient in cancer of the cervix uteri. The SMR is 29 for social class I, but rises to 186 for social class V (see Fig. 13.9 and Table 3.26).

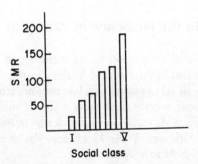

FIGURE 13.9   Mortality from cancer of the cervix uteri in women aged 20–64 years in England and Wales, 1979–80, 1982–83. (Data from ref. 55).

Prevention

Cervical smear testing is of great importance in the prevention of cervical cancers as it can discover a precancerous condition — see Chapter 7, pp. 177–178.

Because of the large variation in incidence of cervical cancer among different social classes in the community, every effort should always be made to test women in social classes IV and V. Smear testing is a good example of where testing smaller numbers of women who are at great risk will discover more precancerous conditions than testing much larger numbers of women from social classes I and II.

CANCER OF THE STOMACH

Cancer of the stomach is the sixth commonest cancer in the UK. In 1991 in England and Wales there were 5122 deaths in men and 3305 in women. Deaths from this cancer are falling steadily. Between 1971 and 1991, the death rates fell in both sexes — by 32.4% in men and by 38.5% in women (see Table 13.10).

TABLE 13.10   Deaths from cancer of the stomach in England and Wales, 1971–91 (rates per 100 000)

Year	Males	Females
1971	30.5	20.6
1976	28.9	19.6
1980	26.7	17.8
1986	24.3	14.7
1991	20.6	12.7

Data from ref. 2.

Factors connected with the incidence of cancer of the stomach

There is a marked geographical connection in the incidence of this cancer in the UK (see Table 13.11). Note that in England and Wales generally the further north, the higher the death rate — all RHAs north of a line roughly from Oxford to East Anglia have a death rate above average, and those south of such a line are below average. In Scotland there is a wide variation — the deaths in Borders being nearly half those in Lanarkshire. Although Table 13.11 does not show this, there is a particularly high death rate in North Wales.

Cancer of the stomach is especially found in persons who have an atrophic gastritis. The incidence of cancer of the stomach is three times higher in those with pernicious anaemia compared with the general population.

Genetic factors may play a part in cancer of the stomach as it has been noted that persons with a blood group A have a 20% greater incidence of this cancer.

Diet almost certainly is connected with the incidence of cancer of the stomach. The high rates of this cancer in Austria (see Table 13.6) is thought to be associated with the more highly spiced foods popular in that country.

TABLE 13.11   Standardized mortality ratios (SMRs) for cancer of the stomach by Regional Health Authority (RHA) in England, 1989, and by Health Board in Scotland, 1980–85

England, RHA	SMR	Scotland, Health Board	SMR
South-west Thames	79	Borders	65
Oxford	81	The Islands	79
East Anglia	82	Dumfries and Galloway	81
Wessex	85	Grampian	86
South-east Thames	86	Lothian	89
North-west Thames	87	Fife	92
South Western	88	Highland	92
North-east Thames	96	Forth Valley	100
Yorkshire	105	Tayside	102
Mersey	110	Ayr and Arran	107
Trent	111	Greater Glasgow	111
North Western	117	Lanarkshire	119
Northern	125		

Data from refs 16 and 46.

Social class

There is a very definite social class gradient in cancer of the stomach as the SMR rises steadily from 50 in men and from 77 in women in social class I to 158 in men and to 161 in women in social class V (see Fig. 13.10).

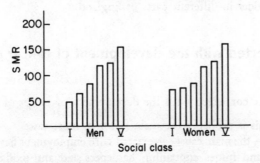

FIGURE 13.10   Mortality from cancer of the stomach in men and women aged 20–64 years in England and Wales, 1979–80, 1982–83. (Data from ref. 55.)

CANCER OF THE BLADDER

Incidence

Cancer of the bladder is commoner in men than in women in the UK in the proportion of 2 : 1. In 1991, in England and Wales, 4880 deaths occurred from this

TABLE 13.12   Standardized mortality ratios (SMRs) for cancer of the bladder in Regional Health Authority (RHA) in England, 1989 (all England = 100)

RHA	SMR
East Anglia	88
North-west Thames	93
Wessex	94
Trent	95
West Midlands	96
Oxford	96
South Western	99
South-west Thames	101
North-east Thames	102
Mersey	106
North Western	107
South-east Thames	108
Yorkshire	111
Northern	115

Data from ref. 46.

cause — 3335 in men and 1545 in women (see Table 13.4).

Table 13.12 shows the mortality differences as expressed by the SMRs in different RHAs in England — this gives an indirect indication of the relative incidence of cancer of the bladder in different parts of England.

Factors connected with the development of cancer of the bladder

The following are connected with the development of cancer of the bladder:

- *Smoking* — this is probably the main factor in most cases.
- *Occupational* — the main causes associated with employment have been identified as the dusts and fumes containing hardeners and anti-oxidants, particularly benzidene, 2-naphthylamines, 3–3 dichlorobenzidine and 4 amonobiphenyl. Approximately 10% of the bladder cancers in men and 5% in women have been traced to these causes. These findings were confirmed by the Employment Medical Advisory Service in 1980.[33] The rubber industry later published a helpful guide to reduce this hazard.[34] After the initial exposure to these chemicals, there usually is a latent period (from 12 to 20 years) before a cancer of the bladder develops. At present, any individual who has been exposed to these chemicals at work is followed up twice a year by urine samples being examined

for any evidence of exfoliated cancer cells in the urine. In this way, it is hoped that very early cancers of the bladder will be discovered.

- *Infestation of the bladder* by *Schistosoma haematobium* has been known to be connected with later development of bladder cancer. This is a common cause of cancer of the bladder in Egypt and Tanzania.

Social class

A quite steep social class gradient exists in cancer of the bladder (see Fig. 13.11). In men the range of SMR is from 80 in social class I to 135 in social class V. In women it is steeper — from 63 in social class I to 142 in social class V.

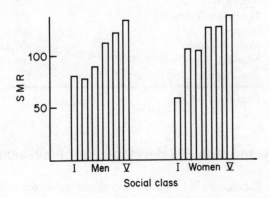

FIGURE 13.11   Mortality from cancer of the bladder in men and women aged 20–64 years in England and Wales, 1979–80, 1982–83. (Data from ref. 2.)

LEUKAEMIA

Incidence

Reference has already been made (see p. 279) to the increase of 10.3% in leukaemia deaths in England and Wales from 1980 to 1991.

The geographic spread in the UK varies (when the SMRs of RHAs in England are compared), but there does seem to be clear differences from the usual trend noted in other cancers (see Table 13.13). In most other cancers, East Anglia and many other RHAs in the south of England tend to have lower SMRs than RHAs in the north. But with leukaemia, the SMRs are more mixed with south-west Thames, Yorkshire and North Western having the three lowest levels and West Midlands, Wessex and East Anglia showing the highest ones.

TABLE 13.13   Standardized mortality ratios
(SMRs) for leukaemia by Regional Health
Authority (RHA) in England, 1988

RHA	SMR
South-east Thames	83
Yorkshire	86
North Western	91
South-east Thames	93
North-west Thames	94
Oxford	99
South Western	99
Trent	102
Northern	103
North-east Thames	103
Mersey	105
West Midlands	106
Wessex	109
East Anglia	111

Data from ref. 46.

Factors connected with the development of leukaemia

Most types of leukaemia, including acute lymphatic leukaemia which accounts for most childhood leukaemia, can be induced by ionizing radiation. Many studies of the incidence of childhood leukaemia have been made to find out whether there is an increased incidence around nuclear installations. The original DHSS enquiry[35] cast considerable doubt that excess radiation was responsible for a small increased amount of leukaemia in the district surrounding Sellafield. But subsequent studies have shown an association between nuclear installations and an increase of childhood leukaemia in the neighbourhood.[36-38]

Exposure to chemicals, such as benzene, in large amounts can cause acute myeloid leukaemia and less frequently acute lymphatic leukaemia.[39]

Certain hereditary diseases have been identified with an increased incidence of leukaemia, the commonest being Down's syndrome where the risk of contracting leukaemia is over 20 times greater than in normal children.[39]

Social class

The differences in mortality in leukaemia between the social classes is very uneven (see Fig. 13.12) and there is no definite trend.

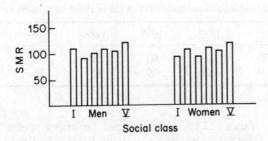

FIGURE 13.12   Mortality from leukaemia by social class in men and women aged 20–64 years in England and Wales, 1979–80, 1982–83. (Data from ref. 55.)

Bronchitis and emphysema

Table 13.14 illustrates how deaths from bronchitis and emphysema fell dramatically from 1980 to 1991 — from 19 244 to 6773 in England and Wales (a reduction of 64.8%).

TABLE 13.14   Deaths from bronchitis and emphysema (ICD codes 490–492) in England and Wales, 1980–91

	1980	1986	1991
Males	14 181	8 456	4 447
Females	5 063	3 663	2 326
Total	19 244	12 119	6 773

Data from refs 21, 48 and 52.

Table 13.14 also shows that deaths from bronchitis and emphysema are consistently more frequent in men than in women. This difference is almost certainly caused by the greater proportion of men than women who have smoked and who still smoke. However, the proportion of women dying from bronchitis and emphysema has risen steadily in this 11-year period — in 1980, deaths in women were 26.3% those of men, in 1986 36.6% and in 1991 52.3%. This change is also most likely to reflect the proportional increase in women who smoke.

Table 13.15 confirms this degree of decline in mortality from chronic bronchitis — the 1980 SMR of 100 falling to 29 in men and to 37 in women by 1989. This calculation has been standardized for age changes in the population over this period.

The incidence within Scotland shows wide variations (see Table 13.16). Note that the mortality during 1980–85 varied from 55 SMR in the Islands to 138 in Greater

TABLE 13.15   Standardized mortality ratios (SMRs) for bronchitis in England, 1980–88

	1980	1983	1985	1986	1987	1988	1989
Males	100	63	60	50	38	35	29
Females	100	82	79	65	51	45	37

Data from ref. 53.

TABLE 13.16   Standardized mortality ratios (SMRs) for bronchitis by Health Board in Scotland, 1980–85

Health Board	SMR
The Islands	55
Highland	70
Borders	73
Dumfries and Galloway	75
Grampian	77
Tayside	85
Fife	90
Forth Valley	96
Lanarkshire	100
Ayr and Arran	100
Lothian	101
Argyll and Clyde	102
Greater Glasgow	138

Data from ref. 16.

Glasgow. This represents a range within Scotland of 2.5 times. Table 13.16 shows an increasing mortality as the degree of urbanization and deprivation rises.[16]

FACTORS CONNECTED WITH THE INCIDENCE OF BRONCHITIS

Cigarette smoking is the main factor, especially when an individual continues to smoke even when suffering from the earliest symptoms of bronchitis. In anyone who smokes, climate can also play a part as a cold damp climate always aggravates this disease. Previously atmospheric pollution was a contributory cause as shown by the infamous smog in London in 1952, which within a week caused just under 4000 deaths in people subject to chronic bronchitis. Such pollution today probably plays a minor role in the UK, although anyone with bronchitis will get fewer complications living in a warmer and drier place.

The dramatic improvement in the last 20 years has undoubtedly followed the reduction of cigarette smoking in the UK — in 1972, 52% of men smoked and

42% of women. These figures had fallen to 31% and 29%, respectively, by 1989 in Great Britain and this rate of fall is expected to continue in the future. Indeed a recent report of the Faculty of Public Health Medicine[40] has suggested that a sensible target to aim at would be a further fall to a 20% maximum in both sexes by the year 2000.

SOCIAL CLASS

There is a steady rise in the mortality from bronchitis in both sexes from social class I, but mortality suddenly increases when social class V is reached (see Fig. 13.13).

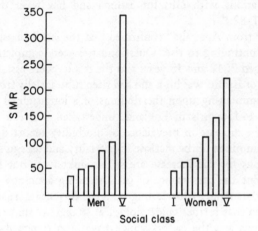

FIGURE 13.13   Mortality from bronchitis by social class in men and women aged 20–64 years in England and Wales, 1979–80, 1982–83. (Data from ref. 55.)

Asthma

Unlike deaths from bronchitis and emphysema, mortality from asthma increased between 1980 and 1986 as illustrated in Table 13.17. However, since 1986 deaths from asthma have decreased slightly. Also deaths in women exceed those in men unlike in bronchitis.

Many papers have recently emphasized that asthma incidence and severity has increased since 1970 in many countries.[41] For instance, the level of asthma in Finland in young men called up for military service increased six-fold from 1961 to 1989.[42] The authors of this study felt this rate of increase must be real and could not be explained by better modern diagnosis.

TABLE 13.17   Deaths from asthma in England and Wales, 1980–91

	1980	1986	1991
Males	611	827	881
Females	869	1163	1073
Total	1480	1980	1884

Data from refs 21, 48 and 52.

From the mid 1970s to the mid 1980s the levels of asthma in the UK for people aged 5–34 years increased markedly, and from 1984 onwards, this increase continued.[43] Consultations with GPs for asthma and hay fever doubled between 1970–71 and 1981–82.[44]

A recent report from Australia[42] confirmed that the levels of asthma in children in Melbourne is continuing to rise. Questionnaires were completed by parents of 10 981 children aged 7, 12 and 15 years and the results were assessed as indicating that the incidence of asthma was high and had risen substantially from 1965 to 1991. Burney et al.[43] commenting upon the findings of a longitudinal study involving 15 000 boys and 14 156 girls in England, undertaken between 1973 and 1986, concluded that 'the increase in prevalence of morbidity reported in this paper is sufficient to explain much of the increase in mortality and uses of services over this period. The reasons for the increase are so far unknown, but large changes in prevalence underline the importance of understanding aetiology in order to formulate an appropriate strategy for dealing with the current international epidemic.'

It is to be hoped that further epidemiological studies are undertaken to unravel the causes of asthma and the factors which have been responsible for the recent increases world-wide.

In England and Wales deaths from asthma have risen from 1480 in 1980 (611 in males and 869 in females) to 1858 (738 in males and 1120 in females) in 1990.

Hypertensive disease

INCIDENCE

During the last 31 years, mortality from hypertensive disease has fallen greatly in the UK as illustrated by Table 13.18. However, the rate of fall is now slowing down. During the 1980s, mortality continued to fall steadily in both sexes (see Table 13.19). There has also been a marked difference in the mortality in different RHAs in England and Wales and in Health Boards in Scotland. This almost certainly reflects a similar difference in the incidence of hypertensive disease in these areas (see Table 13.20).

TABLE 13.18   Deaths from hypertensive disease in England and Wales, (rates per 100 000) 1961–90

Year	Males	Females
1961	31.7	40.5
1966	21.6	27.7
1971	17.6	20.4
1976	14.2	16.8
1980	10.6	12.0
1986	7.5	9.1
1991	6.0	7.1

Data from ref. 2.

TABLE 13.19   Standardized mortality ratios (SMRs) for hypertensive disease in men and women in England, 1980–1989

	1983	1984	1985	1986	1987	1988	1989
Males	81	79	73	69	60	60	56
Females	83	82	81	72	64	50	57

Data from ref. 53.

TABLE 13.20   Standardized mortality ratios (SMRs) for hypertensive disease by Regional Health Authority (RHA) in England, 1989, and by Health Board in Scotland, 1980–85

England, RHA	SMR	Scotland, Health Board	SMR
Mersey	67	Grampian	50
Yorkshire	68	Forth Valley	67
North Western	83	Fife	70
Oxford	89	Tayside	73
Trent	93	Borders	92
Northern	95	Lanarkshire	93
Wessex	96	Argyll and Clyde	93
South Western	97	Highland	108
North-east Thames	104	Lothian	112
East Anglia	109	Dumfries and Galloway	113
North-west Thames	112	The Islands	121
West Midlands	113	Ayr and Arran	126
South-east Thames	116	Greater Glasgow	136
South-west Thames	119		

Data from refs 16 and 46.

SOCIAL CLASS

The usual steep social class gradient from social class I to V exists for hypertensive disease (see Fig. 13.14).

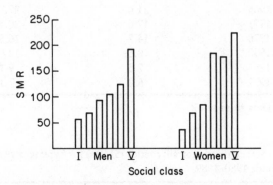

FIGURE 13.14   Mortality from hypertensive disease in men and women aged 20–64 years in England and Wales, 1979–80, 1982–83. (Data from ref. 55.)

FACTORS RESPONSIBLE FOR THE DECLINE IN HYPERTENSIVE DISEASE MORTALITY 1961 TO 1990

There are two main factors responsible for the remarkable reduction in mortality observed between 1961 and 1989. These are:

- *Changes in life style of the population* — during 1961–90 there have been considerable changes in the life-style within the UK. The level of smoking has halved in men, and by 1989 the number of men smoking had fallen to 31% of the population. It is expected that this reduction will continue at a rate of at least 1% per year. It is disturbing that the rate of smoking in women is falling at a slower rate (although it started at a lower level) and by 1989 the rate of smoking in women was 29% — a difference of 2%—whereas in 1971 the difference was 10%. In the youngest age groups, smoking in the UK is now commoner in women than men.
- *Improved treatment* — there is no doubt that the large decrease in mortality in the period 1961–90 has been partly due to improved treatment. It is difficult to quantify the relative effect of life-styles and improved treatment. Probably improved treatment initially played the larger part, but it is clear at present that the improvements in life-style have been equally or more important in the continuing fall in mortality from hypertensive disease in the 1980s.

Diabetes

INCIDENCE

Deaths from diabetes in England and Wales in both sexes rose rapidly from 1980 to 1991 (Table 13.21). Deaths in women have consistently exceeded those in men. The rate of increase in both sexes has been similar.

TABLE 13.21   Deaths from diabetes in England and Wales, 1980–91

	1980	1986	1988	1991
Males	1993	3156	3427	3562
Females	2788	4296	4423	4525

(from OPCS Monitors DH2 83/3, 87/3, 89/2, 92/2)
Data from refs 21, 47, 52 and 54.

SOCIAL CLASS

There is the usual social class gradient with the least mortality in social classes I and II and the greatest in IV and V (see Fig. 13.15). This social class gradient has not always been of such a pattern. Whereas diabetes now shows the lowest death rate in social class I, the opposite was the case in 1921–23 and 1931–32 when the lowest rates were in social class V (Table 13.22).

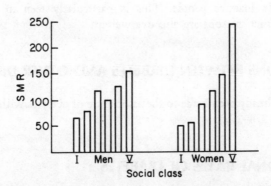

FIGURE 13.15   Mortality from diabetes by social class in men and women aged 20–64 years in England and Wales, 1979–80, 1982–83. (Data from ref. 55.)

TABLE 13.22   Standardized mortality ratios (SMRs) for diabetes for men aged 20–64 years in England and Wales by social class, 1921–83

Social class	1921–23	1930–32	1949–53	1959–63	1970–72	1979–80, 1982–83
I	129	122	134	81	83	67
II	149	155	100	103	93	76
IIIN	93	95	99	100	111	113
IIIM					98	100
IV	75	82	85	98	111	123
V	66	69	105	122	128	155

Data from ref. 55.

FACTORS CONNECTED WITH THE DEVELOPMENT OF DIABETES

The following are the important factors affecting the incidence of diabetes:

- *Heredity* — diabetes has often been shown to have a familial tendency, and if one twin has the disease the chance of the other developing diabetes is five times greater in similar twins than in dissimilar ones.
- *Obesity and overweight* — there is a marked higher incidence of diabetes among persons who are overweight. It has been estimated that 90% of diabetes is related to overweight and obesity, and therefore diabetes is potentially preventable.[45] The milder form of diabetes showed a substantial fall in incidence during 1939–48, almost certainly a reflection of the beneficial effect of food rationing. During these years there was a restriction of the consumption of many attractive foods and sweets and chocolate which made being overweight less likely.
- *Inactivity* — there is a higher incidence of the milder form of diabetes in sedentary and relatively inactive people. This is particularly seen in elderly persons especially if such persons are also overweight.

CONNECTIONS BETWEEN DIABETES AND OTHER DISEASES

Reference has already been made to the association of diabetes with ischaemic heart disease (see pp. 276–277).

INTERNATIONAL RATES OF DIABETES

Mortality from diabetes varies considerably throughout the world. The lowest rates are seen in Hong Kong and Japan, while a particularly high incidence and mortality is seen in Italy (Table 13.23). It is interesting that in all countries diabetes

TABLE 13.23   Deaths from diabetes mellitus per 100 000 population in various countries, 1986 (except where indicated)

Country	Males	Females	Total
Hong Kong	3.3	5.4	8.7
Japan	7.3	7.8	15.1
Ireland[a]	7.4	8.9	16.3
France[b]	10.6	15.1	25.7
England and Wales	13.0	16.8	29.8
USA[a]	12.9	17.2	30.1
Italy[b]	25.6	44.8	70.4

[a] 1984, [b] 1986.
Data from ref. 47.

is one of the few diseases in which there is a consistently higher death rate in women than in men.

In the UK, it has been found that there is a much higher incidence of diabetes in the Indian population living there compared with the indigenous UK population.[45] This has been thought to explain the higher death rates from heart disease recorded in Indians living in the UK.

Cirrhosis of the liver

Although there are many important and serious adverse consequences to alcohol abuse, cirrhosis of the liver and its mortality is one of the most reliable ways to indicate the levels and trends of drinking in any country.

TABLE 13.24   Deaths from cirrhosis of the liver per 100 000 population in various countries

Country	Males	Females	Total
England and Wales (1987)	6.1	4.7	10.8
Netherlands (1986)	6.7	4.2	10.9
Australia (1986)	10.6	4.0	14.6
Scotland (1987)	9.3	6.5	15.8
USA (1985)	14.8	7.8	22.6
Japan (1987)	19.3	8.3	27.6
Spain (1987)	30.7	11.5	42.2
France (1986)	30.9	12.4	43.2
Chile (1985)	46.2	14.7	60.9
Italy (1984)	45.9	20.7	66.6

Data from ref. 50.

INTERNATIONAL LEVELS OF MORTALITY FROM CIRRHOSIS OF THE LIVER

Table 13.24 shows the death rates from cirrhosis of the liver in several countries. It will be seen that the UK countries have low rates of cirrhosis mortality. However, the Scottish figures are 50% higher than in England and Wales. The high rates of Spain, France, Chile and Italy are the result of the population of these countries regularly drinking large quantities of wine.

SOCIAL CLASS AND OCCUPATION

Figure 13.16 illustrates the social class distribution of mortality from cirrhosis of the liver. There is a marked higher level of mortality in social class V, but most of the remaining social classes have a fairly level mortality. Certain occupations have a high mortality, especially those associated with the production and sale of alcoholic drinks. The highest SMR of all occupational groups for all causes of death are brewery and vinery process workers with a SMR of 266 (see Table 3.27). This high death rate is closely connected with cirrhosis of the liver.

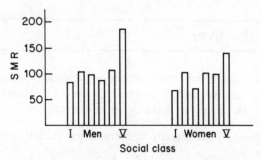

FIGURE 13.16   Mortality from cirrhosis of the liver by social class in men and women aged 20–64 years in England and Wales, 1979–80, 1982–83. (Data from ref. 55.)

Mental disorders

Although it is difficult to quantify accurately, there are many indicators to suggest that the level of mental illness is falling in the UK. The morbidity statistics from general practice show that whereas in the survey carried out in 1971–72, 10.3% of all consultations were for 'mental disorders', in 1981–82 the figure had fallen to 6.8% (see Table 3.18, p. 80). It is certain that the numbers of persons being treated

TABLE 13.25   Mental illness and hospitals for the mentally handicapped – average numbers of beds available daily and patient activity. England, 1979–89/90, thousands

	1979	1982	1984	1986	1987/88	1989/90
Mental illness						
Beds available	89	84	79	72	67	59
Outpatients						
new patients	180	188	198	202	207	207
total attendances	1618	1740	1783	1817	1760	1422
Mental handicap						
Beds available	50	47	44	39	33	26
Outpatients						
new patients	3	3	3	3	4	3
total attendances	20	22	25	31	62	35

Data from ref. 53.

in hospitals for mental disorders continues to be reduced (Table 13.25). However this is mainly due to a change in policy regarding treatment and care of mentally ill people – shorter stays in mental hospitals and more supportive community care are now encouraged, and persons needing continuous care are now mainly looked after outside mental hospitals.

SEX AND AGE INCIDENCE

One of the most striking epidemiological facts about mental illness is the different incidence betwen the sexes – for many years all records have shown that women suffer from mental illness to a greater extent than men. The 1981–82 morbidity survey in general practice carried out by the Royal College of General Practitioners showed that the consulting rate for mental illness was 67.5 per 1000 patients for men but 147.0 for women. For depressive psychosis the sex ratio was 3 : 1 women to men.

In both sexes, the incidence of mental illness increases with age – certainly the chance of anyone being admitted to a mental hospital for the first time increases significantly after the age of 65 years (see Table 13.26). Part of this large increase may be because old people often live alone. This results in hospital admissions for investigation of anyone behaving in an odd way becoming more urgent. However, the increases are so large that they cannot be wholly explained in this way. Many different theories have been put forward to explain the greater incidence of mental illness in women than men, but many of the earlier genetic and biological explanations have recently been shown to be unfounded. The present view is that the most likely explanation for this sex difference is connected with the different social

TABLE 13.26   First admissions to mental hospitals by sex and age, specific rates per 100 000 population in England, 1986

Age group (years)	Males	Females
Under 10	10	4
10–14	24	19
15–19	65	69
20–24	114	108
25–34	118	117
35–44	104	107
45–54	87	102
55–64	89	105
65–74	144	167
75 and over	411	404
All ages	100	119

Data from ref. 56.

environment and to the different social roles of men and women. In persons with learning disabilities (mental handicap) the incidence is similar in both sexes.

SOCIAL CLASS

Figure 13.17 illustrates the SMRs for men and women with mental disorders and shows a steady rising incidence from social class I to V. Note that the incidence of mortality is greater for all social classes in women than in men and provides more indirect evidence to support the finding that there is more mental illness in women.

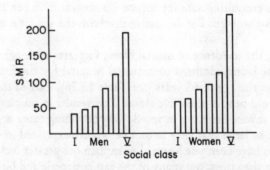

FIGURE 13.17   Mortality by social class for mental disorders in men and women aged 20–64 years in England and Wales, 1979–80, 1982–83. (Data from ref. 55.)

FACTORS ASSOCIATED WITH THE DEVELOPMENT OF MENTAL ILLNESS

The exact cause of most mental illness is not yet fully understood. However, a great deal is known of the factors related to the development of mental illness and these can be divided into:

- intrinsic factors connected with the patient including (a) heredity and (b) phases of his/her development.
- extrinsic factors related to the patient's occupation, home and environment.

Intrinsic factors

These are complicated. Hereditary ones are rather an inherited predisposition to develop mental illness than being born with a mental illness. This predisposition may or may not result in mental breakdown and the likelihood of such illness developing depends on: (a) environmental (extrinsic) factors; (b) certain susceptible stages of his/her life — mental illness is most likely to develop at puberty, pregnancy, middle age (including menopause) or in retirement (old age).

Extrinsic factors

These are even more difficult to assess as each patient is continuously selecting different features from his/her environment. Generally, the more unsatisfactory and insecure the surroundings of any patient, the more likely it is that mental illness will develop but this is not inevitable as each person reacts differently when placed in the same surroundings. Prevention of mental illness is closely connected with early recognition of mental instability. Once a mental illness has started, the longer it lasts the more likely it is to become permanent and so become independent of the detailed circumstances associated with its commencement. It is most important to diagnose the earliest signs of mental illness for this helps treatment.

Many 'functional' disorders are associated with faulty training and upbringing in the home, such as rigid parents who demand too high a standard, or the rejection of a child by a parent. Most GPs meet many such problems in their practices. To assist early diagnosis, preventive psychiatry has been introduced into child health work. It is, of course, impossible to protect any patient from mental and physical trauma in life — in fact, attempts to do this may encourage mental breakdown. But it is usually practicable to alter a patient's environment in some way, and thus help to avoid an impending mental illness.

Balanced advice is always an important environmental factor. Personal counselling can be most helpful in allaying many needless fears which may have been handed down by ignorant parents or relatives and which may otherwise precipitate a mental illness.

Occupation has an important effect on mental stability. Careful medical and psychological testing before persons are placed in various occupations can assist in avoiding subsequent mental breakdowns (personnel management).

FACTORS ASSOCIATED WITH THE DEVELOPMENT OF LEARNING DISABILITIES (MENTAL HANDICAP)

These have been discussed in Chapter 7 (pp. 168–169).

References

1. Doll, R. Social Trends, 1988. London: HMSO.
2. OPCS. Monitors DH2 series. London: OPCS.
3. Rose G, Marmot MG. Social class and coronary disease. Br. Heart J. 1981, 45: 13–19.
4. Coronary Prevention Group. Coronary heart disease and Asians in Britain. London: Coronary Prevention Group. 1986.
5. MacMahon S, Peto R, Cutler J et al. Blood pressure, stroke and coronary heart disease: part 1, prospective observational studies corrected for regression dilution bias. Lancet 1990, 335: 765–774.
6. MacMahon S, Peto R, Cutler J et al.. Blood pressure, stroke and coronary heart disease: part 2, short term reduction on blood pressure; overview of randomised drug trials in their epidemiological context. Lancet 1990, 335: 827–838.
7. Royal College of Physicians of London. Health or smoking: follow up report of Royal College of Physicians of London (Sir Douglas Black, Chairman). London: Pitman Medical. 1983.
8. Royal College of Physicians of London. Obesity. A report. J Roy Coll Physicians London 1983, 17(1).
9. Rose G, Shipley M. Plasma cholesterol concentration and deaths from coronary heart disease: 10 year results of the Whitehall study. Br. Med. J. 1986, 293: 306–307.
10. Stamler J, Wentworth D, Neston JD. Is relationship between serum cholesterol and the risk of premature death from coronary heart disease continuous and graded? J Amer Med Assoc 1986, 256: 2823–2828.
11. OPCS. Dietary and nutritional survey of British Adults. London: HMSO. 1990.
12. Paffinberger RS, Hale WE. Work activity and coronary heart mortality. New Engl. J. Med. 1975, 292: 545–550.
13. Morris JN et al. Vigorous exercise in leisure time. Protection against heart disease. Lancet 1980, 8206: 1207–1210.
14. Padhani A, Dandona P. Diabetes and coronary heart disease in North London Asians. Lancet 1981, 45: 13–19.
15. Mattiason I, Hindgarde F, Nitsson JA, Theorell T. Br. Med. J. 1990, 301: 461–466.
16. Carstairs V, Morris R. Deprivation and health in Scotland. Aberdeen: University Press. 1991.
17. Sigroldason IV, Iniborg I, Stedandottir I, Thorsteinsson I. Decline in ischaemic heart disease in Iceland and change in risk factor levels. Br. Med. J. 302: 1371–1375.
18. Doll R, Peto R. The causes of cancer. Oxford: University Press. 1981.

19. Wold NJ, Namchahal K et al. Does breathing other people's smoke cause lung cancer? Br. Med. J. 1986, **293**: 1217–1221.
20. National Health and Medical Research Council. Effects of passive smoking on health. Canberra: NHMRC. 1987.
21. OPCS. Monitors DH2 83/3: 5. London: OPCS. 1983.
22. Harrison DFN. Dangers of snuff both 'wet' and 'dry'. Br. Med. J. 1986, **293**: 405–406.
23. Parkin DM, Stjersward J. Cancer control, estimates of world frequency of twelve major cancers. Bull. WHO 1984, **62** (2): 163–182.
24. Bristol JB, Emmett PM et al. Sugar, fat and the risk of colorectal cancer. Br. Med. J. 1985, **291**: 1467–1470.
25. Bingham SA, Williams DRR et al. Dietary fibre consumption in Britain: new estimates and their relation to large bowel cancer mortality. Br. J. Cancer, 1985, **52**: 399–402.
26. Boyle P, Zaridze DG et al. Descriptive epidemiology of colorectal cancer. Int. J. Cancer 1985, **36**: 9–18.
27. Pike MC, Ross RK. Breast cancer. Brit. Med. Bull. 1984, 351–354.
28. Merik O, Lund E et al. Oral contraception use and breast cancer in young women. Lancet 1985, ii:650–652.
29. Stadel BV, Rubbin GL et al. Oral contraception and breast cancer in young women. Lancet 1985, ii: 970–973.
30. Singer A et al. Genital warts and virus infections: nuisance or potentially lethal? Br. Med. J. 1984, **288**: 735–737.
31. British Medical Association. Cervical cancer and screening in Great Britain. London: BMA. 1986.
32. Hartveit F, Bertelsen, B, Thurnold S, Maehle B, Christensen J. Risk of intra epithelial neoplasia in women with glomerulonephritis. Br. Med. J. 1991. **302**: 375–377.
33. Employment Medical Advisory Service and Safety Executive. Mortality in the British Rubber Industry 1967–1976. London: HMSO. 1980.
34. Rubber and Plastics Research Association of Great Britain. Clearing the air. London: 1982.
35. Black D. (Chair). Investigation of the possible increase of cancer in West Cumbria. Report of the Independent Advisory Group. London: HMSO. 1984.
36. Heasman MA, Kemp IW. Childhood leukaemia in Northern Scotland. Lancet 1986, i: 266.
37. Cook-Mozaffari PJ, Vincent T et al. Cancer incidence and mortality in the vicinity of nuclear installations, England and Wales 1959–1980. Studies in Medical Population Subjects, no 51. London: HMSO. 1987.
38. Beral V. Cancer near nuclear installations. Lancet 1987, **7**: 556.
39. Wetheral DJ, Ledingham JGG, Warrel DA. Oxford textbook of medicine. Oxford: The University Press. 1983, 4.71.
40. The Faculty of Public Health Medicine of the Royal Colleges of Physicians of the UK. UK level of Health. 1991: 19.
41. Robertson CF, Heycock E, Bish J, Nolan T, Olinsky A, Phelan PD. Prevalence of asthma in Melbourne schoolchildren: changes over 26 years. Br. Med. J. 1991, **302**: 323–326.
42. Haahtela T, Lindholm H, Bjorksten F, Kostenvuo K, Laitinen LA. Prevalence of asthma in young Finnish men. Br. Med. J. 1990, **301**: 266–268.
43. Burney PGJ et al. Asthma mortality in England and Wales: evidence of a further increase. Lancet 1986, ii: 323–326.
44. OPCS. Morbidity Statistics in General Practice, 1981–1982. London: HMSO. 1990.
45. Gatley W, Houston A et al. The prevalence of diabetes mellitus in a typical English community. J. Roy. Coll. Physicians London 1985, **19**(4): 248–250.
46. OPCS. Mortality Statistics: Area. Series DH5 no. 16. London: HMSO. 1991.
47. World Health Annual Statistics, 1987. Geneva: WHO.
48. OPCS. Monitor DH2 92/2. London: OPCS. 1992.
49. OPCS. Mortality Statistics, 1985. Series DH1 no. 17. London: HMSO. 1988.
50. World Health Annual Statistics, 1988. Geneva: WHO.

51. Central Statistical Office. Social Trends 1990. London: HMSO.
52. OPCS. Monitor DH2 87/3. London: OPCS. 1987.
53. Department of Health. Health and Personal Social Services Statistics, 1991. London: HMSO.
54. OPCS. Monitor DH2 89/2. London: OPCS. 1989.
55. OPCS. Occupational Mortality, 1987. London: HMSO.
56. Department of Health. Health and Personal Social Services Statistics, 1990. London: HMSO.
57. Central Statistical Office. Social Trends 1988. London: HMSO.
58. Central Statistical Office. Social Trends 1989. London: HMSO.
59. Smith A, Jacobson B. The Nation's Health. 1988. King Edward's Hospital Fund for London.

14

Food and Nutrition

Introduction

Nutrition and public health are inseparable as a well-balanced and adequate food supply is essential for complete health. There has been much interest and debate in the past two or three decades about the diet and diseases in the western world namely coronary heart disease, obesity, varicose veins, piles, colonic cancer and appendicitis. These diseases are rare in Third World countries. Rich people eat rich food, rich in fat, sugar and alcohol, and lacking the protective action of fibre.[1]

World-wide problems

Many more people die prematurely in the Third World from protein malnutrition, infections (typhoid, tuberculosis, poliomyelitis) and in some areas frank starvation and thirst. As food supplies are increased, improvements in nutrition lead to increases in population which in turn make heavier demands upon the food supply. The solution lies both in limiting the growth of the population and increasing the food supply. This will happen with improvements in agricultural methods, pest control, and production of better and more suitable crops and animal stocks. Most of this is outside the scope of this book, but is clearly connected with public health principles.

Energy and nutrients

All foodstuffs contain energy, nutrients and water, and may contain a variety of other substances such as colourings, flavourings, toxins, etc. Over 40 nutrients are needed for man to survive, namely some 8–10 essential amino acids (in proteins), essential fatty acids, 13 vitamins, and 18 elements in addition to hydrogen, oxygen, nitrogen and carbon. All food contains water. Vegetables contain fibre which undigested helps retain water in the gut. This protects against constipation and diseases such as diverticular disease and haemorrhoids. Third World populations consuming mostly vegetable products eat up to 140 g of fibre a day compared to some 15–20 g in the average western diet.

PROTEINS

Proteins may be of animal or vegetable origin and the best are obtained from milk, eggs, meats, fish, kidney or liver, for such foods contain large amounts of essential amino acids. The amount of protein required varies. A child uses about one third of his protein requirements for growth, but an adult requires relatively little for replacement of tissue. Generally, it is accepted that a man requires a minimum of 70 g of protein daily, although this amount may often be exceeded. Unlike fats and carbohydrates, proteins cannot be stored in the human body. In adults it is possible to obtain large quantities of proteins from vegetable sources, but for the child a high proportion of protein should be of animal origin.

CARBOHYDRATES

These are starches and sugars, e.g. those in bread and potatoes, also cane sugar and glucose. They are the cheapest form of food and the body can metabolize them rapidly to produce energy. As family income diminishes, so the amount of carbohydrate in the diet increases and more bread and potatoes are eaten than fats and meat. Roughly half the energy requirements of the body are obtained from carbohydrates. Fats and carbohydrates are to some extent interchangeable, the latter being necessary for the proper metabolism of fats. Carbohydrates are stored in a concentrated form (glycogen) in the liver and muscles. This can be rapidly broken down into glucose to provide energy in an emergency.

MINERAL SALTS

Many different mineral salts are needed by the body including the following:

- *Calcium* is required for ossification (bone formation), clotting of the blood and for regulating muscular contraction, especially of the heart muscle. It is also important for nerve excitability. The best sources of calcium are milk and cheese. Most vegetables and fruits contain satisfactory amounts. Note that meat, fish, sugars, fats and highly milled cereals are deficient in calcium.
- *Phosphorus* is also required for ossification and for the proper metabolism of fat.

With the exception of butter and sugar, most foods are excellent sources of phosphorus.

- *Iron* is required to form haemoglobin in the blood. Only a few foods — egg yolk, liver, whole grains, beans, kale and some fruits — are satisfactory sources of iron. It is absent in butter and present in only very small quantities in milk.
- *Iodine* is necessary for the proper functioning of the thyroid gland and for preventing goitre. Fish, milk and leaf vegetables are good sources.

In addition, potassium, copper, magnesium, manganese, zinc, boron, flourine, selenium and molybdenum are also required in minute traces. The function of many of them is obscure and they are often referred to as *trace elements*.

VITAMINS

These are organic compounds whose presence in small quantities is necessary for correct growth and health. For convenience they are classified as fat-soluble and water-soluble. Many different vitamins have been isolated, but the most important are the following.

Fat-soluble vitamins

Vitamin A

Present in many animal fats in liver, eggs, fish-liver oils, and is introduced into most butters and margarines. The yellow plant pigment carotene, which is found in green vegetables and carrots, is transformed into vitamin A by the body. Vitamin A deficiency causes a degeneration of surface epithelium. This leads to (a) night blindness, due to a deficiency of visual purple; (b) xerophthalmia, which is a drying and thickening of the cornea and later to (c) keratomalacia, which is a softening and inflammation of the cornea leading to opacity and blindness; (d) hyperkeratosis of the skin. These conditions are very rarely seen in the UK, but are more commonly found in the Middle East.

Vitamin D

This controls the deposition of calcium and phosphorus in bones. The best natural sources of vitamin D are cod and halibut liver oils, but the vitamin can be produced by the action of ultraviolet rays upon ergosterol. Milk will contain vitamin D if the cow has been exposed to sunshine. Vitamin D deficiency in infants leads to rickets and in adults to osteomalacia, a disease where, due to inadequate utilization of calcium, there is a softening of the bones. This condition is endemic in underdeveloped countries and may affect pregnant and lactating women. It is extremely rare in European countries. Rickets has been largely eliminated from this country by the introduction of vitamin D fortification of margarine and butter.

Vitamin E

This occurs in low birthweight babies, and some malabsorption syndromes. Deficiency leads to damage of cell membranes such as the red blood cells so causing a haemolytic anaemia, and nerve cells causing a peripheral neuropathy and ataxia. Despite the claims made for it, it has no effect on athletic success or sexual potency.

Vitamin K

This is necessary for maintaining the prothrombin level of the blood and therefore for promoting clotting. It is synthesized by bacteria in the intestinal tract and is present in many vegetables (e.g. spinach, cauliflower, cabbage, kale). Vitamin K deficiency is seen as a hypoprothrombinaemia in haemorrhagic disease of the newborn due to a deficiency of intestinal synthesis of the vitamin. It is recommended that all babies receive vitamin K at birth.[2]

Water-soluble vitamins

The vitamin B complex contains at least four important factors: (1) vitamin B1 (thiamine), (2) riboflavin, (3) nicotinic acid, (4) vitamin B12 (cyanocobalamin). Folic acid is also clinically a very important vitamin.

Vitamin B1 (thiamine)

This is present in whole grain cereals and acute deficiency (beri-beri) is found in tropical countries. There are two forms, dry beri-beri characterized by a polyneuritis and wet beri-beri with cardiac failure. In this country, thiamine deficiency is usually seen in chronic alcoholics who are taking a high carbohydrate diet with a very low intake of the vitamin. The symptoms usually are those of a peripheral neuritis. There is a slight risk of thiamine deficiency in patients on special diets for coeliac disease, but this is readily corrected by giving a vitamin B supplement.

Riboflavin

This vitamin is found in milk, eggs, liver and kidney. Deficiency of this vitamin shows itself as a dermatitis of the seborrhoeic type affecting the skin around the nose, mouth and ears. There may also be a sore tongue, an angular stomatitis and vascularization of the cornea which may eventually lead to a corneal opacity.

Nicotinic acid

This is found in whole grain cereals excluding maize. Deficiency produces the clinical syndrome of pellagra which is seen in the maize-eating communities of eastern Europe and Asia. Occasionally deficiency is seen in this country in conjunction with chronic alcoholism with steatorrhoea (the passing of large, pale, foul-smelling fatty stools).

Vitamin B12 (cyanocobalamin)

This vitamin is also found in whole grain cereals and deficiency causes pernicious anaemia as, in the absence of *intrinsic factor* from the gastric secretion, vitamin B12 in the diet is not absorbed.

Folic acid

This is a sensitive vitamin which is easily destroyed by over cooking. It is present in foods such as lettuce, raw or lightly cooked green vegetables, fortified breakfast cereals, bread, potatoes, fruit and nuts. Deficiency may occur following upper bowel obstruction, or at time of increased need such as pregnancy or any haemolytic condition, or as a consequence of taking anti-folate drugs such as the antibiotic trimethoprim.

As a result of a randomized trial, reported in the *Lancet* in 1991,[3] the Chief Medical Officer wrote to all doctors in England. Folic acid supplements taken by women who had already experienced one or more pregnancies affected by neural tube defects (spina bifida, anencephaly and encephalocele) reduced the risk of a recurrence by 72%. The folic acid was prescribed in a dose of 4 mg per day, as a single dose and had been started prior to conception. It was recommended that all women be advised to eat foods rich in folic acid.

Vitamin C (ascorbic acid)

This vitamin is present in green vegetables, potatoes, fresh fruit, oranges, tomatoes and blackcurrants. Milk, including human milk, is a very poor source. Deficiency leads to scurvy, in which bleeding occurs in mucous membranes. Today in the UK, vitamin C deficiency is mainly seen in old people living on their own because they often neglect their diet, especially during winter. Spontaneous haemorrhages appear, teeth may become loose and skin purpura may be present. Preventive measures include arranging a varied diet for the elderly containing plenty of fresh vegetables and fruit.

Because of the deficiency of this vitamin in milk it is important to give all babies, whether breast or bottle fed, vitamin C additives. Convenient forms include orange juice or rose hip syrup.

COLOURINGS, FLAVOURINGS AND ADDITIVES

In the UK there are almost 300 permitted flavourings and additives, more than in any other country in Europe. Great concern has been expressed about the role of additives and their function in causing disease. They comprise the following groups with the permitted numbers in brackets:

- *antioxidants (16)* — stop fatty foods going rancid and protect fat-soluble vitamins from the harmful effects of irradiation
- *colours (50)* — enhance the appearance of the food, compensating for colour lost in processing
- *emulsifiers and stabilizers (53)* — enable oils and fats to mix with water in foods; improve the texture of foods, slow baked foods going stale
- *preservatives (35)* — increase storage life of foods, inhibit bacterial growth
- *sweeteners (11)* — sweeten the taste, either with very small amounts (intense sweeteners) or as ordinary sucrose (bulk sweetener)
- *miscellaneous (132)* — include acids, anti-foaming agents, bulking agents, flavour modifiers, flour improvers and bleaching agents, glazing agents, packaging gases, propellants, release agents, sequestrants and solvents.

Virtually none of the above additives have any *nutritional* value whatsoever, 7.4% of people questioned in a survey reported to have recognized a problem with certain food additives.[4] Campaigns for better labelling of food products, which would allow the public to choose for themselves what additives they wish to consume, continue. Several large supermarket chains have taken the lead and put more information on their labels than is required by law, but there are still serious inconsistencies. Packaged meats and bread are required to have such information printed on the packaging, whereas unpackaged foodstuffs are not.

Trends in food consumption

During World War II the concept of the balanced diet, which gave a good variety of the proteins, vitamins and minerals and contained enough fat and carbohydrates for energy, was established in the UK. After 1950, luxury items, such as milk, butter and meat, became more plentiful and were seen as good for you. This new diet, rich in fat, was established and has been seen as one of the major factors in the increase of ischaemic heart disease over the past 40 years or so. In 1984, 14.6% of the total consumer's expenditure was on food (from 18.4% in 1976), 7.4% was on alcohol and 3.4% on tobacco. Low income households allocated a larger proportion of their budgets to food (30%). As the income of the household falls the carbohydrate content of the diet increases and their vitamin C consumption falls. Over the past two decades people have been consuming more cheese, fresh fruit and

TABLE 14.1   Consumption in the home of selected foods in the UK, 1961–88; indices of average quantities per person per week, 1981 = 100

Type of food	1961	1971	1981	1988
Milk and cream	117	116	100	90
Cheese	79	93	100	106
Eggs	127	124	100	73
Beef and veal	131	114	100	91
Mutton and lamb	159	127	100	65
Pork	51	80	100	86
Poultry (uncooked)	33	67	100	107
All other meat/meat products	96	103	100	96
Fish/fish products	116	105	100	103
Butter	168	150	100	54
Margarine	80	77	100	92
All other fats	79	90	100	125
Fresh potatoes	135	117	100	87
Fresh vegetables	103	101	100	98
Other vegetables/vegetable products	58	74	100	114
Fresh fruit	87	101	100	105
Other fruit/fruit products	80	84	100	138
Bread (standard white loaves)	165	137	100	71
All other bread	96	63	100	156
Cakes, biscuits, etc.	128	123	100	98
Sugar	163	143	100	63
Tea	143	121	100	83
Instant coffee	31	85	100	102

Data from ref. 13.

poultry, but less milk, eggs, fish, potatoes, bread, cakes, biscuits and sugar (see Table 14.1). Less tea is being drunk and more coffee (a three-fold increase).

OBESITY

A classic definition of obesity is when the weight of an individual is 120% that of the upper range of normal. Because of different body frames difficulties may exist for any one individual in deciding whether they are obese or not. More recently the measurement of weight/height^2 (Quettalet's Index) or the body mass index (BMI), has been used as a convenient index of relative weight. Table 14.2 demonstrates the relation of the BMI to the build. The incidence of obesity is increasing.

TABLE 14.2   Body mass index; BMI = weight in kg/(height in metres)^2

BMI	Description	Grade of obesity
Under 20	Under weight	
20–24.9	Optimum weight range	0
25–29.9	Overweight, risks not certain	I
30–39.9	Obesity	II
Over 40	Morbid obesity	III

Data from ref. 14.

TABLE 14.3   Guidelines for body weight in adults[a]

Height without shoes		Weight (kg) without shoes			
m	feet, inches	Lower limit optimum weight	Upper limit optimum weight	Obese	Grossly obese
1.45	4'9"	42	53	64	85
1.48	4'10"	42	54	65	86
1.50	4'11"	43	55	66	88
1.52	5'0"	44	57	68	90
1.54	5'1"	45	58	70	93
1.56	5'1"	45	58	70	93
1.58	5'2"	51	64	77	102
1.60	5'3"	52	65	78	104
1.62	5'4"	53	66	79	105
1.64	5'5"	54	67	80	106
1.66	5'5"	55	69	83	110
1.68	5'6"	56	71	85	113
1.70	5'7"	58	73	88	117
1.72	5'8"	49	74	89	118
1.74	5'9"	60	75	90	120
1.76	5'9"	62	77	92	122
1.78	5'10"	64	79	85	126
1.80	5'11"	65	80	96	128
1.82	6'0"	66	82	98	130
1.84	6'0"	67	84	101	134
1.86	6'1"	69	86	103	137
1.88	6'2"	71	88	106	141
1.90	6'3"	73	90	108	144
1.92	6'4"	75	93	112	150

[a] Acceptable weights are W/H^2 20–25; obesity is taken to start at W/H^2 30 and gross obesity at W/H^2 40.
Data from ref. 14.

In 1980, 8% of women and 6% of men were obese. In 1987, the respective figures were 12 and 8%. In addition, 37% of men, and 24% women in 1986–87 were considered to be overweight (BMI 25–29.9).[5]

Diseases associated with obesity and having an increased mortality include diabetes mellitus, coronary heart disease, hypertensive heart disease, strokes and digestive diseases such as gall bladder and colon diseases. Most people with obesity have no obvious medical reason to cause the condition (primary obesity). Various theories exist and are used to explain the cause of obesity. These include the presence of brown fat, lower basal metabolic rates, and disordered appetite regulation. It is known that not all obese people eat more than thin people (but still more than they require to lose weight). Repeated periods on diets may lead to further conservation of energy and lowering of the basal metabolic rate. Table 14.3 shows the guidelines for body weight in adults.

Secondary obesity, as a result of a medical condition, is rare. It may be due to endocrine disorders such as myxoedema or Cushing's syndrome. Obesity may also follow enforced inactivity due to other illnesses such as arthritis, stroke or injury. Some drugs can also increase the appetite; these include steroids, sulphanyl ureas (for diabetics) and oral contraceptives. Psychological causes also may play an important part in causing obesity.

Treatment for obesity

Crash diets do not work and long-term objectives are more important than short-term ones. A loss of 2 kg per week for the first 2 or 3 weeks is encouraging but difficult to maintain, and may reflect just a change of body water. A loss of 0.5 kg per week (a disappointingly small amount for the patient) will result in 25 kg loss (nearly 4 stones) if sustained over a whole year. Obese people can have low self-esteem and in addition may be using their diet as a way to punish themselves. One should try to establish why the person wants to lose weight and, if other problems exist such as with personal relationships, try to address these as well. It is useful to clarify the views of other members of the family.

Special diets are unnecessary. Foods containing empty calories (fats, alcohol and sugars) should be avoided. Three meals should be eaten a day, and snacks avoided between meals. A variety of foodstuffs should be consumed from the four main food groups (fish or meat, cereals, milk and cheese, fruit and vegetables). Calorie counters may be useful with weighings of the portions to show how much or little is indeed needed. Diet sheets can be used and some books are helpful. Some diets may be positively dangerous. A good local slimming club (such as those organized by Weightwatchers) providing group therapy, encouragement and information may be very helpful indeed.

The following simple tips to avoid overeating may also help:

■ eat in one room only

- eat slowly
- put food on a small plate
- avoid buying tempting foods
- understand which foods are high in calories
- count everything that passes the lips (including alcohol).

Exercise must play a part and may have an action beyond that of simply burning up calories. Indeed, calculating how much has been consumed after an hour's moderate exercise can be very disappointing — just the equivalent of two slices of bread and butter!

Drugs have virtually no part to play in the treatment of mildly obese people because of their side effects. If they are to be used, they should be used for very short periods under strict medical supervision.

INFANT FEEDING

The third report from the Child Nutrition Panel DHSS Advisory Committee on medical aspects of food policy[6] covers breast and bottle feeding, solids, vitamins and minerals ingestion, and provides information from the 1985–86 Office of Population of Census and Surveys (OPCS) on infant feeding practices. The percentage of mothers breast feeding has remained unchanged over the last 5 years (64% at birth and 22% at 6 months) but for first babies the figures are down over the past 5 years from 74% to 69%. There is still a large social difference, with 87% of social class I babies being breast fed compared with 43% in social class V. The report suggests that a decline in breast feeding might be starting. Negative influences on breast feeding include lack of education at school, lack of antenatal discussion, provision of milk supplies in maternity units, and few public facilities available for mothers to breast feed when they are out. Regrettably too many mothers see breast feeding as 'too much bother'.

An analysis of bottle feeding trends highlights the high percentage (44%) of mothers who change the type of milk feed within the first 6–10 weeks for a variety of reasons. These include persistent hunger and the baby not being satisfied. The change usually involves changing from a whey-dominant artificial feed to a casein-dominant feed. Maternity units usually provide the whey-dominant milks, supposedly because they are more like breast milks, but the report states there is no evidence to base the choice of one particular formulation as being more suitable than another. Vitamin supplements for healthy full-term infants are probably not now required.

Breast feeding

The statistics show that in 1980, 65% of mothers breast-fed at birth and this had decreased by 1% by 1985 to 64%. However, more significantly whereas 74% of

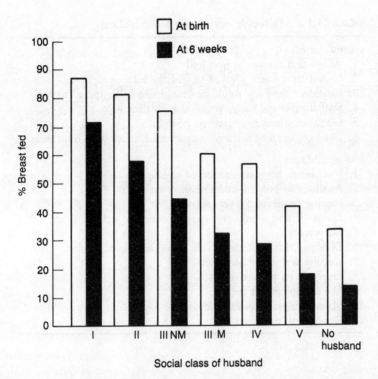

FIGURE 14.1   Proportion of infants put to the breast at birth and proportions of infants being breast-fed at 6 weeks by social class of husband in Great Britain. (From OPCS 1985 survey.)

first time mothers started to breast-feed in 1980, this had dropped to 65% in 1985. The most significant drop was within 1 or 2 weeks, and the proportion stopping within 6 weeks was directly related to social class (see Figure 14.1).

The Joint Breastfeeding Initiative (JBI) was formed in October 1988 by the Department of Health following a meeting to discuss 'the lost 25%', that is the percentage of women who having intended to breast-feed, and started to breast-feed, had already stopped within 6 weeks. The JBI consists of representatives of relevant professional bodies, namely the British Paediatric Association, the Health Visitors Association, the Royal College of General Practitioners, the Royal College of Midwives, and the Royal College of Obstetricians and Gynaecologists and representatives of the three breast-feeding voluntary organizations (La Leche, National Childbirth Trust and Association of Breastfeeding Mothers). It has encouraged regions to develop local breast-feeding policies and to hold educational meetings.

The following characteristics make a woman *less* likely to breast-feed:

TABLE 14.4   Factors in establishing breast feeding

Helpful factors
1. Advice and support at first feed
2. Unrestricted feeds; allowed to feed the baby at night
3. Confident the baby would be brought back if required to feed
4. Staff flexible and midwives good with their help
5. Special care baby unit staff very helpful
6. Good community midwife support for 27 days with difficulties

Unhelpful factors
1. Not shown how; no-one stayed to help
2. Auxiliary in hospital undermining confidence
3. Feeding on demand 'every 4 hours'
4. Unsure if staff would give baby a bottle and did not sleep
5. No privacy
6. Different visiting midwives all giving conflicting advice
7. Regular weight measurement
8. Emphasis on passage of stools
9. Use of supplement feeding
10. Maternal dietary modifications
11. Concept of 'dehydration'

Modified from ref. 8.

- no previous experience
- lower social class or single
- lower education level
- cigarette smoking
- living in Scotland and the Northern England.

Table 14.4 summarizes the factors that have been found to be both helpful and unhelpful in establishing breast-feeding.

Scandinavia has managed to achieve a dramatic improvement in its breast-feeding rates since the 1970s where breast-feeding at 3 months has increased from 30% to almost 90%.[7] This was as a result of deliberate changes in policy. There were changes in maternity ward practice with no supplementary feeding and feeding on demand. Better information was provided, and there was close mother to mother support. There is prolonged maternity leave granted and there is a much smaller commercial market for the manufacturers of formula feeds to have an over-important influence.

Professionals in this country must be consistent with the advice that they give to mothers, but better education must be available from the earliest age, so that a breast-feeding mother is seen as the norm, rather than at times made to feel an outcast. The excellent booklet, *Successful Breastfeeding*,[8] published in 1988 by the Royal College of Midwives, and circulated in 1991 to all general practices

TABLE 14.5   Timetable for introduction of solids

Age (months)	Foods
1–4	Breast milk only
4–6	Cereals
6–7	Vegetables (pureed)
8–9	Finger foods (rusks, bananas and chopped junior foods)
9	Meat, citrus juice (from a cup)
10	Egg yolk (cooked), bite-sized cooked foods
12	Whole egg, most table food, fresh milk

TABLE 14.6   Nutrient content (%) of household diet in the UK by food group, 1989

Food group	Energy	Protein	Fat	Carbohydrate	Dietary fibre	Calcium	Vit A	Vit C
Milk and milk products	14	23	17	7	–	58	16	5
Meat	16	30	26	2	2	3	30	2
Fish	2	5	2	–	–	2	–	–
Eggs	1	3	2	0	0	1	3	0
Fats	14	1	34	–	0	1	19	–
Sugar and preserves	6	–	–	14	–	–	–	1
Vegetables	10	10	4	15	40	7	30	43
Fruit	4	2	1	7	10	2	1	46
Cereals	31	26	12	51	45	25	1	1
Beverages and other foods	3	2	2	3	2	3	1	1

Data from ref. 13.

in England is full of excellent and well-documented advice. A timetable for the ideal introduction of solids is shown in Table 14.5.

CHILDREN

Children should have a balanced diet and eat from the four basic food groups (fish or meat, cereals, milk and cheese, fruit and vegetables) each day — variety is important. Sweet and sugary foods should be rationed and not eaten between meals as a rule. Cereals, bread, vegetables and fruit can be eaten in abundance; milk, cheese, yoghurt, lean meat, fish and eggs eaten in moderation, and butter and margarine eaten sparingly. Since 1980, local authorities are no longer obliged to provide school meals for most children. Whereas the nutritional content of such foods was previously controlled by statute to cover one third of the child's energy needs and 42% of the protein needs, this is no longer the case. Consequently children choose what they like (chips with everything) and the balanced diet suffers. Fast foods and confectionary are eaten instead of proper meals. Soft drinks, often full of sugar and providing only empty calories, replace milk as a convenience drink, thus the intake of calcium is reduced. At peak growth rates some 1300–1400 mg per day of calcium are required in the diet. Other nutrients such as iron, zinc, vitamins A and C, may also be lower than recommended levels.

ADOLESCENTS

Obesity affects about 10% of boys and girls. Of equal concern is the adolescent girl who believes she is not as thin as she would like to be. Dieting and fasting may be attempted, and in a small minority this may go on to anorexia nervosa (1% of middle class girls aged 15–25 years). A young female with a BMI of 18 or less should be carefully watched. A small number of patients with anorexia nervosa do not recover but progress to bulimia nervosa; here the main feature is a cycle of fasting and gross overeating. The prognosis is not good.

THE ELDERLY

The elderly are a particular problem. Several surveys have shown serious deficiencies in their diet. One Department of Health study found that 7% of the elderly, living by themselves in their own homes, were clinically malnourished, and this may be higher in other groups. Nutritional problems are usually secondary to social problems. Risk factors include bereavement, loneliness, isolation, immobility, poverty, ignorance, alcoholism and depression.

Women need to have a high intake of calcium (from milk and cheese) throughout their lives to delay the effects of osteoporosis (see p. 166). Housebound people should be considered for prophylactic vitamin D supplements. Meals-on-wheels and luncheon clubs for the elderly are excellent means of ensuring adequate and well-balanced diets. The nutrient content of the average household diet is shown in Table 14.6.

Food sensitivity

Food allergy is the term commonly used by patients, but technically allergies should be confined to proven immunological reactions. Food sensitivity is a better term.

Intolerance to food additives was first documented in 1959 when tartrazine was shown to cause urticaria. Food additives are added to food for several reasons. Antioxidants prevent oils and fats from going rancid, preservatives stop fungal and bacterial growth, and colours make food more aesthetically pleasing. These substances are not chemically inert and may exert powerful chemical and bio-chemical effects. In affluent countries it has become popular to believe that a variety of symptoms (not just those of classic allergy such as urticaria) are caused by these additives.

Diagnosis of food sensitivity is easy when the response is characteristically early and the food only eaten occasionally (such as shellfish or strawberries), but in delayed reactions involving other systems there are no straightforward tests available. Skin tests are renowned for producing false positive and negative results and are only really useful for urticaria. The radioallergoabsorbent (RAST test) is performed on serum to detect the presence of immunoglobulin IgE specific for the food antigen. False positives and negatives also occur. IgE antibodies may be present for food that the person used to react to as a child but can now tolerate.

Urticaria may be caused by food in four ways: (1) through an IgE-mediated food allergy (peanuts, fish, eggs), (2) through foods containing histamines such as wines, cheese and sausages, (3) foods containing histamine releasing agents such as strawberries, shellfish and pawpaw, and (4) chronic urticaria may result after exposure to salicylates either in aspirin or in naturally-occurring foodstuffs such as dried fruits, berry fruits, oranges, apricots and pineapples. Many herbs, tomatoes and cucumbers also contain salicylates, as do tea, port, wine and liqueurs.

Rhinitis and asthma are more common in childhood. Eggs, chocolates, meat and fish, tartrazine and benzoates have been implicated, as have the preservatives sulphur dioxide and sodium metabisulphide. The stay-fresh spray often used to treat salad and fruit salad in restaurants and hotels contains a high concentration of this.

Eczema may be exacerbated by an IgE-mediated response to milk and eggs. Breast-feeding helps to prevent eczema.

Migraine can be caused by numerous substances including cheese, chocolate, citrus fruits that contain pressor amines, tyramine, phenylethamine and syrephine, respectively. Red wines and other alcoholic drinks, some containing histamines, also commonly produce migraine.

Gastrointestinal diseases. Coeliac disease, first described in 1888, was found in 1953 to be due to gluten, a fraction of wheat. There is much debate as to whether infant colic and irritable bowel syndrome are examples of food intolerance. Intestinal lactase insufficiency is the norm for most Asian and African adults and for a minority of white people. This causes symptoms of diarrhoea, abdominal disten-tion, excess flatus after consuming a cup or more of milk.

HYPERACTIVITY

Feingold in the USA[9] suggested that children (usually boys) with overactivity, short attention spans and impulsive behaviour, might improve on a diet avoiding artificial colourings and salicylates. Evidence is conflicting and not confirmed on double blind testing, but some children in a Great Ormond Street trial with symptoms of urticaria and overactivity did show signs of improvement on an elimination diet.[10]

TREATMENT OF FOOD SENSITIVITIES

The patient should keep a diet diary and attempt temporary elimination of one or a few suspected foodstuffs for about a week at a time. Lamb is the meat least likely to cause reactions, rice the least antigenic cereal, peeled potatoes, carrots and lettuce are the vegetables of choice and pears for fruit. Refined vegetable seed oils such as sunflower oil should be used. The additives most likely to cause problems — those found in brightly coloured soft drinks, cakes and convenience foods — are:

Tartrazine E102	Armaranth E123	Benzoate preserves E210–219
Quinoline yellow E104	Indigocarmine E132	Sunset yellow E110
Green S E142	BHA E320	Carmoisine E122
Annatto E160(B)	BHT E310	

Coloured medicines and confectionery are best avoided as are products stated as containing permitted preservatives. Pollock et al.[11] found that of 2204 drugs tested, 419 different additives were present, of which 52 were colourings and preservatives that had been implicated in causing reactions. Tartrazine has an instance of sensitivity calculated between 1 : 1000 and 1 : 10 000.

Methods of processing foods

The following methods are used to preserve foods. They either kill all bacteria which are responsible for the decay of food, or slow this down to very slow rates:

- *Low temperatures* — by freezing below −4.4°C or chilling between −3 and −1°C
- *High temperatures* — as in canning (using pure water)
- *Ultra-high temperatures (UHT)* — as in long-life milk and fruit juices (above 132°C for at least 1 second)
- *Pasteurization* — used for milk; kills pathogenic bacteria, e.g. tuberculosis bacillus, *Brucella abortus*, streptococci, staphylococci, typhoid, and paratyphoid by being heated to above 71.5°C for 15 seconds and then immediately cooled to below 10°C
- *Sterilization* — e.g. milk is heated to 108.9°C for 10–12 minutes
- *Irradiation* — gamma rays from ^{60}Co can be used on some foodstuffs, but not

on fatty foods or oils because they speed up rancidity; used for white meats, fish and fruit
- *Curing and smoking* — particularly used for ham, bacon and fish; some smoked fish may be painted with a special substance (Brown FK), particularly kippers
- *Drying* — used for fruits (raisins, etc.)
- *Air-conditioning* — carbon dioxide is used in fruit transportation
- *Vacuum packing*.

Inspection of meat

All meat should be examined by an inspector prior to sale, and to facilitate this work notice of intended slaughter of animals must be sent to the local authority. In an emergency, notice must be sent to the local authority as soon as possible after slaughter.

A full examination of the carcass is made, including organs and glands. All serous membranes must be left on the animal for inspection. If there is generalized disease, the whole of the carcass is seized and condemned, but if only part of the animal is affected, a portion only of the carcass may be condemned.

It is usual to condemn carcasses of animals found to be seriously affected by the following diseases: tuberculosis, caseous lymphadenitis, actinomycosis, the cysticercal stages of *Taenia solium*, of *T.saginata* and also of *Trichinella spiralis*. All condemned meat should be clearly stained with a green dye and subjected to heat treatment before it is removed from the abattoir. Careful legal standards are maintained for slaughterhouses, and all slaughtermen must be licensed.

SHELLFISH

Shellfish are often infected with typhoid or paratyphoid bacteria if collected from areas liable to be contaminated with sewage. Many beaches are contaminated by authorities discharging crude sewage into the sea or estuaries, and have been made prohibited areas for the collection of shellfish. Oysters and mussels are cleansed by placing them for 2 weeks in sea water which has been sterilized with chlorine, but from which all traces of chlorine have been subsequently removed.

Food control

Environmental health officers randomly check for adulteration of foods and drinks, and also the premises where food production is carried out. The Food Hygiene

(General) Regulations 1970 aim to eliminate the contamination of food in shops, restaurants and factories. The regulations cover many different aspects of food hygiene including hygiene of personnel, premises, cleanliness of equipment, protection of food from other contamination, carriage and wrapping of foods.

The Food Safty Act came into operation on 1st January 1991 and gives comprehensive powers to deal with new developments in food technology. It also widens the definition of food to include water after it has left the tap and dietary supplements.

Premises must have adequate washing facilities, adequate light and ventilation, and provide first-aid materials. Temperatures at which foodstuffs must be kept are laid down and precautions must be taken to prevent food infections. Any food handler suffering from typhoid or paratyphoid fever, salmonella infection, amoebic or bacilliary dysentery or staphylococcal infection likely to cause food poisoning must notify the local Director of Public Health.

Dietary recommendations

The following proposals were made by the National Advisory Committee on Nutritional Education (1983)[12] set up by the Government to advise on nutrition:

1. Total fats should be reduced from 38%, first to average 34% of calorie intake and eventually 30%.
2. Saturated fat intake should be reduced from the present 18%, first to average 15% of calorie intake and eventually 10%.
3. Polyunsaturated fats may be increased in the medium term from their present 4% to 5% of calories.
4. Sugars should be reduced by 10% during the 1980s, in particular the intake between meals from confectionery and soft drinks.
5. Dietary fibre should be increased from about 20 g per day at present to 25 g (and eventually 30 g) by increasing consumption of whole grain cereals, vegetables and fruit.
6. Salt should be reduced by 10% for a start, mainly by adding less in cooking and at table. Eventually it would be desirable if salt intakes fell by 25%.
7. Alcohol intake should be reduced. The aim should be to reduce to less than four drinks per day.
8. Protein intakes should not be altered, but other recommendations imply that more of the protein should be of vegetable origin.

References

1. Trowell HC Burkitt DP. Western diseases, their emergence and prevention. London: Edward Arnold. 1981.
2. McNinch AW, Tripp JH. Haemorrhagic disease in the newborn in the British Isles. A two year prospective study. Br. Med. J. 1991, **303**: 1105–1109.
3. Medical Research Council. Prevention of Neural Tube Defects. Results of the Medical Research Council Vitamins Study. MRC Vitamins Study Research Group. Lancet 1991, **338**: 131–137.
4. Young E, Patel S, Stoneham M *et al.* The prevalence of reaction to food additives in a survey population. J. Roy. Coll. Physicians London 1987, **21**: 241–247.
5. Health of the Nation. (Cm 1523). London: HMSO. 1991.
6. Department of Health. Present Day Practice in Infant Feeding. London: HMSO. 1988.
7. Helsing E. Supporting breastfeeding. What governments and health workers can do. European experiences. Int. J. Gynaecol. Obstet. 1990, Suppl. 4.
8. Royal College of Midwives. Succesful breastfeeding — a practical guide for midwives (and others supporting breastfeeding mothers). London: Royal College of Midwives. 1988.
9. Feingold BF. Hyperkinesis and learning difficulties linked to artificial food flavors and colors. Am. J. Nursing 1975, **75**: 797–803.
10. Egger J *et al.* Controlled trial of oligoantigenic treatment in the hyperkinetic syndrome. Lancet 1985, **i**: 540–5.
11. Pollock *et al.* Survey of colourings and preservatives in drugs. Br. Med. J. 1989, **299**: 649–651.
12. National Advisory Committee on Nutrition Education. Proposals for nutritional guidelines in Britain. A Discussion Paper. London: Health Education Authority. 1983.
13. Central Statistical Office. Social Trends 1991. London: HMSO.
14. Truswell AS. ABC of Nutrition. London: BMA. 1992.

PART TWO —

PUBLIC HEALTH AND SOCIAL SERVICES

15

History of Public and Community Health and Social Services

The history of public and preventive medicine and social services in Britain is an integral part of the social history of the last 200 years. Before the middle of the 18th century, medicine had been intensely individual and almost completely curative in character. Although there had been repeated epidemics of serious infectious disease, little had been achieved in preventing illness. The first preventive measure came with Jenner's discovery in 1790 that an infection with cowpox protected the individual against smallpox, but the mechanism of this protection was incompletely and imperfectly understood. This was not surprising as Jenner made his discovery 90 years before the first pathogenic bacteria were demonstrated by Koch.

To understand how our system of public preventive medicine and social services developed, it is important to sketch the social conditions in the 18th and 19th centuries. In the UK the one outstanding feature of these times was the tremendous change which occurred in the pattern of life. It was the time of the great inter-related agricultural and industrial revolutions. In the early part of the 18th century (1720–50), England was essentially a rural community in which farming was the main industry and was carried out in many small-holdings. The village was self-supporting, and industry as such was mainly centred in the home, for it was the time of the home craftsman. Spinning of wool served as an occupation for the wife and children of the struggling peasant farmer. There was, however, considerable stability within the village community. Roads were poor and consequently the ordinary villager rarely travelled beyond the town which served as a market centre for the countryside around. This was the pattern of life in England which had hardly altered for many centuries.

Seventy years later (1820), the picture was quite different — the pattern of life and mode of farming in the country areas had changed completely and there had been a great forced migration of country folk to the new, ugly, industrial towns which had mushroomed up in the North, the Midlands, South Wales and the industrial area of Scotland. This remarkable change commenced with advances in farming. The enclosure of open fields developed, forming a system of hedged fields so characteristic of our countryside, allowing for more efficient farming methods with proper scientific rotation of crops. This proved so successful that more and more pressure was brought on Parliament to accelerate this change, which it did by introducing various Enclosure Acts. Small farms amalgamated and the size of holdings greatly increased. However, the significant result on the social conditions of the people was the great reduction in the numbers of independent peasants who could farm. At the same time, important discoveries by Arkwright in 1769 had soon resulted in all spinning being undertaken in workshops or factories, and the profitable work of the peasant's wife and children (spinning at home) was removed.

Industrial revolution

The independence of the country peasant had disappeared and the drift from the countryside began — many seeking a new way of life in the rapidly expanding industrial towns. Very soon it became obvious that these changes in the pattern of agricultural life which had led to much greater efficiency of cultivation were unfortunately producing social problems. There was a great increase in the number of agricultural labourers without any land, who became increasingly more dependent upon the new class of landlord farmers. Soon there was more and more poverty among the peasants and the living conditions of many of them deteriorated.

These changes coincided with a rapid rise in the population — this aggravated the position, as the market price of labour fell. More peasants left the country villages for the new industrial towns. New well-designed roads assisted this exodus and the drift from the countryside became a flood. No longer were the young people content to live all their lives in the village — their ambition was to go to the new industrial towns. The villages, now connected to the towns by better roads, no longer needed to be self-sufficient and many village craftsmen, carpenters and tailors lost their livelihood and had to leave. By 1820–30 the character of social life in England had been completely altered.

The rapid and uncontrolled growth of the new industrial towns in the 19th century produced even more problems, and reforms became necessary and urgent. Alterations in franchise in the Reform Bill of 1832 and other Acts extended the vote. In the industrial towns a new ruling class emerged — those in charge of the new factories — and this class soon showed itself to be harsher and more exacting than the traditional country squire who still ruled supreme in the country areas. Conditions in the new industrial towns were appalling. The migration from the country, which the Industrial Revolution had started, made essential the provision of accommodation for the newly arrived workers as close as possible to the new factories. This was done by large-scale building of overcrowded and ill-designed houses. Every possible expedient was used to crowd in the dwellings, and back-to-back houses (joined at the back as well as sides) were introduced together with many other unsatisfactory devices. Within a few years, vast areas of slums were created in many towns. It is difficult today to understand how such deplorable development was allowed, but there were no effective local authorities or any other form of local control.

The rapidly developing factories demanded large-scale finance from the owners, and a very competitive industrial age had started. It commenced with the ordinary workers of the factories being very ill-organized — later the trade union movement slowly developed in the face of acute opposition. It is easy to be highly critical of many of the factory owners, but it is important to remember that these changes followed closely on the dreadful atrocities of the French Revolution. This was the image always in the minds of those in charge and, although changes were slowly accepted, any signs of organized labour were always looked upon as possibly highly dangerous. This meant that, during 1830–60, changes came slowly and hesitantly.

Problems of poverty

The large-scale migration of peasants from the countryside to the new industrial towns not only produced much overcrowding, but also much poverty. It soon became apparent that the Poor Laws, which had virtually been unchanged since the time of Elizabeth I, were quite inadequate to deal with this problem. These laws had given to the parish the responsibility of relieving poverty, and under the stable self-sufficient village community before the 18th century they had worked satisfactorily, but under the new conditions of mass movement of populations they soon proved inadequate. In 1834 a completely new Poor Law was created by the Poor Law Amendment Act. Although introduced to improve the conditions of those in poverty, it soon produced exactly the opposite effect. Wages at this time were very low — there was no accepted minimum wage — and there was an excess of labour. Hours of work were very long and conditions in industry generally very bad. The new Act created a National Poor Law Commissioner and Boards of Guardians to administer the Poor Law locally over a number of parishes. The overriding principle behind the new Poor Law was to provide an adequate system, but to avoid at all costs making unemployment and the consequent poverty at all attractive. No direct financial help was given, but in its place the workhouse system was created to house those in poverty. Conditions in the new workhouses, built in all the new towns, soon became much worse than in industry, so that no one in the workhouse could ever be in doubt that he or she was living in less attractive circumstances than outside.

These workhouses were grim indeed — families were split up, men to one part, women to another and children to a third. Discipline was harsh and the food bad. Inmates included those who were ill, crippled, mentally disabled or aged and who could not work, and all were badly looked after. It created a loathing of Poor Law by the ordinary person which still exists today in the minds of the oldest members of our community.

Much discussion developed regarding the best way to mitigate the obvious social problems of this period. Two main schools of thought developed — the humanist and humanitarian views. Both were agreed that reforms were urgent, but for different reasons. The humanitarian school advocated reform because it was considered to be immoral to leave unchanged the appalling social conditions of the working populations of the industrial towns. Lord Shaftesbury, who spent so long working to improve conditions, was a leading figure of this group. It is interesting and revealing to see how little help he obtained from the church or the medical profession. It has been a regular feature of social and preventive medical history that reforms are usually vigorously opposed, particularly by the medical profession, and this trend has continued during the 20th century.

But the other view — that of the humanist — proved to be more telling in producing reforms. This school argued that it was unwise to force such a harsh system on the poor and ill because, by doing so, it was more likely that pauperism would be made permanent. Illness was shown to be a greater cause of poverty than laziness. In this case, to deal harshly with a person was to make it much more difficult and perhaps impossible for them to overcome poverty; in fact the humanists preached that the new system of Poor Law and harsh treatment only tended to produce a vicious circle and increase poverty. Slowly the views of the reformers were having an effect. The first changes were shown in the new laws concerning the employment of children and women. In a very halting way, the hours both were permitted to work were reduced, but often the new laws were ignored by unscrupulous factory owners.

Start of medical statistics

In this stormy period of social change, many other important developments were first recorded. In 1837, a great step forward was taken by the appointment of a medical statistician, William Farr. As explained in Part 1, the very essence of preventive medicine is connected with the assessment of the changing problems of health and social conditions of any community. The only way to do this is by careful collection and analysis of records of illness and various vicissitudes of life — births, marriages and deaths. William Farr was the first person to tackle this problem efficiently, and his value in this age of social change was considerable. For the first time it became possible to estimate the extent of disease and this emphasized the deficiencies of the medical services. Farr's careful analysis did a great deal to measure the mortality problems in the country, and his remarkable administrative ability laid the foundation for one of the most efficient government departments — that of the Registrar General. It also soon resulted in a close connection being demonstrated between poor social conditions and ill health.

Establishment of the Board of Health

During 1839–43, Edwin Chadwick, a lawyer who had been very much concerned with Poor Law reform, and a London general practitioner, Dr Southwood Smith, instigated various inquiries into living conditions of the poor. The results were published and contained graphic descriptions of the dreadful plight of many people, and stressed the connection between chronic sickness and poverty. These reports did much to arouse the members of both Houses of Parliament and a Royal Commission to inquire into the Health of Towns was set up in 1843. Its reports advocated many reforms, including the establishment of adequate local control over various sanitary conditions in the towns. A few towns acted quickly; these included Liverpool, where in 1847 a doctor to be responsible for the health of the community was appointed — the first Medical Officer of Health.

In this atmosphere of impending change, the sudden appearance in 1847 of another outbreak of cholera had the immediate effect of forcing the Government to act swiftly. The first Public Health Act was passed in 1848, setting up a central national body — a General Board of Health — for a period of 5 years. Original members included Lord Shaftesbury and Edwin Chadwick, and Dr Southwood Smith was appointed a little later. The Board was given widespread powers to remove public health nuisances and functioned quite separately from Parliament. Chadwick, the salaried officer of the Board, although efficient had the unfortunate habit of making himself extremely unpopular. Although the Board strove hard, it had the great disadvantage of having no well-organized local body to put its recommendations into immediate effect. It was also advising without adequate medical understanding on the method of spread of cholera (this was only worked out by Snow in 1854). Criticism of the Board of Health mounted and when its first 5-year period came to be renewed, Chadwick and Southwood Smith were dismissed and the Board itself was renewed on an annual basis.

DEMONSTRATION OF METHOD OF SPREAD OF CHOLERA

Cholera again broke out in 1854 and in this epidemic Dr (later Sir) John Snow demonstrated epidemiologically that cholera was spread by water. This, coming at least 30 years before the first discovery of cholera vibrio, was to prove highly significant. Before, there had been no general agreement about the method of spread of this disease. Many fanciful and extravagant theories were advanced, but Snow showed that water contaminated with faeces could lead to the spread of cholera. At about the same time William Budd in Bristol also showed that typhoid fever, a much commoner disease in this country than cholera, was also usually spread by water. It so happens that these are the only two infectious bacterial diseases spread in this way, but the effect was very marked. Immediately interest and effort was directed to improve the standards of water supplies and methods of disposal of sewage. In fact, the main efforts to improve the conditions affecting the health of the public were directed to define and set up a minimum standard for such environmental factors.

Development of central and district health authorities

In the meantime, the Board of Health had managed to drag on annually until 1858 when it was finally disbanded and its functions transferred to the Privy Council. In 1855, a young doctor, John Simon, had been appointed to the Board and he was later transferred to the Privy Council. He worked steadily and tirelessly towards improving environmental sanitary matters. In 1871 a new body, the Local Government Board, was created and took over the health functions of the Privy Council. The Local Government Board also became responsible for the national functions of the Poor Law. This amalgamation of Poor Law and health functions nationally was an advantage although locally the Poor Law was administered separately. Shortly afterwards, a national minimum standard of hygiene was laid down in the Public Health Act of 1875, and the basic standards Simon had worked so hard to achieve were created.

Slowly during the 19th century, local bodies were given the responsibility for the health of the local community. The ancient boroughs had this function given to them in 1835, but the absence of effective local authorities in other parts of the country hampered efforts. In 1872, Sanitary Districts were created in both urban and rural areas, and it became obligatory for each to appoint a Medical Officer of Health. Local authorities were created in 1886 consisting of County Councils and County Borough Councils. Urban and Rural District Councils were instituted in 1894 and assumed the public health responsibilities formerly undertaken by the sanitary districts.

The development of community (public) health in the 19th century can conveniently be divided into a period of uncertainty and change until 1875 and then into a period of consolidation until the end of the century. But the emphasis of all development at this time was on the establishment of basic minimum standards of environmental conditions — good water supplies, good sewage systems, adequate roads, etc. It is, however, essential to realize that this stage in the development of the preventive health services had been reached by the end of the 19th century.

Care of children

Public conscience was slowly changing and, towards the end of the 19th century, there was a gradual improvement in the way in which children were treated. Lord

Shaftesbury had worked ceaselessly to improve working conditions with little immediate success. In many ways the great writers, Charles Dickens and Kingsley, achieved more by their novels; *Oliver Twist, Nicholas Nickleby* and *The Water Babies* are good examples of novels which did much to emphasize the plight of children. Other reformers were having their effect too and the Ragged School movement grew up to help educate the destitute child. A young London doctor, Thomas Barnardo, was so impressed with the plight of abandoned London children that he set up the first of the homes for destitute children that were later to become famous as models of their kind throughout the world. The extent of the problem can be understood when it is recalled that one night in 1870, Barnardo found 73 homeless boys sheltering among empty boxes and under tarpaulins in Billingsgate Fish Market. It is interesting to note the pioneering work in the care of children by individuals and voluntary bodies. Statutory responsibility for children came much later — in the 20th century. The strong influence of voluntary bodies such as Barnardos, NSPCC, Shaftesbury Society and National Children's Homes has been very obvious, and various other church-based social services are still most active in helping with the care of children.

By 1870 education was accepted as an essential public service and elective school boards were established at this time. By 1891 education had been made compulsory and free for every child in England.

Personal preventive health services

At the start of the 20th century a completely different stage in preventive medical history commenced — the development of the personal preventive health services. The reasons for this included the many great medical discoveries which took place towards the end of the 19th century. In particular, the discovery by Koch of pathogenic bacteria led to an understanding of the mechanism of infection of many diseases including pulmonary tuberculosis, typhoid fever and streptococcal infections. For the first time, the medical profession knew the nature of the infective agents of the diseases they were trying to avoid and prevent. Very soon remarkable advances were made — in Scotland Lister produced his antiseptic techniques in surgery. These attempted to reduce infection by operating in a spray of carbolic. Although now replaced by the aseptic technique, the results were startling. From a position of almost universal infection of all surgical wounds, Lister soon had results where infection was the exception rather than the rule. As with so many reformers before and after, Lister's efforts were first ridiculed, but his outstanding results finally convinced the profession. The age of elective surgery had started with all its great benefits.

DEVELOPMENT OF IMMUNIZATION

Bacteriology soon became of the greatest importance in diagnosis. In the Boer War, Almroth Wright showed for the first time that it was possible to prevent typhoid fever by prior injection of a mixture of dead typhoid bacilli into the body. Many thousands of soldiers were immunized and so prevented from developing and probably dying of typhoid in South Africa. Another significant stage in the history of preventive medicine had been reached — mass immunization. What had been started quite empirically by Jenner 100 years previously with smallpox was now beginning to be understood and applied. The first advance had been made which 50 to 60 years later was to play such an important part in the eradication of diphtheria and poliomyelitis.

Start of school health service

The Boer War was an important turning point in another type of preventive health development — that of the medical care of the school child. For the first time in war, it had been decided to examine medically all those young men who had volunteered to fight. On a simple clinical examination, over 50% had to be rejected because of some serious medical defect. This finding that over half the young men of the country were unfit for military service shocked the Government and a special investigating committee — an Interdepartmental Committee on Physical Deterioration — was appointed. Its report in 1904 was a remarkable document and suggested, among other recommendations, that there should be: (a) periodic anthropometrical surveys in schools and factories; (b) a system of registration of sickness; (c) special inquiries into the cause and effects of over-fatigue; (d) a systematic medical inspection of children in schools and of young persons in mines, factories and workshops; (e) registration of stillbirths; (f) a special inquiry into the problems of syphilis.

At the same time, the committee recommended that there should be: (i) a central advisory council to help give prominence to public health; (ii) full-time medical officers of health appointed to all districts above a certain population; (iii) proper reports issued locally and nationally covering public health problems; (iv) more co-ordination between medical officers of health and factory inspectors to consider insanitary conditions in factories.

This report marked the starting point of important reforms including the introduction of the school health service. By 1907 education authorities were given the power to provide a medical service, and thus the school health service grew.

Child welfare and health visiting

These changes coincided with many similar ones in child welfare. At the end of the 19th century many different authorities were experimenting with a new kind of visiting service in which a trained nurse went into the infant's home to advise and help the mother to care for her child. Manchester, Liverpool, Birmingham and Huddersfield were all pioneering this work — the beginning of the health visiting services, which was to prove so valuable in the next few decades.

Quite suddenly, research started into the problems of child welfare and child health. The Chief Medical Officer to the Local Government Board (Sir Arthur Newsholme) was a leader in this respect and was responsible for three reports on child mortality. The first report analysed the geographical distribution of infant mortality in England and Wales for 1908 and demonstrated that enormous variations occurred. The second report made a special study of urban areas and showed that the worst mortality occurred in the industrial areas of North England, the Midlands and South Wales. The third report showed that the causes of infant mortality in Lancashire were complicated, but the most important were the living conditions within the home, especially the standards of the mother. It further demonstrated that the most dangerous period was the first month after birth. These investigations encouraged the development of the child welfare services. A further advance was the introduction of the system of notification of the birth of a newly-born child which enabled the preventive health services to give immediate help. By 1907, authorities could insist on notification of births in their area and many did so. In 1915, notification of births became compulsory throughout the country.

The demonstration that poor living conditions had such a serious effect on infant mortality centred attention on: (a) the importance of improving housing conditions especially in the industrial areas — slowly it was realized that uncontrolled building had produced serious problems and that future development must not make the same mistakes, and (b) the length of time it would take to demolish all the unsatisfactory slum houses. Even today in the industrial areas of this country a few still remain. It was, therefore, essential that personal advisory services were introduced to help mothers who had to live in poor conditions; health visiting and child welfare clinics did this by concentrating upon preventive rather than curative medicine.

Midwifery services

In many other fields similar changes were occurring. Much criticism was aimed at the domiciliary midwifery services. It had become quite common for untrained women to attend confinements, often with most unsatisfactory results. Dalrymple-Champneys demanded reforms, but his suggestions that only trained and qualified midwives or doctors be allowed to attend women in childbirth were ridiculed by the medical profession! (Yet another example of how reforms, no matter how necessary, are so often rejected initially.) He persisted in his demands, and in 1902 the Midwives Act was passed which stipulated that all midwives must be qualified and that it was illegal for unqualified persons to attend women in childbirth.

Social reforms 1906–14

With so much consideration being given to personal health services, it is not surprising that new social reforms in other fields were introduced. The Liberal government of 1906–14 passed many outstanding reforms including:

- Education Act (1906)
- introduction of the first old age pensions (1908)
- start of the Borstal system dealing with child offenders and of probation (1908)
- control of hours of work and the introduction of a statutory half day weekly holiday — Shops Act (1911)
- introduction of the first national scheme of health insurance (1911).

The one outstanding omission was that the poor law system was left unchanged. This was surprising as many doubts had been expressed about the workhouse system. A Poor Law Commission was set up in 1905 and its report 4 years later showed opinion was widely divided. The majority view advocated no change, but the minority view of Beatrice and Sidney Webb was a powerful indictment of the injustices of the Boards of Guardians. The Webbs recommended that the administration should pass to large local authorities, but this was not accepted by the government (such a change finally occurred in 1929).

Lloyd George had a major influence in the introduction in 1908 of the first non-contributory old age pensions. By modern standards the pension was very modest, 5 shillings (25 pence) per week for those over 70 years of age whose income was less than 10 shillings (50 pence) per week. Yet it was a major reform and resulted in a classic struggle between the Houses of Commons and Lords which resulted eventually in the Parliament Bill which severely restricted the powers of the House of Lords.

The Borstal system of dealing with child offenders meant that no child under 14 years of age could be imprisoned. The recognition of the importance of prevention of crime was emphasized in the introduction of probation for first offenders.

The minority report of Beatrice and Sidney Webb did result in further active considerations of the health problems of the poor. In 1911 Lloyd George introduced a national scheme of health insurance supported by compulsory contributions from both employers and employees which provided domiciliary medical care. Only the very lowest paid employees were included and their families were not covered by the scheme. But it was the first official recognition that health is too important in any community to leave to the chance arrangements of individuals. The 'panel' system was to remain an important, if limited, part of the medical services of this country for the next 37 years.

Other treatment arrangements were introduced for tuberculosis, venereal disease and ophthalmia neonatorum. It also became obligatory for Medical Officers of Health to be notified of all serious communicable diseases which occurred in their area. Effective preventive health schemes in all parts of the country were rapidly being introduced.

Ministry of Health

The next landmark in preventive medical history was the establishment in 1919 of the Ministry of Health which took over the functions of the Local Government Board. The new Ministry soon published its policy for the future which included developments in: (a) maternity services and a reduction in maternal mortality; (b) child health services and a reduction in infant mortality; (c) school medical services; (d) sanitation in the community; (e) industrial health; (f) prevention of communicable diseases; (g) prevention of non-communicable diseases (rheumatism, heart disease); (h) promotion of health education; (i) research projects; (j) international health control.

The social problems of 1919–39

In the next 20 years (1919–39), the housing problems of the country became acute, and the first steps in slum clearance were undertaken. Following this lead, many thousands of slum houses were cleared between the two world wars and replaced by vast new housing estates. Many old unsatisfactory living conditions were abolished, but the improvement in the health of many persons moved from the slums was disappointing. One survey in Stockton-on-Tees in 1932 actually showed that the health of the persons rehoused deteriorated on moving to new housing estates. This was because the move meant that those rehoused were worse off financially due to higher rents and fares and, with their very low wages, could not afford adequate food and nutrition. This finding demonstrated that the factors affecting the health of any community were multiple and complicated and that soundly built houses are only one factor in good living conditions.

In 1929, the Local Government Act transferred the Poor Law to large local authorities, but in the atmosphere of economic depression which was present in many of the industrial areas at this time, few marked improvements were seen in the local administration of the Poor Law, and the hideous workhouses with their regimes of bureaucratic tyranny remained. All they achieved was to impress on the next generation the need for complete reform of the system. Then followed an unhappy period of development in which much unemployment in the depressed industrial areas created appalling living conditions for the majority of workers, with many associated social and physical ills.

These difficult economic conditions of the 1930s emphasized that nutrition is a major public health factor in any community. Many of those living in the depressed industrial areas of the North, and in South Wales, showed only too clearly the effects of malnutrition.

By 1934 the maternal mortality rate had risen to 441 and was causing great concern. A special committee of the British Medical Association carried out a survey on maternal mortality, and discovered that many of the maternal deaths were due to factors which could have been avoided, resulting from mistakes either by the mother herself or her attendants. This study coined the phrase 'primary avoidable factor' to describe these preventable problems, which even today are present in many maternal deaths. A dramatic improvement in maternal mortality occurred in 1937 with the introduction of chemotherapy which reduced the dangers of puerperal infection. The establishment of a blood transfusion service later, further reduced the hazards of postpartum haemorrhage.

The 1939–45 war period

The problem of nutrition was not forgotten in World War II which followed in 1939. Although housing conditions in the war deteriorated with the destruction of many houses, great care was taken to safeguard the nutrition of the country with special welfare food rationing schemes. As a result, the level of nutrition of the population actually improved. Full employment with the resultant higher wages also greatly assisted and when the war ended in 1945 there was ample evidence that the health of the country as a whole was better than in 1939. Two further spectacular advances were seen in preventive medicine and social services during the war: in immunization and in social security.

- *Advances in immunization.* A large-scale scheme for diphtheria immunization was started in 1942. Within 8 years the annual number of new cases of diphtheria had fallen from over 41 000 to 962. This serious disease which had been responsible for 2700 deaths each year was already becoming rare by 1950. This successful campaign not only virtually wiped out diphtheria, but stimulated a series of further successful immunization efforts which have now almost eliminated poliomyelitis and reduced whooping cough, tetanus and tuberculosis. The diphtheria immunization campaign also showed for the first time the value of mass health education, which was later used widely to popularize immunization.

- *Social security*. In 1943, well before the war was ended, Beveridge published his famous report on social security which was later adopted almost unchanged. This concept was to mark the final stage in the development of the social and health services which had started at the beginning of the century. An essential part of the scheme was the introduction of Family Allowances in 1945 and in 1948 of a comprehensive National Health Service (NHS) in which a full medical service was made available to all people in the country without any payment at the time of need. The finance necessary was provided by an insurance scheme paid for by a special weekly contribution and general taxation.

Children Act, 1948

At the same time as the introduction of the NHS, a new Children Act was passed setting up an independent child care service under the central control of the Home Office and run by the large local authorities. This followed the Curtis report which investigated the deaths of children boarded out and which emphasized the need to have locally an independent committee (Children's Committee) responsible for child care. During the next 23 years, excellent child care services were developed throughout the country, and they remained independent of other local services until amalgamated in 1971 into the work of the new social service departments.

National Health Service Act, 1946

This Act introduced the NHS. The new services, which remained unchanged until 1974, were divided into three parts.

1. *The hospital and specialist services* were run by 20 new Regional Hospital Boards (15 in England and Wales and five in Scotland). Local hospital administration was run by Hospital Management Committees. The large teaching hospitals in England and Wales (but not in Scotland) were run by separate Boards of Governors. Treatment in all hospitals was free although amenity beds (for greater privacy) were introduced.

2. *The general practitioner (GP) service* was run by Local Executive Councils which also looked after the pharmaceutical services, the dental service and the ophthalmic service. Special professional committees were set up locally, Local Medical Committee (for doctors), Local Pharmaceutical Committee (for chemists), etc., and special procedures were laid down by which smaller committees of professionals and laymen dealt with complaints, over-prescribing, etc. Special machinery was set up

to assist in the more equal distribution of doctors throughout the country (it still exists, see p. 26).

3. *The preventive or community health services* remained (until 1974) with the larger local authorities — County Councils and County Borough Councils. These included:

- health centres
- the care of expectant and nursing mothers and young children under 5 years of age (day nurseries transferred to social services in 1971)
- domiciliary midwifery services
- health visiting
- district nursing
- vaccination and immunization
- ambulances
- home helps (transferred to social service departments in 1971)
- prevention of illness, care and aftercare. Under this heading many different functions were included:
  - services to prevent tuberculosis and assist in the rehabilitation from this disease
  - the provision of convalescent care
  - the provision of domiciliary occupational therapy to help the disabled to live with their disabilities and prevent further breakdown
  - chiropody services to help old and disabled people
  - wide health education services.

The first most obvious improvement after introduction of the new NHS was the upgrading of many hospital and specialist services. This was achieved by the training and appointment of consultants, the extension of services and eventually the establishment of regional centres where specialized treatments could be concentrated; neurosurgery, chest surgery, cardiac units and radiotherapy to mention a few examples.

General practice did not improve as expected in the first 17 years of the new NHS because of shortages of GPs and very few new health centres. But since 1966 there has been rapid improvement with the emergence of the primary health care team and many more health centres. There has also been a marked upgrading of the status of general practice.

Many people expressed doubts about the wisdom of keeping the preventive health service with local authorities in 1948. However, the level of the preventive medical services of local authorities was widened with emphasis on maternity and child health, district nursing, ambulance, immunization and home help service. The role of health visitors was extended so that the advantages they had brought to young children were made available to all age groups. Stress was particularly laid on health education and much wider use was made of modern methods of teaching health matters, including radio and television.

Much very effective work has been carried out in improving medical and social services for the elderly and those with disabilities. Services such as meals-on-wheels, chiropody and domiciliary occupational therapy have been developed to a marked degree. In fact, in all fields of health the emphasis has been on developing services within the community wherever possible. This has resulted in the length of stays in hospital becoming shorter. More serious diseases are being fully investigated in out-patient departments. Geriatric services have developed rapidly for the elderly (see pp. 408–409) and many special problems in the elderly demonstrated, e.g. hypothermia.

Improvements in the level of communicable diseases

A national Public Health Laboratory Service (run by the Public Health Laboratory Board) was also introduced in 1948 which made available bacteriological and virological investigations in all areas of the country. Diagnostic facilities have been improved and have hastened the reduction of communicable diseases. Successful trials have led to the introduction of effective vaccines against whooping cough, poliomyelitis, measles, mumps and rubella, and the numbers of cases of these diseases have now fallen — in some instances to very low levels. The improved treatment facilities made possible by the discovery of chemotherapy and antibiotics have continued to prevent disease. The reduction of pulmonary tuberculosis has been most satisfactory; from an average of 52 000 cases with 21 983 deaths in 1948, the level has fallen to 5204 cases with 390 deaths in 1990 in England and Wales. Many new methods of control have assisted in this improvement; mass X-ray services have been used in many ways. From 1957 to 1959 there were several very successful mass X-ray campaigns in Glasgow, Edinburgh and other Scottish cities and in Liverpool in which about 80% of the adult population were X-rayed and many latent cases of tuberculosis discovered, especially in men over 45 years of age. The introduction of BCG vaccination has further assisted in the reduction of tuberculosis and is still used especially for vulnerable family groups including certain immigrants in whom tuberculosis is still fairly common.

One of the most encouraging features of preventive medicine since 1945 has been the improvements in international health control. The World Health Organization (WHO) has developed into a powerful international preventive health service. Indeed, smallpox is no longer present in the world — a remarkable achievement which would have been impossible without world-wide co-ordination. Many successful campaigns to reduce tuberculosis, leprosy, malaria, yaws and various other diseases have been undertaken. WHO has also organized a world-wide system of collecting and disseminating information about the serious infectious diseases in the world.

In food control, numerous improvements have taken place. Tuberculosis has been virtually eradicated from the cattle of the country and, as a consequence, infections of bovine tuberculosis in humans have disappeared. New stringent control methods of handling foodstuffs have reduced the danger of other diseases.

Maternity and child health

Further advances in the early recognition and treatment of toxaemia and of haemorrhage in pregnancy have resulted in a further steady reduction in maternal mortality to a figure of 6.0 per 100 000 in 1989 (representing one maternal death per approximately 16666 deliveries). This compares with one maternal death per 900 deliveries in 1948.

Infant mortality continued to fall, helped by the improved general standard of living. From a figure of 33.9 deaths in the first year of life per 1000 born alive in 1948, the infant mortality rate fell to 7.9 in 1990.

Environmental health

The Clean Air Act, 1956, set out to reduce the dangerous problem of atmospheric pollution, and already more than 80% of its target has been achieved.

Slum clearance has accelerated in the large cities and other methods of improving houses have been tried. Measures designed to improve the conditions of houses let as lodgings, in which large numbers of poor families including immigrants are accommodated, have only been partially successful.

In 1963, the Offices, Shops and Railway Premises Act was introduced and improved the working conditions of many clerical and office workers, a group which had been neglected in the past.

Mental health

The National Health Service Act, 1946, did not alter the out-of-date law relating to mental illness. In 1959 a Mental Health Act was passed to modernize the approach to mental illness and subnormality, now renamed learning disability (mental handicap), with special reference to the prevention of chronic hospitalization of patients by introducing new and extended community mental services. It is hoped that this will lead eventually to a marked reduction in the size and scope of mental hospitals as more and more of the mentally disordered are looked after in the community. These changes are now included in the Mental Health Act 1983.

Since the introduction of the Mental Health Acts, many excellent schemes have been started, especially in the field of employment. But these changes have also demonstrated the urgent need to develop social services for the mentally ill or disordered within the community and especially to develop adequate day care facilities. In 1971, the education of those with learning disability (mental handicap) was transferred from health to education departments, and junior training centres became special schools. This meant that no longer were children with learning disability (mental handicap) segregated from other disabled children, and their education was integrated into the normal education system.

During the latter part of the 1970s, increasing concern was expressed about the need for more safeguards for patients' rights. The government published a Consultative Document in 1976 followed by a White Paper in 1978. The demand for reform continued and, in 1983, a new Mental Health Act was passed.

Social services development

From 1948–70, there had been large-scale developments in the field of social services culminating in 1970 with the passing of the Local Authority Social Services Act. This produced a new unified social service (introduced in April 1971), which deals with the elderly, disabled, homeless and mentally disordered, with child care protection, day nurseries and home help services. The growth of the new social service departments meant that, for the first time, it was possible to develop social services uniformly. Social workers are able at last to deal with all types of social problems rather than be divided into child care officers, welfare officers or mental welfare officers. The development of new 'generic' social workers in this way did much to prevent overlap of functions.

The profession of social workers is rapidly developing and has an important function in the prevention of the adverse social conditions which can lead to illness and disease. In this way, these changes are as significant as those seen at the end of the 19th century when the emphasis suddenly changed from environmental health to personal health control.

In 1977, the care of the homeless was transferred to housing authorities with social service departments still remaining responsible for social work advice.

It is important that every doctor, whether working in hospital or general practice, understands how social work can assist. For these reasons, there is likely to be an increasing link forged between social workers and doctors in the future.

Community problems and unemployment

Since 1965, many community problems became more serious. Much interest has been focused on the difficulties of immigrants and community relations, and new laws have been introduced in an attempt to reduce problems. A Community Relations Council was set up in 1968 and it is steadily extending its scope and usefulness.

Various types of social malaise have been identified. Problems of drug dependence and addiction have led to new legislation to tighten the rules regulating the prescribing of addictive drugs. At the same time, new centres of treatment and prevention have been developed in an attempt to reduce this evil. There has been an increase in crime and especially in vandalism in many cities. Social malaise has shown itself in other ways including an increase in the rate of births outside marriage (from 6% in 1960 to 29.7% in 1991).

Much research has been carried out to find the factors influencing social malaise, and it has shown that the lack of interest by ordinary persons in the conditions in which they live is a contributory factor. A new movement called 'community development' has emerged to encourage more active participation by ordinary people in all types of problems. The movement has grown rapidly, and the Home Office and government departments have set up 5-year research programmes into community development in certain large cities.

Special programmes called Urban Aid were introduced in the late 1960s to assist towns and cities suffering from urban deprivation. In 1977–78, a further Inner Area Partnership was introduced to attempt to halt the decline of certain parts of London and other cities.

In the early 1980s, a number of disturbances and riots took place in Liverpool, Brixton, Bristol and other cities, and considerable analysis, debate and controversy resulted. An official inquiry under Lord Scarman was held and this pointed out the multifactorial causes which existed. Growing unemployment problems following world-wide recession were incriminated as part of these causes, although there is little doubt that there were many different social factors concerned.

Changes in policing methods have been suggested as a means of combating community problems and some areas concentrated upon more policing in the community with greater involvement of local populations and schools.

By 1991, the unemployment levels in the UK had reached new heights — to over 15% for the country as a whole — but there was considerable regional variation: from over 20% in Northern Ireland to just over 10% in south east England. Many different training schemes have been introduced by the Manpower Services Commission and some firms have started 'work sharing'. Some local authorities have extended the use of their recreational and sporting facilities in an attempt to prevent boredom and disillusionment. In addition Enterprise Zones have been introduced by the government in an attempt to encourage new industry to move to some of the worst-hit cities such as Liverpool.

Chronically Sick and Disabled Persons Act, 1970

This Act, coming into operation in 1971, emphasized and extended the responsibilities of local authorities for disabled persons. Its aim was to improve information services, direct services to the public (especially within their own homes), to improve housing for the disabled and to ensure that access to public buildings was improved (see pp. 520–522). The Act resulted in many excellent schemes being developed and in particular many severely disabled people living alone at home have been provided with a telephone. It also emphasized the inequality of services, as a few local authorities have been very slow to respond. In 1974, the Member of Parliament, Alfred Morris, who had introduced this Act, became the first Minister for the Disabled.

Control of population growth

Throughout the world during the 1960s, one of the most discussed problems was the population explosion. In the UK there was a rapid growth in family planning with extension of the powers of local authorities to help in cases of both medical and social need (National Health Service (Family Planning) Act, 1967). In 1972, these services were extended to include vasectomy, and also all female contraceptive methods were made free.

The Abortion Act, 1967, for the first time introduced legal abortion in the UK if it can be shown by two doctors that the mental or physical health of the mother or children would be seriously affected by the birth of the child. Much controversy has followed, and after an initial sharp increase, the number of abortions performed has remained fairly constant (167 360 in England and Wales in 1991). It is, of course, hoped that this Act will reduce markedly the serious problem of illegal back-street abortions.

Immunization

Immunizations for measles (in the late 1960s) and rubella (in 1970) were introduced. The latter is an example of an attempt being made by immunization to prevent damage to the next generation by ensuring that all future mothers will have developed an immunity to rubella and that consequently the accident of infection during the first 3 months of a pregnancy will rarely occur.

Following adverse publicity, immunization against whooping cough fell sharply during 1980–82 and this resulted in a marked increase in the number of cases of whooping cough amounting to an epidemic in 1982.

Further advances occurred in the mid 1980s including the development of a successful vaccine against mumps. From late 1988, a combined inoculation of measles, rubella and mumps (MMR) was introduced in the UK for all children.

Screening (see pp. 176–183)

Much work has been undertaken to perfect simple tests for discovering early abnormalities which may later lead to serious disease. The cytology test for cervical cancer is an example (see pp. 177–178). In the field of paediatrics, congenital dislocation of the hip, phenylketonuria and hypothyroidism are three conditions in which serious after effects can be prevented by early recognition using screening tests. There are now satisfactory screening tests for neural tube defects (see pp. 102–104) and Down's syndrome (see p. 170).

Such new methods have been welcomed by some as representing a very important advance, but others have pointed out that, in many instances, screening tests are disappointing because they require complicated investigations and it may be impossible to treat the early stages effectively. Controversy of this kind has surrounded screening efforts for various cancers, for diabetes, for ischaemic heart disease and for glaucoma. Although screening tests represent promising new methods of preventing disease, caution is needed before making extravagant claims of their value.

Study of congenital abnormalities

Much work has been carried out in the last 25 years into the problem of diagnosis and causes of congenital deformities. Careful records have been collected of all congenital deformities discovered so that epidemiological studies can take place. Interest has centred increasingly on intrauterine development and the factors in pregnancy which may adversely affect the child. This has also led to a new speciality being identified — developmental paediatrics (see pp. 121–122).

Child health and education

In 1976, a special government committee set up to review the health services for children (the Court Committee) reported and its findings are referred to in Chapter 5. Much of the report concentrated upon the continuing problem of perinatal morbidity and particularly was concerned with the need for the development of an integrated service.

Another special government committee set up to review the educational provision for disabled children (the Warnock Committee) reported in 1978, and its findings pointed out the need to consider that group of children, estimated at 20%, disadvantaged by learning difficulties of all types (including social deprivation).

Integration was emphasized, but the report also recommended that certain special school provisions be continued.

The Education Act, 1981, introduced some of the more important principles advocated by the Warnock Committee, especially as regards introducing a new and more logical system of recording the disabled child and his/her needs as well as encouraging more integration in the education of disabled children and co-operation between their parents and local education authorities.

Health service changes

Primary health care has received much emphasis since 1970 with the secondment of health visitors and home nurses to the team based on general practice.

Special training schemes for GPs have been developed including 3-year course of special experience in hospitals and in nearby general practices. By 1982, all new principals in general practice had such training.

Health centres rapidly developed in the 1970s but since then this development has slowed down — by 1988 approximately 30% of all principals in general practice work from health centres. Social workers have also become identified as useful members of the primary health care team.

In 1974, the first massive reorganization of the health services took place, as well as the reorganization of local government. All the health services were unified in area health authorities which, in most cases, instances, were made contiguous with new major local authorities responsible for social services (and education) — the new counties and the new metropolitan districts.

Many difficulties in the new arrangements were highlighted, and in 1976 a Royal Commission was appointed 'to consider in the interests of both patients and those who work in the National Health Service the best use and management of the financial and manpower resources of the National Health Service'. Debate ranged over all aspects such as considering how good the service is, how it should develop in the future, an assessment of the services to patients, the management and financial resources of the NHS.

Generally their report was complimentary to the NHS and stated 'that the NHS is not suffering from a mortal disease susceptible only to heroic surgery'. The Commission felt that, although improvements could be made, the country 'should feel justly proud of their national health service'. They stressed that future improvements in the health of the population would be mainly likely to come through prevention and advocated that the government should adopt a tougher attitude towards smoking, the prevention of road accidents and should take more active steps to prevent alcoholism. There were also many references to administrative changes which were desirable. Subsequently the Department of Health and Social Security (DHSS) introduced a consultative paper 'Patients First' in 1979. This rejected the suggestion that Regional Health Authorities (RHAs) should become directly responsible to Parliament because such an arrangement would be inconsistent with the statutory responsibility of the Secretary of State.

The Commission was also critical of the excessive number of advisory committees in the NHS, and subsequently many of these (and some national bodies) were wound up during 1980–82, including the Health Services Council and the Personal Social Services Council.

In 1982, there were further changes introduced in the NHS. These mainly concerned the replacing of three tiers of health authority by only two. This was achieved by scrapping area health authorities and making the new district health authorities (there are 192 in England and 9 in Wales) responsible for the day-to-day working of the health services other than general practice. This change meant that the principle of coterminicity of area between district health authorities and local authorities responsible for education and social services largely disappeared.

By the mid 1980s, much criticism centred on the effectiveness of concensus management within the NHS, and a special study was commissioned by the Secretary of State. This lead to the Griffith's report which suggested there was a need to have General Managers at regional, area and unit level (within hospitals) and these were appointed in 1986. An interesting innovation was (a) the selection of a variety of professionals to such posts and (b) the introduction of a 3-year 'rolling contract' in an attempt that no one in such an influential post within the NHS is 'appointed for life', but that their continuance in their post should always be dependent on results (an acceptance of the importance of 'output' measurement).

Child abuse

The question of child abuse created considerable public and professional concern in the 1970s. Starting with the Maria Calwell case in Sussex in 1971–72, there have been many similar instances and a number of inquiries have been held including two statutory ones.

At the end of the 1970s, there was a growing realization within the social services that child sexual abuse was a wider problem than had previously been recognized. This was the reason for the change, in 1980, of the title of non-accidental injury to *child abuse* to include both physical injury and sexual abuse. In 1987, considerable public concern was expressed in the county of Cleveland (in the north-east of England) at a sudden marked increase in the number of cases of child sexual abuse being diagnosed in a paediatric department in Middlesborough. This resulted in many children being taken into care. An inquiry was appointed by the Secretary of State under the chairmanship of Lord Justice Butler-Schloss which reported in 1988. (Full details are given in Chapter 23.) This report pointed out that the damage to children who have been sexually abused is often made worse by removing them from their family, and that a less dramatic approach is needed to this very difficult and sensitive subject if permanent harm is to be prevented to such children. Many different factors come to light in the whole range of child abuse (both physical and sexual), but all studies have emphasized: (a) the importance of multiprofessional co-operation; (b) the need to have clear-cut procedures which are fully understood by all professionals and those who later join the services; (c) better training, including the need to give all personnel refresher courses periodically; (d) constant vigilance which involves many different services such as health, education, social services, the police and the probation services through properly organized Area Child Protection Committees.

Replacement surgery

Since 1970 replacement surgery has become increasingly important. Four main areas have developed in: (a) joint replacement, (b) renal transplants, (c) heart and heart/lung transplants, and (d) the replacement of the lens or cornea in the eye. Initially there was considerable controversy about the high cost of early attempts to carry out the more dramatic replacements such as heart transplants. However, there is no doubt that in all four areas there have been remarkable advances which have prevented much chronic invalidism and blindness and which have revolutionized the treatment of some conditions which previously were fatal.

Hip replacements have been the most successful of the joint replacements, but better techniques to replace knees and other joints are being developed. Renal dialysis prolonged the lives of numerous patients with renal failure when introduced, but the quality of life of anyone permanently on such a regime is poor. It is now mainly used in an emergency or in the interval between diagnosis of permanent renal failure and the arranging of a renal transplant.

The most dramatic operations are heart and heart/lung transplants, and there are now many patients alive and well leading normal lives as a result of such surgery. Some of the most encouraging advances have been with young children born with grossly deformed hearts and lungs. In some of these, the combined heart/lung transplant has been more successful and such patients include children with cystic fibrosis of the lungs. The successful cases are excellent examples of *secondary prevention* in which the worst consequences of the disease are avoided and the patient has their quality of life greatly improved.

The replacement of a badly deformed lens in the eye, resulting from a cataract, by a plastic lens is now a relatively simple replacement operation and means that patients with cataract can have their sight restored without the use of either a contact lens or powerful spectacles which only give tunnel vision. A corneal transplant also means that many who otherwise would be at least partially sighted can have their vision restored to normal.

AIDS

The early 1980s saw the emergence of probably the most serious potential health problem since the large-scale poliomyelitis epidemics of the late 1940s and the early 1950s — AIDS. Because this disease process destroys the human immune system, it results in the individual becoming very susceptible to all communicable diseases (whether caused by bacteria or viruses). This means that diseases like tuberculosis often develop, as well as many other relatively unknown conditions. These are called *opportunistic infections* which are usually harmless to humans, but because the body's immune system is damaged, they now become serious and fatal diseases. Unusual forms of cancer are also seen.

The development of AIDS demonstrates another important fact — that the natural history of communicable diseases is not and never will be static because mutations among viruses and bacteria constantly occur. In this instance, the mutation produced a virus — human immune deficiency virus (HIV) — with new properties which, as it attacks the immune system in humans, has immense potential to produce very serious health problems. Initially the spread of HIV was mainly seen in the homosexual populations of the world, but by 1992 the largest increases were occurring in the heterosexual population. Africa, the country where the HIV originally developed, has shown how serious the threat posed by this disease can become.

Work is going on to produce a vaccine and it is hoped that one will be found. However, it is likely to be much more difficult than in 'conventional' infections which do not disturb the normal human immune system. For the time being, it is clear that preventing the spread of HIV and AIDS must mainly depend on everyone understanding the way that HIV and AIDS spread — either by sexual contact (heterosexual or homosexual) or by contamination of blood from someone carrying HIV (not necessarily ill). In practice this means, for the latter case, that both intravenous drug abusers and health staff such as doctors, nurses and dentists dealing with patients who are bleeding, must realize the dangers they could be facing. Too many people still believe that HIV infection and AIDS are mainly confined to homosexuals. This erroneous view is resulting in many more cases being caused by normal heterosexual intercourse.

Health education is, at present, the most important method of prevention. As HIV carriers become more common (as is now occurring in all parts of the UK), it becomes increasingly essential that the methods of spread are better understood so that people can avoid infection. This either means regulating sexual behaviour — limiting this to one constant sexual contact — or by using the protection of condoms.

Reorganization of the Department of Health and Social Security (DHSS)

In 1988, the DHSS, which was then responsible for the health services, the personal social services and for social security was split into:

- Department of Health responsible for the NHS and personal social services
- Department of Social Security responsible for all financial benefits and income support.

This change was a natural development which followed the growth of both the NHS and of the social security system.

Public health development

In 1988, an important report entitled 'Public Health in England' was issued.[2] Following its recommendations, the Department of Health issued a circular[3] which, for the first time, gave health authorities the responsibilities of assessing the health needs of their populations, of allocating resources according to these identified needs and of evaluating the outcome. The circular also required every health authority to appoint a *Director of Public Health* (DPH) to advise them on the discharge of these responsibilities and who must each year provide an Annual Report on the health of the local population. This statutory appointment of a DPH is interesting for until 1974 the Medical Officer of Health for each district had carried out almost precisely the same duties — it is curious how little is really new and how history repeats itself!

Reforms of the NHS

The 1980s produced considerable managerial changes in the hospital services, but the effect of these was disappointing. Much debate followed, and it become clear there was widespread concern about the future development of the hospital and consultant services. Early in 1989 the government finally published a White Paper called 'Working for Patients' which set out plans to reform the NHS. Having first emphasized the achievements of the NHS, it pointed out that there was an urgent need of change and that the reforms should have as their main objective the provision of a better service for patients. The White Paper went on the propose:

- more delegation of responsibility to local level in the hope that this would make the NHS more responsive to the needs of local people

- self-governing hospitals to be created, which should encourage more freedom to develop a particular hospital's services
- new funding arrangements to enable patients to be treated across the rigid boundaries which seemed to have developed gradually within the NHS; one of the aims of this change was the reduction of waiting list times for hospital patients
- the creation of 100 additional consultant posts (to be funded by extra resources provided by the Government) during 1989–92
- GPs budgets to be introduced initially only in the largest general practices
- better audit arrangements.

Although much further debate and controversy followed, new legislation — the National Health Service and Community Care Act 1989 — was introduced and received the Royal Assent in June 1990. At the same time, a new GP contract was published and implemented in 1990. This should provide many opportunities for the family doctor to play a much more important preventive role. Under the new contract, all GPs have to make certain that all of their patients aged 16–74 years who have not seen the doctor during the last 3 years are given an appointment when certain health checks are carried out. Nurses, who work increasingly in general practice, carry out many of these essential health checks. For patients aged 75 years and over, a wider and more extensive health check system was introduced, and if needed a home visit had to be carried out. Other radical changes introduced included child health surveillance examinations and minor surgery.

Another advance was the complete modernization of all patient records in general practice to enable, with the help of computers, more helpful data collection and research to take place in general practice as well as improving methods for the recall of patients for immunization and screening tests. Also, it became possible for a complete medical history to be sent with a patient who is either visiting or being admitted to hospital.

The reforms of the NHS introduced by the National Health Service and Community Care Act 1989 covered many aspects, and those concerned 'with the split between purchasers and providers were especially significant'.[4] The full details of these and the other important changes are fully described in Chapter 1. Medical audit also formed an important part of these changes. The way medical audit can ensure that patient care is constantly being analysed and improved is dealt with in Chapter 2.

The period 1974–91 demonstrated how important it was for the NHS to change to meet the health care needs of local populations. The Chief Medical Officer for the Department of Health in his report in 1991 commented: 'In order to do this, DHAs will have to acquire detailed knowledge of their population's health; obtain information on services known to be effective in addressing health problems; define resources; negotiate contracts for services designed to improve health; and monitor quality and outcome of care. Knowledge about the health needs of a population will be a key feature of public health doctors' contribution to purchasing, as they traditionally have a perspective of health care from a population point of view, and the skills to assess information about the epidemiology of disease and the effectiveness of care'.[4]

Community care development

The community care reforms introduced by the 1989 Act are due to be introduced in stages up to April 1993. The main objective behind this initiative was to enable people, whether they need help because of old age and infirmity, physical handicap or mental disorder, 'to live independently in their homes for as long as they are able and wish'.[4] Local social service authorities should increasingly act as the enablers and the commissioners of services rather than, as in the past, always providing most services. Such arrangements mean that voluntary and private organizations are now playing a greater role in providing many services, especially in the various forms of residential care (see Chapter 18).

Local authorities also had a duty to assess both individual and population needs for social care, just as the health authorities did for health care. Considerable debate took place concerning specific grants from government. The Griffith's Report of 1986 stressed the importance of these for many groups, but government finally decided that such grants would only be made for individuals who either had drug or alcohol abuse or were suffering from mental illnesss. There was considerable disappointment that specific grants were not to be made for other groups, especially for adults with learning disabilities (mental handicap), physical disability and for elderly persons.

Demographic changes

The 1980s showed that earlier predictions of a rapid rise in the UK of the proportion of very old persons in the population were true. In 1978, there were 1 in 104 people aged 85 years and over in the UK, but by 1991 the figure had risen to 1 in 65, and the predictions then made estimated that by the year 2000 the proportion would rise to 1 in 50 and by 2011 to 1 in 44 (see Chapter 18). The inevitable consequence of such a change will be a greater call on all the health and social services. In such a climate of demographic change, efficiency of delivery of these services becomes even more essential.

Further legislative changes

In 1990, further changes introduced included The Human Fertilisation and Emryology Act 1990[5] which brings both the creation and use of human embryos *in vitro*, and the donation and storage of gametes, under legal control. This Act also included an important amendment to the Abortion Act 1967 — in future most abortions will have to take place by 24 weeks gestation.

The Food Safety Act 1990[6] came into operation on 1 January 1991 and gives comprehensive enabling powers to deal with new developments in food technology. The definition of 'food' has been widened to include dietary supplements and water after it leaves the tap.

Health of the Nation

In July 1992, an important White Paper, *Health of the Nation*, was issued by the Department of Health. This set out the strategy for the next decade for improving the health of England. Five key target areas were named — coronary heart disease and strokes, cancers, mental illness, HIV/AIDS and sexual health and accidents. A short summary of its most important parts is given in the Preface (pp. xi and xii).

References

1. Children Act 1989 London: HMSO. 1989.
2. Public health in England; the report of the inquiry into future development of the public health function. (Sir Donald Acherson, Chairman) (Cmd 289). London: HMSO. 1988.
3. Department of Health. Health services management: health of the population: responsibilities of Health Authorities: Health Circular HC(88)64. Heywood(Lancs): Department of Health. 1988.
4. Department of Health. On the state of the public health. Chief Medical Officers Annual Report for the Year 1990. London: HMSO. 1991.
5. Human Fertilisation and Embryology Act 1990. London: HMSO. 1990.
6. Food Safety Act 1990. London: HMSO. 1990.

16

Care of Mentally Disordered Persons

The term 'mentally disordered' includes two main categories of people:

- those suffering from all types of *mental illness*; these include persons with various psychoses (schizophrenia, affective and other types of psychoses), neuroses (anxiety states) and various serious personality disorders
- those suffering from *learning disabilities* (*mental handicap*).

All mental disorders are now dealt with under the same code of practice[1] and under the same law[2], but the features of mental illness and learning disabilities (mental handicap) are quite different.

Mental illness is essentially characterized by emotional stability. It occurs in many forms, at all ages, and in all types of individuals. It is as common in highly intelligent as in unintelligent persons.

Learning disabilities (mental handicap) is, by contrast, essentially a defect of development of the intellect in which the intelligence of the person is seriously retarded. It is usually present from birth, but occasionally may be a complication of certain acute forms of brain disease in young children. Occasionally a person with this condition may also develop mental illness.

The Mental Health Act 1983 (which is the main legislation dealing with mentally disordered persons) introduced two new legal definitions: '*severe mental impairment*' and '*mental impairment*'. Both are similar, but vary in degree. Mental impairment is defined as 'a state of arrested or incomplete development of the mind which includes significant impairment of intelligence and social functioning and is associated with abnormally aggressive or seriously irresponsible conduct'.

Note that all persons who are mentally impaired also have learning disabilities (mental handicap), but only a small proportion of those with learning disabilities (mental handicap) are also mentally impaired. 'Mental impairment' is a legal term and people with this disability are liable to various actions under the Mental Health Act 1983, including, in certain circumstances, compulsory hospital admission.

There are four main aims when dealing with mentally disordered persons:

- to remove the stigma attached to mental disorders

- to bring the medical and social treatment of mental disorders and physical illness onto the same basis
- to simplify hospital admissions when required
- to develop widespread community health and social services so that most persons with mental disorders are treated, if possible, at home or elsewhere in the community.

Removing stigma. This is mainly due to ignorance as to the nature and cause of mental disorders. Although some people feel ashamed or have feelings of guilt when a member of their family develops some form of mental disorder, there is no logical basis for such a reaction. Only a small proportion of mental disorders are hereditary and mental illness is quite common. A recent survey in general practice[3] found that approximately 1 in 14 males and 1 in 7 females consult their general practitioner (GP) each year for some form of mental illness. One way of reducing stigma is to ensure that investigation and treatment is carried out at a special mental health department in a district general hospital and not, as formerly, in an isolated mental hospital. This arrangement has two benefits — the reason for the patients attendance at the hospital is not self-evident, and it creates a better understanding between medical and nursing staffs treating physical and mental illnesses.

The investigation and treatment of physical and mental disorders should be on the same basis. In physical illness, treatment is designed to carry out a full investigation, to correct various pathological processes discovered and, if possible, to restore the patient to full health or, if this cannot be done, to arrest development of the disease and to control problems. Treatment and investigation may take place at home by the general practitioner, or the patient may be referred to hospital either as an out-patient or as an in-patient. Once treatment is completed, *the patient invariably returns home.* Even in a hopeless case (such as a malignant neoplasm with widespread secondaries or a progressive neurological disorder) the patient is sent home and remains there as long as possible. The treatment of mental disorders should be on a similar basis. Occasionally in mental disorders, there is a further problem — that of protecting the patient or others in the community from the effects of some mental disorders, such as the danger of suicide or violent behaviour. This entails having to admit and retain compulsorily a few patients in a mental hospital until it is safe again to return them to the community.

Most long-term treatment and care of people with mental disorders is now carried out, as in the case of physical illnesses, in the community. Hospital admissions are only used for some investigations or in an emergency.

Approximately 90% of cases of mental disorders requiring hospital admission are dealt with in exactly the same way as in physical illness — by arranging with a consultant at the hospital. In the few instances where the admission has to be arranged compulsorily, the procedure has been simplified and involves only a medical decision (see pp. 367–369). Special safeguards are also available — see Mental Health Review Tribunals (p. 369).

All long-term care and treatment should, in most cases, be possible in the community. Ideally this should be at home, but if the individual has no suitable home, in a special hostel and then, when the patient has settled, in normal housing (see pp. 373–374).

To enable community care to succeed, special facilities should be available near the home — these include hostels, training centres, special workshops, occupational therapy, job placement services and after-care social services. Most of these are provided by the local social service departments (see p. 372).

Health and social services for the mentally ill

There has been a remarkable change in the health and social services provided for the mentally ill in the UK from 1969 to 1992. There has been a steady reduction in the number of hospital beds occupied daily, and Table 16.1 illustrates this trend very clearly. The average number of beds occupied by mentally ill persons has been more than halved since 1959. When it is realized that there is no evidence that the incidence of mental illness has changed significantly in this period, it becomes clear that now many more people are being looked after satisfactorily in the community — most return to their own homes, but some need more specialized after-care facilities in hostels, or special housing. Some still need occasionally to return to hospital for a short stay after a temporary relapse or to give relatives a short break. Such a dramatic change in the pattern of care has depended particularly on the development of improved and more comprehensive care and treatment in the community.

TABLE 16.1   Mental illness hospitals: average number of daily in-patients and new out-patients in England and Wales, 1969–90 (in thousands)

	1969	1979	1984	1989/90
In-patients	113	89	79	59
New out-patients	213	180	198	207

Data from ref. 5.

Different types of community care have been developed for mentally ill persons and those with learning disabilities (mental handicap). These are now described separately.

Community care for mentally ill persons

HEALTH SERVICES

Most community care for mentally ill persons is a combination of two types of service:

- improved *community psychiatric care* — this is mainly provided by community psychiatric nurses from the hospital which originally treated the patient
- *special residential services* — for those who have no satisfactory home to return to. These include hostels, day centres to help supervise in the daytime such individuals and specialist supportive housing. These services are mainly provided either by local authority social service departments (see Chapter 20), voluntary bodies or private homes or hostels.

There is no doubt that a multidisciplinary approach is essential if there is going to be a smooth return of any patient to the community. Many psychiatric diseases are chronic and longstanding and there is always a possibility that sudden relapses will occur. It is most important to recognize any relapse early before a serious crisis develops. If this is done and the patient returned promptly to the original hospital for acute treatment, many complications can be avoided. Those continuing to look after such persons in hostels or elsewhere in the community are then likely to be much readier to take back the patient after the relapse, once it becomes obvious that if a further crisis develops, the hospital will respond promptly.

Practical methods of treatment carried out in the community

These include work by GPs and the rest of the practice team (see Chapters 7 and 8) and the community psychiatric nurses (CPNs) already mentioned. CPNs particularly concentrate upon:

- arranging pre-admission psychiatric nursing
- follow-up of patients who have just been discharged from hospital to ensure, as far as possible, that treatment schedules are maintained in an uninterrupted way — one of the commonest factors precipitating a relapse is that the patient either stops taking their medication or only takes it spasmodically. In some cases, it is possible to give medication by injection instead of orally; this has the advantage that the CPN who then gives the injection can be quite certain that the patient is receiving their medication regularly
- liasing with GPs and the primary health care team — in many cases the first symptoms of any impending relapse will be reported to the GP or other member of the primary health care team
- assisting local authority social service departments or voluntary bodies to sort out any psychiatric problems which may develop in their residential homes, hostels or day centres.

New financing arrangements

New specific grants for mentally ill persons to assist with their rehabilitation in the community were introduced in 1991 to help social service departments and voluntary bodies. These are provided under the National Health and Community Care Act 1990[4] and were originally outlined in the White Paper issued late in 1989. Originally it was intended to implement these and other forms of community care by April 1991, but because of the large public expenditure involved, the present plan (outlined by the Secretary of State in July 1990) is to introduce this help in three stages. Under the specific grants introduced in 1991, 70% of the cost of each patient moving to the community (to cover hostel costs, day care, domiciliary staff, etc.) will be transferred from the health budget to social service authorities or voluntary bodies. There is no time limit placed upon these specific grants and, in this way, it is hoped that one of the main difficulties and constraints impeding increasing community care will be removed. One interesting factor that is now emerging is that, in several cases, there is no financial benefit in moving people out of hospital and into the community (i.e. the costs of looking after such patients in hostels and with day care, etc., is more (not less) costly than keeping them in hospital. The real benefit is, of course, in the better quality of life many patients now enjoy because they are now living in more normal surroundings. But this benefit only occurs where there is careful planning before the individuals move into the community. In the past, too many such ex-patients became homeless persons living a miserable life in the inner areas of cities.

Mental illness in elderly persons

More mental illness occurs in elderly persons than in any other section of the community[5] (see Table 16.2).

TABLE 16.2   Mental illness—first admissions in England, 1986

Ages (years)	Numbers	% of admissions	% in general population
All ages	51 673	100	100
25–34	7 877	15.1	15.0
35–44	6 846	13.2	13.7
45–54	4 868	9.4	11.3
55–64	4 958	9.5	10.1
65–74	6 560	12.6	8.8
75 and over	12 609	24.4	6.9

Data from ref. 5.

It will be noticed that up to the age of 65 years the percentage of first admissions to mental hospitals is close to or less than the proportion of that age group in the general population. However, from 65 to 74 years the chance of anyone being admitted for the first time are roughly 50% greater than in the general population.

In persons aged 75 years and over *the incidence of first-time mental hospital admission rises to four times that of the general population.* A proportion of this increase is probably due to an increasing number of persons in this age group who live alone, so that hospital admission becomes more likely even in milder cases when the person might have been able to stay at home if there had been someone to look after them. However, there is no doubt that the general incidence of mental illness is considerably greater in very old people.

Psychogeriatric cases (senile and pre-senile dementias)

Approximately 12% of all first admissions to mental hospitals or departments are caused by senile or pre-senile dementias (see Table 16.3). This proportion rose steeply from 9% in 1976 to 11.7% in 1981, but only increased to 12% by 1986. A further increase is, however, likely because of the demographic changes in the population, especially as the percentage of very old persons in the population is increasing.

There are two special requirements for the care of psychogeriatric cases:

- *The need for special assessment in units staffed by both psychiatrists and geriatricians* — there are certain difficulties of diagnosis because acute confusional states become more likely the older the patient. The diagnosis of confusional states and how they can be differentiated from Alzheimer's dementia is discussed fully in Chapter 18 (pp. 406–407).
- *The need for a few long stay beds* for the worst psychogeriatric cases (mostly Alzheimer's dementia in the late stages). If possible these beds should be located in small units ideally within community hospitals. The latest estimates indicate that about 25–30 long stay beds will be required for every 10 000 elderly persons over the age of 75 years, a total of approximately 10 000–12 000 beds for the UK (based on 1989 population figures). In all psychogeriatric accommodation, it is important that there is always a large day activity area, as the maintenance of daily activities is essential if some forms of dementia are to be slowed down.

Types of mental illness

In England in 1986, the numbers of all admissions to mental hospitals or departments totalled 197 251 (83 865 males or 42.5% and 113 386 females or 57.5%). The seven commonest forms of mental illness are shown in Table 16.3.

Although female cases are generally more often seen in mental illness, there are three forms of mental illness in which the preponderance of women over men is very marked (see Table 16.4). In all three instances, the incidence in females is about twice that of males. For senile dementia, an important factor must be that many more women live to ages over 85 years than men (see Table 3.1, p. 62).

TABLE 16.3   Numbers of all admissions and first admissions to hospital of the seven common forms of mental illness: by diagnostic group, in England, 1976–86

Diagnosis	All admissions			First admissions		
	1976	1981	1986	1976	1981	1986
Depressive disorders not classified elsewhere	45 084	34 578	35 249	16 154	10 689	9 967
Schizophrenia and paranoia	30 947	28 988	29 419	5 413	4 417	3 871
Affective psychoses	23 261	23 220	24 633	5 211	4 164	4 206
Other psychoses including drug induced	13 068	13 143	17 992	6 318	5 105	6 078
Neurotic disorders	22 865	19 476	15 269	8 980	6 880	5 269
Personality and behavioural disorders	18 567	15 473	14 198	5 533	4 786	4 386
Senile and pre-senile dementias	10 238	16 039	20 858	5 207	6 191	6 070

Data from ref. 5.

TABLE 16.4   Forms of mental illness in which there is a preponderance of female cases in England, 1976–86 (numbers)

Diagnosis		1976	1981	1986	1976	1981	1986
Depressive disorders not	Males	16 120	10 922	11 740	6 220	3 701	3 737
classified elsewhere	Females	28 964	23 656	23 469	9 934	6 988	6 230
Neurotic disorders	Males	7 138	6 246	4 978	3 058	2 524	1 976
	Females	15 727	13 230	10 291	5 922	4 356	3 293
Senile and pre-senile	Males	3 115	5 560	7 624	1 587	2 215	2 287
dementias	Females	7 123	10 479	13 234	3 620	3 975	3 952

Data from ref. 5.

Table 16.3 gives some indication of how most hospital admissions must be readmissions following a relapse. Schizophrenia is interesting in that 'first admissions' fell from 5413 in 1976 to 3871 in 1986 (a fall of 28.5%), yet the category 'all admissions' only fell by 5%. This indicates that many such patients, now generally being treated in the community, relapse from time to time and require readmission to hospital for short periods.

Compulsory hospital admissions

Most patients entering a mental hospital or unit are admitted informally in exactly the same way as physically ill people — by the hospital staff agreeing with the GP that admission to hospital is required for treatment or for further investigation. In about 10% of cases, the patient refuses to go to hospital even though such admission is urgently needed because the patient is behaving very abnormally or is a danger to themselves (might commit suicide) or is a danger to other persons (is violent and threatening). There are three reason for compulsory admission of a patient:

1. *Admission for observation in an emergency.* Such an admission is made by following the procedure under section 4 of the Mental Health Act, 1983. This section is mainly used in an emergency and lasts only 72 hours. It requires an application to be made by the nearest relative or a specially trained social worker from the local authority social service department and one medical recommendation. The applicant must examine the patient within 24 hours of making the application, and the doctor must have examined the patient within the last 24 hours. Finally, the admission must be carried out within 24 hours of the medical examination. In many instances the nearest relative is reticent to make the application in case the patient later objects. Usually the application is made by the specialist social worker.

2. *Admission for assessment.* Application can again be made either by the nearest relative or by the specialist social worker. Recommendations of two doctors are now needed, one of whom must be approved as having specialist knowledge of the type of mental disorder from which the patient is suffering. Both doctors must have personally examined the patient at the same time or within a period of 7 days. The medical recommendation must state:

- that the patient is suffering from a mental disorder which warrants detention in a hospital under observation for a limited period
- that the patient ought to be so detained in the interests of his/her own health or safety or with a view to the protection of other persons
- that informal admission is not appropriate.

Admission for assessment is carried out under conditions laid down in section 2 of the Mental Health Act, 1983. Such a patient may be admitted and detained in hospital for a period not exceeding 28 days. There is always an opportunity for the patient to appeal against this action to a Mental Health Review Tribunal (see p. 369) within the first 14 days of detention.

3. *Admission for treatment* (under section 3 of the Mental Health Act, 1983). This is the least commonly used method of compulsory detention and is normally used for patients who have already been admitted to hospital under section 2, but who require to be kept in hospital longer than 28 days in the interests of their own health or safety or with a view to the protection of other persons, and when the patient needs to be kept in hospital for treatment. This method of compulsory admission can be used for

- patients of any age if suffering from mental illness or severe mental impairment or
- for patients under the age of 21 years if suffering from mental impairment or psychopathic disorder.

Two medical recommendations are necessary. Admission under section 3 of the Mental Health Act 1983 lasts for 6 months and then for 1 year at a time. Any patient who has been compulsorily detained for 3 years without a Mental Health Review Tribunal must then be referred to a Mental Health Review Tribunal.

Mental Health Review Tribunals

To ensure that no patient is detained in hospital compulsorily unless absolutely essential, Mental Health Review Tribunals have been set up. These consist of three independent members: (i) a president who must be a lawyer appointed by the Lord Chancellor who acts as chairman. For restricted patients in special hospitals, the president must be a judge or a senior Queen's Counsel, (ii) a psychiatrist who must independently examine the patient before the Tribunal, and (iii) a lay member who has experience in administration, knowledge of social services or other qualifications or experience considered suitable. All appointments are made by the Lord Chancellor and are for 3 years, although they are usually extended up to the age of 72 years.

Applications for the discharge of the patient can be made by the patient or nearest relative. The hearing is informal and it is usual for most patients to be represented by a solicitor. After hearing the evidence the Tribunal decides whether the patient should be discharged. There are strict rules under which Mental Health Review Tribunals operate. In all cases the Tribunal must direct the patient's discharge if they are satisfied that:

- the patient is not suffering from mental illness, psychopathic disorder, mental impairment or severe mental impairment, or
- that it is not necessary in the interests of the patient's health or safety or for the protection of other persons, that the patient should continue to be detained, or
- in the case of a psychopathic or mentally impaired person whose discharge at the age of 25 was barred, that if released he/she would not be likely to act in a manner dangerous to others or himself.

In all cases, the decision of the Tribunal must be communicated in writing to the applicant, the responsible authority and to the patient within 7 days.

Since 1983, there has been an automatic referral to a Mental Health Review Tribunal of any patient who has not exercised their right to apply for a Tribunal in the first 6 months and, as already has been mentioned, has not had a Tribunal in the last 3 years.

Mental Health Act Commission

This Commission was set up after the Mental Health Act in 1983. Its main responsibilities include:

- the exercise of general protective functions for all detained patients
- the visiting and interviewing of detained patients
- ensuring that all patients are informed of their rights
- examining the lawfulness of detention
- investigating complaints.

Members of the Commission also, in carrying out these duties, visit periodically all mental hospital and mental units in district general hospitals.

Special hospitals

There are four special hospitals in England for severely disturbed persons suffering from mental disorders who need to be kept in very secure conditions as many have committed very serious crimes (murder, arson, repeated sexual attacks, etc.). Most of these patients have been admitted to such hospitals by the courts and some may be detained indefinitely if their mental condition indicates they are still a danger to the public or to themselves. The discharge of these patients is under the jurisdiction of Home Secretary and Home Office.

These hospitals are situated at Ashworth Hospital North and South (at Maghull outside Liverpool), at Rampton (near Nottingham) and at Broadmoor (in Berkshire). These special hospitals used to be run directly by the Department of Health, but a new Special Hospitals Service Authority (SHSA) was set up, and this took over responsibility on 1 October 1989. Simultaneously a new system of general management was introduced centrally and within each hospital. The Department of Health is now concerned with: strategic policy and priority setting, approval of long- and short-term plans and the allocation of matching resources, monitoring of standards and progress, and review of performance by means of formal annual accountability reviews. Ministers have, for the first time, set clear government objectives and have provided the SHSA with clear policy guidelines. These arrangements will be subject to further consideration when the SHSA has been in existence for about 3 or 4 years.[7]

PERSONAL SOCIAL SERVICES

Social rehabilitation

Mental illness usually affects the social adjustment of the individual and his/her personal friendships and family relationships. Many people recovering from a mental illness are not able to bear full responsibility for organizing their life in a normal way. Special strains are also imposed on the family who themselves may also require considerable help and support. Most of this social rehabilitation and community supporting services are organized by local authority social service departments (see Chapter 20) and by specialized voluntary bodies. These fall mainly into three categories:

- *social work support* provided by trained professional staff — social workers
- *day care facilities* to assist in the reintegration of the person who is recovering from mental illness; these include all forms of rehabilitation including social rehabilitation, occupational therapy, industrial therapy and workshops
- *residential facilities* for those who have no satisfactory home to return to which would help and support them after their illness.

Social work support

Social work support is provided by social workers based either in the mental hospital or units or within social service (or in Scotland social work) departments. Since 1983, all social workers in the community dealing with mentally ill people must have special training and be approved.

Much after-care and preventive work in the mental health field is concerned with the avoidance of a further breakdown and with general rehabilitation. It is very helpful to develop and organize community support systems run by voluntary bodies and self-help groups. The emphasis should be on measures to support the family and to improve social relationships as well as to increase the general awareness and understanding of mental illness and mental health. In some instances follow-up care will be necessary for many years, and this help is always most effective when provided in close co-operation with those working in the primary health care field.

After-care home visits by CPNs and social workers are always best arranged after discussions with the GP and psychiatrists. Unless social workers have very close working arrangements with members of the primary health care team and CPNs, some patients and some doctors may resent the apparent interference and then after-care and visiting may be refused.

The effects of mental illness are often hidden beneath other problems. In some instances, social problems within the family may result from the mental illness of one member. Early intervention can often prevent more serious crises developing. The family may need much advice and help in a wide range of social problems including financial worries, housing, domestic difficulties and upsets with the children. In many instances, being able to return to employment or, if out of work, obtain a suitable job, is most important.

The value of occupation

A correctly chosen occupation can do much to prevent a person from developing a mental illness or from having a relapse. Help in finding a job is an important after-care service. Mental illness sometimes impairs an individual's ability to work in a constructive way, to keep regular hours or to maintain an adequate output when under pressure. In rehabilitation, therefore, it is important that the rhythm and discipline of working are encouraged — hence the value of special workshops and industrial therapy units.

It is the duty of the Disablement Resettlement Officer (DRO) (see pp. 532–533) to attempt to find employment for all handicapped persons including those with mental disorders. It is rarely easy to find employment for individuals who have had a mental illness; they may have lost their original job and there may be a resistance among employers to re-employ them for fear they will again break down and perhaps disrupt their staff. It is important that the delay in obtaining a suitable post should not be allowed to depress the person. *Occupational therapy* should always be available at any special rehabilitation centre for persons who have been mentally ill, as this will not only help to train the individual in physical skills, but do much to restore self-confidence. Most local authorities and health authorities provide such occupational therapy in their care and after-care services, and most mental hospitals and units at day hospitals operate occupational therapy services.

Day care facilities for mentally ill persons

Day care facilities play an increasing role in the rehabilitation of many former mental hospital patients. Such centres should provide a wide opportunity for the individual to meet many different people and to improve his/her social rehabilitation. Many lack confidence and their self-respect has been shaken by their mental illness. They need to gain confidence by demonstrating that they can manage quite well on their own (when they are away from their families). Daily attendance at such centres, which are usually reached by bus or train, helps them greatly to gain such self-confidence.

The functions of such social service day centres naturally overlap many of the functions of day hospitals. Occupational therapy should be available at day centres and should particularly concentrate upon helping the individual to become more independent. As well as this aspect, day centres can help with cultural and educational activities such as the study of art, music, drama or literature. In all day centres, the ex-mentally ill person should always be encouraged to help in the running of the centre.

Table 16.5 illustrates the steady growth in the number of day centre places for mentally ill persons that were provided by local authority social service departments

TABLE 16.5   Local authority social services day centres for mentally ill persons: by premises and places, in England, 1979–90

Day centres	1979	1984	1986	1988	1989	1990
Premises	128	145	156	171	186	202
Places	4622	5332	5545	6113	6396	6979

Data from ref. 5.

from 1979 to 1990 in England. Similar developments have taken place in the rest of the UK over this period.

Residential facilities

Because of the emphasis being placed on care in the community rather than in hospitals, there has been a marked increase in the number of homes and hostels provided by social service departments, voluntary bodies and private homes in the period 1978 to 1988 (see Tables 16.6).

TABLE 16.6   Number of homes and hostels for mentally ill people in England, 1979–89

Type of home		1979	1984	1985	1986	1987	1988	1989	% increase 1979–89
Local authority homes									
Staffed	Premises	139	151	156	158	166	171	171	23.0
	Places	2310	2523	2563	2646	2676	2661	2703	17.0
Unstaffed	Premises	278	390	427	439	476	473	522	87.8
	Places	1282	1719	1800	1824	1957	1895	1994	55.3
Voluntary homes									
	Premises	67	127	148	174	165	139	162	141.8
	Places	1360	1693	1952	2134	2103	2066	2325	70.9
Private homes									
	Premises	46	62	102	156	208	263	319	471.7
	Places	655	865	1219	1731	2432	3123	3912	497.3

Data from ref. 5.

The largest increase has occurred in the private sector (places have increased from 655 to 3912 or 497.3%) followed by local authority unstaffed homes (from 1282 to 1994 or 55.3%), voluntary homes (from 1360 to 2325 or 70.9%) and local authority staffed homes (from 2310 to 2703 or 17.0%). The overall increase in all homes in England has been from 5607 places to 10 934 (an increase of 95.0%).

It will also be noted that there is now a fairly wide variety in the size of the home/hostel used — from an average of 3.8 persons in unstaffed local authority homes to 15.6 persons in staffed local authority homes. Relatively small homes are still favoured because it is then possible to develop a more personal approach. Many residents have their own room or a double room. In most homes/hostels, it is usual for residents to help with domestic tasks as this encourages independence. The unstaffed homes often act as a half-way stage between the staffed home and completely independent living in rented flats or houses. Even in the most independent accommodation (flats and houses) a certain amount of supervision is undertaken by staff visiting periodically, but once the individual has settled down, this visiting is reduced.

The specific grants under the National Health Service and Community Care Act 1990 (see p. 359) and the other financial help from the government in the past has already enabled large increases in all types of residential care, but particularly in the private and voluntary fields.

Comparing the increase in residential accommodation with the reduction in hospital beds occupied (Table 16.1) over the same period makes it clear that most ex-hospital mental patients have settled down in the community with their families as the numbers of additional home/hostel places is far less than the reduction in hospital beds occupied.

There are also a number of psychiatric hospitals which now have special units of 'independent housing' to encourage patients to achieve full independence, and which, if successful, will pave the way for a permanent move into a rented house or flat, either on their own or sharing with one other similar patient.

Voluntary help

Many persons recovering from a long mental illness have difficulty in re-establishing social ties, particularly if they have no family support. Volunteers can be of considerable value in this respect and many ex-patients in small unstaffed homes or in independent housing rely to a large extent upon the help and support they receive from local volunteers. Many of these work from small local voluntary groups made up of individuals who have had personal experience within their own families of mental illness and who recognize the tremendous help which such volunteers can give to patients trying to re-establish themselves.

Services for persons with learning disabilities (mental handicap)

Most individuals with learning disabilities (mental handicap) are discovered in the first years of life. Three features indicate that the child could have this condition:

- *Lack of normal progress as an infant.* Sitting up, crawling, standing, walking, learning speech, etc. should always be carefully investigated. Much of this can be carried out at home by the health visitor (see Chapter 5). All children with learning disabilities (mental handicap) are slow at learning anything and consequently the 'baby milestones' are always passed late or, in some instances, may never be reached.
- *All types of intelligence test* (see p. 138) *show low results.* The Intelligence Quotient (IQ) indicated by the tests is not a precise measurement of ability as other factors such as deafness or emotional instability may give false low results. Provided

there are no such complications, a consistent IQ in the region of 50 or lower is usually a clear indicator that the individual has learning disabilities (mental handicap).

- *Performance of the child.* This is always the most crucial assessment. A consistently low level strongly suggests that the child has learning disabilities (mental handicap). Therefore performance levels reached at school, in all learning situations, should be studied. An important feature to remember is that even though slow learning may exist, this must never lead to an assumption that such an individual will never learn at all. Most persons can learn but the whole process takes longer. Patient encouragement can succeed, but the levels eventually reached will be limited in comparison to a normal individual.

INCIDENCE

Surveys in Wessex, Newcastle and Camberwell (London) have indicated that approximately 120 per 100 000 population has an IQ of 50 or less and are living at home, while 115 per 100 000 of the population live in hospitals or in other forms of residential care. This indicates an overall incidence of about 235 per 100 000.

MULTIPLICITY OF HANDICAPS

Many surveys have shown that in some children with severe learning disabilities (mental handicap), there were other physical handicaps present. For instance, one in three such children also had epilepsy, one in five had vision defects, and one in 20 were blind. The incidence of multiple handicaps in adults with severe learning disabilities (mental handicap) was slightly less.

HOSPITAL CARE

Table 16.7 indicates (as with individuals with mental illness), that there has been a steady decrease in the numbers of hospital beds occupied in the period from 1978 to 1990. In England in 1979, there were 50 000 beds available daily but this had been reduced to 30 000 by 1990 (a reduction of 40%). At the same time, there was an increase in the numbers of new cases attending out-patients in hospitals for those with learning disabilities (mental handicap). This is a natural increase brought about by follow-up consultations with a number of persons with learning disabilities (mental handicap) now living permanently in the community.

Two types of such individuals need hospital in-patient care:

- about half of those with severe learning disabilities (mental handicap), as some of these also suffer from severe physical abnormalities

TABLE 16.7   In-patient beds available and out-patient attendances at hospitals dealing with persons suffering from learning disabilities (mental handicap) in England 1979–90 (thousands)

	1979	1982	1984	1986	1988–89	1989–90
In-patients	50	47	44	39	30	30
Out-patients						
New cases	3	3	3	3	3	3
Attendances	20	22	25	31	37	35

Data from ref. 5.

- those showing aggressive and seriously irresponsible behaviour — these are also classified as 'mentally impaired' (see p. 361) — and who can be subject, in certain circumstances, to compulsory admission to hospital (see pp. 368–369). A few in this second group show such disturbed behaviour (or even commit serious crimes) that they eventually can only be safely looked after in special hospitals (see p. 370).

COMMUNITY CARE SERVICES

These are mainly the responsibility of local authority social service departments. Three types of community service are provided:

- day care
- social work support
- residential care.

Day care

In many ways day care is the essential foundation for caring for persons with learning disabilities (mental handicap) in the community. Day care should be available to all such people living in the community, whether they are living at home or in hostels/homes. Provided good day care is available, many dedicated parents can manage even difficult individuals, because while the person is being looked after during the daytime at the centre, they can get on with their 'normal' lives and keep abreast of day-to-day tasks in the home or at work. Table 16.8 shows the growth which has taken place in day care in England from 1980 to 1990 (similar trends have occurred in the other countries in the UK).

There is a wide range of day care facilities now available in most local authority areas including:

TABLE 16.8   Local authority adult day centres and adult training centres for adults with learning disabilities (mental handicap) in England, 1980–90 (thousands)

	1980	1984	1986	1988	1990	% increase 1980–90
Premises	451	496	527	577	638	41.5
Places	42 337	47 464	50 374	53 032	55 897	32.0

Data from ref. 5.

- adult training centres
- occupational therapy units
- sheltered workshops
- industrial therapy units
- special care units.

Adults training centres

When any young person with learning disabilities (mental handicap) leaves school at 16 years training is continued in adult training centres run by social service departments. Most are now mixed, but a few single sex centres remain. Problems occasionally arise as puberty develops, and it should always be explained to parents that close supervision must be maintained on activities in and outside the home. In particular, it is important that every parent of a girl with learning disabilities (mental handicap) realizes that her disability will make her more vulnerable to the advances of unscrupulous men. Lax parental control in the past has often resulted in such young girls becoming pregnant.

Training in adult training centres concentrates upon two aspects:

- social training
- preparation for entry into a sheltered workshop.

All receive social training in all its aspects including cooking and how to look after a flat or house. This encourages independence and most should be able to look after themselves initially with supervision. Eventually many will have only slight supervision. Hobbies and recreations of all types are included in the training.

In order to prepare a young person with learning disabilities (mental handicap) to take his/her place in a sheltered workshop, it is necessary to teach them how to work with other persons and to get used to longer hours, as both are important for successful workshop placement. It is an advantage if the adult training centre is sited close to the sheltered workshop so that those in the centre have a target to aim for. Often the individual will spend 6–12 months settling down in the training centre before moving on to the workshop. This period is used to improve such things as a concept of numeracy (often picked up in practical ways when doing woodwork, model making, etc.) and improving muscle co-ordination.

Occupational therapy

In all training centres there should be an occupational therapy complex. Occupational therapy is important for several reasons — these include introducing the young person to handicrafts and other creative activities. The occupational therapist can also help any individuals who may also be physically disabled, especially in method for overcoming their problems when cooking, bathing or any other daily activities.

It is not unusual for the centre to arrange special recreational activities in an evening club once a week. If possible, such a club should be run in such a way that those attending do much of the organization.

Sheltered workshops

All social service departments now run successful workshops for adults with learning disabilities (mental handicap). Once trained and established in the workshop, many remain employed there for much of their life. In these workshops, the younger person is given an opportunity to work on many different tasks. Much of the work undertaken is contracted out from industry and includes several processes which are best done by hand or by some simple hand-operated machine. Other tasks include the manufacture and marketing of 'own product', e.g. production of toys. The workshops are run on 'commercial' lines — they remain open for the whole of the year with the exception of a fortnight's holiday in the summer planned to fit in with the local industrial holidays. The standard of work undertaken is high, as it is all carefully supervised by the staff.

Although the sheltered workshop is a place of employment for a person with learning disabilities (mental handicap), the educational process started in the training centre continues. This is often reflected in the system of payment adopted which is usually based on a points system in which points represent part of the maximum wage and are added for good steady work and high standard of production, and are deducted for bad behaviour, lateness or non-attendance. In this way, the individual employed at the workshop quickly learns the importance of hard work and good behaviour. The usual maximum wage is equal to the amount each may earn without any deductions being made from his/her Income Support.

One of the most encouraging and remarkable changes has been the great improvement in the behaviour and outlook of those with learning disabilities (mental handicap) employed in sheltered workshops. Most working in the workshops obviously feel they have taken a big step forward by showing that they are capable of carrying on a useful occupation.

There is no doubt that the introduction of workshops has done a great deal to improve the opportunities and facilities for many adults with learning disabilities (mental handicap) living in the community.

Industrial therapy units and open industry

The success of sheltered workshops has enabled the best workers to move to special industrial therapy units from where it is hoped that they can be trained to take a job in normal industry. Such industrial therapy units are organized in similar ways to sheltered workshops, but conditions and hours approximate much more to those in normal factories. With these improved methods of training and better liaison, with the assistance of the DRO (see pp. 532–533), with local industry, it should eventually be possible to employ more adults with learning disabilities (mental handicap) in 'open' or ordinary industry. It must be stressed, however, that in only a minority of instances will this be possible, and then only after very careful selection and training. Past experience has shown that up to 10–15% of those now working in sheltered workshops should, in ideal circumstances, be able to leave eventually and take their place in normal industry.

Special care units

Most social service departments have now set up 'special care units' within their training centres. These are designed to look after those with severe learning disabilities (mental handicap), many of whom also have physical disabilities. These persons need to be brought to the centre daily by special transport as most are in wheelchairs and some may not be able to stand. The staff at such units include some with nursing skills to help deal with those persons with special problems — some are incontinent and some may even need 'cot' type beds to rest on during the day. Such special care units are especially valuable to enable parents to get some much-needed respite during the daytime, and have also made it possible to provide community care for some very handicapped persons who previously had to stay permanently in hospital.

Social work support

Social workers, mainly from social service departments, provide continuous social work support for those with learning disabilities (mental handicap) living in the community. It is best if such help starts as, or just before, the young person leaves special school and continues into the adult training centre, workshop and, if reached, open industry. Support will also be needed for the family, and it is always ideal if the social worker can become a trusted person who can be called on in any crisis. As mentioned already, social workers specializing in this task need to work very closely with psychiatrists, GPs and other members of the primary health care team.

Residential care

It is always best for persons with learning disabilities (mental handicap) to live at home. However, in a few instances, the home is quite unsuitable. Social service departments, voluntary bodies and private homes have developed many types of small homes/hostels to help such cases. In the last 10 years, such homes have increased rapidly (see Table 16.9).

TABLE 16.9   Homes and hostels for persons with learning disabilities (mental handicap) in England, 1980–90 (thousands)

		1979	1984	1985	1986	1987	1988	1989	% increase 1979–89
Local authority homes									
Staffed	Premises	504	648	679	720	734	741	776	47.0
	Places	10453	12803	13395	13950	14061	13978	14210	35.9
Unstaffed	Premises	206	373	408	455	606	779	824	300.0
	Places	928	1544	1650	1838	2350	2840	2700	190.9
Voluntary homes									
	Premises	99	200	232	284	330	390	520	425.3
	Places	2120	3996	3991	4693	5038	5505	6846	222.9
Private homes									
	Premises	92	163	231	347	439	507	651	607.8
	Places	1653	2275	3105	3908	5074	6135	7588	359.0

Data from ref. 5.

Note the constant increase which has occurred in all types of residential accommodation in the community during 1980–90. The figures in Table 16.9 refer to England, but a similar increase has taken place in all the other countries of the UK.

It will be seen that the size of homes for such persons is similar to that for mentally ill people — all within the category of 'small homes'. These are ideal because they make it possible to provide home-like conditions. Development from 1978 to 1988 saw a higher proportion of accommodation by voluntary and private homes and this has meant that there is now a better balance to choose from throughout the country.

All residents in these homes should be encouraged to be as self-sufficient as possible. It is encouraging that in England, local authority unstaffed homes for persons with learning disabilities (mental handicap) increased from 719 places in 1978 to 2840 in 1988 — an increase of 295%. As in the case of mentally ill people, these unstaffed homes act as a useful half-way stage between the staffed home the individual enters from hospital to complete independence in rented flats or houses.

It is vital that those persons living in homes/hostels always attend a nearby day centre so that they are encouraged to meet others and can spend a busy useful day.

Such day centres also enable an inconspicuous follow-up to be maintained by professional staff. This should ensure that any complications or crises are recognized early and, therefore, can be dealt with before serious problems develop.

Difficulties facing ageing parents looking after a son or daughter with learning disabilities (mental handicap)

Community care has become much commoner during the last 20–25 years. This is very satisfactory, but a new problem is now emerging — the carers (usually the parents) are getting older and older and an increasing number are very worried about what is going to happen to their son or daughter when they can no longer look after them. This usually happens when the carer reaches their late 60s or 70s. At that time the individual with learning disabilities (mental handicap) is usually aged between 35 and 50 years. The only sensible and practical solution is to anticipate the difficulty before it happens by encouraging the person to become totally independent when aged between 20 and 35 years old. If this can be achieved and the young person settled in an unstaffed home before progressing to a rented flat or house, the parents will have seen real success well before any crises are likely to occur. Otherwise ill health or the death of a parent can leave the young person with learning disabilities (mental handicap) in a very vulnerable situation. The parents can still keep in close touch with their son or daughter and they can perhaps enjoy holidays together. It is never easy for parents who have worked so unselfishly to keep their son or daughter at home to act early enough and to recognize that it is impossible for any parent to care for their son or daughter for ever. Unless sensible action is taken in good time, the likely end result will be such a sudden crisis that admission to some home, which may be unsuitable, becomes almost inevitable, and the parents see all their efforts to keep the son or daughter in the community apparently defeated.

Special problems with mentally disordered persons

CRIMINAL PROCEEDINGS

Courts have power to authorize the admission and detention of a mentally disordered person found guilty of offences by the Courts. A Hospital Order may be made if the Court is satisfied that, on the written or oral evidence of two doctors (one of whom must be specially approved), the offender is suffering from mental illness, severe mental impairment, mental impairment or psychopathic disorder warranting hospital treatment. This order authorizes the removal of a patient to hospital within 28 days. The Court may, if necessary, make an order for the detention of the patient in a place of safety, which includes residential accommodation provided by a local authority, a hospital, including one of the special hospitals (see p. 370), or mental nursing home, a residential home for mentally disordered persons, a police station or any other suitable place where the occupier is willing to receive the patient.

Alternatively the Court may make a Guardianship Order instead of a Hospital Order if it is thought that the client should be cared for within the community. It is usual in such cases for local authorities to assume the office of Guardianship.

The Mental Health Act 1983 altered the criteria for the making of a Hospital Order. The court must be satisfied that the offender's mental disorder is of a nature or degree which makes it appropriate for him to receive medical treatment in hospital and, where he/she is suffering from mental impairment or psychopathic disorder, that treatment is likely to be of benefit.

PROTECTION AND MANAGEMENT OF PROPERTY AND AFFAIRS

Once a person becomes mentally incapable of managing his own affairs, he cannot legally authorize anybody else to do so on his behalf. If power of attorney has been given to another person before the mental disorder, then such authority will probably become inoperable because of the illness.

In such cases, the Court of Protection exists to protect and manage the affairs and property of any person who is mentally incapable of doing so. The Court of Protection usually acts by appointing a receiver — usually a close relative (parent, brother or sister) — to administer the patient's affairs under the direction of the Court after considering medical evidence that the person is not fit to do this.

In all cases, application to the Court of Protection (at 24 Kingsway, London, WC2) can be made by a close relative or by instructing a solicitor to make the approach.

References

1. Department of Health. Code of Practice. London: HMSO. 1990.
2. Mental Health Act. London: HMSO. 1983.
3. OPCS. Morbidity statistics in general practice. 1981–2. OPCS MB 5. London: HMSO. 1990.
4. National Health Service and Community Care Act. London: HMSO. 1990.
5. Department of Health. Health and personal social services statistics. London. 1991.
6. Department of Health. Special Hospitals Service Authority. Starting afresh. London: HMSO. 1989.
7. Department of Health. On the state of the public health. The Chief Medical Officers annual report of the Department of Health for the year 1989. London: HMSO. 1990.

17

Drug and Alcohol Abuse

Drug abuse

It is impossible to know the full impact of drug abuse and drug dependence within the UK. The statistics (see Table 17.1) grossly under-reflect the true incidence. Since 1970, the number of people using opiates regularly has risen, probably at least ten-fold. Very few addicts receive their drugs from drug dependence clinics. The proportion of females among known addicts has increased to 30%. The number of addicts notified in England in 1990 was 16 200; of these 6300 were first notifications and 9900 renotifications.[1] These were increases of 20% and 12%, respectively, compared with 1989. Some of the increase might be accounted for by the better reporting by doctors. As well as the medical problems related to the drugs themselves, approximately two thirds of notified drug addicts were reported to be injecting drugs. However, the problems of drug abuse are not confined to just the notifiable drugs. General practitioners (GPs) are increasingly being asked to provide care for drug misusers. The Guidelines of Good Clinical Practice in the Role of

TABLE 17.1   Numbers of new addicts notified: by type of drug, in the UK, 1973–88

Type of drug	1973	1981	1985	1986	1987	1988
Heroin	508	1660	5930	4855	4082	4630
Methadone	328	431	669	659	627	576
Dipipanone	28	473	223	116	113	124
Cocaine	132	174	490	520	431	462
Morphine	226	355	326	343	250	203
Pethidine	27	45	34	33	37	44
Dextromoramide	28	59	104	97	101	80
Opium	0	0	14	23	17	18
Others	2	4	7	4	5	2
Total notified addicts	806	2248	6409	5325	4593	5212

Data from ref. 16.

Drug Misuse were sent to all doctors in 1984.[2] A Specific Grant of £2 million was introduced in 1991 under the National Health Service and Community Care Act, 1990, for local authorities to initiate, expand or improve voluntary sector provision for people with drug and alcohol related problems.

The medical use of drugs is ingrained in our behaviour, as clearly shown by the colossal expenditure on self-remedies sold yearly 'over the counter'. Society's apparent ambivalence to the harmful drugs nicotine and alcohol adds to the problems of education when dealing with abuse of drugs. There is no such thing as a *safe* drug.

Much concern at dependence on the barbiturate group of drugs was expressed during the early 1970s, and their prescription subsequently dramatically fell. The benzodiazepine group of drugs had been introduced, with apparently clear advantages, but in the 1980s these too gave rise to concern about their potential for harmful addiction. In 1978, 25 million prescriptions for sedatives and tranquillizers and 17 million prescriptions for hypnotics were given, but by 1988 there had been a reduction of over half for the number of prescriptions issued for the first group (12 million prescriptions) and a 7% reduction for the second group (16 million).

DRUG DEPENDENCE

Use of the term addiction is no longer recommended, having been replaced by the term drug dependence. This is defined by the World Health Organization (WHO) as a state, psychic and sometimes physical, resulting from the interaction between a living organism and a drug, characterized by behavioural and other responses that always include a compulsion to take the drug on a continuous or a periodic basis in order to experience its psychic effects and sometimes to avoid the discomfort of its absence. Three types of such dependence are recognized:

- *Type 1*. Intermittent consumption *without* development of tolerance. There are no physical withdrawal effects. (NB, not strictly dependence as defined by the WHO as compulsion is usually absent.)
- *Type 2*. Daily use of drugs, often by injection to obtain psychic effect. Tolerance often occurs with other drugs used in the attempt to maintain the psychic effect. Withdrawal symptoms would occur if supplies stopped.
- *Type 3*. Often the drug has been prescribed therapeutically, and is consumed *without* noticeable effect. The need to continue taking the drug is primarily to avoid psychological or physical withdrawal symptoms. The barbiturate group of drugs gives the most problems, but much recent attention has been focused on the more widely prescribed benzodiazepine tranquillizers and hypnotics.

REASONS FOR THE MISUSE OF DRUGS

There is no one single cause for drug dependence. Reasons include:

- *Personality*. Often difficult to assess in retrospect, the drug abuser may show signs of an inadequate personality, instability and immaturity. Type 2 drug users often report broken family background, unhappy childhood, with adolescent problems such as truancy and criminal behaviour. Depression may be an effect of the drug taking rather than cause.
- *Peer pressure*.[4] The pressure to conform to one's friends' behaviour and not appear to be the 'odd one out' may prove very difficult to withstand.
- *Life experience*.[4] The need to experiment as part of personal development, and be curious about new experiences, may be too strong a temptation. It may be used as an escape from boredom, or as a hope of 'instant happiness'.
- *Availability of drugs*.[4] Certain subcultures see the use of drugs as normal, and drugs are freely available. The medical profession itself has a higher incidence of drug abuse than average, mostly due to the accessibility of drugs, but partially due to the strains and stresses of the job.

However, it is important to realize that those with drug dependency problems come from all walks of life, and exhibit very different patterns of behaviour.

DRUGS ABUSED

Specific agents regularly abused include narcotics (such as heroin, methadone and morphine, amphetamines, cocaine, lysergic acid diethylamide LSD), barbiturates, cannabis (pot, hash, marijuana, grass); solvents; tranquillizers; and others including pencyclidine (PCP or 'angel dust').

Narcotics

It is estimated that there are 100 000 addicts in the UK abusing opiates and other notifiable drugs. Heroin first appeared as a problem in the 1960s in the UK. Since the late 1970s the incidence and prevalence of heroin use and addiction as recorded by the Home Office has increased significantly. Official statistics regarding the number of dependent patients abusing narcotics (12 500 in 1984), may under-estimate the true number perhaps up to five-fold. Increased availability has been particularly noticeable in the large urban conurbations outside London such as Merseyside, Manchester, Edinburgh and Glasgow. Imported heroin (and seizures) have increased significantly, and intermittent recreational use (sometimes smoked not injected) has also increased. Relative to inflation, the price of heroin has halved since 1978.

Very few addicts now receive heroin on prescription from drug dependence units. The GP is increasingly being turned to for help.

Amphetamines

These drugs speed up the action of the brain, but rapidly cause irritability and insomnia. Physically the pupils become dilated, the blood pressure increases and the mouth becomes dry. When the drug is stopped there is a 'come down', phase which is exemplified by poor concentration and depression. Large dose ingestion may be associated with quite marked violent behaviour or a paranoid state.

Cocaine

This has a shorter duration of effect than amphetamines. Cocaine is usually sniffed (snorted), but may be injected intravenously. In the USA there has been a most dramatic increase in the use of cocaine in the past few years. In some circles it has become a very fashionable drug. Regular users with adequate resources may use 1–2 g per day. It is being increasingly used in Britain, particularly in London and the south of England. The purified form Crack has particular problems with its use. It is said that dependence can occur after just one or two experiences.

Lysergic acid diethylamide (LSD)

This drug was widely used in the 1960s and early 1970s and recently has again increased in use. The onset of action is from up to 2 hours and lasts for 8–14 hours. Return trips or flashbacks may return without any further use of the drug. Feelings produced when LSD is used unsupervised may be so strong (either beautiful or terrifying), that completely unpredicted effects may ensue (attempts to fly, etc.).

Barbiturates

Changes in prescribing practices have reduced their availability, but barbiturates remain a problem with some heavy drug users. Marketed commonly in capsules, they may be dissolved and injected. Chemically they are a depressant and when used, particularly with alcohol, may cause death by respiratory depression. Dependence occurs relatively quickly and vomiting, restlessness and even epileptic fits may occur on withdrawal. Planned withdrawal should probably be carried out in hospital.

Cannabis (pot, hash, marijuana, grass)

Produced from the Indian hemp plant with the active principles, $^1-3$, 4 *trans* and $^6-3$, 4 *trans* tetrahydrocannibinol, cannabis is a drug which produces a feeling of well-being and laziness. Most consumption of this drug appears to be of Type 1, namely occasional and intermittent use. Medically it may be used in counteracting the nausea produced by radiotherapy and may have value in the treatment of glaucoma. The danger to society is from the change in the subject's judgement and reaction time, important when driving a motor car and operating machinery. Its use in the UK is illegal.

Tranquillizers

When used therapeutically symptoms may only be produced on attempts at withdrawal (Type 3). These symptoms (anxiety and insomnia) ironically may be the very symptoms for which the drugs were initially prescribed. Slow reduction of dosage, substitution for benzodiazepines with a longer half-life, and the use of other drugs such as beta blockers to help the somatic withdrawal symptoms may be successful. More rational and responsible prescribing and use of such drugs will hopefully prevent problems in the future.

Volatile substances such as solvents

There are many accounts of the use of solvents as drugs over the past 200 years. Recently there has been much publicity and concern at the increase in their abuse. The toxic effects of the chemicals may not in themselves be serious, but when used in restricted spaces, or with the use of a plastic bag placed over the head may put the user at serious risk of asphyxia or inhalation with vomiting. There were 130 estimated deaths in the UK in 1990. Most were under the age of 20 years, and males outnumber females 4:1. Glue is no longer the main substance used. The inhalation of lighter fuels such as butane (from lighter refills) is the main substance, with aerosols being the second most commonly used. Nearly 20% of the deaths occurred in apparent first time users. Chronic long-term usage may be associated with lung, liver or heart damage.

Recognition of the problem

Patients may present in a variety of ways with the problem of drug dependence, or a diagnosis of dependency may be made opportunistically. New patients may be given a questionnaire which should contain details of drugs, smoking and alcohol intake. Certain patients may be considered to be at risk; these would include people with a known personal or family history of dependence, frequent attenders for minor ailments, frequent requests for certification, patients with crime-related problems, homeless, unemployed, and those in high-risk occupations. Other members of the family will often be the ones to present the problem and seek help (both for the patient and the family). Performance at work may be the first clue to there being a problem. Absenteeism, change in work practice, and mood changes may well alert the occupational health service to the problem.

Certain presenting symptoms may also suggest drug dependence or abuse. These include malnutrition with possible signs of vitamin deficiency, insomnia, anxiety, blackouts or fits, symptoms of liver disease, recurrent infections and trauma and peripheral neuropathies.

Management of drug dependence

All who deal with people with drug dependence problems must never take a moralistic or judgemental attitude. The person with the problem seeking help must be able to do so, fully trusting the helpers, and feel encouraged to come forward for help. A full social and family history should be obtained. A clear management policy must be drawn up, with a contract made with the patient. A doctor dealing with a person dependent on a notifiable drug has a duty in law to notify the Home Office[3] (see below). The Chief Medical Officer (CMO) reminded all doctors in 1990 of this statutory obligation, and notification should be made if the doctor knows or even suspects addiction. Referral to special drug dependency clinics may be appropriate, but the GP and other members of the primary health care team are increasingly involved in the management of such problems. Patients injecting drugs are at particular risk of HIV infection and hepatitis B (see Chapter 11). The workload dealing with such patients can be very considerable.

If an addict successfully comes off drugs, close follow-up and support are essential. Self-help agencies such as Narcotics Anonymous and Families Anonymous may be of great help.

NOTIFICATION OF DRUG ADDICTS

The Misuse of Drugs Act 1971 was introduced at a time when opiate misuse had become more widespread. The Misuse of Drugs Regulations 1985 reclassified controlled drugs as follows:

- *Schedule 1* includes mind-altering drugs and hallucinogens such as cannabis, with very limited use in medicine
- *Schedule 2* includes opiates and cocaine, with strict rules as to their safe keeping
- *Schedule 3* includes amphetamines and barbiturates
- *Schedule 4* includes the benzodiazepines
- *Schedule 5* includes controlled drugs in preparations of such a dilution to make them exempt from restrictions of supply, possession and prescription.

Any doctor *who suspects* that he/she is treating an addict must notify the CMO, Home Office Drugs Branch within 7 days, preferably using the specially designed form HS2A/1. This reporting is required to be repeated on an annual basis. The name, address, date of birth and the NHS number of the patient must also be stated. Doctors failing to notify the Home Office, or prescribing prohibited drugs irresponsibly, may be referred to the Misuse of Drugs Tribunal, which can recommend that a doctor be prohibited from possessing prescribing and administering specific controlled drugs.

NOTIFIABLE DRUGS

Table 17.2 shows the drugs which at present are classified as notifiable drugs.

TABLE 17.2   Notifiable drugs, 1991

Cocaine	Hydromorphone (Dilaudid)	Oxycodone (Proladone)
Dextromoramide (Palfium)	Levorphanol (Dromoran)	Pethidine
Diamorphine (Heroin)	Methadone (Physeptone)	Phenazocine (Narphen)
Dipinanone (Diconal)	Morphine	Piritramide
Hydrocodone (Dicodid)	Opium	Papavertum (Omnopon)

PREVENTION OF DRUG ABUSE

All doctors should be actively concerned with the prevention of drug abuse, especially when considering Type 3 dependence. Recognition of developing dependence may be difficult, and the doctor must always keep a high awareness of a potential drug abuse problem, being ready to counsel and substitute other drugs if appropriate. Elderly people metabolize drugs less efficiently than younger people, and may have increased side effects. Consumption of alcohol, even in small amounts, may aggravate dependency and compound the effects of the drugs. The Advisory Council on the Misuse of Drugs published a report in 1984 called 'Prevention'.[4] They concluded that the most helpful educational programmes for young people were those that put legal and illegal drugs into a realistic social and cultural context. Mass media campaigns could even be counter-productive encouraging experimentation.[5]

It is with the increasing numbers of young persons involved that the main problem lies as regards notifiable drugs. The influence of the family is paramount. There is a greater incidence of problems in broken families and those where parents go their own ways and take less personal interest in their children. This can happen across the social classes. Health education is important, but is of greatest value when reinforced in the life-style of the parents, and in the helpful atmosphere of a caring interested school. Once started, the drug abuse habit will soon be likely to lead to criminal behaviour in young persons, mainly because of the urgency to obtain money to fund more purchases of the drug. In many cases these criminal activities will lead to the first recognition of the drug problem.

Young persons who run away and gravitate towards the big cities are at great risk. Many voluntary organizations have played a significant part in providing hostels, day centres, counselling and information services. Improved communication between doctors in such areas (whether in hospital or general practice) and these voluntary groups and local social service departments is of the utmost importance. Rehabilitation of those who become dependent on drugs is a lengthy process and failure is not unusual. This often makes it difficult for those working in this field to maintain their drive to prevent drug abuse.

Alcohol abuse

Dependence on alcohol, previously known as alcoholism, can be defined as dependence upon alcohol to such a degree that the individual shows noticeable mental disturbance or an interference with bodily or mental health. It is a medicosocial problem in both its origins and manifestations as it interferes with interpersonal relationships and with the normal economic and social functioning of the person and their family.

CONSUMPTION

There has been a doubling in the amount of alcohol consumed over the past 30 years in Great Britain. Alcohol consumption in 1989 was 9.29 litres per head of

TABLE 17.3   Average number of units of alcohol consumed 7 days before interview by sex and household social class in persons aged 16 years and over, 1987

Household social class	Units of alcohol	
	Men	Women
I	11.4	4.3
II	15.4	6.1
IIIN	14.0	5.3
IIIM	15.4	4.6
IV	12.5	3.4
V	17.3	3.7
Total	14.3	4.8

Data from ref. 17.

population aged 15 years and over, an increase of 0.6% compared with the previous year. Beer consumption has increased by 30% since 1950, spirits by 200% and wine by 500% (to 1981). In 1964 it took a manual worker 6 hours of work to earn the price of a bottle of whisky. By 1984 this had been reduced to 2 hours. Table 17.3 shows the weekly average consumption, for each social class, in England and Wales in 1987. Over the same period, deaths from chronic liver disease and cirrhosis increased by 6.7% in England and Wales.

DEFINITIONS

The term alcoholic is now no longer used, mainly because it implied a separate disease state, whereas in fact any one may be susceptible to the adverse effects of alcohol. For the purpose of deciding how much one drinks, a unit of alcohol is that amount present in a half pint of beer, or a glass of wine, a single measure of spirit or an aperitif. Hence two pints of beer measure 4 units and a treble whisky 3 units. The Royal College of Physicians defines four types of drinkers:

- *Social drinker*. Someone who drinks usually not more than 2–3 units of alcohol a day, does not become intoxicated and is not likely to harm him/herself or family through drinking. The amount that can be drunk without harm varies widely between individuals, but greater amounts than this are associated with an increasing risk of harm.
- *Heavy drinker*. Someone who regularly drinks more than 6 units of alcohol a day, but without *apparent* harm.
- *Problem drinker*. Someone who experiences physical, psychological, social, family, occupational, financial or legal problems attributable to alcohol.
- *Dependent drinker*. Someone who has a compulsion to drink, takes roughly the same amount each day, has increased tolerance to alcohol in the early stages and reduced tolerance later. The person suffers withdrawal symptoms if alcohol is stopped, which are relieved by drinking more. Drinking takes precedence over other activities and is resumed after a period of abstinence.

The Office of Health and Economics [6] estimate that some 8% of the adult population may be defined as heavy drinkers (3 000 000), 2% as problem drinkers (700 000) and 0.4% as dependent drinkers (150 000). Men outnumber women in these studies by approximately 5: 1, but more recently the evidence is that this ratio is reducing.

PROBLEMS OF ALCOHOL ABUSE

It has been estimated that there are between 5000 and 40 000 premature deaths a year as a result of alcohol abuse;[7] 500 below the age of 25 years. The overall cost to the country has been estimated at £1600 million. Between 8 and 15 million working days are lost each year as a result of alcohol. In 1989, there were 93 000 findings of guilt and cautions for offences of drunkenness in England and Wales.[8] The peak age of offender was 20 years, both for men and women.

In the UK in 1988 there were 22 700 deaths or injuries following road traffic accidents where the driver/rider had a blood alcohol level of greater than 80 mg per 100 ml. This, however, did mark a decrease over the period 1979–88; 32% of drivers involved in accidents had illegal levels in 1979 , but the figure had dropped to 20% of drivers in 1988. The corresponding figure for adult pedestrians was 70% with similarly high levels.

Half a million acute admissions a year to hospital are as a result of alcohol ingestion, including some 14 000 psychiatric admissions. Eighty per cent of deaths in fires, 65% of serious head injuries, 50% of murders, 40% of road traffic accidents, 30% of fatal accidents, 30% of domestic accidents and 14% of drownings are alcohol related. Alcohol contributes to one in three divorces and one in three cases of child abuse.[9] Some of these figures may be quite serious under-estimates. Table 17.4 summarizes the conditions commonly associated with alcohol abuse.

TABLE 17.4   Conditions commonly associated with alcohol abuse

Physical	Social	Psychological
Liver damage	Family problems	Insomnia
Hepatitis	Divorce	Depression
Cirrhosis	Homelessness	Anxiety
Cancer	Unemployment	Amnesia
Gastritis	Financial problems	Attempted suicide
Pancreatitis	Fraud	Suicide
Cancers of mouth, pharynx,	Debt	Personality changes
larnyx, breast, colon	Vagrancy	Delirium tremens
Malnutrition	Drink/driving	Hallucinations
Obesity	Accidents	Dementia
Diabetes		Misuse of other drugs
Heart disease		
High blood pressure		
Stroke		
Impotence		
Infertility		
Fetal damage		

CAUSES OF ALCOHOL ABUSE

There is no one cause of alcohol abuse/dependence. The greater the amount of alcohol drunk, the more likely that problems will occur. Social factors are important and there is a significantly higher proportion of alcohol abuse in persons who are single, divorced or widowed. The mean age for men involved is the mid forties, while in women it is higher. The greatest incidence is in social classes I and V.

No particular type of personality is especially susceptible, although both excessively shy people and the gregarious extrovert show a higher incidence of alcohol abuse. People in certain occupations are at particularly high risk. This can be seen from studies of the incidence of cirrhosis of the liver. Publicans have a 15-fold increase in cirrhosis mortality, armed forces personnel a 3.5-fold increase, and doctors a 3-fold increase (see Chapter 13).

RECOGNITION AND DIAGNOSIS

Early recognition and diagnosis are important in helping patients with alcohol related problems. Increasing absenteeism, decline in job efficiency with helpful colleagues covering, increasing marital disharmony and self-neglect are suggestive. The inability to keep to a limit, drinking more than companions, missing meals, blackouts, nocturnal sweating and early morning drinking are more progressive signs of alcohol dependence. Heavy drinkers consult their GPs more often than moderate drinkers. A high index of suspicion by the GP is important. Very often problems may be presented by other members of the family.

The CAGE questionnaire was first described in 1972[10] and asks the four simple questions:

1. Have you ever thought you should **C**ut down on your drinking?
2. Have you ever been **A**ngry when someone has criticized your drinking?
3. Have you ever felt bad or **G**uilty about your drinking?
4. Have you ever had or felt the need for an early morning drink to steady your nerves or get rid of a hangover (**E**yeopener)?

If two or more questions are answered positively, there is a likelihood of there being an alcohol dependence problem. The CAGE questionnaire is very little known and is underused; it is very simple and quick and deserves much wider usage. Other questionnaires also exist such as the MAST questionnaire (Michigan alcoholism screening test).[11]

Patients' drinking problems may also come to light when they are admitted to hospital.[12] Occasionally this may be in the most dramatic form of an acute withdrawal, with the development of the delirium tremens (DTs), or more usually with tremor, sweating, insomnia and anxiety. Very rarely seizures can occur or Wernicke's encephalopathy develops, which is associated with thiamine deficiency.

All hospital doctors (and all other health care workers) should be looking out for such problems.

Opportunistic blood screening

An increased mean corpuscular volume (MCV) discovered on a routine blood test, or abnormal liver function tests (LFTs), or raised serum alcohol levels in patients, may strongly suggest a problem.

TREATMENT

Treatment involves co-operation of the patient who needs in the first instance to admit that there is a problem. Education and explanation of safe quantities, in conjunction with drinking diaries may be used. (In such diaries the patient logs exactly how much is being drunk to show both the extent of the problem and to monitor progress.) It is important to involve close members of the family. Referrals to other agencies such as the district community alcohol team, Alcoholics Anonymous (AA) and Al-Anon (for relatives) may be helpful. Individual counselling or group work may also prove beneficial.

Treatment is aimed at (a) reversing the damage done to the physical, mental and social life of the patient, (b) attempting to deal with the underlying problems and (c) rehabilitating them in society. If there is need for admission to hospital, there are 18 special alcoholism units in the country. There recently has been much progress made with home detoxification with the GP co-ordinating the care with the relatives.

Primary care has been shown to be effective and efficient both with identifying those at risk, but also in assisting them to reduce their alcohol consumption. Anderson[13] has described that intervention at primary care level leads to reduction of alcohol consumption of around 15%, and reductions in the proportions of excessive drinkers of around 20%, and is one twentieth of the cost of specialist services. Under the 1990 GPs new contract, such work may be classified as a health promotion activity, and attract a separate payment, thereby helping with the provision of staff.

In Scotland, the Scottish Health Education group has pioneered a minimal intervention programme for problem drinkers in general practice.[14] This scheme has been called the DRAMS scheme (drinking reasonably and moderately with self-control).

REHABILITATION AND AFTER-CARE

Once successful treatment has been completed relapses are common unless careful follow-up is instituted. Doctors, social workers, other primary health care personnel and voluntary bodies such as AA and Al-Anon all play an important part. Special hostels and day centres may be used. For those who have lost their jobs, attempts, with the possible co-operation of the Disablement Resettlement Officer (DRO), should be made to gain other employment, ideally in an alcohol-free environment. All the agencies involved should attempt close co-operation and co-ordination of their efforts.

PREVENTION OF ALCOHOL ABUSE

Overall the aim must be to reduce the total levels of consumption across all sectors. WHO has recommended three main methods of achieving these aims:[15]

- *Fiscal measures* — the price of alcohol, and its increase, should remain above that of inflation
- *Availability controls* — licensing restrictions should be imposed
- *Public and professional education* — prevention of alcohol problems depends on sensible understanding of the dangers of alcohol abuse, (see below).

For the individual, the following hints may be of help:

- Avoid drinking alone.
- Ration the amount of time for drinking. The earlier in the evening a drink is taken the greater is the likelihood of more alcohol being consumed.
- Substitute non-alcoholic drinks at times where alcoholic drinks are freely available, as at parties and in the pub, etc. Drinks such as bitter lemon are useful as it is impossible at a glance to see if they are non-alcoholic. It cannot be stressed too strongly that most alcohol abuse starts with social drinking.
- Strictly adhere to the no drink and drive principle. As society rightly demands control over the drinking and driving problem, public opinion changes and the pressure to drink alcohol diminishes.

The example of parents can be crucial in influencing the drinking habits of young persons. Sensible control in parents can do much to mould the subsequent drinking habits of their children and vice versa.

Doctors and other health care workers must be vigilant in attempting to recognize the problem and dependent drinker at an early stage when it may be possible to reverse the process. Recently, industry has begun to examine this problem in the workplace, and occupational health departments can play a key role in the early identification of problems.

Education

The key for the future must largely lie with education. The introduction of the National Curriculum requires that 7- to 11-year-olds know about factors which contribute to good health and body maintenance, including '. . . avoidance of harmful substances such as . . . alcohol'; 11- to 14-year-olds must 'understand the risks of alcohol . . . abuse and how (it) affects body processes'.

For the general population, there is a great ignorance. In a survey by the Health Education Council in 1985 the majority of the public thought that alcohol only harmed those who were dependent and there was little understanding about the concept of units of alcohol. Most did not understand that 1 unit of beer was no different from 1 unit of whisky or wine. National Drinkwise Days have been introduced, but are not as well publicized as the no smoking days. Booklets such as *That's the Limit — a guide to sensible drinking* published by the Health Education Authority, are very informative and helpful, when used in conjunction with counselling.

Each RHA has created the new post of the Regional Alcohol Misuse Coordinator. These have been funded by the Department of Health through the Health Education Authority. Some are based within local Departments of Health. These co-ordinators work closely with the Directors of Public Health.

Overall though the money spent on education is minute when compared to the money spent on advertising. Every opportunity must be taken to be on the look out for problems related to alcohol, both in the patient and the family.

References

1. Home Office. Statistics of the misuse of drug addicts notified to the Home Office, United Kingdom 1990. Home Office Statistical Bulletin 1991. London: Home Office. 1991.
2. Department of Health and Social Security. Report of the medical working group on drug dependence. Guidelines of good clinical practice in the treatment of drug misuse. London: DHSS. 1984.
3. Misuse of Drugs Act 1985. London: HMSO.
4. Advisory council on the misuse of drugs. Prevention. A report. London: HMSO. 1984.
5. Bandy P, President PA. Recent literature on drug abuse prevention and mass media: focussing on youth, parents, women and the elderly. Drug Education 1983, **13**: 255-271.
6. Office of Health Economics. Reducing the Harm. London: Office of Health Economics. 1981.
7. Royal College of Physicians. The medical consequences of alcohol abuse. A great and growing evil. London: Tavistock. 1987.
8. Home Office. Offences of drunkenness. England and Wales 1989. Statistical Bulletin 40/90. London: Home Office. 1991.
9. Social habits and health. Social Trends, vol. 19: 123. London: HMSO.
10. Mayfield D *et al*. The CAGE questionnaire: validation of a new alcoholism screening instrument. Am. J. Psychiatry 1974, **131**: 121-123.
11. Pokorny AD *et al*. The brief MAST. A shortened version of the Michigan alcoholism screening test. Am. J. Psychiatry 1972, **129**: 342-345.
12. Alcohol problems in the general hospital. Drugs Ther. Bull. **29**(18): 69-71.
13. Anderson P. Managing alcohol problems in general practice. Br. Med. J. 1985, **291**: 1873-1875.
14. Robertson I, Heather N. So you want to cut down on your drinking. Edinburgh: Scottish Health Education Group. 1986.

15. WHO. Problems related to alcohol consumption. Report of a WHO expert committee. Technical report series no 650. Geneva: WHO. 1980.
16. Central Statistical Office. Social Trends 1991. London: HMSO.
17. OPCS. Drinking in England and Wales in 1987. London: HMSO.

18

Care of Elderly Persons

In the UK, the numbers and proportions of people aged 65 years and over has steadily risen over the last 90 years. By 1989, in England and Wales there were 7 999 000 people aged 65 years and over — this represents 15.8% of the total population. There were 3 203 000 males (40.1%) and 4 796 000 females (59.9%). The proportion of women to men rises as ages are greater and, by age 85 years old, there are 75% women and by 90 years old this rises to 80%.

The really significant change occurred from 1976 to 1992 — during these 16 years the proportion of those aged 85 years and over rose from 1 in 104 of the population to 1 in 65. Table 18.1 shows the projections of population changes expected for England and Wales up to the year 2021.[1]

Table 18.2 groups the ages over 65 years into 65–74 years, 75–84 years and 85 years and over and shows the proportion of the population aged 85 and over.

TABLE 18.1   Projections of persons aged 65 years and over: by age groups and sex in England and Wales, 1989–2021 (thousands)

Age groups (years)	1989		1996		2001		2011		2021	
	Males	Females	Males	Females	Males	Females	Males	Females	Males	Females
65–69	1215	1423	1096	1226	1073	1166	1265	1362	1324	1438
70–74	785	1051	945	1178	921	1106	946	1090	1249	1452
75–79	648	1023	657	971	718	1004	708	911	854	1076
80–84	366	734	406	767	431	755	479	748	509	749
85–89	144	392	185	471	208	494	258	519	269	486
90+	45	172	63	234	82	276	116	316	141	321
Total	3202	4796	3352	4847	3433	4801	3772	4946	4346	5522
65+	7 999		8 194		8 234		8 618		9 868	
Total population	50 562		51 749		52 527		53 310		54 411	

Data from ref. 1.

TABLE 18.2   Projection of persons aged 65–74, 75–84, 85 years and over in England and Wales, 1989–2021 (thousands)

Age groups (years)	1989	1996	2001	2011	2021
65–74	4 474	4 445	4 265	4 663	5 463
75–84	2 771	2 801	2 908	2 846	3 189
85+	754	853	1 060	1 209	1 217
	(1 in 67)	(1 in 62.5)	(1 in 50)	(1 in 44)	(1 in 45)
Total population	50 562	51 749	52 527	53 510	54 411

Data from ref. 1.

Note that from the 1992 level of 1 in 65, the proportion of persons aged 85 years and over progressively rises to 1 in 62.5 in 1996, 1 in 50 by 2001 and 1 in 44 in 2011. It then steadies and drops very slightly to 1 in 45 by the year 2021.

Another way of expressing the change is to emphasize that:

- from 1989 to 1996 there will be an increase of 99 000 or 13.1%. in those aged 85 years +
- from 1989 to 2001 there will be an increase of 306 000 or 40.5%. in those aged 85 years +
- from 1989 to 2011 there will be an increase of 455 000 or 60.3%. in those aged 85 years +.

In the past, the Office of Population Census and Survey (OPCS) projections have turned out to be very accurate. Such an increase in the numbers of elderly people over the age of 85 years will probably produce many problems. Some of the problems will be economic, but this chapter only considers the likely effect in terms of care difficulties in both the health and the social service fields.

Probable consequences of expected demographic changes

The most likely consequences of these demographic changes are connected with the fact that many individuals aged 85 years and over have much higher levels of disability and their mobility may be limited. Therefore they have a greater need for health and social services of various kinds.[2]

Another difficulty which may follow is that, for many years, families have become smaller, which means that elderly people are less likely to receive help and support from their family.[3] However this group of the population is extremely varied and many such individuals react quite differently to the problems of ageing.

It is quite wrong to assume most old persons aged 85 years and over will produce the same problems.[4]

Research into characteristics of elderly persons

Much research has attempted to study and classify the problems of elderly people and especially those who determine the success or relative failure of their retirement. A comprehensive and fascinating study was carried out by Taylor and Ford in 1980 in Aberdeen on a random sample of non-institutionalized elderly persons.[5,6] The results of this research are extremely interesting and useful because they emphasize:

- the marked differences between many elderly persons living in the community;
- how individual problems are not necessarily a direct consequence of their health or social conditions, but depend more on their attitude and approach.

Three main 'risk groups' were identified in this study. They included those:

- *at high risk*:
  - the very old (aged 80 years and over) — 15% of the sample
  - those who have recently been discharged from hospital — 13% of the sample
  - those who have recently moved house — 13.7% of sample
- *at moderate risk*:
  - those on low incomes
  - those recently widowed
  - those living alone
  - those in social class V
- *at low risk*:
  - those living in isolated situations
  - those who have never married
  - childless persons.

It is interesting that those found to be at greatest risk did not coincide with the popular view that elderly people living alone or in poor financial circumstances or those living in isolated situations would always be in a precarious situation.

The second part of this research was even more fascinating. Here subgroups or clusters were drawn up according to their similarities across a range of variables.[6] Ten clusters were identified as follows:

- *Elderly elite* — highly favoured persons who were very successful in retirement. There were more men than women in this group and most were middle class.
- *Family shielded* — this group had one dominant variable — their family was readily available and were living close by. Many were active outside the home, but they had few friends although they had a high degree of support and help from the family.

- *The supported* — these all had one main variable — all had a great deal of visits from friends and family. This group is highly sociable within their own home. It had a high proportion of individuals who lived alone and were generally older than most groups.
- *Ill and unsupported* — this group find their retirement difficult and unsuccessful. Most are in poor health, have little psychological well-being, and are relatively inactive. It contains a high proportion of middle class widows.
- *Exclusive couplehood* — this curious name refers to their one main characteristic — the husband and wife very much depend on each other. Outside their spouse they have little social support and often a low degree of activity. It is a successful group, but would seem to be especially vulnerable if their spouse were to die.
- *Health optimists* — this is a group of elderly persons who are generally in poor health, yet have many friends and maintain a high morale. They have many hobbies and interests. The group is older than many others, contains mainly women. In spite of their health problems it is a successful group with an extremely positive approach to life.
- *Psychologically fragile* — this could be said to be a group of people who are almost the opposite to the above group. In poor psychological health, they have a low confidence in themselves, they worry a great deal and are very insecure.
- *Socially isolated but defended* — these have few family members available and spend a lot of time on their own. They have above average health, at least average psychological well-being, do not worry much and have an above average income. They have few friends and score badly on intimacy.
- *Inadequately housed* — this cluster is almost entirely defined in poor housing terms. A group of inner city tenement dwellers, they have a low income, have few interests and yet seem highly satisfied with their lives.
- *Poor souls* — these have a multitude of problems — poor health, poor psychological well-being, low confidence, isolated, working class and mainly consist of women. They tend to be older than most groups and do have visits. The authors of the research appropriately describe them 'in the Scottish vernacular, they would be called poor souls'.

This excellent study has been described in considerable detail because it emphasizes one very important point — the error of assuming that 'the elderly' make up a homogeneous group. Almost the only characteristic that is similar to all old people is their age. Apart from that, they represent a completely mixed group of the population. Although this may seem only to state the obvious, many professionals make the mistake of believing that old people share many similar difficulties, and therefore the solutions are likely to be fairly similar. This is not the case for the various difficulties faced by old people are always highly individual. As can be seen from the cluster analysis in the Aberdeen research, most problems depend not only on the physical characteristics connected with the old person's immediate environment, but on their attitude and on the positive or negative way the individual reacts to any difficulty.

Preparation for retirement

Short 2–3 day courses are becoming increasingly popular in the UK to assist people who are due to retire in the next few years. The usual course is arranged in the following way:

- it is best if each course is not too large — 15–30 persons is an ideal number as this encourages participation and discussion amongst those attending
- the employee and their partner should attend (husband, wife or close friend), this is important for the retirement of anyone always affects their partner
- ideally seminars should be residential to enable the group to mix freely and to discuss topics informally.

The subjects that are covered in such courses include:

- discussions on the *correct approach to retirement* which should always be positive and optimistic as well as discussing the opportunities that retirement can bring
- *social security*, including the state retirement pension and unemployment benefit if applicable
- *company pensions*, explaining exactly what each employee will receive; courses held at least 3–4 years before retirement are ideal as this enables the employee to enhance his/her pension by making additional voluntary contributions (AVCs) which can be a very efficient method of saving because of the tax benefits
- *the home in retirement* which should always include three topics — the facilities and structure of the home (such as the importance of having a downstairs toilet and, if at all possible, a shower or bath), security in the home, and also personal relationships; the correct facilities can make the management of any later disability or serious illness in the home much easier to cope with
- *health aspects*, both physical and mental health in all their aspects; advice should be given explaining how to help persons to remain healthy and active
- *work and leisure in retirement*, this should deal with all relevent aspects of both subjects including voluntary, part-time or even full-time work, as well as recreations and pastimes; note that anyone retiring from full-time work will find that they have to fill an extra 2000 hours each year
- *financial advice*, this should cover taxation, AVCs, pensions, and particulary whether a lump sum should be taken in lieu of a portion of the pension (commutation), mortgages, inheritance and capital gains tax and investments.

The ideal way to arrange such courses is to do it in two stages:

- a 1-day course about 10 years before retirement; this deals mainly with long range financial planning covering social security, AVCs, pensions and investments and savings

- a 2–3 day course containing all the subjects mentioned above about 3–4 years before the employee is expected to give up work.

Health problems in elderly persons

Special features that affect the incidence and treatment of illnesses in old persons include:

- *Social conditions*. The cause of ill-health in elderly persons is often connected with their poor living conditions (cold, damp accommodation or steep stairs can be very detrimental). The benefits from treatment may equally be reduced by poor housing.
- *Multiple diseases* (the incidence at the same time of more than one disease in the same person). This is relatively common in elderly people but rare in other age groups. For instance, an old person may present with heart failure but the real cause may be chronic bronchitis, ischaemic heart disease or a combination of both. This means that not only is diagnosis made more difficult, but treatment can also be more complicated as the two diseases may require a different approach — one may need rest and the other a more active regime.
- *Rehabilitation*. The motivation to return to normal activity is often absent in old people or may not be very marked. Therefore treatment should include special emphasis on rehabilitation at either a day centre or specialist unit.
- *Limitation of function*. This can become the worst handicap, therefore every effort must be made to keep the old person as active as possible. Limitation of activity for even a few days can be very detrimental, especially in very old persons. Hence, it is often better to treat an old person over 85 years in a chair, as serious complications (such as pneumonia or even pressure sores) are then less likely to develop than if the individual is treated in bed.
- *Signs and symptoms of disease in an old person may be different*. For instance, in various infections in old people, fever is often absent, whereas in younger age groups fever is almost invariably present. However, an old person in such cases may show mental confusion. For this reason, for any old person who suddenly develops mental confusion, the doctor should always make certain that there is not an acute infection present.
- *Prevention of accidents*. This is most important in elderly persons because an accident can often be the start of rapid deterioration. Early diagnosis can be equally important as the gradual development of any illness, which could be curtailed by specific treatment, may be the starting point of a steady decline in health. Therefore, early recognition and effective treatment of illnesses are always important in elderly persons.

Because of these six differences, the diagnosis, care and treatment of illness in elderly persons is variable and complicated, and so a special branch of medicine has evolved — *geriatric medicine*. Because most elderly people are considerably susceptible to poor social conditions, a close link has been developed between geriatic medical services and local social services in the community. This link should also be fostered in all primary health care when dealing with elderly persons (see pp. 181–182, 412).

COLD-ASSOCIATED ILL HEALTH

Severe hypothermia only affects a small proportion of elderly persons.[7] Recent research has, however, drawn attention to the much larger problem of 'cold-associated diseases'.[8] It has recently been demonstrated that 80% of the weekly fluctuation in the deaths of old people can be explained by changes of air temperature. From this figure, it has been estimated that there are between 40 000 and 75 000 cold-associated deaths in the UK each year. Respiratory diseases, heart diseases and strokes are the main illnesses falling into this category.[9]

In the UK, approximately 500–600 deaths are caused each year by severe hypothermia. This is most likely to be found in persons over 75 years old who are incapacitated in some way, which has reduced their mobility, or in individuals who at that time are ill. Certain drugs, including tricyclic antidepressants and phenothiazines, can make the development of hypothermia more likely. Clinical conditions which predispose to hypothermia include hypothyroidism, diabetes, Parkinsonism, strokes, confusional states and alcohol dependence.

Living rooms and bedrooms should be kept between 18°C and 24°C, and sick and immobilized persons should be kept even warmer. Efficient automatic heating is important, but insulation of windows and lofts is equally necessary.

The early signs of hypothermia include the following:

- the elderly person does not usually look cold and does not shiver
- the hands and face often appear warm and are red or reddish-purple in colour, but feel cold
- the person is often drowsy and very inactive and his/her *speech may be slow and slurred*
- body temperature is usually below 35°C (95°F).

Once the condition is recognized, emergency treatment must be started quickly, although this may produce further difficulties. Rapid warming must be avoided and warming limited to about 0.7°C per hour. The room should be kept warm, but no direct heat should ever be applied to the patient.

MENTAL ILL-HEALTH

Reference has already been made in Chapter 16 to the greater incidence of mental disorders found in elderly persons (see p. 365).

Various forms of confusional states found in elderly persons

There are three forms of confusional states found in elderly persons:

- chronic Alzheimer's dementia
- multi-infarct type of dementia
- acute confusional states

Alzheimer's dementia

It is estimated there are at least half a million people in the UK suffering from Alzheimer's disease. The disease has a gradual and insidious onset and is characterized by:

- a significant slow and progressive decline in the ability of the individual to understand the common features of life; there is clear cognitive impairment
- this lack of understanding is general (there are no local areas where understanding is different)
- there is a general deterioration of higher cortical function although the patient remains alert
- patients become obviously confused, but anxiety is usually absent and the individual is not therefore worried; the patient has no clear insight into what is really happening; this is in sharp contrast to the acute confusional states.

Alzheimer's dementia can be difficult to diagnose with certainty early in the syndrome. Its differential diagnosis includes other dementias which are part of a widespread neurological disorder, such as Huntingdon's disease or the extra pyramidal features of Parkinson's disease. Note that in younger persons, HIV testing should always be carried out as AIDS is becoming an increasingly important cause of dementia.

There is a familial form of Alzheimer's disease which is an autosomal dominant disease. The gene associated with this form is located on chromosome 21. This is the same chromosome as that involved in Down's syndrome, and probably explains why Alzheimer's dementia is considerably commoner than normal in persons with Down's syndrome who are over the age of 40 years.

Care and treatment

The prospects for the treatment of Alzheimer's dementia are limited. There is no known cure. In the early stages, Alzeimer's dementia is best looked after at home, if this is practicable, although it does throw an increasing strain on the supporting relatives. It is therefore always important that *some form of respite care is available for relatives*. There is usually a gradual deterioration which eventually makes it difficult for the family to cope safely at home. Such late terminal cases require constant care in psychogeriatric units. Eventually patients fail to recognize even their closest relatives.

Vascular or multi-infarct types of dementia

This type of dementia has been estimated to account for 20% to 30% of all forms of dementia.[10] It usually develops slowly and is characterized by sudden intellectual deterioration followed by a period of improvement. There is an obvious day-to-day fluctuation in the individual's condition. Usually some neurological symptoms are present from an early stage. The gait of the patient often becomes abnormal and muscular weaknesses may occur, which may suggest a possible minor hemiparesis. However, there is no obvious loss of power although co-ordination is poor.

Progress is uneven and, in some, there may be quite long periods of improvement. However, most patients gradually deteriorate. Many can stay at home for quite a long time provided they can be looked after, but eventually most will need constant psychogeriatric care.

Acute confusional states

Acute confusional states usually have a rapid onset, occur in old people over the age of 70 years, and are connected with a variety of causes. The patient suddenly becomes confused and, although this can be very distressing for the close relatives (who may wrongly believe that it is the start of Alzheimer's dementia), once the cause has been identified and corrected, the person quickly returns to normal.

The following are the commonest precipitating causes of acute confusional states:

- *dehydration* — if some very old persons do not drink enough fluid they can become dehydrated and then they can become confused
- *infections* — in very old people these can be quickly followed by a confusional state (see p. 403); in such cases, as soon as the infection has subsided, the individual quickly returns to their normal lucid self
- *hypoxia* — lack of enough oxygenation of the brain, perhaps caused by cardiac failure or respiratory insufficiency, and some anaemias can all lead to a confusional state developing in old persons over the age of 75 years
- *development of uraemia*

- *medicines/drugs* — many commonly prescribed medicines can produce confusion in old persons over the age of 75 years. Another name for this condition is iatrogenic disease (doctor induced); examples include beta blockers, cimetidine, anticholinergics, many tranquilizers (particulary benzodiapezines and barbiturates)
- *depression* — some patients with psychotic depression who are old also become confused
- *alcohol and alcohol withdrawal*
- *intrinsic brain damage* — cerebral tumours, strokes and trauma may be accompanied by an attack of confusion in the patient
- *carcinomatosis* — advanced cancer patients with secondaries can produce a sudden confusional state.

It is always important to recognize the acute confusional states promptly as many can be quickly and effectively treated. This can often prevent considerable anxiety from developing among close relatives. There has usually been a short history (often only days). The level of consciousness varies, although it is usually clouded and much anxiety and agitation is present. The patient realizes that something is wrong and is extremely worried.

Delusions and hallucinations are common and often these are visual or auditory. There is also much disruption of speech or thought.

Once the correct diagnosis has been made, specific treatment should be started at once. Keeping the patient at home is important, if possible, as it is always best to have the patient surrounded by people and objects they know well. It is essential for the close relatives to understand fully the nature of the confusional state, and that, in most cases, because there is a specific cause, it is likely to be short-lived and the patient should probably make a full recovery. Reassurance of spouses in this way always seems to help the patient indirectly.

Expert nursing is important, especially in drowsy patients if pressure sores are to be avoided. Maintenance of hydration (i.e. fluid intake) is more important than nutrition, provided that vitamin B_1 deficiency is not the cause. Most acute confusional states do well once the main cause has been found and rectified.

Recognition of mental deterioration in an elderly person

It is always important to recognize promptly impending mental deterioration in an elderly person at home, as it makes early treatment possible and may prevent a serious or final mental breakdown. Danger signs include:

- *change in outlook* — the change may be towards either apathy or agitation
- *change in eating habits* — this takes the form of the old person becoming very fussy and eating very little
- *depression* — this becomes more common and may also be accompanied by outbreaks of verbal aggression making the old person difficult to live with

- *memory loss* — all elderly people notice difficulty in memorizing names; occasionally, however, this may be associated with the old person mislaying things and then accusing others of stealing them
- *talking* — the usual tendency for old people to talk a lot disappears
- *worries* — these may become morbidly increased; often the old person becomes quite excessively concerned that their income will be insufficient for their needs although this is clearly not the case.

In addition there may be quite marked swings in the *behaviour pattern* of an elderly person showing early signs indicative of mental deterioration. A visitor, such as a doctor or social worker, is very liable to see the old person at his/her best as a special effort may be made, only for the individual to become abnormal within half an hour of the end of the visit.

Hospital care for elderly persons

Old people use hospitals about twice as much as those under the age of 65 years. The Department of Health normally considers about 10 beds per 1000 of the elderly population should be provided (about 30% of these should be in the District General Hospital). The aim is that each geriatric unit should have a reasonable turnover of patients — at least five patients per bed per year.[11] In Hull, a turnover of nine patients per year has been achieved.[12]

Although old people are often admitted to ordinary wards in acute hospitals, it is better if they are admitted to a *geriatric unit*. This may be a separate hospital or part of a general hospital. In such units, a complete medical and social investigation can take place, and there are also the special rehabilitation facilities necessary for successful treatment. The great difference between hospital care for the elderly and other age groups is that, with the elderly, there is often more than one system of the body diseased and producing symptoms. The investigation is, therefore, usually more involved and is further complicated by the fact that social circumstances of the patient do much to determine the outcome. There must be, therefore, co-ordination between those working in the geriatric unit and the social service departments of neighbouring local authorities. The geriatric unit is concerned with initial diagnosis and treatment and rehabilitation; it therefore relies more on its physiotherapy section than most other hospital units. Another essential stage is the assessment of the more chronic cases to decide whether they should be discharged: (a) home, often with special assistance such as attendance at a day hospital or day activity area within a hospital for physiotherapy and occupational therapy; (b) to special residential accommodation (either hostels or sheltered housing); (c) to hospital chronic sick accommodation. Such units deal with two types of cases: first bedridden elderly persons suffering from a chronic illness in which there is no likelihood of marked improvement, and second severe psychogeriatric patients.

Geriatric day hospitals (or day activity areas) help with the rehabilitation of elderly patients. They act as a half-way stage between hospital and home, patients being brought there by ambulance transport and returned home in the evening. Attendance may be daily or on a specified number of days per week, and physiotherapy and occupational therapy services are provided for old persons attending.

The main value of day activity areas is that they:

- enable an elderly person to be discharged home earlier
- assist with the rehabilitation of the patient
- increase co-operation between the geriatric unit and the local social service department as social workers usually attend such units regularly.

Strategy for future care of elderly persons

It is clear that from 1992 to 2011 there is going to be a massive increase in the proportion of very old people over the age of 85 years in the UK. It is therefore important to consider the strategy that will be necessary to maintain and improve the health and welfare services for this potentially vulnerable group. Muir Gray[13] has ably defined the following strategy:

- keep elderly persons in their own homes for as long as possible
- slow down functional decline
- maintain the quality of life by every possible method
- recognize the immense value of all forms of carers, particulary unpaid ones — families, friends, neighbours, etc. — to support them
- help old people to have a good death as well as a good life.

MAIN NEEDS OF ALL PERSONS AGED 65 YEARS AND OVER

The main needs of all elderly people include the following; all should have:

- an adequate income well above subsistence level
- good physical and mental health, ideally until very close to the end of their life
- suitable accommodation — this includes being able to maintain easily their home and garden (if they have one)
- congenial friends and neighbours
- one or more absorbing interests and hobbies
- a positive (i.e. optimistic) approach to life; this is particulary important when the inevitable difficulties begin to obtrude — stiff arthritic joints that are painful, decreased mobility, illnesses and disabilities of various kinds
- assistance at times of crisis especially when illness occurs, when death of the spouse occurs and in any other sudden emergency within the home

- a sensible philosophy about life in general (this of course may be a religious faith) so that as the person reaches the late stages of retirement, they can face the end of their life calmly.

SOCIAL SERVICES AVAILABLE FOR ELDERLY PERSONS

Many special services are supplied by local social service departments and voluntary bodies to assist elderly persons living in their own homes. In all instances, the main objective is to ensure that the old person remains as independent as possible. Advice may be needed about many aspects of life — retirement pensions, additional income support (if this is needed). Practical help may be required to enable the old person to continue to manage at home. Many different individuals — a doctor, a health visitor, district nurse, clergyman, friendly visitor or neighbour — may discover an elderly person in difficulty. The main initial reference point is the local social services area office. If this is not known, the Citizens' Advice Bureau will be able to indicate its location. Arrangements will then be made for a social worker to call to find out exactly what is the problem, give advice and, if needed, arrange special help. The social worker is there to act as an advocate for the elderly person in difficulty, and will therefore be able to follow-up and sort out the problem. It may well be that a type of 'follow-up' care will be required periodically as further crises threaten or develop. Examples of the type of community services available include the following:

Care assistants (formerly home helps)

In the UK approximately one in 10 elderly persons are receiving assistance from the care assistant services (see p. 413).

Meals-on-wheels

Meals-on-wheels is a service whereby a hot meal is taken to the old person at home. A modest charge is made towards the cost of the meal, the content of which is specially planned to suit the elderly (see later, p. 415).

Luncheon clubs

Another excellent way in which social service departments help an elderly person living at home is to provide lunch clubs to which old people can go for a meal say on three or four occasions a week. In many cases, the local branch of Age Concern provide helpers who serve the meals. These arrangements have the added value that the old person is encouraged to leave home, get exercise and keep mobile, as well as benefiting from the social contacts at the centre. Some lunch clubs are held in specially built centres, but many are arranged in buildings such as church halls. A similar charge to that for meals-on-wheels is usually made.

Home care programmes

Recent surveys have shown that one of the most critical times for many old people occurs when they are discharged home from hospital after an illness. Elderly persons living on their own are particularly susceptible to rapid deterioration at such a time. New home care programmes are being experimented with to support old people at such times. One such programme aims at providing home help and meals services plus home nursing services for 20% of elderly persons discharged from hospital (selected to include those at greatest risk) for at least 4 weeks following discharge. A feature of such schemes is that consultants and hospital social workers select the cases to be helped and give a few days' notice of discharge so that the care assistant and other services can be waiting for the old person on discharge. At the end of the 4-week period, those in need of further help are assisted through the normal care assistant services enabling the special home care programme staff to care for new discharges.

Further experimental schemes are linked with special geriatric teams (of doctors and nurses) to treat an old person at home in the case of an acute illness, in the hope that the person can be rapidly improved within 4–5 days, and thus prevent the need for admission to hospital (which in itself is very unsettling for old people and can become the starting point of deterioration).

Clubs and handicraft centres

Many old people enjoy the social life at a club or rest centre, where they are in the company of others. Some elderly people also attend a handicraft centre at which they can carry out some recreational hobby — the value of this provision is mainly the interest it creates. Recent research has emphasized the usefulness of handicrafts in arresting the development of early mental deterioration. Clubs, rest centres and handicraft centres are provided both by social service departments and by voluntary bodies. In many instances, there is a joint arrangement whereby the local authority provides the building and pays the running costs, while the voluntary staff run the centre.

Day centres

Many social service departments and voluntary bodies provide day centres which elderly people can visit during the day. Simple meals are usually served at such centres, and in some various handicrafts are also encouraged.

Day care centres

These provide an entirely different service and have often been referred to as 'hostels without beds' as they are intended to care for frail elderly people requiring the kind of care and attention which is provided in hostels. The old person is brought to the day care centre daily by transport and is provided with all meals and other services usually found in hostels. In the evening, transport takes the old person back again to their home. This form of care is particularly useful where a frail old person is living with younger relatives who both go out to work during the day, and means that the elderly person can be looked after during the day without the need to be admitted permanently to a hostel. It also has been used to help old people living alone by taking them to a day centre 2–3 days per week so that they do not lose contact with the community outside. Problems do arise in some of these instances where the old person has to return to an empty, and perhaps cold, house in the evening. For this reason, it is best to link such arrangements with help from a good neighbour scheme.

Visiting

Regular visiting of old people living at home is an important function of social service departments. The numbers of old people are so large that only those needing special attention can be visited regularly. Social workers concentrate upon those elderly people who urgently need special accommodation and determine the priority for admission to hostels and make adequate arrangements for those who cannot immediately be accommodated. This will include the arranging of care assistants or meals-on-wheels. Health visitors are continuously visiting many families and will also be seeing many elderly persons living at home. Special arrangements are usually made for a link between geriatric hospitals, social workers, district nurses and health visitors to assist in the after-care of elderly persons recently discharged from hospital. They also visit those elderly persons being investigated in out-patient departments and those in need of after-care. Voluntary visiting is also very important and is increasingly arranged by community councils and other neighbourhood groups. In many instances, it is possible for a friendly visitor to be found who will call on the old person regularly.

Financial help

In many cases, financial problems still arise, for many elderly persons worry excessively about money and may stint themselves trying to economize, even when their financial circumstances are quite sound. This anxiety about money increases with age. The visitor must repeatedly explain pension entitlements, the true nature of Social Security and to what extra help the old person may be entitled. Aid may be needed to complete pension and other forms.

Help with heating costs

Considerable concern has been expressed recently about the sharp increase in fuel prices which have affected the elderly more than any other group. Quarterly gas and electricity bills have caused difficulties, and wherever possible pay-as-you-go schemes have been introduced to help the elderly on low budgets. Pensioners are now largely protected against disconnection of gas and electricity under the Code of Practice. Local authorities have started loft insulation schemes in their council houses and priority has been given to the elderly.

CARE ASSISTANTS (HOME HELPS)

Local authorities, who run the personal social services, have a duty to provide care assistants (formerly called home helps) through their Social Services Committee and Director of Social Services. The main objective of this service is to provide assistance in the home for elderly persons who cannot look after their home adequately because of chronic illness or frailty. Approximately 900 000 persons (approximately 1 in 10) are helped each year in the UK by care assistants. Elderly persons make up the largest group helped in this way (approximately 90%) and the remainder are those who need such assistance because of mental disorder or serious physical disability.

Duties of care assistants

Most care assistants in the UK work part-time, usually for 20 hours per week. The duties of each include many of the usual tasks carried out in the home — cleaning rooms, preparing food and meals, cooking, shopping, lighting fires, etc. Service can be provided for a client on a full-time or part-time basis and varies from a few hours a week to full-time attendance. In most cases, and especially in those receiving help for a long time, help is provided for two to three sessions per week. In this way, it is possible for the care assistant to help more people and, at the same time, encourage the elderly person to continue to do quite a lot of the housework and to keep as active as possible. By sensible use of this service, together with the meals services, it is often possible to keep an elderly person living at home for some years longer than would otherwise be the case.

The care assistant soon gets to know the elderly person who is being looked after very well, and learns a great deal about their personal problems. For this reason it is important that care assistants work in close contact with social workers, for the care assistant can act as a very useful source of information about an elderly person living alone at home. Most care assistants are women aged 25–65 years but recently a few men have been recruited in some areas. Male assistants generally undertake especially dirty or heavy work. They also have been used successfully to help difficult old persons whose behaviour is odd. Occasionally specialized cleaning equipment is taken to the home in a specially equipped van to clean up very dirty houses in readiness for someone about to be discharged from hospital.

Organization of care assistant services

Most social service departments have a senior care assistant organizer directly responsible to an assistant director of social services (see Fig. 20.3, p. 445). Although the senior care assistant organizer is responsible for recruitment and training, the day-to-day control is linked with the area teams of social workers; in this way, the close links are maintained between the two services. In each area social work team, there is usually an assistant care assistant organizer to help with the assessment of need, distribution of services and with the supervision of the care assistants.

Referrals

Referrals for care assistants' services come from the health services and from social workers and others (clergymen) working in the community. An increase in demand for care assistants has been noticed from primary health care teams and especially from those with health visitor attachments. Hospital referrals still account for many new cases and the increase in hospital geriatric departments has swelled the demand for these services. For the individual GP (or hospital doctor, especially geriatrician) who wishes to arrange care assistance for his/her patients, a request should be made locally to the area social work office.

Good neighbour schemes

There is usually a waiting list for those requiring care assistant services and a few authorities have experimented with an official good neighbour scheme in which a local volunteer is sought who will agree to carry out a number of the lighter duties of care assistants — shopping, lighting a fire, cooking, etc. Such good neighbour schemes are different from the voluntary schemes of visitors. Often an individual recruited as a good neighbour lives close to the old person requiring assistance so that no travelling is involved. It is usual to pay the good neighbour a small honorarium based on the number of tasks undertaken per week; for service involving some help on most or all days per week, the honorarium would be about £5–£7 per week.

MEALS SERVICES

This is a developing service, which, although designed mainly to help the elderly, also assists many severely disabled persons living at home. In England, approximately 44 million meals are provided each year, 70% being delivered to the client's home (meals-on-wheels) and 30% being served in various day centres and luncheon clubs (see Table 18.3). The growth of meals services has been most marked in London and the large provincial cities where much of the expansion has been provided by direct development by social service departments, and has been made possible by greater use of frozen foods and packing each meal in a foil disposable pack. In the rural and country areas and in smaller towns, the service still largely depends on the help of voluntary bodies such as the WRVS. In the large towns, special delivery vans are used, and in many instances lunch and a light supper can be provided (to different clients) to ensure that maximum use is made of the cooking and delivery services. In country areas many of the meals are still delivered by volunteers in private cars.

TABLE 18.3   Meals services: main meals provided in England, 1976–90 (millions)

	1976	1981	1984	1986	1987	1988	1989	1990
Meals provided	40.5	41.5	42.4	44.1	45.4	46.4	46.4	46.3
In recipients home	24.3	27.0	28.8	30.9	32.0	33.0	33.0	32.9
In centres, etc.	16.2	14.4	13.6	13.2	13.4	13.4	13.4	13.4

Data from ref. 23.

Surveys carried out recently have shown that in approximately 44% of cases, meals are delivered twice a week, about 18% for either 3 or 5 days a week, 8% have a meal on 1 or 4 days a week while 2% have a meal either on 6 or 7 days a week.

Referral for meals

Referrals for meals come from the health services (especially geriatric hospitals and primary health care teams with health visitor attachment) and from area social service teams. Most social service departments arrange for meals to be prepared and distributed centrally, but increasingly all referrals for new meals are being dealt with directly by area teams of social workers. Any doctor wishing to arrange for a meals service for patients should contact the local Area Social Services Officer.

THE COMMUNITY CARE APPROACH – THE KENT COMMUNITY CARE PROJECT

An interesting and practical project was developed in Kent because research had shown that frail elderly people living in the community have wide and varied needs. These tend to be met by 'traditional' social services (both from social service departments and from voluntary bodies) in a fragmented way with very little integration.[14] Another problem is that such help tends to be 'service orientated' rather than 'client orientated'.[15] In other words, no special effort is made to analyse the individual needs of any frail old person. Help is given in many instances that is not really appropriate to the most important requirements of that old person.

The Kent scheme has developed in a number of local authorities in that area and in Gateshead and:

- provides an organizational framework in which social work staff and other fieldworkers can develop sensitive and different alternatives to long-term hospital or residential care
- resources are decentralized to individual fieldworkers
- case loads are defined and expenditure limits set (within these the social staff are encouraged to develop care services to match the individual needs of an old person)
- attempts are made to integrate the various care services into a more practical and effective individual care service
- aims at building closer links with the local health care services (both in the primary health care section and in hospitals).

Organization of the community care service

An essential starting point in the Kent Community Care Project is the identification of the most urgent needs of the individual old person in an approach which is quite different and separate from any consideration as to how these needs may be met.[16] One of the important and unusual methods adopted in this scheme was that the extra finance made available was often used to recruit local people as helpers. Each of these helpers when being introduced to their clients was given a contract of care making quite clear what was needed. Another innovation was the use of small day care groups (four or five people) who meet in a helper's home to undertake various social and rehabilitative activities. This was often arranged for elderly persons living on their own who had just been discharged from hospital. In this way, frail elderly persons who were fearful of falling and therefore wanted to go into a residential home, found that with this help they could overcome their fear and remain at home quite satisfactorily.

Many types of frail elderly have been helped by this scheme including:

- hesitant and fearful frail elderly people apprehensive of living alone
- minor psychiatric cases
- elderly persons who have excessive drinking problems
- even some demented elderly persons.

In particular, it was found that support for carers was more readily provided in ways that were very appropriate — relief on particular days or evenings. A visitor might be arranged who then helped both the elderly person and the carer. Realistic limits were devised making more certain that carers would not be overburdened. This can easily happen when a willing and unselfish member of the family takes all the strain alone. This scheme has helped especially when the carer has been working with mentally ill old people.[16]

Results and effects of the Kent Community Care Scheme

A follow-up of 74 matched pairs of elderly persons over 1, 2, and 3 years was made to see if there was a difference between those frail elderly persons looked after by the Kent Community Care Scheme (CCS) and those cared for by the standard social service department (see Table 18.4). It is clear from Table 18.4 that the frail elderly people cared for by CCS did considerably better in most of the variables studied. This shows that flexible community care is a greater help to frail old people living at home than the usual social service care. This should be expected bearing in mind the large variety of problems old persons can face (see pp. 400–401).

TABLE 18.4   Location of 74 matched cases over 1, 2 and 3 years receiving the Community Care Scheme (CCS) and standard social services in Kent

	Year 1		Year 2		Year 3	
	CCS	Std services	CCS	Std services	CCS	Std services
At home	51	25	37	15	26	9
Residential	9	20	15	25	16	23
Hospital care	3	4	2	2	6	1
Moved away	1	1	1	2	2	2
Died	10	24	19	30	24	39
Total	74	74	74	74	74	74

Reproduced from ref. 15.

Similar results were found in the scheme set up in Gateshead.

One important feature in this project is that it shows that individual delegation to fieldwork staff to make decisions about the form of care is essential if there is ever to be a matching of the needs of frail elderly persons with the services provided. This matching of needs and services will not occur easily if the decisions about clients are made centrally; the assessment of needs is better left to the fieldworker who knows the old person well.

OTHER SOCIAL SERVICES FOR ELDERLY PERSONS

Outings and holidays

Most social service departments arrange special summer outings for old people and this is also supplemented by voluntary bodies. One important provision is for holidays for the elderly living alone or for those living with a family, as a separate holiday may be of value both to the old person and the family. Some local authorities own holiday homes while others may make block bookings at a seaside resort.

Rent rebates

Local authority housing tenants can obtain a rent rebate when the gross income is below a certain level.

Help with the community charge

There are special national arrangements to help elderly persons on a low income with their community charge. There is a personal allowance which depends on the age of the applicant and the allowance is further increased for elderly people. Savings are only taken into account if these exceed £3000. The help is progressively reduced between £3000 and £16 000 in savings on a sliding scale. Anyone with savings greater than £16 000 will not receive any help with their community charge. Leaflet CCB 1 issued by the Department of Social Security gives more details of the scheme of financial help.

Bus passes or concessionary fares

Most local authorities have introduced special schemes by which elderly persons can obtain special free passes or concessionary fares on their buses. These schemes vary in different parts of the country, but in an increasing number of authorities are available to women over 60 and men over 65 years of age who are in receipt of a pension. Most schemes enable the old person to travel free in non-peak periods of the day (9.30 a.m. to 4.30 p.m.). The value of these schemes is very great because they encourage independence in the elderly and remove any constraint on travelling to visit relatives and friends. Previously the high cost of bus fares prevented many elderly people from travelling and led to their isolation. British Rail also offers reduced fares for persons 60 years and over (Senior Rail Card).

Accommodation

Houses, flats, bungalows or flatlets

All authorities provide special housing accommodation for the elderly. The type of dwelling varies with the district. In urban areas, small flats and flatlets are popular and these should be compactly planned with all accommodation on one floor and easily reached by lift. An ideal arrangement is a bedsitting room with kitchenette and small bathroom. Heating should be automatic — either gas, electric or central heating. In rural areas, bungalows are ideal.

Collective homes

There is an increasing need for a combination home to be provided along the pattern of the collective home so popular in Denmark, and local authorities have planned similar projects. Flatlets are provided in conjunction with a small old persons' home and large restaurant. The old people live in the flatlets and are provided with a regular midday meal in the attached restaurant, the charge for which is included in their rent. They stay in the flatlets for as long as possible, but if they become too frail to remain in them they have priority to enter the old persons' home. This means that the old people need never leave the district and, when they become very frail, are cared for by the staff already known to them.

Sheltered housing

Many different types of sheltered housing have been provided during the last 10 years. The essential feature of 'sheltered housing' is specially built or adapted accommodation often in a flatlet or flat for old people with a resident warden in attendance to ensure that the old person can get help in an emergency. Old people living in such accommodation are all capable of looking after themselves, but can remain safely in such accommodation much longer if there is a resident warden to help. The housing accommodation is provided by housing authorities (district councils in county areas or metropolitan districts or in accommodation built by housing trusts or voluntary bodies).

The Social Services Committee usually pays a varying sum annually to those providing sheltered accommodation, dependent upon the facilities provided, as a contribution towards the cost of providing the resident warden, the alarm system, telephone installations, or other communal facilities (midday meals, lifts, TV room, central heating, etc.). In this way, encouragement is given to the provision of extra facilities which will help to enable the old person to remain independent as long as possible.

Many social service departments are now concentrating on rapidly developing more different types of such sheltered accommodation rather than extending their hostel provision. This is because sheltered housing provides a better and more normal answer and is more popular with the elderly since it encourages independence. Sheltered housing is also cheaper to provide (an important feature at a time when new capital development is difficult). New schemes of community support (visiting, care assistants, good neighbours, meals services, various care programmes) are being rapidly developed to enable frail old people to stay longer in such accommodation. In particular, it is important to concentrate upon times of great stress when the old person is at special risk, such as during illness or on returning home after a stay in hospital (see home care programmes, p. 411).

Supportive housing

An additional new provision is supportive housing (sometimes called very sheltered housing). This is essentially the best type of sheltered housing plus an arrangement whereby the frail old person receives as part of the rental some daily domestic help plus a warm midday meal. Some of these units are run by social service departments and others by housing authorities, but it is most important that they are only used for very frail old people. Also, if the arrangement does not work, there must be immediate admission to an old persons' hostel (see below).

RESIDENTIAL ACCOMMODATION FOR ELDERLY PERSONS

There have always been three types of residential accommodation available to elderly persons who no longer can live at home — provided by:

- large local authorities (county councils, metropolitan districts and London boroughs) and are administered by their social service departments
- private individuals
- voluntary bodies.

Until the 1980s, most old persons homes were provided by local authorities, but a rapid growth has occurred since 1978 in private homes for the elderly as shown in Table 18.5. Note that local authorities in 1978 provided 67.7% of the residential places in England for elderly persons, private homes provided 16.2% and voluntary

TABLE 18.5   Residential home places for elderly persons aged 65 years or over

Type of home	1978	1983	1986	1988
Local authority	102 804 (67.7%)	103 598	101 704	97 380 (44.4%)
Private	24 657 (16.2%)	42 142	77 557	96 162 (43.9%)
Voluntary	24 526 (16.1%)	26 468	25 121	25 633 (11.7%)
Total in residential homes	151 987	172 208	204 382	219 175

Data from ref. 24.

bodies provided 16.1% (similar changes have taken place in the rest of the UK). By 1988, the overall number of places had risen from 151 987 to 219 175 (an increase of 67 188 or 44.2%). The whole of this increase was due to a very rapid expansion in the numbers of places in private homes which now have a similar number to local authorities. Indeed, local authority places contracted slightly — they had 5424 less places available in 1988 than in 1978. This trend is likely to continue with the main further increases all taking place in the private sector (see Fig. 18.1). In Fig. 18.1

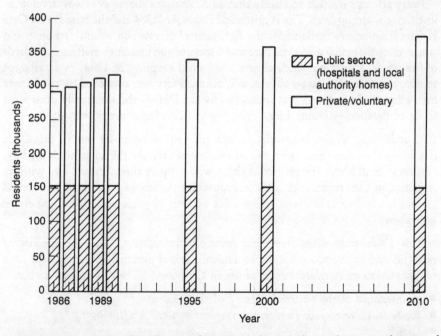

FIGURE 18.1   Projected residents aged 65 years and over in hospitals, nursing homes and residential homes in England, 1986–2010. Note: Derived by application of 1986 age-specific rates of occupation to Office of Population Censuses and Surveys population projections assuming static public sector provision. (Reproduced from ref. 25.)

the places for persons aged 65 years and over in NHS hospitals and local authority residential homes have been grouped together as 'public sector' and the remainder are in the private/voluntary group.

Most local authority homes are now modern, specially designed buildings, but a few have been converted from large houses. Private homes and many voluntary homes are usually converted large houses. The size of each home varies — the modern purpose-built homes of local authorities mostly cater for 40–55 persons. Accommodation is mainly in single rooms in the best of them, but some have a number of double rooms. There are lounges of various types, usually on each floor, a lift is always provided so that all the accommodation can be reached without climbing stairs (this type of accommodation is often referred to as 'ground floor type'). A resident matron and her/his staff look after the home and all meals are taken in a dining room usually at a table with four places. The private and voluntary homes are usually smaller — up to 35–40 places, and the sharing of bedrooms is commoner, although some single rooms are usually available.

Medical care of the residents is provided by a local GP, and usually minor illnesses can be looked after for a few days, although serious illness cannot normally be coped with and the elderly person has to be admitted temporarily to hospital.

Every attempt is made to ensure that an old persons' home does not develop an institutional atmosphere. The Registered Homes Act 1984 and the Residential Care Homes Regulations made under the Act, control private and voluntary homes and concentrate particulary on structure and fitness of the building, staffing, standards of fire safety, sanitation, medical care and record keeping. In 1984, in an attempt to encourage the right type of care, a Working Party was convened by the Centre for Policy on Ageing and was sponsored by the DHSS, and eventually drew up a Code of Practice — Home Life.[17] The report in its introduction stated:

. . . underlying all the recommendations and requirements set out in this Code is a conviction that those who live in residential care should do so with dignity; that they should have the respect of those who support them; should live with no reduction of their rights as citizens (except where the law so prescribes), and should be entitled to live as full and active a life as their physical and mental condition will allow.

This Code emphasizes five basic principles intended to improve the life of residents and to introduce a more individualistic and personal approach with little regimentation or standardization of life in the home.[18] These principles include:

- maintenance of the personal dignity of the resident
- access to private space (which the resident can call her/his own)
- choice
- autonomy — the principle that, as far as possible, residents should have a say in the way the home is run and controlled; instructions and rules should be kept to an absolute minimum (i.e. fire, safety, etc.) and should be similar to those in a good hotel

- responsible risk-taking — this means that overprotection should be avoided; when dealing with very old people, some minor risks can only be eliminated by excessive overprotection and this is what adds to the frustration of the resident.

What is really intended by the Code of Practice, which has the full support of the Department of Health, is that although emphasis on environmental factors (fire prevention, sanitation, etc.) is necessary, these features are not the most important to those living in the home. The residents want to live reasonably normal lives and this entails being able to control their lives.[19] They want:

- to eat their meals when they want to (within reasonable limits)
- to heat their rooms as they wish
- to open or shut windows
- to watch television or not
- to go to bed when they want, e.g. to live normally as if they were in their own home.

Many authors since Townsend's[20] classic description of the harsh realities of institutional living have confirmed that although conditions have improved, many residents in homes have little privacy or choice either in local authority homes[21] or in private homes.[22]

One of the difficulties which is likely to continue is the large proportion of very old, very frail people who now live in these homes. A high proportion are in their 80s and 90s, mostly women (at least a 3 : 1 ratio women to men in most homes). A number are often mildly confused and some may be partly incontinent. The increasing numbers of elderly persons with mental disorders presents special problems, for some can be difficult and verbally aggressive. A few homes now segregate the very confused from other more normal residents, and special homes for mentally disordered elderly persons are now being developed.

In the local authority homes, every resident contributes to the cost of their accommodation. Each home has a standard charge which represents the economic weekly cost of keeping a resident in the home. Every person entering the home is asked if they can afford this charge. If they can, they do so. If not, each resident must pay a proportion of her/his retirement pension leaving pocket money for personal spending. The local authority is then responsible for any additional cost. Such an arrangement ensures that every old person (even if her/his only income is the retirement pension) contributes to the cost. Capital below £3000 is ignored. If capital is greater than £3000 the full cost must be paid until the capital falls to this amount. The type and standard of the accommodation provided for the elderly person is the same for all regardless of the amount paid. In private and voluntary homes, many receive a subsidy towards the cost of the accommodation from the Department of Social Security. The same rules apply about any capital the old person has (see above).

Because of all these features, it will always be likely that most elderly persons will prefer, if at all possible, to remain in their own homes. This is why this remains one of the most important strategies which should be adopted to cope with the future increase in the numbers of very old people in the community.

The frailest old people local authorities can care for in their homes are those who can do all the following: (1) get up daily, (2) dress even if only with assistance, (3) make their way across a room with help, (4) eat a meal without assistance.

Emergency compulsory admission of old people

Under section 47 of the National Assistance Act, 1948, and the Amendment Act, 1951, power is given for the compulsory removal of aged and certain other persons to hospital or other institutions.

Those who can be compulsorily removed must be: (a) suffering from grave chronic disease or being aged, infirm or physically incapacitated, are living in insanitary conditions; and (b) are unable to devote to themselves, and are not receiving from other persons, proper care and attention.

The local community physician and another doctor must certify that it is in the interests of the person to remove him/her from the dwelling. This being so, the local authority (through the social services department) applies to a magistrate (or court) for removal. If the magistrate (or court) is satisfied, then the order for removal to hospital or institution is made.

Only very few elderly people are removed in this way as most readily agree or can be persuaded, but occasionally action is necessary. Such cases are old people who have neglected themselves badly or who are very ill, such as those suffering from late neoplastic disease, and who are afraid to go into hospital. If a GP meets with such a case and cannot persuade the patient, it is best to apply to the Director of Social Services who will arrange the necessary medical examinations and, if necessary, compulsory removal.

References

1. OPCS. Monitor PP2 91/1, p. 6. London: OPCS. 1991.
2. OPCS. Surveys of Disability in Great Britain, Report 1: The prevalence of disability in adults. London: HMSO. 1988.
3. Hunt A. The elderly at home. A study of people aged sixty-five and over living in the community in England and Wales in 1976. A survey carried out on behalf of the DHSS by the Social Survey Division of OPCS. London: HMSO. 1978.
4. Rowe JW, Kahn RL. Human ageing: usual and successful.
5. Taylor RC, Ford G. Inequalities in old age: an examination of age, sex and class differences in a sample of community elderly. Ageing and Society 1983, 3(2): 183.
6. Taylor R. In Wells N, Freer C (eds). The ageing population. Macmillan Press. 1988, pp. 119-128.
7. Alderson MR. Season and mortality. Health Trends Vol. 17, London: HMSO. 1985, pp. 87-96.

8. Collins KJ. Low indoor temperatures and morbidity in the elderly. Age and Ageing 1986, **15**: 212–220.

9. Grut M. Cold-related deaths in some developed countries. Lancet **i**: 212.

10. Mulley GP. Differential diagnosis of dementia. Br. Med. J. 1986, **292**: 1416–1418.

11. Woodford-Williams E. The efficiency and quality of the service. *In* Coakley D (ed) Establishing a geriatric service: London: Croom Helm. 1982, pp. 106–112.

12. Bagnell WE, Datta SR, Knox J *et al*. Geriatric medicine in Hull: a comprehensive service. Br. Med. J. 1977, **2**: 102.

13. Gray JAM. *In* Wells N, Freer C (eds) The ageing population. Macmillan Press. 1988, pp. 217–218.

14. Challis DJ, Davies BP. The community care approach. An innovation in home care by social service departments. *In* Wells N, Freer C (eds) The ageing population. Macmillan Press. 1988, p. 191.

15. Challis DJ, Davies BP. Case management in community care. Aldershot: Gower Press. 1986.

16. Ratna L; Davies J. Family therapy with the elderly mentally ill: some strategies and techniques. Br. J. Psychiat. **145**: 311. 1984.

17. Centre of Policy on Ageing. Home life: a code of practice for residential care. Report of a working party (Kine, Lady Avebury, chair). 1984. London.

18. Peace S. Living environments for elderly. *In* Wells N Freer C (eds) The ageing population. Macmillan Press. 1988, pp. 217–221.

19. Willcocks DM, Peace SM, Kellaher LA. Private lives in public places: a research-based critique of residential life in local authority old persons homes. London: Tavistock. 1986.

20. Townsend P. The last refuge. London: Routledge and Kegan Paul. 1982.

21. Willcocks DM, Peace SM, Kellaher CA, Ring AG. The residential life of old people: a study of 100 local authority homes, Vol. 1 Research Report No 2. Polytechnic of North London. 1982.

22. Weaver T, Willcocks D, Kellaher L. The business of care: a study of private residential homes for old people. Research Report No. 1, Centre of Environmental and Social Studies in Ageing. Polytechnic of North London. 1985.

23. Department of Health. Health and Personal Social Services Statistics, 1991. London: HMSO.

24. Department of Health. Health and Personal Social Services Statistics, 1990. London: HMSO.

25. Laing W. Environments for the Elderly — A Mixed Economy in Long-term Care in the Ageing Population. Macmillan. 1988.

19

Hospital Social Work

In the treatment and management of all illness, the reaction of the patient to the various social factors (the family, job, etc.) is often quite crucial. Where the illness is largely produced by the psychological reaction of the patient (i.e. psychosomatic diseases), successful diagnosis and treatment is dependent upon the ability to understand, change or influence for the better the patient's reaction and adjustment to these social aspects.

This is particularly so in any long-standing or permanent illness such as a congenital abnormality, or a disabling condition such as rheumatoid arthritis, multiple sclerosis or hemiplegia or a sudden serious accident. Also, the reaction of the patient and family is often most important in a terminal illness (leading to the death of the patient), and this is especially so in some incurable cancers appearing suddenly in middle age.

In hospitals, the unravelling of many of the more complicated social features in disease is undertaken at the request of the consultant by a trained social worker — the *hospital social worker*. This work in all its aspects forms part of a team approach and assists and complements that of the consultant and medical team.

The number of hospital social workers has steadily increased in the last 40 years. Their tasks have altered considerably since their predecessors were appointed as 'almoners', who were among the earliest social workers and were functioning in some hospitals at the end of the last century.

In England and Wales there are approximately 2300 hospital social workers. Most of these work in district general hospitals or in geriatric and paediatric units. Those who work in psychiatric hospitals and are specially qualified are called *psychiatric social workers*.

There are four main areas of work for hospital social workers:

1. *Medical casework* — concerned with the adjustment of the patient and his/her family to their disease. This is the largest and most important aspect of hospital social work. It mainly involves working with the patient in hospital (including in-patient and out-patient work), but may also necessitate the hospital social worker visiting the patient's home.
2. *Environmental help* — arranging how the patient's home can be assisted to help cope with the illness. This may involve complete rehousing of the patient or the

adaptation of the home either structurally or by the introduction of certain aids.

3. *Arrangements of immediate assistance to the patient or relatives* — this includes financial help, convalescent arrangements, provision of escorts and accommodation for relatives.

4. *Liaison with various other social work agencies* — to enable long-term care and assistance to be provided for the patient.

The nature of hospital social work, its value and its limitations can best be illustrated by the following series of examples.

Medical casework

Casework by hospital social workers is undertaken for most types of patients and for most ages. There is, however, a greater need in certain age groups who are potentially more vulnerable. Hence more work is done with children, elderly persons and certain groups who are obviously going to face more social problems — unmarried mothers, patients who show signs of maladjustment (anxiety states, suicides, those with alcohol abuse), the homeless and any other patient who obviously has an acute difficult personal problem — marital difficulties would be an obvious example.

Another important group to the hospital social worker is the long-standing or chronic patient, especially if he/she has a disability. After the acute treatment of any such patient has been carried out, the next stage — successful rehabilitation back into the patient's own home and normal life (back to employment) — may depend on solving as many social problems as medical ones. For instance, mobility is of paramount importance for anyone who is going to return successfully to work. The hospital social worker is expected to know how these can be best dealt with and has the responsibility of arranging all the various solutions — special transport, industrial training, special housing, etc. (see below).

HOSPITAL SOCIAL WORK WITH CHILDREN

A particular problem seen in paediatric work is connected with congenital disabilities of all kinds. Their recognition, diagnosis and treatment are obviously tasks for health visitors, district nurses, midwives, paediatricians and all their specialized teams, which will include hospital social workers. Many parents find it very difficult to accept and may always do so. There is a natural tendency for all such parents to disbelieve the paediatrician and not to accept the true position. Very often the parents will rationalize this natural disbelief by suggesting that the doctor is wrong or that there must be some treatment which will help. Any tendency on the part of the medical team to become impatient with such an attitude can quickly result in the parents seeking other medical help — perhaps privately in another part of the country or even abroad. They may even, in extreme cases, spend large sums of money which they cannot afford (and which they will need later) in a futile attempt to find someone who will 'cure their child'.

Much of this fruitless effort can be avoided if the medical team recognizes that most parents find it very difficult to accept reality at once and that many need support for a long time before they will finally accept the true situation. But the immediate problem can be helped by a sympathetic hospital social worker who can quietly assist the parents by discussion, listening and practical advice, and by arranging the special aid such parents need — how to help their child to develop more normally. Many such children suffer from the disadvantage of isolation (because the child is unable to mix in normal ways) and this can be overcome by attending a special day nursery or playgroup. If the hospital social worker sees the parents and child regularly and arranges for health visitors, teachers or social workers to meet them too, slowly the parents begin to accept the diagnosis and will be better able to face the various difficulties. Similar problems are often seen with parents of children with learning disabilities (mental handicap). In all these cases, it is often very helpful if the parents can meet other parents who have older children who are disabled in the same way. It is for this reason that local associations for many congenital disabilities have developed, and hospital social workers in paediatric hospitals can often introduce the parents to such a group. Many parents, in a curious way, feel guilty or ashamed about their congenitally disabled child (although many would never admit it) and may be stubbornly resentful of meeting similar parents. Patient persuasion can overcome this and can make a great difference to the eventual acceptance of the problem and its solution.

Home accidents

These are a serious problem in paediatric work (see p. 127). In many instances, the question may arise whether the accident could have been prevented if only some precaution had been taken. Studies of children with burns show in some cases that this is the second case in the same family or even in the same child. This may be coincidental, but usually there is a reason for this — the home circumstances may not be satisfactory and children may be left on their own for long periods at home or in the care of an older child. Occasionally the question of serious neglect may arise and the accident may be the only means of bringing this to light. For these reasons, hospital social workers often undertake further investigations on behalf of the paediatrician to see whether the home can be made safer and therefore reduce the chance of further accidents. In most instances, the hospital social worker would discuss the case with the health visitor who is visiting the home.

In some instances, the question arises whether the injury which the child has suffered is the result of an accident at all or whether it may not be a case of *child abuse*. Suspicion in such cases usually starts with the doctor seeing the child recognizing that the injuries are not consistent with the parents' story, the type of injury or the attitude of the parent (see p. 504). As soon as reasonable suspicion occurs, the hospital social worker will help arrange a 'case conference' with the doctors and local social service department officers (see p. 502). The hospital social worker will also help follow up the consequent treatment of child abuse, and possible sexual abuse cases and, in this respect, will work very closely with social workers, health visitors and voluntary bodies in the community.

HOSPITAL SOCIAL WORK WITH THE ELDERLY

The elderly are a very important section of the community in whom any serious illness may often be accompanied by many social problems (see Chapter 18). It therefore follows that any serious illness in an old person necessitating admission of that individual to hospital should be followed by inquiry into the home circumstances to see whether the old person, when medically fit for discharge, can safely go home, e.g. whether there is suitable supportive help at home. For most old people living in a family, home discharge is quite safe provided that nursing and medical care is available. Many elderly people live alone and home discharge in such cases calls for special arrangements — the provision of a care assistant, or a meal being delivered, or arrangements made for some friend or relative to help temporarily in the period immediately following discharge — until the old person is completely fit again and able to cope alone. Most geriatricians, physicians and surgeons treating elderly patients in hospital will usually refer those who live on their own to the hospital social worker so that provision can be made to ensure that the old person will be looked after properly on discharge. Some local authorities have set up special home care programmes (see p. 411) to help such cases, but all can arrange for a care assistant to be available.

A further problem which hospital social workers have to consider is that some elderly people, although in urgent need of such help, may refuse to accept it. In many instances, the real reason for refusal is financial. The old person feels he/she cannot afford such help. Careful explanation that no charge is made for care assistant services to the elderly whose only income is their retirement pension may help. There can still be a few difficult cases of elderly persons able to afford to pay for help, but who are so conscious of rising costs that they still refuse. Such elderly patients usually rationalize their refusal by firmly stating they do not need such help. Careful co-operation between the doctor and social worker will help, particularly if the old person clearly realizes, before admission if possible, that this form of support is all part of the necessary treatment.

TERMINAL ILLNESS

Obviously many problems will have to be faced in a terminal illness, and these will depend on the age of the patient, his or her family responsibilities and the likely length of the terminal illness (short terminal illnesses usually provide fewer social problems than illnesses which last many months).

Carcinoma of all kinds, especially in younger adults with family commitments, often calls for a considerable amount of social casework. An infinite variety of problems occur. First there is the initial treatment and the support, reassurance and anxieties of the patient to be faced. Any adult with a family to support — such as a mother with a family still at school with, for example, a carcinoma of the breast or ovary — has a greater chance of success with treatment if natural anxieties about how the family are going to cope without them are reduced by sympathetic and effective practical help. In all instances, the problems faced by the family immediately will depend on the attitude of the spouse and other adult relatives and on the age of the children. In many instances, the family may be able to cope but, in a number, help will be needed at once or may become necessary as the family perhaps, later, begins to show signs of strain or of being unable to manage. Many types of assistance are possible — social service departments will be able to do much to enable the family to stay together by providing a care assistant. In other instances it is best to arrange for a young child to go into a day nursery so that the parent can leave the child there on the way to work and collect him/her on the way home, knowing that the child will be properly looked after. In some cases, such arrangements might not be possible and it may be necessary for the children to be provided with accommodation in a children's home until the parent has had their treatment and is fit again to look after them. In some cases a mixture of care may be appropriate — one or two children being provided by the local authority with accommodation and one (or two) staying with the other parent.

The hospital social worker will need to work very closely with other social workers in the community and also with health visitors who may already be well known to the family from their ordinary home visiting of young children. The hospital social worker must be able to see the patient in hospital and to discuss with the doctors, nurses and other staff the prognosis and the assistance required.

In some terminal cases, other types of problems will have to be faced. In many elderly patients with a fatal illness, the type of home they live in and the health of their spouse may be crucial in deciding whether to discharge the patient home at all, and what further supportive services will be required. Within the hospital, the consultant medical and nursing staff usually will refer such cases to the hospital social worker to investigate the home circumstances. Most hospital social workers will not carry out a home visit in such instances, but will depend on the views of the primary health care team (general medical practitioner, health visitor, district nurse) and the local social worker.

In some cases, the solution is unlikely to be permanent. The patient may return home for a period and then may suddenly deteriorate and need either readmission to hospital or admission into a nursing home dealing with such illnesses. Obviously the closest co-ordination is necessary between the hospital social worker and the primary health care team. In many instances admission may finally be arranged into one of the many excellent nursing homes or hospices run by charitable or religious bodies. Hospital social workers will have a local list available and help choose the one most suitable.

SINGLE PARENT FAMILIES

In single parent families, any illness in that parent will usually produce many social problems. Lone parent families are increasing rapidly. During the 1970s and 1980s, there was a marked increase in the proportion of families with dependent children where there was a sole parent in Great Britain — from 8% in 1971 to 13% in 1981 and to 19% in 1990.[1] (About 95% are lone mother families.) Obviously the care of the children will depend upon their age, but in many instances unless the family can help, the younger children will need to come into the care of the local social services department. If the illness is long and protracted, such children may need a family placement (see p. 483) and the hospital social worker will initiate the arrangements. The number of births outside marriage reached 29.7% of all births in England in 1991.[2] Some of these births present special problems which usually fall to the hospital social worker to solve. Many mothers will wish to keep their child, and fortunately there are many excellent schemes to help with housing accommodation (the local social services department should be able to help find places). In some instances, the mother may wish to have her baby adopted and, if the mother decides early enough, the hospital social worker arranges for this to be undertaken by either the local social services department or by a voluntary adoption agency (see pp. 493–495).

GYNAECOLOGICAL CASES

In gynaecology departments, many special social problems have to be sorted out. Many women have deep-rooted fears about gynaecological conditions which need careful explanation. Much of this is carried out by the consultant and medical staff, but the multidisciplinary team approach is being increasingly used in such hospital departments, and the hospital social worker is expected to deal with these problems. A variety of marital difficulties may have to be tackled by the hospital social worker especially in the rehabilitation of hysterectomy patients. Some of the troublesome symptoms may be connected with marital or sex difficulties. Hospital social workers need special training and must work closely with the medical team in the hospital and the primary health care team in the community.

Many gynaecology departments have to deal with questions such as abortions and hospital social workers must know all the alternative arrangements which are available if an abortion is either refused or cannot take place in hospital because of shortage of beds.

ACCIDENT CASES

In accident cases involving adults, many social problems occur. Some of these are due to the suddenness of the injury and to the period of doubt which follows concerning the outcome, especially if the patient remains unconscious. There may still be a very difficult period for the family and patient to face until it is clear that there is no permanent brain damage. Not only is it necessary for the hospital social worker to help support the family but he/she will also need to help with rehabilitation and with employment problems and perhaps with industrial retraining. In most instances, the hospital social worker acts as the co-ordinator between the doctors in hospital and with those responsible for industrial retraining including the Disablement Resettlement Officers (see pp. 532–533).

In accident cases involving paralysis (such as paraplegia), there may be a period of doubt about the outcome as it may be weeks before it is possible to know whether the paralysis is permanent (due to a division of the spinal cord) or whether it is temporary (due to severe bruising). If the case turns out to be one of permanent paraplegia, then a great deal of social work needs to be undertaken by the hospital social worker in conjunction with social workers in the community, and with occupational therapists to ensure that the home will be suitable as the patient will be in a wheelchair on discharge. Many adaptations and modifications will probably be necessary, but these will take a long time to arrange and therefore it is most important that the hospital social worker starts such arrangements (which will necessarily involve many outside agencies) early in the stay of the patient in hospital. It is for this reason, that many regional hospitals looking after paraplegic patients arrange for their hospital social workers to discuss each patient's home conditions in detail with a social worker from the local social services department shortly after the admission of the patient.

RHEUMATOID ARTHRITIS AND SIMILAR CHRONIC DISABLING DISEASES

Many serious disabling conditions which develop suddenly in adult life (but which are not fatal) such as rheumatoid arthritis always provide a range of social problems. Some of these may be obvious, like the care of young children if the mother is affected and has to be admitted to hospital for a long period. But others may be related to the difficulty of adjustment which many patients find. If an active young adult suddenly develops a crippling and painful condition such as rheumatoid arthritis, the initial reaction is usually one of incredulity. Much patience is needed by professional staff to overcome this, and the hospital social worker backed up by other social workers and health visitors in the community can play a major part by casework and counselling (by sympathetic listening, explanation and encouragement) to enable the patient to accept the limitations of the illness and therefore to help the rehabilitation process.

In other diseases such as multiple sclerosis and muscular dystrophy, there is usually a general slow deterioration and progression, although there will be periods of remission and relapses and, in some cases, the disease will suddenly abort. Crises are bound to occur in some of these cases as the effects of the disease produce their social problems. Many of these have to be dealt with by those working outside hospital such as social workers, primary health care teams, but in some instances hospital admission becomes inevitable and the hospital social worker has to help solve any difficulty. This will vary from complete family breakdown if a married partner leaves the home, to more minor problems connected with various aids and adaptations which need to be fitted to help the partially paralysed patient.

MENTAL DISABILITY

Social workers employed in mental hospitals form an important part of the psychiatrist's team. The successful discharge of most patients depends upon not only the correct psychiatric treatment, but also on the home conditions and family support. All psychiatric patients are influenced adversely by unsatisfactory living conditions. In fact the 'extrinsic' conditions (see p. 307) are always an important predisposing factor in sudden deterioration or breakdown in mental illness. It therefore follows that success or failure will often depend on the social conditions surrounding the patient on discharge — the home, family and the availability of suitable employment.

Follow-up of all discharged mentally ill patients is also most important and the hospital social worker should help the psychiatrist to assess how the patient is managing after discharge. This can only be satisfactorily undertaken by the hospital social worker if there are excellent links with the primary health care team and the social worker undertaking the after-care. The provision of day care facilities in the community is also important (see p. 372) and reports should always be available from such units. In the past, many psychiatric social workers in hospitals undertaking after-care work did many visits themselves. With the larger number of discharges being arranged from psychiatric hospitals, this is now rarely possible, and arrangements are made for the social workers in the area teams in the community to visit the hospital regularly, to attend weekly conferences on patients about to be discharged and to act as the visiting after-care force for the hospital treatment team.

In the case of persons with learning disabilities (mental handicap) many social problems occur. Reference has already been made to the difficulties many parents have in accepting the diagnosis. In many instances, hospital social workers will not be involved as most of these persons live at home. But sometimes, the person with learning disabilities (mental handicap) is also physically disabled in some other respect (about 48% of those with cerebral palsy also have learning disabilities) and the hospital social worker may be involved in helping and advising during a stay in hospital or on attendance at out-patient or assessment clinic.

GENERAL MEDICAL, SURGICAL AND ORTHOPAEDIC CASES

In a few such cases, the hospital social worker will be brought into the diagnostic and treatment team in hospital by the consultant because of special difficulties connected with social problems of the patient at home or at work. Any illness which may become long-standing is more likely to produce social problems. For this reason diabetes, epilepsy, chronic bronchitis and ischaemic heart disease (coronary thrombosis), hemiplegia, tuberculosis and many other diseases often involve the hospital social worker either during the initial illness or during a relapse. The uncertainty of outcome (prognosis) adds to the various social problems to be faced by such patients and their families.

Arrangements of immediate assistance

A further function of hospital social workers could be classified as arranging features which facilitate medical care. It includes a wide range of functions many of which might be described as routine or superficial services for patients and their relatives, which do not involve social casework. They include arranging for financial help, convalescence, provision of escorts and accommodation for relatives.

FINANCIAL HELP

Many patients will need advice about their 'welfare rights' — what financial help they are entitled to — sickness benefit, invalidity benefit and the various industrial injury benefits. Many of these are extremely complicated and are constantly changing and most patients find them confusing. For accidental injuries, the hospital social worker must explain that compensation may be available through civil action in the courts and stress the importance of the patient and relatives seeing a solicitor at the earliest possible moment, to ensure that proper advice is received. If the patient belongs to a professional organization or trade union, that body usually will be most helpful in such cases.

There are also special financial grants available through the local social security office to assist with the visiting of children and others who are patients in hospital. The hospital social work department has to undertake this type of work.

CONVALESCENT ARRANGEMENTS

Convalescent arrangements of various kinds are made by hospital social workers. These include a range of facilities within the health service, e.g. transfer to special convalescent hospitals and/or a convalescent type of holiday. In addition there is a wide variety of other convalescent homes available which are run by industrial concerns, nationalized bodies and trades unions which assist with convalescence for those working in the corresponding industry. There are also many voluntary organizations which have bought or built convalescent homes. The hospital social worker therefore has a wide range of convalescent facilities to choose from when helping any individual patient.

PROVISION OF ESCORTS

In some instances, an escort has to be arranged to travel with a child or elderly person leaving hospital and the hospital social worker is responsible for doing this. The escort is usually from a panel of voluntary helpers or a local voluntary organization.

Accommodation for relatives

In some cases, the patient has been admitted to a hospital a long way from home and close relatives find it very difficult or impossible to visit unless they can arrange to stay for a short time near the hospital. The hospital social worker usually has a list of suitable addresses — covering a range of accommodation and price — and will assist relatives to find accommodation. This is particularly important if the patient is dangerously ill or is due to have an operation and the relatives wish to be close to hand.

References

1. OPCS. Monitor SS91/1. General Household Survey 1990. London: HMSO 1991.
2. OPCS. Population Trends 1991. London: HMSO.

PART THREE –

SOCIAL SERVICES

20

Personal Social Services and their Management

The 'social services' cover three main groups:

1. *Social services departments provided by the local authority* which include a wide range of statutory, community and residential services for the elderly, children, physically disabled, mentally disabled and homeless. The hospital social work services are also provided in this way although working entirely within a hospital setting. Centrally these services are the responsibility of the Department of Health.

2. *The probation and after-care service* which is attached to the courts and works mainly with adult offenders who, as part of their sentence, are placed on probation. In addition, much of the after-care work for discharged prisoners is undertaken by this service. The probation service is quite separate from the services in the first group given above and, like the Prison Service, is centrally the responsibility of the Home Office. This book is not intended to deal with this service.

3. *Voluntary bodies.* There are many well-established voluntary bodies providing social services both on a national and local basis. They include Family Service Units, Women's Royal Voluntary Service, the various bodies working for children (NSPCC, Barnados, National Children's Homes, the Family Welfare Association), Age Concern for the elderly and the various bodies working for the disabled including The Royal Association for Disability and Rehabilitation, and locally through Councils of Social Service and Rural Community Councils. These local voluntary bodies often undertake a co-ordinating function in respect of smaller local voluntary bodies or local branches of the large national bodies.

   As many of these voluntary bodies are undertaking responsibilities which could also be covered by social services departments, it is essential that very close working arrangements are made. In many instances, some of the local finance necessary for their functions is provided by the Social Services Committee of the local authority.

   The government minister who works most closely with these voluntary bodies is the Secretary of State for Health. In some instances, special financial grants are paid by the Department of Health to large voluntary bodies to promote research (e.g. into alcohol abuse) and develop certain specialized social services (e.g. work with deprived children).

Further voluntary bodies are the Citizens' Advice Bureaux. These bodies were first developed in the World War II to help with various queries about rationing, missing relatives, etc. Their role has now widened, especially in the field of consumer protection, the provision of legal advice and the explanation of various pension rights. They are particularly valuable in helping families who may be unwilling to seek statutory assistance from social service departments or social security offices because they feel aggrieved for some reason – they may have been evicted for rent arrears or generally are resentful of the way they have been treated by local authorities and other statutory services. For this reason, some Social Services Committees provide financial grants to Citizens' Advice Bureaux to enable them to help such clients who otherwise would be unlikely to seek help. Centrally there is a National Association of Citizens' Advice Bureaux linked to local bureaux by a regional committee.

Functions of the Secretary of State for Health

The Secretary of State for Health has overall responsibility for the wide range of social services run by Social Services Committees of local authorities and also for helping to promote similar services by the voluntary bodies mentioned above. The Secretary of State is a member of the Cabinet and, of course, is responsible for the health services and is therefore in an ideal position to co-ordinate these services nationally and to ensure that their individual developments are balanced.

METHOD OF CONTROL EXERCISED BY THE DEPARTMENT OF HEALTH ON THE DEVELOPMENT OF SOCIAL SERVICES BY LOCAL AUTHORITIES

There are three main ways in which the Department of Health exercises control of local social services:

1. *In an advisory capacity* – important advisory memoranda are issued giving advice in detail on the development of certain services. Sometimes such memoranda deal with the need to develop services in a co-ordinating way with other services – examples were the circulars on child abuse and in the development of services for the elderly. In some cases, advisory memoranda deal only with items of immediate concern to social services departments. Occasionally joint memoranda are issued both by the Department of Health and another department.
2. *Planning and policy* – this is an essential function of the Department of Health and is becoming more important with the trend towards developing more

services for people within the community, for these can only succeed if balanced provision is made by social and health services. The development of community care for the mentally ill is a very good example of the need for the planning and policy to be carefully balanced and co-ordinated so that the needs of those mentally ill persons are provided by social services departments to enable the health and hospital services to discharge their patients from hospitals. The central structure of the Department of Health has been reorganized to assist the integration of planning between the social and health services. A central planning division has been established alongside a central regional division, and in both the social service and the health service professional officers are closely working with their linked administrative officers. There is also a Social Work Service based centrally and within the 10 regions of the Department of Health (see Fig. 20.1). The function of this service is mainly advisory and to assist in developing better social services. Its regional staff assist, advise and help the social

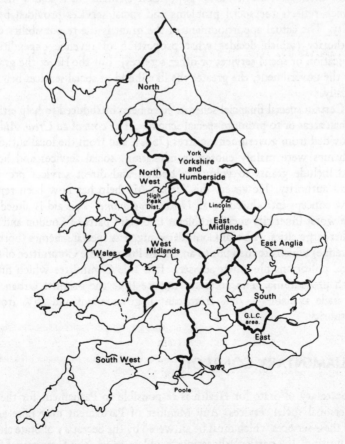

FIGURE 20.1   Department of Health regions of England and Wales.

services departments in their areas. These staff carefully study suggested capital developments and advise the Central Department. They also act as the local adviser to Directors of Social Services and their staff in the region.

3. *Financial* — this is an important method by which the Department of Health can control the development of social services. It is more apparent as regards new capital development than revenue expenditure because local authorities must obtain loan sanction from the Department of Health for all new buildings (capital). This means that all new residential accommodation (e.g. day centres, day nurseries, workshops) can only be built with government permission (key sector finance). Office accommodation is not covered by this as it is provided from a block grant called locally determined schemes.

Revenue (or costs of running day-to-day services) is financed by means of a grant from the government and from the local council. The government grant is the large block grant of money made to local authorities to assist them with their services. It has a 'population element' in it and a 'needs' element which reflects the social problems and social services provided by that authority. The actual apportionment of the grant is the responsibility of each local authority (which decides what proportion of revenue expenditure goes to education or social services or other services). But the larger the grant provided by the government, the greater the likelihood of social services being developed locally.

Certain special financial schemes have been introduced to help either deprived urban areas or to promote special schemes. The cost of an *Urban Aid Scheme* was provided from government sources (75%), and from the local authority (25%). Schemes were mainly chosen in education, social services and housing areas and include grants to voluntary bodies, and direct services provided by the local authority. However, this Urban Aid help has now been replaced and a new concept introduced — an *Urban Programme*. This aid is aimed at assisting the worst inner city social problems in certain parts of London and some of the other large cities. A Local Committee suggests special schemes (both capital and revenue) which are then put to an Urban Programme Committee of national and local politicians plus their advisers. It is this Committee which finally decides each programme. The necessary finance (like the original Urban Aid grants) is made available — 75% from central government and 25% from the local authority.

PARLIAMENTARY CONTROL

The Secretary of State for Health is responsible to Parliament for the conduct of the personal social services. Any Member of Parliament may raise any question about these services which must be answered by the Secretary of State either verbally or in writing. If a particularly serious problem arises, the Secretary of State can set up an inquiry to consider all aspects relating to it and to issue a report. An example was the inquiry held into sexual abuse in children in Cleveland in 1987.

Training of social workers

THE CENTRAL COUNCIL FOR EDUCATION AND TRAINING IN SOCIAL WORK

This Council is responsible for the promotion of training in all fields of social work — in field and in residential work — and also approves and reviews courses leading to a professional qualification in social work. Most courses are held at polytechnics and universities and last usually from 1 to 2 years depending upon the qualification and the standard of the candidates. At present there are two main ways to train to become a social worker:

- by obtaining a relevant degree in Social Sciences and then taking a 1-year course
- by taking a 2-year course (with or without any other type of degree).

Candidates may be either sponsored or seconded to training courses from social services departments or apply for an educational grant.

Local authority social services

Comprehensive social services are provided by all major local authorities (county councils and metropolitan districts and London boroughs) under the Local Authority Social Services Act, 1970. Figure 20.2 shows the local authorities in England.

Each authority has a Social Services Committee which controls services and in each authority there is a Director of Social Services who is the chief officer in charge of the department administering all these social services.

TYPES OF SOCIAL SERVICES

The following are the services provided by the social services department:

- care of the elderly (Chapter 18)
- care of the physically handicapped, including the blind, deaf, spastic, epileptic and paraplegic (Chapter 24)
- care of the homeless (Chapter 25)
- child care protection including child care supervision, acceptance of parental

FIGURE 20.2   Social services authorities in England.

responsibility of children committed into the care of the local authority, control
of children's homes, admission units, reception centres, boarding out arrangements, community homes, special community homes (with education on the
premises) and those acting as assessment centres, remand homes and services for
adoption; these services are provided under the Children Act 1989 (see Chapters
22 and 23); social work and family casework with the mentally disordered
including provision of social workers; also included are day centres, adult training centres, workshops and residential accommodation (hostels) for the mentally
disordered
- day care of children under five years of age, day nurseries and child minding
- the provision of care assistants (formerly home helps)
- care of unsupported mothers, including residential care.

SOCIAL SERVICES DEPARTMENTS

A typical layout of the social services department is given in Fig. 20.3. It will be
noted that there are five main parts of the department:

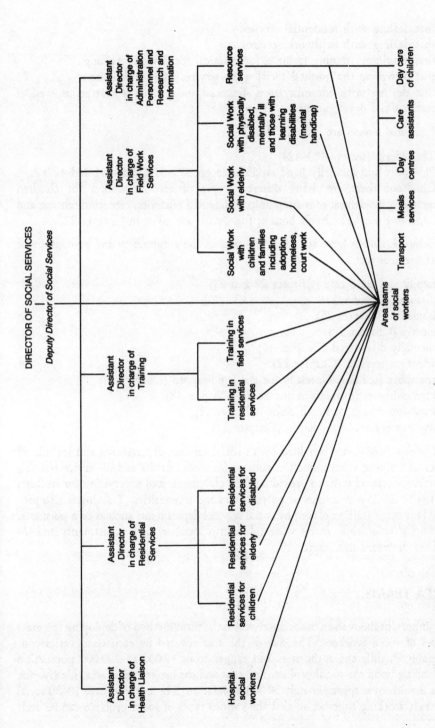

FIGURE 20.3   Structure of a social services department.

- that dealing with residential services
- that dealing with fieldwork services
- that providing training facilities for practical social work training
- that providing the hospital social work services and health liaison
- that dealing with administration, financial and personnel matters as well as research and development.

Residential services are provided for:

- The elderly (see pp. 420–424)
- Physically and mentally handicapped (see pp. 373–374, 380–381 and 427)
- Children: there are many different types of accommodation for children including residential admission units, residential nurseries, reception centres, and large and small children's homes; full details are given in Chapter 22.

Fieldwork services look after facilities within the community and provide social work services for:

- family and child care (Chapter 22 and 23)
- disabled (Chapter 24)
- homeless (Chapter 25)
- elderly (Chapter 18)
- mentally disordered (Chapter 16)
- adoption services (Chapter 22)
- transport facilities, especially for the handicapped (Chapter 24)
- care assistants (formerly home helps) (Chapter 18)
- meals-on-wheels or lunch clubs (Chapter 18)
- day nursery accommodation (Chapter 22)

Training facilities are provided by all social services departments and include all types of training from induction courses for new recruits and in-service training courses for trained staff, to providing field placements and supervision for students on the 1- and 2-year courses at polytechnics and universities. Training is also provided for other staff employed by social services departments such as care assistants.

Hospital social work services were taken into social services departments in 1974 and are described in Chapter 19.

AREA TEAMS

An important innovation in social services is the team method of deploying the main forces of social workers. The size of the area covered by each team varies considerably in different authorities and ranges from 40 000 to 100 000 population depending upon the social problems present and the geographical area. Ideally each area should cover approximately 50 000 population. The aim is to have 10–30 social workers working together so that the various types of social problem can be dealt with quickly and without overlap. In each of these teams are social workers who specialize in either child care, welfare work with the elderly and handicapped or mentally disabled, all of whom work closely together under the leadership of a senior officer. The aim is that most types of social problems will eventually be dealt with by each social worker although a certain amount of specialization is inevitable and desirable. The main object of these teams is to provide a balanced social service which can quickly deal with any problem. Therefore the doctor whether in general or hospital practice should refer any social problem directly to the senior officer in charge of the area. The Director of Social Services will be able to indicate who this individual is and how he/she can be located.

It is usual in social work to refer to persons requiring help from the social services as clients, and this term is used by social workers when discussing their patients with doctors.

Because social workers need to use many different specialist services to resolve problems with their clients, most area teams will have attached to them the main community resources. Examples of area team responsibility include the allocation of care assistants to clients or the ordering of meals-on-wheels for elderly or handicapped people requiring them. The doctor needing this sort of help can obtain it through the senior officer in charge of the area team. For this reason, it has become increasingly usual to arrange for a social worker from the area team to attend health centres and other practices regularly to ensure direct and easy communication with the medical staff working there.

A close link is also maintained between the area social workers and the hospital social workers stationed at the local hospitals.

Liaison between community health services and social services

The co-operation between health services and social services is most important, and the reorganization of both during the past decade has been planned to facilitate co-ordination as far as possible. Thus, the health services provide medical advice to the social services and the local social services provide the hospital social work services and any social work advice and help required by doctors working within the community. It is, however, very important that liaison between the two services is good. On the health side, a community physician is appointed with responsibility for liaison and on the social services side a senior officer is appointed (usually an Assistant Director of Social Services) to take charge of the hospital social work service and be responsible for integration.

Whenever possible there should be similarity between the District Health Authority and a number of social services areas so that officers from both services work in similar geographical divisions (there will often be four to six social services area teams to each DHA). It is also important that close working relationships should be built up between GPs and social workers from the local social services department. This can best be achieved by social workers being attached part-time to the primary health care teams. Eventually it is hoped that such an arrangement will be general and that whenever hospital admission is arranged for an individual who is 'at risk' of social deprivation (perhaps because he/she is elderly and living alone) the team in hospital will be alerted by the social worker.

Close liaison between the two services is important in all problems, but particularly in the case of children, the severely physically or mentally disabled and the elderly. Many individual examples illustrate the need for such arrangements, especially the instances of child abuse. More details of the way such co-ordinated arrangements are ensured are given (i.e. pp. 511–512 where joint Area Child Protection Committees are described).

JOINT CONSULTATIVE COMMITTEE (JCC)

The Joint Consultative Committee provides a permanent statutory committee between the local authority providing social services and the matching DHA. The constitution and role of such committees have been described on p. 17. They play an increasingly important part in assisting coordination between the social and health services through Joint Financing arrangements and Joint Care Planning Teams (see p. 17).

21

Social Problems – Their Measurement and Assessment

There are many ways of assessing social problems in a community and these are often referred to as 'social indicators'. It is possible to measure certain factors known to be associated with the development of social difficulties and then to demonstrate how such conditions have contributed to and affected the problem. For instance, very poor housing conditions and overcrowding are known to be connected throughout the world with high levels of crime and social deprivation. Some of the worst of these are to be found in very large urban communities, and generally inner city areas have some of the worst reputations in this respect. Yet although rural areas rarely produce such concentrations of social deprivation, sometimes their remoteness may limit the range of employment and educational facilities. Indeed, in many countries, social deprivation develops because people migrate from their homes in rural districts to large cities in search of employment only to find work still very difficult to obtain and to discover living conditions, especially housing, to be very expensive.

By measuring a whole range of such factors such as unemployment, job stability, housing conditions and amenities available, education, levels of crime, prevalence of disease, dependence of families on social security benefits (an indicator of how poor a family is), and various groups (such as social class) (see p. 61), an indirect measure and indication of social problems and difficulties can be obtained. These are called *objective social indicators* in comparison with *subjective social indicators* which are dealt with later in this chapter (see pp. 474–475).

Objective social indicators

Chapters 3, 10 and 13 have already considered the general effects on the incidence and mortality of various communicable and non-communicable diseases, how many of these are also connected with social class groupings, and how these can affect the levels of disease in any community. These studies include successive periodic measurements, e.g. variability of the incidence of a disease over the decades. Such studies always emphasize the *inequalities in health*, which are often as great now as when the welfare state began in the UK in the late 1940s.[1] Levels of health have generally improved a great deal since 1946, but the inequality between different sections of the community largely remains.[2-4] This chapter will make no further reference to health problems, but will concentrate upon social difficulties and their consequences.

SOURCES AND METHODS OF STUDYING SOCIAL PROBLEMS IN THE UK

There are three main sources of information on social problems within the UK:

- individual research projects
- continuous government studies and publications
- specialized studies into specific social problems initiated by government departments of by professional organizations.

Individual research projects

Many of these have concentrated upon either a specific topic such as crime or unemployment or have involved a study of a whole range of social problems in a local area. An interesting example of the latter was the Social Malaise Study of Liverpool (1970)[5] which studied 36 different indices including:

Children in care	Education grants for clothing
School absenteeism	Job instability
Physically handicapped children	Unemployment
Educationally subnormal children	Possession orders
Adults who were mentally ill	Debtors
Adults who had learning disabilities	Homeless families case conferences
(mental handicap)	Higher education grants
Illegitimacy	Electricity Board entry warrants
Dysentery levels	Crime, mainly assault, sexual
Children deloused	immorality, burglary, theft, fraud
Dwellings disinfested	and malicious damage
Adults in receipt of free	Infant mortality
meals-on-wheels	

In this study correlation analysis was used to test the likely levels of connection between two of the various indices, and the results were published as a matrix of correlation.

There was a very high association between unemployment and assault, a high association between unemployment and debtors, homeless family cases, electricity warrants, burglary, theft, but a low association between unemployment and higher education grants.

Although such a study often only states the obvious, such analyses do attempt to measure and compare the spread of social problems in a city and to unravel the many causative factors responsible.

Illegitimacy was found to have a high connection with children coming into care, a moderate association with school absenteeism and educational subnormality, but less obvious connections with most of the other social indicators.

It is revealing to analyse the different levels of social problems or malaise within a large city like Liverpool. This survey showed a greater degree of variation than was expected. The usual collection of statistics had not brought to light the wide range of variations. For instance, illegitimacy varied between 3.4% and 23.2% (at that time the total illegitimate rate for Liverpool was 11.4%). There was a similar range of finding for children classified as educationally subnormal — from 0.6% to 4.7% in different wards of the city. The exact figures are not as important as the range of social problems they represent.

These types of research and the information they provide are very useful to social services departments to identify areas with a profusion of problems and difficulties. Some departments have Research and Information Units working continuously collecting similar data to enable local problems to be identified in detail. Such information is invaluable in helping to determine priorities of development. They help to identify the groups within the population that are at special risk of further deprivation. Resources (such as staff, playgroups, day centre facilities of all kinds, voluntary help initiatives, etc.) can then be concentrated where they are most needed — in the areas with the greatest social problems. To make such studies really effective, they must be repeated periodically as needs do change within any large urban area.

Continuous government studies and publications

Government Departments (Home Office, Department of Health, Department of Environment, Department of Education and Science, Office of Population Censuses and Surveys (OPCS)) carry out a continuous collection and analysis of various kinds of social statistical data from many sources and areas (such as information on population, migration, employment, housing, education, social services, transport, crime, drug problems, etc.). The publication 'Social Trends' produced annually by the Central Statistical Office summarizes the more important pieces of information and gives an excellent starting point for anyone wishing to study various social problems. It also contains two or three articles on subjects of topical interest. It also occasionally includes population projections based on the latest census results and other information collected, enabling accurate estimates to be made of the likely levels of future problems. For instance, it is known that the proportion of very old people in the UK is increasing rapidly, and this is bound to lead to many more social problems as such persons will need more and more help from various support services irrespective of their financial resources (see Chapter 18).

Methods of study of objective social indicators

One of the main difficulties of the various social indicators is that so many factors are inter-related and connected. This leads to 'double counting' (see below).

The Department of the Environment (DOE) has devised a measure of social deprivation which includes the following factors:

- persons unemployed
- overcrowded households
- single parent families
- households lacking exclusive use of basic amenities
- pensioners living alone
- residents with the head of the family born in the New Commonwealth or Pakistan.

Many of these are used to 'weight' central government grants to local authorities. Unfortunately, neither car ownership nor low social class have been included.[6] Most of the social indicators chosen in various surveys and research projects have some reservations attached to them. Most methods of assessing social deprivation include special demographic sub-groups such as 'elderly persons living alone', and it is then assumed that any district which contains a larger proportion of elderly persons living alone must suffer from a greater degree of social deprivation. The Jarman score which calculates the so-called 'underprivileged areas' and which is used to 'weight' general practitioners (GPs) remuneration is an example.[7] The problem is that there will be many persons in such a definition who do not fall into a deprived social category. For instance, there are some affluent retirement areas where there is a high proportion of elderly persons living alone. It so happens that, in the case of the Jarman category, many such patients, particularly if they are over the age of 80 years, do make more demands on the services of their GP, but this is not social deprivation in the usual sense.

In a recent publication dealing with social deprivation and health in Scotland, Carstairs and Morris[8] used a classification which has much to recommend it. They use only four variables:

- *overcrowding* — persons in private households living at a density greater than one person per room as a proportion of all persons in private households
- *male unemployment* — proportion of economically active males seeking work

- *low social class* — proportion of all persons in private households with the head of the household in either social class IV or V
- *no car* — proportion of all persons in private households with no car.

This classification is simple and also has the merit that it avoids double counting. Carstairs and Morris[8] then calculated the standard deviation for each of the four variables and then multiplied the standard deviation by the proportion of each variable, e.g. the proportion of overcrowding, male unemployed, low social class and no car. They then devised a 'deprivation score' which is the summation of all four variables expressed as the product multiplied by the standard deviation. The resultant score is either a positive or negative score — the positive figures representing the deprived part of the population studied and the negative figure the affluent part. The greater the negative figure obtained, the greater the affluence and the greater the positive figure the greater the deprivation.

Such 'deprivation scores' were then calculated for various parts of Scotland using either post-code districts (there are 1010 of these in the country each representing approximately 5000 persons), or local government districts and by Health Boards. Each 'deprivation score' was then subdivided into seven categories — 1 to 7. Categories 1–3 represent the more affluent sections, category 4 is roughly the mean, while categories 5–7 are the socially deprived groups. In this classification, the further from the mean the greater the deprivation or affluence. Thus category 7 represents the greatest social deprivation and category 1 the most affluent. The resultant distribution for Scotland as a whole is shown in Table 21.1.

TABLE 21.1 Deprivation categories for Scotland, 1980–85

| Category | Affluent ⟶ Deprived | | | | | | | |
	1	2	3	4	5	6	7	All
No car	13.3	23.4	30.8	41.8	50.4	61.9	79.4	41.3
Male unemployment	4.0	5.8	8.3	11.5	15.9	20.3	30.6	12.5
Low social class	5.2	13.7	20.2	25.2	29.0	34.0	42.7	24.0
Overcrowding	8.0	14.1	19.6	25.0	31.2	38.4	48.4	25.4
Deprivation score	−6.02	−3.86	−2.01	−0.24	+1.96	+4.28	+8.36	

Data from ref. 8.

TABLE 21.2 Range in deprivation scores by area level

	Most affluent	Most deprived
Post-code sectors	−7.3	+12.3
Deprivation categories	−6.02	+8.36
Local government districts	−5.65	+4.07
Health Boards	−1.95	+2.50

Data from ref. 8.

Table 21.2 illustrates the range of deprivation scores throughout Scotland by post-code sectors, local government districts and Health Boards. Note that the range is greatest for post-code sectors and least for Health Boards, although this is mainly a reflection of the greater degree of variation in the smallest groups and the least in the largest ones.

Comparison between Scotland and England and Wales

It is very interesting to see the deprivation scores of Scotland compared with England and Wales classified under the system devised by Carstairs and Morris[8] (see Table 21.3).

TABLE 21.3   Population living at differing levels of deprivation in England and Wales, and Scotland (percentage)

Deprivation category	England and Wales	Scotland
1 Affluent	21.6	6.1
2	30.4	13.7
3	21.7	21.8
4	14.6	25.5
5	7.6	14.8
6	3.6	11.4
7 Deprived	1.0	6.8

Data from ref. 8.

Table 21.3 clearly shows the greater degree of social deprivation in Scotland — 6.8% of the population fall into the most socially deprived section of the country in Scotland compared with only 1.0% in England and Wales. At the other end of the scale, only 6.1% of the population in Scotland are in the most affluent category, whereas 21.6% are so classified in England and Wales.

Comparison of urban and rural areas

Many observations in the past have shown that social deprivation is highest in urban areas, especially within inner city districts compared with rural areas. Levels of crime, for instance, are well known to be greatest in overcrowded urban areas. The deprivation scores evolved by Carstairs and Morris[8] confirm this trend even though crime figures do not form part of their indicators. In their analysis Carstairs and Morris[8] also emphasized:

- owner occupation increases with rurality
- cars per household increase with rurality and that public transport declines as a means for getting to work

- unemployment is highest in urban areas
- the percentage in the population of social class I and II is highest in rural areas and lowest in most urban areas with little variation in between.

Importance of a balanced combination of different methods of assessing social problems

It is important, especially for anyone working in the field of personal social services whether in local authorities or with voluntary bodies, to realize that no one method of studying and assessing social problems will ever meet every need. Therefore, this chapter is aimed at introducing and describing a variety of well-tried ways of approaching the task. So far, an attempt has been made to consider ways of determining whether an area, district or group has a high or low level of social deprivation. If a balanced approach is made and different methods studied, then a good idea is gained about the general levels of any social deprivation present. It is always important to quantify the results as far as possible. This enables the findings to be compared from district to district or from group to group within the community. It also allows changes over any time period to be studied; in this way trends can be forecast and it also makes it easier to assess the success or failure of any services introduced in an attempt to reduce levels of social deprivation. The value of the comparative methods introduced by Carstairs and Morris[8] in their study in Scotland (see above) is obvious, for such an approach enables a base line to be determined at any moment of time as well as making it possible to compare the levels of social deprivation in Scotland and in England and Wales (even though there are bound to be recognizable limitations).

SPECIFIC TOPICS WHICH CAN ASSIST IN THE STUDY OF SOCIAL PROBLEMS

Brief descriptions follow several specific topics which can usefully be studied and researched in the field of social factors. These include:

- *population statistics* — particularly changes, trends and predictions
- *households* — their make up, type of accommodation, characteristics of the people living there and their social needs
- *employment statistics* — including job stability, type of job, distribution of the sexes in employment, trend in all aspects
- *ethnic minority information* — the proportion of an ethnic minority in any area, particular problems they face including education, language, accommodation, employment and social mixing
- *marriage and divorce statistics* — this is a changing topic as trends have rapidly

altered since 1971; it also involves the consequences of divorce, especially on any children of the marriage
- *lone parent families* — this is an increasing group in society and is often associated with social problems
- *education statistics* — these include such topics as preschool education, special education for children with special educational needs, higher education with special reference to the proportion who gain qualifications (the levels of unemployment are lowest in those with good qualifications and highest in those with none)
- *suicide and parasuicide* — there are a number of social factors involved
- *life-styles and their effect on social deprivation* — many changes have occurred in life-styles since 1950, including a large increase in couples living together outside marriage, a changing emphasis in family life-styles, greater independence especially for young persons, increased drug abuse, changes in alcohol abuse. All individuals now have a greater range of choice, especially young persons. This is generally welcomed, but if choices rapidly lead to great changes in life-styles, this can produce many secondary social problems.

Population — trends and predictions

The population predictions published by the Office of Population Censuses and Surveys (OPCS) highlight considerable changes that will occur in the proportion of various age groups in the population of England and Wales in the early part of the next century — from 1989 to year 2029.[12] During this period, it is expected that the population of England and Wales will rise to 55 million (a rise of 9%). However, this increase will be spread very unevenly throughout the age groups. The following changes are predicted:

- the number of children will rise until a peak is reached by 2003 and then fall gradually during the next 10 years; from 2013 to 2029 the numbers will rise again and by 2029 the total rise for the period 1989–2029 will be 14.9%
- the working population will first rise and then fall slightly; it is predicted there will be a total rise of 841 000 persons from 1989 to 2029 (an increase of 2.5%)
- persons of pensionable age (60 years for women and 65 years for men) will rise during 1989 to 2029 from 9.3 million to 12.8 million, a rise of 37%.

However, the largest rises will occur in the older age groups within those of pensionable age. Those over 75 years will rise from 3.5 million to 5.1 million by 2029 (a rise of 44%), but the most dramatic rise will be seen in persons aged 85 years and over. In 1989 there were 754 000 people of this age in England and Wales, but it is predicted that by 2029 the numbers will have risen to 3.0 million — a rise of 2.24 million or 298%. This very large increase comes immediately after a 40% increase from mid 1981 to mid 1989,[9] so the trend is quite unmistakable.

The significance of this increase mainly lies in the many social problems which always tend to occur in very old persons, many of whom live alone. Social problems are likely to be further increased because a large proportion of elderly women have long-standing chronic handicaps (see Chapters 18 and 24).

Economic problems

A further serious economic difficulty will be added to the social problems of caring for so many very old people by the year 2029, in that the number of persons of working age will fall proportionately as is clearly illustrated by Table 21.4. It will be seen that the numbers of dependent persons (e.g. children under the age of 16 and persons of pensionable age) per 100 people of working age increases progressively from 1989 to 2029. In 1989 there were 62 such dependent persons per 100 of working age, but this figure will rise to 65 by 2001, to 69 by 2021 and to 76 by 2029.

TABLE 21.4   Projected number of dependent people per 100 population of working age during 1989–2029 in England and Wales

Age group	1989	1991	2001	2011	2021	2029
Children under age 16	32	33	35	33	33	35
Pensionable ages (years)						
Total	30	30	30	32	36	41
65/60ª–74	19	19	17	20	22	25
75 and over	11	12	12	13	14	16
Total dependants	62	63	65	65	69	76

ª Age 65 years for men, 60 years for women.
Data from ref. 12.

Further discussion of the social problems likely to be created by the increasing numbers of very old persons is given in Chapter 18.

Households

Size

The type of household people live in is important as it may indicate the possible social problems which can follow. Figure 21.1 shows the types of household in Great Britain from 1911 to 1981 (the last fully analysed census at time of publication). Note that, by 1981, 20% of households contain only one person, and this trend towards a larger proportion of households with only one person in them is known to have continued during the 1980s. If one-person households are further

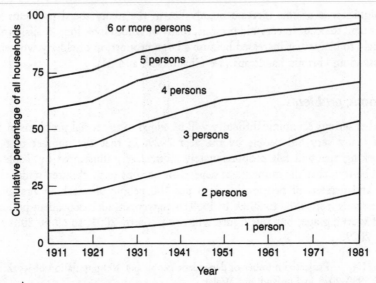

FIGURE 21.1   The size of households in Great Britain, 1911–81. (Data from ref. 10.)

analysed, about two thirds contain a person of pensionable age – it is also a measure of the increasing incidence of more elderly persons living alone. In certain districts such as Hove, Worthing and Eastbourne, more than 30% of all households in 1981 were in this category, and this emphasizes the special social problems potentially present in such areas in relation to caring for the elderly.[10]

Tenure

There is a marked difference between the forms of tenure of households in Great Britain (whether they are owner-occupiers or rented) in different socio-economic groups in the population (see Fig. 21.2).

Figure 21.2 shows how in 1988 in Great Britain, 89% of households headed by someone from the professional socio-economic group were owner-occupied compared with 35% of households headed by unskilled manual workers. The opposite trend occurs for rented accommodation where the highest group is composed of unskilled manual workers and the lowest by professionals. Economically inactive (including many elderly persons) also represent a large group (53%) of the people who live in rented accommodation. Note that the rented group (from either local authority or the new towns) makes up the largest group outside owner-occupation. Although social problems occur in all types of households, some of the most persistent tend to be concentrated in the rented group – homelessness, high proportion in social class V with consequent low earning capacity, largest numbers of single parent families, etc.

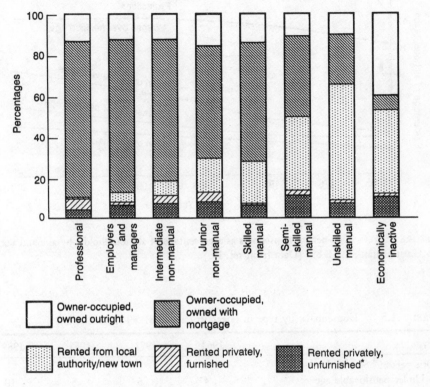

FIGURE 21.2   Tenure by socio-economic group of head of household in Great Britain, 1988. * Includes those renting from a housing association and those renting with a job or business. (Data from ref. 13.)

One-person households

The proportion of households containing only one person increased steadily from 1971 to 1988. The types of people now occupying one-person households and the projected projections are clearly shown in Fig. 21.3. Note that approximately 25.5% of all households in 1988 were occupied by one person, but that this is expected to rise to approximately 30.7% by the year 2001. As some of these persons are over retirement age, the potential number of social problems is likely to rise.

Table 21.5 shows how the make-up of households has changed from 1961 to 1989 in Great Britain. It illustrates that the proportion of elderly persons over retirement age who occupy one-person households (e.g. live alone) has increased from 7% in 1961 to 16% by 1989. There has also been a similar increase in the proportion of younger persons living alone − from 4% to 10%.

It is clear that the opportunity for close family support for both retired persons

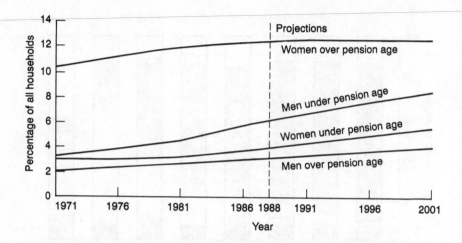

FIGURE 21.3   One-person households as a percentage of all households; by age and sex in Great Britain, 1971–89. (Data from ref. 11.)

TABLE 21.5   Households: by type in Great Britain, 1961–89 (percentages)

Type	1961	1971	1981	1989
One person households				
Under pensionable age	4	6	8	10
Over pensionable age	7	12	14	16
Two or more unrelated adults	5	4	5	3
One family households				
Married couple with				
No children	26	27	26	27
1–2 dependent children	30	26	25	21
3 or more dependent children	8	9	6	5
Non-dependent children only	10	8	8	9
Lone parent with				
Dependent children	2	3	5	5
Non-dependent children only	4	4	4	4
Two or more families	3	1	1	1
All households	100	100	100	100

Reproduced from ref. 11.

and younger people has also been reduced in this period, which has probably contributed to a number of additional social problems.

Employment and unemployment

Since 1971, there has been a marked change in the proportion of men and women in employment. Figure 21.4 illustrates that the proportion of men in the category of 'economically inactive' has increased slightly from 9% to 12% whereas in women the proportion has decreased sharply from 50% to 23%.[11] Unemployment rose very sharply in the UK in 1980 and 1981 and then increased further until 1986 (see Fig. 21.5).

The association between unemployment and various social problems is well known and is not only connected with the consequent financial difficulties, but especially with a low personal esteem and a lack of a sense of purpose. It is interesting to compare the unemployment rates of different countries. As definitions vary in various countries, the Organization for Economic Co-operation and Development (OECD) has introduced a standard set of concepts. Table 21.6 compares these for most developed countries. Note that, apart from Germany, the UK had the lowest unemployment rate of the European Community (EC) countries.

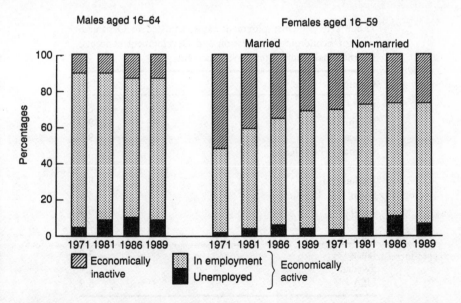

FIGURE 21.4   Population of working age: by sex and economic status in Great Britain, 1971–89. (Data from ref. 11.)

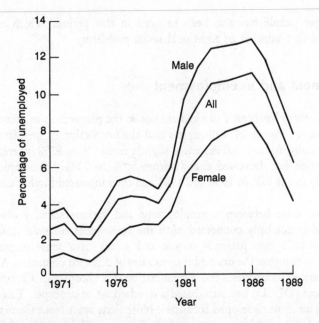

FIGURE 21.5   Unemployment rate (percentages): UK annual averages, 1971–89. (Data from ref. 11.)

TABLE 21.6   Unemployment rates, adjusted to Organization for Economic Co-operation and Development concepts: international comparisons, 1989 (percentages)

Country	%
UK	6.4
Belgium	9.0
France	9.5
Germany (Fed. Rep.)	5.5
Italy	10.9
Netherlands	8.3
Spain	16.9
Australia	6.1
Canada	7.5
Finland	3.4
Japan	2.3
Sweden	1.4
USA	5.2

Data from ref. 11.

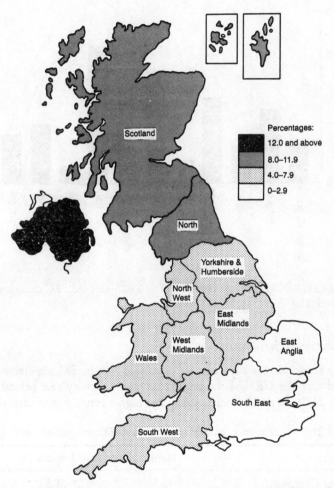

FIGURE 21.6   Unemployment rate: by region in the UK, 1990. (Data from ref. 11.)

Elsewhere in the world, Japan and Sweden have exceptionally low rates.

In the UK, unemployment by region is an important indicator of potential social problems in any area (see Fig. 21.6). Note that there is a marked difference in unemployment rates in different regions of the UK. The highest rates are in Northern Ireland (13.7%), the North (8.7%) and in Scotland, and the lowest rates are in East Anglia and the South East (3.9%).

Unemployment in young persons is another useful indicator of potential social problems. Figure 21.7, which illustrates unemployment rates for EEC countries in 1989, shows that there is marked variations in the unemployment among under 25-year-olds. The rate for the UK in 1989 was 9.9% which is substantially below the EC average of 17.4%.[11]

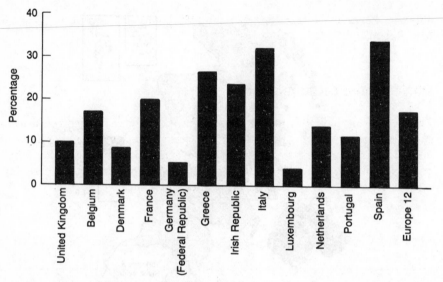

FIGURE 21.7   Unemployment rates of under 25-year-olds: EC comparison, 1989. (Data from ref. 11.)

Economic activity rates

If the economic activity rates are calculated for the EC population in 1988, it is found that the UK had the highest economic activity rate behind Denmark (see Table 21.7). In all 12 countries men had higher activity rates than women, but the

TABLE 21.7   Economic activity rates:[a] by sex, EC comparison, 1988 (percentages)

Country	Males	Females	All
United Kingdom	75.5	51.5	63.0
Belgium	62.0	36.7	48.9
Denmark	75.2	61.0	67.9
France	67.0	47.2	56.7
Germany (Fed. Rep.)	70.7	42.0	55.6
Greece	69.0	36.3	51.8
Irish Republic	73.6	35.4	54.2
Italy	66.9	35.0	50.4
Luxembourg	69.9	34.7	51.7
Netherlands	70.4	42.3	56.2
Portugal	71.6	47.0	58.6
Spain	67.0	32.5	49.1

[a] The civilian labour force aged 16 years and over as a percentage of the population aged 16 years and over.
Reproduced from ref. 11.

difference between the sexes ranged from 14% points in Denmark to 38 in the Irish Republic.[11]

Ethnic related social problems

There are many indicators which suggest that the race of the individual has a bearing on the number of potential social problems which may be met. For instance, unemployment levels are lower in the white population than for other ethnic groups (see Table 21.8). Note that at all qualification levels, the highest unemployment rates are in the Pakistani/Bangladeshi ethnic groups.

TABLE 21.8   Unemployment rates:[a] by highest qualification, ethnic origin and sex in Great Britain, 1987–89

| Origin and sex | Highest qualification[b] | | | |
	Higher qualification	Other qualification	No qualification	All persons[c]
Males[d]				
White	3	7	15	9
West Indian or Guyanese	–	15	25	18
Indian	–	10	15	10
Pakistani/Bangladeshi	–	–	30	25
Other[e]	–	11	–	11
Females[d]				
White	4	8	11	8
West Indian or Guyanese	–	18	–	14
Indian	–	–	–	13
Pakistani/Bangladeshi	–	–	–	–
Other[e]	–	–	–	11
All persons[d]				
White	3	7	13	9
West Indian or Guyanese	–	17	20	16
Indian	–	11	15	11
Pakistani/Bangladeshi	–	20	30	25
Other[e]	–	12	–	11

[a] Definition of unemployment — OECD concepts.
[b] Qualification level.
[c] Includes those who did not state whether they had a qualification.
[d] Males aged 16–64 years, females aged 16–59 years.
[e] Includes African, Arab, Chinese, other stated and mixed.
Reproduced from ref. 11.

TABLE 21.9   Economic activity rates: by age, sex and ethnic origin in Great Britain, 1987–89 (percentages)

Ethnic origin	Age			All of working age[a]	
	16–24	25–44	Females 45–59 Males 45–64	Male	Female
White	80	84	74	89	70
West Indian or Guyanese	73	83	83	85	76
Indian	58	80	68	84	58
Pakistani or Bangladeshi	44	53	56	77	21.
Other[b]	56	70	75	74	59
All[c]	78	83	74	88	70

[a] Males aged 16–64 years, females aged 16–59 years.
[b] Includes African, Arab, Chinese, other stated and mixed.
[c] Includes ethnic group not stated.
Reproduced from ref. 11.

If economic activity rates are compared by age, sex and ethnic groups, the results again indicate certain ethnic groups (such as Pakistani or Bangladeshi) are at a disadvantage (see Table 21.9).

Divorce

Following the Divorce Reform Act 1969, the number of divorces in the UK has more than doubled (see Table 21.10).

TABLE 21.10   Divorce in England and Wales, 1961–89

	1961	1971	1976	1981	1986	1989
Decrees absolute granted (thousands)	25	74	127	146	154	152
Persons divorcing per 1000 people	2.1	6.0	10.1	11.9	12.9	12.7
Percentages of divorces where one or more partners had been divorced previously	9.3	8.8	11.6	17.1	23.2	24.7

Data from ref. 11.

Many EC countries have also experienced a similar large increase in divorce. Denmark is the one other EC country with a divorce rate greater than 10 per existing marriages (see Table 21.11).

It is difficult to compare the divorce rates of different countries, not only because of existing religious constraints, but also because cohabitation is commoner in

TABLE 21.11 Annual divorce rates in EC countries, 1961–88

Divorces per 1000 existing marriages	1961	1971	1981	1985	1989
UK	2.1	5.8	11.5	13.2	12.6
Belgium	2.0	2.8	6.1	7.3	8.6
Denmark	5.7	10.8	12.1	12.6	13.6
France	2.9	3.5	6.8	8.1	8.4
Germany (Fed. Rep.)	3.6	5.2	7.2	8.6	
Greece	1.5	1.7	2.5		
Irish Republic					0.0
Italy		2.5	0.9	1.1	2.1
Luxemburg	2.0	2.6	5.9	7.2	10.0
Netherlands	2.2	3.7	8.3	9.9	8.1
Portugal	0.4	0.3	2.8	3.7	

Data from ref. 11.

many EC countries than in the UK. However, cohabitation is also changing in the UK, with many young couples now living together without becoming married (see Table 21.12).

TABLE 21.12 Percentage of women cohabiting: by age in the UK, 1979–88

Age group (years)	1979	1981	1986	1988
18–24	4.5	5.6	9.0	12.4
25–49	2.2	2.6	4.6	6.3
18–49	2.7	3.3	5.5	7.7

Data from ref. 14.

For men, cohabitation is more prevalent at ages 25–29 years (in 1988, 13% of men were cohabiting in this age group), whereas in women the most prevalent age for cohabiting is the age group 20–24 years (14% of women in 1988 were cohabiting at these ages).

Divorce and children

One of the most difficult and distressing social problems of divorce is connected with the children of the marriage. By 1986, approximately 56% of divorcing couples had 150 000 children, of which about 30% were under the age of 5 years, 40% between 5 and 11 years and 30% between 11 and 16 years (see Fig. 21.8).
The instability and trauma surrounding any marriage breakdown usually

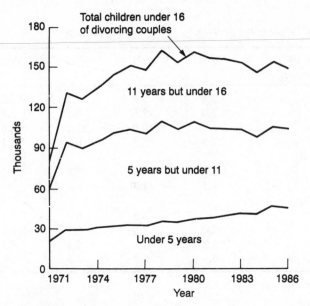

FIGURE 21.8   Children under 16 years of age of divorcing couples in England and Wales, 1971–86 (thousands). (Data from ref. 15.)

produces a number of extra problems for the children of the marriage. This is often shown in different ways — difficult behavioural problems, poor educational attainment, insecurity, etc. A further long-term effect, which is not always recognized, is that the children of divorced couples often themselves make disastrous marriages which end in divorce. In this way, divorce can be self-perpetuating for the children, who then have similar difficulties to their parents.

Lone parent (or one parent) families

Reference has already been made to the increase in one parent households and families (see Fig. 21.3 and Table 21.5). A further social problem is that there is now an increasing number of these lone mothers with dependent children whose situation has been caused by divorce or separation rather than by widowhood. There is at present also a smaller increase in the numbers of single women with dependent children (see Fig. 21.9).

The social problems of lone parents also include, to a much smaller degree, lone fathers with dependent children. The proportion of all families headed by lone mothers and lone fathers has increased from 8% in 1971 in Great Britain to 14% in 1987 as illustrated in Fig. 21.10.

These various statistics emphasize the increasing social problems faced by lone parents (mostly mothers). Child care sections of social services departments (see

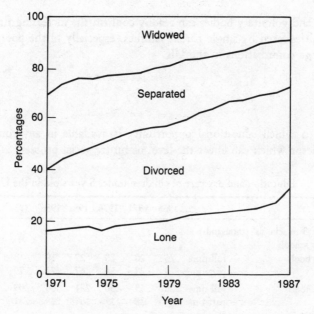

FIGURE 21.9   Lone mothers with dependent children: by marital status in Great Britain, 1971–87 (percentages; 3-year moving averages used apart from 1971 and 1987). (Data from ref. 11.)

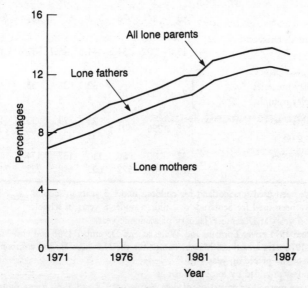

FIGURE 21.10   Proportions of all families with dependent children headed by lone mothers and lone fathers in Great Britain (percentages; 3-year moving averages used apart from 1971 and 1987). (Data from ref. 11.)

Chapter 22) and voluntary bodies can readily confirm the increasing financial and social difficulties faced by single parent families, especially in the poorer parts of cities and large conurbations in the UK.

Education

The extent to which educational opportunity is available in any country is an important factor which can effect the level of future social problems.

TABLE 21.13   Education and day care of children under 5 years old in the UK, 1966–89

		1966	1971	1976	1981	1986[a]	1987[b]	1988	1989
Children under 5 in schools[c] (thousands)									
Public sector schools									
Nursery schools	— full-time	26	20	20	22	19	18	18	17
	— part-time	9	29	54	67	77	79	80	65
Primary schools	— full-time	220	263	350	281	306	309	314	317
	— part-time	—	38	117	167	228	231	243	273
Non-maintained schools	— full-time	21	19	19	19	20	21	23	26
	— part-time	2	14	12	12	15	16	17	18
Special schools	— full-time	2	2	4	4	4	4	4	4
	— part-time	—	—	1	1	2	2	2	2
Total		280	384	576	573	671	681	700	722
As a percentage of all children aged 3 or 4		15.0	20.5	34.5	44.3	46.7	47.6	48.4	49.1
Day care places[d] (thousands)									
Local authority day nurseries		⎱21	23[c]	35 ⎰	32	33	33	34	34
Local authority playgrounds		⎰		⎱	5	5	5	6	4
Registered day nurseries		⎱75	296	401 ⎰	23	29	33	40[g]	49[g]
Registered playgroups		⎰		⎱	433	473	477	479	480
Registered child minders[e]		32	90	86	110[f]	157	174	189	216
Total		128	409	522	603[f]	698	722	747	783

[a] Data for 1985 have been used for Scotland for children under 5 years in schools.
[b] Data for 1988 have been used for Scotland for children under 5 years in schools.
[c] Pupils aged under 5 years at December/January of academic year.
[d] Figures for 1966 and 1971 cover England and Wales at end-December 1966 and end-March 1972, respectively. From 1976 data are at end-March, except for the Northern Ireland component which is at end-December of the preceding year.
[e] Includes child minders provided by local authorities.
[f] Because of a different method of collection of data between 1978 and 1981, these figures are less reliable.
[g] No figures are available for registered nurseries in Scotland. An estimate has been made for the purposes of obtaining a UK total.
(Data from ref. 11.)

Education and day care of children under the age of 5 years

The educational and day care facilities for children under 5 years of age is important in any community where the proportion of women working is increasing. The large increase from 1966 to 1989 in all forms of education and day care for children under the age of 5 years in the UK is clearly shown in Table 21.13.

In EC countries, France provides almost 100% of under 5-year-olds with a nursery school place. The relative position of the UK is shown in Fig. 21.11.

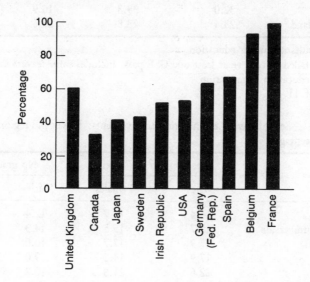

FIGURE 21.11   Participation of 3- to 5-year-olds in education (excluding day care): international comparisons, 1987 (at January except for Canada (June) and USA and Japan (October); 1988 for Sweden and 1985 for Irish Republic). (Data from ref. 11.)

School leavers examination results

Although the academic attainment of school leavers does not indicate specific social problems, it does emphasize certain potential difficulties — unemployment levels are always highest in persons with no qualifications. Considerable variation is seen in the levels of examination results for school leavers between the different constituent countries of the UK (see Table 21.14). Note that generally Scotland and Northern Ireland have the highest proportion of school leavers with at least one 'A' level result (or SCE in Scotland). In Scotland, Northern Ireland and Wales, females had better results than males — in England, the sexes were fairly similar. As regards the poorest results, e.g. school leavers with no graded results, England was best followed by Scotland, Wales and Northern Ireland. Generally, females faired better than males. There is also considerable variation between the various regions of England (see Table 21.15).

TABLE 21.14   School leavers' examination achievements:[a] by sex and country in the UK, 1987–89 (percentages)

Country	One or more 'A' levels or SCE highers (Scotland)		No graded results[b]	
	Males	Females	Males	Females
England	19.0	18.4	11.1	7.9
Wales	16.7	19.1	20.5	14.1
Scotland	32.0	39.8	16.9	12.9
Northern Ireland	23.4	28.8	26.6	15.9

[a] Excludes results in further education.
[b] Those who failed to achieve at least one GSE pass. Includes some leavers in Wales with certificate of education examination.
Data from ref. 11.

TABLE 21.15   School leavers' examination achievements:[a] by sex and region in England, 1987–89 (percentages)

Region	One or more 'A' levels		No graded result[b]	
	Males	Females	Males	Females
North	14.4	15.7	12.4	7.9
Yorkshire/Humberside	15.7	15.5	14.3	9.9
East Midlands	17.9	17.7	10.0	7.3
East Anglia	17.9	14.2	9.0	5.1
South East	22.6	21.6	10.2	7.6
West Midlands	17.2	16.7	11.4	8.9
South West	18.1	19.1	6.8	4.9
North West	18.3	16.8	13.9	9.6

[a,b] See comments under Table 21.14.

Between 1971 and 1981, the number of students in further education fell by 61 000, but from 1981 to 1989 it rose by 333 000.[11] In 1971, there were more males than females in further education, but since 1981 this trend has been reversed, and by 1989 there were 110 000 females to 100 000 males in further education in the UK (see Fig. 21.12).

Low incomes

Those whose household income is very low usually have to face many social problems. Although there is no single accepted measure of what constitutes a low

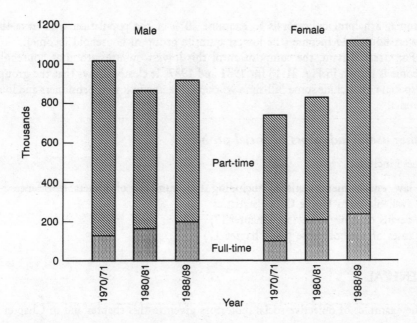

FIGURE 21.12   Students in further education: by sex and type in the UK, 1970–71 and 1988–89 (thousands). (Data from ref. 11.)

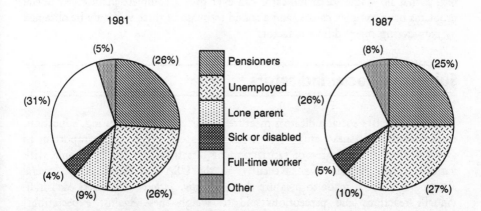

FIGURE 21.13   Composition of the lowest quintile group of household income (unit of analysis is the individual, and the income measure is their net equivalent household income) by economic status of the family head (individuals are classified according to the economic status of the head of their social security benefit unit; where more than one description applies they are allocated to the first named) in Great Britain, 1981 and 1987. (Data from ref. 11.)

income, a helpful indicator is to examine 20% of the population who have the lowest household income (the lowest quintile group of household income).

For Great Britain, the composition of this lowest quintile group of household income is shown in Fig. 21.13 for 1981 and 1987. It clearly shows that the groups at special risk include some full-time workers, the unemployed, pensioners and lone parents.

Other useful indicators of social problems

These include:

- law enforcement statistics including the numbers of indictable offences — available from Home Office statistics
- details of drug abuse (see Chapter 17)
- cases of alcohol abuse (see Chapter 17).

GENERAL

The examples of objective social indicators given in this chapter and in Chapter 3 are not in any way intended to be comprehensive. They do, however, illustrate the way social conditions and problems can be measured. Unless the social services being provided in any area are constantly being checked against needs, it is very easy for them to become partly irrelevant. Any professional using such indicators must realize that no single social indicator can ever give a complete picture. All social problems have complex causes, and a sound estimate of these will only be obtained by considering many different factors.

Subjective social indicators

Whereas objective social indicators measure conditions such as housing, education, employment lawlessness, etc., there is another aspect which is also important to assess — that is the degree of satisfaction or dissatisfaction felt by people with various aspects of their lives. Recently, in the USA and this country, several attempts have been made to measure these *subjective factors* — to assess each individual's reactions and perceptions and to weigh these against expectations, experiences, attitude and present circumstances. Such measurements are spoken of as *subjective social indicators*.

These studies were developed because many people pointed out that objective social indicators are crude measurements and, although useful to give a general background picture, have many limitations. For instance, the quality of life in a community depends very much on the life which people lead — their participation in community events, their concern for the community they live in, racial equality, etc. Small communities, villages and small towns are well known to be pleasanter places to live in than cities, and often this is principally because the person is more integrated into that community and is therefore more useful and feels needed.

The method of carrying out these surveys is interesting. An 11-point scale was used to indicate 'satisfaction ratings'; levels 0 and 1 represent very low satisfaction, 9 and 10 very high satisfaction. Each person interviewed was asked to classify his/her satisfaction rating at the time, for 4–5 years ago and what he/she thought it would be in 4–5 years, under the following headings (or domains): marriage, family life, health, standard of living, housing, job, education, spare time, district, religion, democracy.

First, each person was asked to say which of these items was most important in determining his/her satisfaction or dissatisfaction with life in general.

The results, in order, were: marriage, family life, health, standard of living, housing, job, spare time, district, religion, democracy, education.

Next persons were asked to put in order their satisfaction levels in these features and the order then was: marriage, family life, job, district, health, spare time, housing, standard of living, education received, religion, and democratic standards.

Most said that marriage, family life and health were very important, and also that their levels of satisfaction in these aspects were high. But in two of the features, standard of living and housing, there was a marked disparity between the levels of importance (both were considered important) and the levels of satisfaction (both were scored low).

Studies of this type introduce a completely new dimension into the ways of measuring social problems. Although such researches are subjective (they depend on the assessment of the people tested) they are measuring features which everyone recognizes as most important. Social problems follow dissatisfaction, and it is well known that satisfaction is not the inevitable sequence of a high standard of living and an excellent house to live in. If objective conditions such as salary levels or housing standards alone are studied, only very crude indications are given into how many social problems exist. If, however, subjective social indicators are studied as well, a much deeper impression is gained of what people themselves consider important and how far their hopes and expectations are met.

It is hoped that further subjective social surveys will be carried out to ensure that, in measuring social problems, the satisfaction people themselves feel is accepted to be as important as any of the other well-tried objective factors described earlier in this chapter.

References

1. Inequalities in health. Report of a research working group (Sir Douglas Black, Chairman). London: Department of Health. 1980.
2. Whitehead M. The health divide. Inequalities in health. London: Penguin. 1988.

3. Pamuk E. Social class inequalities in mortality from 1921 to 1972 in England and Wales. Population studies 1985, **39**: 17–31.
4. Marmot MG. Mortality decline and widening social inequalities. Lancet 1986, **ii**: 274–276.
5. Amos J. Social malaise study in Liverpool. Liverpool: City Council. 1970.
6. Department of Environment. Urban deprivation. Information note no 2. London: Department of Environment. 1983.
7. Jarman B. Identification of underprivileged areas. Br. Med. J. 1983, **286**: 1705–1709.
8. CarstairsV, Morris R. Deprivation and Health in Scotland. Aberdeen: University Press. 1991.
9. OPCS. Monitor PP1 90/1. London: OPCS. 1990.
10. OPCS. Census Guide No 4 London: OPCS. 1986.
11. Central Statistical Office. Social Trends **21** London: HMSO. 1992.
12. OPCS. Monitor PP2 91/1. London: OPCS. 1991.
13. OPCS. General Household Survey, 1988. London: HMSO.
14. OPCS. General Household Survey, 1990. London: HMSO.
15. Central Statistical Office. Social Trends, 1988. London: HMSO.

22

Children In Need

All major local authorities through their social services departments have responsibility for providing all forms of child care services for children and young persons under the age of 18 years. There are many reasons why children need special help — because they are orphans, or they have been abandoned by their parents, or their parents have been found incapable of providing adequate care.

The main principle in looking after children is to settle the child in as normal a home as possible. This is why a family placement is the method of choice. If this proves difficult for any reason then every effort is made to look after the child in small groups — in homes as similar as possible to a child living in a large family.

Day care for children

The Children Act, 1989, imposed new duties on local authorities to provide appropriate day care for *children in need* (see pp. 478–479) in their area who are aged 5 years and under and not yet attending schools.[1]

Local authorities must also provide care and supervised activities outside school hours and during the school holidays for children in need of any age who are attending schools (Children Act, section 18(5).[1] Local authorities also have powers to provide either of the above services for children in their area who are not in school (Children Act, section 18(2).[1]

Of children under the age of 5 years, 706 277 were provided with some form of day care by social services departments, education departments, voluntary or private care in England in 1989 (see Table 22.1).

DAY NURSERIES

Day nurseries are provided by local authorities to help care for young children who, due to social circumstances, cannot remain at home during the daytime. Such day nurseries are a great help to:

TABLE 22.1   Numbers of day nurseries, playgroups, child minders and nursery education for children under the age of 5 years in England, 1989

Type of day care	Number	(%)
Local authority day nursery	32 585	(4.6)
Local authority playgroup	2 717	(0.4)
Registered day nursery	45 026	(6.4)
Registered playgroup	399 460	(56.5)
Registered childminder	186 222	(26.4)
Children under 5 years in school (full- or part-time)	40 267	(5.7)

Data from the Department of the Health and the Department of Education and Sciences.

- the unmarried mother who has to go out to work
- a single parent (widow or widower or divorced person) with a young family to support
- the mother of a family who is suddenly taken ill and has to be admitted to hospital
- a family with either a mild or more severely handicapped child.

Day nurseries are open 5 days a week from about 0730 hours to 1730 hours. Children from a few weeks old to 5 years can be admitted, and the parent usually brings the child to the nursery on the way to work. The child normally has all meals at the day nursery and will be completely looked after there during the day. A small charge is usually made for this service. Most day nurseries care for about 50 children who are usually looked after in 'family groups' consisting of eight to ten children aged from 6–8 months to 5 years, as it is thought that this gives a more homelike life and enables the children from the same family to be kept together with the two nursery nurses who care for them. The babies are usually cared for in a separate nursery.

A qualified matron and a deputy matron are in charge of the nursery and, to assist them, there are a *number of trained nursery nurses*. The health of the children is carefully supervised — usually a doctor from the child health services does this by making regular visits to the nursery to see and examine the children. Care is taken to ensure:

- every child is well when admitted
- every child is fully immunized
- that any case of communicable disease is fully investigated.

Any child with diarrhoea should be immediately excluded until a bacteriological examination is normal. It is important that any case of dysentery is recognized promptly as this disease can spread rapidly throughout a day nursery.

PLAYGROUPS

Most playgroups are provided by voluntary bodies or by groups of mothers. All must be registered with the local authority. In addition, a few playgroups are run by local authorities. Playgroups mostly provide sessional care for children between $2\frac{1}{2}$ years and 5 years of age. Local arrangements vary and playgroups may meet two to five times a week and are mainly used to help mothers, especially in deprived areas, by giving the mothers a break and by involving them and, in this way, using the playgroup as a means of teaching mothers more about the care of their children. This can often help parents to provide a better home environment for their children. Many playgroups are linked to various community groups and can help reduce the isolation felt by many mothers, especially where they have recently been rehoused in an area where they know very few people.

PRIVATE DAY NURSERIES

Places in private day nurseries now exceed those provided by local authorities.[2] All must be registered with the local authority, which then specifies the number of children who can be looked after, as well as laying down standards of equipment, fire precautions and staff. A number of local industries provide these private day nurseries for their staff — formerly these were called 'creches'.

CHILDMINDERS

These look after young children under 5 years of age in their own homes. All people looking after more than one child in this way in their home must be registered with the local authority. As shown in Table 22.1, childminders now provide a significant number of places for children under 5 years of age — in 1989 in England childminders looked after 26.4 of all children helped with day care.

EDUCATIONAL PROVISION

In 1989, in England, 11 048 children under the age of 5 years attended full-time and 29 219 part-time at nursery schools. Since 1973, there has been a steady increase in the numbers of 3- and 4-year-olds who attend at either maintained or non-maintained schools. The latest estimation (in 1989) indicated that approximately 57% of such children now attend some form of nursery education (Children Act, section 18(2).[1]

CO-ORDINATION

Although day care facilities for children under 5 years of age are provided by both social services and education departments of the local authority, it is important that every local authority plans its day care work in such a way that maximum co-ordination is achieved between both services and the voluntary field.

In the training of nursery nurses, the syllabus now recommends that every student spends some time training in both day nurseries and in nursery schools. It is hoped that, in this way, better day-to-day co-operation and understanding will develop between day nurseries and nursery schools.

Child care services – the Children Act, 1989

The Children Act, 1989, which was implemented in October 1991, primarily aims to improve the care, upbringing and protection of children. The Act is based 'on the belief that children are generally best looked after within the family with both parents playing a full part and without resort to legal proceedings'.[3] That belief is reflected in the following changes introduced by the Act:

- there is a new concept of 'parental responsibility' which replaces the former parental rights
- it is now possible for unmarried fathers to share parental responsibility by agreement with the mother
- there is a duty on local authorities to give support to children and their families
- local authorities also have a duty to return a child looked after by them to his/her family unless this would be against his/her interests
- there is a duty for local authorities for the first time to ensure contact is maintained with the parents of the child who is being looked after by them away from home.

CHILDREN IN NEED

The Children Act, 1989, identifies clearly the type of children (in future to be called 'children in need') for whom the services provided by social services departments of local authorities are designed.

Children in need include the following groups:

- if the child is unlikely to achieve or maintain, or have the opportunity of achieving or maintaining, a reasonable standard of health or development without the provision of the services of the local authority
- if the health or development of the child is likely to be significantly impaired,

or further impaired, without the provision of the services of the local authority
- if the child is disabled.

The Act defines when a child is considered disabled 'if he/she is blind, deaf or dumb or suffers from mental disorder of any kind or is substantially and permanently handicapped by illness, injury or congenital deformity or such other disability as may be prescribed'.

The child's welfare is paramount, and in all cases, the first consideration is *the need to safeguard and promote the welfare of the child*. This means that, while the Courts should take into consideration all the relevant surrounding circumstances, including the wishes of the parents, ultimately the Court must do what is best for the child. This part of the 1989 Act underlines that there should be no change from the position concerning the child's interests being paramount.

PARENTAL RESPONSIBILITY

Parental responsibility covers all the duties, rights and authority which any parent has in respect of their child. All decisions about parental responsibility, in future, must be made by the Courts (either Magistrates, County or High Courts). It is not now possible, as formerly was the case, for *a local authority to assume parental authority as any question about 'parental responsibility' must be now determined by the Court*. This ensures that there will always be an opportunity for any decision on parental responsibility to be challenged, questioned and properly discussed.

Generally, parental responsibility will be conferred on both parents if they are married and on the mother if they are not. But the Act makes it easier for unmarried parents to obtain parental responsibility. An unmarried father, for instance, can share parental responsibility provided both parents agree by a simple agreement and without going to Court, which previously was the case.

CHILDREN AWAY FROM HOME

When the local authority has to arrange for a child to live away from home (for any period) because the natural parents are unable to look after him/her properly or need respite, it is preferable that voluntary arrangements are made. In such instances, the parents retain their parental responsibility and act as partners with the local authority or with those caring for their child. The parents should participate in the child's care and in the decision made. They should also keep in contact with the child so that the child can return to them as soon as possible.

All administrative measures to exercise compulsion on a child being looked after, whether to limit contact with a parent or to prevent a parent recovering a child, were abolished by the Children Act, 1989. A range of *contact orders* has been introduced by the Act for any situation where a child needs protection from his/her parents.

Even when a child is under a Care Order (i.e. being looked after by a local authority) the Act provides for the parents to retain their parental responsibility (although the local authority may limit its operation). The parents must be involved in local authority decision and must have reasonable contact with the child unless the courts provide otherwise.

SAFEGUARDING AND PROMOTING CHILDREN'S WELFARE

There is a general duty imposed by the Children Act, 1989, on local authorities to provide a range and level of services which are appropriate to the needs of children in their area, who are in need, to:

- safeguard and promote the welfare of children in need
- so far as is consistent with that aim, promote their upbringing by their families.

This duty does, of course, not interfere with the overriding principle, already mentioned, that the child's best interests are paramount. Factors such as the racial origin, culture and language are important and the Act makes its quite clear that these should be taken into account by the local authority which is looking after the child. Every local authority must prepare the child in need for the time he/she leaves school up until the age of 21 years.

Main duties of local authority social services departments in relation to children in need including the changes introduced by the Children Act, 1989

The main changes introduced by the Children Act include:

- abolition of 'voluntary care' — this has been replaced by a duty placed on the local authority 'to provide accommodation' (see below)
- compulsory powers of a local authority can now only be granted by a Court Order (and even then the parents retain their parental responsibility)
- the only time that a local authority can obtain parental responsibility for a child is by a Court Order granting them a Care Order
- a local authority must provide accommodation for a child in need in their area who requires accommodation because:
  (1) there is no person who has parental responsibility for the child
  (2) the child is lost or has been abandoned
  (3) the person who has been caring for him/her is prevented (whether permanently or not and for whatever reason) from providing him/her with suitable accommodation or care (Children Act, section 20(1).[1]

- if the person with parental responsibility removes a child from the accommodation, the only way that the local authority can keep the child is for them to obtain a Court Order which states that it is in the best interest of the child to remain with the local authority.

Types of accommodation indicated by the Children Act, 1989, to be provided by a local authority social services department

The Children Act, 1989, indicates the options a local authority should consider and use when providing accommodation for children in need. These include:

- *A family placement* — this means the child should, if at all possible, always be placed with a family, a relative or other suitable person. Under previous legislation this was referred to as 'boarding out', but this term is no longer used. Any person with whom a child is placed, becomes a '*local authority foster parent*' unless he/she is the child's parent, or anyone having at that time parental responsibility for the child (i.e. a guardian) or a person in whose favour a court has made a *Residence Order* (see below).
- Placements in a community home, a voluntary or registered childrens home or a home provided by the Secretary of State.
- *Other appropriate arrangements* — such as in an older young persons hostel for semi-independent living or in rental accommodation.

An interesting further innovation introduced by the Children Act, 1989, is that where a person fosters more than three children (who are not siblings) he/she will be treated as if he/she runs a childrens home and therefore must be registered with the local authority.

Often the local authority only provides accommodation for a child for a short time, e.g. during some family crisis such as an illness. In such cases the most appropriate method of care should be used — family placement or where the child stays in a small childrens home. Children rarely suffer any deprivation in such instances. It is usual if the local authority looks after more than one child from the same family, that all the children are accommodated together.

New duty for local authority to promote contact between any child being looked after by them and those who are usually connected with the child

Under the Children Act, 1989, a new duty has been imposed upon a local authority who is looking after the child and providing him/her with accommodation to promote contact between the child and those who are usually connected with him/her. This is a positive duty and means that the local authority must do everything in its power to ensure that the child keeps in contact with his/her parents or anyone else with parental responsibilities for the child. This duty to promote contact also includes relatives and friends of the child.

This duty extends even if a Court Order has been made giving the local authority a Care Order. Reasonable contact with the child's parents, any guardian or other person with whom the child was living immediately before the Care Order was made must be encouraged by the local authority. The only time that a local authority can refuse reasonable contact between a parent, guardian or anyone with parental responsibility and the child is when:

- a Court directs no contact (e.g. such action is in the best interests of the child)
- in an emergency.

INDEPENDENT VISITORS

Under the Children Act, 1989, where it would be in a child's best interests, an independent visitor must be appointed. Such a visitor can be a relative or friend of the child, but must be independent and no one connected with the local authority. The circumstances when an independent visitor or visitors must be appointed include those when a parent or person with parental responsibility has not visited the child for 12 months or where all communication has been infrequent.

COURT ORDERS

The Children Act, 1989, gives powers to a Court to make the following orders.

Care Orders and Supervision Orders

These are to determine parental responsibility. The sole ground for a Care Order is one of 'harm' or likely harm to the child.

The preconditions for Care and Supervision Orders are that the child is suffering from or is likely to suffer from significant harm because of a lack of reasonable parental control or because he/she is beyond parental control. Reasonable parental care is that care which a reasonable parent would provide for the child concerned. Thus, a standard of care which would be reasonable for a normal healthy child may not be reasonable if the child has special needs because, for example, he/she has brittle bones, or is asthmatic or mentally disabled.[3]

It is not relevant that particular parents suffer from limitations such as a low intelligence or physical disablement. It follows that if a parent, for any reason, cannot cope with the child, he or she is acting unreasonably if help is not sought.

Such help woulde include the local authority social services providing accommodation for the child.

The preconditions also cover cases where the child has been looked after and the parents now want him/her back. As in all other instances, if there seems to be any conflict of interest between the interests of the child and his/her parents, the interests of the child must be the top priority.

For all interim Care and Supervision Orders, the preconditions are exactly the same as for the full Care or Supervision Order.

Supervision Order

— a Supervision Order puts a child under the supervision of a local authority or a probation officer. The supervisor is required to advise, assist and befriend the child and to take steps which are reasonably necessary to give effect to the order.

The supervisor appointed can require the child:

- to undergo education and training
- to receive counselling and guidance
- to take part in local schemes such as 'intermediate treatment' (see p. 493)
- to submit to a medical or psychiatric examination.

Residence Orders

— to decide with whom the child will live.

Contact Orders

— to decide what form of contact the child is to have with other people.

Specific Issue Orders

— to deal with any other particular matter in relation to the child.

Prohibited Steps Orders

— to prohibit anything being done in relation to the child, for example to ensure that a parental responsibility order by the Court is carried out.

Additional Court Orders which can be made include those dealing with the protection of children (see below), Education (see p. 489) and Family Assistance (see p. 488).

Court Orders for the protection of children

The Children Act, 1989, created three new Court Orders to protect children.

Emergency Protection Order

— this is a short-term order enabling a child to be made safe in an emergency. Such an order can only be made when the Court is satisfied that the child is likely to suffer significant harm if either:

- he/she is not removed to accommodation provided by a local authority or to that of the applicant for the order (e.g. in child abuse, see p. 505)
- he/she does not remain in the place in which he/she is then being accommodated (e.g. if he/she is removed from suitable safe accommodation). An Emergency Protection Order will have an effect as long as the Court specifies, subject to a maximum of 8 days. The local authority or authorized person can ask the Court to extend the period by a further 7 days in certain circumstances.

A Child Assessment Order

— this may be made on the application of a local authority or a person who is authorized to apply for a Care Order or Supervision Order (i.e. NSPCC Officers) if the Court is satisfied that:

- there is reasonable cause to suspect that the child is suffering, or is likely to suffer, from significant harm
- that an assessment of the state of the child's health or of the way he/she has been treated is required to determine whether or not the child is suffering or likely to suffer significant harm.

A Recovery Order

— this order can be made when there is reason to believe that a child:

- has been unlawfully taken away or is being unlawfully kept away from the person who for the time being has care for him/her by virtue of a Care Order or Emergency Protection Order or is in police protection (see below) (Children Act, sections 49(2) and 50(2).[1]
- has run away or is staying away from the responsible person or
- is missing.

The effect of a Recovery Order is to:

- compel the person who is in a position to do so to produce the child on request to an authorized person or
- authorize the removal of the child by an authorized person or
- authorize a constable to enter premises specified in the order and search for the child, using reasonable force if necessary, or
- require any person who has information as to the child's whereabouts to disclose that information if asked to do so to a constable or to an officer of the Court.

In addition, Courts can make *Private Law Orders* — these may be made by a Court altering the arrangements concerning with whom the child lives, regulating his/her contacts with other people, determining any particular matter relating to his/her upbringing and prohibiting any particular step being taken.

Other important changes introduced by the Children Act, 1989, in relation to the protection of children

There are two further important powers introduced by the Children Act, 1989, aimed at protecting children from harm:

- Duties of a local authority to protect children
- police protection.

Duties of a local authority to protect children

A local authority has a duty to investigate the case fully in five circumstances:

(1) where they have reasonable cause to suspect that a child who lives or is found in their area is suffering or is likely to suffer significant harm
(2) where they have obtained an Emergency Protection Order in respect of the child
(3) where they are informed that a child who lives or is found in their area is subject to an Emergency Protection Order or is in police protection
(4) where a Court in family proceedings directs them to investigate a child's circumstances
(5) where a local education authority notifies them that a child is persistently failing to comply with directions given under an Education Supervision Order (see below).

The duty of the local authority in all of the above circumstances is to make inquiries and investigate (or to arrange for such inquiries to be made, e.g. by another agency such as the NSPCC. In particular the aim of the inquiry is to find out whether the local authority should exercise any of its legal powers to protect the child.

If the local authority decides not to apply for legal protection (i.e. for an Emergency Protection Order), it then must decide whether to review the child's case later. If it decides to do this, it must then fix a date on which the review is to begin.

Police protection

The immediate powers of the police in child protection cases has been changed by the Children Act, 1989. The power of a police constable to take a child to a place of safety has been replaced by the power to take a child into police protection. Such a power may be exercised where the constable has reasonable cause to believe that a child would otherwise be likely to suffer significant harm (Children Act, section 46(1)).[1]

The police constable either:

- removes the child to suitable accommodation (i.e. that run by the local social services department) or
- takes reasonable steps to ensure that the child is removed to a hospital or other suitable place

Police protection cannot last longer than 72 hours. As soon as is reasonably practicable, the constable must ensure that the case is further investigated by an officer designated for that purpose.

Further powers of the courts

Family Assistance Orders

Under the Children Act, 1989, a Court may make a Family Assistance Order in family proceedings. This enables a social worker or probation officer to be made available to give advice and assistance and, where appropriate, befriend the person named in the order — this may be the child, a parent or guardian of the child or any person with whom the child lives. Before such an order may be made, each person named in it must give his or her consent. Such an order may last up to 6 months and is designed to give expert advice to families, especially in separation and divorce cases.

Private Law Orders

The Court may use Private Law Orders to protect children and to help resolve disputes between parents. These are available to anyone who can show they have a proper interest in the child and can be a useful alternative to the other Court Orders mentioned above. It is usual for such Private Law Orders to be limited to parents and others who have some legal responsibility for the child or who may have cared for him/her for a substantial period.

Age limit

In all cases where parental responsibility has been transferred to a local authority, this ceases when the young person reaches the age of 18 years.

Education Supervision Order

An Education Supervision Order can be made by a Court to ensure that a child will be properly educated. When an Education Supervision Order is made, the supervisor appointed is required to advise, assist and befriend, and give instructions to the child concerned and his parents in such a way as will, in his/her opinion, secure that the child will be properly educated.

If these directions are not complied with, the supervisor can either:

- make new directions or
- refer the case to the local authority and apply for the discharge of the order.

When an Education Supervision Order is discharged, the Court may direct that the local authority investigate the child's circumstances.

TABLE 22.2   Children in care of local authorities by age group, and manner of accommodation in England, 1979–89 (thousands)

		1979	1984	1985	1986	1987	1988	1989
Children in care	Total	95.1	74.8	69.6	67.3	65.8	64.4	62.1
Age groups (years)								
Under 5		9.9	8.0	7.5	8.6	9.5	10.1	10.4
5–15		61.7	46.7	42.8	40.8	39.4	37.9	36.1
16 and over		23.6	20.2	19.2	18.0	16.9	16.3	15.6
Manner of accommodation								
Placed with foster parents (family placement)		34.2	36.1	35.0	35.1	35.0	34.9	34.2
In lodgings or residential employment		1.9	2.0	2.0	1.9	2.0	2.1	2.0
In community homes provided, controlled or assisted by local authorities:								
with observation and assessment facilities		4.6	3.1	2.9	2.9	2.8	2.5	2.2
with education on the premises		5.5	2.7	2.2	1.9	1.8	1.3	1.1
other homes		19.2	10.7	9.7	9.1	8.6	8.5	7.7
Voluntary homes and hostels		3.6	1.7	1.5	1.3	1.3	1.0	1.0
Accommodation for children with special educational needs		3.0	2.1	1.8	1.7	1.7	1.4	1.2
Under charge of parent, guardian, relative or friend		17.5	12.8	11.3	10.3	9.0	8.8	8.8
Other accommodation		5.6	3.7	3.2	3.2	3.5	3.8	4.0

Reproduced from ref. 2.

Children in care

The numbers of children in care fell steadily from 1978 to 1988 (see Table 22.2). It will be seen that the majority (43 000 or 69.2%) were in a family placement — 34 200 were living with local authority foster parents and 8800 with parents and guardians. Some 7700 were accommodated in local authority community homes (12.4%), 2200 (3.5%) were in special community homes for observation and assessment and 1100 (1.75%) were in community homes with education on the premises. The remainder were in lodging, voluntary homes or other accommodation.

TYPES AND METHODS OF CHILD CARE

Reference has already been made to the types of accommodation suggested by the Children Act, 1989 (see p. 483). Most of these are widely used by social services departments. It is usual for every child given accommodation to be carefully assessed initially and then for the child to be placed in the most appropriate way. In some large local authorities, a special admission community home is used for this period of assessment. It is important that every effort is made to keep siblings (brothers and sisters) together, unless there are exceptional reasons against this. In practice there are five main ways a child can be looked after:

- *In a family placement.* This is where the child lives with a family just as if this was his or her own home. This can be ideal and is always the first choice as there is substantial evidence that children in family placements do best. The local authority foster parents who look after such children are always very carefully chosen. It is best if they can come from the same background as the child — from the same race, culture and religion. All children in any family placement must be visited by a social worker regularly and at least every 6 weeks. It is best if the same social worker does the visiting of any family placement so that the child gets to know him/her well and the foster parent likewise can be assessed effectively.
- *In a small family group home.* This is a very small community home in which four to six children are looked after. Such homes are best scattered throughout the area and are made as inconspicuous as possible so that the children living in them will be leading as normal a life as possible.
- *In a community home.* These should never be large, 12–18 children are the maximum number presently accommodated in community homes in the UK. This type of care is only used when the child, for some reason, cannot settle into a family placement immediately or where a child has already been in a family placement, but has absconded or is unhappy. Many such children after a period in such a community home move on to a successful family placement.

- *In the child's own home under supervision.* If a child has had to come into care and then the home problems improve, this method of rehabilitation is often used. This enables a check to be made whether the time has arrived when the child can safely return to his/her own home. The supervision in such cases should make certain that, if conditions in the child's own home suddenly deteriorate, that the child can be removed promptly.
- *In a community home run by a voluntary body* such as the National Children's Homes or Barnardos.

SPECIAL COMMUNITY HOMES

Some of the largest social service departments run special community homes. These include special units for very disturbed children and young persons who may have already committed serious offences and are being held on remand before a Court appearance. Such homes often contain children from a number of local authorities. Such special community homes include:

- *Reception centre.* This is particularly designed for children who may be quite disturbed and require a long period of assessment and observation. As some of these children are maladjusted, psychiatric sessions are usually arranged regularly. Psychological investigation is also needed and therapy sessions may be required.
- *Community homes with education on the premises (CHEs).* These homes particularly look after children on remand or those who require a long period of treatment. Assessment plays a very important part in any such community home. Expert staff are needed in such homes as many of the children in them are maladjusted and disturbed, having come from very unsatisfactory homes. Highly trained staff are needed and full psychiatric and psychological support is essential. Entry to such a home often follows a Court appearance for some serious offence. After an assessment has taken place, a period of treatment is started. Many such children benefit from the support and security in a community home with education on the premises, and although few return to their homes (because many have broken homes or most unsatisfactory ones) some children do return to normal life in either a small community home, and if this is successful, eventually to a family placement. After-care for these young persons is very important (see below).

EDUCATION FOR ALL CHILDREN IN CARE

For children in reception centres and CHEs, education is always provided in the community home. The usual arrangement is for the local education authority to run one or two classes at the home. All children in a family placement or in a community home attend normal schools in the community and, if this is still practicable, the same school that they attended before coming into care.

AFTER-CARE

When any child ceases to be looked after by the local authority, that authority must continue to advise, assist and befriend the child with a view to promoting his/her welfare (Children Act, section 24(1)).[1] Steps should always be taken to prepare the child for the time when he/she is no longer looked after.

Local authorities are empowered to assist any person who has been in care by providing assistance in kind and, in exceptional circumstances, in cash. Assistance may include the local authority making a grant to assist with the cost of education and training.

Juvenile proceedings

The Children Act, 1989, introduced some important changes in relation to how a child or young person can be treated — Care Orders may no longer be imposed as a sentence in criminal proceedings. However, the fact that a child or young person has committed an offence may be evidence that he/she is suffering from or is likely to suffer from significant harm so that a local authority may apply for a Care or Supervision Order. 'Harm' includes impairment of behaviour or social development (Children Act, section 31(9)).[1]

Supervision Orders can still be made in criminal proceedings, but there is a difference between a criminal and a civil Supervision Order. In criminal proceedings, a Supervision Order can:

- impose requirements on those with parental responsibility or on other people with whom the child or young person is living
- insist that the child or young person shall live in accommodation provided by or on behalf of the local authority for a period of up to 6 months
- stipulate that the child or young person shall not live with a named person during that period.

The intention of this residence requirement is that, in a repeat offender, who has committed a serious offence and whose criminal behaviour has been attributed to the circumstances in which the child or young person is living, that risk should not be allowed to continue. A 'serious offence' means an offence which, if it had been committed by someone over the age of 21 years, would have warranted a prison sentence. The serious offence must also have been committed while there was in force an earlier Supervision Order.

The power to remand a child or young person to the care of a local authority has been replaced by the Children Act, 1989 'to remand to accommodation provided by a local authority'. This means that any remanded child or young person is no longer to be treated as if he/she was under a Care Order. The child or young person will just be looked after in accommodation by the local authority who will *not* have parental responsibility for him/her.

INTERMEDIATE TREATMENT

A Juvenile Court can place a child or young person on a Supervision Order and then attach to the order a condition that the child or young person must attend a local scheme of intermediate treatment. The main reason for the Court to do this is that, wherever possible, it is better to keep the young offender within the community and family rather than attempt to resolve problems away from the environment in which they arose. Intermediate treatment aims at the following:

- attempting to avoid the problems of institutionalization which can easily follow a period in which a young person is confined to a secure type of residential care, as in a community home with education on the premises (CHE)
- providing a more interesting, practical and realistic method of working with young persons rather than removing him/her from their home surroundings
- avoiding the difficulties of re-integration back into the community after a young person has been sent away for some months living in a CHE.

During the last 5 years, intermediate treatment has often been chosen as an alternative to admitting the individual to a CHE. The usual arrangement in intermediate treatment is to place the young person so that he/she can undertake useful and practical tasks such as learning some trade or occupation. This should channel the energies of the young person into the development of industrial skills which later could be crucial in leading to a full-time job that interests the child or young person.

Adoption services

In the UK, every Social Service Authority (County Councils, Metropolitan Districts and London Boroughs) must establish an adoption service. This should be done in close conjunction with voluntary social services for children and with other approved societies (adoption agencies) in its area.

The responsibility for the approval and registration of adoption societies in England and Wales is that of the Secretary of State for Health in England and Wales.

The legal status of an adopted child is now exactly the same as that of a child born to the adopters. Unless the child is related to the adopters or has been placed with them by the High Court or an adoption agency, an Adoption Order cannot be made unless the child has resided with the applicants for at least 12 months.

The most important requirements for adoption are briefly as follows:

- legal adoption is by an Adoption Order made by a Court of Law
- persons who can adopt include the mother and father of the child
- either can only adopt singly if
  - the other parent is dead or cannot be found or
  - there is some other reason justifying the exclusion of the other natural parent
- a married couple can adopt where each has attained the age of 21 years (this is the sole exception to the general rule that an Adoption Order may only be made to one person)
- an Adoption Order may be made on the application of one person where he or she is 21 years of age or over and is:
  - not married or
  - the spouses have separated and are living apart and the separation is likely to be permanent
  - the spouse is, by reason of ill health (physical or mental) incapable of making an application to adopt
- a child who has been married cannot be adopted
- a male person normally cannot singly adopt a female child
- the Court hearings must be in private
- the child must have been in the care of the applicant for at least three consecutive months
- an Adoption Order may contain such terms and conditions as the Court thinks fit; a change that has been made by the Children Act, 1989, is that if, in adoption proceedings, the Court considers that it may be appropriate to make a Care or Supervision Order, it may direct the local authority to investigate the child's circumstances
- the applicant must notify the local authority if the adoption has not been arranged through an adoption society
- the persons whose consent is necessary must fully understand the nature of the consent; parental consent to adoption may be dispensed with where a parent cannot be found or is incapable of giving agreement or where a child has been seriously ill-treated
- the adoption must be in the best interests of the child
- the adoption must *not* be arranged for reward
- prospective applicants must be visited by a social worker during the 3-month period
- cohabiting couples cannot jointly adopt a child
- if the parents agree to the adoption, the Court will appoint a Reporting Officer

who visits the parties and reports back to the Court; where there is no agreement, the Court appoints a *Guardian ad Litem* who is an officer who safeguards the interests of the child on behalf of the Court

- parental consent to adoption is now given before an Adoption Order is made; this procedure frees the child for adoption and allows the parent to give early consent which can be less traumatic; the Children Act, 1989, has made the following change — in future, an adoption agency will not be able to apply for a freeing order without the consent of the parent or guardian
- foster parents and others who have looked after the child continuously for 5 years can apply to adopt the child without any fear that the child can be removed before the Court hearing; this enables foster parents who have satisfactorily cared for a child for 5 years to apply for adoption without being worried that the local authority or natural parent can remove the child from their care
- adoptions may only be arranged through an adoption society unless the person wishing to adopt the child is a close relative of the child.

HEALTH CONSIDERATIONS

It is important for doctors and nurses to realize that there are important health considerations in adoption proceedings relating both to the child and to the adopting applicants. The applicants should know all about the general health of the child and of any defects of sight, speech or learning disabilities (mental handicap). Serological tests for syphilis and HIV infection should always be carried out. At the same time, the *adopting person should be in good general health and be temperamentally and psychologically fit to care for a child* and have a good family history. Circumstances which should always be considered include mental illness, learning disabilities (mental handicap), epilepsy, tuberculosis and any other serious chronic illness.

ACCESS TO BIRTH RECORDS

Adopted persons over the age of 18 years have a legal right to information about their birth records. The Children Act, 1989, made some changes to the procedure. The Registrar General is required to set up an Adoption Contact Register to enable adopted people to contact their birth parents and other relatives. It is only open to people aged 18 and over. Before anyone can use the register, the Registrar General has to be satisfied about the identity of the applicant and of the relationship with the adopted person. A fee will now be charged.

Persons adopted after 12 November 1975 must be given an opportunity to see a counsellor, but need not do so. Those adopted before 1975 must see a counsellor before being given the information that they seek. Since the Children Act, 1989, the counselling interview may be held either in the UK (formerly this was the only method) or outside the UK by a body which has notified the Registrar General that it is willing to provide counselling and has satisfied the Registrar General that it is suitable to do so.

References

1. Children Act, 1989, London: HMSO.
2. Department of Health. Health and Personal Social Services Statistics. London: HMSO. 1991.
3. An introduction to the Children Act 1989. London: HMSO. 1991.

23

Child Physical and Sexual Abuse

Since 1970, greater emphasis has been given to child abuse. There are two main categories of child abuse:

- *physical abuse* — this is the deliberate injury to a child (formerly this was called 'non-accidental injury'.
- *sexual abuse* — this is sexual interference with a child usually in his/her home surroundings; most child sexual abusers are men or youths, and very often it is a male relative who is involved (i.e. father, step-father, cohabitor or brother); very occasionally a woman is involved, either as the abuser or in consenting to or arranging for the abuse to take place.

The research and investigation into child abuse from 1970 to 1990 has brought to light the serious nature and degree of this problem. It is, however, difficult to compare the present and former levels of child abuse because so little investigation took place before 1970. Undoubtedly both child physical and sexual abuse have

TABLE 23.1   Children and young persons on Child Protection Registers: by sex and age in England and Wales, 1990 (Numbers and rates)

Age (years)	Boys	Girls
Number (thousands)		
Under 1	1.5	1.4
1–4	7.7	6.9
5–9	7.5	7.3
10–15	4.9	6.6
16 and over	0.5	1.1
All children	22.6	22.9
Rates (per 1000 population in each group)		
Under 1	4.2	4.2
1–4	5.7	5.6
5–9	4.6	4.7
10–15	2.7	3.8
16 and over	0.7	1.7
All children	3.8	4.2

Data from ref. 11.

existed for a long time and the increased levels now recorded, and which are still increasing, may be partly apparent.

Table 23.1 shows the number of children and young persons on the Child Protection Registers in England and Wales in 1990 — a total of 45 500. There were 22 600 boys and 22 900 girls (this compares with a total of 30 900 in 1988 which was the first year detailed statistics were collected in this form. The 1990 figures represent a rate of 4.0 children per 1000 population aged under 18 years; the rate was 4.2 for girls and 3.8 for boys.[1]

Table 23.1 emphasizes that younger children are more likely to be on the register than older ones. The highest rates were found in the 1–4 year age group for both boys and girls. Under the age of 5 years, the incidence in both sexes is similar. From age 5 years upwards girls are more likely to be abused. From age 16 years and over, girls are over two times more likely to be abused than boys.

Types of child abuse (physical and sexual)

Five types of sexual abuse were classified in the Department of Health publication *Working Together* in 1988.[2]

These include:

- *Neglect.* The persistent or severe neglect of a child (for example by exposure to any kind of danger, including cold and starvation) which results in severe impairment of the child's health or development, including non-organic failure to thrive.
- *Physical abuse.* Defined as physical injury to a child, including deliberate poisoning, where there is a definite knowledge or reasonable suspicion, that the injury was inflicted or knowingly not prevented.
- *Sexual abuse.* This includes the involvement of dependent, developmentally immature children and adolescents in sexual activities they do not fully comprehend, to which they are unable to give informed consent, or that violate the social taboos of family roles.
- *Emotional abuse.* This is the severe and adverse effect on the behaviour and emotional development of a child caused by persistent ill-treatment or rejection. All abuse involves some emotional ill-treatment. This category should only be used where it is the main or sole form of abuse.
- *Grave concern.* This includes children whose situations do not currently fit the above categories, but where social and medical assessments indicate that they are at significant risk of abuse. These could include cases where another child in the household has been harmed or the household contains a known abuser.

The distribution of these five types on the Child Protection Register is shown in Fig. 23.1. The figures for 1990 are very similar to those for 1988 (shown in the

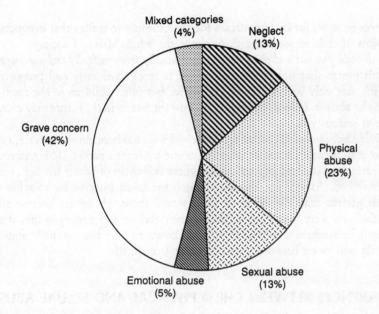

FIGURE 23.1   Children on child protection registers: by reason in England and Wales, 1990 (percentages). (Data from ref. 11.)

parentheses): grave concern was the commonest abuse at 40% (37%), followed by physical abuse at 24% (28%), sexual abuse at 15% (14%), neglect at 13% (13%) and emotional abuse at 5% (4%).

Characteristics of child abuse

There are striking similarities and differences between child physical and child sexual abuse.

SIMILARITIES BETWEEN CHILD PHYSICAL AND CHILD SEXUAL ABUSE

The similarities include the following:

■ *Both forms of child abuse, physical and sexual, are found in all types of families and social classes.* Although cases are commoner in certain social groups in society, many instances of child abuse will be missed if it is assumed that cases never occur in those families usually described as the 'pillars of society'. Such judgements should never be used, for it is important for professionals to realize that instances of all forms of child abuse occur throughout the whole strata of society.

- *Both child physical and child sexual abuse usually start gradually and are progressive.* This means that unless the child abuse is recognized early and properly dealt with, not only will the abuse get worse, but other children in the family may also be abused. Indeed, children born into the family in the future may eventually be at serious risk.
- *Child abuse can be self-generating.* Any child who has been abused is more, not less, likely to become an abuser when he or she becomes a parent. This characteristic is often seen in child physical abuse where this chain of events has been carefully researched. As yet, not enough research has taken place to see to what extent this pattern may also occur in child sexual abuse. However, because all individuals are very much influenced by their earliest experiences in life, it should never be assumed that anyone who is known to have been sexually abused as a child will never become a sexual abuser later in life.

DIFFERENCES BETWEEN CHILD PHYSICAL AND SEXUAL ABUSE

The differences between child physical and child sexual abuse are most obvious when the effects on the child are studied.

In cases of *child physical abuse*, progressive injury to the child is likely to occur and therefore any such child may be in acute danger. This means that delay over diagnosis and effective treatment can lead to severe injury and even death in some children. Therefore, in the investigation and treatment of child physical abuse, *the safeguarding of the child is paramount at all times*, but particulary early in the development of the syndrome. This is why short-term separation of the child from the family is justified in serious cases of physical abuse.

In most cases of *child sexual abuse*, the damage to the child is primarily emotional. It is important to investigate all suspected cases, but there is never the degree of urgency to protect the child by immediate separation from the family except in serious cases of child physical abuse. Indeed, routine removal of a child who has been sexually abused from the family may increase the child's emotional problems. It was this action in Cleveland in 1987 — the removal of many children from their families following suspected sexual abuse — that produced so many disturbing factors. The very suspicion of child sexual abuse is a very emotive accusation that can easily destroy a marriage and family life, particularly if accompanied by the removal of the child, which usually publicizes the problem. Even if the suspicion is later shown to have been unfounded, irreparable damage may already have occurred to the relationship between the husband and wife.

Stages in the investigation and management of child abuse

There are three stages in the recognition and management of child abuse:

- recognition and investigation
- assessment and planning
- treatment and review.

RECOGNITION AND INVESTIGATION

In recognizing both physical and sexual child abuse the most important factor is that the professional — doctor, nurse or social worker — must be aware that there is always a possibility that the explanation for the various signs and symptoms may be child abuse. Many of the most serious mistakes occur because this possibility has never been considered. It therefore follows that in such cases, this possibility should always be carefully and seriously considered. Once this has been done and rejected, then other causes can be investigated in depth. When this procedure is not followed, it is always possible to miss cases of child abuse which seem quite obvious with hindsight. This is particularly the case in child sexual abuse.

The detailed diagnostic signs of child physical abuse and child sexual abuse are different and are therefore described separately (see pp. 503 and 508.)

In both forms of child abuse, once any professional suspects that child abuse may be occurring, it is essential to refer this concern immediately to either the local authority social services department, the police or to the National Society for the Prevention of Cruelty to Children (NSPCC). Whenever any person alleges child abuse, a full investigation must be undertaken immediately. Every allegation must be considered serious unless proved otherwise.

Once the facts have indicated that this is probably a case of child abuse, the question of whether the child is still in danger must be asked. If this is likely, an Emergency Protection Order must be obtained from a Court (see p. 486). If this is not immediately practicable (e.g. at a weekend), then Police Protection should be sought at once (see pp. 487–488). Any procrastination can prove to be disastrous.

Once the child is no longer in immediate danger, the next step in all cases is to call a case conference. This should be set up as quickly as possible (within 24 hours) either by the social services department or by the NSPCC (in those areas where this body acts as the main specialist for child abuse). Any professional can request a case conference.

Case conference

Every case conference should include all those already concerned with the case. This will include the paediatrician, the family doctor, the health visitor, the social worker (both the specialist social worker, see p. 509, and the general social worker from the district concerned), a teacher from the school (if the child or sibling is still at school), the NSPCC inspector and, if relevant, the probation officer. Parents should also be invited, where practicable, to attend part, or if appropriate, the whole of the case conference unless, in the view of the chairman of the conference, their presence will preclude a full and proper consideration of the child's interests. Parents should also be informed of the outcome of a case conference as soon as is practicable, and this information should be confirmed in writing.

The case conference discusses the case in detail and then decides whether the case is child abuse and, if so, what should be the next action. If there is still doubt, then the case conference orders further investations and meets later to decide the outcome. In all case conferences it is most important that all decisions are made jointly and not by any individual professional. In the past it has often been shown that this is the only way to ensure the wisest decision is made as sharing information within the case conference often emphasizes the true nature of the events. In the past, many mistakes have been attributed to failure to follow this principle.

Once a case conference decides that a case of child abuse has occurred (either physical or sexual) the name and address of the child and family must be entered on the local *Child Protection Register* (see p. 510) and the parents informed that this has been done.

ASSESSMENT AND PLANNING

Once any child has been identified by a case conference as having been abused (physically or sexually) and his/her name entered on the Child Protection Register, then either the local authority social services department or the NSPCC should be responsible for all future child care in the case.

The next stage is for a *key worker* to be appointed to the case. This professional has three main responsibilities:

- to carry out all aspects of care for the child and family
- to prepare a multidisciplinary plan for the child and family, this should include comprehensive social and medical assessments. The next stage is for the key worker to suggest short-term and long-term objectives
- to act as the leading professional for all inter-agency work; the key worker should indicate exactly what role, if any, the other agencies should undertake in the proposed treatment and care; each agency should then clearly indicate in writing whether they accept the suggested role; once this comprehensive plan has been drawn up and accepted, it should be recorded in the notes of the case conference.

TREATMENT AND REVIEW

As the treatment for the two forms of child abuse are different, these are now considered in detail separately.

Child physical abuse

Incidence and characteristics

Child physical abuse is usually caused by close relatives — parents, brother, stepparents and cohabitors — and occurs in children of all ages, although most serious cases are found in children under the age of 8 years. Men cause most cases — just over 70%, but women, especially those living alone, are responsible for a surprisingly large number. Some of the worst cases of criminal neglect occur in problem families in whom other forms of anti-social behaviour are found, e.g. assaults, drunkenness, frustration and bad living conditions. There is a higher proportion of child physical abuse found in single parent families. Many of these inevitably have to accept unsatisfactory and overcrowded living conditions where unsympathetic neighbours or landlords are constantly complaining about babies and infants who cry.

Three groups of parents show a higher incidence of child physical abuse:

- *those who were physically abused themselves when a child*
- *those who are young and under the age of 20 years*; many of these have to face very unsatisfactory living conditions and poverty; they are also very immature and consequently much less tolerant of all the inherent problems that all young children produce
- *those who are suffering from some mental disorder* which is characterized by their inability to cope with everyday problems and especially those of infants and young children.

Diagnosis and early recognition

Any additional stress will always tend to aggravate child physical abuse. Often moving house results in much loneliness and strain and child abuse may start or, if already present, get worse.

Any child physical abuse is always repetitive and progressive, so it is always important to look for signs which may be the result of earlier incidents of abuse — bruises that obviously occurred earlier, healed fractures of bones or a history of a marked change in the demeanour or behaviour of a child. Children who are being abused become quiet and watchful, particulary of strangers and adults. A health visitor who has been visiting and seeing an infant since birth should notice such a change which may develop quite quickly after the child abuse has started.

Early recognition and diagnosis of child physical abuse are all important as the next assault and abuse on the child is likely to be worse than earlier ones and may be devastating. Hence delay in making a diagnosis can be disastrous.

Early diagnosis of child physical abuse depends upon the alertness of many types of professional staff including general practitioners (GPs), paediatricians, health visitors, district nurses, midwives, social workers and the staff of voluntary organizations especially the NSPCC. Because physical injury to the child is always a dominant feature, all those working in casualty departments of hospitals should be especially vigilant.

Child physical abuse can present itself in many ways, but usually starts by one or both parents, a step-father or cohabitor slapping, hitting, punching or severely shaking the child, causing bruises and occasionally more serious injuries. The following signs are commonly seen:

- minor bruises which may show that the child has been gripped too tightly or shaken
- minor injuries (especially facial bruises) usually caused by slapping or hitting the child; the type of injury is often similar — 70% are soft tissue injuries to the head and face; there may be 'finger bruising' in which the outlines of the fingers which slapped the child can clearly be seen within the bruised area; such bruising tends to pick out the bony prominences; often the child's lips are thick and bruised and there is a torn upper lip frenum; ribs are frequently bruised or broken and X-rays often indicate that these injuries have been caused in the past; occasionally small burns such as cigarette burns may be present
- an unexplained failure of any child to thrive
- unusual behaviour by the parents — this may take many different forms — over-anxiety and frequent attendance with the child at the casualty departments or at surgeries; a mother who has witnessed abuse often does this as she is likely to be in a dilemma — she is torn between not wanting to incriminate her husband or partner, yet she realizes, because of the repeated abuses so characteristic of child physical abuse, that her child is probably at serious risk of permanent injury — if the correct diagnosis is made, many such mothers are relieved; another, although less common attitude, of a parent may be an unnatural lack of concern for the child's condition.

It is known that parents who commit child physical abuse often start taking their child to a hospital for treatment in a neighbouring town or district to reduce the chance of being discovered. Therefore, any child attending an unusual hospital (i.e. one outside their usual area) should always be examined with extra care.

Action to be taken when there is a reasonable suspicion of child physical abuse

Once there is a reasonable suspicion of child physical abuse, the following action should always be taken:

- the child should be admitted immediately to hospital for diagnosis, assessment and for the child's own safety
- an Emergency Protection Order should be sought from a Court; the social services department will do this (see p. 486)
- the child may be just 'provided with accommodation' while investigations proceed, but this does not prevent either parent suddenly turning up at a childrens home and demanding that the child immediately goes home
- a case conference should be arranged immediately unless this has already been done (see p. 502); even if the suspicion is not firm enough to justify immediate admission to hospital, a case conference should still be held.

If suspicion is very slight, in every instance the professional should at least:

- consult the family doctor
- discuss the details of the case with a senior colleague and make a note that this has been done
- make enquiries to find out if the child or his/her family are on the Child Protection Register.

Treatment and rehabilitation

In all instances the aim of treatment is to ensure that the short-term and long-term interests of the child are met as far as possible. Although there are certain serious cases of intentional injury and neglect that can only be properly treated by permanent removal of the child from his/her parents, most cases are quite different. In these, the physical abuse has been caused and/or influenced by many other factors such as bad living conditions, unemployment, poverty, threat of eviction (especially where small infants cry repeatedly) and by minor psychiatric illnesses. These parents urgently require help and if this can be satisfactorily given they may be able to be assisted to develop into perfectly satisfactory parents and families. However, the causative factors must be discovered. In same instances, it may be necessary to provide accommodation for the child while the parent is treated.

Day care can be a very useful form of treatment. Many people, particulary young mothers who have been found to ill-treat their children, are often very isolated and lonely. In some cases the mother herself had an unhappy childhood or was brought up in a broken home and suffers from a great deal of insecurity.

A very useful method of helping this kind of case is to admit the child to a day nursery or playgroup, and then to arrange for the mother to help with the group. In this way the mother will be encouraged to make new friends and thus to obtain the support she needs. She will also be taught to improve her relationship with her own child from the example she will see in the nursery or playgroup.

Education by example is being used increasingly in this way. Older children in the same family come along to the day unit after school as well as many senior girls who help periodically in playgroups and day nurseries. In this way, these girls learn at first hand the correct methods of care of young children. This is particulary important as the incidence of child abuse is highest in teenage mothers. Some day nurseries tend to specialize in taking children who have been abused regularly. This can be quite helpful, not only because the staff in such units naturally become experienced and expert at dealing with the problem of child abuse, but also because special links can then be created between nearby paediatric units and these centres and nurseries. Such an arrangement enables all types of students in training — doctors, health visitors, nurses, social workers — to attend for training and to see for themselves some of the best methods of treating most child abuse cases. Day care in a special day nursery also enables the staff to keep a careful watch on children who have been abused. Not only can the children be examined (if new bruises appear then the staff can question the mother about them), but any unexplained absence from the nursery can be followed up immediately. This is important because if another episode of physical abuse has occurred, the child will undoubtedly be kept at home on some pretext to conceal any new injuries the child may have received.

Periodic review of long-term cases

Some of the more difficult problems occur in long-term cases of child physical abuse. It is important not only to follow-up any children known to have been abused in the past, but to realize that new children born into the family can easily present a new set of risks with the cycle of child abuse starting again. Health visitors are in an especially good position to carry out this kind of surveillance, as the health visitor will receive a notification of all new births in the area. Where such a birth occurs in a family in whom child abuse has occurred before, a special and careful watch must be maintained.

Such observation should involve many professional staff normally concerned with children — GPs, teachers, school nurses, health visitors, education welfare officers, social workers (including those working in child guidance clinics), as well as appropriate voluntary agencies.

In all older children (in whom some of the worst cases of child abuse occur), it is important that there is a sound level of communication established with the teaching staff in the area. Most good teachers know a great deal about those local families who have constant problems (including child abuse), and can, therefore, help considerably in spotting new potential danger signs so that effective preventive action can be taken to avoid new outbreaks of child abuse.

The Department of Health has made it quite clear in a recent publication[2] that the Director of Social Services must be informed (or the NSPCC in those few areas where this organization acts as the main specialist in child abuse) when any case of child physical abuse is suspected. Unless locally there is an effective sharing of information between all staff working with children in the education, health, or social service fields, delays will be inevitable and intervention may only be started when it is too late. This is the reason why no long-term case is 'written off' and removed from the Child Protection Register until a case conference agrees to this action. Unless this multidisciplinary team approach is always used, the mistakes of the past will be repeated.

If a doctor or nurse comes across a case which could be child physical abuse, the child should be admitted to hospital immediately and the Director of Social Services for the area immediately notified (see p. 505). If access to the child is denied, then the help of the police should be sought at once as, under the Children Act, 1989, the police have powers 'to take a child into police protection' (see pp. 487–488), and this power lasts up to 72 hours thus enabling further examinations and investigations to take place.

Child sexual abuse

Incidence and characteristics

Few people dispute the fact that the sexual abuse of children has always existed. Yet detailed studies have only recently been widely undertaken in the UK. Undoubtedly in the UK, interest in child sexual abuse has increased markedly since, in Cleveland in 1987, an alleged 464 cases were reported in a period of 4 months. This was in a population of 550 000 (giving a rate of 84 per 100 000). Not all of these were confirmed cases. This incident attracted great interest and a special government inquiry was set up presided over by Lord Justice Butler-Schloss.[3] The recommendations were included in the DHSS booklet *Working Together*[2] which laid down guidelines for the recognition, investigation and treatment of child sexual abuse, as well as child physical abuse.

In the past, much research has confirmed the traditional view that 80% of sexually abused children are females[4] and 95% of the abusers are male.[5] However, in 1990 Wilkins pointed out that increasing evidence is accumulating that women may be responsible for 13% of the sexual abuse in girls and nearly 25% in boys.[6,7] In another study, Faller[8] found that four fifths of the women perpetuators were the mother to at least one of their victims. The commonest forms of sexual abuse by women in this study were fondling of a child's genitals, oral sex, digital masturbation and actual sexual intercourse in that order.

Child sexual abuse is an extremely emotive subject and it is never easy to involve the parents in any investigation without risking the complete destruction of their own personal relationships. In physical child abuse, any parent may inadvertently raise suspicion by overstepping the mark by the natural discipline of any child, but to introduce a sexual element into the affection given by one parent or by another adult to the child of either sex is to suggest something which most parents would find very offensive. Certainly there is no doubt that most people feel a greater abhorrence towards anyone who has been found to abuse a child sexually compared with physical abuse, especially if the physical abuse has been of a minor nature and there are extenuating circumstances.

Diagnosis and recognition

The diagnosis of child sexual abuse is always very difficult. Apart from the few cases where a child unequivocally alleges sexual abuse in the clearest terms, the diagnosis is rarely clear-cut and is usually only reached after a lengthy period of assessment. Even when a child has initially made an unambiguous accusation, this is often retracted later when the seriousness of the disclosure is realized and this, of course, introduces such an element of doubt that it may be impossible to be certain that sexual abuse has taken place.

There is no single conclusive diagnostic sign that child sexual abuse has occurred,[9] except when semen is found or blood from a different group than that of the child.[3] Careful assessment, observation and investigation by a multi-professional team is always important to ensure that a balance is maintained between over-enthusiasm and zeal and the failure to act in time. Different doctors, nurses, health visitors, teachers and the police all have a contribution to make. Because of the complexity of these issues prompt diagnosis is almost impossible.

The usual starting point in any diagnosis of child sexual abuse is the raising of suspicion that it may be occurring. The following guidance is taken from the 1988 DHSS publication,[2] which suggested three types of suspicion — serious, moderate and mild:

- *Serious suspicion* should always be raised in the following instance — when a child makes clear verbal allegations of sexual abuse. If the allegation is spontaneous, it would be most unusual for it to be a fabrication.
- *Moderate suspicion* is justified in the following instances:
    - if the child makes an allegation of sexual abuse in ambiguous terms and therefore does not make absolutely clear precisely what happened
    - if a child is sexually provocative to adults or discloses detailed knowledge of sexual matters in conversation, fantasy or drawings
    - if a child responds to questioning by describing sexual abuse, but has not made a spontaneous allegation
    - if a child shows a specific fear of a father, step-father or sexually mature older brother
    - if a child is living in overcrowded conditions and the mother is known to be a prostitute; however, it must be emphasized that a particular family setting should never, on its own, be grounds for serious suspicion.
- *Mild suspicion* should always be aroused in the following circumstances:
    - if a child shows behavioural or emotional disturbance for which no other cause can be found
    - if a child shows unexplained changes in behaviour
    - if a child makes a suicide attempt

— if a child runs away from home when there is no obvious cause to do so
— if there is an unusually close relationship between the father or step-father and the child and, at the same time, there is marital discord in the home.

Management and treatment

The most marked difference between child physical and sexual abuse is that, in child sexual abuse, an emergency response such as the immediate removal of the child from the household is not necessarily called for. The one exception is where the child is liable to assault or intimidation — *then care away from the home must be provided promptly*.

As in all child care work the interests of the child are the most important feature. The main problems a child has to face after sexual abuse are emotional ones and this means that often it is best to keep the child within the family. Initially it is often better for the abuser to leave the family home for at least a period.

All circumstances must be considered and perhaps the most important is whether one should always strive to keep the family together. Often that would be ideal, but there are exceptions and therefore the decision of whether to adopt a particular line of action is always a very individual one. The final decision should, as in physical abuse, be taken by a case conference, but it is always a great help if the key worker understands the paramount need to support the parents and family and to get their confidence. Equally it is most important to obtain the views of the child. The final answer will depend on the individual circumstances of each case.

As the Butler-Schloss inquiry[3] suggested, the development of a specialist team in each area would be a great advantage. Such a team would always include a social worker, a doctor and a specialist police officer. Those making up the team should have a genuine interest in the topic and must attempt to approach the problem without any prejudice and on preconceived ideas. Child sexual abuse is an emotional subject, and produces in many people an overwhelming revulsion. This, of course, makes a rational approach difficult for many individuals, including some professionals. What is urgently needed is the gradual and logical development of successful methods of treating child sexual abuse and one therefore needs:

- more research
- careful trial and error, e.g. a careful evolution based on the experience of different successful methods of dealing with sexual abuse in children; certainly the model of treatment already worked out for physical abuse is not appropriate for many forms of child sexual abuse
- an individual approach, as the various factors in each case may be quite different
- to make every effort to prevent the child victim from later developing long-term effects
- the encouragement of love and support for the child within the family; this may even mean that the bond of affection between the child and his/her abuser may need to be maintained once abuse has ended

- the avoidance of any kind of implied criticism that the child, in some way, is partly to blame; one of the most damaging long-term effects can be the accumulation of guilt feelings in the child that in some way he/she has been responsible for the breakdown between husband and wife and the rest of the family.

Much successful treatment will involve counselling and support for the child, the parent who is innocent, the abuser and the rest of the family. Even in the most promising cases, this is likely to take a long time — months at least — and precipitate judgements are likely to be harmful in some cases. What may be needed is the patient introduction of a series of models of treatment until some are shown to have the best chance of success. The test of success must always be in the long-term results, e.g. when a child who is known to have been sexually abused grows up into a normal loving and caring adult and parent capable of happy personal and sexual relationships, who is then living a contented life with his or her own family and children.

Child Protection Registers

Reference has already been made to the value of the Child Protection Register. The up-to-date keeping of such a register is essential for each area/district to ensure there is an effective means of recording and sharing information about child abuse. The register is usually maintained by the local authority social services department, but in a few areas where the NSPCC acts as specialists for child abuse, the latter organizes the register. The following information is always recorded in the register:

- name of the child and family and details of any other children known to live in the household
- the nature of the child abuse
- the name of the key worker and the core group
- in addition, a record is kept of the name of the child's GP, the health visitor, name of the school the child attends, details of the original referral, investigations carried out, treatment plans and the review; the date of deregistration if applicable (the date when the child's name was removed from the register) would also be recorded.

IMPORTANCE OF CONFIDENTIALITY OF ALL DETAILS ON THE REGISTER

Child Protection Registers and the information in them is absolutely confidential. Special arrangements must be made to ensure complete confidentiality. Any queries are always dealt with on the 'ring back' principle. If any professional rings up and asks to indicate if a certain child or family are on the register, their name is taken and telephone number and they are told that the official in charge of the register will ring them back. This allows their position and phone number to be checked and, if everything is genuine, a return phone call is made to provide the information requested.

Arrangements should also be made to share information on the registers with neighbouring social services departments. Further features about the management of Child Protection Registers are that:

- they should be readily available at all times — it should be possible for nurses, doctors and social workers to check the information at least on a 14-hour basis every day;
- they must be carefully kept up-to-date;
- notes of all referrals to the register should be kept and, where two different professionals make enquiries within 18 months, the two professionals should be informed and put in touch with each other; this is designed to help in the sharing of information between professionals who are obviously concerned about the child.

Note that the discovery that a particular child or family is already on the register does not, of course, prove that the present incident which prompted the enquiry is child abuse, but does call for extra special care and vigilance.

Inter-agency co-ordination in child abuse

Most of the official inquiries set up to consider very serious cases of child abuse during 1972 to 1990 (many instances in which the abused child died as a result of their injuries) emphasized in the report that the most consistent mistake made locally was a lack of co-ordination between the social services, health services, education services, police and voluntary bodies working in this field (almost invariably the NSPCC). Because effective co-ordination is so important, the various memoranda and guidelines issued by the Department of Health insist that a special co-ordinating committee, now called the Area Child Protection Committee, must be set up locally.

This Area Child Protection Committee should always include the Director of Social Services, who usually acts as the convenor and secretary of the committee, the Director of Education (or representative), the District Medical Officer, a senior paediatrican, District Nursing Officer, specialists in community medicine who deal with social services and child health, a senior police officer, senior inspector of the local NSPCC and a representative of the Chief Probation Officer.

The Area Child Protection Committee should meet regularly and at least four times a year, should act as a policy-forming body to ensure that all the administrative and training arrangements for dealing with both forms of child abuse (physical and sexual) are satisfactory. The detailed duties of the Area Child Protection Committee include the following:

- review local practice and procedure for dealing with such cases (child abuse) with special reference to inter-agency guidelines to be followed
- ensure that immediate hospital admission for children at risk is accepted
- approve written instructions defining the exact duties and responsibilities of professional staff in connection with child abuse
- provide education and training programmes for staff in the health and social services
- review the work of case conferences
- inquire into the circumstances of cases which appear to have gone wrong and from which lessons could be learned
- ensure that procedures are in operation to safeguard continuity of care between neighbouring areas and in those instances when families move to another area
- agree arrangements for the operation of the Child Protection Register.

Training

Since the publication of *Working Together*[2] there has been a great deal of joint training carried out for social services staff and the police. However, as a recent article noted 'training for doctors has been patchy.'[9] In 1989 a short booklet was published by the British Medical Journal[10] which contains 18 helpful articles by medical experts and is edited by Professor Roy Meadow. All aspects of both forms of child abuse are covered, and the booklet contains figures and coloured plates. Its contents should certainly be studied by any doctor in training for general practice and for all aspects of child health. It particulary points out 'that the concept of a single, conclusive diagnostic sign of sexual abuse is invalid'. As the official inquiry into the Cleveland child sexual abuse episode in 1987 pointed out in a discussion on the test of reflex anal dilatation in a child (which had been taken in many cases to indicate sexual abuse in a child), that 'there is no proof of a direct link between reflex anal dilatation and the diagnosis of sexual abuse' although its presence does raise the level of suspicion.

References

1. Central Statistical Office. Social Trends London: HMSO. 1988.
2. Department of Health and Social Security. Working together. London: DHSS. 1988.

3. Department of Health and Social Security. Inquiry into child abuse in Cleveland in 1987. London: DHSS. 1988.
4. Kendall-Tackett KA, Simon AF. Perpetrators and their acts: data from 365 adults molested as children. Child Abuse Negl. 1987, **11**: 237–245.
5. Mrazek P, Lynch M, Bentovim A. Recognition of sexual abuse in the United Kingdom. *In* Mrazek P, Kempe CH (eds) Sexually abused children and their families. Oxford: Pergamon Press. 1987, pp. 35–50.
6. Wilkins R. Women who sexually abuse children. Doctors need to become sensitized to the possibility. Br. Med. J. 1990, **300**: 1153–1154.
7. Finkelhor D, Russel D. Women as perpetrators. *In* Finkelhor D (ed) Child sexual abuse: new theory and research. New York: Free Press. 1984, pp. 171–185.
8. Faller KC. Women who sexually abuse children. Violence and Victims 1987, **2**: 263–276.
9. Miles M. Cruel truths. Br. Med. J. 1990, **300**: 1598.
10. Meadow R (ed). ABC of Child Abuse. London: Br. Med. J. 1989.
11. Central Statistical Office. Social Trends. London: HMSO. 1992.

24

Care and Rehabilitation of Disabled Persons

The care and rehabilitation of disabled persons is an important function of local authority social services departments. Because of the diverse nature of these handicapped persons (blind, partially sighted, deaf, hard of hearing and all types of physically handicapped people), the help and assistance given by social services departments should always fit closely within a range of other services including:

- all the health services (hospitals, primary health care, and many specialized units such as regional spinal injury units and other rehabilitation day centres)
- many voluntary bodies covering the whole range of specialized voluntary bodies who provide services for specific groups of disabled persons
- central government departments responsible for training and provision of employment for disabled people (mostly the Department of Employment)
- social security departments providing special financial benefits for disabled and handicapped persons
- local education departments who have been responsible for educating and training many seriously handicapped children and young persons who, having reached school leaving age, are about to leave their care.

Registration of disabled persons

Social services departments arrange for the local registration of disabled persons. Table 24.1 gives details of the number and type of disabled persons registered in England in 1987 and 1990. The number registered has risen steadily for many years, but this is most likely to be due to more disabled people taking the trouble to register (many for the first time) rather than a true increase in incidence.

Table 24.2 gives a further breakdown of the group of 'general classes', e.g. the first four groups in Table 24.1 by age group. Note that the incidence of disability and handicap rises significantly as the age group rises, and that at least 65% of all disability occurs in those aged 65 years and over.[1]

TABLE 24.1   Persons registered as substantially and permanently disabled by type and degree of disability, England, 1987 and 1990 (thousands)

	1987		1990	
	All ages	65 years and over (%)	All ages	65 years and over (%)
Very severely disabled	76.1	42.9(56.4)	75.9	42.5(56.0)
Severely disabled	516.1	338.5(65.6)	544.5	364.0(66.8)
Other registered persons	638.5	425.2(66.6)	645.0	438.8(68.0)
Blind persons	133.9	104.5(78.1)	–	–
Partially sighted persons	79.0	60.1(76.1)	–	–
Deaf persons	37.9	12.3(32.6)	37.9	12.3(32.6)
Hard of hearing persons	70.9	55.6(79.1)	70.9	55.6(79.1)

Data from ref. 1.

TABLE 24.2   Persons registered as substantially and permanently disabled, general classes: by age group in England, 1987 and 1990 (thousands)

Age group (years)	1987		1990	
	Number	%	Number	%
Under 16	23.4	1.9	21.8	1.7
16–64	400.6	32.6	398.3	31.5
65 and over	804.1	65.5	845.3	66.8
Total	1227.6	100.0	1265.4	100.0

Data from ref. 1.

Incidence of real disability

These registration figures are not only limited because it is known that a large proportion of disabled people never register, but also because registration figures can never give an indication of the true incidence of real handicap – i.e. of the problems which the disabled person suffers from and has to overcome if he/she is to lead a reasonably normal life. The figures in Tables 24.1 and 24.2 are always subdivided into various groups, and the largest of these are the 'general groups'. Such a classification is based on diagnosis rather than on an assessment of function (e.g. they give no measure of the real problems any disabled person faces and which will tend to significantly lower their quality of life. These include many features such as mobility, disfigurement, behaviour, dexterity, etc.).

This type of assessment was made in a series of surveys carried out by the Office of Population Censuses and Surveys (OPCS) between 1985 and 1988 in Great

Britain[2]. These surveys covered adults and children living in both private house-holds and communal residential establishments; 100 000 persons were first screened by a postal survey covering all parts of Great Britain. This was then followed by 2824 personal interviews with people living at home, and a further 11 424 postal enquiries. The next stage was holding 3533 personal interviews with disabled persons living in residential homes or nursing homes/hospitals.

The survey focused on disability, and this was defined as an inability to perform normal activities because of 'an impairment of the structure or function of the body or mind'. Disability was considered as a continuum which varied from very slight to very severe. A relatively small degree of disability was used as the starting point of the survey and 13 different types of disability were included in the classification including:

Locomotion	Continence	Behaviour
Reaching and stretching	Seeing	Intellectual function
Dexterity	Hearing	Consciousness
Personal care	Communication	Eating, drinking and digestion
	Disfigurement	

This approach to classification of disabled persons has considerable advantages to the ones used in earlier surveys such as the 1971 survey carried out by Harris in Great Britain.[3]

In this survey most disabled adults were found to have more than one of the 13 types of disability. The three commonest were (in order):

- locomotion
- hearing
- personal care.

In those living at home, the commonest disabilities found were musculo-skeletal complaints, especially arthritis. The second commonest conditions included ear complaints, eye problems and diseases of the circulatory system.

For those living in residential establishments, mental complaints especially forms of dementia, were most commonly found, followed by arthritis and strokes.

DEGREE OF SEVERITY OF THE DISABILITIES DISCOVERED

One of the most interesting features of this survey is the degree of severity discovered. Ten different levels of severity were used — category 10 was the most severe and category one the least severe. From the results of the sample, an estimate was made of the likely numbers of each category on the assumption that the levels found were used for the whole population of Great Britain. The estimates are given in Table 24.3 classified in the 10 categories of severity.

Note that the total figure of disabled persons in Great Britain was estimated to

TABLE 24.3   Estimates of numbers of disabled adults in Great Britain: by severity, 1985–88. Thousands.

Severity category	In private households	In residential establishments	Total population of disabled adults
10	102	108	210
9	285	80	365
8	338	58	396
7	447	39	486
6	511	34	545
5	679	29	708
4	676	27	704
3	732	19	751
2	824	16	840
1	1186	13	1198
Total	5780	422	6202

Data from OPCS survey.[2]

be about 6.2 million people (or approximately 10.8% of the total population). Of these, 93.5% live at home and the remainder in various residential establishments. Table 24.3 shows that:

- for those living at home, the numbers with the most severe disablement (categories 9 and 10) represent the smallest proportion (6.7%)
- the opposite is true of those living in residential establishments where the most severe categories make up the largest proportion (44.5%).

In the whole of Great Britain the survey suggests there are 210 000 very severely disabled persons and just under half (48.5%) live at home.

DISABILITY AND AGE

One of the most striking findings in this survey is the large numbers, in both sexes, of disability in persons aged 60 years and over (see Fig. 24.1). Note that, in both men and women, the rate of disability rises very sharply after the age of 60 years. In women 65% of disability occurs in persons aged 75 years and over and 29% in ages 60–74 years. In men the proportions are very similar — 63% for ages 75 years and over and 32% for ages 60–74 years.

Earlier surveys had shown that the greatest concentrations of disability occurred in retired people,[3,4] but this study emphasized that it is in the very old age groups that the major concentrations occur.

Because generally women live longer than men (see Table 3.2, p. 62) one would expect that there would be more disabled women than men in the population,

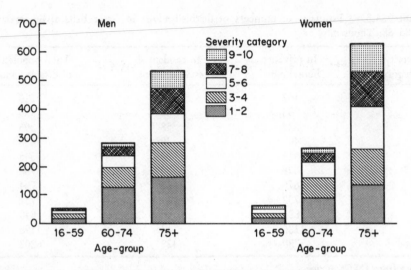

FIGURE 24.1   Estimates of prevalence of disability among adults: by age and severity category for men and women in Great Britain, 1985–87. (Data from ref. 2.)

but Fig. 24.1 is a measure of the rate of disability, and clearly shows that elderly women are more likely to be disabled than men. Bearing in mind the population predictions until 2011 (see Table 18.2, p. 399) there are bound to be large increases in the numbers of disabled people in this section of the population over this period.

REGIONAL INCIDENCE OF DISABLED PERSONS

The OPCS survey also analysed regional differences in the incidence of disability in England and Wales. This showed that the highest rates were in the North (particulary Yorkshire and Humberside) and in Wales, while in the southern regions (including London), there were lower than average rates of disability.

General principles for caring for disabled persons

In the rehabilitation and training of disabled people, there are four basic principles which are always important:

- difficulties and problems are highly personal and individual
- usually the best solution is the one which is as normal as possible
- much improvization is necessary

- great determination and singleness of purpose are always important for success.

FACTORS AFFECTING INDIVIDUAL PROBLEMS OF DISABLED PEOPLE

Factors which affect the potential difficulties and problems of any disabled person include:

- The age of the person. Obviously someone who is disabled from birth because he/she is born blind, deaf or is physically disabled in some way has to live all their lives as a potentially handicapped individual. The person must be educated and trained and hopefully be gainfully employed, as well as coping with the problems of growing old with the same disability. Anyone who becomes disabled in their late 50s or 60s has only their retirement to consider.
- The attitude of the person is crucial. Any disabled person who has a positive approach always does better than someone who is negative. This is because anyone who is positive will tend to adapt to overcome their problems, while a negative person will probably use the disability as an excuse for not doing things.
- The approach and attitude of the professional (doctor, nurse, social worker etc.) who is looking after the disabled person can equally affect the problems to be faced later. This is especially the case in the early stages of any disability, because a positive attitude at this time is very important. Frequently, the best approach is a fairly tough one which promises the disabled person little and many hard struggles and disappointments. At all costs, *self-pity must be avoided*.
- If the disabled person is the main wage earner in the family problems usually increase. Thus a family in which both husband and wife are employed is less at risk. One-parent families are always at special risk, and many require extra help and support.
- The family can do much to determine the likelihood of success or failure. A sensible, sympathetic and supportive family is always an advantage. A caring family can be equally helpful unless they are so concerned that they overprotect the disabled person.

It is always important to look upon the family as a single unit for social problems will often involve all members of the family. Children can become handicapped by the disability of a parent. But, equally, the birth of a disabled child or the development in any child of a disabling condition, can quickly lead to serious problems for the parents and even to the break-up of their marriage. Tew and Laurence[5] in their controlled survey in Bristol of the family and spina bifida, found there was a marked increase in marital breakdowns in families with an affected child. Only one in four families were free from marital difficulties, and the relationship between the parents tended to deteriorate over the years. The divorce rate was twice that in the control group.

NORMALITY

There is always a very simple rule to follow in determining what should be the advice to any disabled person: *the best solution is always the one that is as normal as possible*. This is true for educational, employment or recreational problems. Thus, a normal person works in industry or in an office and is in no way protected, and this is equally the best solution for anyone who is disabled. This means that 'open industry' is better than 'sheltered workshops', which in turn are preferable to home workers' schemes (see pp. 535–536). When it becomes difficult to suggest the next stage in the rehabilitation of any individual, the 'as near normal' rule is a valuable guide.

IMPROVISATION

Just as the problems and difficulties of any disabled person differ, so will the solutions. Hence an ability to improvise in overcoming difficulties is most important, and no professional working with disabled people can ever afford to be rigid or inflexible. All the most successful people working with disabled people are resilient and often unconventional individuals to whom improvisation comes naturally.

DETERMINATION AND SINGLENESS OF PURPOSE

It is usually easy to find an excuse for failure when working with disabled people. Therefore, to succeed, it is important to concentrate solely upon success, however remote this might seem to be. If possible, the disabled person and those immediately around him/her should be fired with an enthusiasm to succeed irrespective of the difficulties and inevitable disappointments. A complete singleness of purpose should be encouraged, for this often helps to overcome difficulties.

The Chronically Sick and Disabled Persons Act, 1970 (as amended by the Disabled Persons (Services, Consultation and Representation) Act, 1986 and the Disabled Persons Act, 1981)

The Chronically Sick and Disabled Persons Act, 1970, gives many special responsibilities to local authorities in respect of those who are substantially and permanently disabled (including those with learning disabilities (mental handicap)). Their main duties are:

- *Information*. Local authorities must ensure (a) that they are adequately informed of the numbers and needs of disabled persons so that they can properly plan and develop their services, and (b) that disabled people and their families know what help is available to them by general publicity and personal explanations.
- *Provision of services* (section 2). Local authorities, when satisfied that the services are necessary to the disabled person, can provide the following:
  - practical assistance in the home (such as the provision of social-workers, care assistants, occupational therapists)
  - wireless, television, library or similar recreational facilities in the home
  - recreational facilities outside the home (access to parks, sports centres and gymnasia and all club activities), and assistance in taking advantage of educational facilities
  - travelling facilities for handicapped persons (group transport), i.e. help with mobility
  - assistance in carrying out adaptations to the home
  - facilitating the taking of holidays
  - meals at home or elsewhere
  - a telephone and any special equipment necessary for its use (usually installation and rental).

The Disabled Persons (Services, Consultation and Representation) Act, 1986, aims at improving the effectiveness and co-ordination of services for persons with learning disabilities (mental handicap). It improves section 2 of the Chronically Sick and Disabled Persons Act, 1970, by:

- ensuring the disabled person does not fall between the various services (such as the social, educational and hospital services), this Act introduces an 'advocacy' service where a representative of the disabled person can be appointed when the disabled person cannot represent him/herself because of mental or physical incapacity; voluntary bodies are expected to play an active part in providing 'advocates' when none other is available
- the social services department must assess the needs of any disabled person when requested to do so and must send a written report of the results of that assessment to the person or to the parents of a child
- all proper help (such as assistance to a deaf and dumb person) must be given by a social services department so that any assessment will be adequate
- if the social services department considers that a disabled person has no needs, it must say so and give a full explanation
- the social services department can refuse a particular need, but must give its reasons in writing and consider every case on its merits
- the presence of a 'carer' (who is looking after the disabled person) is never an excuse for a social services department not looking critically at the needs of that disabled person and for not providing the support which otherwise would have been given if there had been no carer present

- the social services department must publish periodically general information as to its services for disabled persons.

Housing

Every local housing authority must consider the special needs of disabled persons, and any new houses planned must show that special provision has been made. This clearly gives housing authorities a duty to plan and provide special housing accommodation for disabled persons.

Premises open to the public

There is a series of requirements for public buildings including:

- providing means of access to and within the building and in the parking facilities and sanitary conveniences for the disabled; such provision must be considered before planning permission is given
- need for a local authority to provide public sanitary conveniences for disabled persons
- need for anyone providing sanitary conveniences in premises open to the public for accommodation, refreshment or entertainment, to make provision, as far as is practicable, for disabled people and adequate sign-posting for the above provisions from outside
- need to provide facilities for access, parking and sanitary conveniences suitable for disabled persons as far as is practicable at school, university and other educational buildings.

In addition, there are special clauses about Advisory Committees considering problems of disabled persons either nationally or locally and these insist that members of such committees must include persons with experience of work for the disabled and persons who are themselves disabled.

Other needs of disabled people

Local authorities must now, when building any new public convenience, include facilities for disabled persons. Under the Act, new increased powers are given to local authorities to enforce the provision of satisfactory sanitary appliances in places of entertainment.

The Act also requires all local authorities to ensure that there is adequate sign-posting of facilities for disabled people including the route of travel between specially reserved parking spaces and the entrance to the car park.

The Act also contains powers (not yet implemented) to place a requirement for all developers to make satisfactory provision in every case for disabled people unless a body which the Secretary of State may prescribe in regulations is satisfied that in the circumstances of the cases it is not practicable or reasonable for such provision to be made.

The Disabled Persons Act, 1981, further strengthened the powers of the Chronically Sick and Disabled Persons Act, 1970 in respect of:

Highways and road traffic

Local authorities under the 1981 Act are under a duty to consider:

- the needs of disabled and blind people when carrying out street works
- where they place lamp-posts, bollards, traffic signals and other permanent obstruction so that they are not a potential hazard to blind and disabled people; footway widths must not be narrowed so that they would impede wheel chairs
- placing kerbed ramps at all crossing places
- where there are openings in the carriageway and footways, that they are suitably fenced off (not just by using ropes) so that a blind person using a stick would become aware of the hazard at a safe distance.

There are also additional penalties introduced for able bodied persons who use a parking space reserved for disabled persons.

Planning facilities

Additional measures have been added to the Town and Country Planning Act, 1970, to ensure that in future developers will be better informed about their statutory duties under the Chronically Sick and Disabled Persons Act, 1970, and the various British Standards Codes of Practice for access for disabled people to all types of buildings (including schools and colleges, factories and shops).

In addition local planning authorities are urged to consider attaching conditions of access for disabled persons when granting planning permissions (this in future will include such places as multi-level shopping centres).

The Secretary of State when considering appeals against the decisions of local planning authorities takes into consideration the means of access for disabled persons.

Under the 1981 Act, all local authorities are urged to designate one of their officers as an *access officer* to provide a single clearly identifiable point of contact for disabled people.

Domiciliary services for disabled persons

Among the domiciliary workers visiting handicapped people at home are social workers, specially trained workers for the blind and deaf and dumb, occupational therapists and health visitors. Much domiciliary visiting by social workers is concerned with assessment of individual problems. Occupational therapists particularly concentrate on teaching clients to live with their disabilities rather than on instruction in craftwork. Those working in special centres for disabled and mentally handicapped people include occupational therapists, social workers, handicraft instructors and voluntary workers. Health visitors are especially useful in maintaining a close link with hospital services or with GPs. Social workers usually play an active part in the administration of these services and in arranging residential accommodation. Care assistants (see p. 413) and meals-on-wheels (see p. 415) are also provided for some seriously disabled persons living at home.

Day centres

Occupational therapy and rehabilitation centres

Most social services departments run occupational therapy and rehabilitation centres for disabled persons where training is given with the assistance of various aids and machines, including knitting machines, fretsaw machines, various looms, etc. Many crafts — rug making, simple carpentry or basketry — are taught. There is also a training kitchen which helps the disabled person to become more independent. Usually special transport collects disabled persons from their homes, and this makes it possible to extend the range of those who can be helped.

The rehabilitation centre is open for people to attend either for half a day or a full day and one of the valuable features of these units is the social one, whereby various disabled people meet other persons. In many long and chronic illnesses there is a tendency for the person to become more and more withdrawn as he/she stays permanently at home meeting only family or close friends. Attendance at an occupational therapy rehabilitation centre and travelling to it greatly increases self-confidence and does much to prevent permanent invalidism.

Community or domiciliary occupational therapy may also be run by DHAs. Thus, some community occupational therapy services in England at present are run by DHAs and others by the local social services department.

Handicraft centres

Handicraft centres for disabled people (including the elderly) are provided by local authorities and staffed by handicraft instructors. The aim of such centres is to help those who are disabled to maintain an interest and to enjoy recreational facilities even when rehabilitation is not practicable.

Social centres and clubs

Most local authorities run clubs for disabled persons or give financial support to such centres provided by voluntary bodies.

Housing for disabled persons

The design of the home is important for many severely disabled people. Doors may have to be widened to allow free access to wheelchairs and bathrooms may have to be provided at ground level. The Chronically Sick and Disabled Persons Act, 1970, encourages help with housing for such persons and many local authorities now build special houses or bungalows, as it is more satisfactory to do this than adapt existing premises, especially if many alterations are needed. Housing Associations also build special flats and bungalows for disabled people.

Adaptations

An important function of social services departments is to arrange and assist with the adaptations of any disabled person's home. Such adaptations include minor additions such as handrails or ramps, but may involve much more radical alterations to the home such as the building of a downstairs bathroom and lavatory, the widening of doorways or passages. In most instances, the local authority will either pay all the cost of the adaptations or a substantial portion of them provided that permission to carry out such adaptations is first obtained from the social services department.

In such cases, there is usually a contract signed so that if within a reasonable period (usually 5 years), the house is resold at a profit, a proportion of the costs of the adaptations has to be repaid.

In England in 1987, 76 400 adaptations were made to private dwellings. In addition, 17 400 adaptations where the whole cost was met by social services departments were undertaken in local authority dwellings.[1]

Aids and gadgets

Under the Chronically Sick and Disabled Persons Act, 1970, local authorities are given power to provide a wide range of aids for the disabled. These include the following:

- *hoists* in bedrooms and bathrooms for those paralysed in the legs so that they can become more independent and mobile
- *lifts and stair lifts*
- *modifications to table implements*, knives, forks and spoons, to make them more easily used by those whose grip is weak or whose hands are deformed

- *various kitchen fitments* for disabled persons; these include many gadgets for one-handed people or those who have power only in one hand; other aids are provided for those whose balance is poor (slings are fitted to sinks to support the individual while standing)
- *kitchen management and planning* are important, including the heights of various working surfaces and the design of kitchen furniture
- various *personal dressing aids* to encourage independence in the client; the occupational therapist also attempts to increase the mobility of disabled persons; special walking aids are provided and the handicapped person is trained in their use; whenever rehabilitation has reached a certain stage, the individual should be encouraged to attend a rehabilitation centre
- an extensive range of *special clothing* is now available for disabled people; many garments have special arrangements for fastening to enable a disabled person with a poor grip to dress and to be completely independent.

During 1987, 448 100 personal aids were provided with the help of social services departments in England.[1]

Aids centres

Permanent aids centres containing a wide range of equipment suitable for the disabled have been established in London by the Disabled Living Foundation and in 17 other areas including Liverpool, Newcastle, Birmingham, Southampton, Wakefield, Leicester, Edinburgh, Glasgow and Caerphilly.

These aids centres enable severely disabled persons to see for themselves the range of equipment and to compare the various facilities available. It is usual to staff such units with experienced occupational therapists and to run the centre on an appointment system as it usually takes $1\frac{1}{2}$ to 2 hours to demonstrate all the appropriate equipment.

Disabled persons or their families wishing to visit such centres should contact either the Disabled Living Foundation, 380 Harrow Road, London W9 2 HU, or the local Director of Social Services.

Holidays and outings

Outings in summer and special holidays for disabled persons may be arranged and many of these are in seaside hotels or holiday camps at the start or end of the season. It is usual to send special staff with such holiday groups to assist with wheelchairs and help those who are severely disabled. In this way, many disabled people are able to enjoy a holiday who otherwise could not do so. There has been a wide exten-

TABLE 24.4 Numbers of disabled persons sent on holidays with the help of social services departments in England 1987 (thousands)

Age (years)	Number
Total all ages	54.6
65 +	39.6
16–64	14.1
Under 16	2.9

Data from ref. 1.

sion in the range of holidays (see Table 24.4) and more and more disabled people can now enjoy what has become normal to many ordinary persons — an annual holiday abroad.

Telephones

Telephones can be provided for very severely disabled persons *living alone or left on their own for long periods of the day*. Criteria vary slightly in different areas, but usually include a minority of *medical reasons* (usually a medical condition which might require urgent medical help) and many social reasons where:

- the individual cannot go out of his/her home in normal weather conditions and
- where the person lives alone or is left alone for long periods.

It is usual for the social services department to pay the installation and rental charges and for the disabled person to pay for the calls made.

In 1987 in England, 99 500 disabled people had their telephone rentals paid and 14 800 also had telephones installed. In addition, 3800 persons had special telephone attachments provided and 6100 had other types of communication equipment provided.

Special homes or hostels for handicapped and disabled persons

Many voluntary bodies and a number of local authorities have built hostels for handicapped persons. Examples of the former are the Cheshire Foundation Homes for seriously disabled persons. It is usual for local authorities to pay the *per capita* charge for any of their residents living in such homes. In addition, a number of sheltered housing units for disabled people have been developed to encourage independence.

Mobility and transport for disabled persons

Apart from disabled war pensioners, for whom a small car is provided, the usual method of helping with individual transport is by the mobility component of the *Disability Living Allowance* (see below) and by the government supporting a voluntary organization called *Motability* which assists disabled people to obtain a car either by leasing or by a special hire-purchase scheme (see p. 531). In addition, for those persons who are permanently disabled and therefore relatively immobile, many different types of wheelchairs are available through the local Artificial Limb and Appliance Centre.

Local authorities provide wheelchairs on a temporary basis, but this aid does not normally last longer than 6 months.

Group transport for disabled persons

Personnel carriers of various types and small buses may be provided to take disabled people to day centres, clubs and so on. Most of these vehicles have hydraulic lifts attached so that a wheelchair and occupant can be easily loaded.

Financial assistance

DISABILITY LIVING ALLOWANCE

In April 1992, a new Disability Living Allowance[6] was introduced for persons whose disability starts before the age of 65. This brought together the former Attendance Allowance and Mobility Allowance for this age group and extended and improved the range of financial benefits available to disabled persons. For those whose disability starts after the age of 65 years, the former Attendance Allowance remains unchanged except that for those with a terminal illness, they automatically qualify for the top rate and there is no waiting period. Also such persons benefit from the new adjudication and assessment process (see below).

The Disability Living Allowance has two components:

- a care component
- a mobility component.

The *care component* is available from age 3 months to 65 years. Children must need substantially greater help and care than a normal child of that age. This allowance is tax-free and is payable to anyone who, because of severe physical or mental disability has needed, for 3 months or more, frequent attendance throughout the day and/or night. The requirements which have to be met are:

By day: frequent attention throughout the day in connection with his/her bodily functions *or* continual supervision throughout the day in order to avoid substantial danger to himself/herself or others.

By night: prolonged or repeated attention during the night in connection with his/her bodily functions *or* continual supervision throughout the night in order to avoid substantial danger to himself/herself or others.

For example, the following conditions would quality, if a person needs a lot of help with:

- walking and getting about
- using the toilet
- washing, dressing or undressing or shaving
- using a kidney machine at home.

Also if someone must constantly remain with the seriously disabled person to prevent a serious accident or other dangers, this would qualify.

A higher rate of allowance is paid if one of the day requirements and one of the night requirements are satisfied for at least 3 months (unless the disability is caused by a terminal illness when the allowance is paid immediately). A lower rate is paid if one of the day or night requirements is satisfied for a period of 3 months.

Claims are made by completing a form from the Benefits Agency. All claims are decided at Norcross House, Blackpool.

The care component is payable at one of three rates. The top two rates have already been described plus a new lowest rate. This will go to persons who need self-care during the day but less frequently than is necessary to qualify for the middle rate. The main test is based upon a person's ability to prepare a main meal — if the claimant cannot do this then he/she qualifies.

The *mobility component* is payable at one of two rates. The higher one is equivalent to the former mobility allowance, the new lower rate is paid to those who are not independently mobile but do not meet the criteria of the former mobility allowance, i.e. the individual must be unable, or virtually unable, to walk because of the disability which must be likely to persist for at least 12 months. The person must be able to make use of the allowance and a person who, for medical reasons, cannot be moved, or who is in a coma, does not qualify. The lower rate of the mobility component goes to those who are not independently mobile but who *can* walk but who require guidance and supervision from another person for most of the time.

Persons can qualify for either or both care and mobility components. Only one claim form is needed and there is only one assessment. Where a person qualifies for both components, they are paid together.

Individuals who before April 1992 were receiving the Attendance Allowance or the Mobility Allowance were automatically transferred with no change of benefit. Such disabled persons may also claim any extra help to which they are entitled under the new benefits.

Once awarded, the Disability Living Allowance continues to be paid irrespective of age.

Other changes introduced following the Disability Living Allowance

The mobility component has been extended to include people who are both deaf and blind (this change operated from April 1990).

There has also been an extension of the mobility component to all double amputees automatically (from April 1992).

A new assessment and adjudication procedure has been introduced involving the Disability Appeals Tribunal. Since 1992, the use of medical examination to obtain information about any claimant's capacities and needs is avoided as far as possible. Instead, there is a much greater reliance on self assessment backed up by evidence from professionals (such as social workers, occupational therapists and physiotherapists) who are familiar with the case.

It is estimated that 300 000 disabled persons in the UK, who before 1992 received no additional benefit, will qualify for the lowest benefit for the care and mobility components of the Disabled Living Allowance.

Information about Disability Living Allowance

There is a free telephone service in the UK to answer all queries about the Disability Living Allowance and Attendance Allowance (for these over 65). The number is 0800 882200.

VEHICLE EXCISE DUTY EXEMPTION

Recipients of the mobility component of the Disability Living Allowance (or persons nominated to receive the allowance on their behalf) no longer have to pay vehicle excise duty on a vehicle used by or for the purpose of a disabled person. This vehicle excise duty exemption can also be claimed for those whose disability started after the age of 65 and therefore cannot claim a Disability Living Allowance provided they are:

- unable to walk
- have a car registered in their own name
- need to be driven.

MOTABILITY

This is a voluntary organization formed on the initiative of the government to help disabled persons to get maximum value for money using their Disability Living Allowance when acquiring a car for their use. It offers two types of schemes:

- a leasing scheme
- a hire purchase scheme.

The leasing scheme is based on a 3 to 4-year term and provides for the whole of the mobility component to be surrendered in return for a new car to be made available, plus full maintenance. Initially a 'once and all' down payment has to be made for some of the larger cars but the smallest are exempt. The lease includes arrangements for the full cost of maintenance as well as the cost of new tyres, when needed, for most of the cars in the scheme. The lease is based on an annual mileage of 10 000 miles. If this is exceeded, then an additional payment must be made. A block comprehensive insurance scheme has been arranged with the Zurich Insurance Company and the disabled person must pay the premium. The disabled person also has to pay the cost of petrol and oil. At the end of the lease the car has to be returned, but the disabled person may then lease another new car. It has proved to be a very valuable scheme.

For those disabled people who require major adaptations to a car, the special hire purchase scheme is likely to prove more useful. Full details of both schemes can be obtained from Motability, 61 Southwark Street, London SE1 0TK.

DISABILITY WORKING ALLOWANCE

This will be an income-related benefit and will be available to two groups of people who have a physical or mental disability which puts them at a disadvantage in getting a job. These include:

- those who are getting long-term incapacity benefit (Invalidity Benefit, Severe Disablement Allowance, or a disability premium with Income Support, Housing Benefit or Community Charge Benefit) before they started work
- those persons getting the Disability Living Allowance.

Anyone considering whether they qualify for any of the new benefits should either obtain the press release issued with the Bill, or ask for full details from the Benefits Agency, Department of Social Security (Freephone 0888 666 555) or obtain an up-to-date pamphlet on the Disability Living Allowance from the Benefits Agency, published by the Central Office of Information for the Department of Social Security.

INVALID CARE ALLOWANCE

This is a taxable Social Security benefit paid to help people who look after someone who gets the Disability Living Allowance (care component), Attendance Allowance or Constant Attendance Allowance. It is paid to the carer. To qualify, the carer has to:

- be at least 16 years old but under 60 years for a woman and 65 years for a man
- look after someone for at least 35 hours a week
- the person being looked after must receive the Disability Living Allowance (care component), Attendance Allowance or the Constant Attendance Allowance
- normally live in Great Britain.

In addition the carer must not be:

- on a full-time education course (i.e. 12 or more hours of supervised study per week)
- on holiday from a full-time education course
- earning more than £30 a week (after deducting allowable expenses).

Claims should be made on an Invalid Care Allowance Pack (DS700).

Employment and training for disabled persons

The employment and training of disabled persons of all ages is complex. Careers guidance and assessment at school is mainly the responsibility of the specialist careers officers of the local education authority.

For adults, the main government department is the Department of Employment. Training is promoted through the Industrial Training Boards on which local employers are widely represented. Employment Rehabilitation Centres (ERCs) are also maintained by the Department of Employment to offer special courses for people who, after a serious injury or illness, disablement or prolonged unemployment, find it difficult to obtain a job. These ERCs have three main functions:

- the assessment of an individual for employment
- the selection of the most suitable employment for the individual
- the completion of the rehabilitation regime.

The key local officer is the *Disablement Resettlement Officer* (DRO) who is mainly engaged on assisting and placing disabled persons into occupations. There are two main ways a disabled person can be placed in employment:

- *In 'open industry'*. This refers to ordinary occupations and working conditions where the disabled person works with and under exactly the same conditions as normal people receiving full wages. This is always the most satisfactory solution.

It is, of course, not possible for many seriously disabled persons to do this as they may not be able to keep up with the pace and standard of ordinary work. Yet this should always be the first objective, and the DRO is constantly helping to select, train and introduce disabled people into open industry. In some instances, it may be possible to train a disabled person in a workshop within a day centre or in a sheltered workshop to such a standard that the individual can successfully move on into open industry. Mobility may be a problem, but often this can be solved and the person can become independent. Then, provided that the disabled person is determined enough and has proper training and qualifications, he/she may be able to carry out normal work alongside ordinary people. In the case of blind persons, especially trained officers (Blind Persons Resettlement Officers) are employed to assist in the successful placement of suitable blind persons in ordinary work (see p. 535).

- *Sheltered employment.* This is subsidized, full-time employment of disabled persons either in a workshop or on a home workers' scheme. Remploy factories are examples of sheltered employment and are spread throughout the UK in centres of employment for mainly a general group of disabled people. A minimum standard of work must be maintained, but special arrangements can be made during the rehabilitation phase after a long serious illness or accident. Skilled doctors are always available to advise the disabled person on medical problems or difficulties.

Special workshops for blind persons are available (see p. 536) and there are usually home workers' schemes in remote areas to help blind people who cannot reach a sheltered workshop. Special subsidized wages are paid in suitable cases (see p. 536).

Various voluntary bodies also help disabled persons, especially those who only want part-time work. In these cases, help is given with supplying suitable materials, in training and in the marketing of finished products (often in special shops staffed by volunteers). In all cases of part-time employment, no financial subsidy is paid.

Links between the health, education, employment and social services

With disabled persons of all ages, it is essential that there are effective links between the health, education, employment and social services. For congenitally disabled children, the health visitor usually plays an important role and is assumed to be the person to act as a key worker. The satisfactory education of such a child depends largely on the co-operation between the health, education and social services. In particular, these links become even more important during that difficult period of transition from school to adult life. The Warnock Committee in its report emphasized how vulnerable many disabled youngsters and their families were at this critical period. The specialist careers officer of the local education authority also plays a crucial role in advising the disabled young person about what further training and careers are most suitable.

Any individual disabled person who is having difficulty in obtaining or retaining a job, can often be helped by a brief case conference between the Disablement Resettlement Officer, the social worker, the occupational therapist and doctor to ensure that all the difficulties and potentials are fully understood. It is very easy to assume that seriously disabled persons are unemployable, but this is rarely so. However, if such individuals are allowed to remain at home just idling away time, they can soon become disillusioned and may never reach their true potential. For this reason, day centres, education and training of all kinds are so important in rehabilitation because the individual handicapped person is given some clear sense of purpose as regards the future.

Detailed social services for different groups of disabled persons

THE BLIND

Registration

Each person suspected of being blind must be examined by a consultant ophthalmologist who carries out a complete examination of the eye and indicates, in the report, the degree of sight and prognosis. A person is considered blind if 'unable to perform any work for which sight is essential'. In practice, this means that any person with vision less then 3/60 (Snellen), with a full visual field, is blind; if the field is considerably contracted then visual acuity up to 6/60 may come in this category. Those whose vision is better than these standards, but still defective, are partially sighted.

There were 133 700 blind people in England in 1988; 78% were aged 65 years and over and 10% were aged 45–59 years. Thus, blindness is mostly found in older and retired people.

Individual assessment

The age of onset of blindness is an important factor in relation to the social problems created. A child born blind must be educated and employed as a blind person as well as facing the problems of old age with the same handicap. But a very old person going blind has only a few years of blindness to face. Age, personality, past training, intelligence and home conditions have a marked effect on either reducing or increasing difficulties.

Each blind person must, therefore, be carefully and individually assessed by expert social workers (home teachers for the blind). With newly blinded people aged 20–50 years, assessment is never easy for the sudden onset of blindness often leaves the person uncertain and full of bitterness and self-pity. The Royal National Institute for the Blind runs a special assessment centre at the Queen Elizabeth Homes of Recovery at Torquay for newly blinded men and women, to enable them once again to look forward to a future in commerce or industry. For those who need training for daily living as a blind person, there is Clifton Spinney at Nottingham where the newly blinded person can go, usually for a 13-week course. After visits to these centres, most lose any self-pity and return home with a new and essential spirit of hope.

Periodic visiting should be carried out by social workers to continue observation of current problems in an unobtrusive way.

Employment

Approximately 10.1% of blind people are aged between 16 and 50 years, and it is in this group that the problem of employment occurs. Full-time employment is undertaken either in 'open industry' or in sheltered employment in workshops or home workers' schemes.

Employment in 'open industry'

There are many different types of occupation in which the intelligent, highly trained blind person can succeed and these include a number of industrial processes such as capstan lathe operatives, telephone operators, piano tuners, etc. Two essentials are needed for the successful placing of blind people in industry: (a) a helpful and sympathetic employer who is prepared to try one or two blind people in the factory, and (b) proper training of the blind person before and during early employment.

In both respects, the Blind Persons Resettlement Officer of the Department of Employment is invaluable. He/she is usually a highly trained blind person who acts as liaison officer with industry, finding suitable vacancies for blind people. This officer assesses the potential of each blind person, trains those who are selected and then introduces each to their new post and helps with the training on the job. Later follow-up visits are made to ensure there are no problems.

In general, the aim should always be to place as many blind people as possible in open industry. In many areas, up to 70% of employable blind persons are working in open industry. No special arrangements are made as regards remuneration.

Occupation in sheltered employment

Sheltered employment is specially subsidized full-time occupation and there are two main types:

Workshops

A blind worker needing sheltered employment should, if possible, be sent to a special workshop for blind persons where, after training, he/she is employed in one of the traditional trades including basket making, chair caning, rug making, brush making or machine knitting. Sighted foremen help with the finishing off of the articles and also arrange for the marketing of the products.

Each blind worker receives the usual wage for the occupation although, because of their handicap, it is unlikely this could be earned on 'piece rates'. The difference between what is actually earned and what he/she is paid is called 'augmentation' and is provided by the local authority, which receives a large grant form the Department of Employment.

Home workers' schemes

In rural areas or small towns, it is never possible to collect together enough blind people to run a workshop. Home workers' schemes are then used. The blind worker is trained in an occupation, supplied with materials at home and makes a certain quota of goods which are later collected and marketed. Provided the blind person averages a certain agreed minimum output, augmentation is paid as in the workshop scheme. Although home workers' schemes are valuable, they are not as satisfactory as sheltered workshops. Difficulties include inadequate supervision and consequently the quality and quantity of work are usually lower.

Part-time employment

Arrangements are made to help other blind people wishing to do some part-time employment and the home teacher for the blind assists with the provision of materials and with the marketing of finished products. No augmentation is paid for part-time employment.

Other services for blind persons

Learning to read

Braille is the best method of reading used by blind people. It is taught to all children and younger adults and others who have the ability and desire to learn. Home teachers instruct with the aid of a widespread library maintained by the Royal

National Institute for the Blind. It usually takes an intelligent person at least 6 months' concentrated study to learn Braille and is, therefore, beyond the scope of many who have recently lost their sight. A useful indicator of the likelihood of an elderly person being suitable to learn Braille is given by inquiring about reading habits before sight was lost. Avid readers should always be taught Braille, but others find reading substitutes more useful.

Substitutes for reading

A large lending library of tape-recorded books is maintained by the Royal National Institute for the Blind and a tape recorder is lent to each blind person wishing to take advantage of this service. By borrowing these, the blind person can have a continuous and changing supply of books read aloud to him. Each local authority makes a financial contribution to the Royal National Institute for the Blind in respect of each blind person making use of this service.

Radios for blind people

The radio is most useful and is greatly enjoyed by many blind people. There is a special voluntary society (Wireless for the Blind Fund) financed by the traditional radio appeal each Christmas Day, whose object is to ensure that every blind person has a radio. Maintenance of the radio is arranged by most social services departments.

Special aids

There are many special aids in the home available for the blind. An example is the special Braille form of 'regulo' which can be fitted to gas stoves.

Provision of guide-dogs for blind people

A society exists which provides and trains special guide-dogs for use by blind people. The selection and training of the dogs and the blind person is lengthy and limits the number who can be helped in this way. Guide-dogs are especially useful to those blinded in early adult life and those living on their own. Local authorities assist with the cost of training.

Holidays and hostels

There are a number of special holiday homes for blind persons adapted to make it safe for them to go on holiday alone, and many of these are run by voluntary bodies, but local authorities assist with the running costs on a *per capita* basis.

For elderly blind persons, it is better to look after them in an ordinary elderly persons' home (perhaps two to three per home) than to provide special homes.

Voting

A blind person has the right to vote by post in parliamentary and local elections or to have his ballot paper marked with the help of a sighted person.

Free postage is allowed for a number of 'articles for the blind' including embossed literature, paper for embossing and recordings acting as an alternative to an embossed book.

THE DEAF AND DUMB

Because normal speech is learnt by imitation, in the past the congenitally deaf have been unable to speak. Today, with special instruction methods, it is usually possible to teach some speech to most congenitally deaf children. Deaf and dumb people often suffer from isolation and communicate by a mixture of lip reading, sign and finger language. They benefit from club and recreational facilities where they can meet others with similar problems.

There are few employment problems provided interpreter services are available to help with interviews. Skilled trained social workers who freely speak sign and finger language are employed usually by a voluntary society financed by local authorities. Many of these societies are connected with church bodies — a legacy from the past when the main object of welfare services was to provide special church services for the deaf and dumb.

THE HARD OF HEARING

People who become deaf, having in the past enjoyed good hearing, are usually referred to as 'hard of hearing'. Such persons have normal speech and this is the usual method of communication although a hearing aid and lip reading may be used. Most of the hard of hearing are elderly persons as deafness, like blindness, often accompanies old age (78% of the hard of hearing are aged 65 years and over[1]).

The difficulty of communication, leading to loneliness and isolation, is the biggest problem. It is essential that the fullest use is made of any residual hearing which should be correctly assessed by pure tone audiometry and the fitting and maintenance of a hearing aid. In many instances, medical social workers of departments of audiology in large general hospitals organize clubs and recreational facilities. This arrangement helps surveillance, as does periodic home visits by social workers or health visitors to check that the deaf person is managing any hearing aid. As most hard-of-hearing persons are elderly, employment problems are not great and sheltered workshops not required.

THE PHYSICALLY DISABLED

This large and diverse group contains many conditions which are chronic and sometimes progressive, such as hemiplegia, paraplegia, multiple sclerosis, rheumatoid arthritis, osteoarthritis, poliomyelitis and muscular dystrophies.

The rehabilitation of those with paraplegia was greatly advanced by the establishment in World War II of special regional hospital spinal centres, the largest being at Stoke Mandeville. Insistence on the importance of independence for paraplegics whenever possible has completely changed the outlook of this group and now 85% of such patients are capable of gainful employment.

By careful training, it is usually possible for bladder functioning to be either controlled by abdominal muscles or, in higher lesions, to become automatic. With development of arm and shoulder muscles, many functions can be carried out by paraplegics including raising the weight of the body when climbing into chairs. Various motor vehicles are used making the patient even more independent. Recreational and sporting facilities have been developed extensively for paraplegics and include archery, basket ball and swimming and many clubs have been formed to encourage these activities. Local authorities help in this work by providing gymnasia and swimming baths. Reference has already been made to the types of wheelchairs and special motorized transport that are available (see p. 528).

For the very severely disabled persons many additional facilities are available. The full range of district nursing services is used together with specialized lifting equipment — hoists, and special beds which are lent by the local authority to the patient. It is essential to encourage such patients to be as active as possible even if they are bedridden or the eventual prognosis is poor, and they should be visited by the occupational therapist at home and taught various crafts and handicrafts, a most valuable local authority service.

In many serious cases where the patient is almost completely paralysed, an electronic machine operated by sucking or by blowing into a mouthpiece or by similar light pressure has been developed. It is called Patient Operated Selector Mechanism (POSSUM) and enables a tetraplegic or completely paralysed person to make a telephone call, turn on and off a radio or television, switch off lights and use a typewriter, etc. This machine adds much to the independence of a grossly paralysed person. It is now available on the NHS, but the local authority is expected to undertake the electrical fitments needed and to provide a stand. Inquiries should be made to the DHA who will send out a consultant to assess each client individually.

For persons crippled with rheumatoid arthritis or osteoarthritis there is a large range of gadgets now available to assist with everyday tasks of cooking, dressing and life at home. Such individuals should attend the occupational therapy or rehabilitation centres (see p. 524) where their needs can be expertly assessed.

CEREBRAL PALSY

The incidence of cerebral palsy in the UK is about 2 per 1000 schoolchildren. This means there are approximately 27 500 persons with some form of cerebral palsy under the age of 20 years. About 88% are caused by prenatal or intranatal conditions, while the remainder are of postnatal origin (anoxia, meningitis). In the prenatal groups, 20% have a history of prematurity. Lack of oxygenation of the brain is an important cause. There is a marked increase of learning disabilities (mental handicap) in celebral palsy (in one survey, 48% of such patients had IQs below 69 compared with 3% of the normal population). But there is much variation, and the mildest cases usually have a normal IQ, although there are few instances of very severely disabled persons with a normal IQ. Accurate and early diagnosis is important, so that full benefit can be obtained from special education.

In early adult life, assistance may be required to find suitable employment. It is of value to designate a social worker to help with co-ordination with the Disablement Resettlement Officer and with the specialist careers officer (see p. 534). In those with learning disabilities (mental handicap), many of the services available to that group are helpful. The value of a good home is important and, if this is lacking, young adults should, if possible, be placed in a hostel and given special industrial training.

EPILEPSY

Persons with epilepsy present many problems not found in other disabled people. This is not due to the difficulties of treating epilepsy, but to ill-informed public opinion which, quite wrongly, may consider that persons with epilepsy are usually dangerous. The truth is that most epileptics are well controlled, and can quite satisfactorily be educated and employed normally. Adverse public reaction results in many persons concealing the fact that they have had occasional epileptic seizures, because they fear if it becomes known they may lose their jobs or find it difficult to obtain employment. This in turn leads to considerable strains which produce other difficulties including minor anxiety states.

In order to help the person with epilepsy, it is important to realize these environmental pressures and to arrange for an employer or prospective employer to be told the full facts, and particularly that epilepsy, if properly controlled, is no problem. Many have some warning of an impending attack and, apart from avoiding a few dangerous occupations in which those with epilepsy will rarely want to work, there are few jobs which are not suitable. But a watch should be maintained to en_ure that the disease is being controlled. This surveillance can be carried out by a specially trained health visitor who maintains a close liaison with the person's doctor. The social aspects, which are so important to successful treatment, should always be carefully considered — including conditions in the home and occupation — so that problems can be avoided or corrected before they have a serious effect.

Occasionallly, it is necessary to admit the individual to an epileptic colony which mainly deals with those rare cases whose illness cannot easily be controlled by treatment and with those who show anti-social behaviour. Those in such a colony may remain there permanently and, if possible, do some productive work on a farm or in a small workshop. Most colonies are run by voluntary bodies with local authorities meeting the *per capita* cost.

ISCHAEMIC HEART DISEASE

This disease has become an increasing problem (see p. 271) and it is important to consider how the rehabilitation of the person can be assisted. There is a danger of too much overprotection of the convalescent patient and many families show too much anxiety. In rehabilitation it is important to encourage the patient early and to concentrate on normality. Extra rest may be needed, but moderate exercise, walking, golf, swimming, horse riding or cycling are valuable. It is best to avoid competitive sports because of the emotional stress involved. Rehabilitation will vary with the age of onset. In the younger person who has had a coronary thrombosis, return to work is desirable as soon as the convalescence is over. Most can return to their former occupations with the exception of those in heavy unskilled occupations. Smoking should always be given up and overweight corrected, but it is a mistake to stress particular diets for they tend to make the individual introspective and afraid to go out for meals.

Even for those who have symptoms, a light job should be found. Occupational therapy should always be encouraged for any unable to find work.

JOSEPH ROWNTREE MEMORIAL TRUST

A special fund for the families of handicapped children — the Joseph Rowntree Memorial Trust — was fully set up in 1973 to help the parents of severely congenitally disabled children under the age of 16 years in the UK. It aims to help in relieving stress in families by complementing the provision of services and cash benefits from both statutory and voluntary sources. Application forms can be obtained from the Trust at its offices at Beverly House, Skipton, Yorks.

Further details of services for disabled persons will be found in the textbook *The Disabled Child and Adult*[8] and in *Rehabilitation of the Physically Disabled*.[7]

References

1. Department of Health. Health and Personal Social Services Statistics. London: HMSO. 1991.
2. Survey by OPCS. 1985–1988
3. Harris AI. Handicapped and impaired in Great Britain. Part I. OPCS. London: HMSO. 1971.
4. Bradley EM, Thompson RP, Wood PHN. The prevalence and severity of major disabling conditions — a reappraisal of the Government Social Survey of the handicapped and impaired in Great Britain. Int J Epidemiol 1987, 7: 145–151.
5. Tew B, Laurence KM. Mothers, brothers and sisters of patients with spina bifida. Dev. Med Neurology 1973 (Suppl) 29: 69–76.
6. Disability Living Allowance and Disability Working Allowance Bill. London: HMSO. 1990.
7. Meredith Davies. Social factors in disability. In Rehabilitation of the physically disabled; Ch. 3, pp. 24–34. Goodwill CJ, Chamberlain MA (eds). London: Croom Helm. 1988.
8. Meredith Davies B. The Disabled Child and Adult. Eastbourne: Baillière Tindall. 1982.

25

Homelessness

Homelessness is a very complex subject. It is found in young persons, families with young children, in adults living on their own and in elderly people. Usually it is the end result of a series of family or economic disasters, but can occur by choice in persons described as 'rootless'. Homelessness is often referred to as only a social problem, yet it has serious effects on the health of those unfortunate enough to find themselves in such circumstances. In many instances, homelessness typifies the inequalities in any society. In the UK, homelessness is a growing problem even at a time of affluence.

In the UK, homelessness is divided into two types:

- *legal homelessness* — as defined by the law; the housing (Homeless Persons) Act, 1977, defines five categories of legal homelessness (see below)
- *'unofficial' homelessness* — this covers persons who clearly have no home and do not fit into the five legal categories of homelessness. Some of these people have very obvious social and medical problems such as mental disorder, alcohol abuse or drug abuse. Many within this group drift towards big cities, especially London, and many have no fixed abode, spending some nights in various 'night refuges' set up by voluntary bodies, charities or the churches, or they sleep rough.

Drug abuse is not infrequently found in some rootless young persons, and crime and prostitution may also develop in some homeless people desperate to find the money to buy more drugs, etc.

In this short chapter, there will first be an explanation of the legal homeless and how the complicated problem of homelessness is resolved. Then follows a description of the various priority groups — those with a priority need. The question of intentional homelessness is also explained. The chapter ends with a section on 'unofficial' homelessness with special reference to homelessness in:

- young persons
- mentally ill people.

The number of homeless in both these groups is increasing in the UK, and there is a general concern that further problems would seem to be inevitable. The consequences that are likely to follow are that these difficulties become self-generating and progressive. The fact that both groups are especially vulnerable to exploitation, adds to the potential dangers of these homeless persons. Unless this vicious circle can be broken, the future for many of these individuals must be very bleak.

Legal homelessness

This is defined by the Housing (Homeless Persons) Act, 1977, in the following manner. A person is legally homeless if that person:

- has no accommodation which can be occupied in the UK or cannot secure entry to it
- has a home, but is threatened with violence from someone living there and it is clearly not reasonable for that person to go on living in the same household
- is part of a family (who normally live together), but the individual and members of the family are now living in separate homes because they have nowhere to live together
- is living in accommodation meant only for an emergency or a crisis
- is living in a mobile home (a caravan or houseboat) and has nowhere to put it.

People are said to be 'threatened with homelessness' if they are likely to become homeless within the next 28 days.

ACCEPTANCE OF HOMELESSNESS

The first stage in a person being officially recognized as being legally homeless is for an application to be made to the local authority claiming that the individual person or family is homeless. The law then requires the local authority to make enquiries to check this claim. Then follows a series of enquiries and stages to determine:

- whether that person comes into one of the five categories mentioned above; if that is so, then there may be a duty on the local authority (or appropriate local authority) eventually to offer permanent accommodation to the applicant
- whether the applicant is in *priority need*
- whether the homelessness is *intentional* (if this is found to be the case, then the local authority only has a duty to offer temporary accommodation (see below)
- whether the individual has a *local connection* (if so, then that local authority has a legal duty to offer *permanent accommodation* to the applicant. If not, then the local authority where the applicant normally lives has the legal authority to offer permanent accommodation).

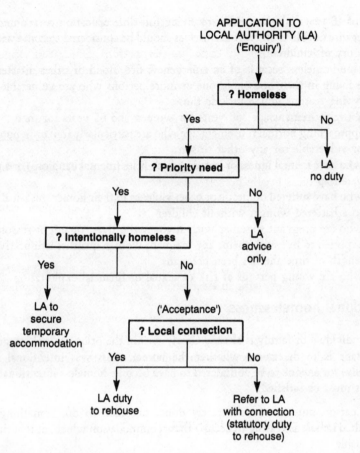

FIGURE 25.1   The operation of the Housing (Homeless Persons) Act, 1977 to determine whether a local authority has a duty to provide permanent accommodation for someone claiming to be homeless. (Data from ref. 1.)

All these stages are illustrated in Fig. 25.1 which comes from an excellent report published in 1991 on 'Housing or Homelessness'.[1]

Priority need

Once it has been confirmed that the individual or family is 'legally' homeless, then the next stage is for enquiries to determine whether there is a priority need. There are three main categories of priority need and these include those who:

- have dependent children living with them; (the Code of Guidance issued with the 1977 Act states that all those under the age of 16 years and others under the

age of 18 years who are either receiving full-time education or training or are otherwise unable to support themselves should be considered to come within the category of 'children')
- become homeless because of an emergency: fire, flood or other disaster
- have living in their household one or more persons who are vulnerable for the following reasons which include those:
  - above retirement age; 60 years for women and 65 years for men
  - approaching normal retirement age who are particularly frail or in poor health or vulnerable for any other reason
  - who have mental illness or learning disabilities (mental handicap) or a physical handicap
  - who have suffered domestic or other violence in their home; this usually refers to a battered woman without children
  - who are pregnant together with anyone who lives, or might reasonably be expected to live with them; any pregnant woman qualifies irrespective of the length of time she has been pregnant
  - who are young persons at risk of sexual or financial exploitation.

Intentional homelessness

If the individual or family is already clearly within the priority need category, the next stage is to determine whether the homelessness was intentional or not. Generally, for anyone to be considered to have become homeless intentionally three features must be satisfied:

- the person must have deliberately done, or failed to do, something which resulted in he/she ceasing to occupy the accommodation which, at that time, was available
- it must have been reasonable for the individual to occupy the accommodation
- the person must have been aware of all the relevant facts — an act of omission in good faith on the part of someone unaware of any relevant fact is *not* regarded as deliberate; this means that a person who is unaware that he/she is entitled to rent allowances or rebates or other welfare benefits, and therefore gets into debt and rent arrears and then may be evicted would not be classified as 'intentional homelessness'.

Local connection

The final stage in the enquiry into an applicant who is legally homeless, has a priority need and is not intentionally homeless, is to determine if the applicant has a local connection. This usually means the family or individual has lived within the local authority's area for a specified time or has close relatives living there. If this is so, that local authority has a legal duty to rehouse the household or person in permanent accommodation. If there is no local connection, then the applicant must be referred to the local authority with whom they do have a local connection for rehousing. That authority then has a legal duty to offer them permanent accommodation.

DIFFICULTIES IN THE GENERAL APPLICATION OF THE HOUSING (HOMELESS PERSONS) ACT, 1977

One would expect from analysing Fig. 25.1 that the whole process of determining those who are legally homeless and in dealing with them would be reasonably straightforward. Unfortunately, the interpretation throughout the UK of the Code of Guidance varies, and some authorities determine that certain families and individuals are not 'vulnerable', and this has resulted in much confusion and difficulty. Occasionally, evidence suggests that some local authorities are, in practice, largely ignoring the advice in the Code of Guidance.[1] Unfortunately, the standards laid down in the Notes of Guidance are discretionary, and have no statutory power to force a local authority to adopt them. It is expected that a revised Code of Guidance will be published shortly, but what is clearly required is that it should be mandatory on local authorities.

INCIDENCE OF HOMELESSNESS

The number of persons accepted by local authorities as legally homeless increased dramatically in the UK from 1978 to 1990. This is illustrated in Table 25.1. Note that the figures for England include those of Greater London. These are, however, shown separately as homelessness is an especially large problem in the

TABLE 25.1   Households accepted as homeless: each year 1978 to 1988–89 in England, Scotland and Wales

Year	England	(Greater London)	Scotland	Wales
1978	53 110	(14 430)		
1979	57 200	(16 650)		
1980	62 920	(17 480)		
1982	74 800	(21 110)	9 486	
1984	83 550	(25 180)	12 387	4 999
1986	103 560	(29 740)	14 896	5 465
1988	117 550	(29 320)	24 335	6 818
1989	126 680	(33 610)	28 926	6 648
1990	145 800	(37 240)		

Source of data: ref. 1.

capital. In 1990, 25.5% of all the legal homeless were from Greater London. The present trend is for the proportion from London to fall in the future.[1,2] A further breakdown and analysis of these official figures shows that homelessness is not only a problem in large conurbations — 43% of official acceptances originated in small towns and rural areas. Homelessness is therefore clearly a national problem within the UK.

CHARACTERISTICS OF LEGALLY ACCEPTED HOMELESS HOUSEHOLDS

Although official statistics are not published, all investigations agree that most homeless households are made up of families with children. In one survey in 1985–86, 70% of the homeless were found either to be unemployed and/or in receipt of supplementary benefit (now Income Support) or suffered from some disability. Only 21% were in any form of paid employment.[2] Another study carried out in 1988 found that 32% of homeless households contained a full-time worker.[3] Another feature was that single parents and childless households who were homeless were unlikely to contain anyone in work.[4]

CAUSES OF HOMELESSNESS

Official statistics only allow limited analysis of the reasons for legal homelessness, but several research projects and studies have indicated that there is no one single cause responsible.[2,4,5,6] The commonest cause of homelessness in about 60% of cases are disputes with relatives, spouses or partners.[7,9] This is then followed by defaults of payments of various kinds, particularly defaults of mortgage payments (about 14% of cases).

TEMPORARY ACCOMMODATION

Temporary accommodation is used in two ways to house homeless families:

- to accommodate temporarily those in priority need whose homelessness has been found to be intentional; the housing authority (local authority) has a duty to offer temporary accommodation to allow such individuals and families to find permanent accommodation on their own
- to provide accommodation as an emergency measure for homeless persons with a priority need for whom the local authority has accepted responsibility; this group will then be offered suitable accommodation as soon as it is available.

There are three main types of temporary accommodation provided by local authorities:

- hostels
- bed and breakfast accommodation — usually in specified hotels
- short-term housing.

The growth of all forms of temporary accommodation is shown in Fig. 25.2. Note that there was a marked increase in bed and breakfast accommodation used by local authorities from 1981 to 1986. After that date, there was a more gradual increase in Greater London, but a continued steady increase in the rest of England.

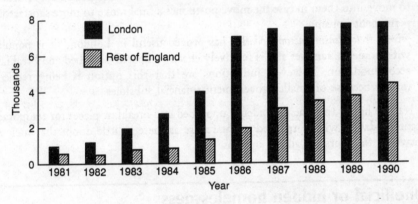

FIGURE 25.2   Numbers in bed and breakfast accommodation at the end of each year in London and the rest of England, 1981–90 (for 1990, to end of 3rd quarter) (thousands). (Data from ref. 1.)

Hostels

Hostels have changed since the 1970s. Every effort is now made to house families in accommodation in which the following are provided:

- safe warm accommodation which is reasonably independent of the other homeless families housed in the hostel
- skilled help and supervision to attempt the practical training of homeless families so that, when rehoused, they are unlikely to make the same mistakes and end up facing the same problems again.

Bed and breakfast accommodation

These are used by local authorities to provide about 65% of the temporary accommodation. This facility is usually provided in cheap, run down hotels and is never satisfactory. The Code of Guidance under the 1977 Act referred to them 'as a last resort'. They are totally unsuitable for family life, costly and ineffective.[4,5]

Short-term housing

This is made up of two types:

- *poor 'hard-to-let' permanent housing* in run down areas; these do provide relatively independent accommodation and can be useful for short periods; however, some applicants who have been accepted for permanent accommodation are reluctant to move into them in case the move postpones a final move to more satisfactory permanent housing
- *private sector leasing accommodation* has proved useful in London,[1] it is popular with homeless families and is relatively cheap compared with bed and breakfast accommodation; however, indications are that this option is being reduced mainly because of smaller government financial subsidies.

It is to be hoped that the dependence upon bed and breakfast places for temporary accommodation will be reduced in the future as there is little doubt that such an answer is the worst of all the options.

Unofficial or hidden homelessness

Another term widely used to describe persons who are homeless, but who do not come within the legal definition of 'homelessness' is 'hidden homelessness'. This covers a very diverse group of people of all ages from young persons who have left home for any reason (including those virtually forced to leave because of some form of serious abuse) to some very inadequate mentally disordered people and to a few old persons.

It is difficult to be certain of the size of the problem. Most estimates have been centred on studies in London where the following seem to be the best figures currently available:

- 4000 are sleeping rough;[10]
- 10 000 are occupying night shelters run by charities and churches
- 3000 are squatters[11]
- 10 000 are living as unauthorized tenants[12]
- 7500 have self-referred themselves to bed and breakfast accommodation.[11]

This adds up to 60 000 households in London alone.

In addition, those in receipt of board and lodging supplementary benefits in the UK rose from 49 000 in 1979 to 164 000 in 1984. The rules for receipt were then changed and removed many young persons from receiving benefit, and the 1985 figure was down to 127 000.[1] It therefore seems clear that the total number of people who would generally be accepted as being unofficially homeless on any common sense judgement must exceed 200 000. This figure is, of course, in addition to those known to be 'legally' homeless.

Within the various groups of 'unofficial' homeless, two are of special interest because they are very vulnerable, either because of their age or their mental condition: young persons and mentally ill people.

YOUNG PERSONS

The Code of Guidance published by the government at the time of the passing of the Housing (Homeless Persons) Act, 1977, specifically mentioned that one of the groups of vulnerable persons who should be considered as being in priority need are 'homeless young persons who are at risk of sexual and financial exploitation'. Yet there is considerable evidence that this is not being carried out. The National Childrens Home (NCH) carried out research and reported on this in 1989.[13] They circulated local housing authorities in the UK to find out what their practice was as regards 'vulnerability' in young people. They had a good response to their questionnaire, and 20% of housing authorities reported they would not classify as vulnerable a girl under the age of 18 on the grounds that she was open to sexual and financial exploitation if she was sleeping rough. Twice that proportion (40%) said they would definitely deal with such a girl as legally homeless, and the remainder indicated that it would depend on the circumstances and evidence.

Two fifths of the local authorities replied they would not even consider a young homeless person with serious family problems as vulnerable. It is interesting to note in the same survey, that local authorities in the Metropolitan Authorities (the large conurbations in cities and towns), in London Boroughs and in Scotland were generally more sympathetic than the rural areas of England.

One worrying feature was the erroneous view expressed that any young person under the age of 18 must be the sole responsibility of the social services authorities. This view, and its different approach in rural areas, may be because in the conurbations (including London), the housing and social services departments are run by the same local authority, but in the country areas these are separate.

The NCH concluded its report by stating 'the picture that emerges from this survey is bleak. The vulnerability safety net in the homeless legislation is failing to protect young single homeless people at risk'. This statement is re-emphasized by Shelter who estimate that between 100 000 and 150 000 young people sleep rough at some time during the year.[14]

MENTALLY ILL PEOPLE

Concern has been expressed by many professionals that evidence is accumulating that a substantial proportion of the single homeless (those who are homeless on their own) are mentally ill persons, many of whom formerly lived in mental hospitals. Reference has already been made in Chapter 16 to the development of better community services for mentally ill persons to enable them to live within the community, either with their families or independently, receiving help and support from community psychiatric nuses (CPNs) and social and voluntary services. Much has been achieved, but there is no doubt that a proportion of mentally ill people are living from hand to mouth, either sleeping rough or dependent on direct-access hostels (such as the Salvation Army hostels). A recent study highlighted the problem.[15] A sample of men newly arriving at a Salvation Army hostel from September 1986 to April 1987 situated in Waterloo, London were studied. The findings showed that there was a high proportion of psychiatric disorders in the group:

- 25% had a history of schizophrenia
- 14% had alcohol dependence
- 11% had personality disorders
- 6% had mood disorders.

The study went on to analyse also a sample of long-term men who had lived in the hostel for more than a year and found that the incidence of schizophrenia was even more striking at 37%. What was more surprising was that this mental condition was the only significant one found in the group. The authors of the study, who are practising consultant psychiatrists in central south London hospitals referred to this degree of schizophrenia as 'a massive over-representation' as the prevalence for schizophrenia in South London was 0.2%. This incidence of schizophrenia in hostel inmates is higher than the one reported in 1971, which then discovered in a similar hostel population, that 15% of the residents had schizophrenia and 8% affective mental disorders.[16] It seems probable that this increase must be connected with the intervening emptying of many mental hospitals (following the community care initiatives) of many of their chronic mentally ill persons. Such individuals often do well where they can be supported by a caring family, but all too often, without such support, they become homeless and dependent upon hostels.

Another interesting study which was carried out in Bloomsbury, an inner London district, compared the features of two different groups who were being visited by CPNs. The groups were 642 home-based patients/clients and 342 homeless ones. The homeless group was made up of 61.3% who lived in Salvation Army hostels, 15.5% were squatters, 12.1% lived in bed and breakfast accommodation and 11.1% were sleeping rough. The CPNs found that in many ways, there was no great difference between the two groups except that in the homeless, more had been diagnosed as schizophrenics — 26.8% compared with 17.8% in the home-based group. The home-based group also had a higher proportion of affective disorders (14.8% compared with 5%) and dementia (5% in the home-based group compared with nil in the homeless group).

A revealing observation in one of these reports[15] asked the question of how it is possible for large direct access hostels (such as those run by the Salvation Army) to cope with this high level of psychiatric morbidity? Perhaps it is because they exhibit two features which are strikingly reminiscent of the old mental hospitals:

- the wide range of bizarre behaviour tolerated
- the general non-intrusiveness of other residents and staff.

A further study[17] looked at whether those who referred themselves to the psychiatric services differed significantly from the main group of homeless persons. It found that alcohol abuse and personality disorders were more common in those who referred themselves, while schizophrenia was more common in the common lodging house group.

As has already been suggested, the movement towards community care has been partly responsible for the present high level of mental illness in the single homeless. In the USA, this movement was started earlier than in the UK, and similar problems have been reported, with up to 3 million individuals — who have been discharged from mental hospitals — said to be living on the streets, making homelessness a national scandal.[18, 19]

These findings must, of course , be balanced with the undoubted benefits which are being enjoyed by many former mental hospital patients who are now living with their families or in well-supported independent accommodation in the community. These surveys and many others do point out, however, that any community care solution has clear hazards as well as advantages unless:

- there is practical support for very vulnerable people such as ex-mental hospital patients with no immediate family support or other well-organized assistance
- that one of the most important factors of support is satisfactory housing of some kind
- there is far better co-ordination between the mental hospital health services and those responsible for providing housing services, especially for those who are vulnerable and often difficult to deal with.

The constant and repeated finding that schizophrenia is so often found in homeless people raises the question of why this mental condition should be so dominant in this group. One suggestion is that schizophrenia can lead to what are referred to as 'negative symptoms',[20] in which the ability of anyone to motivate themselves becomes greatly reduced.

Whatever the factors, one feature is unchanged — the situation is getting worse. The 1972 study of Tidmarsh[21] of the Camberwell Centre in London showed exactly the same type of problems but to a lesser degree. Timms and Fry[15] conclude their excellent paper on the subject with a particularly interesting comment which seems to suggest a sensible and practical next step: 'This study demonstrates an analogous situation regarding patterns of psychiatric morbidity and service use in a hostel for the homeless. It would therefore seem reasonable that special hostel-based psychiatric services should be established, as has been done in the USA. If this is not possible, psychiatric services should at least acknowledge the role that hostels for the homeless play in caring for their ex-hospital patients, by providing them with suitable support from specialist multi-disciplinary teams in the area.

References

1. Faculty of Public Health Medicine of the Royal Colleges of Physicians of the United Kingdom. Housing or homelessness: a public health perspective. Report from a working group on housing and health of the Committee of Health Promotion. Royal Colleges of Physicians of the United Kingdom: London. 1991.
2. Evans A, Duncan S. Responding to homelessness: local authority policy and practice. London: HMSO. 1989.
3. London Research Centre/London Housing Unit. One in every 100. A special survey of 1000 acceptances as homeless. London. 1989.
4. Niner P. Homelessness in nine local authorities: case studies of policy and practice. London: HMSO. 1989.
5. Audit Commission. Housing the homeless: the local authority role. Report. London: HMSO. 1989.
6. Institute of Housing. Who will house the homeless? Report. London 1988.
7. The experience of homelessness in London (Jeffers S and Miriea (eds) Bristol: School for Advanced studies. 1987.
8. Lawton J, Bonnerjea. Homeless in Brent. A report by the Policy Studies Institute. London: PSI. 1986.
9. Speaking for ourselves: Families in Bayswater Bed and Breakfast. London: The Bayswater Hotel Homelessness Project. 1987.
10. Canter D et al. Homelessness in West Central London. Department of Psychology, University of Surrey Research report.
11. London Housing Unit. Another disastrous year for London's homeless. Report. December. London: London Housing Unit. 1989.
12. The London Housing Survey. 1986–1987. Full report of results. London: London Research Centre. 1989.
13. National Childrens' Homes. Housing vulnerable young single homeless people. Research Report. London: NCH. 1989.
14. Randall G. Homeless and hungry. A sign of the times. Central Office, Centrepoint Soho, London. October 1989.
15. Timms PW, Fry AH. Homelessness and mental illness. Health Trends, Vol. 21. London: HMSO. 1989, pp. 70–71.
16. Lodge Patch IC. Homeless men in London: demographic findings in a lodging house sample. Br. J. Psychiat. 1971, 118: 313–317.
17. Priest RG. Proceedings of the Royal Society of Medicine 1970, 63: 437.

18. Brickner PW *et al*. Homeless persons in health care. Ann. Inter. Med. 1986, **104**: 405.
19. Bassuk EL. The homeless problem. Sci. Am. 1984, **251**: 40.
20. Crow TJ. Positive and negative schizophrenic symptoms. Br. J. Psychiat. 1980, **139**: 379.
21. Tidmarsh D. The Camberwell Reception Centre. London: DHSS. 1978.

INDEX